WITHDRAWN

CURIOSITIES
OF
STREET
LITERATURE

CHARLES HINDLEY

CURIOSITIES

OF

STREET

LITERATURE

**NEW FOREWORD BY
MICHAEL HUGHES**

AUGUSTUS M. KELLEY, PUBLISHERS
NEW YORK 1970

First published in 1871. This edition published in the
U.S.A. in 1970 by Augustus M. Kelley, 1140 Broadway, New York,
N.Y.10001.
Foreword © Michael Hughes, 1970.
L.C.C. card No. 70-111203
SBN 678 08012 7

**Reproduced and Printed in Great Britain by
Redwood Press Limited
Trowbridge & London**

FOREWORD

The *Curiosities of Street Literature* is a collection of broadside ballads and prose broadsides which were sold, sung and recited in the streets of England between 1800 and the 1860's and 70's. Broadsides (single, unfolded sheets of paper printed on one side only) and broadsheets (printed on both sides) originated during the first quarter of the sixteenth century and were the first medium of mass communication. They were simple pieces of paper on which was printed the news of the day, sermons, politics, satire, public events, proclamations, romantic and humorous tales, descriptions of murders—anything, in fact, which would excite popular interest and be saleable. For two and a half centuries, at first printed in gothic 'black letter' and later in roman or 'white letter', they were the most widely circulated, most enduring source of news and entertainment for the poorer classes. And in form, style, subject matter and tone they remained astonishingly unchanged from their birth with the printing press to their demise on the streets of Victorian England.

THE PRE-VICTORIAN BROADSIDE

Broadsides were an urban product, born of the printing press, nurtured on literacy and reflecting the ethos of the town. As the most elementary printed form they could be produced rapidly and cheaply, qualities which determined their journalistic function and ensured them the unsophisticated, relatively poor readers with whom they found continuing favour. But although essentially urban they were born and flourished during periods when oral, folk traditions were meaningful, and their subject matter and its treatment reflected this and assumed similar functions. The mass of tales, romances, moralities, superstitions, credulities, dire events and wondrous happenings which comprises so much of their early subject matter was in large measure drawn from oral tradition, while their reporting of topical events was greatly coloured by the assumptions and perspectives of a folk culture.

In two other respects the influence of oral tradition was fundamental to the broadside: in its use of the verse ballad as the most characteristic form of expression, even above prose, and the fact that the ballads were sung, not read or recited. The ballad pattern was taken over from the traditional ballad, a folk music genre which had evolved during the late Middle Ages and which provided the rhymed, narrative verse form which was used almost exclusively on broadsides, although with its own very different style and subject matter. The musical aspect was likewise an influence from the traditional ballad, which provided the general example and in many cases the actual tunes to which broadside ballads were composed, although the importance of music and song in popular culture and the skill and fondness for music of the people of the time were important general influences. These characteristics—the ballad set to a tune—had clearly evolved by about 1525; three centuries later they were still the hallmark of the Victorian broadside.

The broadsides were immensely popular with the lower classes, partly through the magical quality which printed matter had for the newly literate and partly because their use of familiar tunes guaranteed popularity. Of great importance for their widespread circulation were the activities of the itinerant sellers of fancy goods, chapbooks and broadsides known as chapmen, who cried the ballads in the streets, fairs and market places of towns and carried them into the lanes, villages and ale houses of the countryside. The chapman was the main link between the ballad author and his rural public, carrying the songs of the city into the remotest country areas and was for most people the main source of reading matter. The chapman's importance cannot be over estimated and is attested to by his frequent appearance in contemporary literature. Shakespeare's Autolycus in *The Winter's Tale* is a gently satirical portrait of a purveyor of fictions and romances; Ditty in *The London Chanticleers* (1659) provides a more rounded picture of a chapman and his wares:

> *DITTY:*"...All sorts of ballads and pleasant books! *The Famous History of Tom Thumb and Unfortunate Jack, A Hundred Goodly Lessons,* and *Alas, Poor Scholar, whither wilt thou go? The second part of Mother Shipton's Prophesies, newly made by a gentleman of good quality,* foretelling what was done four hundred years ago, and *A Pleasant Ballad of a bloody fight seen i'th'air,* which the astrologers say, portends scarcity of fowl this year. *The Ballad of the Unfortunate Love.* I have *George of Green, Chivy Chase, Collins and the Devil;* or, *Room for Cuckolds, The Ballad of the London 'Prentice, Guy of Warwick, The Beggar of Bethnal Green, The Honest Milkmaid;* or, *I must not wrong my Dame, The Honest Fresh Cheese and Cream Woman.* Then I have *The Seven Wise Men of Gotham, A Hundred Merry Tales, Scroggin's Jests;* or, *A Book of Prayers and Graces for Young Children.* I have very strange news from beyond the seas. The King of Morocco has got the black jaundice, and the Duke of Westphalia is sick of the swine pox, with eating bacon; the Moors increase daily, and the King of Cyprus mourns for the Duke Saxony, that is dead of a stone: and Presbyter John is advanced to Zealand; the sea ebbs and flows there but twice in four-and-twenty hours, and the moon has changed but once the last month."

The ballad authors were invariably anonymous poets producing pot-boiling verse set to popular tunes. Some are remembered by name, like Elderton "of the ale-crammed nose", Thomas Deloney, "the balleting silk-weaver", the royalist Martin Parker, and Henry Carey—authors whose verse is still read with pleasure and respect. But the majority were nameless professionals, 'tavern poets and gutter versifiers', men whose skill was their sympathy with the public's tastes and whose craft was their ability to readily and mechanically churn out ballads to meet them. Their milieu was the market place. They wrote to make money, mediocre practitioners of the first mass medium whose limited poetic abilities were judiciously supplemented with bawdy, sensation and deceit to entice and hold their barely literate readers.

Rarely did their verse rise above uninspired competence and they invariably lacked poetic intuition and dramatic sense; indeed, they probably shunned such subtleties for their main concern was to tell a story, which they did directly and without frills. Sometimes their ranks were dignified by educated writers, especially during the eighteenth century when statesmen and men of letters brought wit, classical manners and polemical concerns to the broadside. But although broadside authors and their audience had always in part been drawn from lettered people these qualities were alien to the main tradition, which was of the streets, not the study or the coffee house.

Fashionable and sophisticated contempories regarded broadside authors with ridicule and contempt, both for the crudity of their verses and the alacrity with which they produced them on every possible subject and occasion. "A poet should detest a ballad-maker" said Ben Jonson, it being a deadly insult to confuse one with the other, and Shakespeare, who with other Elizabethan dramatists displayed considerable familiarity with broadside ballads, generally slighted them. Those who considered them vulgar and cheap thought their judgements confirmed when they were immensely popular as well! Henry Chettle wrote in 1592 "that ballads are abusively chanted in every street; and from London this evil has overspread Essex and the adjoining counties", and he complained "of idle youths, loathing honest labour, and despising lawful trades, (who) betake themselves to a vagrant and vicious life, in every corner of cities and market towns of the realm, singing and selling ballads". In the same year the author of *Martin Mar-sixtus* observed that "scarce a cat can look out of a gutter, but out starts a halfpenny chronicler, and presently a proper new ballet of a strange site is indited", and Massinger spoke for many when he wrote:

> let but a chapel fall, or street be fired,
> A foolish lover hang himself for pure love,
> Or any such like accident, and before
> They are cold in their graves some damned ditty's made
> Which makes their ghosts walk.

Most references to broadsides during their golden age before 1700 were hostile to the ballads, their authors and the people who bought them in a way subsequently to become familiar for other media. A new form of communication had become enormously popular with an audience not generally embraced by conventional doctrines of culture and literacy. The form and the audience it commanded were excluded from accepted assumptions and were believed to undermine or threaten those assumptions and their self-appointed guardians. The broadside ballad was therefore deemed unworthy of serious attention, except perhaps to attack and revile.

But the broadside, like the drama and the novel and later cultural forms was to disprove judgements which denied worth to a whole medium, without attempting to discriminate within it. From the middle of the seventeenth century broadsides began to receive the serious attentions of collectors and scholars, and from this period date the great collections of Selden, Harley, Pepys, Roxburghe and others. It was realised that ballads provided a picture of the opinions and imaginative life of the common people which was not otherwise represented in literature; that, to quote John Selden, the earliest major collector, "...you may see by them how the wind sits. As take a straw and throw it up into the air, you shall see by that which way the wind is, which you shall not do by casting up a stone. More solid things do not show the complexion of the times so well as ballads".

As scholars and antiquarians began to interest themselves in a social class whose culture was largely expressed in ritual, sport, dancing and oral tradition, the broadside ballad assumed a primary importance as almost the only cultural form which lived beyond the moment of expression and which directly reflected the tastes and attitudes of ordinary people. Steele wrote of an Elizabethan politician who "had all manner of books and ballads brought to him...and took great notice how much they took with the people; upon which he would, and certainly might, very well judge their present disposition". And as interest and respect for the disposition of ordinary people became more common then judgements on the broadside ballads began to be revised.

LITERARY INFLUENCES

The major revaluation of the broadside ballad came with the eighteenth century's interest in them as literature rather than social history or antiquarian lore, a revaluation which was to contribute an important strand to the Romantic Revival. Considering that the poetry most favoured during the early eighteenth century was typified by the artificial, mannered elegancies of Pope and Dryden it is perhaps surprising that the crude simplicities of the broadside ballad should have attracted fashionable favour. But behind eighteenth century urbanity lay a belief that Nature had granted men reason and taste in equal measure, and from this it was deduced that those whose reason and tastes were least corrupted by the artificiality and sophistication of polite society were likely to produce the most pure, most natural art. This belief in the instinctive taste and simplicity of the common people was influentially advanced, in the ballad context, by Joseph Addison in *The Spectator* during 1711 in a favourable discussion of the ballad *Chevy Chase,* where he argued that the poetry of the lower classes possessed virtues which had been lost by, and could well redeem, the poetry then preferred by the sophisticated, concluding that "It is impossible that anything universally tasted and approved by the Multitude, tho' they are only the Rabble of the Nation, which hath not in it some peculiar Aptness to please and gratify the Mind of Man". Addison's *Spectator* articles touched off a storm of argument and abuse concerning the nature of poetry and the value of popular verse which continued for decades, but they marked the beginning of a movement which was to transform English poetry.

The history of this is complex, but one of its main themes is the penetration of sophisticated poetry by the forms, style and feeling of the poetry of 'the Rabble of the People'. Two landmarks in this history should be mentioned—the publication in 1765 of Percy's *Reliques of Ancient English Poetry,* a collection of 'ancient' popular poetry of folk and broadside origin which had more influence on eighteenth century literary taste than any other publication or event. And the 1798 *Lyrical Ballads* of Wordsworth and Coleridge which were much influenced, particularly in the case of Wordsworth, by *The Reliques.* Wordsworth later wrote that "I do not think that there is an able writer of verse today who would not be proud to acknowledge his obligation to *The Reliques",* which had "absolutely redeemed" English poetry. Although folk or traditional ballads predominated in Percy's collection, which was a foundation study for distinguishing these from the broadside ballads, the latter were strongly represented and Wordsworth's debt to them was considerable. His poetic philosophy was buttressed with examples taken from broadsides and much of his early verse copied their style and feeling. Wordsworth was not the first poet to draw on broadside ballads for his own work, but he was perhaps the greatest and he was certainly the most influential.

It is interesting and significant that the eighteenth century's revaluation of the broadside ballad was in terms of the older, black letter ballad and largely ignored the white letter ballads which were then being sold in great numbers, and which in many instances were identical with, or derived from, older versions. Percy had been rather apologetic about the broadside texts in *The Reliques* and had always emphasised their black letter origins and obscured their relation with contemporary street ballads. When William Dicey, the most prolific eighteenth century printer of chapbooks and broadsides presented him with one hundred and eleven currently sold white letter broadsides of historical interest, Percy made use of them in *The Reliques* but did not disclose his sources. His attitude was fairly typical. Age and a superceded typography conferred a spurious dignity on the earlier ballads, which allowed them to be valued and idealised in terms which might be applicable to the common people of previous centuries but which could not be accepted as applying to the common people of their own day.

Between Addison and Percy writers influenced by the popular ballad had sought to 'improve' it towards the literary level of their own poetry; after Percy they sought to refine their own poetry towards the simplicity of the ballad. Wordsworth, although he came at the end of the movement, clarified and magnified this tendency in his imitations—they were hardly more than this—of the street ballad and conferred on them the imprimatur of a great poet. After him the poetry of the people was conclusively a respectable source of inspiration for poets good and bad. The traditional ballad was the more generally approved model and the broadside ballad was still regarded with some distaste, but it had gained considerable acceptance and was soon to become an established feature of the literary landscape, its devices a commonplace of poetic craft and vocabulary, its texts collated and analysed by scholars of learning and eminence.

THE VICTORIAN BROADSIDE

The broadsides collected in the *Curiosities of Street Literature* are the direct, white letter descendants of those whose history has been briefly described, and they illustrate how the salient characteristics of the earlier broadsides survived almost unchanged into the Victorian era. This was a second golden age for them in which more titles were more widely circulated in greater numbers than ever before. Yet although the broadside was extremely lively and reached a vast audience its standing with the cultural establishment was either low or non-existent, for in general Victorian official culture either ignored contemporary broadsides or was unaware that they existed.

In part this attitude stemmed from a hardening and exaggeration of the eighteenth century's distinction between black and white letter broadsides, so that while the major black letter collections were being edited and republished by eminent scholars in multi-volumed editions, white letter broadsides were pouring off the presses unnoticed. Also influential was the movement, initiated in *The Reliques,* to distinguish traditional, orally preserved ballads from their print based counterparts, which produced a reaction against broadside texts. This became the dominant interest in folk music studies, culminating in Francis James Childe's monumental, five volume *The English and Scottish Popular Ballads,* the definitive winnowing of the traditional ballads and their variants. Childe took some of his traditional texts from broadsides, but broadside ballads in general he considered to be "veritable dung-hills, in which, only after a great deal of sickening grubbing, one finds a very modest jewel". Childe's somewhat extreme opinion was written in 1872 but his sentiments would have been accepted as applicable to the contemporary broadside long before this.

But probably the most important reason why most Victorians ignored the broadsides of their own day was that under the pressure of an expanding and changing pattern of literacy they had become almost wholly a working class cultural form. Their circulation had always been predominantly among the 'lower classes' (a phrase which before the Industrial Revolution denoted a fairly broad spectrum of society) but had always reached a minority in other classes; as the growth of literacy incorporated whole new areas of society into the reading public, and as new, more sophisticated forms developed for those fairly skilled in reading, so the broadside readership increased numerically but contracted socially. With the working class stamp distinctly on them, the social tensions of the early nineteenth century almost guaranteed the flight of their respectable readers.

BROADSIDES AND LITERACY

The first half of the nineteenth century saw greater changes in English society than in any other fifty years. In 1800 the population was round about eleven million people; by 1850 this had climbed to twenty-one million, more than half of whom lived in towns. The consequences of this flood of people to the cities are well known and do not need repeating, but without wishing to minimise the appalling conditions in which the city poor lived—and remember that the lot of the rural poor was hardly better—it should be said that the transformation of rural society and culture upon which the cities fed was a condition for the political and material liberation of the mass of the people. Mastery of the printed word was an important part of this liberation, and the struggle for literacy, the manner in which rudimentary reading skills were used and improved, owed a good deal to the popular reading tradition which the broadside dominated for the first half of the century.

By 1850 a probable 60% to 70% of the British population could read and, possibly, write to a useful degree. The efforts of the dame schools, the voluntary associations, the sunday schools, the adult schools movement, the British and Foreign Schools Society and the many other philanthropic and self-interested bodies which set out to educate the working class, created a nation eager for print and reading, and many charitable bodies and entrepreneurs exerted themselves to meet this demand. The foundations of 'mass produced' literature for the working classes had been laid in the eighteenth century by propagandists like Sarah Trimmer and Hannah More, who had bombarded the nation with magazines and tracts "designed", as Mrs. Trimmer put it, "to convey to the lower orders of the people many instructive lessons...in order to correct many of the faults peculiar to their humble station in life". These improving doctrines were inevitably extended to publications intended for the more numerous nineteenth century working class readers, and organisations like the Society for Promoting Christian Knowledge, the Religious Tract Society and their secular rivals such as the Society for the Diffusion of Useful Knowledge, published great quantities of literature intended to instruct and improve. Many of these publications, issued in weekly parts, sold in surprising numbers: the circulation of the eight page *Penny Magazine* was estimated at 200,000 in 1832, and *Chambers' Edinburgh Journal,* the *Saturday Magazine* and other imitative weeklies of the 'cheap literature movement' achieved similarly substantial circulations. These were fairly sober, unobtrusively didactic magazines, retailing history, useful knowledge and simplified science and mechanics to the higher class of artisan; between 1832 and the mid 1840's they provided a major portion of working class reading matter.

The 'weekly romances' which supplanted them in popular favour during the 1840's retained something of this educational role but owed their enormous success to melodramatic serials of romance, seduction and improbable adventure. Their balance of fact and fiction proved a money-winning formula, a more accurate judgement of popular tastes than the improving magazines which they replaced. The more popular of these weeklies achieved astonishing circulations: in the 1850's that of the *London Journal* was estimated at half a million, that of the *Family Herald* at 300,000, that of *Reynold's Miscellany* at 200,000, and there were hundreds of others with lesser circulations.

The cheap literature movement and the weekly romances were an outstandingly successful response to the needs of the millions of ordinary people who had been newly incorporated into literary citizenship, but while these new forms and styles achieved their astronomical sales the older forms were also expanding and enjoying unprecedented growth. Newspapers, although burdened by taxes, increased in numbers and readership, particularly the sensationalist Sundays like the *News of the World,* which was selling 50,000 copies a week by the end of the 1840's. Political weeklies, tracts, pamphlets of every description, the Radical press, the penny dreadfuls of Salisbury Square, almanacs like *Old Moore's,* which untaxed after 1836 achieved annual sales of over half a million copies: these and many other forms contributed to the ever rising flood of print which engulfed the first half, no less than the second half, of the nineteenth century.

This was the background to the broadside renaissance, and although one would expect broadside circulation to increase in an expanding market one should remember that the chapbook, its 'rival' traditional form, which had dominated popular reading during the eighteenth century, sharply declined with industrialism, while the broadside not only survived into the industrial age but achieved phenomenal popularity. The extent of this popularity is difficult to estimate as broadsides were inherently ephemeral and unlikely to be preserved, while the lack of contemporary interest has left little in the way of evidence. On the few occasions when they were seriously noticed in contemporary journals their popularity was generally a cause for amazement, Charles Manby Smith going so far as to write in 1857 that their sales "far exceeds that of any other production of the press throughout the world".

The Baring–Gould Collection in the British Museum contains approximately twelve thousand broadside titles, most of them from the nineteenth century, and to these can be added many thousands more preserved in other collections in the Museum, in public, university and institutional libraries, and in the great public and private collections in America. The total extant can only be guessed at and would include many duplicated titles, but these are only the survivals of these commonplace, flimsy pieces of paper, which must be but a small proportion of the total printed.

Other evidence comes from the broadside printers. Not all of them added their names to the sheets, and the same ones freqently circulated under different imprints, but in London alone over fifty printers have been identified as regularly producing broadsides, and the provinces offer as many again. Catnach's successors in Seven Dials advertised four thousand different broadsides for sale and another London printer "upwards of five thousand different sorts of ballads". But it is from the researches of Charles Hindley, almost the sole contemporary investigator, that we get the hardest evidence of their vast circulation.

The murder and gallows literature had a powerful hold on the public imagination and heavily outsold the other types of broadside. When John Thurtell murdered William Weare at Elstree, Hertfordshire in October 1823 the crime became a national sensation. To profit from this James Catnach, the prince of Seven Dials printers, set up four presses and by working eight formes day and night for a week produced 250,000 broadsides on the crime; for Thurtell's trial he doubled the number of presses and printed 500,000. The murder and burial of Maria Marten in the 'Red Barn' (p.189) was another Catnach best seller to the extent of 1,166,000 sheets; he bettered this with his various execution papers on the Greenacre–Gale murder (p.192) which numbered 1,650,000. In 1848–49 broadsides printed on the Rush murder (p.196) totalled 2,500,000, as did those on the murder of Patrick O'Connor by the Mannings (p.198).

While these figures must be treated with caution we should remember that the first three examples refer to the output of one printer only, James Catnach, and that dozens of other printers would be active on the same murders; also that they relate to a mere five of the tens of thousands of broadside titles produced during the half century. However gingerly one treats the figures it is obvious that a phenomenal number of broadsides celebrated these crimes and that the total output of broadsides, numbering many millions, must have been a very significant factor in the growth of the mass reading public.

The broadsides won their tremendous sales by occupying the vacuum in reading tastes which more sophisticated forms didn't seriously exploit until almost mid-century. The improving, broadly educational literature was one important response to the new literacy which was widely read for its interpretation and guidance to the new urban world, but it was sober, didactic and uplifting and largely ignored man's desire for the romantic, the political or the sensational, particularly in contemporary terms. The broadsides, their authors, publishers and salesmen from the class they appealed to, were produced for no reason other than to sell, and without social or moral inhibitions were directly tailored to interest, amuse, scandalise, horrify or in any other way *entertain* their readers. This does not mean that they were without seriousness—the minutely described details of a public hanging are serious enough—but that they were conceived to give the public what it wanted, rather than what somebody else thought it ought to want. They were also cheap, convenient to circulate, immediately topical if required to be and not too difficult or too long to read. And the ballad form, although giving way to or sharing the sheets with prose, was still a potent ingredient of their appeal, unavoidably as declaimed by the innumerable street singers or more usefully as a musical mnemonic for faltering readers.

Their success undoubtedly owed a good deal to the heavy taxes imposed on newspapers by governments anxious to contain the reading of the lower classes. Until 1836 a Newspaper Stamp Duty of 4d a copy (1d thereafter) and a duty of 3/6d on each advertisement kept newspaper prices at around 7d a copy. Until the mid 1850's these taxes, including Paper Duty from 1836, maintained newspapers as the preserve of the wealthy, except, significantly, certain sensational Sundays which in style and content imitated the broadsides. It was only in 1855 when the taxes were removed that newspapers were able to challenge broadsides for their traditional markets. From this date the new penny dailies, aided by technical developments and written to a formula based on the broadsides and the still expanding romance weeklies, began to occupy the territory hitherto commanded by the broadsides; and within ten years they had almost conquered it. Broadsides lingered on beyond the end of the century, a few printers making a living at the business, the occasional antiquarian collecting them, the infrequent street singer prolonging the tradition, and as late as 1904 Ralph Vaughan Williams heard two street singers from his house in Barton Street, Westminster, from whom he bought a broadside of 'William and Phyllis' in a version taken from Catnach. (Ironically, Cecil Sharp had collected two oral versions to the same tune in Somerset the previous year). But 'William and Phyllis' was a romantic, untypical survival. In real terms the broadside died during the 1860's with the arrival of the penny newspaper and other cheap fiction forms. Popular taste had become more sophisticated and demanding for detailed, accurate news; Victorian street life and activity altered, assisted by the laws against hawking and singing in the streets; the abolition of public executions in 1868, and the spirit which brought this about, worked against the broadsides. For many and complex reasons the broadsides lost their appeal as a mass reading form, there was a steep decline in their production and sales, the hoarse voices of the street singers were stilled and by 1870 the broadside's three hundred and fifty year old history was all but over.

BROADSIDES AND POPULAR CULTURE

The broadsides were, first and foremost, commercial products conceived and published to satisfy public demand by people largely indifferent to their content. This is not to say that their publishers might not have some sympathy with their subject matter or that some were not written with commitment or sympathy, but they were primarily fictions, imaginative compositions written, with little regard for the truth, for a competitive market in which the tastes and fashions of prospective purchasers counted for more than publisher's principles. This is illustrated by the murder and execution sheets, a staple of the trade from its beginning, on which we are given names and dates which are accurate and verifiable, and graphic, detailed descriptions of the executions, absolutely convincing in the personal detail and horror of these events, written by someone who must assuredly have been present. Alas, many of these were written before the executions which they purport to describe, and when written subsequently they were composed from rumour and press reports with as much artistry and disregard for the facts as any novel. The 'Execution of James Rutterford' (p.237) provides an example of this; we read of the man's behaviour in his cell and on the gallows and of his execution, poorly written but fundamentally no different from any other broadside; we then read in an editorial note that the broadside was never sold because, in fact, Rutterford was reprieved on account of a throat malformation!

So convincing and powerful are most of the execution sheets that it is hard to believe that they are skilful concoctions, but literal truth is of secondary importance in this context, what characterises genuine popular culture is its truth to the imaginative, emotional and social realities of its audience. That Rutterford did not hang is unimportant (except that it destroyed the basic illusion), what matters is whether the evocation of the circumstances of his fictional death enlarged, enriched or confirmed the emotional or imaginative experience of those who read about it.

English law during the heyday of the Victorian broadside was severe, brutal and operated on the assumption that the protection of property was more important than the protection of persons. Until 1826 felonies were punished by hanging, and a felony was the theft of anything valued at more than twelve pence. Up to 1868 executions were held in public and provided a spectacle-cum-holiday at which tens of thousands might watch the death struggles of the criminal.

The executions were an ever present part of lower class consciousness. When one could be hanged for the pettiest of crimes awareness of the gallows was perpetual, and this was constantly reinforced by the personal involvement, rumour, awful stories and sheer horror of these ghastly public rituals. This was the consciousness to which the execution broadsides appealed. Commercialised fictions they might be, using sensationalism, brutality and horror for their appeal, but they were a response to popular social experience which by confirming common meanings, by permitting vicarious participation, made the horrific concrete and tolerable, even, by their stylised, ritualistic descriptions, giving it dignity and controlled passion.

The 'Esher Tragedy' (p.199) relates the story of Mary Brough who killed her six children on 9 June 1854, and afterwards attempted suicide. The broadside prints the customary moralising verses and a prose description of the actual murders:

"On Friday last, I was bad all day; I wanted to see Mr. Izod, and waited all day. I wanted him to give me some medicine. In the evening I walked about, and afterwards put the children to bed, and wanted to go to sleep in a chair.—About nine o'clock, Georgy (meaning Georgianna) kept calling me to bed. I came up to bed, and they kept calling me to bring them some barley water, and they kept calling me till nearly 12 o'clock. I had one candle lit on the chair—I went and got another, but could not see, there was something like a cloud, and I thought I would go down and get a knife and cut my throat, but could not see. I groped about in master's room for a razor—I could not find one—at last I found his keys, and then found his razor. I went up to Georgy, and cut her first; I did not look at her. I then came to Carry, and cut her. Then to Harry—he said, 'don't mother'. I said, 'I must' and did cut him. Then I went to Bill. He was fast asleep. I turned him over. He never awoke, and I served him the same. I nearly tumbled into this room. The two children here, Harriet and George were awake. They made no resistance at all. I then lay down myself".

I have not found in records of the trial or in contemporary newspaper reports that May Brough ever used those words or any at all like them. They were made up by a hack. They are a fairly typical description in that the full, gruesome details are given and the maximum horror is extracted from the terrible situation. But it is also, to my mind, sincere and moving, an honest response to a situation not unfamiliar or ever far from the minds of harrassed, Victorian lower class wives. In spite of the horrific intentions, the feeling it creates is of tragedy and compassion. Contemporary readers, initially attracted by the classic horror situation, would recognise kinship with Mary Brough; her tragedy would reach them at the level of common meanings and shared experience. For them it could never be just a cautionary tale or a shocking story, for the anonymous author, motivated by commercial pressures though he was, shaped it from experience to satisfy public taste, and put into it imaginative and social meanings which he held in common with his readers. It affects us today because those meanings—the pathetic murder of her children by a distraught, depressed mother—are ones we can easily share. We cannot so easily enter the world of the public executions. We may feel horror when reading of them but it requires a serious, conscious effort to try and appreciate the complex, subtle effects—the common meanings—which these would have had in a society permeated by public executions, on those for whom the gallows was an ever present threat.

I have dwelt on the execution papers not because they were so popular but because they illustrate an important point about broadsides and popular culture in general: that cultural forms which enjoy immense and sustained favour, however humble or debased they or their audience might be, embody social and individual experience worthy of serious attention. The political broadsides, also 'commercial' although apparently representing considered political viewpoints, those illustrating the popular attitude to Popery, the broadsides on the Royal Family, even the 'cocks' and 'catchpennies', they all tell us something about the nature and experience of the Victorian lower classes. They are not great, or even good art; indeed they represent a different order of experience which is not amenable to such criteria. And they have little to offer if culture is conceived of as one wholly aesthetic order of artistic merit, ranging, perhaps, from Shakespeare down to an unspeakable nether world which includes broadsides.

But if one honestly and profoundly accepts what is obvious: that different levels and orders of experience and sophistication produce and require different levels of culture, then the way is open for evaluating broadsides and popular culture, not against Shakespeare or other 'high' art, but against the common experiences and needs of people. It is in this spirit that *Curiosities of Street Literature* is offered to the reader.

Michael Hughes.

LONG-SONG SELLER.

(From a Daguerreotype by BEARD.*)*

" Three yards a penny ! Three yards a penny ! Beautiful songs !
Newest songs ! Popular songs ! Three yards a penny !
Songs, songs, songs !"

CURIOSITIES

OF

STREET LITERATURE:

COMPRISING

"COCKS," OR "CATCHPENNIES,"

A LARGE AND CURIOUS ASSORTMENT OF

STREET-DROLLERIES, SQUIBS, HISTORIES, COMIC TALES IN PROSE AND VERSE,

BROADSIDES ON THE ROYAL FAMILY,

POLITICAL LITANIES, DIALOGUES, CATECHISMS, ACTS OF PARLIAMENT,

STREET POLITICAL PAPERS,

A VARIETY OF "BALLADS ON A SUBJECT,"

DYING SPEECHES AND CONFESSIONS.

TO WHICH IS ATTACHED THE ALL-IMPORTANT AND NECESSARY

AFFECTIONATE COPY OF VERSES,

AS

"Come, all you feeling-hearted Christians, wherever you may be,
Attention give to these few lines, and listen unto me;
It's of this cruel murder, to you I will unfold,
The bare recital of the same will make your blood run cold."

"What hast here? ballads? I love a ballad in print, or a life; for then we are sure they are true."—SHAKESPEARE.

"There's nothing beats a stunning good murder, after all."—EXPERIENCE OF A RUNNING PATTERER.

LONDON:

REEVES AND TURNER,

196, STRAND.

1871.

NOTICE.

The "Execution Paper" of John Gregson, for the Murder of his Wife, at Liverpool—page 235 of CONTENTS—is CANCELLED, and Eight Pages, "THE HEROES OF THE GUILLOTINE," supplied instead.

196, STRAND,
December 30th, 1870.

INTRODUCTION.

In selecting and arranging this collection of "Street Papers" for publication, every care has been taken to print them *verbatim et literatim*. They all bear the printer's name and address were such is used, and, in many cases, the wood-cuts have either been borrowed or purchased for the purpose of presenting them in their original style. The real object being to show, in the most genuine state, the character and quality of the productions written expressly for the amusement of the lower orders by street-authors. The general instruction given to our printer has been to "set up word for word from copy, with the exception of qunɹǝd lǝʇʇǝɹs *(sic)* and those of a WʀOng FoNт (?)"—it being thought quite unnecessary to repeat these *convenient* and at that time *compulsory* "Errors of the Press," and which were very common in former days with the printers and publishers of street and public-house literature; arising alike from a want of skill in the art, a deficiency of capital, and the hurried manner in which they were prepared and worked off to meet the momentary demand.

Old "Jemmy" Catnach—whose name is ever associated with the literature of our streets—was a man who hated "innowations," as he used to call improvements, and had a great horror of buying type, because, as he used to observe, he kept no standing formes, and when certain sorts run short, he was not particular, and would tell the boys to use anything which would make a good shift. For instance, he never considered a compositor could be aground for a lowercase l while he had a figure of 1 or a cap. I to fall back upon ; by the same rule, the cap. O and figure 0 were synonymous with "Jemmy ;" the lower-case p, b, d, and q, would all do duty for each other in *turn*, and if they could not always find roman letters to finish a word with, why the compositor knew very well that the "reader" would not mark out ita*lic*.

At the time Catnach commenced business, "Johnny" Pitts,* of the Toy and Marble Warehouse, No. 6, Great St. Andrew Street, was the acknowledged and established Printer of Street-Literature for the "Dials" district ; therefore, as may be easily imagined, a powerful rivalry and vindictive jealousy soon arose between these "two of a trade"—most especially on the part of "Old Mother" Pitts, who is described as being a coarse and vulgar-minded personage, and as having originally followed the trade of a bumboat woman at Portsmouth : she "vowed vengeance against the young fellow in the court for daring to set up in their business, and also spoke of him as young "Catsnatch," "Catblock," "Cut-throat," and many other opprobrious terms being freely given to the new comer. Pitts' staff of "bards" were duly cautioned of the consequences which would inevitably follow should they dare to write a line for Catnach—the new *cove* in the court. The injunction was for a time obeyed, but the "Seven Bards of the Dials" soon found it not only convenient, but also more profitable to sell copies of their effusions to both sides at the same time, and by keeping their own council they avoided detection, as each printer accused the other of buying an early sold copy, and then reprinting it off with the utmost speed, and which was in reality often the case, as "Both Houses" had an emissary on the constant look-out for any new production suitable for street-sale. Now, although this style of "Double dealing" and competition tended much to lessen the cost price to the "middle-man," or vendor, the public in this case did not get any of the reduction, as a penny broadside was still a penny, and a quarter sheet still a halfpenny to them, the "street-patterer" obtaining the whole of the reduction as extra profit.

The feud existing between these rival publishers, who have been somewhat aptly designated as the Colburn and Bentley of the "paper" trade, never abated, but, on the contrary, increased in acrimony of temper until at last not being content to vilify each other by words alone, they resorted to printing off virulent lampoons, in which Catnach never failed to let the world know that "Old Mother Pitts" had been formerly a bumboat woman, while the Pitts announced that—

> "All the boys and girls around,
> Who go out prigging rags and phials,
> Know Jemmy *Catsnatch*!!! well,
> Who lives in a back slum in the Dials.
>
> He hangs out in Monmouth Court,
> And wears a pair of blue-black breeches,
> Where all the "Polly Cox's crew" do resort
> To chop their swag for badly printed Dying Speeches.

At length Catnach, from the possession of greater capital and business acumen, became—to use the words of our informant —"the Cock of the Walk," and continued so until his retirement in 1839. In his Will—or Last Dying Speech—which was proved April, 1842, "James Catnach, of Dancer's Hill, South Mimms, in the county of Middlesex, gentleman, formerly of Monmouth Court, Monmouth Street, printer, bequeathed the whole of his estate to his sister Anne, the widow of Joseph Ryle, in trust, nevertheless, for her daughter, Marion Martha Ryle, until she obtain the age of twenty-one years. Witnesses—William Kinsey, 13, Suffolk St., Pall Mall, Solr. Wm. Tookey his clerk."

The present street literature printers and publishers are Mr. W. S. Fortey (Catnach's successor), of 2 and 3, Monmouth Court, Seven Dials. Mr. Henry Disley (formerly with Catnach), 57, High Street, St. Giles's. Mr. Taylor, Brick Lane, Spitalfields. Mr. H. Such, 177, Union Street, Borough ; and Mr. J. Harkness, 121, Church Street, Preston. From whose "establishments" upwards of two thousand street "papers" and "ballads" have been obtained, and from which—together with a private collection —we have made our selection to form "The Curiosities of Street Literature."

With such a vast amount of "material" to hand, it is somewhat difficult to know which to retain and which to reject. It being utterly impossible to reproduce the whole, the only thing to be done is to make the attempt to divide them into something like classes. We have, therefore, arranged our collection into four divisions, which may be briefly alluded to as—I. "Cocks," or "Catchpennies." II. Royalty and Political. III. Ballads on a Subject. IV. Dying Speech and Confessional Papers.

During the progress of our "Collection" through the press, we had, by a special appointment, an interview with Mr. John Morgan, a street author, and who may be said to be the oldest of his peculiar class. "I'm the last one left of our old crew, Sir," he observed during our conversation. He is now upwards of 70 years of age, and formerly wrote for "Old Jemmy" Catnach,

---

* Pitts, a modern publisher of love garlands, merriments, penny ballads,—
"Who, ere he went to heaven,
Domiciled in Dials Seven !"—G. Daniel's "Democritus in London."

with whose personal history he is well acquainted, and still continues to write for the " Seven Dials Press." A street ballad from his pen will be found at page 103 of our work. In allusion to Mr. John Morgan, the writer of an article on " Street Ballads " in the *National Review* for October, 1861, makes the following remarks :—

"This ballad—'Little Lord John out of Service'—is one of the few which bear a signature. It is signed 'John Morgan' in the copy which we possess. For a long time we believed this name to be a mere *nom-de-plume* ; but the other day, when making a small purchase in Monmouth Court, we were informed, in answer to a casual question, that this is the real name of the author of some of the best comic ballads. Our informant added, that he is an elderly, we may say old, gentleman, living somewhere in Westminster ; but the exact whereabouts we could not discover. Mr. Morgan followed no particular visible calling so far as our informant knew, except writing ballads, by which he could not earn much of a livelihood, as the price of an orginal ballad, in these buying-cheap days, has been screwed down by publishers to somewhere about a shilling sterling. Something more like bread-and-butter might be made perhaps by poets who were in the habit of singing their own ballads, as some of them do, but not Mr. Morgan. Should this ever meet the eye of that gentleman (a not very probable event, we fear), we beg to apologise for the liberty we have taken in using the verses and name, and hope he will excuse us, having regard to the subject in which we are his humble fellow-labourers. We could scarcely avoid naming him, the fact being that he is the only living author of street ballads whose name we know. That self-denying mind, indifferent to worldly fame, which characterised the architects of our cathedrals and abbeys, would seem to have descended on our ballad-writers ; and we must be thankful, therefore, to be able to embalm and hand down to posterity a name here and there, such as William of Wykeham, and John Morgan. In answer to our inquiries in this matter, generally we have been told, 'Oh, any body writes them" and with that answer we have had to rest satisfied. But in presence of that answer, we walk about the streets with a new sense of wonder, peering into the faces of those of our fellow-lieges who do not carry about with them the external evidence of overflowing exchequers, and saying to ourselves, 'That man may be a writer of ballads.' "

With regard to illustrations, a ballad-printer is in the habit of buying up old wood-cuts which have been engraved for any other works, and of applying them to his own purposes ; disregarding alike their age, rudeness, and condition. Most of those adopted are repeatedly employed over and over again. The printers of " broadsides " seldom care whether an ornament of the kind used is, or not, appropriate to the subject of the ballad, so long as it is likely to attract attention. Many examples will be found in this collection, and we are indebted to Mr. H. Disley and others for the use of the same.

"The authors and poets who give this peculiar literature, alike in prose or rhyme to the streets, are all in some capacity or another connected with street-patter or song ; and the way in which a narrative or a 'copy of verses' is prepared for the press is usually this:—The leading members of the 'schools'—some of whom refer regularly to the evening papers—when they hear of any out-of-the-way occurrence, resort to the printer and desire its publication in a style proper for the streets. This is usually done very speedily, the school—or a majority of them—and the printer agreeing with the author. Sometimes an author will voluntarily prepare a piece of street-literature and submit it to a publisher, who, as in case of other publishers, accepts or declines, as he believes the production will or will not prove remunerative. Sometimes the school carry the manuscript with them to the printer, and undertake to buy a certain quantity to insure publication. The payment to the author is the same in all cases—a shilling ; but sometimes if the printer and publisher like the verses he "throws a penny or two over." And sometimes also, in case of a great sale there is the same "over-sum." The "Dials" and its immediate neighbourhood is the chief residence of these parties, as being nearest to the long-established printer they have made it the 'head meet' of the fraternity.

"It must be borne in mind that the street-author is closely restricted in the quality of his effusions. It must be such as the patterers approve, as the chanters can chant, the ballad singers sing, and—above all, such as the street buyers will buy."*

We have recently met, near the Strand, the street ballad singer of our youth, and, from whom we procured, "Wait for the Turn of the Tide," and " Call her back and Kiss Her," and the following information—" Oh, yes, I remember you, remember you well; particularly when I see you down at Brighton ; when you treated me to that hot rum and water ; when I was so wet and cold, at a little snug public-house in one of the streets that leads off the main street. I don't remember the name on it now, but I remembers the rum and water well enough ; it was good. You said it would be, and so it was, and no mistake. How old am I now ? Why, 59. How long have I been at it ? Why, hard on fifty years. I was about nine or ten year old—no, perhaps I might have been 12 year old, when I come to think on it. Yes, about 12 year old ; my mother was a widow with five children, and there was a boy in our street as used to go out singing ballads, and his mother said to my mother, 'Why don't you let your boy (that's me) go out and sing ballads like my boy.' And I said I didn't mind, and I did go out, and I've been at it ever since, so you see it 'aint far short of 50 year. How many do I sell in a day ? Well, not so many as I used to do, by a long way. I've sold me four and five quires a-day, but I don't sell above two and three dozen a-day now. That's all the difference you see, sir—dozens against quires. How do I live then ? Why, you see I am now so well-known in different parts of London, that lots and lots of people comes up to me—like you always do—and says—'How do you do, old fellow ? I remember you when I was a boy, if its a man, and when I was a girl, if its a woman.' And says, 'So you are still selling songs, eh ?' Then they give me a few coppers ; some more and some less than others, and says they don't want the songs. Some days—very often—I've had more money giving me than I've took for the ballads. Yes, I have travelled all over England—all over it I think—but the North's the best—Manchester, Liverpool, and them towns ; but down Bath and Cheltenham way I was nearly starved. I was coming back from that way, I now remember, when I met you, sir, at Brighton that time. I buy my ballads at various places—but now mostly over the water, because I live there now and it's handiest. Mr. Such, the printer, in Union-street in the Borough. Oh ! yes, some at Catnach's—leastways, it ain't Catnach's now, it's Fortey's. Yes, I remember 'old Jemmy Catnach' very well ; he wa'n't a bad sort, as you say ; leastways, I've heard so, but I never had anything of him. I always paid for what I had, and did not say much to him, or he to me—writing his life of him, are you indeed ? No, I can't give you no more information about him than that, because, as I said before, I bought my goods as I wanted them, and paid for them, then away on my own account and business. Well, he was a man something like you—a little wider across the shoulders, perhaps, but about such a man as you are. I did know a man as could have told you a lot about 'old Jemmy,' but he's dead now ; he was one of his authors, that is, he wrote some of the street-ballads for him, and very good ones they used to be, that is, for selling. Want some old 'Dying Speeches' and 'Cocks,' do you indeed ; well, I a'nt got any—I don't often 'work' them things, although I have done so sometimes, but I mostly keep to the old game—'Ballads on a Subject.' You see them other things are no use only just for the day, then they are no use at all, so we don't keep them—I've often given them away. You'd give sixpence a piece for them, would you, indeed, sir ; then I wish I had some of them. Now I come to think of it I know a man that did have a lot of them bye him, and I know he'd be glad to sell them. I don't know where he lives, but I sometimes see him. Oh ! yes, a letter would find me. My name is Samuel Milnes, and I live at No. 81, Mint-street, that's in the Borough ; you know, Guager is the name at the house. Thank you, sir, I'm much obliged. Good day, sir."

It will be seen that our street-ballads and "papers" come down to the latest period, several being issued during the printing of this collection ; in fact, any public affair seems of sufficient importance to write a ballad about. We have, therefore, placed some blank leaves between each division, for the purpose of mounting other examples that may be from time to time published by the printers of Street Literature.

*"Mayhew's London Labour and the London Poor."

CONTENTS.

DIVISION IV.

The "Gallows" Literature of the Streets.

"For that cruel murder he's doomed to die
On Norwich fatal sad gallows high."

"I am doomed to die, my glass is run,
For the murder of my darling son."

A COLLECTION

OF

"COCKS," OR "CATCHPENNIES."

"The common people are to be caught by the ears as one catches a pot by the handle."

CURIOSITIES

OF

STREET LITERATURE.

DIVISION I.

A COLLECTION

OF

"COCKS," OR "CATCHPENNIES,"

STREET DROLLERIES, SQUIBS, HISTORIES,

COMIC TALES IN PROSE AND VERSE.

"Cocks—fictitious narratives, in verse or prose, of murders, fires, and terrible accidents, sold in the streets as true accounts. The man who hawks them, a patterer, often changes the scene of the awful event to suit the taste of the neighbourhood he is trying to delude. Possibly a corruption of Cook, a cooked statement, or, as a correspondent suggests, the Cock Lane ghost may have given rise to the term. This had a great run, and was a rich harvest to the running stationers."—Hotten's Slang Dictionary.

"Few of the residents in London—but chiefly those in the quieter streets," says Mr. Henry Mayhew, in his exceedingly amusing work of "London Labour and the London Poor,"—"have not been aroused, and most frequently in the evening, by a hurly-burly on each side of the street. An attentive listening will not lead any one to an accurate knowledge of what the clamour is about. It is from a 'mob' or 'school' of running patterers, and consists of two, three, or four men. All these men state that the greater the noise they make, the better is the chance of sale, and better still when the noise is on each side of the street, for it appears as if the vendors were proclaiming such interesting or important intelligence, that they were vieing with one another who should supply the demand which must ensue. It is not possible to ascertain with any creditude *what* the patterers are so anxious to sell, for only a few leading words are audible, as 'Horrible,' 'Dreadful,' 'Murder,' 'One penny,' 'Love,' 'One penny,' 'Mysterious,' 'Seduction,' 'Former crimes,' 'Nine children,' 'Coal-cellar,' 'Pool of blood,' 'One penny,' and the like, can only be caught by the ear, and there is no announcement of anything like ' particulars.' The running patterers describe, or profess to describe, the contents of their papers as they go along, and they seldom or never stand still. They usually deal in murders, seductions, crim.-cons., explosions, alarming accidents, ' assassinations,' deaths of public characters, duels, and love-letters. But popular, or notorious murders are the 'great goes.' The running patterer cares less than any other street-sellers for bad weather, for if he 'work' on a wet and gloomy evening, and if the work be 'A COCK,'—which is, a fictitious statement,—there is less chance of anyone detecting the *ruse*. Among the old stereotyped 'cocks' are love-letter. One is well known as a Married Man caught in a Trap." And being in a dialogue and an epistolary form, subserves any purpose: as the 'Love-Letters,' that have passed between Mr. Smith, the butcher, baker, grocer, draper, &c.—' the decoyer of female innocence'—and Mrs. Brown, Mrs. Jones, or Mrs. Robinson, or Miss A—, B—, or C—, not 100 yards off—'And the very image of his father,' &c., &c.—and can be fitted to any real or pretended local scandal.

When the patterer visits the country, he is accompanied by a mate, and the " copy of verses" is then announced as being written by an "underpaid curate" within a day's walk. " It tells mostly, sir," said one man ; " for its a blessing to us that there always is a journeyman parson what the people knows, and what the patter fits." Sometimes the poetry is attributed to a sister of mercy, or to a popular poetess ; very frequently, by the patterers who best understand the labouring classes, to Miss Eliza Cook. Sometimes the verses are written by a "sympathising gent" in that parish, " but his name wasn't to be mentioned, or any nobleman or gentleman," whose name is before the public in connection with any recent event, or an assumed account of "A Battle between Two Ladies of Fortune." The patterers have only to stick a picture in their hat to attract attention, and to make all the noise they can.

Occasionally, the running patterer transmigrates into a standing one, betaking himself to "board work," as it is termed in street technology, and stopping at the corners of throughfares with a large pictorial placard raised upon a pole, and glowing with highly-coloured exaggerations of the interesting terrors of the pamphlet he has for sale.

When there are no "popular murders" the standing patterer orders of the artist a new and startling "cock-board" and sells his books or pamphlets, the titles of some of which are fully set forth and well displayed ; for example : "Horrible murder and mutilation of Lucy Game, aged 15, by her cruel brother, William Game, aged 10, of Westmill, Hertfordshire. His committal and confession, with a copy of a letter sent to his affectionate parents." "Full particulars of the poisonings in Essex,—the whole family poisoned by the female servant. Confession of her guilt.—Was seduced by her master.—Revenged herself on the family." Another is—"Founded on facts"—The Whitby Tragedy, or the Gambler's Fate, containing the lives of Joseph Carr, aged 21, and his sweetheart, Maria Leslie, aged 18, who were found dead, lying by each other on the morning of the 23rd of May. Maria was on her road to town to buy some ribbon and other things for her wedding day, when her lover, in a state of intoxication, fired at her, then run to rob his prey, but finding it was his sweetheart, reloaded his Gun, placed the Muzzle to his Mouth, and blew out his Brains, all through the cursed Cards and Drink. With an affectionate copy of verses."

A popular street-book for "board work" is entitled "Horrible Rape and Murder !!! The affecting case of Mary Ashford, a beautiful young virgin, who was diabolically Ravished, Murdered, and thrown into a Pit, as she was returning from a Dance. including the Trial of Abraham Thornton for the Wilful Murder of the said Mary Ashford ; with the whole of the Evidence, Charges to the Jury, &c., with a Correct Plan of the Spot where the Rape and Murder were Committed."

This "street-book" is founded on a fact, and, in reality, gives the salient points of a memorable circumstance which took place in 1817, when Abraham Thornton was charged at the Warwick Assizes, before Mr. Justice Holroyd, for the murder and violation of Mary Ashford, at Erdington, near Birmingham. The prisoner was found—after a consultation of the jury of five minutes— Not Guilty, to the utmost surprise and disappointment of all persons assembled. The second charge of committing a rape on the body of the said Mary Ashford was abandoned by the prosecution. The case created the greatest possible sensation at the time, and the trial and subsequent appeal were printed and published in a separate form, and occupies 120 pages in double columns, "with a correct plan of the spot where the rape and murder were committed, and a portrait of Thornton drawn and engraved by G. Cruikshank."

The acquittal of Thornton in the atrocious rape and murder of Mary Ashford excited the most undisguised feelings of disappointment in all classes of persons throughout the kingdom, and various provincial newspapers began to canvass the subject with vigour, freedom, and research. This aroused most of the London papers, and the *Independent Whig* on Sunday, August 17th after fully commenting on the case, cited several instances where individuals, who, after having been arraigned under the charge of murder and acquitted, were tried a second time for the same offence, in consequence of an appeal by the next of kin of the deceased against the verdict of the jury, and wound up their remarks by that,—"If ever there was a case of brutality, violation and murder, that had greater claims upon the sympathy of the world than another, and demands a second trial, we think it is exhibited in that of the unfortunate Mary Ashford." This gave the "key-note," a very large section of the press adopted the same view of the case, and a subscription was immediately set on foot—Mary's friends being in indigent circumstances—to defray the necessary expences. And Abraham Thornton was apprehended a second time, on a Writ of Appeal, for the murder of Mary Ashford, which excited an interest in the public mind altogether unprecedented—an interest that was heightened by the unusual recurrence of the obsolete proceedings necessary in the case by the Saxon Writ of Appeal, together with the staggering fact of Thornton having challenged his appellant—William, the eldest brother of the deceased Mary Ashford—to a solemn trial by battle, and avowing himself ready to defend his innocence with his body.

The challenge was formally given by throwing down a glove upon the floor of the Court of King's Bench, whence the case had been removed by "Writ of Habeas Corpus," to be heard before Lord Ellenborough. But the combat did not take place, and the prisoner escaped. An Act of Parliament was then passed abolishing the trial by battle in any suit, as a mode unfit to be used.

Mary Ashford was buried in the Churchyard of Sutton Colefield, and over her remains is placed a stone with the following inscription, written by the Rev. Luke Booker :—

"As a warning to female virtue, and a humble
Monument to female chastity,
This stone marks the grave of
MARY ASHFORD,
Who, in the 20th year of her age,
Having incautiously repaired to a
Scene of amusement, without proper protection,
Was brutally violated and murdered
On the 27th of October, 1817."

The artist who paints the patterers' boards, must address his art plainly to the eye of the spectator. He must use the most striking colours, be profuse in the application of scarlet, light blue, orange—not yellow—that not being a good candle-light colour—and must leave nothing to the imagination. Perspective and back-grounds are things but of minor considertion, everything must be sacrificed for effect. These paintings are in water colours, and are rubbed over with a solution of gum-resin to protect them from the influence of rainy weather.

The charge of the popular street-artist for the painting of a board is 2s. or 3s. 6d., according to the simplicity or elaborateness of the details ; the board itself is provided by the artist's employer. The demand for this peculiar branch of street art is very irregular, depending entirely upon whether there has or has not been perpetrated any act of atrocity, which has rivetted, as it is called, the public attention. And so great is the uncertainty felt by the street-folk whether "the most beautiful murder will take or not," that it is rarely the patterer will order, or the artist will speculate, in anticipation of a demand, upon preparing the painting of any event, until satisfied that it has become "popular." A deed of more than usual daring, deceit, or mystery, may be at once hailed by those connected with murder-patter as "one that will do," and some speculation may be ventured upon, as it was in such cases as Greenacre, Rush, Tawell, and the Mannings, but these are merely exceptional, so uncertain, it appears, is all that depends, without intrinsic merit, on mere popular applause.

It is stated that Catnach cleared over £500 by Weare's murder and Thurtell's trial and execution, and was so loth to leave it, that when a wag put him up to a joke, and showed him how he might set the thing a-going again, he could not withstand it, so about a fortnight after Thurtell had been hanged "Jemmy" brought out a startling broad-sheet, headed "WE ARE ALIVE AGAIN !" He put so little space between the two words "WE" and "ARE," that it looked at first sight like "WEARE." Many thousands were bought by the ignorant and gullible public, but those who did not like the trick called it a "CATCHPENNY," and this gave rise to this peculiar term, which ever afterwards stuck to the issues of the "Seven Dials Press."

For the use of the first two wood cuts in our collection of "Cocks" and "Catchpennies" we are indebted to the kindness of Messrs. Charles Griffin and Co., of Stationers' Hall Court, the present proprietors of Mayhew's *London Labour and the London Poor* —a work which, of all others, gives by far the best description of LONDON STREET-FOLK ; and is of itself a complete cyclopædia of the condition and earnings of—those that *will* work, those that *cannot* work, and those that *will not* work. We had intended to have used the originals of "Jemmy" Catnach, but Mr. W. S. Fortey, his successor, writes to inform us that, after a lengthened and active service, the cuts in question were worked and worked until they fell to pieces.

With these remarks we now introduce our readers to a genuine Catnachian "Cock," and one that is said to have "fought well in its day," entitled, "Horrid Murder Committed by a Young Man on a Young Woman."

HORRID MURDER,

Committed by a young Man on a young Woman.

George Caddell became acquainted with Miss Price and a degree of intimacy subsisted between them, and Miss Price, degraded as she was by the unfortunate step she had taken, still thought herself an equal match for one of Mr. Caddell's rank of life. As pregnancy was shortly the result of their intimacy, she repeatedly urged him to marry her, but he resisted her importunities for a considerable time. At length she heard of his paying his addresses to Miss Dean, and threatened, in case of his non-compliance, to put an end to all his prospects with that young lady, by discovering everything that had passed between them. Hereupon he formed a horrid resolution of murdering her, for he could neither bear the thought of forfeiting the esteem of a woman who he loved, nor of marrying one who had been as condescending to another as to himself. So he called on Miss Price on a Saturday and requesting her to walk with him in the fields on the following day, in order to arrange a plan for their intended marriage. Miss Price met him at the time appointed, on the road leading to Burton, at a house known by the name of "The Nag's Head." Having accompanied her supposed lover into the fields, and walked about till towards evening, they sat down under a hedge, where, after a little conversation, Caddell suddenly pulled out a knife and cut her throat, and made his escape, but not before he had waited till she was dead. In the distraction of his mind he left behind him the knife with which he had perpetrated the deed, and his case of instruments. On the following morning, Miss Price being found murdered in the field, great numbers went to take a view of the body, among whom was the woman of the house where she lodged, who recollected that she said she was going to walk with Mr. Caddell, on which the instruments were examined and sworn to have belonged to him. He was accordingly taken into custody.

J. Catnach, Printer, Monmouth Court.

CRUEL AND INHUMAN MURDER
Committed upon the body of Captain Lawson.

It is with surprise we have learned that this neighbourhood for a length of time, was amazingly alarmed this day, by a crowd of people carrying the body of Mr James Lawson to a doctor, while streams of blood besmeared the way in such a manner, that cries of murder re-echoed the sound of numerous voices. It appears that the cause of alarm, originated through a courtship attended with a solemn promise of marriage, between him and Miss Lucy Gurd, a handsome young lady of refined feelings, with the intercourse of a superior enlightened mind, who lived with her aunt, who spared neither pain, nor cost, to improve the talents of Miss G. these seven years past, since the death of her mother in Ludgate Hill, London, and bore a most excellent character, until she got entangled by the deluding allurements of Mr L., who after they mutually agreed and appointed the nuptial day, not only violated his promise, (on account of her fortune being small,) but boasted thro' the neighbourhood of the unbecoming manner he had triumphed over her virtue (which left her in a languishing situation those six months past) while he chanted his eloquence to another young lady, of a stamp more adequate to a covetous mind, (namely of a great fortune) who took such a deep impression in his heart, that he advanced the most energetic gallantry, and obtained her consent, got the banns published in London, and on the point of getting married to her, with a rapturous prospect of holding a rural wedding, yet we find that the intended bride had learned that Miss Gurd held certain promissory letters of his, and that she determined to enter an action against him for a breach of promise, which moved, clouded and eclipsed over the variable Mr Lawson, who knew that Miss Gurd had letters of his, sufficient to substantiate her claim in a Court of Law. However, he was determined to remove that obstacle, at all events, which was not likely to diminish the only idol which the twofold miscreant so faithfully worshipped — namely, gold and that

nothing should prevent his intended wedding, but it appears, when he comes to traverse his imagination, that two unexpected obstacles greatly embarrassed his proceedings. He demanded from her his letters at the peril of her life, which Miss G. like a distinguished young lady, refused, and prepared herself with unequal fortitude, and after stating to him the consequences of his unmanly conduct she cautiously ordered him to quit the premises, where to confirm his ambition (which crowned his reward) he readily attempted to get near her trunk, through which a sturdy scuffle ensued, and while she screamed for assistance, he attempted to commit an outrageous violation on her person, when to protect her virtue, she drew a large carving knife, and stabbed him under the left breast (which quickly brought him to subjection), his vehement cries alarmed the neighbours, who came to her assistance, and found them both in a contest at the door, while she thrusted him out in a gore of blood, which exhibited a scene of such momentary confusion, that the most anxious conjecture was unable to draw the slightest idea on the wanton provocation, yet it appears that though the skillful physicians succeeded in stopping the blood, that they can form but little hopes of his recovery, as they are doubtful as to the knife having separated an artery, and should thus prove to be the case, they are decidedly of opinion, that it will put a certain period to his existence, which leaves the intended bride to bewail her disappointment, while the valiant victress was forced to submit to judicial decorum in the 19th year of her age, where sufficient sponsors voluntary offered to join her recognisance, to await the issue. The whole of her evidence being bound to appear on her final trial (which will gratify the curious where we expect the judge of equity will give an electrical oration, on amorous gallantry, passionate affection, breach of promises, &c., when Cupid's private Ambassadors, or the precious Love Letters will appear unmasked at Chelmsford ensuing Assizes.—*Epping Telegraph.*

J. Catnach, Printer, Monmouth Court, Seven Dials.

The Life, Trial, Execution, Lamentation, and Letter written by the unfortunate man

James Ward,

Aged 25, who was hung in front of the Gaol,

For the Wilful Murder he committed on the body of his Wife, near Edminton.

TRIAL.

At an early hour on the morning of the trial, the court was crowded to excess, the Judge taking his seat at nine o'clock. The Prisoner, on being placed at the bar, pleaded 'Not Guilty' in a firm tone of voice. The trial lasted many hours, when, having been found 'GUILTY,' the learned Judge addressed the prisoner as follows:—

"Prisoner, you have been found guilty of a most cold-blooded murder, a more deliberate murder I never heard of. You and your wife had been to a neighbouring town, and were returning home, when you did it. She was found in a ditch. I cannot hold out the slightest hope of mercy towards you in this case." During this address the whole court was melted into tears. His Lordship then put on the black cap and passed the sentence as usual, holding out no hope of mercy to the prisoner.

Letter written after his Condemnation.

Dear Sister,   Condemned Cell.

When you receive this you will see that I am condemned to die; my Father and Mother are coming to take their last farewell, and I should very much liked to have seen you, but knowing that you are on the eve of bringing into the world another to your family, I beg that you will refrain from coming; if that you do serious may be the consequences, therefore, dear Sister, do not attempt to come. I hope that no one will upbraid you for what I have done; so may God bless you and yours; farewell! dear sister for ever.   J WARDE

EXECUTION.

The Execution of the above prisoner took place early this morning at eight o'clock, the people flocking to the scene at an early hour. As the period of the wretched man's departure drew near, the chaplain became anxious to obtain from him a confession of the justice of the sentence. He acknowledged the justice of his sentence, and said he was not fit to live, and that he was afraid to die, but he prayed to the Lord for forgiveness, and hoped through the merits of his Saviour that his prayer would be heard. Having received the sacrament, the executioner was not long in performing his office. The solemn procession moved towards the place of execution, the chaplain repeating the confession words, "In the midst of life we are in death." Upon ascending the platform he appeared to tremble very much. The cap being drawn over his eyes and the signal given, the wretched man was launched into eternity. He died almost without a struggle. After the body had hanged the usual time it was cut down and buried according to the sentence, in the gaol.

LAMENTATION.

Come all you feeling hearted christians, wherever you may be,
Attention give to these few lines, and listen unto me;
Its of this cruel murder, to you I will unfold,
The bare recital of the same will make your blood run cold.

Confined within a lonely cell, with sorrow I am opprest,
The very thoughts of what I've done deprives me of rest;
Within this dark and gloomy cell in the county Gaol I lie,
For murder of my dear wife I am condemned to die.

For four long years I'd married been, I always lov'd her well,
Till at length I was overlooked, oh shame for me to tell;
By Satan sure I was beguiled, he led me quite astray,
Unto another I gave way on that sad unlucky day.

I well deserve my wretched fate, no one can pity me,
To think that I in cold blood could take the life away;
I took a stake out of the hedge and hit on the head,
My cruel blows I did repeat until she were dead.

I dragged the body from the stile to a ditch running by,
I quite forgot there's One above with an all-seeing eye,
Who always brings such deeds to light, as you so plainly see,
I questioned was about it and took immediately.

The body's found, the inquest held, to prison I was sent,
With shame I do confess my sin, with grief I do repent;
And when my trial did come on, I was condemned to die,
An awful death in public scorn, upon the gallows high.

While in my lonely cell I lie, the time draws on apace,
The dreadful deeds that I have done appear before my face;
While lying on my dreadful couch those horrid visions rise,
The ghastly form of my dear wife appears before my eyes.

Oh may my end a warning be now unto all mankind,
And think of my unhappy fate and bear me in your mind;
Whether you are rich or poor, your wives and children love,
So God will fill your fleeting days with blessings from above.

Rocliff, Printer, Old Gravel Lane, London.

SHOCKING RAPE AND MURDER OF TWO LOVERS.

Showing how John Hodges, a farmer's son, committed a rape upon Jane Williams, and afterwards Murdered her and her lover, William Edwards, in a field near Paxton.

This is a most revolting Murder. It appears Jane Williams was keeping company, and was shortly to be married to William Edwards, who was in the employment of Farmer Hodges. For some time a jealousy existed in John Hodges, who made vile proposals to the young girl, who although of poor parents was strictly virtuous. The girl's father also worked on farmer Hodges's estate. On Thursday last she was sent to the farm to obtain some things for her mother, who was ill; it was 9 o'clock in the evening when she set out, a mile from the farm. Going across the fields she was met by the farmer's son, who made vile proposals to her, which she not consenting to, he threw her down, and accomplished his vile purpose. In the meantime her lover had been to her house, and finding she was gone to the farm, went to meet her. He found her in the field crying, and John Hodges standing over her with a bill-hook, saying he would kill her if she ever told. No one can tell the feelings of the lover, William Edwards. He rushed forward, when Hodges, with the hook, cut the legs clean from his body, and with it killed the poor girl, and then run off. Her father finding she did not return, went to look for her; when the awful deeds were discovered. Edwards was still alive, but died shortly afterwards from loss of blood, after giving his testimony to the magistrates. The farmer's son was apprehended, and has been examined and committed to take his trial at the next Assizes.

Thousands of persons followed the unfortunate lovers to the grave, where they were buried together.

Copy of Verses.

Jane Williams had a lover true
  And Edwards was his name,
Whose visits to her father's house,
  Had welcome now became.

In marriage soon they would be bound,
  A loving man and wife,
But John Hodges, a farmer's son,
  With jealousy was rife.

One night he met her in the field,
  And vile proposals made ;
How can I do this wicked thing ;
  Young Jane then weeping said.

He quickly threw her on the ground,
  He seized her by surprise,
And did accomplish his foul act,
  Despite her tears and cries.

Her lover passing by that way,
  Discovered her in tears,
And when he found what had been done
  He pulled the monster's ears.

Young Hodges with the bill-hook,
  Then cut young Edwards down :
And by one fatal blow he felled
  Jane Williams on the ground.

There side by side the lovers lay
  Weltering in their blood :

Young Jane was dead, her lover lived,
  Though ebb'd away life's flood.

Old Williams sought his daughter dear,
  When awful to relate,
He found her lifeless body there,
  Her lover's dreadful fate.

Now in one grave they both do lie,
  These lovers firm and true,
Who by a cruel man were slain,
  Who'll soon receive his due.

In prison now he is confined,
  To answer for the crime.
Two lovers that he murdered,
  Cut off when in their prime.

J. Catnach, Printer, Monmouth Court.

d

FULL PARTICULARS

OF THIS

DREADFUL

MURDER.

A scene of bloodshed of the deepest dye has been committed in this neighbourhood, which has caused a painful and alarming sensation among all classes in this place, in consequence of its being committed by an individual that is well known to most of the inhabitants who are going in great numbers to the fatal spot where the unfortunate and ill-fated victim has met with this melancholy and dreadful end.

On the news arriving at our office, we at once dispatched our reporter to the spot, and on his arrival he found the place surrounded by men, women, and children, gathered around where the vital spark had fled, which was never to be regained on the face of this earth. Deep was the conversation among the accumulated persons, as to how a fellow creature could be guilty of committing such a revolting and diabolical act upon one, who, it appears, was much respected in this neighbourhood.

The reporter states that on the police authorities arriving at the place, they had some difficulty in preserving order; but after a short lapse of time this was accomplished. They then proceeded to the spot where the lifeless corpse laid, and took possession of the same, and which presented one of the most awful spectacles that has been witnessed for many years.

What could have been the motive for such a cold-blooded and wanton murder being committed we are at a loss to conceive; without it was in consequence of some disagreement having taken place between the unfortunate victims and their assailants, and then ending in the depriving their fellow-creatures of life, which we are forbidden, according to the commandments, to take away; but this seems to be entirely violated in many instances by our dissipated and irregular habits which tends to the committal of such serious things, and through disobeying the scriptural advice brings the degraded creatures to an untimely end. According to the Scriptures, " He that sheddeth man's blood, by man shall his blood be shed," which we entirely agree with in these instances, and fully acknowledge the just sentence that is often obliged to be carried into effect; and certainly must say, that were it not for the rigidness of those laws, many of us would not be able to proceed on our journey at heart. So, therefore, we are in duty bound to call upon those laws being fully acted up to, for it is our opinion that those crimes are very seldom committed without there is some disregard or ill feeling towards their unfortunate victims, and thereby end their days in a dreadful manner.

The unfortunate persons being so well known and so much respected, every one feels anxious to know all particulars, and it is the constant enquiry amongst them to know if there is any one apprehended for the murder, or if there is anything more known as to lead to the suspicion who it has been committed by, all being very desirous to hear of the perpetrators of this diabolical and horrid deed. We feel much for the family, who are thrown into the greatest affliction through this dreadful circumstance, and which has cast a gloom over the circle of friends in which they moved.

As a member of society, there will be no one that we know of who will be more missed; one who was often known to relieve the wants of his fellow creatures as far as his circumstances would permit, and whose society was courted by all. As a member, of the family to which they belonged, none will be more deeply regretted, but those who are now remaining will feel the loss and deplore the lamentable death of their respected and worthy friends.—Just as we are going to press, we have received information from our reporter, that something has been elicited from a party that has thrown a light on this subject, and which has led to the apprehension of one of the principal offenders, and who, if proved guilty, will, we hope, meet with that punishment due to his fearful crime.

London: J. Lucksway, Printer and Publisher, High Street, Westminster.

THE COMMITTAL OF
W. THOMPSON,

To the County Gaol at Oxford for the

MURDER OF HIS WIFE

AND THREE CHILDREN,
On the 12th instant.

This morning, the 12th inst., the neighbourhood of Queen-st., Banbury, was thrown into a state of excitement at hearing the cries of murder between the hours of 12 and 1, at the house of Wm. Thompson. Several of the neighbours arose from their beds and knocked at, and tried the door, but all was silent, when Sarah Cope said, some efforts must be made to enter, and two Policemen were quickly on the spot, and about 2 o'clock they forced the door open, when a most awful sight presented itself. The wife lay weltering in her blood and with her head literally knocked to pieces, and the prisoner, who was drunk, was quickly apprehended. Up stairs the two youngest were found lying in a pool of blood on the chamber floor, and the eldest boy, Thomas, four years old, was found a lifeless corpse on the bed, and the clothes covered with blood.

Two surgeons pronounced life to be extinct. An inquest was held at the Blue Boar, and after a post-mortem examination of the bodies, and the whole of the Evidence heard by the Jury, a Verdict of Wilful Murder was returned against William Thompson.

The Prisoner was calm during the whole of the proceedings, and did not attempt to deny his guilt. Since his committal he has made the following Confession.

THE CONFESSION.

On the 12th ultimo, I left my wife and family and went to the house of Sarah Potts, and during the day when we were drinking, she asked me to leave my family and live with her; I gave her no decisive answer at that time. At midnight I returned home and found my wife and children were gone to bed, but she got up and let me in without speaking an angry word; but I got hold of an iron bar and struck her a fatal blow on the head, and repeated the blows until she was dead. I then proceeded to the bed-room, where the children were. My eldest son, Thomas, four years of age, begged for mercy, but I was deaf to his cries and tears; I then raised the bar of iron and struck him three times on the head; the two youngest are twins, I beat their heads against the chamber floor, and I hope the Lord will forgive me.

A COPY OF VERSES.

ALL you that have got feeling hearts, I pray you now attend,   (lend,
To these few lines so sad and true, a solemn silence
It is of a cruel murder, to you I will unfold—
The bare recital of the tale, must make your blood run cold.

'Twas in the town of Banbury, all in fair Oxfordshire,
One William Thomson did reside, by trade a Carpenter,
He had a kind and loving wife, likewise three children dear,   (hear,
Who victims fell unto his rage, as shortly you may

The one it was a little boy, just turned two years old,
The other two were lovely boys, the truth I now unfold,
Long time he kept his family, in credit and renown,
Until he was led astray, by a woman on the town—

One Sarah Potts it was her name, who first did him betray,   (astray,
And from his wife and children, caused him to go
At rest from her he ne'er could be, by day nor yet by night,   (quite.
Until her false deluding tongue, had proved his ruin

It was on the 12th day of the month, unto her house he went   (intent;
A drinking, for to spend the day, it was his chief
She says, come leave your house and home, your family also,
And to some other country, along with you I'll go.

About the hour of twelve at noon, he homeward did repair,   (share—
And found his poor deluded wife, waiting his love to
One angry word she never spoke, though he unkind had been   (in.
But with the meekness of a lamb, she rose to let him

Soon as the house he entered, he straightway locked the door,   (floor;
Soon seized upon an iron bar, and threw her on the
With which he beat her on the head, as she lay on the ground,   (around.
Her brains most awful for to view, lay scattered all

Oh then he seized those lovly twins, whilst sleeping on the bed,   (ther said—
Now with your mother you shall die, the wretched fa-
He seized them by their little legs, and dashed them on the floor,   (more.
And soon their tender lives were gone, alas! to be no

The eldest child seeing what was done, upon his knees did rise,   (his eyes—
And loud for mercy he did call, whilst tears were in
Oh, Dadda dear, oh, Dadda dear, and asked me for a kiss,
Why are you going to murder me, what have I done amiss?   (fall,

Again for mercy he did plead whilst pearly tears did
The cruel father's hardened heart, was deaf unto his call—
Again took up the iron bar, and beat him on the head,
And soon the blood of the dear boy, was spilt upon the bed.

It was early the next morning, before the break of day,
He by Policemen taken was, and to prison sent straightway,   (stand,
Where till the Assizes he must lie, his trial for to
When blood for blood will be required, by the laws of God and man.

[Smith, Printer, High Street, London.

A REMARKABLE PUNISHMENT

OF

MURDER.

The following melancholy account was given by a very worthy man, Mr. Thomas Marshall, a Church-warden well-known and respected by all.

Some years ago, a young gentleman and lady came out of Scotland, as is supposed, upon a matrimonial affair. As they were travelling through the country, they were robbed and murdered, at a place called the Winnetts, near Castleton. Their bones were found about two years ago, by some miners who were sinking an Engine-pit at the place.

One James Ashton, of Castleton, who died about a fortnight ago, and who was one of the murderers, was most miserably afflicted and tormented in his conscience. He had been dying, it was thought, for ten weeks; but could not die till he had confessed the whole affair. But when he had done this, he died immediately.

He said, Nicholas Cock, Thomas Hall, John Bradshaw, Francis Butler, and himself, meeting the above gentleman and lady in the Winnets, pulled them off their horses, and dragged them into a barn belonging to one of them, and took from them two hundred pounds. Then seizing on the young gentleman, the young lady (whom Ashton said was the fairest woman he ever saw) entreated them, in the most piteous manner, not to kill him, as she was the cause of his coming into that country. But, notwithstanding all her intreaties, they cut his throat from ear to ear! They then seized the young lady herself, and, though she entreated them, on her knees, to spare her life, and turn her out naked! yet one of the wretches drove a Miner's pick into her head, when she dropped down dead at his feet. Having thus dispatched them both, they left their bodies in the barn, and went away with their booty.

At night they returned to the barn, in order to take them away; but they were so terrified with a frightful noise that they durst not move them: and so it was the second night. But the third night, Ashton said it was only the Devil, who would not hurt him; so they took the bodies away and buried them.

They then divided the money: and as Ashton was a coal carrier to a Smelt Mill, on the Sheffield Road, he bought horses with his share; but they all died in a little time. Nicholas Cock fell from a precipice, near the place where they had committed the murder, and was killed. Thomas Hall hanged himself. John Bradshaw was walking near the place where they had buried the bodies, when a stone fell from the hill and killed him on the spot, to the astonishment of every one who knew it. Francis Butler, attempted many times to hang himself, but was prevented; however, he went mad, and died in a most miserable manner.

Thus, though they escaped the hand of human justice (which seldom happens in such a case), yet the Invisible Hand found them out, even in this world. How true then it is, that He art about our path, and about our bed, and spiest out all our ways!

Evans, Printer, Long Lane.

THE LIFE, TRIAL, CHARACTER, AND CONFESSION

OF

The Man that was Hanged

IN FRONT OF NEWGATE, AND WHO

IS NOW ALIVE!

WITH FULL PARTICULARS OF THE RESUSCITATED.

"There are but two classes of persons in the world—those who are hanged, and those who are not hanged; and it has been my lot to belong to the former."

THERE are few men, perhaps, who have not a hundred times in the course of their life, felt a curiosity to know what their sensations would be if they were compelled to lay life down. The very impossibility, in all ordinary cases, of obtaining any approach to this knowledge, is an incessant spur pressing on the fancy in its endeavours to arrive at it. Thus poets and painters have ever made the estate of a man condemned to die one of their favourite themes of comment or description. Footboys and 'prentices hang themselves almost every other day, conclusively—missing their arrangement for slipping the knot half way—out of a seeming instinct to try the secrets of that fate, which —less in jest than in earnest—they feel an inward monition may become their own. And thousand of men, in early life, are uneasy until they have mounted a breach, or fought a duel, merely because they wish to know, experimentally, that their nerves are capable of carrying them through that peculiar ordeal.

Now *I* am in a situation to speak from experience, upon that very interesting question—the sensations attendant upon a passage from life to death. I have been HANGED, and am ALIVE—perhaps there are no three other men at this moment, in Europe, who can make the same declaration.

Before this statement meets the public eye, I shall have quitted England for ever; therefore I have no advantage to gain from its publication. And, for the vanity of knowing, when I shall be a sojourner in a far country, that my name—for good or ill—is talked about in this,—such fame would scarcely do even my pride much good, when I dare not lay claim to its identity, But the cause which excites me to write is this—My greatest pleasure, through life, has been the perusal of any extraordinary narratives of fact. An account of a shipwreck in which hundreds have perished; of a plague which has depopulated towns or cities; anecdotes and inquiries connected with the regulations of prisons, hospitals, or lunatic receptacles; nay, the very police reports of a common newspaper—as relative to matters of reality, have always excited a degree of interest in my mind, which cannot be produced by the best-invented tale of fiction. Because I believe, therefore, that to persons of a temper like my own, the reading of that which I have to relate will afford very high gratification ;—and because I know also, that what I describe can do mischief to no one, while it may prevent the symptoms and details of a very rare consummation from being lost; for these reasons I am desirous, as far as a very limited education will permit me, to write a plain history of the strange fortunes and miseries to which, during the last twelve months, I have been subjected.

I have stated already, that I have *been* hanged and *am* alive. I can gain nothing now by misrepresentation —I was GUILTY of the act for which I suffered. There are individuals of respectability whom my conduct already has disgraced, and I will not revive their shame and grief by publishing my name. But it stands in the list of capital convictions in the Old Bailey Calendar for the Winter Sessions of 18—

Hodges, Printer (from the late J. Pitt's) Wholesale Toy Warehouse, 31, Dudley Street, 7 Dials.

THE LIVERPOOL TRAGEDY.

Showing how a Father and Mother barbarously Murdered their own Son.

A few days ago a sea-faring man, who had just returned to England after an absence of thirty years in the East Indies, called at a lodging-house, in Liverpool, for sailors, and asked for supper and a bed; the landlord and landlady were elderly people, and apparently poor. The young man entered into conversation with them, invited them to partake of his cheer, asked many questions about themselves and their family, and particularly of a son who had gone to sea when a boy, and whom they had long given over as dead. At night the landlady shewed him to his room, and when she was leaving him he put a large purse of gold into her hand, and desired her to take care of it till the morning, pressed her affectionately by the hand, and bade her good night. She returned to her husband and shewed him the accursed gold : for its sake they mutually agreed to murder the traveller in his sleep.

In the dead of the night, when all was still, the old couple silently creaped into the bed room of their sleeping guest, all was quiet : the landlady approached the bedside, and then cut his throat, severed his head from his body; the old man, upwards of seventy years of age, holding the candle. They put a washing-tub under the bed to catch his blood. And then ransacking the boxes of the murdered man they found more gold, and many handsome and costly articles, the produce of the East Indies, together, with what proved afterwards, to be a marriage certificate.

In the morning, early, came a handsome and elegantly dressed lady and asked, in a joyous tone, for the traveller who had arrived the night before. The old people seemed greatly confused, but said he had risen early and gone away. "Impossible!" said the lady, and bid them go to his bed-room and seek him, adding, "you will be sure to know him as he has a mole on his left arm in the shape of a strawberry. Besides, 'tis your long lost son who has just returned from the East Indies, and I am his wife, and the daughter of a rich planter long settled and very wealthy. Your son has come to make you both happy in the evening of your days, and he resolved to lodge with you one night as a stranger, that he might see you unknown, and judge of your conduct to wayfaring mariners."

The old couple went up stairs to examine the corpse, and they found the strawberry mark on its arm, and they then knew that they had murdered their own son, they were seized with horror, and each taking a loaded pistol blew out each other's brains.

Printed by J. Catnach,—Sold by Marshall Bristol. Just Published—A Variety of Children's Books, Battledores, Lotteries, and a quantity of popular Songs, set to Music. Cards, &c., Printed cheap.

5

THE MASSACRE

OF THE WHOLE OF THE

PASSENGERS AND PART OF THE CREW
OF THE SEA HORSE,

On her Homeward Passage from Sydney, and the Plunder of 18,000 ounces of Gold by the Murderers.

We have just received intelligence of one of the most daring cases of plunder and wholesale murder on the high seas that it is our duty to make public for many years. It appears that the crew and thirteen passengers of the ill-fated ship, the Sea Horse, some of whom had been seeking to better their condition by toiling at the diggings of Ballarat, Bendigo, and the several numerous diggings of the surrounding country, whilst others had gained a respectable position in life by mercantile and other pursuits, all returning light-hearted and elated by their good success to the land of their birth, and to look on the dear faces, and gladden the hearts of the dear ones they had left at home, but whom they were doomed never to meet no more on earth. Among the crew was a Spaniard known by the name of Digo Salvesata, and three others, who were tempted by a love of gold to gain possession of the valuable cargo, to do which, they conceived the horrid idea of putting the whole of the passengers and that part of the crew who would not join them to death. The following are the facts of this demon-like outrage :—It appears that the Sarah Ann, of North Shields, on her passage home, was driven by the gales into the German ocean, and it was in sight of the white cliffs of Old England that these horrible murders were committed. As the Sarah Ann was laying at anchor on the morning of the 12th, at day break they saw through the fog the ill-fated vessel, and not seeing any one on deck they hailed her, and on receiving no answer a boat was immediately lowered, and they went on board, and on getting below a shocking sight met their gaze, with one exception the whole of the passengers and the remainder of the crew were in their berths stiff and cold, with their throats cut, and otherwise dreadfully disfigured. One poor man had a piece of dirty sheet tied tightly round his throat, and about eight inches of it stuffed tightly into his mouth. On this being removed, there was a large wound in the throat four inches in extent from right to left; there were five incisors on the right side ending in one deep one on the left. The windpipe was cut through and the muscles of the neck on the left side; the forehead was contused and scratched. The hair was covered with blood. On the back part of the right hand there were several scratches. Most of the victims were more or less mutilated. On going to the Captain's cabin another shocking sight presented itself, he was laying completely hacked to pieces, his tongue was completely cut out at the root, and his entrails strewed on the cabin floor, showing that there had been a terrible struggle; it appears from the statement of a man who had stowed in the hold to escape the slaughter, that the second mate, who is one of the murderers, treated the passengers and the rest of the crew with some grog in which some laudnum was mixed, which rendered them senseless, and while in that helpless state murdered them in the manner described, they afterwards went to the Captain's cabin, who fought bravely but was overpowered by numbers, they then took all the gold they could find and lowered the long boat and made off with their ill-gotten gains. The tiller of the boat has been found, so whether they have escaped and sent the boat adrift is not known, but search is being made after the murderers, and we hope they will soon be taken, and meet with their just reward.

COPY OF VERSES.

You landsmen and you seamen bold,
   Attention give to me,
While I a tragedy unfold,
   Upon the briney sea;
In the German ocean it occurred,
   Near the sight of land,
Twenty-eight fell victims
   To the cursed murderers hands.

The Sea Horse it from Sydney sailed,
   Bound for Old England's shore,
With crew and thirteen passengers,
   Whose fate we now deplore;
Returning home with hard earned gold,
   Across the briney main,
But alas! the ones they loved at home,
   They ne'er will see again.

Four of the crew they laid a plan,
   The passengers to slay,
And with the gold they dearly earnt,
   O'er the seas to bear away;

These murderers were led away,
   All by their thirst for gold,
And their victims they did cruelly slay,
   Most shocking to unfold.

In some grog they mixed some laudanum
   And soon they fell asleep,
And then these wretched monsters
   To their victim's berths did creep;
Then to the Captain's cabin,
   Intent on blood did steer,
And mangled his poor body,
   How dreadful for to hear.

The Sarah Ann from North Shields,
   As by the facts appear,
Saw the poor ill-fated ship,
   And boarded it we hear;
And found the gory victims—
   How shocking for to read,
May the murderers soon be taken
   And suffer for their deeds.

Walton, Printer, Mary Street, Limehouse.

FULL PARTICULARS

OF THE

HORRIBLE & DREADFUL

GREAT FIRE IN LONDON.

[Few public calamities recorded in our annals can bear a comparison, in point of distress, with the tremendous conflagration which reduced the greater part of the British metropolis to ashes, in the 1666. Of this dire catastrophe, all our histories give a general, and some of them a detailed, account; but no relation hitherto published is so minutely descriptive as that written at the time, and as it were on the smoking embers of the city, by the ingenious John Evelyn; from whose memoirs we have therefore extracted the whole narration.]

September 2. This fatal night about ten began that deplorable fire near Fish Street, in London.

Sept. 3. The fire continuing, after dinner I took coach, with my wife and son, and went to the bank side in Southwark, where we beheld that dismal spectacle, the whole city in dreadful flames near the waterside; all the houses from the bridge, all Thames street, and upwards towards Cheapside down to the Three Cranes, were now consumed.

The fire having continued all this night (if I may call that night which was light as day for ten miles round about, after a dreadful manner), when conspiring with a fierce eastern wind in a very dry season; I went on foot to the same place, and saw the whole south part of the city burning from Cheapside to the Thames, and all along Cornhill (for it kindled back against the wind as well as forward) Tower street, Fenchurch street, Gracious street, and so along to Bainard's Castle, and was now taking hold of St. Paul's Church, to which the scaffolds contributed exceedingly. The conflagration was so universal, and the people so astonished, that from the beginning, I know not by what despondency or fate, they hardly stirred to quench it, so that there was nothing heard or seen but crying out and lamentation, running about like distracted creatures, without attempting to save even their goods, such a strange consternation there was upon them, so as it burned both in breadth and length, the Churches, Public Halls, Exchange, Hospitals, Monuments, and ornaments, leaping after a prodigious manner from house to house and street to street, at great distances one from the other, for the heat with a long set of fair and warm weather had even ignited the air and prepared the materials to receive the fire, which devoured after a most incredible manner, houses, furniture, and every thing. Here we saw the Thames covered with goods floating, all the barges and boats laden with what some had time and courage to save, as, on the other, the carts, &c., carrying out to the fields, which for many miles were strewed with moveables of all sorts, and tents erecting to shelter both people and what goods they could get away. Oh the miserable and calamitous spectacle! such as haply the world had not seen the like since the foundation of it, nor to be outdone till the universal conflagration. All the sky was of a fiery aspect, like the top of a burning oven, the light seen above forty miles round about for many nights. God grant my eyes may never behold the like, now seeing above ten thousand houses all in one flame; the noise and cracking and thunder of the impetuous flames, the shrieking of women and children, the hurry of people, the fall of towers, houses, and churches, was like a hideous storm, and the air all about so hot and inflamed that at last one was not able to approach it, so that they were forced to stand still and let the flames burn on, which they did for near two miles in length and one in breadth. The clouds of smoke were dismal and reached upon computation near fifty miles in length. Thus I left it this afternoon burning, a resemblance of Sodom, or the last day. London was, but is no more!

H. Jones, Printer, Smith Street, London.

7

AN ACCOUNT

OF THE

FATAL THUNDERSTORM,

Which happened in these parts, and the

SINGULAR DREAM OF A YOUNG MAN,

Well known in this Neighbourhood.

On the first day of this month there was a dreadful storm of thunder and lightning in these parts. Its most fatal effects occurred about three miles from this town. There was a young shepherd, about twenty-three years of age, who had always entertained a remarkable dread of such storms; on that day, as it began to grow cloudy, his mother would have dissuaded him from going out, but he said he must go, as certain of his sheep absolutely required his attendance. This was agreeable to a tenderness of temper which, from his childhood, had been remarkable in his character. Quickly after he got into the fields, the storm arose; he was then in an open valley of greensward, and upon the neighbouring land there were two places of shelter equally distant; the one a stack of beans where some men were employed in thrashing, the other a rick of hay where nobody was. Humanly speaking, his life depended upon the choice he made between these two places, and he unhappily chose the rick. Quickly after, the thrashers at a small distance saw it take fire! They immediately ran to extinguish it, which they did without any great difficulty, as stacked hay burns but slowly; but they found the shepherd dead! His heels were stuck up, and his back rested against a part of the rick which had not been on fire. On a more careful examination, they found that his coat was singed on the right shoulder; his waistcoat did not appear to be burnt; but his shirt was reduced to tinder, not only on the shoulder, but all over the back. The skin under it appeared a little blistered, but the flesh not at all torn. His right leg was blistered round the outer ankle, and his shoe-buckle shattered almost to perfect powder. There was no wound on any part of the body which could be thought the cause of his death. About a month before this accident he told his mother a dream which struck deeply upon his imagination for a considerable time. He said he fancied himself surprised by a storm of thunder, and that he fled for shelter to the wall of a house, when a great flash of lightning came directly upon him, and that immediately he fancied himself strangled for want of breath.

About three months previous to this melancholy occurrence the same young man, who is well known in these parts, and whose name and address we withhold out of respect to his surviving relations, dreamt that as he sat on a fragment of St. John's Castle, romantically situated on the shores of Loch-Ree—one of those many ruins that are to be found in desolated parts of this county! The scene around him was one of age and sublimity: he felt its imposing effect and was filled with the solemnity of its aspect! The winds were sweeping their sullen murmurs through the broken walls of the gigantic pile; the "voice of Time-disport-ing towers" fell with a sad sound upon the ear, and he could fancy, in the pauses of the hollow blast, that he saw spectral shapes of other days peeping from the dark passages and broken windows, and then suddenly disappearing like night-birds, that, having wakened too early for their dusky evening flight, shrink back aghast to their gloomy bowers, from the offensive glare of a lingering sunset! Melancholy and romance were in the hour, and he insensibly yielded to their powerful influence.

As his half-closed eyes were carelessly fixed upon a little chasm in the vaulted floor, that lay some fifty feet beneath him, he perceived, with a surprise not unmixed with terror, that the long grass which partly concealed it began to move with more than the wind-motion. He thought a thin blue smoke issued from the widening aperture, and a confused murmur of hollow voices arose. He would have fled from the place, but his companions had, at his own request, left him to indulge in melancholy, and had taken his boat for a short sail to some islands farther up the lake; besides, he had no means of quitting the almost insulated ruin, but by passing the mysterious vapour, which crossed the only path to a strip of land that connected the basement of the castle with the main shore. This he was determined not to do. He therefore quietly remained in the watch-tower with mingled feelings of curiosity and dread!

The blue mist at length disappeared—the murmur of hollow voices died away—all was silent again save the beach-wave and the moaning of the wind through the caverns of the ruin. He began to think he had imagined the scene, and was just about to quit his hiding-place, when suddenly the vapour issued again, and, thunder-struck with astonishment and admiration, he beheld a female figure slowly rising from the vault like a spirit from earth's tomb on its way to immortal blessedness! she was lightly clad—lightly enough to betray a form of beauty, half-woman, half-child, that he had never before contemplated, even in his dreams! It was loveliness even beyond his ideal conceptions, and seemed to be of that age when childhood usually gives her last portion of innocence to youth, and fearfully resigns her little charge to approaching maturity.

She ascended, with the rapidity of a winged creature, up a curtain-wall that shut out the northern view of the lake from the interior of the castle, when, having gazed long and wistfully (as he thought) upon the dim sail of his little bark in the hazy distance, she descended with the same careless activity, to a mound of ivy and wild flowers that sprung up spontaneously in the ruin, like sweet, but unbidden recollections of happy days gone by in a broken heart.

THE SCARBOROUGH TRAGEDY.

Giving an Account how Susan Forster, a Farmer's only Daughter, near Scarborough, was seduced by Mr Robert Sanders, a Naval Officer, under promise of Marriage. How she became Pregnant, and the wicked hardened, and cruel Wretch appointed to meet her at a well-known retired spot, which she unhappily did, and was basely Murdered by him, and buried under a Tree, and of the wonderful manner in which this base Murder was brought to light, and he was committed to Gaol.

YOUNG virgins fair of beauty bright,
　　And you that are of Cupid's fold,
Unto my tragedy give ear,
　　For it's as true as e'er was told.
In Yorkshire, liv'd a virgin fair,
　　A farmer's only daughter dear,
And young sea-captain did her ensnare,
　　Whose station was her father near.

Susannah was this maiden's name,
　　The flower of all that country,
This officer a courting came,
　　Begging that she his love would be.
Her youthful heart to love inclin'd,
　　Young Cupid bent his golden bow,
And left his fatal dart behind,
　　Which prov'd Susannah's overthrow.

Ofttimes at evening she would repair,
　　Close to the borders of the sea,
Her treach'rous love would meet her there,
　　The time it passed most pleasantly,
And while they walked the sea-banks over,
　　To mark the flowing of the tide,
He said he'd be her constant lover
　　And vow'd that she should be his bride.

Within the pleasant groves they walk'd,
　　And vallies where the lambs do play,
Sweet pleasant tales of love they talk'd,
　　To pass away the summer day.
My charming lovely Susan, said he,
　　See how the pleasant flowers spring,
The pretty birds on every tree,
　　With melody the groves doth ring.

I nothing want for to delight
　　My soul, but those sweet charms of thine,
My heart is fix'd, therefore my dear,
　　Like the turtle-dove let us combine,
Let me embrace my heart's delight,
　　Within this pleasant bower here ;
This bank of violets for our bed,
　　Shaded with these sweet roses fair,

She said, what can you mean, I pray,
　　I am a farmer's daughter born.
What signifies my beauty bright,
　　A trifle, when my honour's gone.
My parents they will me disdain,
　　Young virgins they will me deride,
Oh ! do not prove my overthrow,
　　If you love me stay till your bride.

Sweet angel bright, I here do vow,
　　By all the powers that are divine,
I'll ne'er forsake my dearest dear,
　　The girl that does my soul confine.
And if that you will me deny,
　　This sword shall quickly end my woe,
Then from her arms he ran straightway
　　In fury, out his sword he drew.

Her hands as white as lilies fair,
　　Most dreadfully she then did wring
She said, my death's approaching near,
　　Would I pity take and comfort him
It only brings my fatal fall,
　　'Tis I who must receive the wound
The crimson dye forsook her cheeks,
　　At his feet she dropp'd upon the ground.

Thus innocence he did betray,
　　Full sore against her chaste desire ;
True love is a celestial charm,
　　The flame of lust a raging fire.
But when her senses did revive,
　　He many vows and oaths did make,
That he'd for ever true remain,
　　Her company would not forsake.

Now virgins in the second part,
　　Observe this maiden's fatal end,
When once your virtue is betray'd,
　　You've nothing young men will commend.
After the traitor had his will
　　He never did come near her more,
And from her eyes both day and night,
　　For his sake the crystal tears did pour,

Into a mournful valley she crossed,
　　Would often wander all alone,
And for the jewel she had lost
　　In the bower would often mourn.
Oh ! that I were some pretty bird,
　　That I might fly to hide my shame ;
O silly maid, for to believe
　　The fair delusions of a man.

The harmless lamb that sports and plays,
　　The turtle's constant to his mate,
Nothing so wretched is as I,
　　To love a man that does me hate.
I will to him a letter send,
　　Remind him of the oaths he made
Within that shady bower, where
　　My tender heart he first betray'd.

Her trembling hand a letter wrote,
　My dearest dear, what must I do?
Alas! what have I done, that I
　Forsaken am now by you!
I could have wedded a worthy farmer,
　Who little knows my misery;
I did forsake a wealthy grazier,
　All for the love I bore to thee.

And now my little infant dear
　Will quickly spread abroad my shame,
One line of comfort to me send,
　E'er I am by your cruelty slain.
This answer he to her did send,
　Your insolence amazes me,
To think that I should marry one
　With whom, before, I have been free.

Indeed I'll not a father be
　Unto a bastard you shall bear,
So take no further thought of me,
　No more from you pray let me hear.
When she this letter did receive,
　She wrung her hands and wept full sore:
And every day she still would range,
　To lament within the pleasant bower.

The faithless wretch began to think,
　Her father's rich, as I do hear,
He said, I sure shall punished be,
　Soon as the story he does hear.
The devil then he did begin
　To enter in his wretched mind;
Her precious life he then must have,
　Thus he to act the thing did find.

He many times did watch her out,
　Into the pleasant valley, where
One day he privately did go,
　When he knew she was not there.
And privately he dug a grave
　Underneath an oaken tree.
Then in the branches he did hide,
　To act his piece of cruelty.

Poor harmless soul she nothing knew,
　As usual she went there alone,
And on a bank of violets
　In mournful manner sat her down.
Of his unkindness did complain;
　At length the grave she did espy,
She rose indeed to view the same,
　Not thinking that he was so nigh.

You gentle gods so kind, said she,
　Did you this grave for me prepare?
He then descended from the tree,
　Saying, strumpet now thy death is near.
O welcome, welcome, she replied,
　As long as by your hand I die,
This is a pleasant marriage bed,
　I'm ready, use your cruelty.

But the heavens bring to light
　Thy crime, and thus let it appear,
Winter and summer on this grave,
　The damask rose in bloom spring here.
Never to wither though 'tis cropped,
　But when thy hand do touch the same,
Then may the bloom that minute blast
　To bring to light my bitter shame.

More she'd have said, but with his sword,
　He pierc'd her tender body through;
Then threw her in the silent grave,
　Saying, now, there is an end of you.
He fill'd the grave up close again,
　With weeds the same did overspread;
Then unconcerned, he straight went home,
　Immediately went to his bed.

Her parents dear did grieve full sore, at
　The loss of their young daughter,
Thinking she was stole away, as
　To all their riches she was heir to.
Twelve months after this was passed,
　Thousands for a truth do know,
According as she did desire,
　On her grave a damask rose grew.

Many wonder'd at the same,
　For in the winter it did spring,
If any one did crop the rose,
　In a moment it would grow again.
The thing it blazed the country round,
　And thousands went the same to see,
This miracle from heaven shew,
　He 'mong the rest must curious be.

To go and see if this was true,
　But when unto the plant he came,
The beauteous rose he saw in bloom,
　And eagerly he cropp'd the same.
The leaves did fall from off the bush,
　The rose within his hand did die,
He cried, 'tis fair Susannah's blood,
　That spring up from her fair body.

Many people that were there,
　Took notice of what he did say,
They told him he'd a murder done,
　He the truth confess'd without delay.
They dug and found the body there,
　'Twas but this month that it was known,
Before a magistrate he went,
　And now in prison lies forlorn.

Till he his punishment receives,
　No doubt but he will have his due;
Young men by this a warning take,
　Perform your vows whate'er ye do.
For God does find out many ways,
　Such heinous sins to bring to light,
For murder's a most horrid sin,
　And hateful in his blessed sight.

TRAGIC VERSES.

COME all fair maids both far and near and listen
    unto me,
While unto you I do relate a dreadful Tragedy,
A deed of blood I will unfold which lately came to light,
When 'tis made known, you'll surely own you never
    heard the like.

'Tis of an honest farmer's child, a damsel fair and
    young,   (tongue,
Who was in tender years beguil'd all by a flattering
The finest lady in the land could not with her compare,
Her dimpled cheeks and rosy looks how charming sweet
    they were.

Crowds of admirers flocking came, to gain fair Susan's
    love;   (move,
But none her favour could obtain, nor her affections
Till by mischance a youth she met, as fate would have
    it so,   (overthrow.
Who caught her heart in Cupid's net and prov'd her

A naval Captain of renown, beguil'd her tender youth,
Deceit and lies he did disguise with air of seeming truth,
He prais'd her looks, her shape, her air, vow'd she
    should be his wife,   (life.
And thus did vilely her ensnare—then took her precious

When he had thus her ruin prov'd by many a solemn
    vow,
The very maid he vow'd to love was hateful in his view.
With bitter tears she did implore that he'd his vows
    fulfil;   (his will.
But all in vain—she charm'd no more now he had had

She wrote a letter which she thought would grieve his
    heart full sore,   (swore,
And tenderly she him besought, to mind the vows he
T'was you that did my heart trepan, which now in tears
    I rue—
Slighted many an honest man all for the love of you.

I wish that my young babe was born and on the nurse's
    knee,   (over me.
And I myself was dead and gone and the grass grown
When he this letter through had read, which expos'd
    his villainy,
A deadly thought came in his head her butcher for to be.

With seeming kindness in his face which made poor
    Susan gay,
He did appoint a lonely place to meet with her next day.
The hour arriv'd, she hasten'd there to the appointment
    true,
Where the deceitful murderer the lovely damsel slew.

When she beheld his deadly knife she rais'd her lovely
    face,   (to disgrace,
Crying, Oh! spare, Oh! spare my life and leave me
Have pity on your unborn babe tho' you have none for
    me;
Alas! a dark untimely grave, my bridal bed will be.

Her lovely face, her beauteous eyes, for mercy plead in
    vain,
Of no avail were tears or cries unmov'd he did remain,
He rais'd his arm,—a deadly plunge, and down she
    weltering lay,   (dying breath did say.
And while her heart's-blood stain'd the ground, with

" Monster, the fearful crime you've done heaven's LORD
    will bring to light,   (sight.
" No human eye is looking on—none sees the cruel
" Yet righteous KING of heaven and earth my blood
    doth cry to thee,
" To visit my untimely death that all mankind may see."

Now when this deed of blood was done he dug a hole
    so deep,   (retreat,
And thrust her murdered body in, then homeward did
But vengeance did his crime requite for to his great
    dismay,
The horrid murder came to light all in a wond'rous way.

He did confess—they dug the ground while hundreds
    came to view.   (lov'd so true,
And here the murder'd corpse they found, of her who
In irons now in Prison strong lamenting he does lie;
And, by the laws condemn'd ere long, most justly he
    will die.

J. Catnach, Printer, 2, Monmouth-court, 7 Dials.

THE NAKED TRUTH,

OR

DIAMOND CUT DIAMOND,

BEING THE FULL ACCOUNT OF

AN EXTRAORDINARY WAGER OF £5000,

Laid between Lord ——— and the Duke's Son,

TWO MEN OF FASHION.

To Miss C———
When—fiercest storms are gone to rest,
Shall—mild and gentle calms succeed,
I—'m told, to ease the heart opprest,
Sleep—is the only balm we need.
With—these few lines, by nature taught,
You—will a simple question find;
My—meaning's plain, so find it out,
Love—will direct you, tho' he's blind.

Miss C———'s answer.
To—bless you is my soul's desire,
Night—brings in dreams my flame,
If—you can feel an equal fire,
You—'ll find me still the same.
Will—you be still of tender mind;
Bring—love not light, but constant kind,
The—world would ne'er see such a couple;
Parson—'s can conquer every scruple,

A few nights since, at a fashionable *hell* in the western part of this *well policed* metropolis, the following extraordinary wager was laid and decided. Lord ——— bet £5000 with the eldest son of the Duke of ——— who had frequently distinguished himself by his eccentricities, that he would carry him on his shoulders nine times round St. James's square after the business of the house was finished. At three o'clock in the morning, the parties, attended by their friends, repaired to the spot; but here Lord——— observed that his bet was to carry his opponent, but *not his clothes also.* However, the young hero of joking and smoking celebrity, was not to be done by his cunning adversary, and he actually, at that hour of the morning, with the wind sharp as a "serpent's tooth," stripped himself to the *buff.* Yes, gentle, refined, or rheumatic reader! he, this son of the Duke of ———, divesting himself of shame (if ever he had any), stripped himself of *all*, even to the most minute parts of his dress, and won £5000. And then covering himself, not with glory, but his clothes, went to finish at a bagnio, with the notorious and accommodating Miss C——— of ——— Square, not a hundred miles off.—**"These are the Men of Fashion!!"**

Batchelar, Printer, Long Alley.

EXTRAORDINARY & FUNNY DOINGS
IN THIS NEIGHBOURHOOD.

It is —— is a comical place,
    And you'll find from one end to the other,
And all classes of persons through life,
    Can daily find fault with the other.
Some can gossip and tattle about,
    And fill every person with dizziness,
What an excellent thing it would be,
    If people would mind their own business.

Did you see Mrs Bubble-and-squeak,
    Walk out with her young daughter Sally,
She has got on a new bonnet and shawl,
    And a nice handsome gown on the tally.
Such a bustle, oh ! dear, she does wear,
    Why cut up with pride I am sure she is,
Some can always see other folks' faults,
    But they never can mind their own business

Mrs Stradle has just gone along,
    Don't you think she's a queer sort of creature
She owes tenpence for chandler's shop score,
    Besides eighteen pence for the baker.
And she can drink gin like a fish,
    Which oft fills her head with dizziness,
But you know that is nothing to me,
    For I always do mind my own business.

Mrs Thingembob, what do you think,
    You know Mrs and Miss Carbuncle,
Last night took the pillows and sheets,
    Their flat irons and gowns to my uncle.
I think between you and me,
    It can be nothing more than laziness,
I wish you'd take my advice,
    Look at home and mind your own business,
And we shall all find enough for to do.

Madam,

The love and tenderness I have hitherto expressed to you is false, and I now feel that my indifference towards you increases every day, and the more I see you the more you appear ridiculous in my eyes, and contemptible—I feel inclined and in every respect disposed and determined to hate you. Believe me I never had any inclination to offer you my hand. Our last conversation I assure you left a tedious and wretched insipidity which has not possessed me with an exalted opinion of your character, your inconstant temper would make me miserable, and if ever we are united, I shall experience nothing but the hatred of my parents, added to the everlasting pleasure in living with you, I have a true heart to bestow, but however I do not wish you for a moment to think it is at your service, as I could not give it to one more inconstant and capricious than yourself, and one less capable to do honour to my choice, and my family. Yes, Madam, I beg and desire you'll be persuaded that I think seriously, and you will do me a great favour to avoid me.   I shall excuse you taking the trouble to give me an answer to this, as your letters are full of nonsense and impertinence, and have not a shadow of wit and good sense. Adieu, and believe me truly, I am so averse to you, that it is impossible I should ever be, Madam, your Affectionate Servant and Lover. R. G.

Sir,

The uniform tendency of your behaviour from the natural brutality of disposition evinced by you since the period of our acquaintance, has possessed me with a sovereign contempt of your understanding, without the most exalted opinion of your politeness and integrity, believe me, I have considered you a despisable being, and could I ever be induced to change my condition, you are the last person I should choose ; nay, I despise you you are only capable of inspiring in me such ideas. Though it has lowered me in my opinion, nevertheless your letter has afforded me satisfaction by convincing me I am not so contemptible a character as I should be did I possess your esteem. With respect to your heart I believe it to be quite as worthless as your letter, and did it offer me a refusal some difficulty might occur to decide whether to throw it on the dunghill or the fire. Matrimony is a union not to be formed without due care, my knowledge of you has redoubled caution on this point, and I should prefer you on such an event taking place, if like Polita I wish to deal in monkeys and apes— I cannot conclude without giving thanks for your candour, though in it you may have violated every rule of decency, and I shall follow your example by assuring you I am resolved never to subscribe myself what I really am not your well-wisher and sincere friend, E. H. M.

By reading every other line of the above letters the true meaning will be found.

THE LOVE LETTER,

The Lady's Maid!! The Secret Found out!!! Or

A MARRIED MAN CAUGHT IN A TRAP.

"Good morning, Sir."

"The same to you, Miss! Very happy to meet you here; how far are you going?"

"Not far, Sir; but I should be proud of your company for a short time."

"Thank you, Miss, I hope we shall be better acquainted e're long."

"I hope, Sir, you're unmarried?"

"Happy to say at present—I am!"

"Very well, Sir, I am at present without a sweetheart who has possession of my heart."

"My dear, I will endeavour to try to gain you."

"Excuse me, Sir, I am poor."

"My dear, I am only a theatrical gentleman, but very fond of the fair sex."

"Do you think, my cherub, that you will be able to keep us when we are wed?"

"Yes, my dear, for I will feed you on oysters, beef-steaks, and all such fattening and strengthening things as are necessary for our conjugal happiness and comfort."

"But, Sir, can I really depend upon you?"

"Yes, my dear, shall we name the day for our marriage?"

"Suppose we say, my love, the day after to-morrow."

"Agreed; until that, adieu."

On the morning appointed for the wedding, the young woman received the following epistle :—

"My Dearest Fanny.—I have thought on your proposal since last we met, but from circumstances that have transpired, I beg leave to postpone our marriage to a future day. I thought on our conversation and your delightful company ever since, and have enclosed a copy for your perusal.

"I am,
"Yours for ever,
"HENRY J.N.S.

"Light of my soul! by night and day,
I'll love thee ever;
Light of my soul! list to my lay,
I'll leave thee never.
Light of my soul! where'er I go,
My thoughts on thee are hov'ring;
Light of my soul! in weal or woe—
Send by the bearer a sovereign!"

The young woman read this letter with disdain, and wrote back the following answer :—

"Sir,—I return your note with disgust, having been informed that you are a married man, and I hope you will bestow the trash you offered me upon your wife. So pray trouble me no more with your foolery."

Poor H. took this so much to heart, that he went and drowned his senses in wine, and then returned home; undressing himself, the letter fell from his bosom, his wife picked it up, read it, and beat him about the head with a dish-cloth.

There are two ways of reading this to discover the parties. Henry ——— lives in THIS STREET, and Fanny ——— at the ——— shop round the corner, and is said to be no better than she should be. The child's name we understand is to be Anthony.

ALL FOUND OUT AT LAST,

Or the SECRET DISCOVERED,

After having been carried on in a curious manner for a long time.

"Most adorable Mary—

"Why have you left me, and deprived me of those pleasures of beholding the most charming face that nature ever made? How shall I find words to express the passion you have inspired me with? Since the day I first beheld your form I have felt the sharpest pangs of love, which have worked me up to the utmost pitch of distraction. But, alas! such a shock I felt as is impossible to express. The dearest object of my heart is locked in the embrace of Robert E—— that vile monster and decoyer of female innocence. Oh! never should I have thought that after so many pleasant hours we have passed together, and promises pledged on either side, that you would have slighted me in the manner you have, and find your heart callous to one who adores you, and even the ground your angelic form walks upon. Oh, my adorable angel, do not forsake me and the welfare of yourself; drop all connection with that vile deceiver, R. E., and once more reinstate me to that pleasure which none but lovers know. My fluctuation of fortune shall never abate my attachment, and I hope the day is not far distant, when I shall lead you to the altar of Hymen. Oh! soon may the time arrive when I may call thee, dearest Mary, my own. Oh! my dearest angel, consent to my request, and keep me no longer in suspense; nothing on my part shall ever be wanting to make you happy and comfortable. My engagement will expire in two months from hence, when I intend to open a shop in the small-ware line, and your abilities as a seamstress and self-adjusting

crinoline maker, with the assistance of a few work girls, shall be able to realize an independence; and, moreover, I will indulge you in all things needful in the marriage state, and show my regard for you by cleaning your shoes, lighting the fire every morning, buying crumpets, new butter, and so forth; besides, my dear Mary, we will live merrily upon beef-steak, oysters, and other tasty articles necessary for our conjugal happiness, and upon my bended kness I pray for it, and may earthly friendship and confidence, with truest love, continue to the end.

> "You are the first, I freely own,
> That raised love in my breast,
> Where now it reigns without control,
> But yet a welcome guest.
> Ah! must I drive the cherub hence,
> In sorrow to regret,
> And will you join to foster me,
> And me no more neglect."

"Most adorable Mary,—I have to repeat my former request, that is, quit R. E.'s company, and place yourself under the protection of me, only in whom you will find all the comfort that wedded life can bestow.

"I remain, dear Mary, yours till death,

"JOHN S——

"P. S.—Favor me, my angel, with an answer by return of post; if not, I shall start off directly for Liverpool, and embark for America."

THE YORKSHIRE KNIGHT,

OR THE

FORTUNATE FARMER'S DAUGHTER,

IN THREE PARTS.

PART I.—Showing how a noble Knight was riding by a farmer's house, when his wife was in travail. The Knight knowing the signs and planets, and looking on a book, read that the farmer's daughter that was born that hour was to be his lady and bride. And how the cruel Knight got the child from her parents, and flung it into a river; but by good fortune, the child was taken up by a poor fisherman alive, and brought home till she was eleven years old.

PART II.—How the fisherman was at an inn with some gentlemen, the cruel Knight being in the same company, and seeing the young girl come in, he asked the fisherman if she was his own daughter, who told the story of his taking her up, &c. How the cruel Knight got this poor girl away, and contrived her death a second time, and how he was prevented.

PART III.—How the Knight contrived her death a third time; but her life was saved, by showing the Knight a ring that he flung in the sea; when the Knight saw it, found it in vain to strive against his fortune, so he married her, and made her his lady; with other things worthy of note.

PART I.

In York fair city a farmer did dwell,
Who was belov'd by his neighbours full well;
He had a good wife who was virtuous and fair,
And by her he had a child every year.
In seven years time six children they had,
Which made both the father and mother's heart glad
But a little time after as we do hear say,
This farmer in money and stock did decay,
Although at one time he had riches in store,
But a little time after he quickly grew poor,
He strove all he could, but alas! could not thrive,
Nor hardly could keep his poor children alive.
But children came faster than silver or gold,
For his wife she conceived again as I'm told,
And when her time came in hard travail she fell,
But if you will mind, a strange wonder I'll tell;
A rich noble knight did chance to ride by,
And hearing this woman to shriek and to cry,
He being well learned in planets and signs,
Did look on a book which much puzzled his mind.
For the more he did look, still the more he did read,
And found that fate this young child had decreed,
Who was born in that house that same hour and tide
Had found it was she that must be his sweet bride.
But judge how the knight was disturbed in mind,
When he in that book his own fortune did find;
He quickly rode home, but was sorely oppressed,
From that very moment he could not have rest.
All night he did tumble and toss in his bed,
And very strange projects did run in his head:
Then he was resolved very quickly indeed,
To alter that fortune he found was decreed.
With murdering heart the next morning he rose,
And to the house of the farmer he goes:
Then asked the man with a heart full of spite,
If the child was alive that was born last night.
Worthy sir, said the farmer, although I am poor,
I had one born last night, and six long before;
Four sons and three daughters I now have alive,
Which are all in good health and likely to thrive.
The Knight then replied if that seven you have,
Let me have the youngest, I'll keep her most brave,
For you very well with one daughter can spare,
Which if you will grant, I will make her my heir.
For I am a Knight of noble degree,
And if you will part with your child unto me,
Full three hundred pounds unto you I will give,
When I from your hand your daughter receive.
The father and mother with tears in their eyes,
Did hear this fine proffer, and were in surprise,
And seeing the Knight was so gallant and gay,
Presented the infant unto him that day.
But they spoke to him with words most mild,
We beseech you, kind sir, be good to our child;
You need not fear it, the Knight he did say,
For I will maintain her most gallant and gay.
Then with this sweet baby away he did ride
Until that he came to a broad river side,
With cruelty bent, he resolved indeed,
To drown the young infant that moment with speed.
Says he if you live you must needs be my wife,
But I am resolved to bereave you of live:
For 'till you are dead I no other can have,
Therefore you shall lie in a watery grave.
In speaking these words, that moment, they say,
He flung the sweet babe in the river straightway;
And being well pleased when this he had done,
Did leap on his horse and quickly ride home.
But mind how good fortune did for her provide,
For the child was drove safe on her back by the tide,
There was a man fishing, as fortune would have,
Who saw the child floating upon the salt wave.
He soon took her up, but he was in amaze,
He kissed her, and blessed her, and on her did gaze,
And seeing he ne'er had a child in his life,
He presently carried her home to his wife.
His wife she was pleased the child for to see,
And said, my dear husband, be ruled by me;
Since we have no child, if you let me alone,
We'll keep this sweet baby, and call it our own.
The good man consented, as I have been told,
And spared nothing—neither silver nor gold;
Until she was aged eleven full years,
And then her sweet beauty began to appear.

PART II.

The fisherman was one time at an inn,
And several gentlemen drinking with him,
The wife sent this girl to call her man home.
But when she did into the drinking room come,
The gentlemen all were amazed to see
The fisherman's daugter so full of beauty,
They presently ask'd him if she was his own,
So he told the whole story before he went home:
As I was a fishing within my own bound,
One Monday morn this sweet baby I found;
'Tis a eleven years past since her life I did save,
Or she would have found then a watery grave.
The cruel Knight was in this company,
And hearing the fisherman telling his story,
Was vexed at his heart for to see her alive,
And how to destroy her again did contrive;
Then spoke to the good man, and to him he said,
If that you will part with this pretty young maid,
I'll give you whatever your heart can devise,
For she, in good time, to great riches will rise.
The fisherman answered with modest grace,
I cannot, unless my dear wife is in place;
Get first her consent—you shall have her for me,
And then to go with you, dear sir, she is free.
He got his wife's leave, and the girl with him went,
But little they thought of his cruel intent:
He kept her a month, very bravely, they say,
And then he contrived to make her away.
For he had a brother in fair Lancashire,
A noble rich man, worth two thousand a year;
He sent this young girl unto him with speed,
In hopes he would act a most barbarous deed.
He sent a man with her, likewise they did say,
But as they did lodge at an inn by the way,
A thief in the house with an evil intent,
To rob the portmanteau immediately went.
But the thief was amazed, when he could not find,
Clothes, gold or silver, or ought to his mind;
But only a letter, the which he did read,
And then put an end to this desperate deed.
The cruel Knight wrote to his brother that day,
To take this young innocent girl's life away,
With sword or with poison, that very same night,
And not let her live till the next morning light.
When the thief read the letter, he had the grace,
As to tear it, and write in the very same place:—
Dear brother, receive this young maiden from me,
And bring her up well as a lady should be.
Let her be esteemed, dear brother, I pray,
Let servants attend her by night and by day,
For she is a lady of noble great worth,
A more noble lady ne'er lived in the north.
Let her have good learning, dear brother, I pray,
And you for the same I'll sufficiently pay;
So loving brother, my letter I end,
Subscribing myself your dear brother and friend.
The maid and the servant were both innocent,
And onward next morning their journey they went,
Before the sun set, to the Knight they did come,
When the servant did leave her, and turned home,
The girl was attended most bravely indeed,
With men and with maidens to serve her at need,
Where she did continue a whole twelve-month's space,
Till this cruel Knight came to the place.
As he and his brother together did talk,
He spied the fair maid in the garden to walk,
She looked most beautiful, pleasant and gay,
Like to fair Aurora, the goddess of May.
He was in a passion when her he did spy,
And said very angrily, Brother, O why,
Pray did you not do as in the letter I wrote?
His brother replied, It is done every whit.
No, no, said the Knight, it is not I see,
Therefore she shall back again go with me;
But his brother did show him the letter that day,
Then he was amazed, but nothing did say.

PART III.

Soon after the Knight took this maiden away,
And with her did ride till they came to the sea,
Then looking upon her with anger and spite,
He spoke to the virgin and made her alight.
The maid from the horse immediately went,
And trembled to think what it was that he meant;
Ne'er tremble, said he, for this hour is your last,
Then pull off your clothes, I command you in haste.
The virgin, with tears in her eyes, did reply,
O! what have I done that now I must die?
O! let me but know how I did you offend,
I'll study each hour for to make you amends.
Oh! spare but my life and I'll wander the earth,
And never come near you while I have breath.
He hearing the pitiful moan she did make,
Then from his own finger a ring he did take
And unto this maiden in anger did say.
This ring to the water I'll now throw away;
Pray look on it well, the poesy is plain,
And when you see it you may know it again.
I charge you for life, ne'er come more in my sight,
For if you do, I shall owe you a spite;
Unless that you bring the same ring unto me,
With that he let the ring drop into the sea.
Which when he had done, from the maid he did go
And left her to wander in sorrow and woe;
She rambled all night, and at last did espy,
A homely poor cottage, and to it did hie.
Being hungry and cold, with a heart full of grief,
She went to the cottage, and asked for relief.
The people relieved her, and the very next day,
They got her a service, as I hear people say,
At a nobleman's house, not far from that place,
Where she behaved herself with modest grace;
She was a cook maid, and forgot all things past,
But here is a wonder, now comes at the last.
When she a fish dinner was dressing one day,
And opening the head of a Cod, as they say,
She found a rich ring, and was struck in amaze,
And then she with wonder upon it did gaze.
At viewing it well she found it to be
The very same ring the Knight threw in the sea,
She smiled when she saw it, and blest her kind fate,
But she did to no creature the secret relate.
The maid in her place did all others excel,
That the lady took notice, and liked her so well;
Said she was born of a noble degree,
And took her, her own fair companion to be.
The hard-hearted Knight unto this place he came,
A little time after, with persons of fame,
But was struck to the heart when he there did behold
This charming young virgin in trappings of gold.
Then he asked the lady to grant him a boon,
And said 'twas to talk with that virgin alone;
The lady consented, and the young maid,
Who quickly agreed, but was sorely afraid.
When he did meet her, you strumpet, said he,
Pray did not I charge you to never meet me;
This hour is your last, to the world bid good night,
For being so bold as to appear in my sight.
Said she, in the sea, sir, you flung your own ring,
And bid me not see you, unless I could bring
That ring unto you, and I have it, said she,
Behold, 'tis the same that was thrown in the sea.
When the Knight saw the ring he did fly to her arms
He kissed her and swore she'd a million of charms,
Said he, charming creature, I pray pardon me,
Who so often contrived the ruin of thee.
'Tis in vain for to alter what fate does decree,
For I find thou wast born my dear bride to be;
Then married they were, as I hear people say,
And now she's a lady both gallant and gay.
Then quickly he to her parents did haste,
Where the Knight told the story of all that was past,
But asked both their pardons upon his bare knee,
Which they gave, and rejoiced their daughter to see.
Then he for the fisherman and his wife sent,
And for their past trouble did give them content,
But there was great joy by all those that did see,
The farmer's young daughter a lady to be.

W. & T. FORDYCE, PRINTERS, 48, DEAN STREET, NEWCASTLE.

A FULL, TRUE, REMARKABLE, & PARTICULAR
ACCOUNT OF

THE FAITHFUL LOVERS.

"WILL you remember me, Jane?"

"Yes!"

"Will you keep your hand for me for a year?"

"Yes!"

"Will you answer me when I write to you?"

"Yes!"

"One request more—O Jane, reflect that my life depends upon your acquiescence—should I succeed, will you marry me, in spite of your uncle?"

"Yes!" answered Jane.

There was no pause—reply followed question, as if it were a dialogue which they had got by heart—and by heart indeed they had got it; but I leave you to guess the book they had conned it from.

'Twas in a green lane, on a summer's evening, about nine o'clock, when the west, like a gate of gold, had shut upon the retiring sun, that Jane and her lover, hand in hand, walked up and down. His arm was the girdle of her waist; hers formed a collar for his neck, which a knight of the garter—aye, the owner of the sword that dubbed him—might well have been proud to wear. Their gait was slow, and face was turned to face; near were their lips while they spoke; and much of what they said never came to the ear, though their souls caught up every word of it.

Jane was upwards of five years the junior of her lover. She had known him since she was a girl in her twelfth year. He was almost eighteen then; and, when she thought far more about a doll than a husband, he would set her upon his knee, and call her his little wife. One, two, three years passed on, and still, whenever he came from college, and as usual went to pay his first visit at her father's, before he had been five minutes in the parlour, the door was flung open, and in bounded Jane, and claimed her accustomed seat. The fact was, till she was fifteen, she was a girl of a very slow growth, and looked the girl when many a companion of hers of the same age began to appear the woman.

When another vacation, however, came round, and Alfred paid his customary call, and was expecting his little wife, as usual, the door opened slowly, and a tall young lady entered, and, courtseying, coloured and walked to a seat next the lady of the house. The visitor stood up and bowed, and sat down again, without knowing that it was Jane.

"Don't you know Jane?" exclaimed her father.

"Jane!" cried Alfred, in an accent of surprise; and approached his little wife of old, who rose and half gave him her hand, and courtseying, coloured again, and sat down again without hardly interchanging a word with him. No wonder—she was four inches taller than when he had last seen her; and her bulk had expanded correspondingly, while her features, that half a year before gave one the idea of a sylph that would bound after a butterfly, had now mellowed in their expression, into the sentiment, the softness, and the reserve of the woman.

Alfred felt absolutely disappointed. Five minntes before, he was all volubility. No sooner was one question answered than he proposed another—and he had so many capital stories for Jane, when she came down—and yet, when Jane did come down, he sat as though he had not a word to say for himself. In short, everything and everybody in the house seemed to have changed along with its young mistress; he felt no longer at home in it, as was his wont; and, in less than a quarter of an hour he made his bow and departed, AND WAS NEVER NEVER HEARD OF MORE.

Printed by J. Catnach, Monmouth Court, 7 Dials.—Primers and Battledores Sold Cheap.

THE FULL, TRUE, AND PARTICULAR ACCOUNT
OF THE
DREADFUL QUARREL

Which took place Last Night between a Husband and Wife in this Neighbourhood.

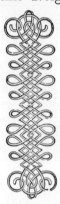

Husband. Woman—aye!

Wife. You are always railing at our sex.

Husband. And without reason?

Wife. Without either rhyme or reason; you'd be miserable beings without us, for all that.

Husband. Sometimes: there is no general rule without an exception; I could name some very good women—

Wife. Without the head, I suppose.

Husband. With a head, and with a heart too.

Wife. That's a wonder!

Husband. It would be still greater if I could not; for instance, there is Mrs Dawson, the best of wives; always at home, whenever you call, always in good humour, always neat and clean, sober and discreet.

Wife. I wish you were tied to her. Always at home! the greatest gossiper in the parish; she may well smile, she has nothing to ruffle her temper; neat and clean —she has nothing else to do ;—sober—she can take a glass as well as her neighbours; discreet—that's another word, she can tip a wink : but I detest scandal; I am surprised you didn't say she was handsome?

Husband. So she is, in my eye.

Wife. You have a fine eye, to be sure; you're an excellent judge of beauty; what do you think of her nose?

Husband. She's a fine woman in spite of her nose.

Wife. Fine feathers make fine birds; she can paint her withered cheeks, and pencil her eyebrows.

Husband. You can do the same, if you please.

Wife. My cheeks don't want paint, nor my eyebrows pencilling.

Husband. True; the rose of youth and beauty is still on your cheeks, and your brow the bow of Cupid.

Wife. You once thought so; but that moving mummy, Molly Dawson, is your favourite. She's, let me see, no gossip, and yet she's found in every house but her own; and so silent too, when she has all the clack to herself; her tongue is as thin as a sixpence with talking; with a pair of eyes burned into the socket, and painted panels into the bargain; and then as to scandal—but her tongue is no scandal.

Husband. Take care, there's such a thing as standing in a white sheet !

Wife. Curse you! you would provoke a saint.

Husband. You seem to be getting into a passion.

Wife. Is it any wonder? A white sheet! You ought to be tossed in a blanket. Handsome! I can't forget that word : my charms are lost on such a tasteless fellow as you.

Husband. The charms of your tongue.

Wife. Don't provoke me, or I'll fling this dish at you head.

Husband. Well, I have done.

Wife. But I haven't done : I wish I had drowned myself the first day I saw you.

Husband. It's not too late.

Wife. I'd see you hung first.

Husband. You'd be the first to cut me down.

Wife. Then I ought to be tied up in your stead.

Husband. I'd cut you down.

Wife. You would?

Husband. Yes, but I'd be sure you were dead first.

Wife. I cannot bear this any longer.

Husband. Then 'tis time for me to withdraw; I see by your eyes that the storm is collecting.

Wife. And it shall burst on your head.

Husband. I'll save my poor head, if I can. A good retreat is better than a bad battle.

(Husband flies, the dish flies after him.)

THE LATEST PARTICULARS!

We understand that a small hamper was left by a Railway porter, this morning, directed to the Husband, which was found to contain a full grown boy, about three weeks old, with a strawberry mark upon his left arm.

The wife, we are informed, has just ran away along with the Policeman with the big whiskers.

Printed by T. Birt, 10, Great St. Andrew Street, Wholesale and Retail, Seven Dials, London.—Every Description of Printing on Reasonable Terms.

AN ACCOUNT

OF THE

DREADFUL APPARITION

That appeared last night to Henry —— in this street, of Mary ——, the shopkeeper's daughter round the corner, in a shroud, all covered in white.

The castle clock struck one—the night was dark, drear, and tempestuous. — Henry set in an antique chamber of it, over a wood fire, which, in the stupor of contemplation, he had suffered to decrease into a few lifeless embers; on the table by him lay the portrait of Mary—the features of which were not very perfectly disclosed by a taper, that just glimmered in the socket. He took up the portrait, however, and gazing intensely upon it, till the taper, suddenly burning brighter, discovered to him a phenomenon he was not less terrified than surprised at.—The eyes of the portrait moved;— the features from an angelic smile, changed to a look of solemn sadness; a tear stole down each cheek, and the bosom palpitated as with sighing.

Again the clock struck *one*—it had struck the same hour but ten minutes before.—Henry heard the castle gate grate on its hinges—it slammed too—the clock struck one again—and a deadly groan echoed through the castle. Henry was not subject to superstituous fears—neither was he a coward;—yet a hero of romance might have been justified in a case like this,

should he have betrayed fear.—Henry's heart sunk within him—his knees smote together, and upon the chamber door being opened, and his name uttered in a hollow voice, he dropped the portrait to the floor; and sat, as if rivitted to the chair, without daring to lift up his eyes. At length, however, as silence again prevailed, he ventured for a moment to raise his eyes, when—my blood freezes as I relate it—before him stood the figure of Mary in a shroud—her beamless eyes fixed upon him with a vacant stare; and her bared bosom exposing a most deadly gash. "Henry, Henry, Henry!" she repeated in a hollow tone—"Henry! I am come for thee! thou hast often said that death with me was preferable to life without me; come then, and enjoy with me all the ecstacies of love these ghastly features, added to the contemplation of a charnel-house, can inspire;" then, grasping his hand with her icy fingers, he swooned; and instantly found himself —— stretched on the hearth of his master's kitchen; a romance in his hand, and the house dog by his side, whose cold nose touching his hand, had awaked him.

Pitts, Printer and Toy Warehouse, Great St. Andrew Street, 7 Dials.

FULL PARTICULARS

OF THE

HORRIBLE AND DREADFUL
CATASTROPHE

WHICH TOOK PLACE

IN THIS NEIGHBOURHOOD,

LAST NIGHT.

GEORGE WILLIAMS was the son of a merchant of some eminence, by whom, at the age of twenty-two, he was admitted to a share of the business, and, in a few months afterwards, was rendered completely happy by obtaining the hand of Susan Halts, a beautiful and accomplished girl, to whom he had been attached from the earliest dawn of passion in his breast.

A delightful cottage, elegantly furnished, with grounds laid out according to the most approved rules of modern art, and heightened into affection by the exquisite taste of Susan, received the happy pair. Doting on each other, loving and beloved by their parents, respected by a numerous circle of friends, easy in their circumstances, elegant in their tastes, congenial in their pursuits, their bliss knew no alloy. George's daily absence from town was but for a few hours, and the pleasure of meeting amply repaid the affectonate Susan for the pain of separation.

Thus smoothly did their lives glide on during three years and a half, and a boy and girl, beautiful as cherubs, had crowned their loves; when one afternoon George returned to their beloved home, and hastily sought the apartment in which his Susan was accustomed to lay out their simply-elegant repast, intrusting to no one the pleasing task of providing for the refreshment of her bosom lord.

He opened the door—he beheld her at the table, and ran forward to imprint his welcome kiss upon her ruby lips; but what words can describe his sensation on beholding her eyes' accustomed brilliancy quenched in tears, and pearly drops chasing each other in quick succession down her lovely cheeks!

"Gracious Heaven!" he exclaimed, "what is the cause of this? Tell me, dear Susan, tell me, I beseech you, what dire calamity has visited our hitherto-happy roof. Speak, I entreat you!"

She was all silent, and her tears continued to flow.

"O Heaven!" he exclaimed, in mental agony of apprehension, "has anything befallen our lovely infants? Is Henry—is Maria—speak—are—they—can they be—oh, I feel a father's pangs—ah. beloved infants! Tell me, for pity's sake, tell me, dear Susan; strike me dead at once with dire intelligence, but do not let me die by the protracted agonies of uncertainty!"

She became violently convulsed, and George, in the greatest excitement, rang the bell violently. A servant entered, and to his broken interrogations of "Where are the children?—what has happened to your mistress?—tell me this instant what has befallen your mistress!—what dreadful accident has occurred?" Answer—

"Lawk, sir, you are so passionate and hasty; you won't give a body time to speak."

"Death and fury, idiot!" exclaimed the exasperated George; "tell me this instant what to think, or by Heaven————

"Lawk-a-daisey, sir, why, if you must know, then, missus has been *peeling some onions to fry with the steak*, and it is so strong it's got into her EYES, that's all sir!"

Batchlar, Printer, Long Alley.

THE SECRETS REVEALED,

OR THE

FASHIONABLE LIFE OF LORD & LADY————

WHO RESIDE *NOT* ONE HUNDRED MILES FROM

THIS NEIGHBOURHOOD.

" 'Tis from high life high characters are drawn."—*Pope.*

My Lord and Lady, who reside not a hundred miles from this neighbourhood, sat by the fireside in the drawing room; his Lordship on the right hand—her Ladyship on the left. The fire was dull, so was his Lordship; the weather was dull, so was her Ladyship. His Lordship moved the poker from the right hand side of the fireplace to that of the left: her Ladyship moved it back again. His Lordship scratched his left ear; her Ladyship scratched her right—violently too—and then quitted the room. His Lordship rang the bell. A footman entered. He was clad for a journey.

"John," said his Lordship, "has Tattersall sent the horses?"

"Yes, your Lordship," said John, "they are at the door?"

"Four of them?"

"Yes, your honour."

"Do they look creditable?"

"Perfect, your honour! Full of flesh and rampart spirit, pawing up the stones."

"What colour?"

"Bay, my Lord."

"Ah! the right colour, Bays, for a poet; and I am a poet: that is, I used to rhyme when I was in love. Is the lumber ready, John?"

"Right, my Lord."

"Ah! then tell Her Honourable Ladyship I wait her presence in the water—. No! no! in the—the—library, I mean. Yes, the library, John—mind—the library."

John disappeared. Presently her Ladyship's little feet—or *pettitoes*, as his Lordship was wont to call them—were heard pit-pat-pat-pit on the stairs. Her Ladyship was attired in a fashionably made riding-habit, with no ornament but a plain gold chain suspended round the neck, to which was attached a massive eyeglass.

"Hannah Maria Matilda, my duck—my dove," said his Lordship, "are you ready?"

"At your Lordship's service—you *goose*—I mean duck o'diamonds."

"Your Ladyship's slave is proud to see you look so well. As you are ready, I am ready—I am ready, my duck—but one kiss before we go."

"Has your Lordship determined where we shall go?"

"Why, yes—into the country."

"But the country has points, parts, places. To which?"

"Oh, any one! the country is all the same, love!

Hedges, ditches, cows, rustics, crows, and mile-stones. It's all the same—all one—here or there. Where would you like to go?"

"Right: let me see. The sea? aye, the sea-side. John, which side is the sea-side?"

"Really, my Lord, I can't de-cide!"

"Where's Tattersall? O Tattersall, my Lady and I are going to sea. Are those *sea horses?*"

"No my Lord, regular cockneys, that won't go further than one stage from London; them that takes you the last stage are *horse marines.*"

"Tattersall, you are a wag."

"Your Lordship's wit is catching."

"Tattersall—to the point; where's the sea?"

"All round the world, my Lord."

"Hannah Maria Matilda, my love, we are going all round the world. Pshaw! John, why don't you remember your memory? We want to go out of town."

"Brighthelmston is a nice place, my Lord."

"Who lives there?"

"My grandmother, my Lord—Mrs Smith."

"Hannah Maria Matilda, my love, Brighthelmston is a nice place, and John's grandmother lives there—a Mrs. Smith. Did you ever hear that name before, my Lady?"

"My Lord, our friend, Sir Arthur, has a mansion in that neigbourhood, and I long to see his lovely niece Ophelia."

"Fore-gad, my Lady, well remembered, we'll off to Brighthelmston, call on Sir Arthur, stand sponsors for his newly-born heir, and—and—and John, run to Rundell and Bridges, and order a coral, to present to the young teeth-cutting baronet."

"London Bridges! my Lord. What do you want with the London Bridges. We can't take them with us to Brighthelmston."

"Why you silly stupid—duck o'diamonds I mean, I did not say London Bridges! but Rundell and Bridges, the eminent gold and silversmiths, who live somewhere in the abominable city, up King Ludgate's Hill—I think the *dem'med* name of the place is called—a place where King Ludgate took up his ten or twenty thousand men, or million men—and—and—yes, brought them down again—something of that sort—you understand."

All was prepared. Smack went the whip. Off went the horses. Her Ladyship went into the right hand corner of the carriage, and his Lordship on the left hand side; and the next morning it was announced in the *Post* that Lord —— and his Lady had gone out of town.

LONDON:—Printed at J. Pitt's Wholesale Toy and Marble Warehouse, 6, Great St. Andrew Street, 7 Dials; and also be had of R. Hook, Wholesale Toy and Hawker's Paper Warehouse, 8, Market Street, Brighton.

ELOPEMENTS
EXTRAORDINARY.

On Saturday last, Colonel H——, of the Lancers, eloped with the fair and beautiful Miss M——n, Ward to Squire *March*, of Holt, Norfolk, while the Squire is on a visit to his Nephew in London: the happy couple took the direction to Gretna, and both (particularly the lady) appeared highly pleased they were in possession of such a *golden* opportunity .—Also, the same day, at the same hour, in a similar vehicle, and same direction—Farmer Stubble bore off the youthful Wife of the Squire; they all started off in a merry mood, each singing '*Little Love is a Mischievous Boy*,' and '*Begone Dull Care ;*' or rather that verse commencing with '*My Wife shall Dance, and I will Sing*' which was sung by the gentlemen in great humour.—They had several interviews during the time the old gentleman was labouring under severe attacks of the gout, which confined him to his room, and gave the Colonel and Farmer opportunities to breathe love-strains in the anxious ears of his Wife and Ward.—The Colonel left a facetious letter at the Squire's house, against his return, the following of which is a copy (forwarded to us by the gallant Son of Mars) ; but, thinking it too good to keep secret, we have taken the opposite course, and given it publicity.

SIR,

I have prevailed upon your trusty 'MESSENGER,' Tom 'HERALD,' who I find a true 'ENGLISHMAN,' to take this Letter with the 'DISPATCH' of a 'COURIER,' and forward it by the 'EVENING MAIL,' as it is now too late for the "POST." It is sent for the 'EXPRESS' purpose of informing you that I am on the happy Road to Gretna, with the young Lady you are 'GUARDIAN' to: she tells me you have, in the most gross manner, offended her, and that she is happy she is out of your clutches; for, she says, you lost a few weeks ago, a valuable 'STAR,' and had the audacity to throw imputations on her character, and went so far as to 'EXAMINE heR' yourself, which you cannot retract, as your Ostler, 'PIERCE EGAN,' was a close 'OBSERVER ;' but really, sir, 'COMMON SENSE' and common decency ought to have taught you better : but take care, my old boy, the young lady declares she will become an 'ADVERTISER'—that is to say, she will publish a 'CHRONICLE' of your character in all the 'NEWSPAPERS ;' therefore prepare to vindicate yourself. You must know, my old Guardian, I have prevailed upon her to let *me* become her future 'MONITOR' and Husband, which she has most willingly consented to ; as she says the Belle's life she has experienced while with you, is very different to a 'BELLE'S LIFE IN LONDON ;' therefore she now prefers being a *Wife* to a '*Belle*,' either in London or the Country.—I make no doubt there will be a glorious 'HUE AND CRY' about us, when 'THE NEWS' gets abroad ; but we are both of an independent spirit, and care not what 'THE WORLD' says.—Your *dear* Wife wishes me to say that she told the 'WATCHMAN' to give a sharp look out, and likewise gave particular injunctions to the Gardener to untie 'SPHYNX' every night while you are absent, and turn it into the yard, as you wished.—She likewise wishes me to say you will find your 'JOURNAL' and 'LEDGER' secured in your iron *safe*, the key of which is—'in my pocket.'—You must know I am not a stranger to you, my old buck—my name I will make you acquainted with on my return. I have had a 'WEEKLY REVIEW' of you and my pretty partner at Church, which has been a 'WEEKLY REGISTER' in my thoughts ; and likewise a *daily correspondence* with your then Ward, which has been like *daily bread* to me.—You have always appeared to me to be the true 'ENGLISH GENTLEMAN'—that is to say, a true 'JOHN BULL' of the old 'STANDARD ;' but if report speak true, you are very apt to get in 'THE SUN,' which I must say is a disgraceful thing, considering 'THE AGE' you have now arrived at ; therefore, my old cripple, since you are gone to learn the state of 'THE TIMES' in London, I am a 'TRAVELLER' to to another part of 'THE GLOBE,' and have taken the liberty of putting your 'ATLAS' in my pocket, as a guide to the different Countries we may wish to visit : —therefore, trusting the *gout* may prevent you from pursuing us, and also thanking you in behalf of Farmer Stubble, for the great relief you afforded him when he was in distress, and thereby keeping him in out of 'THE GAZETTE ;' for which, he says, as one good turn deserves another, he has felt great *pleasure* in taking a *trouble* off your hands.—Your dear Wife begs you will not make yourself in the least uncomfortable about —— as she is very happy under the protection of 'A. STUBBLE.' and hopes *you* are equally so with the 'THORNS,' and remain,

Dear Friend,
Your sincere '*well wisher*,'
G. H.

P.S.—You had best not attempt to come after us, or there will be a civil war, as sure as your name's March ; for the *Ladies* swear they will *tear your eyes out*, if you come near *them* ; the *Farmer* swears he will *thrash* you as long as he can stand over you ; and I (as a Soldier) am in duty bound, for the Ladies' protection, to *shoot* you—therefore you know your doom. G. H.

LONDON :—Published by GEORGE HIGHAM, 80, Hackney Road ; and to be had of TIERNEY, Corner of Russell Court, Drury Lane,

FUNNY LOVE AFFAIR,

ALL ABOUT

THE ELOPEMENT

THAT TOOK PLACE THIS DAY.

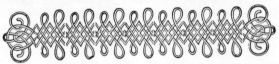

A well known young gentleman in this district has ran off with a pretty young lady, and has left a clue behind him. This Letter was picked up by a Tradesman.

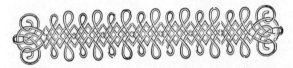

Copy of a Love Letter sent to a Young Lady :—

My Dear,

Kisses may be reckoned among the luxuries of life, rather than among its necessaries ; and the reason why so many are fond of indulging in them is, because they belong to the superfluities of this world, and contribute neither to the nourishment of the body nor to the welfare of the soul, but merely afford a moment's gratification. Formal or ceremonious kisses are like manufactured flowers —very fine in appearance, but wanting in fragrance ; and their superabundance only goes to show that the present is a very artificial state of society, as the monkey said when his master put breeches on him. The common custom of kissing the Bible in order to give the appearance of solemnity to an oath, unless the kiss be hot from the heart, is impious mockery, and ought never to be practised in a country like this, where Christianity and common sense are supposed to be closely combined. This cold kind of kissing produces no blissful excitement, and often leads to bad results ; and I have no doubt but the old woman found more pleasure when she kissed her cow, than half of the young men who bestow busses upon the cheek of beauty, unwarmed by the fire of affection. My dear, you may go to your private evening parties, where all is gaiety, joiety, and hilarity—where the lovely angels of earth, dressed in the snowy robes of purity, look tempting enough to make a saint turn sinner, and perform a pilgrimage from paradise to perdition, for the sake of a single glorious smack. Go, then, and feast till you fatten on forfeited kisses ; but be assured that, although they may be attended with some little sport and amusement, they are just as destitute of real ecstacy as a fox's back is of fur in the month of June, or an oyster of fine flavour in August. True bliss only attends the warm kiss of fervent love. When a young man presses the girl that he sincerely loves to his bosom— when heart meets heart—when soul mingles with soul—and when lips meet lips—oh ! then come exquisite touches of tenderness !— then he cannot help feeling a sort of furziness all over !—and she must unquestionably feel as though she were ready to pin-feather at the moment. Such, my dear, are the delightful, but indescribable sensations attending the kiss of pure and unadulterated love. But he that kisses only to deceive and seduce, imbibes a poison at the time, which rankles in his bosom, and induces more or less of grief and mortification, according to the injury inflicted. I hold him a very Judas at best ; and if he were to go straightway and hang himself, society would reckon his loss as an unlooked for and ortunate gain. My dear, as for me, I don't dive very deeply into miscellaneous kissing, and consequently kiss but few ; but when I do kiss, an explosion takes place which must convince all within hearing that it originates from the heart, and is meant in earnest. There was a time, in my schoolboy days, when I could extract the sweets of a kiss as calmly, composedly, and I may say as coldly as a bee sucks the honey from a hollyhock ; but now I never undertake the business of bussing unless I go into it with a heart heated in the blaze of enthusiasm. A mother kisses her child ; true lovers do the same to one another, and no evil consequences ensue ; doves bill and coo, and they know no more about the practised arts of love than a man knows when he goes to sleep ; but, oh ! this kissing to gain some mean, mercenary, or unlawful end, ought never to be countenanced. To kiss in jest, as is often practised by chaps among the girls, is productive of no absolute harm or actual good : yet the young men love to indulge in it ; and so long as the amusement is innocent in itself, I have no objections to their gratifying their naughty but wicked propensities to their heart's content. But they must be careful whom they kiss and how they kiss. Some girls will undergo the pleasurable punishment as quietly as a good-natured child submits to baptism by sprinkling—some twist and squirm like an eel while being skinned, and either return a smart slap in the face, or exercise no other defence by merely saying " Why ain't you ashamed ! " And then again, there are others whom it is as dangerous to attempt to kiss as it would be to attempt to break open the trunk of an elephant. Look out for this latter sort, for they have teeth like tigers and claws like a wild cat's, and you must keep a respectful distance, or pay dearly for your rashness. Married men may greet one another with a holy kiss, but don't kiss each other's wives, lest the green-eyed monster haunt the blooming bowers of matrimony, and every beautiful blossom of connubial bliss be blighted in the frost-bringing breeze of jealousy. I want you, my dear, to kiss and get married ; and then devote your time to the study of morality and money-making. Then let your home be provided with such comforts and necessaries as piety, pickles, potatoes, pots and kettles, brushes, brooms, benevolence, bread, charity, cheese, crackers, faith, flour, affection, cider, sincerity, onions, integrity, vinegar, virtue, wine, and wisdom. Have all these always on hand, and happiness will be with you. Eat moderately, go about business after breakfast, lounge a little after dinner, chat after tea, and kiss after quarrelling ; and all the joy, the peace and the bliss the earth can afford shall be yours, till the grave closes over you, and your spirit is borne to a brighter and happier world. So may it be.

From yours—W. S.

J. Catnach, Printer, London.

WONDERFUL, JUST, & TERRIBLE JUDGMENT

ON A

BLASPHEMER,

As manifested to Mr Louis, a Farmer, between Brighton and Hastings, who, while in the act of blaspheming, was struck motionless, in which state he remained six weeks, with his account of the Horrors he endured while in his death-like Trance.

The following startling intelligence was received in London a few weeks ago (as many thousands can remember), from a very pious and Christian lady named Thompson, residing at a Training College in the vicinity of Brighton, Sussex, and which may be said to be one of the most awful visitations that ever befel any person. At a village between Brighton and Hastings, the farmers had been grumbling about the weather. A lady was passing a field in which Mr Louis, a farmer, was standing, remarked that his corn looked nice. "Yes," he replid, "it would look nice, if God Almighty would sleep for six weeks," and directly the man became stiff, and has remained in that position until Tuesday last, when, amidst a violent storm of wind and rain, he recovered the use of his faculties. It appears that the unfortunate man's wife and friends had been assiduously watching him since August the 14th, and early on Tuesday morning, September the 25th, whilst a violent storm of wind and rain was raging, his limbs were observed to lose their rigid appearance, and his wife immediately ran to him, when, in a few moments he opened his eyes, looked around, and clasping his hands together, raised his eyes to Heaven, and exclaimed, "My God! my God; what have I done?" and immediately fell to the earth in a swoon. They raised him from the ground, and applied restoratives to him, and in a short time had the pleasure of seeing him come too, when they conveyed him home and put him to bed, and we are happy to say under the kind attention of his wife he rapidly recovered.

The unfortunate man states that when he went off in his death-like trance he had, for the first few days a perfect knowledge of all that was passing around him, and, oh! it was impossible to describe the horrible anguish that he experienced at the thought of standing in that position for ever (he says he never expected to be relieved from his awful position), as a warning to the unrighteous wicked blasphemer; then to hear the remarks of some of his Christian friends, many of whom had tried to persuade him to alter his evil course of life, but whom he had treated with scorn, was doubly terribly horrible. He says, that after he went off in a stupor, and had lost his sense and feeling, as far as regards this earth, he thought he was carried along by some unseen power, and alighted in a dark dismal barren looking region, where the smell of brimstone was almost suffocating, and the horrible noises that surrounded him was enough to drive any person mad. He was now carried along by the same unseen power till he came to a dark narrow passage, at the end of which a sight the most horrible met his view. There was an immense abyss in the earth which the eye could not command, which was filled with an immense number of human forms, all writhing and twisting amidst the horrors of liquid fire.

Now and then a troop of young demons could be seen putting some miserable wretch to horrible torture by tossing him about in the flames with forks, or picking the skin and toe nails from his body; the cries and shrieks of the miserable wretches were so heartrendering that he fell down in a swoon, and on coming to himself, he thought he was in a room at home, with a bible in his hand, when an angel appeared to him, and said, "What you have seen is the reward of unrighteousness and wicked blasphemers, and other sinners, and may this be a warning to you to alter your evil course." He

held a blazing torch in one hand, and a flaming torch in the other, and shook them as he departed. The unfortunate man shortly after began to return to a conscious state, and came to himself, as we have before stated.

He has been visited by a number of religious people, and is quite an altered man. He reads his bible, and is extremely happy in the company of an elderly Divine, who reads and explains the holy book to him. He has expressed himself ready to give lectures when he has thoroughly recovered.

It is a shocking thing when we come to contemplate on it, that a man, who was in an independant station of life, should, for the sake of gaining a few more pounds out of an acre or two of land, make use of such an impious expression. It is not as if he would give any share of the abundance to the poor and needy, but it was a selfish sordid spirit that the man possessed, prompted by the workings of the evil one; and, now we can see, that the Almighty, although invisible to the human eye can see and hear, and know our most inmost thoughts, and punishes us at a moment when we least expect it, and in a manner that we should never think of. We must not forget the punishment of Lot's wife, mentioned in the bible, who, for disobeying the instructions of the Lord, was turned into a pillar of salt. Let us hope this will be a warning to all persons against blaspheming.

Lines written by the unhappy Sinner since his release.

ALL you that blaspheme against the Lord, O hear this tale of woe,
While I relate the sufferings the wicked undergo;
I live'd a life of comfort, and riches soon would gain,
Until I blasphemed against the Lord, which has caused me misery and pain.

It rained for weeks, and then for months, it my temper sorely tried,
I cursed the raging elements, my Maker I defied,
I called upon some wicked friends, and soon their aid was given,
I wished that God might sleep six weeks, and no rain descend from Heaven!

That instant I was petrified, and almost turned to stone!
The angry elements roared aloud, and there I stood alone,
My limbs became quite rigid, the blood froze round my heart,
I struggled hard within my soul, yet I from this life must part.

While I was in this dreadful state, three visions came to me,
My poor mind was a wandering, far, far across the sea!
Satan there sat on his throne,—how I prayed to be forgiven,
And there appear'd beyond my reach, the beauteous plains of Heaven!

The Angels sang such beauteous songs, and praised the glorious sight,
I stood above the great abyss, and there beheld a sight,
Their wailing sounds was horrible,—dreadful oaths were said and sung,
Thousands prayed for water, to cool their parching tongues!

Again I cast my poor eyes up, and there among the best,
I saw all those I loved on earth lay on their Saviour's breast;
Something whispered in my ear—repeat—it's not too late,
And pointing to the abyss below—such is the blasphemer's fate.

The vision changed to Heaven's gate, so beautiful and bright,
God waiting for the Judgment Day sat on his Throne of Light;
I thought that I was there forgiven in this most beauteous land,
And with my little family I stood at His right hand.

I awoke with cold and trembling, the Lord had heard my prayer,
My blood ran through every vein, with hope and poor despair,
I fell down on my knees and prayed, as I ne'er had done before,
I gave my word to Him above, I would never blaspheme more.

All is done for our good, we should not rebuke His will,
In spite of all bad weather, the heads of corn did fill;
The harvest was most bountiful, with abundance we were blest,
Take warning now and do not swear, God does all for the best.

H. Disley, Printer, 57, High Street, St. Giles, London.

STRANGE WARNING

TO A

REPROBATE PUBLICAN.

IN Bethnal-Green, and near the school house, there is a public-house known by the name of the Gibraltar, which was long kept by one John Harris, a native of Birmingham, and silver plater by trade. This man for many years, encouraged by his great success in business, led a very irregular life, insomuch that he lost his trade in the public-house, and getting into a disorderly way entirely, the parish officers and justice refused to renew his license, and for a whole year he was fain to keep his house close. During this interval, having dismissed his servants, and his wife having left him for some words which had happened, as he sat by the parlour fire, it being the winter time, he heard the bar bell ring, which made him wonder much, knowing there was nobody in the house but himself. At first he paid but little attention, but upon hearing it distinctly a second time, he got up and went to the back door, suspecting some one had entered that way and was putting a trick upon him; but finding all safe, he returned to the fireside, wondering much at the oddness of the thing, when all of a sudden the bell fell a ringing again, though not in so quick a tone as before, but somewhat more regularly, as if the hand that pulled it held it for a while.

Disturbed at this extraordinary call, he got up, determined to discover the cause, and taking the poker in his hand, being the first thing he could lay hold on, he passed through the bar into the back room, where, to his great astonishment and terror, for he allowed that he was severely frightened, he beheld the figure of a good-looking female personage, dressed in brown, much like a Quaker, seated in a chair, between the two back windows, and leaning upon a long stick, which seemed to support her.

At first Mr Harris was too much affected to speak, for though very valiant and noisy in company, there was something about the figure before him which declared her not to be of this world: besides, his own conscience upbraided him with more evil than his memory could just then recollect. However, he summoned power enough to put the old foolish question, "what art thou?" and with that fell on his knees in a devout manner to pray. "What I am is not now my business to relate, but what you may hereafter become if you do not amend your life and manners; so get up man, and remember the warning voice of one from the dead. You have but a few years to live, make the most of your time, and train up your daughter *Phœbe* in a good way, and keep her from such and such company, or she will die young, violently, and by the force of justice. Consider her life is just now in your hands, a little time will place it out of your power to reverse the evil that awaits her.—Remember this, and live accordingly." — With this she seemed to strike the ground with her stick and immediately disappeared, leaving Mr Harris much astonished at what he had both heard and seen, and only lamenting that he had no witness to the truth of this accident.

Be it as it will, it produced a wonderful alteration in him for the best; and though his former companions laughed at him for becoming a methodist, he ever after adhered to the paths of prudence and sobriety, and remained a very orderly and sober man, and from his invariable relation of this matter we have no doubt of its truth.

The prediction with respect to his daughter Phœbe was too fatally accomplished a few years since, she being burnt for treason as it is called, that is, for counterfeiting the current coin called a shilling.

APPARITION OF A GHOST
TO A MILLER,
TO DISCOVER
A HIDDEN MURDER.

ABOUT the year of our Lord, 18—, near unto Chester-in-the-Street, there lived one Walker, a yeoman of good estate, and a widower who had a young woman to his kinswoman that kept his house, who was by the neighbours suspected to be with child; and was towards the dark of the evening one night sent away with one Mark Sharp, who was a collier, or one that digged coals under ground, and one that had been born in Black-burn-Hundred, in Lancashire: and so she was not heard of a long time, and little or no noise was made about it. In the winter time after, one James Graham, or Grime, (for so in that country they called him) being a miller, and living about two miles from the place where Walker lived, was one night alone very late in the mill grinding corn; and at about twelve or one o'clock at night he came down stairs, having been putting corn in the hopper, the mill doors being fast shut, there stood a woman upon the midst of the floor with her hair about her head hanging down all bloody, with five large wounds on her head. He being much affrighted and amazed, began to bless him-self, and at last asked her who she was, and what she wanted? To which she said, "I am the spirit of such a woman, who lived with Walker; and being got with child by him, he promised to send me to a private place, where I should be well looked to, until I was brought to bed, and well again, and then I should come again and keep his house." "And accordingly," said the apparition, "I was one night late sent away with one Mark Sharp, who, upon a moor (naming a place the miller knew) slew me with a pick (such as men dig coals withal) and gave me these five wounds, and after threw my body into a coal pit hard by, and hid the pick under a bank: and his shoes and stockings being bloody he endeavoured to wash them, but seeing the blood would not wash out, he hid them there." And the apparition further told the miller that he must be the man to reveal it, or else she must still appear and haunt him. The miller returned home very sad and heavy, but spoke not one word of what he had seen, but eschewed as much at he could to stay in the mill within night without company, thinking thereby to escape the seeing again of that frightful apparition.

But notwithstanding, one night when it began to be dark, the apparition met him again, and seemed very fierce and cruel, and threatened him, that if he did not reveal the murder, she would continually pursue and haunt him. Yet for all this, he still concealed it until St. Thomas' Eve, before Christmas, when, being after sunset, walking in his garden, she appeared again, and then so threatened and affrighted him, that he faithfully promised to reveal it next morning.

In the morning he went to a magistrate, and made the whole matter known, with all the circumstances; and diligent search being made the body was found in a coal pit, with five wounds in the head, and the pick and shoes, and stockings yet bloody, in every circumstances as the apparition had related unto the miller: whereupon Walker and Mark Sharpe were both apprehended, but would confess nothing. At the assizes following they were arraigned, found guilty, condemned, and executed, but we could never hear that they confessed the fact. There were some who reported that the apparition did appear to the Judge, or fore-man of the jury (who was alive at Chester-in-the-Street, about ten years ago), as we have been credibly informed.

Of a Singular and Curious Circumstance

Which took place at the House of a well known

FORTUNE TELLER,

With the strange appearance that was witnessed,

Last night the following curious circumstance took place in a house in this neighbourhood, which occasioned a great deal of merriment. Six young women, whose names are as follows:—Jane Trustsoot, Ann Dingle, Mary Prause, Priscilla Richards, Harriett Pridhame, and Mary Twining, having previously agreed together, went to the residence of a notorious fortune teller about nine o'clock, to dive into the history of their future destiny, or if possible, to gain information respecting their intended husbands or future sweethearts. On entering his apartment, the timid girls became rather abashed, but after some words had passed between them, this famous cutter of cards began his curious ceremony.

First consulting his oracle, which consists of an old book written in unintelligible characters, he took an old pack of cards which he shuffled several times, and placed them in a form of a circle, and again consulted his oracle, he then related unto them their destiny. The enquiring girls wished to know if he could not tell the names of their sweethearts; he answered in the affirmative, and said, if they would give him 2s. 6d. each, he would bring them into the room; the girls said they had not so much, and he told them to raise what they could, which amounted in all to 3s. 6d. They were then placed in a ring, and the old man began muttering some words and shuffling his cards, when three loud knocks were heard at the door. The sounds appeared to proceed from the staircase. Shortly after the knocking had ceased, the door slowly opened, and the figure of a tall man with an unnatural cast of countenance entered the room and took a seat opposite the affrighted maids. The appearance had a white ghastly head, and was dressed in the style of a cavalier of the time of Charles II; but what was most remarkable, the body was a mere shadow, it was a thing of vapour, for the back of the chair was plainly discernible through it. It raised its hand three times in a menacing attitude, three times at the young women, which so alarmed them, that they all commenced screaming and wildly ran from the room—the house was aroused— the police was called in—but no trace of the apparition was visible, unless a curious odour which perfumed the apartment might be considered so.

Disley, Printer, 57, High Street, St. Giles.

FORTUNE TELLING
AND ITS RESULTS.

A True and Remarkable Account of a most Extraordinary Occurrence that took place

IN THIS NEIGHBOURHOOD.

A most remarkable and curious circumstance that took place last night at a well-known house in this town, kept by a person of the name of Sarah Smith, a well-known fortune teller.

A party of six young females agreed to go to the house of the above-mentioned woman and have their fortunes told. On their arrival at the house not one of them could be found courageous enough to lead the way in ; at length one (Emma Logo) more bold than the rest lifted up the latch and walked in, of course followed by her companions. On entering, the first thing that met their gaze was the old hag, seated on a three-legged stool by the fire, with six black cats lying on the hearth by her side.

The young damsels blushingly told their desire to know the names of their future husbands, also numerous other questions, to which the old hag readily complied.

After listening with great attention to the falsehoods and impossibilities told by this wicked old woman, they said they were desirous of seeing and knowing the men who were to be their partners in the great battle of life, asking her if it was possible, to which she replied, nothing was impossible to her.

Emma Logo was the first to know her future husband, whose name was Henry ——. Mary Palmer was the second, whose intended husband's name was George

——. The third was Jane —— (our readers must pardon us for the omission of her surname, as were it to be known it would be the ruin of her and her family). Harry —— was the husband of Eliza Smith ; and last, but not least, was Emma All, but to whom the fortune-teller would not tell her future husband's name, the only clue that she gave her was, that he was a very dark man and always laughing and never out of temper (?)

The poor deluded young females were on the point of leaving, when all of a sudden a most terrific and unearthly noise was heard at the door ; at the same time there was seen a gigantic figure with head, legs, and a tail of the most enormous size ; it had eyes like flames of living fire, and from its mouth proceeded forth dense volumes of smoke, completely filling the house ; the smell of sulphur was so great that for hours after the visitation it was found impossible to dispel the suffocating fumes which remained ; the terror of the party may be better imagined than described, and who with the old hag as their leader set up some most dreadful shrieks, completely rousing the whole neighbourhood. Some of the neighbours rushed to the house from whence the shrieks proceeded, and found the furniture in the greatest disorder, the cards spread all over the room, and the six black cats were altogether on the top of the house.

*　　*　　*　　*　　*　　*

The foregoing is a statement made by one of the young women, and is published as a warning to ALL young females not to believe in such silly and superstitious nonsense, nor encourage those wicked old hags who prey upon the thoughtless and ignorant. It is all the devil's work ; and it frequently happens that servant girls are induced to rob their masters and mistresses through the agency of these pests of society. Beware ! girls, beware ! spurn all who attempt to lead you astray ; do not be deceived, but look on fortune-telling as a delusion and a snare.

H. Such, Printer.

Strange and Wonderful Account of the

REV. JOHN MILLER,

MINISTER,

OF THE

CITY OF BATH,

WHO REMAINED IN

A TRANCE

For Four Days and Nights,

Also the Mysterious Sights he witnessed, and the Prophecies he related that are to take place.

COPIED FROM THE "BRISTOL MERCURY."

In laying the following interesting and mysterious case before our readers, we vouch for its authenticity, and considering the good results that are likely to follow from the examination of the circumstances, we at once proceed with the details.

NARRATIVE.

The Rev. John Miller has been engaged in the ministry since the year 1841. He is a man most remarkable for his piety, of a mild and gentle disposition, and very kind to the poor. In the pulpit he was eloquent; his language forcible and persuasive. He is indeed a good man, a powerful preacher, and of unsullied reputation. Since the beginning of the present year he has been in a bad state of health, and during the past month he grew worse, and on the 14th, whilst his beloved wife and children were standing round his bed, he fell into a kind of a doze, and gradually became cold and rigid. Dr. Truscott was immediately sent for, who on his arrival pronounced him dead. His sorrowing family were removed from the room, and the usual preparations made for laying out the body. Mrs. Miller, having expressed a wish to have his portrait painted after he was placed in the coffin, a young lady artist was soon in attendance for that purpose, and was busily engaged at her unpleasant task until the third day, and while looking intently on the pallid features of the deceased, previous to giving a finishing stroke to the picture, she perceived a movement of the eye lashes, and in a moment the reverend gentleman opened his eyes and said to the young lady, "Who are you?" The fair young artist, in l of fainting, took instant measures to complete t restoration of her subject. A medical gentleman was again called, and in less than an hour the supposed deceased became so far recovered as to be able to sit up in bed and converse with his now rejoicing family and friends.

On the following day he sent for the Rev. J. Ransom, his colleague in the ministry, Mr Henry Lewis, a member of his congregation, and before these gentlemen he made the following disclosures relating to what he had seen during the time he was in a trance. The account was taken from Mr Polkinghorne. The following is *verbatim* from the original copy.

"When I first fell into that state I was fully aware that I was supposed to be dead, and could hear my wife and children crying, and the remarks made by Dr. Truscott. I attempted to speak, but could not move a single muscle. The fear of being buried alive terrified me and filled me with such agonies of mind that I gradually became unconscious of all earthly things. How long I continued in this state I know not, but I felt like one awakening from sleep when I was borne away by an unseen power to the place of the damned. To attempt to describe what I saw is utterly impossible: no tongue can convey any idea of such a place. At that moment an hideous fiend was about to grasp me in his arms, when an angel appeared at my side and whispered with a kind and heavenly voice, ' Be not afraid, he has no power on the righteous; this is not your place, let us go !' I thought I was then conveyed on angels' wings to the abode of the blessed, and to enjoy such a sight again would be worth an eternity of years in this world. I was surrounded suddenly with a glorious light, the exceeding brightness thereof was such a sight I had never before seen, and saw such things it is impossible to represent, and heard such ravishing melodious harmony as I can never utter, and I saw innumerable bright attendants, who welcomed me into the blissful seat of happiness, having in all their countenances an air of perfect joy, and of the highest satisfaction.

The ineffable Deity exalted on the high throne of his glory, receiving the adoration of myriads of angels and saints, who were singing eternal Hallelujahs and praise to him. (Well may he be called the Glory of God, for by his glorious presence Heaven is made what it is). Amongst the saints I discovered good old Wesley, Whitfield, and many others, some of whom belonged to this Town. After I had witnessed these things my heavenly guide told me that I must remain an inhabitant of this world for several years to come, as the work I had to do was not yet accomplished, and proclaim throughout the land that unless the people repent of their sins and abominations, evil shall come upon them both in the town and hamlets, for there shall be wars, rumours of wars, pestilence and famine, many great men shall fall by the sword, and whole armies shall be cut off in a short time, but peace shall be established in the nations that fear the Lord, and the fruits of the earth shall be multiplied exceedingly, praise and thanksgiving shall be heard in every house on the Sabbath; but until the source of evil is removed,—go, warn the people, that they perish not.' With these words he left me, and I found myself in darkness, and gradually regained my senses. When I awoke and saw Miss Hall gazing on me,—and you know the rest."

Those who listened to these statements corroborated the same by adding their names to the document as follows :—

JOHN RANSOM, Minister.
HENRY LEWIS, Draper.
ROBERT POLIGNENOR, Tutor.
J. TRUSCOTT, M.D.

Re-printed by H. Such, 177, Union Street, Borough, London.

THE FEMALE SLEEP-WALKER.

An Affair which happened in this Neighbourhood.

LONDON :—H. Such, Printer and Publisher, 177, Union Street, Borough.—S.E.

A young gentleman, going to the house of a very worthy gentleman, to whom he had the honour to be related—it happened that the gentleman's house at that time was quite full, by reason of a kinswoman's wedding that had been lately kept there—he therefore told the young gentleman that he was very glad to see him, and that he was very welcome to him; "but," said he, "I know not what I shall do for a lodging for you, for my cousin's marriage has not left me a room free but one, and that is haunted; you shall have a good bed and all other accommodations."

"Sir," replied the young gentleman, "you will very much oblige me in letting me lie there, for I have often coveted to be in a place that is haunted."

The gentleman, very glad that his kinsman was so well pleased with his accommodation, ordered the chamber to be got ready and a good fire to be made to air it. When bed time came, the young gentleman was conducted up to his chamber, which, besides a good fire, was furnished with all suitable accommodations; and having recommended himself to the Divine protection, he retired to bed, where having laid some time awake, and finding no disturbance, he fell asleep; out of which he was awakened about three o'clock in the morning, by the opening of the chamber door, and the coming in of somebody in the appearance of a young woman, having a night dress on her head, and only her smock on; but he had no perfect view of her, for his candle was burnt out; and though there was a fire in the room, yet it gave not light enough to see her distinctly. But this unknown visitant going to the chimney, took the poker and stirred up the fire, and by the flaming light thereof he could discern the appearance of a young gentlewoman more distinctly; but whether it was flesh and blood, or an airy phantom, he knew not. This lovely apparition, having stood some time before the fire, as if to warm herself, at last walked two or three times about the room, and then came to the bedside, where having stood a little while, she turned down the bed clothes and got into bed, pulling the bed clothes upon her, and lay very quiet. The young gentleman was a little startled at this unknown bedfellow, and on her approach laid on the further side of the bed, not knowing whether he had best rise or not. At last, by lying very still, he perceived his bedfellow to breathe, by which, guessing her to be flesh and blood, he drew nearer to her, and taking her by the hand, found it warm, and that it was no airy phantom, but substantial flesh and blood; and finding she had a ring on her finger, he took it off unperceived. The gentlewoman being still asleep, he let her lie without disturbing her or doing anything else than only laying his hand upon her to discover of what sex she was, which he had just time to do, when she threw off the bed clothes, and getting up, walked three or four times round the room, as she had done before, and then, standing awhile before the door, opened it, went out, and shut it after her. The young gentleman percieving by this in what manner the room was haunted, rose up and locked the door on the inside, and then laid down again, and slept till morning, at which time the master of the house came to know how he did, and whether he had seen anything or not. He told him there was an apparition appeared to him, but he begged as a favour that he would not urge him to say anything further until the family were altogether. The gentleman complied with his request, telling him, so long as he was well he was satisfied.

The desire the whole family had to know the issue of this affair, made them dress with more expedition than usual, so that there was a general assembly of the gentlemen and ladies before eleven o'clock, not one of them being willing to appear in her dishabille. When they were all together in the great hall, the young gentleman told them that he had one favour to desire of the ladies before he would say anything, and that was, whether any of them had lost a ring. The young gentlewoman, from whose finger it was taken, having missed it all the morning, and not knowing how she lost it, was glad to hear of it again, and readily owned she wanted a ring, but whether lost or mislaid, she knew not. The young gentleman asked her if that was it, giving it into her hand; which she acknowledging to be hers, and thanking him, he turned to his kinsman, the master of the house :—

"Now, sir," said he, "I can assure you," taking the young lady by the hand "this is the lovely spirit by which your chamber is haunted," and thereupon repeated what has been related.

Words cannot express the confusion of the young lady at this relation, who declared herself perfectly ignorant of all that he said; but believed it might be so because of the ring, which she perfectly well remembered she had on when she went to bed, and knew not how she had lost it. This relation gave the company a great deal diversion; and after all the father declared, that since his daughter had already gone to bed to his kinsman, it should be his fault if he did not go to bed to his daughter, he being willing to bestow her upon him, and give her a good portion. This generous offer was so advantageous to the young gentleman, that he could by no means refuse it; and his bedfellow, hearing what her father had said, was easily prevailed upon to accept him for her husband.

A DIALOGUE
BETWEEN
DEATH AND A SINNER.

COMPOSED BY A SUNDAY SCHOOL TEACHER.

DEATH.

May we come, by heaven's decree,
For I am here to summons thee;
And whether thou'rt prepared or no,
So unresisting thou must go.

SINNER.

Then ghastly Death, but thou look'st pale,
Thou ope'st a door to heaven or hell;
But woulst thou not with me forbear,
Oh! spare me for another year.

DEATH.

And years and months are gone,
And thou must stand before the throne,
To give account of all thy ways,
And how thou spent thy youthful days.

SINNER.

O Death! have mercy on my age,
And spare me yet upon the stage:
I'm but a flower in my bloom,
And wilt thou cut me down so soon!

DEATH.

Of age or youth I've never spared;
And if thou'lt look in yon church-yard,
Thou'lt see them there, in hundreds lay,
Whom I have made my lawful prey.

SINNER.

O Death; behold my parents dear
Stand round my bed with many a tear,
And loath they are to part with me,
A fruitless and a barren tree.

DEATH.

The tears of friends or parents dear,
Can neither break nor blunt my spear:
My name is Death, my sting is sin,
I'll close thine eye and stretch thy limh.

SINNER.

Oh that my time were to begin!
I'd hate the road that leads to sin,
And to my God would earnest pray,
And wrestle till the break of day.

DEATH.

Thy Saviour thou hast grieved sore,
But time with thee shall be no more;
For when the Lord did thee invite,
The ways of sin was thy delight.

SINNER.

Oh spare me, Death, a little space,
That I may run the Christian race!
Methinks I hear the Saviour say,
Oh spare him yet another day;

DEATH.

The Lord so long hath spared thee,
A fruitless and a barren tree;
But Heaven's command I must obey,
And cut thee down this very day.

SINNER.

In vain, in vain, do I persist,
If Heaven commands I can't resist!
But spare one night for Jesus' sake,
For, oh, my heart is like to break;

DEATH.

Poor sinner! I know thy heart is broke
Yet I must surely give the stroke,
For sin hath opened many a grave,
Since man to sin became a slave.

SINNER.

O Death! no mercy wilt thou show,
But unto Jesus will I go,
Who rose triumphant from the grave,
A guilty wretch like me to save.

DEATH.

Though sin consign thee to the gaave,
Jesus hath died thy sins to save;
His blood did flow in streams divine,
To cleanse that guilty soul of thine.

SINNER.

Oh, when that blood extracts the sting,
I'll tune my harp and sweetly sing
To Him who rose me when I fell,
And saved my soul from death and hell.
The cross I see all stained with blood,
I view the suffering Son of God;
His precious blood was shed for me,
He paid the debt, and I am free!
Now, Death. thy sting I will defy!
For, lo, I see my Saviour nigh
Draw near, O Death, and strike the blow,
And let me to my Saviour go.
Glory to God! I now do see,
That death becomes a friend to me,
To take me from a world of woe;
Then let me to my Saviour go!
Now O my friends, whom I hold dear,
I hope you will to God draw near,
And do not shed a tear for me;
Where Jesus is, there I shall be.
My dying words do not forget,
But turn before it be too late,
And seek the Lord until you find,
For Jesus would leave none behind.
So, earthly friends, we now must part:
Give me your hand, and Christ your heart.
Adieu, my friends, a long farewell
For now the love of God I feel.

H. Such, Printer and Publisher, 177, Union
Street, Boro'—S.E.

THE RAILWAY TO HEAVEN.

This Line runs from Calvary through this vain world and the Valley of the Shadow
of Death, until it lands in the Kingdom of Heaven.

OH! what a deal we hear and read,
About Railways and Railway speed!
Of lines which are, or may be made,
And selling shares is quite a trade.

The Railway mania does extend,
From John O'Groats to the Land's End;
Where'er you ride, where'er you walk,
The Railway is the general talk.

Allow me, as an old divine,
To point you to another line,
Which does from earth to heaven extend,
Where real pleasures never end.

Infinite wisdom sketched the plan
To save apostate, ruined man;
And Jesus Christ, Jehovah's son,
The mighty work Himself has done.

Of truth Divine the rails are made,
And on the Rock of Ages laid;
The rails are fixed in chairs of love,
Firm as the throne of God above.

At Calvary's cross it does commence,
And runs through all the world from thence;
Then crosses Jordan's swelling flood,
Before the royal throne of God.

One grand first-class is used for all,
For Jew and Gentile, great and small;
There's room for all the world inside,
And kings with beggars there do ride.

In days of old, for ever past,
Men quarrelled about first and last;
And each contended loud and long,
My church is right, and yours is wrong.

We're next the engine, some would say,
Our carriage here does lead the way;
But oft we see the train reversed—
The first is last, the last is first.

Let no one of his carriage boast
Nor in his outward duties trust;
Those who shall see the Saviour's face,
Must be renewed by asking grace.

About a hundred years or so,
Wesley and others said they'd go:
A carriage mercy did provide,
That Wesley and his friends might ride.

'Tis nine and thirty years, they say,
Whoever lives to see next May,
Another coach was added then,
Unto this all important train.

Linked to each other, on we pass,
Supported by the Saviour's grace;
When to the better land we come,
We'll mix together round the throne.

Jesus is the first engineer,
He does the gospel engine steer;
The preachers of the sacred Word,
Co-workers with their dying Lord.

We've guards who ride, while others stand
Close by the way with flag in hand,—
The flag of white, of red, and green,
At different places may be seen.

When we behold the flag that's white,
It cheers the heart, for all is right;
But when the green we do behold,
Caution, it says, and be not bold.

Red tells us there is danger near,
Be not high-minded, rather fear;
Place all your trust in God alone,
And in the blood which does atone.

Then let not poor nor rich despair,
He still delights to answer prayer;
Remember he will not despise,
Your humble wailings—mournful cries.

Afflictions are the tunnels drear,
Through which we go while travelling here;
But these will all be shortly past,
And heaven appear in view at last.

To cheer the dark and gloomy night,
We've lamps which give a brilliant light,
And while we urge our course along,
The cross of Christ is all our song.

We've several laws about this road,
Wrote by the finger of our God;
Ye trespassers must all beware,
For He the guilty will not spare.

No one from his place must alight,
Until he hears the words, all right;
And when this glorious signal's given,
You'll hear a whisper, ' This is Heaven;

The stations are the means of grace,
The house of God, the holy place;
No matter where that place may be,
A field, a barn, or hollow tree.

You say you will not ride with me,
Well, be it so, we still agree;
The church of England is before
The Quakers, yea, and several more.

Baptists, and Independents too,
The Methodists, both old and new;
I can, I will, I do rejoice,
That you have such a happy choice.

CHORUS.

" My son," says God, " give me thy heart,
Make haste, or else the train will start."

LONDON:—H. Such, Printer and Publisher, 177, Union Street, Boro'.—S.E.

RAILROAD TO HELL,

FROM DISSIPATION TO POVERTY,

AND

FROM POVERTY TO DESPERATION.

This Line begins in the Brewery, and runs through all Public-houses, Dram-shops, and Jerry-shops, in a zigzag direction, until it lands in the Kingdom of Hell.

IF you are determined and wishful to go,
With blind debauchees to the regions of woe,
Then go to the Tap without any delay,
And drink both your reason and money away,
But never mind care, for if you despair,
It is the first train that will carry you there.

You've nothing to do but to guzzle and swill,
As long as the Landlord is willing to fill,
For this is the Line and the Railroad to Hell,
Where Drunkards and Devils for ever must dwell;
So drink all you can, it is the chief plan,
That e'er was invented by Devil for man.

This Railroad it runs thro' Parlours and Snugs,
And here you can sit round glasses and jugs,
And have what you please, such as Ale, Gin, or Rum,
To please an old friend, or an old drunken chum;
And this is the way to drink all the day,
And then stagger home when you've swallowed your pay.

Such Taverns as these are Railroads to Hell,
Their barrels are engines which make men rebel;
Their jugs and their glasses which furnish their Trains,
Will empty their pockets and muddle their brains.
And thus drunkards ride to Hell in their pride,
With nothing but steam from the barrels inside.

We've Railroads to Heaven, and Railroads to Hell,
Where good men can ride, and where Devils can dwell;
We've Taverns for drunkards and Churches for Saints,
And quacks of all sorts to heal our complaints;
So now we can ride to Hell in our pride,
On Railroads of sin with blue Devils inside.

Old Swilltub the doctor and guard of the Trains,
He filches your pockets and fuddles your brains;
But when he's got all from the poor silly man,
He then sends him home to do as he can,
With all his old chums, his badgers and bums,
Who sue him for money he owes in great sums.

But let us not ride on these Railroads of sin,
Nor drink either Brandy, Ale, Porter, or Gin;
And then we shall ride into Heaven with joy,
Where no drunken quacks can our vitals destroy
With poisonous drugs, sold to us in jugs,
In either their Bars, their Parlours, or Snugs.

The number of vaults which we have in Town,
Have robbed the poor lass of her bonnet and gown,
Her topknots and feathers have gone to the Pop,
And many have lost both credit and shop;
Both young men and maids of very good trades,
Have drunk all they earned, and gone down to the shades.

We've plenty of signs, both Horses and Bulls,
Of Lions and Dragons, to serve drunken Trulls;
We've signs too of Angels, of Warriors and Kings—
Yes, plenty of signs of good and bad things.
But what's their design? Why Gin, Rum, and Wine,
Sold here to intoxicate puppies and swine.

We've White and Black Bulls and two Suns in one street,
One Swan and two Lions which never taste meat,
And here you see women with bottles and jugs,
Roll into these taverns and dram-drinking snugs,
As brazen as brass to get an odd glass,
In some of these shops where a fool cannot pass.

No wonder that Pop-ticket women and wags,
Are dressed up in nothing but patches and rags.
Their dresses and shawls for strong liquor they'll swop,
Yes, Tagrag and Bobtail must go to the pop;
And when this is done, away they will run,
To either a Lion, a Bull, or a Sun.

Such poor sorry women who pledge their old rags,
Are known by their petticoats hanging in jags;
You'll see them at night with their heads wrapt in shawls
Not far from the Dram-shop, or sign of Three Balls,
With bonnets and hats, old dresses and brats,
Made up into bundles as you have seen Pat's.

LONDON:—T. Such, Printer, Union street, Boro'

F

PRETTY MAIDENS BEWARE!

A LOVE LETTER from SARAH to CHARLES.

The following epistle was written by a girl at Deal to her sweetheart, a sailor on board a man of war in the Downs. The lieutenant of the ship found it on board, twisted up with tobacco in it, by which it seems our seafaring spark had as little regard for his mistress, after enjoyment, as if he had been of a more illustrious rank.

Lovin Der Charls,

This mi kind love to yow is to tell yow, after all owr sport and fon, I am lik to pay fort, for I am with child; and wors of al, my sister *Nan* knos it, and cals me hore and bech, and is redy to ter my sol owt, and curs *Jack Peny* lies with her evry tim he cums ashor; and the saci dog wold have lade with me to, but I wold not let him, for I wil be always honest to yow; therfor der Charls com ashor, and let us be mared to safe my vartu: and if yow have no munni, I will paun my new stais and sel mi to new smoks yow gave me, and that will pay the parsen and find us a diner; and pray der lovin *Charls* cum ashor, and der *Charls* dont be frad for wont of a ring, for I have stole mi sister *Nans*, and the nasty tod shall never have it no mor; for she tels abot that I am goin to have a bastard, and God bles yowr lovin sol cum sune, for I longs to be mared accordin to yowr promis, and I will be yowr der vartus wife til deth,

SARAH JOHNSON.

Feb 19th.

P.S.—Pray dont let yowr mesmat Jack se this, if yow do hel tel owr *Nan*, and shel ter mi hart owt then, for shes a devil at me now.

A Poetical Version of the foregoing.

Dear object of my love, whose manly charms
With bliss extatic fill'd my circling arms;
That bliss is past, and nought for me remains
But dire reproach, and sharp unpitied pains:
For (Death to me, and food to others pride)
My sister has my growing shame descry'd,
Ev'n she assails me with opprobious name,
When the prude's conscious she deserves the same
Her loose associates, sated, from her flies,
And vainly to seduce my virtue tries:
True, as a wife, I only want the name;
O! haste and wed me, and preserve my fame.
Unlike most modern matches ours shall be, ⎫
From settlement, the lawyers fetters free; ⎬
I'll quit my All, and be content with thee. ⎭
Then haste away, and strike detraction dead;
The nuptial feast awaits you, and the bed;
Nor fear the hand that will endure for life,
With me, your loving and your faithful wife.

POSTSCRIPT.

These earnest dictates of my anxious heart
I beg you will not to your friend impart;
For oft beneath fair friendship's specious show,
The traitor lurks, the undermining foe.

R.A.

Printed by John Andrews, Portsmouth.

THE VERY PRETTY MAID OF THIS TOWN,
AND THE
AMOROUS 'SQUIRE,
NOT ONE HUNDRED MILES FROM THE PLACE.

"I do not seek to quench your love's hot fire, but qualify the fire's extreme rage, lest it should burn above the bounds of reason."—*Shakespeare.*

A pretty maid both kind and fair,
    Dwells in this very town,
Her pleasant smiles and easy air,
    Engages fop and clown.

Being accosted t'other day,
    By a clumsy 'squire,
Who ask'd her if she knew the way
    To quench a raging fire.

Water, Sir, reply'd the maid,
    Will quench it in a trice,
O no, said he, you little jade,
    I've try'd that once or twice.

Then Sir, said she, 'tis past my skill,
    To tell you what will do;
I'm sure, said he, you know what will;
    There's nothing can but you.

Alas-a-day, what do you mean,
    Reply'd the pretty fair;
I'd have you try it once again,
    You never should despair.

Despair I cannot, cry'd the 'squire,
    While you are in my sight,
'Tis you must quench the burning fire,
    You set it first alight.

Then strait he clas'p her round the waist,
    And forc'd from her a kiss;
Ho! ho! said she, is that your tale,
    Then pray you, Sir, take this.

And with a pail, placed at the door,
    She sluic'd the amorous 'squire;
You're welcome, Sir, to this and more,
    To quench your raging fire.

Printed by W. H. TICKLE, at his General Printing Office, Croydon, Surrey.—An extensive assortment of Songs, Recitations, Shop Window Bills, &c.—Printing of every description readily performed cheap as in London.

E 2

35

THE FULL PARTICULARS

OF

"TAKING OFF"

PRINCE ALBERT'S INEXPESSIBLES.

IN THE BOROUGH COURT OF REQUESTS.—THIS DAY.

Had that love-sick young lady, Miss Juliet, lived in these un-romantic, matter o' fact times, when puffery and humbug lead men on to fame and fortune, instead of integrity, honesty and fair dealing,—when ignorant and worthless foreign quacks are fostered and encouraged, and native merit and native talent left to starve,— she would certainly have become duly impressed with the importance of a "name." "The Queen's name is a tower of strength," and so think the enterprising commercial geniuses of the present day, inasmuch as the patronymic of our gracious Sovereign is applied to all imaginable purposes. We have *Victoria* washing tubs, mouse-traps, and mustard-pots, and *Albert* toasting-forks, shaving-brushes, and dung-barges, and last, though by no means least, "Albert inexpressibles." However, as the young lady alluded to above says, "a rose by any other name would smell as sweet."

Timothy Shaw, a bandy-legged "ninth part," with a mouth sufficiently capacious to admit the largest cabbage that ever flourished in field or garden, summoned a knowing-looking specimen of the *genus homo*, named Gilpin, before the commissioners, for the sum of 7s, for work and labour performed in the manufacture of a certain pair of "*kicksies*," for the wear of a certain Mr Gilpin.

The defendant, an "artful card," was described by the plaintiff as a "'buss cove out of luck," that is, he had been in the habit of doing the amiable at the door of a Walworth omnibus, but had lost his place. The tailor, having blown his nose in that peculiar and primitive manner which gave rise to a certain riddle tending to show that the poor man often throws away what the rich man puts in his pocket, proceeded to "open his case" as follows :—" Please yer vorship, I'm a tailor by trade." And here we must slightly digress to remark that a disciple of the bodkin and shears, upon being asked to describe himself, invariably says, "I'm a tailor by *trade*." A celebrated author is of opinion, that this is to prevent his being considered a *tailor by nature*. "I'm a tailor by trade," said the plaintiff, "and von't turn my back on the best vorkman in the wicinity of Tooley street for a slap up fit in the first stile of fashion, 'causc I regularly takes a trip to the vest-end to pick 'em up. Twigged the 'Prince' t'other day with a new pair of trousers on,—had the cut on 'em all right in the turn of a bodkin."

Commissioner : Really you must be a very clever person to "take off" the Prince's inexpressibles so very expeditiously.—Plaintiff : Beg pardon, yer vorship, but I vouldn't be guilty of any sich indelicate hact, as to "take off" anybody's breeches.

The Commissioner finding that "snip" had the laugh on his own side, adjusted his wig, and requested him to keep to the question.— Tailor : So I do, yer vorship ; I'll swear I never tuck not nobody's breeches off but me own.

Commissioner : Well, what have you to say about Prince Albert ? I suppose he wears his clothes like other people ?—Tailor : Ah !

that's all a mistake, 'cause I've heerd that some knowing Jarman has hinwented new fashioned unmentionables, wot all—

Commissioner : There, there, we don't want to hear any more of this nonsense. What have you got to say against the defendant ?— Plaintiff : Vy, my lord, it's "a plain unwarnished tale." Master Gilpin steers himself into my shop, and ses to me, "Tim, old feller, I vant you to make me a hout-and-hout pair of *kicksies*, 'cause I vonts to show off a bit at *Court* in 'em." In course, me lord, I vos regularly flabbergasted to hear a kiddy as vos only a "buss cove" talk in sich a way, but it soon comed out as he vos a going to lodge in Pennyvinkle-court, vich is close in our neighbourwood, me lord ; and then he said he vos a goin to be married. "Poor devil," ses I, "you're a goin to tie a knot as I should be werry glad to untie." As bad luck 'ud have it, my old woman heard me, and didn't I cotch it nicely.

Commissioner : Well, did you make him any trousers after all ? —Plaintiff : Oh ! yes ; and arter altering 'em three times the war-mint vouldn't pay a farden.

Commissioner : What did he complain of ?—Plaintiff : 'Cause they didn't fit tight to his legs, though I told him it warn't the fashion.

The Commissioner told the defendant that he was ready to hear anything that he might have to say about the matter.—Defendant : I was fool enough to let this old spooney have some cloth to make a pair of trousers, and when I came to try them on, I found them so tight at the top that I couldn't button them, and the legs were large enough to have admitted my whole body. He pretended to alter them—they were worse than before.—Plaintiff : I made them in the "Albert style," yer vorship, so that shows the wagabone's bad taste.—Defendant : If Prince Albert ever wore sich a pair of *kicksies* as them I'll eat my hat.

Commissioner : How much are you willing to allow him for his trouble ?—Defendant : Not the ghost of a mag ; why should I ?— ar'n' he spoiled my breeches ?—Plaintiff : Some people as is werry ugly, thinks the tailor ought to make 'em look handsome. Now, my lord, 'cause this pig-headed hobgoblin didn't look a regular *cock wenus* in the breeches, he lays it all to me.

Commissioner : Now if you had contented yourself with making him look like a "buss cove," as you describe him, instead of trying to *Albertise* him, you would, in all probability, have given satisfaction. You should never try to make a silk purse out of a sow's ear. —Plaintiff : That's very true. It is labour in vain to try to make a gemman out of sich a wulgar blackguard.—Defendant : Keep a civil tongue in your head, old bandy legs.—Plaintiff : Take a fit, young gallus. You arn't no sich a *cock wenus*, pug-nose, arter all.

Commissioner : We cannot allow this. The defendant will **pay** 5s and the costs.

PRINTED BY THE ROYAL AUTHORITY of Messrs March Winds and April Showers.

BATTLE OF PEA SOUP,

FOUGHT ON THE

FIFTY-TWELFTH DAY OF ROTTENSTICKS

This memorable battle took place on the Ocean of Sprats, situated on the Continent of Green Peas, within half a mile of a Donkey; where Bobby the Ratcatcher swallowed the Monument, and the poor old soldier was killed by being drowned in a bog of buttermilk: such an unseasonable battle was never known before.

It took place on the Fifty-twelfth day, on London Bridge, between 15 and 160 o'clock in the night.

Arthur Mc Kelly's nose was knocked into eighteen thousand pieces and converted into a cheese knife, and sold in Plum pudding court, going up to Christmas on the top side of little Bobby the Ratcatcher; the regiment was commanded by General Pigsfry, and Colonel Beefsteak, the bone polisher, who lived one thousand and ninety-nine miles beyond mutton chops, in the parish of Blackberry pudding, a robust strong man, well fed upon marrow bones, and Darby O'Daud, Judy Saggin's son, was mortally wounded, his second hand coat that was made and mended by Patrick Mc Patch, three calendar months beyond the city of Cork. The back buttons were turned before, and a mail coach could have gone through the button holes, the sleeves were massacred and murdered, his waistcoat suddenly took fright, jumped aside off his back, and tumbled into the trap of great Calamity, which was fixed within a quarter of an inch of bad luck. This made him roar out "potatoes" loud enough to be heard sixteen hundred miles beyond Buttermilk, and Selim O'Blunder, the second son of Teddy Humbug, a son to Mr. Nonsense, was terribly wounded in the understanding by the frightful appearance of the blade of a slug, his remembrance was knocked against the corner of his consideration, which capsized

his wisdom out of his Knowledge. His ability was rocking in the cradle of Lamentation, which was fixed between joy and sorrow, where Lamentation fell asleep, and Billy Riley received three dreadful wounds—both his elbows were put out of joint, the shin bones of his knee breeches were transmogrified into a woolpack, and his stockings were made to rue the day his legs were born. Billy Gobbles, the dish licker's son, was accidentally wounded in different parts, first in his constitution, and then in his feelings. After which a piece of plum pudding stuck in the stomach and knocked his appetite asunder, and the sons of buttermilk were all put to the rout, and never stopped till they went and rode the bull, and started off to the land of potatoes, where buttermilk is sold by the yard—to plaster their wounds with potatoes, and the humbugging hospitals of both nations in Dublin is filled with all the buttermilk sons that were killed and wounded in this terrible battle of Pea Soup.

There is one hundred and forty-ten thousand nine hundred and sixty-twelve pounds reward for whoever will give the least information of the author of this battle. The money to be paid down to the informant by Mr Jack Neverfind, who lives at the top of Toleration street, three doors below the bottom, near the corner of Humbug lane, in the days of Tantonybobus, when Adam will be a young man, three hundred and sixty-five miles beyond the remembrance of the Antediluvians, in the reign of our Lord and Sovereign, Queen Richard, by the grace of Candlesticks, Queen of Potwollopers, such as velveteen plum puddings, calico dumplings, and leather apple pies.

The Full & True Particulars

OF THE GREATEST

FANNY.

The fields were gay,
And sweet the hay,
Our gang of gypsies seated
Upon the grass,
Both lad and lass,
By you we all were treated.

Young chicken, geese,
With ducks and pease,
And beans and bacon dainty;
With punch and beer,
The best of cheer,
You gave us them in plenty.

'Twas all to cheat poor silly Fan,
And pilfer that same jewel;
You're sworn to be my perjur'd man,
Tho' now so false and cruel.

You stole some cloaths,
And caps and hose,
From sister Pat last Easter,
To make me fine,
You gave me nine-
Pence and a silver teaster.

OLD

An apron too,
Tho' not quite new,
And good as from the needle;
And once, I own,
You gave a crown,
To save me from the beadle.

'Twas all to cheat poor silly Fan,
And rifle that same jewel;
You're sworn to me, you perjur'd man,
Tho' now so false and cruel.

Whene'er we'd meet,
With kisses sweet,
And speeches soft you won me;
The hawthorn bush
Shou'd make you blush,
'Twas there you first undone me.

What signifies
Your shams and lies,
Your jokes no more shall jeer me;
A licence bring
With golden ring,
Or never more come near me.

For you have cheated silly Fan,
And pilfer'd that same jewel;
You're sworn to me, you perjur'd man,
Tho' now so false and cruel.

IN THIS NEIGHBOURHOOD.

It is pretty well known among the circle of his acquaintances, and the townspeople generally, that Mr————, the old established and highly *respectable* tradesman of THIS NEIGHBOURHOOD is much addicted to wenching, and that he is known to nearly every boy and girl in the town, big or little, as the "OLD RAM," or "BILLY GOAT." And it is also well-known that his wife, who is as nice and amiable a little body as ever laid on a husband's shirt-tail—can never keep a maid-servant with a tolerable agreeable face, but he is sure to be in pursuit of her; and only this year they have had in their service Mary Carter, Jane Baker, Martha Price, Jemima Smith, Harrietta Johnson, Sarah Tompkins, and Betsy Rogers, all of whom have left at a short notice in consequence of the *rumbustiousness* of Mr ————. A few weeks ago Mrs ———— engaged with a very pretty girl named Fanny H————, but no sooner did "The Old Ram" behold her than he was smitten with her charms, considering her as a domestic treasure, of which, he flattered himself, he should soon be possessed. Accordingly, Mr ———— took every opportunity in the absence of her mistress to say civil things, which so tormented the girl, that she soon gave her mistress warning. Mrs ————, the tradesman's wife, having taken a great liking to this servant, was very sorry to part with her, offered to increase her wages, and diminish her labour; but these kind overtures had no effect, the young woman saying it was impossible for her to stay. This peremptory declaration excited Mrs ————'s curiosity to know what could give the girl so great a disgust of the place, when, upon being interrogated closely upon the subject, she replied, "Why then, Madam, to tell the truth, my master teazes me so much in your absence that I have no comfort of my life. I would not mind, continued the girl, if he was a handsome and a young man, but to be tormented by such *an ugly fellow* is insupportable." "An ugly fellow! resumed Mrs ————, with great warmth,—what, call my husband *an ugly fellow?* Get out of the house this instant, you jade,"—then stamping her foot in great rage, she immediately discharged the girl.

Printed by J. Pitts, Wholesale Toy Warehouse, Great St Andrew Street, Seven Dials.

THE WONDERFUL

Adventures of Mr. O'Flynn in Search

OF

OLD MOTHER CLIFTON.

UNDERSTANDING that old Mother Clifton's house was blown away 366 miles above the moon, I went in search of her. I was searching nine days, running hard as I could with my two shin bones in my pocket, and my head under my arm, by order of Old Joe Buck, the Pensioner, who lost his middle eye at the Battle of Waterloo, chewing half-boiled stirabout. I then got upon a buck-flea's back, which carried me over large hills of skilligalee and bog holes of butter-milk, till I met Jarvis the coachmaker driving two dead horses under an empty post-chaise loaded with 18 milliners, 2 tambour workers, 5 loads of apples, a roasted milestone, and half-a-dozen grenadier cock magpies, belonging to the French flying artillery, drinking tea till they were black in the face. I asked Mr Jarvis did he get any account of the Old Woman of Ratcliffe Highway, who was drowned in a shower of feathers last night about three weeks ago, and he told me he had got no account of her whatever, but if I went to John Ironsides I'd get some intelligence, and where John Ironsides lived he told me was two miles beyond all parts of the parish, up and down a street where a mad dog bit a hatchet next week, and pigs wrestle for stirabout: I thanked him for his information and bid him good night. I than began to run as fast as I could sit down by the side of a ditch with my two shin bones and my head in my pocket, till I met a gentleman with the custom-house of Dublin on his back, the Manchester exchange in his pocket, and Lord Nelson's pillar in London stuck in his eye for a walk-ing-stick. The Lord help you, poor man, said I, I am sorry for you, and the devil skewer you, why had you no better luck? I asked him what was the matter, and he told me he was bad with the gravel in his eye, the daddy grumble in his guts, and the worm cholic in his toe. I then put him into a coach and drove him into a druggist's shop and ordered him two pennyworth of pigeon's milk, three ounces of the blood of a grasshop-per, a pint of self basting, the head and pluck of a buck flea, the ribs of a roasted chew of tobacco, and the lights and liver of a cobbler's lapstone, boiled separately altogether in a leather iron pot.

Immediately after taking the mixture he was de-livered of a pair of blacksmith's bellows, and a small tomb-stone only a ton weight. Then proceeding on to Johnny Gooal's house, said I to him, John, did you get any account of Mother Clifton's house, that was blown 366 miles above the moon by a gale of wind from a sow gelder's horn. I got no account, says Johnny, only I wrote a letter to her to-morrow night, when I was snoring fast asleep with my eyes open, knowing her father to be a smith and farrier to a pack of wild geese, and her mother nurse to a nest of young monkies that was held in the said parish of Up-and-down, where pigs wrestle for stirabout; but John told me I should not go till I had dined with them; we then sat down, and what should be brought up but a dish of stewed paving stones,, well mixed with tho oil and ribs of a chew of tobacco, and two quarts of the blood of a lamplighter's snuff-box. The next great wonder she showed me, she brought me into a fine garden and placed me by a cab-bage-stalk, which only covered 52 acres of ground, and where I saw ten regiments of artillery firing a royal salute of 21 guns.

The next wonder she showed me was a big man standing upon a small table made of heath, dressed in a scarlet black cloak, who made a very great sermon, but a north country buck flea bit him in the pole of the neck, and made him roar murder. The next great wonder I saw was a small boy only a thousand years old, thrashing tobacco into peas, and one of the peas started through a wall eighteen feet thick, and killed a dead boy on the other side. Then there was the London privateer and the Channel royal mail coach in a desperate engagement; firing boiled oyster shells, stewed lapstones, and roasted wigs one at the other, one of the lapstones struck Mother Clifton over the right eye and delivered her of the old woman of Ratcliffe Highway, who was sister to Mother Clifton, who had nine rows of bees-wax teeth and a three cocked hat made of the right side of a crab's nostril. I then took the Old Hag and made a short leap from Liverpool to Naas in the North of Ireland, where I saw a French frigate coming with Nelson's monument on the top of her mainmast. So now to bring my story to an end this Old Woman and me stepped out of the vessel into the port-hole; I made my escape, but the Old Woman was always tipsy with drinking Chandler's tobacco, so she sunk to the bottom, and if you go there you will find her making straw hats of deal boards.

London:—H. Such, Printer & Publisher, 177, Union-street, Borough, S.E., and sold at 83, White-cross-street, St. Luke's.

SALE OF A WIFE

IN THIS NEIGHBOURHOOD --- MRS. YOU - KNOW - WHO.

Come all you lads and lasses gay, and banish care and strife,—In the market-place, a mason did by auction sell his wife;—Thirteen shillings and a penny for the lady was the sum,—And to see the curious spree, some thousands soon did run;—In the market-place, I do declare, it's true upon my life,—A mason did the other day, by auction sell his wife. This man and wife, good lack-a-day, did often disagree;—For she often pawned her husband's clothes to go upon the spree. So he led her to the market, with a halter, I am told,—And there she was, so help my Bob, by public auction sold. When the auctioneer began the sale, a jolly farmer cried,—Here's five and fourpence half-penny for the mason's lushy bride; a tanner cried out seven and six, and then a butcher said,—I'll give you ten and sevenpence, besides a bullock's head. She's going, cried the auctioneer, she's going, upon my life;—Tinkers, coblers, sailors, will you buy a charming wife? Such fighting, scratching, tearing too, before no one did see;—Such roaring, bawling, swearing, O! blow me, it was a spree. At length a rum old cobler did give a dreadful bawl,—Here's thirteen and a penny, with my lapstone and my awl. Thirteen and a penny, when down the hammer dropt,—With whiskers, apron, bustle, shawl, stays, petticoat, and —— A lushy mason's lady was this blooming damsel gay,—She did unto the hammer come upon a market day;—Bakers, butchers, masons, did bid for her, we hear,—While a lot of rum old women pitched into the auctioneer. Young men and maids did halloa, while married folks did sneer, They frightened the old cobler and knocked down the auctioneer. The cobler took the lady up just like a Scotchman's pack, and the funny mason's lady rode upon the cobler's back. Some laughed till they bursted, while others were perplexed, But the cobler bristled up his wife with two big balls of wax; The cobler sat her on his knee, and joyfully did bawl,—While the lady knocked about the seat the lapstone and the awl. Then the mason he did sell his wife, as you shall understand, And thirteen and a penny was popt into his hand; he whistled and capered, for to banish care and strife,—He went into a gin-shop, singing, I have sold my wife; So the divorced mason he may go, to banish care and strife,—Unto the market place again and buy another wife. Now the cobler and the lady are both in a stall, While the cobler works the bristle, and the lady works the awl. And they upon the lapstone do so merry play together,—Singing, heel and toe, gee up, gee woe, big balls of wax and leather. And day and night in sweet delight, they banish care and strife,—the merry little cobler and his thirteen-shilling wife.

THE PERPETUAL ALMANACK,

OR

GENTLEMAN'S PRAYER BOOK.

Showing how one Richard Middleton was taken before the Mayor of the City he was in, for using cards in church during divine service; being a droll, merry, and humourous account of an odd affair that happened to a private soldier in the 6th Regiment of Foot.

The sergeant commanded his party to the church, and when the parson had ended his prayer, he took his text; and all them that had a Bible pulled it out to find the text, but this soldier had neither Bible, Almanack, nor Common Prayer book; but he put his hand in his pocket and pulled out a pack of cards, and spread them before him as he sat. While the parson was preaching, he first kept looking at one card and then at another. The sergeant of the company saw him, and said, "Richard, put up your cards; for this is no place for them." "Never mind that," said the soldier, "for you have no business with me here."

When the parson had ended his sermon, and all was over, the soldiers repaired to the church-yard, and the commanding officer gave the word of command to fall in, which they did. The sergeant of the city came and took the man prisoner. "Man, you are my prisoner," said he. "Sir," said the soldier, "What have I done that I am your prisoner?" "You have played a game of cards in the church." "No," said the soldier, "I have not play'd a game, for I only look'd at a pack." "No matter for that, you are my prisoner." "Where must we go," said the soldier? "You must go before the mayor," said the serjeant.

So he took him before the mayor; and when they came to the mayor's

house, he was at dinner. When he had dined, he came to them and said —"well serjeant, what do you want with me?" "I have brought a soldier before your honour, for playing at cards in the church." "What! that soldier." "Yes." "Well, soldier, what have you to say for yourself?" "Much sir, I hope." "Well and good, but if you have not you shall be punished the worst that ever man was." "Sir," said the soldier, "I have been five weeks upon the march, and have but little to subsist on, and am without either Bible, Almanack, or Common Prayer book, or anything but a pack of cards. I hope to satisfy your honor of the purity of my intention."

Then the soldier pulled out of his pocket the pack of cards, which he spread before the mayor, and then began with the ace.

"When I see the ace," said he, "it puts me in mind that there is one God only; and when I see the deuce, it puts me in mind of the Father and the Son; when I see the tray, it puts me in mind of the Father, Son, and Holy Ghost; When I see the four, it puts me in mind of the four Evangelists that preached the gospel, viz., Matthew, Mark, Luke, and John; when I see the five, it puts me in mind of the five wise virgins that trimmed their lamps; there were ten, but five were foolish, who were shut out; when I see the six, it puts me in mind that in six days the Lord made Heaven and Earth; when I see the seven, it puts me in mind that the seventh day God rested from all the works which he had created and made, wherefore the Lord blessed the seventh day and hallowed it; when I see the eight, it puts me in mind of the eight righteous persons that were saved when God drowned the world, viz., Noah, his wife, three sons, and their wives; when I see the nine, it puts me in mind of nine lepers that were cleansed by our Saviour, there were ten, but nine never returned God thanks; when I see the ten, it puts me in mind of the ten commandments that God gave Moses on Mount Sinai on the two two tables of stone.

Here he took the knave and laid it aside.

"When I see the queen, it puts me in mind of the queen of Sheba, who came from the furthermost parts of the world to hear the wisdom of King Soloman, and who was as wise a woman as he was a man; for she brought fifty boys and fifty girls, all clothed in boys' apparel, to show before King Solomon, for him to tell which were boys and which were girls; but he could not until he called for water for them to wash themselves; the girls washed up to their elbows, and the boys only up to their wrists, so King Solomon told by that. And also of Queen Victoria — THE QUEEN OF *our* HEARTS—to pray for her. And when I see the King, it puts me in mind of the great King of heaven and earth, which is God Almighty."

"Well," said the mayor, "you have given a very good description of all the cards except one, which is lacking." "Which is that?" said the soldier. "The Knave," said the mayor. "Oh, I can give your honour a good description of that, if your honour won't be angry. "No, I will not," says the mayor, "if you will not term me the knave."

"Well," said the soldier, "the greatest that I know of is the serjeant of the city that brought me here." "I don't know, said the mayor, "that he is the greatest knave, but I am sure he is the greatest fool."

"I shall now show your honour how I use the cards as an Almanack." "You certainly are a clever fellow," said the mayor, "but I think you will have a hard matter to make that appear."

"When I count how many spots there are in a pack of cards, I find there are three hundred and sixty-five, there are so many days in the year."

"Stop," said the mayor, "that's a mistake." "I grant it," said the soldier, "but as I have never yet seen an almanack that was thoroughly correct in all points, it would have been impossible for me to imitate an almanack exactly, without a mistake." "Your observations are very correct," said the mayor; "go on." "When I count how many cards there are in a pack, I find there are fifty-two; there are so many weeks in the year; when I count how many tricks there are in a pack, I find there are thirteen: there are so many lunar months in the year; there are four suits in the pack, which represent the four seasons of the year. You see, sir, that this pack of cards is a Bible, Almanack, Common Prayer book, and Pack of Cards to me."

Then the mayor called for a loaf of bread, a piece of cheese, and a pot of good beer, and gave to the soldier a piece of money, bidding him to go about his business, saying he was the cleverest man he had ever seen.

Taylor, Printer, 92 and 93, Brick Lane, Spitalfields.

THE

FAR FAMED FAIRY TALE

OF

FENELLA.

A Famous Fish Factor Found himself Father of Five Fine Flirting Females, Fanny, Florence, Fernanda, Francesca, and Fenella. The First Four were Flattering, Flat Featured, Forbidden Faced, Freckled Frumps; Fretful, Flippant, Foolish, and Full of Fun. The Fisher Failed, and was Forced by Fickle Fortune to Forego his Footman, Forfeit his Forefather's Fine Fields, and Find a Forlorn Farmhouse in a Forsaken Forest. The Four Fretful Females, Fond of Figuring at Feasts in Feathers and Fashionable Finery, Fumed at their Fugitive Father, Forsaken by Fulsome, Flattering Fortune hunters, who Followed them when Fish Flourished. Fenella Fondled her Father, Flavoured their Food, Forgot her Flattering Followers, and Frolickled in Frieze without Flounces. The Father, Finding himself Forced to Forage in Foreign parts For a Fortune, Found he could afford a Fairing to his Five Fondlings. The First Four were Fain to Foster their Frivolity with Fine Frills and Fans, Fit to Finish their Father's Finances. Fenella, Fearful of Flooring him, Formed a Fancy For a Full Fresh Flower. Fate Favoured the Fish Factor For a Few days, when he Fell in with a Fog. His Faithful Filly's Footsteps Faltered, and Food Failed. He Found himself in Front of a Fortified Fortress. Finding it Forsaken, and Feeling himself Feeble and Forlorn, with Feasting, he Fed upon the Fish, Flesh, and Fowl he Found, Fricasseed and Fried, and when Full, Fell Flat on his Face on the Floor. Fresh in the Forenoon he Forthwith Flew to the Fruitful Fields, and not Forgetting Fenella, he Filched a Fair Flower, when a Foul, Frightful, Fiendish Figure Flashed Forth. "Felonious Feller, Fingering my Flower, I'll Finish you! Go! Say Farewell to your Fine Felicitious Family, and Face me in a Fortnight!" The Faint-hearted Fisher Fumed and Faltered, and Fast was Far in his Flight. His Five daughters Flew to Fall at his Feet, and Fervently Felicitate him. Frantically and Fluently he unfolded his Fate; Fenella, Forthwith Fortified by Filial Fondness, Followed her Father's Footsteps, and Flung her Faultless Form at the Foot of the Frightful Figure, who Forgave the Father, and Fell Flat on his Face; For he had Fervently Fallen in a Fiery Fit of love For the Fair Fenella. He Feasted and Fostered her, till Fascinated by his Faithfulness, she Forgot the Ferocity of his Face, Form, and Feature, and Finally, Frankly, and Fondly Fixed Friday, the Fifth day of February For the affair to come off. There were present at the wedding, Fanny, Florence, Fernanda, Francesca, and the Fisher; there was Festivity, Fragrance, Finery, Fireworks, Fricaseed Frogs, Fritters, Fish, Flesh, Fowls, and Furmity, Frontinac, Flip, and Fare, Fit For the Fastidious, Fruit, Fuss, Flambeaux, and Flowers, Four Fat Fiddlers and Fifers, and the Frightful Form of the Fortunate and Frumpish Fiend Fell From him, and he Fell at Fenella's Feet, a Fair Favoured, Fine, Frank Freeman of the Forest. Behold the Fruits of Filial affection!!

SECRETS,
FOR LADIES DURING COURTSHIP.

TEASING MADE EASY.
ADVICE TO LADIES.
HOW TO TEASE THE GENTLEMEN.
HOW TO GET A LOVER,
And a mass of Information on
LOVE, COURTSHIP, & MATRIMONY.

Let the lady, on some occasions, appear devotedly attached, and unusually fond, particularly at parting in the evening.—The next day, let her meet her lover with a frown of hatred, and repulse his advances with a look of ineffable scorn. If he dare to demand a reason for such conduct on her part (which he will hardly venture to do for some hours), let the reply be, " I am surprised, sir, YOU should think of addressing me, after what has past. Oh! I never! " This will SETTLE him for the rest of the day, during which time you can throw in a variety of sly HINTS, to make him COMFORTABLE, and cause him to wish that he had never been born. At parting, hold out your hand to him, coolly, and say, " Farewell, cruel man! " but deign no further favor. The next morning, if he call on you—which he certainly will,—relax somewhat of your austerity—burst out into tears, and throw yourself into his arms, sobbing as if your heart would break. This will produce a fine effect! He will accuse himself, inwardly, of a thousand faults he never committed, and acknowledge them for the sake of forgiveness, which you must gradually bestow.

Another very delightful method of teasing a man if he is very fond of you, is to propose taking a walk with some friends, and then after making yourself look " provokingly handsome," accompany him to the door and then, apparently without design, take the arm of some gentleman of the party, then on your return, say, " I was so delighted with my walk! I did so enjoy myself; did not you, DEAR? " Repeat these and other doses during courtship, and if you be skilful you make him fit for a husband, and he will ever let you have your own way and do what you please.

43

THE
TRADESMAN'S
NEW HYMN.

WHEN Nature in a voice of pain,
    Speaks of want and woe,
The voice is heard—but heard in vain,
    As our misfortunes show.

For many weaks we work have sought,
    But work we can't procure,
Sad distress has been our lot,
    To go from door to door.

How does the wretched parent feel,
    When children cry for bread,
How keen the pain of sorrow then,
    They surely must be fed.

Look then on us in our distress,
    Nor think us much to blame,
In God alone we put our trust,
    For poverty's no shame.

May want upon you never frown,
    Nor in your dwelling come ;
May Heaven pour its blessing down,
    On every friendly soul.

Lord give us grace, that we may be,
    Closely united unto thee ;
On thee we call, for thou alone hast power,
    To raise us friends in this distressing hour.

Thou, Lord, can make the meanest soul,
    An object of thy care,
Regard the feelings of my heart,
    And hear the Tradesman's prayer.

The Saviour died upon the cross,
    My sins and grief to bear,
For his sake, Lord, turn not away,
    But hear a sinner's prayer.

My lot seem'd hard, but 'twas ordained,
    My faithfulness to prove,
The child was taken far from home,
    To learn a Saviour's love.

In darkness long my soul remained,
    A rebel bold was I,
But love subdued my stubborn heart,
    And proved that God was nigh.

And if thy Son has made me free,
    Then I am free indeed ;
My soul is rescued from its chain,
    For this did Jesus bleed.

Lord, send Thy Word to that far land,
    Where my poor brethren dwell,
Teach them the way, the truth, the life,
    That saves from death and hell.

Oh, that my father and mother dear,
    Might there thy mercy see,
Tell what Christ has done for them,
    What he has done for me.

Lord, Jesus thou hast shed thy blood,
    For thousands such as me,
Many despise poor Tradesmen's lot,
    But to thy cross I flee.

FRIENDS,—It is with feelings of the deepest regret that we are at present compelled, for the support of ourselves and families, to offer you these few but simple verses to your notice, trusting that you will be pleased to purchase this paper, it being the only means left us at present, to support the tender thread of our existence and to keep us and our families from the utter starvation which at present surrounds us.

E. Jackson, Printer, 15, High Street, Stockport, & Sold by H. Such, 177, Union-st., Boro.'—S.E.

A COPY OF THE REGISTER

OF THE

MANOR OF DUNMOW,

Certifying the truth of the late

CLAIM OF A GAMMON OF BACON

By Thomas Shakeshaft, and his Wife Ann.

On the 20th of June, 1751.

Dunmow. *late the Priory.* THE Court Baron of Mary Hallett, Widow, Lady of the said Manor, thus holden for the said Manor, on Thursday, the twentieth day of June, in the five and twentieth year of the reign of our Sovereign Lord George the Second, by the Grace of God of Great Britain, France, and Ireland, King, defender of the faith, and so forth ; and in the year of our Lord, 1751. Before John Comyns, Esq. ; Steward of the said Manor.

William Townsend, Mary Cater, John Strutt, Martha Wicksted, James Raymond, Elizabeth Smith, } sworn.

Daniel Heckford, Catherina Brett, Robert Mapletoft, Elzbth. Haselfoote, Richard Birch, Sarah Mapletoft, } sworn

At this court it was found and presented by the homage aforesaid, that Thomas Shakeshaft, of Weathersfield, in the county of Essex, weaver, and Ann his wife, have been married for the space of seven years last past, and that by reason of their quiet, peaceable, tender, and loving cohabitation during all the said time : They are fit and qualified to be admitted by the court to receive the antient and accustomed oath whereby to entitle themselves to have the bacon of Dunmow delivered unto them, according to the custom of the said Manor.

Whereupon the said Thomas Shakeshaft, and Ann his wife being present here in court in their proper persons, humbly pray'd that they might be admitted to take the oath aforesaid : And thereupon the said steward, with the jury, suitors, and other officers of the court, proceeded with the usual solemnity to the antient and accustomed place for the administration of the oath, and delivering the bacon aforesaid (that is to say) to the great stones lying near the church door within the said Manor ; where the said Thomas Shakeshaft, and Ann his wife, kneeling down on the said stones, the said steward did administer unto them the following oath (to wit)

You shall swear by the custom of our confession,
That you never made nuptial transgression,
Since you were married man and wife,
By household brawls or contentious strife ;
Or otherwise in bed or at board,
Offended each other in deed or word ;
Or since the parish clerk said amen,
Wished yourselves unmarried again,
Or in a twelve month and a day,
Repented not in thought any way ;
But continued true and in desire,
As when you joined hands in holy choir :
If to these conditions without all fear,
Of your own accord you will freely swear :
A gammon of bacon you shall receive,
And bear it hence with love and good leave ;
For this is our custom at Dunmow well known,
Tho' the sport be ours, the bacon's your own.

Upon which a gammon of bacon was delivered to the said Thomas Shakeshaft, and Ann his wife, with the usual solemnity.

45

THE RENT DAY;
OR, BLACK MONDAY MORNING.

Oh, black Monday morning dread I'm sure,
The landlord is coming, he's just at the door;
With his book in his hand he seems fully bent
To have from his tenants the whole of his rent.

Well, Mrs. Longface, have you got any rent ready—let me see, there's 5s. on the book, and 3s. this week makes 8s., now I have brought a receipt for the whole.—I am very sorry, sir, but I have no money till next week!—Next week! why your husband was drunk last Saturday night, and he earns 50s. a week, and can't pay 3s, this won't do; If I can't get my rent I shall bring the bailiff on Monday morning, so I tell you what you have to trust to.

So away then he goes, and with a black look,
And under his arm he puts his rent book;
He knocks at the next door, and his looks are so sour,
He will turn all the milk in the town in an hour.

Well, Mrs. Paywell, have you got any rent for me?—Yes, sir.—You are the best tenant I have got; let me see, 20s., here's your receipt.—Stop, sir, before I pay you this money, you must send a bricklayer and a carpenter; there's the top of the house wants repairing, the stairs are all to pieces, and the privy door is off, and I am desired by my husband not to pay you a farthing till you have put the whole in complete repair.—No. I won't repair it at all, so if you don't like it leave it.—Yes, but I am not agoing to give you 20s. When it rained the other night we were obliged to get up, and move the children into the middle of the room, and my husband and I were compelled to keep up all night with an umbrella over our heads to keep the rain off. I think if landlords were as fond of sending carpenters and bricklayers as they are of sending bailiffs, it would be more to their advantage.—But, Mrs Paywell, where's your husband, I must speak to him about it.—Why, he's at work, and he can't afford to lose a day to wait on you, so as soon as you get the repairs done here's your money.

Away then he goes, for he's quite in the dumps,
And at the next door he gives some hard thumps;
But on looking up you'd have thought he'd have swooned,
For his tenants were gone by the light of the moon.

Now, I'll call on Mother Lushy. Well, my little girl, is your mother at home?—No, sir, she popped out as you popped in.—Has she left any rent for me?—Yes, sir, she has left 9d. in the teacup on the mantlepiece.—What, 9d. out of two months. Why your mother must think I'm a fool.—No, sir, mother says you're an old rogue.—Well, tell her I shall send the broker.—She says you have broke her of the last 9d. she had.—Has your mother left any money in the teapot?—No, sir, there's only a quartern of gin in it that mother was going to drink, but she went out in a hurry.—Ah, I suppose she knew I was coming.—Yes, Mrs. Longface told her the old rogue of a landlord was coming.

You see how the tenants the landlords abuse,
If you ask for your rent you're sure to get abuse;
They'll pester your brains about lots of repairs,
But who pays the rent, there is nobody cares.

Well, Mrs Meek, have you got my rent ready this morning. Let me see, two weeks is 8s., and I'll write you a receipt.—Sir, I am sorry, extremely sorry, very sorry, indeed, sir, but—if—Oh! hang your ifs and your buts, I suppose you mean to say that you have got no money for me?—No, sir, you seem quite out of temper this morning.—Temper! enough to make any man out of temper. I've been to a dozen houses, and can't get no money. If I can't get the rent next Monday I shall put a bailiff in and sell all off.—Stop! sir, stop, not quite so fast about selling; I am an old woman and can tell you a little about these houses, yes, I have lived many years in this neighbourhood, and can tell you that they are not yours at all.—Not mine! bless my soul the woman's mad.—Not so mad as you may imagine, for I'll tell you, your father was errand boy to old Mr Neasy. When he grew up he suffered him to gather his rents. To make long and short of the story, old Neasy and his wife died, and the son being abroad, your father claimed the houses, but I—Stop! stop! I don't want to hear any more, but come over the way and have a drop of gin, and I'll cross out the 8s. and you shall live rent free; but don't say a word to the other tenants.

So home he goes and thumps down his book,
Makes his wife and his children begin for to lock;
Confound all the houses, they all shall be sold,
And the old bricks and mortar I'll turn into gold.

TAYLOR,
PRINTER, 92 & 93, BRICK LANE, SPITALFIELDS.

HOW TO COOK A WIFE.

While MEN spare no pains in obtaining the BEST MATERIALS for this superlative DISH, they are often totally regardless after the first MOUTHFUL, of the necessary precautions to render it permanently SWEET, and if through neglect it turn sour they invariably slander the Dish, while the fault is in themselves. To MAKE the wife a sweet companion, but to keep her so, this may be accomplished in the following manner: —Obtain an adequate supply of the pure water of affection, and gently immerse her therein: should the water during this process become ruffled, a little of the original balm of courtship will soon restore it to its usual smoothness. The fire should be composed of true love, with a few sighs to increase the flame, which should not be too warm, nor yet suffered to abate entirely, as that would spoil the dish. Coolness is often the ruin of this dish, erroneously asserted by some cooks to be necessary, which cooks add also sprigs of indifference, but this is a very dangerous practice, as a good wife is exquisitely delicate and susceptible. A few evergreens, such as industry, sobriety, and fondness, are necessary, and a moderate quantity of the spirit of coaxing and oil of kisses may be added, giving the whole a most delectable flavour. Garnish with flowers of endearment and kindness, and you will then fully appreciate the delights of a dish, compared with which all others sink into insignicance; namely

A GOOD WIFE.

47

ALARMING SACRIFICE!!!

SALE BY AUCTION,

ON MONDAY NEXT, APRIL THE FIRST,

OF THE

FURNITURE & EFFECTS

OF

HOOKEY WALKER, Esq.,

Consisting of a Glass Bedstead, Iron Feather Bed and Copper Hangings, a pair of Tin Sheets, two Catgut Pillows and Lead Bolster, eight Portland Stone Night Caps, and a Green Baize Looking Glass; a brass Wire Mop with cork handle, six pounds of Moonshine, three quarts of Pigeons' Milk, four pounds of the Report of a Gun, six patent blue Buckskin Wigs lined with cold tripe; three barrels of Roasted Snow, twelve yards of Sun's Rays, a mahogany Set of China, with six Oilskin Tea Spoons, and a Muslin Milk Pot; a Sealing Wax Copper, eight Wooden Saucepans, without bottoms, sides, or tops; six pairs of Oak Gloves, a Double-Distilled Moonbeam, Flannel Tea Caddie, four pounds of Patience, six Crape Decanters with carrot corks, twelve Spider Web Wine Glasses, a Worsted Pianoforte, with Barley Sugar Keys; a Dimity Slop Pail, four Dogskin Tooth Brushes, three wings of a Lion, a case of Spiders' Eyebrows, artistically arranged; Photographs of the Buoy at the Nore, Tommy Dodd, and the Cove of Cork playing a three-cornered game of chess, a pair of Brass Boots with Leaden Straps, a pasteboard chest of Drawers, and a Tombstone made of the best pigtail Tobacco, six sky-green Shirts, a Beeswax Stove Grate with satin wood Fireirons, a Plaster of Paris Carpet, Cambric Washing Tub; two butter toasting Forks, and a decayed New Moon,

A SPLENDID OIL PAINTING,

" William the Conqueror Smoking his First Pipe of Tobacco."

And three pairs of Cotton Candlesticks, two bottles and a half of Smoke, a Calico Ale Barrel, a Brass Toad-in-the-hole, a yard of Rum-steaks cut from the Bulwarks, a set of Brown Paper Knives and Forks and a Cork Gridiron, a Paper Frying Pan, Ivory Cabbage Net, a German Sausage Watch Chain with Stilton-cheese Trinkets, a Whalebone pair of Breeches lined with Slates, a splendid pair of Gauze Bellows, a quantity of Pickled Gingerbread, two Empty Bags filled with Sand marked A.B. with the letters rubbed out, a Tallow Cheese-board, a Sable Black Horse covered with White Spots, the second-hand Report of a Cannon, a quantity of Public Opinion, in lots to suit purchasers.

UNREDEEMED PLEDGES,

The Property of several Members of Parliament, a real Live Hobby Horse, a Green Jew's Eye, some Live Butterflies stuffed with Straw, the Bower of Beauty, Six Eggs that the Ship laid-too of in the Hatchway, the name weight and colours of the Man that paid the Income Tax with pleasure, three yards of Railway Jams, a Policeman's " Move on there ! " (nearly new), the Autograph of the Man in the Moon, and other articles, too numerous to mention.

Sale to Commence at half-past 5 and 20 minutes past One hour and a half.

For further particulars make an early application to the Bung-hole of the Tub with the bottom out. Conditions as usual. Carriages ordered at 13 o'clock. Horses heads to be turned inside out, and Tails made to cut their Lucky—by order of the MAYOR.

THE GENUINE THING

OR

The Last of the "Cocks," or "Catchpennies."

When at Brighton in the month of August, 1869, and winding our way through a maze of small streets laying between Richmond and Albion Hills, in the northern part of the town, our ears voluntarily "pricked up" on hearing the old familiar sounds of a "street, or running patterer" with the stereotyped sentences of "Horrible,"—"Dreadful,"—"Remarkable letters found on his person,"—"Cut down by a labouring man,"—"Quite dead,"—"Well-known in the town,"—"Hanging,"—"Coroner's Inquest,"—"Verdict,"—"Full particulars,"—"Most determined suicide,"—"Brutal conduct," &c., &c., *only a ha'penny! Only a ha'penny!* Presently we saw the man turn into a wide court-like place, which was designated by the high-sounding name of "SQUARE," and dedicated to RICHMOND; hither we followed him, and heard him repeat the same detached sentences, and became a purchaser for *only a ha'penny!* when to our astonishment we discovered a somewhat new phase in "Cock" selling, inasmuch as our purchase consisted of the current number (253) of the *Brighton Daily News*—a very respectable looking and well printed Halfpenny Local Newspaper, and of that day's publication, and did in reality contain an account of a most determined suicide.

Being at the time engaged in arranging the materials for THE LITERATURE OF THE STREETS, we ventured upon a conversation with the "street patterer" in the following form: "Well, governor, *how does the cock fight?*" "Oh, pretty well, sir; but it ain't a 'cock,' it's a genuine thing—the days of cocks is gone bye—cheap newspapers 'as done 'em up." "Yes; we see this is a Brighton newspaper of to-day." "Oh, yes, that's right enough—but it's all true." "Yes; we are aware of that; but you are vending them after the old form." "That's all right enough —you see, sir, I can sell 'em better in that style than as a newspaper: I've sold ten or twelve dozen of 'em to-day." "Yes; but how about them to-morrow?" "Oh, then it will be all bottled-up—and I must look for a new game. I'm on my way to London, but hearing of this suicide job, I thought I'd work 'em." To our question of "Have you got any old *real* 'cocks' by you?" he replied, "No, not a bit of a one; I've worked 'em for a good many years, but it ain't no go now. Oh, yes, I know'd 'Old Jemmy Catnach' fast enough—bought many hundreds, if not thousands of quires of him.—Not old enough? Oh, ain't I though; why I'm turned fifty, and I've been a 'street paper' seller nearly all my life. I knows Muster Fortey too very well; him as is got the business now in the Dials —he knows his way about, let him alone for that." Having rewarded the man with a few half-pence to make him some recompense for having detained him during his business progress, we parted.

On a perusal of the newspaper "Particulars" of the case, of which we subjoin a condensed copy, it will be found to contain all the necessary material for a clever and experienced "Patterer" to work upon, and that—

"'Tis strange—but true; for truth is always strange, stranger than fiction!"

The Determined Suicide of an Aged Artist.
REMARKABLE LETTERS OF THE DECEASED.

Yesterday, at noon, an inquest was opened at the Race Hill Inn, Lewes Road, before J. A. Freeman, Esq. (deputy coroner), and a highly respectable jury, on the body of Mr. John Baldey, an aged artist, who committed suicide in a most determined manner early on the morning of the previous day. During the inquiry, which was a lengthy one, some remarkable letters, proved to be in the handwriting of the deceased, were read. They were written in a clear, and rather bold round hand, the caligraphy particularly, for so old a man, being exceptionally good.

John Salter said—I am a labourer; yesterday morning about twenty minutes to six o'clock, I was going to my work to the building, I saw a man hanging, and that made me go in. The house is unfinished, and is at the corner of Park Crescent Road and Upper Lewes Road. I found the deceased hanging from one of the joists in the back room on the ground floor. I did not know the deceased. I at once cut him down. His feet were about 18 inches from the ground. There was a ladder close to his left hand. When I cut him down he was quite dead; he appeared to have been dead for hours. There was a man passing at the time, and, as I was going into the house, I called to him to assist me. He helped me with the deceased, and I afterwards went for a policeman.

John Bannister said—About ten minutes past nine o'clock on Monday evening I saw the deceased come out of Park Crescent and go into the unfinished house at the corner of Park Crescent. There was nothing particular about the deceased to attract my attention. I did not see the deceased come out of the house again that evening. The next time I saw the deceased was about ten minutes to six o'clock on Tuesday morning. I saw him lying on the ground in the unfinished house into which I had seen him go the previous night. That was after he was cut down. He was quite dead.

Mrs Ann Colwell said—The deceased lodged at my house. He had lodged with me about five years. He was about seventy years of age. I last saw him alive on Monday afternoon about half-past four o'clock. I spoke to him, and he seemed about as usual. During the last three weeks or a month he had complained to me of his circumstances, and told me he must get cheaper lodgings. Generally, he was of a cheerful disposition. I did not notice any particular change in his manner except that he occasionally sighed. In consequence of what he said I let him have his lodgings a shilling a week cheaper. He was an artist, and used to go out to sell his water-colour drawings. Last week he went out for that purpose, and when he came he said it was of no use, but that he would have one more trial to sell his pictures, and when he returned he said he had done no good. One lady had promised to come and look at his pictures. He suffered from chronic affection, which caused him acute pain. His last attack was about a week ago. He had been an invalid for a long time. The affection under which he laboured disturbed his rest. He was desponding about his future—his general conversation led me to think that he very much feared poverty, but on the whole he was a taciturn man. I did not think he was more desponding during the last week than he had been previously. He did not tell me much about his affairs, but I understood some small source of income had recently ceased. Last Saturday he brought in two eggs for his dinner, and he provided nothing for Sunday. That was unusual. I asked him on Sunday morning what he was going to have for dinner, and he said he only wanted a knife and fork. I think he had a small pie for dinner, but I don't know. There was a bag on the table containing 6d.—that was all the money that has been found. Two of the letters produced were found on the mantel-piece—they are in the handwriting of the deceased.

The Coroner read the letters. The first was addressed to his brother, and was as follows:

"You will regret dear Charles my untimely end. I have not the heart to say more than love to all. Your affectionate brother JOHN."

"You will find in the deal box my rent book—2 weeks rent is due, a trifle to the laundress, and 10s. on Mr. Verrall's acc't—that is all I owe."

The second letter was in the following terms:—

"16 St. George's St
"Augt 23—1869.

"to the humane,
"let my body be taken direct to the receiving house of the parochial cemetery I wish to be placed in the earth at the least possible expense and inconvenience at the inquest this writing will shew that I caused my own death, being, at the same time quite serene and composed. I wish my remains to be placed in a deal coffin, and when the darkness of night has closed in to be intered (*sic*) in the catholic burial ground the catholics are larger and warmer hearted than protestants, I trust and hope these my wishes may be conceded and fulfill'd

"JOHN BALDEY
"aged 70 years 37 days."

In answer to further questions,

Mrs. Colwell said—I don't think the deceased went to any place of worship. He was not a drinking man—he never drank to any excess.

Mr. W. Hamilton Brown Ross, retired surgeon-major in the Indian army, said—I live at 149, Upper Lewes Road. Yesterday morning, soon after six o'clock, I was called by a policeman. I dressed as quickly as possible and came to this house. I found the deceased in one of the lower rooms, and from the appearance and temperature of the body—the coldness of the body and limbs, and the general surface, and the surface mark round the neck, and the ecchymosis or extravasation of blood round the mark, and the parchment-like appearance of his shrivelled skin, the cadaverous rigidity of the limbs and neck, usually denominated *rigor mortis*, I am decidedly of opinion the man must have been dead six hours or more. The expression of countenance was haggard and depressed in the extreme—it had altogether a worn and wretched appearance. The characteristics of hanging were so strongly marked, so apparent, that I considered a *post mortem* examination perfectly unnecessary, and the more so as the morbid appearances of the brain had been so much modified by the long period the body had been·suspended, that any indications of congestion, or other brain disease, would have been merged in those produced by hanging so long. I have heard the evidence hitherto given, and the letters read, and I say this,—that, although nothing could be more deliberate and determined than the act of suicide, I am of opinion

that his mind was so overcharged and thrown off its balance by the dread of approaching inevitable poverty, that he was driven in a moment of despair to put an end to his existence; and, therefore taking all these things into consideration, I am further of opinion that he committed the deed while labouring under an attack of suicidal monomania. I think that suicidal monomania is consistent with his having written the letters which have been read, for it is a peculiarity of that disease to be quite sane on all other points.

P.C. Bassett said—I was called to the deceased, and found him lying on the ground in the unfinished house. He was quite dead. Part of the rope I produce was round his neck. I searched the body then and there, and found in the left-hand coat pocket the letter I produce. It is addressed to Mrs. Colwell.

The Coroner read the letter, which was as follows:—

"Mrs. Colwell,
"Dear Madam,
"I have long felt should I outlive my means and be reduced to want—I could not have the heart or know how to plead poverty, that state of things has come to pass, with my health and strength utterly prostrate my heart sinks with despair, as I am unworthy and but little known. I feel I have no claim on society or to be supported by others, the thought of the future has heavily overcome me. I end my days rashly and sadly, do not censure me, but make allowance for the frailties of human nature, consider it to be an act of weakness and want of manly fortitude.—Your's truly with best wishes.

"JOHN BALDEY.
"August 23, 1869."

P.C. Bassett further said—In the right-hand waistcoat pocket I found the small bag produced. I afterwards removed the body to this house.

Superintendent Crowhurst said—I had known the deceased a good many years—by name and by sight. I knew Dr. Baldey, the brother of the deceased, who lived in Bartholomews, and was a parish doctor twenty-four or twenty-five years ago. He committed suicide by taking prussic acid. There was no inquest, but an inquiry by the police.

Mr. Charles Baldey said—I am a grocer, and live in Chichester Place, Kemp Town. The deceased was my brother, and was seventy years of age. I last saw him alive last Wednesday. He came up to my house and dined with me. He appeared rather low, and complained that nothing had passed through him for a long time past, and he suffered great pain in consequence; and that he must go to the doctor. That morning, at three o'clock, he had suffered extremely. I asked him whether he would take any ale. He said he dared not —he had not taken any for two years. He had about half a glass of gin. He received a sum of £10 about a couple of months ago. He sold a reversion three or four years ago for about £150 or £170. We—my brother and myself—knew he was in poor circumstances, and intended to provide for him. We were only waiting for him to come to us. Nothing had ever directly passed between the deceased and myself as to his poverty. He was a man of few words, but very excitable, and we were obliged to be careful what we said to him. He had not been to my house previous to Wednesday since Christmas. I remember my brother, Dr. Baldey—it is true he committed suicide about twenty-four years ago. I don't know what religion my brother was, for I have seen so little of him, but we are not a Roman Catholic family.

The Deputy-Coroner shortly left the case to the jury, who, after consideration, found that the deceased destroyed himself while suffering from "suicidal monomania."—*Brighton Daily News.*

DIVISION II.

A COLLECTION OF BROADSIDES

ON

The Royal Family.

POLITICAL LITANIES, DIALOGUES, CATECHISMS,

ACTS OF PARLIAMENT,

AND

VARIOUS STREET BALLADS & PAPERS ON POLITICAL SUBJECTS.

To "work a litany" in the streets is considered one of the higher exercises of professional skill on the part of the patterer. In working this, a clever patterer—who will not scruple to introduce anything out of his head which may strike him as suitable to his audience—is very particular in his choice of a mate, frequently changing his ordinary partner, who may be good "at a noise" or a ballad, but not have sufficient acuteness or intelligence to patter politics as if he understood what he was speaking about. I am told that there are not twelve patterers in London whom a critical professor of street elocution will admit to be capable of "working a catechism" or a litany. "Why, sir," said one patterer, "I've gone out with a mate to work a litany, and he's humped it in no time." To 'hump,' in street parlance, is equivalent to 'botch,' in more genteel colloquialism. "And when a thing's humped," my informant continued, "you can only 'call a go.'" To 'call a go,' signifies to remove to another spot, or adopt some other patter, or, in short, to resort to some change or other in consequence of a failure.

The street-papers in the dialogue form have not been copied nor derived from popular productions—but even in the case of Political Litanies and Anti-Corn-law Catechisms and Dialogues are the work of street authors.

One intelligent man told me, that properly to work a political litany, which referred to ecclesiastical matters, he "made himself up," as well as limited means would permit, as a bishop! and "did stunning, until he was afraid of being stunned on skilly."—*Henry Mayhew's London Labour and the London Poor.*

BROADSIDES ON ROYALTY,

POLITICAL LITANIES, &c.

OUR KING

IS A

TRUE BRITISH SAILOR.

Too long out of sight have been kept Jolly Tars,
　In the ground-tiers like huts stow'd away,
Despis'd & contemn'd were their honour'd scars
　And Red Coats were Lords of the day.
But Britannia now moves as a gallant first-rate
　And with transports the Blue Jackets hail
　　her;
For William's right hand steers the helm of
　　the State,
　And our King is a true British Sailor.

No danger the heart of a seaman appals,
　To fight or to fall he is ready,
The safeguard of Britain is her wooden walls,
　And the Helmsman cries " steady ! boys,
　　steady !"
Cheer up, my brave boys, give the wheel a new
　　spoke,
　If a foe is in view we will hail her,
For William the Fourth is a sound heart of oak,
　True Blue, and a bold British Sailor.

The wild winds around us may furiously whistle
　And tempest the ocean deform,
But unite the red rose, the shamrock, & thistle,
　With King William we'll weather the storm;
Hard up with the helm, Britannia's sheet flows
　Magna Charta on board will avail her,
And better she sails as the harder it blows,
　For her Pilot's a King and a Sailor.

Co-equal with red be the gallant true blue,
　And nought can their glories o'erwhelm,
Whilst Sydney & Freemen direct the brave crew,
　And William presides at the helm;
Then fill up a bumper, Britannia appears
　New rigg'd, and with joy we all hail her,
Here's a health to the King, with three times
　　three cheers,
　And long life to the first British Sailor.

(ENCORE VERSES.)

As a Beacon on high with a glorious blaze,
　Our Monarch, our Admiral, and Friend,
A staunch crew of heroes on deck can soon raise
　Britannia's just rights to defend.
Steady, always be ready, he cries at the wheel,
　Making justice and mercy prevail here;
With a hand that can guide and a heart that
　　can feel,
　Our King's heart and soul is a Sailor.

Fore and aft fill the glasses and make the
　　decks ring,
　We are loyal and true one and all;
Prepar'd to support our lov'd Country & King
　And with liberty stand boys, or fall.
Our Sweethearts, our Wives, & our Children
　　combine,
　For Britannia there's no one will fail her;
As laurels the temples of William entwine,
　Our King ! and a bold British Sailor.

Printed by T. BIRT, No. 10, Great St. Andrew Street, Seven Dials.

53

KING WILLIAM IV.

AND HIS MINISTERS FOR EVER!

TUNE.—" *All Nodding, nid, nid, Nodding.*"

YOU heroes of England draw near awhile,
    The Isle of Great Britain will ne'er fail to smile,
For William and his Ministers will never look with scorn,
They are every one determin'd to struggle for Reform.
    And they are all conversing about Parliament Reform. .

Pray what do you think of William and his Queen?
A better in Great Britain there never can be seen,
Conquered by the Tories, they'll never be, we're told,
For the rights of the people they'll fight like heroes bold.
    And they're all struggling to obtain the nation's rights.

What do you think of brave Russell, Brougham, & Grey,
They have boldly beat the Tories now they have got fair
    play,
To fight for your liberties they eager do resolve,
And his Majesty on Friday last did Parliament dissolve.
    And they're all trembling, they'll not get in again.

What do you think of the Blacking man of Wilson and
    others ?
Why like a set of turn-coats they'll go to h— like brothers
Into the House of Commons they will never go again,
They may cry and pray, lord ! lack-a-day, it will surely
    be in vain.
    And they're all lamenting because their seats they must
    resign.

What do you think of Hobhouse and Sir Frank ?
I think they're men of honour, & can play a pretty prank.
They've done the best you must allow to crush a desperate
    evil,
While Blacking men and Soldiers both will ramble to the
    devil
    And they're all conversing about Parliament Reform.

What do you think of the agitator Dan ?
For the rights of Great Britain he stuck up like a man.
The state of the nation he told the tories blunt,
And if I may be believ'd he's not deceived like foolish
    Harry Hunt.
    And they're all conversing about Parliament Reform

What do you think of Waithman and of Wood ?
They've done their best endeavours to do the people good,
They stuck to William & his Ministers, rumours could not
    be afloat,
That they like many others will never turn their coat.
    So we're all rejoicing the dissolution's taken place.

What do you think of the Rat-catcher Bob ?
I think he had a sneaking to get into a job,
Along with the old Soldier, but mark what I do say
The King will never part with Russell, Brougham, or Grey
    So they're all praying, the tories are praying for the
    death of all the three.

Now what do you think about the Dissolution ?
If William had not closed the house, there'd have been a
    revolution.
In every part of England there's been some funny stories
So success to Russell & to Grey, the devil take the Tories,
    Who are all lamenting the places they have lost.

Pray what do you think of the Boroughmongers now ?
Each day and every hour they've been kicking up a row.
They've endeavoured the whole nation to fill with dis-
    content,
But they never more will have a chance to get into Par-
    liament
    So they're all lamenting because they are turned out.

I'm certain every Briton owns it was to gain their right
King William and his Ministers did so boldly fight ;
Turn-coats, Boroughmongers and Tories you will see
King William take by the heels and drown them in the sea
    So we're all laughing at the Boroughmongers fall.

Here's a health to King William and his Ministers so true,
We are certain they will never flinch, their courage is
    True Blue ;
Turn-coats, Boroughmongers, and Tories too may grunt,
But the devil will drive them in a van, with Wilson and
    with Hunt.
    And they're all lamenting.

Printed by T. BIRT, No. 39, Great St. Andrew Street, Seven Dials.

QUEEN VICTORIA.

WELCOME now, VICTORIA!
   Welcome to the throne!
May all the trades begin to stir,
   Now you are Queen of England;
For your most gracious Majesty
May see what wretched poverty
Is to be found on England's ground,
   Now you are Queen of England.

CHORUS.

Of all the flowers in full bloom,
   Adorn'd with beauty and perfume,
The fairest is the rose in June,
   Victoria, Queen of England.

While o'er the country you preside,
Providence will be your guide,
The people then will never chide,
   Victoria, Queen of England.
She doth declare it her intent
To extend reform in parliament,
On doing good she's firmly bent,
   While she is Queen of England.
     Of all the flowers, &c.

She says, I'll try my utmost skill,
That the poor may have their fill;
Forsake them!—no, I never will,
   While I am Queen of England;
For oft my mother said to me,
Let this your study always be,
To see the people blest and free,
   Should you be Queen of England.
     Of all the flowers, &c.

And now, my daughter, you do reign,
Much opposition to sustain,
You'll surely have, before you gain
   The blessings of Old England,
O yes, dear mother, that is true,
I know my sorrows won't be few,
Poor people shall have work to do,
   While I am Queen of England.
     Of all the flowers, &c.

I will encourage every trade,
For their labour must be paid,
In this free country then she said—
   Victoria, Queen of England;
That poor-law bill, with many more,
Shall be trampled on the floor—
The rich must keep the helpless poor,
   While I am Queen of England.
     Of all the flowers, &c.

The Royal Queen of Britain's isle
Soon will make the people smile,
Her heart none can the least defile,
   Victoria, Queen of England;
Although she is of early years,
She is possess'd of tender cares,
To wipe away the orphan's tears,
   While she is Queen of England.
     Of all the flowers, &c.

With joy each Briton doth exclaim,
Both far and near across the main,
Victoria we now proclaim
   The Royal Queen of England;
Long may she live, and happy be,
Adorn'd with robes of royalty,
With blessings from her subjects free,
   While she is Queen of England.
     Of all the flowers, &c.

In every town and village gay,
The bells shall ring, and music play,
Upon her Coronation-day,
   Victoria, Queen of England.
While her affections we do win,
And every day fresh blessings bring,
Ladies, help me for to sing
   Victoria, Queen of England.
     Of all the flowers, &c.

W. & T. Fordyce, Printers, 48, Dean Street, Newcastle.

CORONATION

OF

HER MAJESTY, QUEEN VICTORIA.

AROUSE! arouse! all Britain's isle,
   This day shall all the nation smile,
And blessings await on us the while,
   Now she's crown'd Queen of England—
Victoria, star of the Brunswick line,
Long may she like a meteor shine,
And bless her subjects with her smile,
   Victoria, Queen of England.

Then let England, Ireland, Scotland, join,
And bless thy name in every clime—
In unison we all combine
   To hail the Queen of England.

CHORUS—Then hail, Victoria! Royal Maid,
     For it never shall be said,
     Thy subjects ever were afraid
     To guard the Queen of England.

Thy lovely form, with smiles so gay,
Just like the sun's meridian ray,
Shall cheer thy subjects on their way,
   Whilst thou art Queen of England.
Whilst thou the sceptre still dost sway,
Britannia's sons, cheerful and gay,
Shall bless thy Coronation-day,
   Victoria, Queen of England.

Then let England, Ireland, Scotland, join,
And bless thy name in every clime—
In unison we all combine
   To hail the Queen of England.

     Then hail, Victoria, Royal Maid, &c.

From every clime, from every shore,
All nations shall their treasures pour,
In humble tribute to our shore,
   Victoria, Queen of England.
Then may Heaven, with its smiles divine,
This day upon Victoria shine,
And a thousand blessings attend the reign
   Of Victoria, Queen of England.

Then let England, Ireland, Scotland, join,
And bless thy name in every clime—
In unison we all combine
   To hail the Queen of England.

     Then hail, Victoria, Royal Maid, &c.

There is Portugal, and likewise Spain,
Each govern'd by a youthful Queen,
But of all the Sov'reigns to be seen,
   None like the Queen of England:
Her virtues are so very rare,
The poor shall ever be her care,
And all her generous bounty share,
   Victoria, Queen of England.

Then let England, Ireland, Scotland, join,
And bless thy name in every clime—
In unison we all combine,
   To hail the Queen of England.

     Then hail, Victoria, Royal Maid, &c.

All hail her Coronation-day,
Long o'er us may she bear the sway,
And all her subjects still shall say,
   God bless the Queen of England.
Then Britons join both hand and heart,
That Heaven may all its joys impart,
And still protect and ever guard
   Victoria, Queen of England.

Then let England, Ireland, Scotland, join,
And bless thy name in every clime—
In unison we all combine
   To hail the Queen of England.

     Then hail, Victoria, Royal Maid, &c.

                T.H.

W. & T. Fordyce, Printers, 48, Dean Street, Newcastle. Sold also at No. 42, Myton Gate, Hull.

SAILOR JACK
AND
QUEEN VICTORIA.

You've heard of Sailor Jack, no doubt,
Who found our good King William out—
To Windsor Castle, too, he'd been,
A visiting the King and Queen.
     Ri tooral, &c.

Now Jack, who'd travell'd far away,
Returned to port the other day—
He turn'd his bacca o'er and o'er,
For he found the Sailor King no more.
     Ri tooral, &c.

"Shiver my timbers! here's a breeze!
We've got a woman now to please—
So straight to London I must go,
To see who's got the craft in tow.
     Ri tooral, &c.

Then to the palace soon he came—
He'd got no card, but sent his name.
"Go back," said they, "she won't see you!"
Said Jack—"No damme if I do!"
     Ri tooral, &c.

"Stand back, you lubbers! not see me,
The friend of his late Majesty?"
He floor'd them all, sprung o'er the stair
And got where the court assembled were.
     Ri tooral, &c.

They in amazement view'd the scene—
Says Jack, "I want to see the Queen!"
When smiling, seated from afar,
Says she—"Well, here I am, old tar."
     Ri tooral, &c.

"All right!" says Jack on hearing this,
"I've come here just to warn you, Miss,
Don't you by courtier sharks be led—
For, d'ye see, I likes your *Figure Head*
     Ri tooral, &c.

"Don't fear me, Jack—it's true, indeed,
But I'm British-born, and take good heed;
And if against my peace they strike,
I'll give 'em, Jack, what they wo'n't like."
     Ri tooral, &c.

"Hurrah!" says Jack, "your Majesty!
Just like your noble family!
You knows what's what, and I'll repeat
What you have said to all the fleet."
     Ri tooral, &c.

"I like your manners," answered she,
"An admiral you soon shall be."
The lords in waiting there, said "No!"
The Queen—"Why, can't I make him so?"
     Ri tooral, &c.

"You jealous swabs, what are you at?
I knows I am too old for that--
So one request instead I'll make,
Off pigtail you'll the duty take."
     Ri tooral, &c.

The Queen, who quite enjoyed the fun,
Soon promised Jack it should be done,
Says he, "I've one thing more, and 'tis,
To ax you how your mother is?"
     Ri tooral, &c.

"Why, hark ye, Jack," the Queen replied,
"The old 'un's still her country's pride."
"She is—and if you'll view my ship,"
Says Jack, "for both I'll stand some flip."
     Ri tooral, &c.

Then to his messmates soon he hied,
"I've seen her—it's all right," he cried,
"I'll prove to you she's wide awake—
She's a trim built craft, and no mistake."
     Ri tooral, &c.

They ordered grog to crown the scene,
And drank—"The Navy and the Queen!"
Says Jack, "our toast shall ever be,
'God bless her gracious majesty!'"
     Ri tooral, &c.

THE

QUEEN'S MARRIAGE.

A subject I want for a song, do you see,
So Her Majesty, look ye, my subject shall be;
Nay, there I am wrong, so my muse here avers,
My "subject" she can't be because I am *her's!*
Forgive me I beg, if with words I do play,
And "hear a plain man in his own queer plain way,"
And still to my errors in mercy pray lean,
While the wedding I sing of our glorious Queen!
   Our cups to the dregs in a health let us drain,
   And wish them a long and a prosperous reign;
   Like good loyal subjects in loud chorus sing
   Victoria's wedding with Albert her King.

Many suitors the Queen's had of class, clime, and creed,
But each failed to make an impression, indeed;
For, for Albert of Coburg the rest off she packs—
Thus "giving the *bag* each" and keeping the "SAXE!"
A fortunate fellow he is, all must say,
And right well his *cards* he has managed to play;
The *game* he has won, and no wonder, I ween,
When he play'd "speculation" and turn'd up "*The Queen.*"
   Our cups to the dregs, &c., &c.

A hundred thousand a year he may get
For taking the Queen, which is something to wit;
I myself had "propos'd," had I known it that's flat,
For I'd willingly take her for much less than that.
Even yet, if Her Majesty *should* chance to scoff
At the bargain she's made, and the matter break off,
I'll instantly seek her, and lay my mind down,

And offer to take her at just—*half-a-crown*!
   Our cups to the dregs, &c., &c.

Since the Queen did herself for a husband "propose,"
The ladies will all do the same, I suppose;
Their days of subserviency now will be past,
For all will "speak first" as they always did *last*!
Since the Queen has no equal, "obey" none she need,
So, of course, at the altar, from such vow she's freed;
And the women will all follow suit, so they say—
"Love, honour," they'll promise, but never—"obey."
   Our cups to the dregs, &c., &c.

"Those will now wed who ne'er wedded before—
Those who always wedded will now wed the more;"
Clerks will no time have to lunch, dine, or sup,
And parsons just now will begin to *look up*!
To churches, indeed, this will be a God-send,
Goldsmiths be selling off *rings without end*;
For now, you'll not find from castle to cot,
A *single* man living who *married* is not!
   Our cups to the dregs, &c., &c.

But hence with all quibbling, for now I'll have done,
Though all I have said has been purely in fun;
May the Queen and the King shine like Venus and Mars,
And heaven *preserve* them without any *jars!*
Like Danae of old may we see it plain,
'Till time is no more, these bright *sovereigns rain*;
May pleasure and joy through their lives know no bounds,
So let's give them a *toast*, and make it *three rounds.*
   Our cup to the dregs, &c., &c.

ATTEMPT TO ASSASSINATE
THE QUEEN
AND PRINCE ALBERT.

PARTICULARS.

About six o'clock on Wednesday evening the Queen and Prince Albert left Buckingham Palace by the garden gate opening upon Constitution hill. Her Majesty and the Prince were seated in a very low German drotschky followed by the equerries in waiting, Colonel Buckley and Sir Edward Bowater, and the usual attendants. A number of respectable people had assembled outside the gate to witness her departure, and were ranged in two lines to admit of the carriages passing through. After the carriage had issued from the gate, and had preceeded some short distance up Constitution hill, so as to be quite clear of the crowd, a young man, who it is said had come from the Green park, and was standing with his back to the railings, presented a pistol and fired it directly, either at Her Majesty or Prince Albert, there being no person between him and the carriage. The Prince, who, it would seem, had heard the whistling of the ball, turned his head in the direction from which the report came, and Her Majesty at the same instant rose up in the carriage, but Prince Albert as suddenly pulled her down by his side. The man then drew from behind his back a second pistol, which he discharged after the second carriage, which proceeding at the ordinary pace, had by that time passed him a little. The reports of both pistols were very loud, and at the discharge of the second several of the female spectators screamed loudly. Several persons rushed towards the perpetrator of this gross outrage, and he was immediately seized, first by a person having the appearance of a labouring man, and then by Mr. Beckham, one of the Queen's pages, and another bystander, by whom he was handed over to two of the metropolitan police, who conveyed him to the Queen square Police Court. By some it is alleged that the miscreant stood with his arms folded, apparently waiting for the arrival of the carriage; others state that he was crouching down, as if endeavouring to escape observation; and, after firing the first shot, he changed the second pistol into his right hand in order to fire it. The discharge of the pistols and the seizure of the offender scarcely occupied a minute. Her Majesty's carriage sustained no delay, and moved on up Constitution hill at the usual pace, and by half-past six had arrived at the Duchess of Kent's Ingestrie-house, Belgrave-square, where her Majesty stopped for a short time, but neither her appearance nor that of Prince Albert evinced any inclination of alarm or excitement at the deadly attack from which they had so providentially escaped.

NAME OF THE MISCREANT.

The name of the ruffian who has been guilty of this atrocious attack is Edward Oxford; his address is No. 6, West-street, West-square, and he is said to be a servant out of place. His appearance is that of a mechanic, from 18 to 20 years of age, and rather below the middle height. We have been informed that on searching him a list of the names of twenty-six individuals was found, which he admitted that he had intended to have burnt or destroyed, and some circumstance has transpired which leads to a belief that the persons whose names are contained in the list above-mentioned are in some way connected with the prisoner for some sinister purpose. On searching his lodgings a sword was also found, and some crape arranged for the purpose of being worn on a hat or cap in such a way as to conceal the face of the wearer, and the crape is also stated to be folded in a peculiar manner, so that the crape which was intended for the prisoner would distinguish him from the rest of the gang with which it is said he is connected, and who were to be similarly disguised.

We have also heard that on being taken to the police-station the following conversation took place:—

"What are you?—I have been brought up to the bar.

"Do you mean to say as a lawyer?—No; to the bar, to draw porter.

"Are you a pot-boy?—No, I'm above that.

"Are you a publican?—No, I'm not so high as that."

We cannot vouch for the authenticity of this conversation, but merely give it as it reached us. The conduct of the prisoner throughout his examination manifested great self-possession.

The pistols are described as small pistols of Birmingham manufacture, rather well finished. They were loaded with balls, one of which struck the wall opposite to where the prisoner stood, and the other ball is said to have lodged in one of the trees.

The charge against the prisoner entered on the charge sheet is—"With maliciously and unlawfully discharging two pistols at Her Majesty and Prince Albert on Constitution-hill."

[London: Printed by J. Wilson, New Cut.

ACCOUCHEMENT OF HER MAJESTY.

BIRTH OF A PRINCESS.

GOD SAVE THE QUEEN!!!

At ten minutes before two yesterday afternoon, her Majesty was SAFELY DELIVERED OF A DAUGHTER. The Queen, we rejoice to say, is, to all appearance, as well as her subjects can desire, and that the illustrious infant bids fair for life.

At five-and-twenty minutes to three a royal salute from the Tower and other guns announced the joyous intelligence to her Majesty's subjects in the metropolis.

Her Majesty's marriage, it will be remembered, took place on Monday, the 10th of February, nine months and eleven days since.

The Lord Chancellor was presiding in his Court with the intention of pronouncing some judgments, but he instantly locked up his papers and repaired to Buckingham Palace, as his presence is officially required on these occasions.

"EXTRAORDINARY GAZETTE,

"SATURDAY, Nov. 21, 1840,
"Buckingham Palace, Nov. 21.

"This afternoon, at ten minutes before two, the Queen was happily delivered of a Princess, His Royal Highness Prince Albert, Her Royal Highness the Duchess of Kent, several Lords of Her Majesty's Most Honourable Privy Council, and the Ladies of Her Majesty's Bed-chamber being present.

"This great and important news was immediately made known to the Town, by the firing of the Tower guns; and the Privy Council being assembled as soon as possible thereupon, at the Council Chamber, Whitehall, it was ordered that a Form of Thanksgiving for the Queen's safe delivery of a Princess be prepared by his Grace the Archbishop of Canterbury, to be used in all churches and chapels throughout England and Wales, and the town of Berwick-upon-Tweed, on Sunday the 29th of November, or the Sunday after the respective ministers shall receive the same.

"Her Majesty and the young Princess are, God be praised, both doing well."

LATEST PARTICULARS.

The following official bulletin was issued during the afternoon, a copy of which was forwarded to the Lord Mayor :—

"Buckingham Palace, Nov. 21, 1840.
"Quarter-past Three o'clock.

"The Queen was safely delivered of a Princess this afternoon at ten minutes before two o'clock.

"Her Majesty and the Royal Infant are both doing well.

(Signed)   "JAMES CLARK, M.D.
            "CHARLES LOCOCK, M.D.
            "ROBERT FERGUSON, M.D.
            "R. BLAGDEN.

A BABY BALLAD.

Of course you've heard the welcome news,
    Or you must be a gaby,
That England's glorious Queen has got
    At last a little baby?
A boy we wanted—'tis a girl!
    Thus all our our hopes that were
To have an *heir unto the Throne*,
    Are all *thrown to the air!*

How could folks think she'd have a boy?
    To me it seem'd all fun—
For in a dark November *fog*
    We seldom have *a sun!*
Yet after all I'm wrong myself
    To reason so, perhaps,
For we all know what winter is
    The time for having CHAPS.

Doctors Locock, Blagden, Clark,
    They made the great *diskivery*,
And having brought the goods to town,
    Were "paid upon delivery!"
Prince Albert for a nurse sent off,
    To tend his babe and spouse—
One living at the *Isle of Wight*,
    As *milk is best from* COWES!

From eve till morn, from morn till eve,
    The pretty infant prattles,
Gives hope strong of life being leng,
    Though oft it has the RATTLES!
These sprigs of royalty may soon
    Be plentiful as sermons—
Prince Albert possibly may have
    A lot of these SMALL GERMANS!

John Bull must handsomely come down
    With something every year,
And he may truly to the child,
    Say, "You're *a little dear!*"
Sad thoughts will fill his head whene'er
    He hears the infant rave,
Because when hearing a *wight squall*
    It brings *a notion grave!*

Howe'er let's give the Princess joy,
    Though now's her happiest lot,
For sorrow tends a *palace* more
    Than e'er it does a *cot!*
If in some years a son appears,
    Her claim to rule were vain,
And being near the *court* she'll have
    To *stand out of the* REIGN!

QUICK, Printer, 42, Bowling Green Lane, Clerkenwell, and at 8, Little Paternoster Row, Spitalfields.

QUEEN'S WANTS

At Child Birth; or, what a bother

IN THE PALACE.

London, November 21st, 1840.

Come all good people list to me,
I will tell you of a jovial spree,
News from London has come down,
That a young princess has come to town.

CHORUS.

What a bother in the palace,
In the month of November,
Such a bother in the palace
You never did see.

Now all those things, as I heard say,
The Queen did want upon that day,
Night-caps, gowns, frocks, and frills,
And old John Bull must pay the bills.

I must get all things I can,
A child's chair and a small brown pan,
Nine hundred and forty gallons of rum,
And a sponge to wash her little bum.

A great deal of money I want,
You must put it down to my account,
Tops and bottoms, and sugar plums,
And a ring to rub her little gums.

I want a copper to make pap in,
And fifty-three dozen of napkins,
And when she's christened, oh, dear me !
Wont we have a jovial spree.

I cannot help thinking, oh, what fuss
There was in calling in the nurse,
Run for a napkin, open the door,
The child has dirtied on the floor.

At three months old she'll learn to walk,
Italian, Dutch, and Spanish, talk,
She'll jump Jim Crow and catch the flies,
We'll whip her bottom if she cries.

When Albert and I goes out to ride,
We'll have our darling by our side,
And on her head we'll place a crown,
I'll beat her well if she wets my gown.

At the christening we'll have such joys,
Sour crout, palonies, and saveloys,
There'll be all my friends from Germany,
Coburghs and all the bugs to tea.

When she was born there was a pull,
On the purse of old John Bull,
With fair promises, I will be bound,
They'll coax him out of ten thousand pounds.

There was such work I do suppose,
For to put on the baby's clothes,
Oh, nurse, look here, how very silly,
You've run a pin in the little girl's belly.

God bless the Queen, we wish her joy,
And may the next one be a boy,
And if they both should crave for more
Let's hope they will have half-a-score.

MAY

THE QUEEN

LIVE FOR EVER.

Whilst the bright star of glory in Liberty's rays,
Over the face of Great Britain resplendently shines,
Where's the power upon earth can Victoria dismay,
Whilst her true British Subjects together combine.

Huzza, may the Queen live for ever, &c.,
Shall we ever see her like, no never ;
Here's her health in a bumper of wine.

Let the voice of her people re-echo the strain,
And her fame thro' the trumpet extend thro' the World,
May the sun over her throne ever shed its bright rays,
While her Banners of Justice and Mercy's unfurl'd.

We'll sing, too, in praise of Old England our Isle,
Who hath succour'd all Nations imploring her aid,
May that Omniscient Eye look down with a smile,
On our Queen and all who at her Mercy are laid.

John Harkness, Printer, Preston.

A STRANGER IN HER MAJESTY'S BEDROOM.
THE BOY JONES AGAIN!
"What will Mrs. Grundy say—Mrs. Lilley?"

On Wednesday, shortly after 12 o'clock, the inmates of Buckingham Palace were aroused by an alarm being given that a stranger had been discovered under the sofa in her Majesty's dressing-room. The domestics and officers of the household were immediately in motion, and it was soon ascertained that the alarm was not without foundation. The daring intruder was immediately secured, and safely handed over to the custody of the police.

The inquiry into this mysterious circumstance has created the most intense interest at Buckingham Palace and the west-end of the of the town, where the report spread with the rapidity of lightning. At first it was not generally believed, but when it was known that the prisoner was under examination at the Home Office public curiosity was at its height, and inquiries into the most minute particulars were made in every place where it was likely to obtain information respecting an event which might, under present circumstances, have been attended with most dangerous effects to the health of our beloved Queen.

Shortly after 12 o'clock one of her Majesty's pages, attended by other domestics of the royal household, went into her Majesty's dressing-room, which adjoins the bed-chamber in which the Queen's accouchement took place. Whilst there they imagined that they heard a noise. A strict search was commenced, and under the sofa on which her Majesty had been sitting only about two hours before they discovered a dirty, ill-looking fellow, who was immediately dragged from his hiding-place, and given into the custody of Inspector Stead, then on duty at the Palace. The prisoner immediately underwent a strict search, but no weapon of any dangerous nature was found on his person. He was afterwards conveyed to the station in Gardener's Lane, and handed over to Inspector Haining, of the A division of police, with instructions to keep him in safe custody until he received further orders from the Home Office. We understand that as soon as the prisoner was handed over to the police he was immediately recognised as the same person who effected such an extraordinary entrance into Buckingham Palace about two years since, for which offence he was tried at the Westminster Sessions and acquitted, the jury being of opinion that he was not right in his mind. It may here be stated that the name of the daring intruder into the abode of royalty is Edward Jones; he is 17 years of age. In person the prisoner is very short of his age, and has a most repulsive appearance; he was very meanly dressed, but affected an air of great consequence; he repeatedly requested the police to address him in a becoming manner, and to behave towards him as they ought to do to a gentleman who was anxious to make a noise in the world.

At 12 o'clock on Thursday the prisoner was brought in custody of the police to the Home Office, and shortly afterwards taken before the Council, when, we understand, he was interrogated as to his motives for such extraordinary conduct, and particularly as to the mode by which he obtained an entrance into the Palace. He (the prisoner) told their lordships that he was willing to point out to the police the way he effected an entrance, and to state all particulars. Their lordships, on this statement, directed the police immediately to convey Jones to Buckingham Palace, and obtain the information he promised to give, and adjourned the inquiry until half past two o'clock.

The prisoner was taken to the Palace, and brought back again to the Home Office at two o'clock. At half-past two the Council re-assembled, when we understand the prisoner made the following extraordinary statement :—

On Monday night he scaled the wall of Buckingham Palace garden, about half-way up Constitution Hill; he then proceeded to the Palace and effected an entrance through one of the windows. He had not, however, been there long before he considered it unsafe for him to stay, as so many people were moving about, and he left by the same mode as he entered. The next day he again effected an entrance in the same manner as on the previous night; and he went on to state that he remained in the Palace the whole of Tuesday night, the whole day on Wednesday, and up till one o'clock on Thursday morning, when he was discovered under a sofa in her Majesty's dressing-room, as above described. The prisoner pointed out all the passages and places he had gone through previous to his arrival at the room in which he was discovered, and there appears no reason to doubt his statement. The hiding place of the intruder was first discovered by one of her Majesty's pages, and when he was asked what brought him there, he replied, that he wanted to see what was going forward in the Palace, that he might write about it, and if he was discovered he should be as well off as Oxford, who fared better in Bedlam than he (prisoner) did out of it. He was also asked if, during the time he was in the Palace, he saw the Queen or the infant Princess, and he replied that he did not,

but that he had heard a noise, which he thought came from her Majesty's room.

Her Majesty's page, who discovered the prisoner, and the constable who took him to the station-house, were then examined.

The Council came to the decision that, as no property or dangerous weapon was found on the prisoner, it would be better to inflict a summary punishment; and a warrant was accordingly made out, and signed by Mr. Hall, committing the prisoner to the House of Correction, Tothill Street, as a rogue and vagabond, for three months.

The prisoner was immediately afterwards conveyed in a cab to Tothill Street.

LATEST PARTICULARS.

The sensation caused by the late mysterious entrance of the boy Jones into Buckingham Palace, appears to be even greater than that produced by his apprehension in the same place in December, 1838. The object which prompted so daring a proceeding is still involved in the utmost doubt; but it was not probable that it was his intention to do any personal injury to her Majesty, for had such been his purpose abundant opportunities of carrying it into effect presented themselves during his concealment in the chamber where he was secured. From a well informed source, we have heard the sofa under which Jones was found is in the ante-room in which the Princess Royal and Mrs. Lilley, her Royal Highness's nurse, repose. On the night in question the latter had not long retired to rest ere she fancied she heard a noise similar to that likely to be caused by a person who was endeavouring to prevent his presence from being discovered, and was moving in a stealthy manner. Mrs. Lilley at first treated the matter as of no moment, thinking probably that the noise might have been imaginary. Its renewal, however, created an alarm, and she instantly summoned those of the attendants who were on guard in the adjoining ante-chamber. On their arrival the offender was quickly discovered and drawn from his place of hiding. The statement then goes on to say that her Majesty, who but three hours previously had been sitting on this particular sofa, having been disturbed by the confusion to which the event had given rise, called out and desired to be informed as to its cause. As an apprehension was, however, entertained that the sudden communication of the occurrence might be attended with an unfavourable effect on her Majesty, the attendants gave an evasive answer. The Queen repeated her command, and then the fact of the boy's concealment and subsequent apprehension were made known to her.

The circumstances at that time appeared not to produce any very visible effect on her Majesty, but on Thursday symptoms of other than a satisfactory character were apparent. It affords us the highest gratification to be able to add that a few hours of quietude tended to the restoration of her Majesty.

It would appear that there is now no doubt but that the account given by Jones as to his having effected his entrance into the Palace by scaling the garden wall from Constitution Hill is correct. Upon being asked whether he had not met some of the attendants in the course of his progress along the corridor and staircase, he replied, "Yes," but that, when he saw any one coming in his direction, he hid himself behind the pillars, or behind any piece of furniture which happened to be near. Hitherto he has been silent as to the motive which induced him to take so extraordinary a step as that of forcing his way a second time into the royal apartments, and when asked on Friday morning, after he had been upon the tread-wheel, how he liked his punishment, his answer was to the effect that he had got into the scrape, and must do the best he could.

There does not appear to be the slightest ground for the rumour that he is insane.

Many circumstances have transpired to show that Jones was in the Palace the whole of Wednesday. The delinquent states that during the day he secreted himself under different beds and in cupboards, until at last he obtained an entrance into the room in which he was discovered. Not much reliance can be placed in his statements, but, as such general curiosity exists on the subject, we may state that, in answer to interrogatories, he said, "that he had sat upon the throne, that he saw the Queen, and heard the Princess Royal cry."

Prince Albert was in the room with her Majesty taking leave for the night when the miscreant was discovered under the sofa.

The fellow's shoes were found in one of the rooms of the ground-floor. The sofa under which the boy was discovered, we understand, is one of most costly and magnificent material and workmanship, and ordered expressly for the accommodation of the royal and illustrious visitors who call to pay their respects to her Majesty.

MR. FERGUSON

AND

QUEEN VICTORIA.

TUNE—"Jim Crow."

Come all you Britons high and low,
  And banish grief and care,
There's a proclamation insued out,
  " You don't lodge here!"

CHORUS.

  They ran away without delay,
    To the Queen to banish fear,
  But she said,—my chaps, its very fine,
    But you don't lodge here.

There was an Orange merchant.
  As you shall understand,
So she started him to Hannover,
  To cumber up the land.

The next it was a soldier,
  And he wore scarlet clothes,
So the queen took up the poker,
  And hit him on the nose.

The next was Bobby Orange Peel,
  She thought he was a flat,
In his right hand was a truncheon,
  And in his left a trap.

The next was Frank from Wiltshire,
  She put him to the rout,
She wopp'd him all round Windsor park,
  And cured him of the gout.

The next it was a leg of Lamb,
  He thought to make things right,
Says the Queen, my lord, it's very fine,
  But you don't lodge here to-night.

The next man was from Bedford,
  A little chap that's never still,
You don't lodge here to-night says she,
  'Till you have burnt the Poor Law Bill.

There Springed a little man from Cambridge,
  Rice was his name you know,
So she made him dance and reel about,
  And jump Jim Crow.

The next was Mr. Broomstick,
  With him she play'd a rig,
She wopped him with the Poor Law Bill,
  And choked him with his wig.

Then up came Dan O'Connel,
  Saying I'll befriend the people,
With a great Shillalah in his hand,
  As big as Salsbury steeple.

Old women three hundred and ninety five,
  To petition her did begin,
Crying,—Please your gracious Majesty,
  Take the duty off the gin.

Says the Queen to do old women good,
  I'll strive with great delight,
Its all right Mrs Ferguson,
  But, you don't lodge here to-night.

Then toddled up old Joey Hume,
  Saying sufferings I have had many,
The villains knock'd me all the way,
  From Brentford to Kilkenny.

Says the Queen, I am going to Brighton,
  So quiet let me be,
For if you come to trouble me,
  I'll drown you in the sea.

And when I open Parliament,
  Then you'll find I'll do enough,
I'll take the duty off the tea,
  Tobacco, gin, and snuff.

I will make some alterations,
  I'll gain the people's right,
I will have a radical parliament,
  Or, they don't lodge here to-night.

I must tell both wigs and tories,
  Their tricks I do not fear,
Their sayings all are very fine,
  But they don't lodge here.

About the wigs and tories,
  There has been a pretty bother,
I think I'll give the devil one,
  To run away with the other.

Birt, Printer, 39, Great St. Anderw Street, Seven Dials.
Printing of every description done cheap.

ACCOUCHEMENT OF HER MAJESTY.

Birth of a Prince of Wales.

THE
ROYAL BIRTH.

"The Queen was safely delivered of a Prince this morning at 48 minutes past 10 o'clock.

"Her Majesty and the Infant Prince are perfectly well.
"JAMES CLARK, M.D.,
"CHARLES LOCOCK, M.D.,
"ROBERT FERGUSON, M.D.,
"RICHARD BLAGDEN.
"Buckingham Palace, Tuesday, November 9, 1841,
"Half-past 11 o'clock, a.m."

Dr. Locock and Prince Albert, with the nurse, were the only persons in the Queen's chamber, situated in the north-west angle of the palace. The Duchess of Kent and the Lady in Waiting were in an apartment immediately adjoining, and close to where Sir James Clark and his medical colleagues were assembled. The Ministers, Privy Councillors, and Great Officers of State occupied one of the state rooms. It has been stated that these all wore the Windsor uniform; such is not the fact; not one of them did so. The Duke of Wellington wore the dress of Constable of the Tower, Earl Jersey the official dress of Master of the Horse, the Earl of Liverpool, Earl Delawarr, and the Marquis of Exeter wore their household uniforms, and the Ministers their official dresses.

The birth took place at 12 minutes to 11 o'clock, and was duly announced to the great functionaries of the kingdom assembled by Sir James Clark, and they were soon afterwards gratified with a sight of the royal infant.

The Archbishop of Canterbury, Lord Wharncliffe, Lord President of the Council, and Lord Stanley, Secretary of State for the Colonies, were too late, arriving at the palace a few minutes after the birth had taken place. It is an error in some of the accounts which have been published which stated that the Archbishop of Canterbury was present at the birth. The Bishop of London was the only prelate present.

GAZETTE EXTRAORDINARY.

The following is the official announcement from the *London Gazette Extraordinary*, published early in the afternoon:—

"Buckingham Palace, Nov. 9, 1841.

"This morning, at twelve minutes before eleven, the Queen was happily delivered of a Prince, his Royal Highness Prince Albert, her Royal Highness the Duchess of Kent, several Lords of Her Majesty's Most Honourable Privy Council, and the Ladies of Her Majesty's Bed-chamber, being present.

"The great and important news was immediately made known to the town by the firing of the Park and Tower guns; and the Privy Council being assembled as soon as possible thereupon, at the Council Chamber, Whitehall, it was ordered that a Form of Thanksgiving for the Queen's safe delivery of a Prince be prepared by his Grace the Archbishop of Canterbury, to be used in all churches and chapels throughout England, Wales, and the town of Berwick-upon-Tweed, on Sunday, the 14th of November, or the Sunday after the respective ministers shall receive the same.

"Her Majesty and the Infant Prince are, God be praised, both doing well."

The auspicious event, although daily anticipated for the last fortnight, has come upon the country with a pleasurable sudden surprise.

Her Royal Highness the Duchess of Kent remained with the Queen throughout the day until six o'clock in the afternoon, when Her Royal Highness returned to Clarence House.

The nobility and gentry thronged during the afternoon to Buckingham Palace.

THE BIRTH
OF THE
PRINCE OF WALES.

Tune—King and the Countryman.

You've heard of Sailor Jack, no doubt,
Who found our Queen Victoria out,
Who ev'ry time ashore he went,
On visiting the Queen was bent.
Ri tooral, &c.

Now Jack, who'd travell'd far away,
Returned to port the other day—
He left his messmates all behind,
For he heard the Queen had been confin'd.
Ri tooral, &c.

'Shiver my timbers! here's a breeze
She's got a young 'un now to please—
So straight to London I must go,
To see who's got the craft in tow.'
Ri tooral, &c.

Now Jack he to the Palace came—
He'd got no card, so he sent his name.
'Go back!' says they, 'she wont see you!'
Says Jack—'No, damme, if I do!'
Ri tooral, &c.

'Stand back, you lubbers! Not see me,
The old friend of Her Majesty?'
He floored them all—'mid shout and din—
And got where the Queen *was lying in.*
Ri tooral, &c.

Each in amazement viewed the scene—
Says he 'I'm comed to see the Queen!'
The Queen she threw the curtains back—
Says she—'What's that my old friend Jack?'
Ri tooral, &c.

Jack turned his quid, and scratched his tail,
When he saw the Queen looked rather pale—
Says she, 'Jack, don't you be dejected—
They say I'm as well as can be expected!'
Ri tooral, &c.

Says Jack, when he beheld the boy,
'Your Majesty, I wish you joy!
Some day he'll rule us in your stead,
For damme, I likes his figure head!'
Ri tooral, &c.

The folks at Court enjoyed the scene,
To see the sailor with the Queen,
For he took the Prince upon his lap,
And gave him lots of royal pap.
Ri tooral, &c.

Says Jack, 'So long I've been to sea,
That ev'ry fish is known to me—
I've seen their heads, I've seen their tails,
And now I've seen a Prince of *Wales.*'
Ri tooral, &c.

It was really quite a treat to see
Jack dance the Prince upon his knee—
But, finding what he was about,
He *held his Royal Highness out!*
Ri tooral, &c.

The nurse his Royal Highness took,
And gave to Jack a knowing look—
And with the rest, to crown the scene,
Jack took his caudle with the Queen!
Ri tooral, &c.

Then Jack he to his shipmates went,
On fun and frolic still intent—
Our standing toast shall be, he cries,
'God bless his little Royal eyes!'
Ri tooral, &c.

John Marks, Printer, 206, Brick Lane, Whitechapel.—Country Dealers and the Trade supplied.

A NEW SONG

ON THE

BIRTH

OF THE

PRINCE OF WALES

Who was born on Tuesday, November 9th, 1841.

John Harkness, Printer, Church Street, Preston.

There's a pretty fuss and bother both in country and town,
Since we have got a present and an heir unto the crown,
A little Prince of Wales so charming and so sly,
And the ladies shout with wonder, what a pretty little boy.

CHORUS.

So let us be contented and sing with mirth and joy,
Some things must be got ready for the pretty little boy.

He must have a little musket, a trumpet, and a kite,
A little penny rattle and silver sword so bright,
A little cap and feather with scarlet coat so smart,
And a pretty little hobby horse to ride about the park.

Prince Albert he will often take the young Prince on his lap,
And fondle him so loving while he stirs about the pap,
He will pin on his flannel before he takes his nap,
Then dress him out so stylish with his little clouts and cap.

He must have a dandy suit to strut about the town.
John Bull must rake together six or seven thousand pound,
You'd laugh to see his daddy, at night he homeward runs,
With some peppermint or lollipops, sweet cakes and sugar plums.

He will want a little fiddle, and a little German flute,
A little pair of stockings and a pretty pair of boots,
With a handsome pair of spurs and a golden headed cane,
And a stick of barley-sugar as long as Drury Lane.

An old maid ran through the palace, which did the nobs surprise,
Bawling out he's got his daddy's mouth his mammy's nose and eyes
He will be as like his daddy as a frigate's like a ship,
If he had got mustachoes on his upper lip.

Now to get these little nicities the taxes must be rose,
For the little Prince of Wales wants so many suits of clothes,
So they must tax the frying pan, the windows and the doors,
The bedsteads and the tables, kitchen-pokers and the floors.

Now all you pretty maidens, mind what the story says,
And try to get a son in nine months and eleven days,
That's what folks call industry, so damsels young and fair,
Be quickly rolling on the straw with a pretty little dear.

K

A NEW SONG

ON THE

BIRTH

OF THE

PRINCE OF WALES

J. Harkness, Printer, 121 and 122 Church Street Office,
North Road, Preston.

Come all you bold Britons, and list for awhile,
And I will sing you a song that will make you to smile,
A young Prince of Wales is come to town,
The pride of all the nation, and heir to the crown,
On the ninth of November, 'tis true 'pon my life,
All Buckingham Palace was bustle and strife,
The nurses stared at each other with joy,
Bawling, our queen she has got a most beautiful boy.

CHORUS.

The bells they shall ring, and the music shall play,
The ninth of November, remember the day,
Through England, Ireland, Scotland, and Wales,
Shout long life to the Queen and the young Prince of Wales.

It was on the ninth, about eleven in the morn,
When the young Prince of Wales in the palace was born,
Little Vic. she was there, as you all may be sure,
Besides doctors, nurses, and gossips—a score,
Says Vic. I declare he is the image of me,
And there's my dear Albert's nose to a tee,
One and all declared, when he grew up a man,
He would drub all the foes that infested the land.

Then Albert he stepped in with a face full of glee,
And danced and he dandled his son on his knee,
When all in an instant his countenance fell,
And he cried "don't I see a most terrible smell!"
"Mine Cot," says Al., "oh Lord what a mess!
He has completely spoilt my new morning dress,
Be quick go fetch me some napkins or towels,
For my son, the young Prince, is relaxed in his bowels."

Of friends and relations there came such a crew,
Of Lords, Dukes, and Ladies, and Germans a few,
Each one bringing presents, the young Prince to please,
They all were as brisk as a cart load of fleas;
Lady Melbourn she brought him a neat little lamb,
With lollipops he was by Miss Russel cramm'd,
There were cradles and pap, boots, and rattles complete,
And lots of small chairs with large holes in the seat.

The head nurse Miss Peel, declared with much joy,
She never saw such a sweet little boy,
She'd clap him she said at the head of the police,
That is if his mamma would give him that leave,
Says old Waterloo Nell, it shall be no such thing,
For the Prince he was born to become a great king;
When the child to decide the question let fly,
With a basin of pap knock'd out Betty Peel's eye.

The young Prince was set at the end of the room,
And instead of a sceptre he shouldered a broom,
His great uncle Ernest swore he could whack,
And he gave him in earnest a most devilish crack,
They all were as merry as grigs I declare,
Each one seem'd determin'd to drive away care,
One and all took a glass and drank with much joy,
Long life to the Prince, he's a fine little boy.

THE OWDHAM CHAP'S VISIT

TO

TH' QUEEN.

It happen'd t'other Monday morn, while seated at my loom, sirs,
Pickin' th' ends fro, eaut o'th yorn, eaur Nan pop'd into th' room sirs,
Hoo shouted eaut, aw tell thee, Dick, aw think thour't actin shabby,
So off to Lunnon cut thy stick, and look at th' royal babby.

Every thing wur fun an' glee, they laugh'd at o aw tow'd em,
An' ax'd if th' folk wur o like me, ut happen'd t' come fro' Owdham.

Then off aw goes an' never stops, till into th' palace handy,
Th' child wur sucking lollypops, plums, and sugarcandy;
An' little Vic i'th nook aw spied, a monkcy on her lap, mon,
An' Albert sittin' by her side, a mixin' gin an' pap mon.
                    Everything wur, &c.

When Albert seed me, up he jumps, an' reet to me did waddle;
An' little Vicky sprung her pumps wi' shakin' o' my daddle;
They ax'd to have a glass o' wine, for pleasure up it waxes;
O yes, says aw, six eight or nine, it o' comes eaut o'th taxes.
                    Everything wur, &c.

They took the Prince of Wales up soon, an' gan it me to daudle;
Then Albert fotch'd a silver spoon, an' ax'd me to taste at t' caudle,
Ecod, says aw, that's good awd buck, it's taste aws ne'er forget mon,
An' if my owd mother'd gan sich suck, 'cod aw'd been suckin yet mon.
                    Everything wur, &c.

They ax'd me heau aw liked their son, an' prais'd both th' nose an eyes on't,
Aw towd 'em though 't were only fun, 't wur big enough for th' size on't,
Says aw your Queenship makes a stir (hoo shapes none like a dunce mon
But if eaur Nan lived as well as her hoo'd breed 'em two at wonce mon,)
                    Everything wur, &c.

They said they'd send their son to school as soon as he could walk mon,
And then for fear he'd be a foo, they'd larn him th' Owdham talk mon,
Says aw there's summut else as well, there's nout loik drainin th' whole pit,
For fear he'll ha' for t' keep hissell, aw'd larn him work i'th coal pit.
                    Everything wur, &c.

Then up o'th slopes we hod a walk' to give our joints relief sirs,
And then we sat us deun to talk, 'beaut politics and beef sirs,
Aw towd 'em th' corn laws wur but froth, an' th' taxes must o drop mon,
That when eaur Nan wur makin broath, some fat might get to th' top mon,
                    Everything wur, &c.

So neau my tale is at an end but nowt but truth aw tells sirs,
If ever we want the times to mend we'll ha' for t' do 't eaur sells sirs,
So neau yo seen aw've towd my sprees, and sure as aw am wick mon,
If my owd wife and Albert dees aw'll try for 't wed wi Vic mon.
                    Everything wur, &c.

J. HARKNESS, Printer, 121, Church Street, Preston.

THE OPENING
OF THE
ROYAL EXCHANGE.

TUNE.—"*Great Meat Pie.*"

ON Monday, October twenty-eight,
    The Queen, you're all aware,
Opeu'd the Royal Exchange in state,
    And lunch'd with the great Lord Mayor;
A holiday all London made,
    At least there were many that stole one,
While *half* a sovereign was gladly paid,
    To get a sight of a *whole* one !
                                Ri fol, &c.

Shop fronts of articles were bared,
    To make way for those who'd chink,
While a label over their heads declar'd
    Them ' warranted uot to shrink.'
At a furrier's shop close by, a sight
    Of human mugs did grin, sirs,
With a bill above, in black and white,
    " A stock of *muffs* within, sirs ! "
                                Ri fol, &c.

The state procession pass'd by quick,
    A very spicy state in,
There were Lords of the Gold and Silver Stick,
    And other *sticks* in waiting.
The Master of the Hounds, of course,
    (A·regular *buck*) was there,
And the noble Master of the Horse,
    Who went to see the *mayor !*
                                Ri fol, &c.

At Temple Bar, Lord Magnus Mayor,
    Perform'd King Dick that day,
And offer'd Vic. his sword so bare,
    In a werry *cutting* way,
" Of such fine looking bla les," cries Vic.,
    " In the City there but few are,
So take it back again, old flick,
    I'm not so sordid (*sworded*) as you are."
                                Ri fol, &c.

The aldermen made quite a fix,
    Their nags so frisk'd and play'd did,
Ducrow could never do such tricks
    On horseback such as they did.
They reach'd the 'Change, quite pleas'd, no doubt,
    When the trnmpeter, clever elf !
Gave his trumpet a good *blow out*,
    Though he didn't get one *himself.*
                                Ri fol, &c.

The Address was read to her apace,
    Though they minded all their stops,
They thank'd her for coming to *open* the place,
    Though she *shut* up all their shops.
When Mr. Tite was introduc'd,
    Says the Queen, with much affection,
" Well, Mr. Tite, with much delight,
    I admire the fine erection."
                                Ri fol, &c.

When Lambert Jones kiss'd hands, so coy,
    Says Vic., but not with malice,
" I wonder, Al., if that's the *boy*
    That got inside my palace ? "
Just then the bells began to ring,
    And the band began to play,
While Magnay whistled, for he couldn't sing,
    " It is our op'ning day."
                                Ri fol, &c.

To luncheon now they went full tear,
    For splendour naught could beat it,
And as it was a *game* affair,
    They were game enough to eat it.
The wine and toasts went round, so Vic.
    Gave, " Here, success to trade is,"
Says Albert, " Well, I'll be a brick,
    I'll give ' The charming ladies.' "
                                Ri fol, &c,

For Alderman Gibbs no small amount
    Of enquiries folks were making,
'Twas thought he had gone to his long account,
    The reckoning day mistaking.
But Michael went another way
    To the banquet so inducing,
For though he expected duck that day,
    He didn't want a *gaosing.*
                                Ri fol, &c.

The royal pile they now walk'd round,
    When they reach'd the merchants' space,
At the brazen trumpet's martial sound,
    Her Majesty open'd the place.
Thus clos'd the door with great eclat,
    (As a few remark'd, so witty,)
" Sho help ma *cot,* I never *shaw*
    Chit a sphlendid *chite* in the *chitty.*"
                                Ri fol, &c.

LONDON.—Published by J. FAIRBURN, Commercial Place, City Road.

PRINCE OF WALES' MARRIAGE.

Everybody stop and listen to my ditty,
And let the news spread from town to city,
The Prince of Wales has long enough tarried,
And now we know he has got married.

For he went to sleep all night
    And part of the next day,
The Prince of Wales must tell some tales,
    With his doo dah, doo dah, day.

His pastime for a week there's no disputing,
For the first three days he went out shooting,
He's like his father I don't deceive her,
And she like Vick is a good feeder.

The next two days, so it is said, sir,
He began to dig out the parsley bed, sir,
Like his dad he does understand,
And knows how to cultivate a bit.

The first day over he laid in clover,
And just alike he felt all over ;
At fox-hunting he's clever and all races,
Yet she might throw him out of the traces.

He must not go larking along with the gals,
Keep out of the Haymarket and Pall Mall ;
And to no married woman must he speak,
She'll stand no nonsense or half-crowns a-week.

In November next she must not fail
But have a little Prince of Wales,
Young Albert he must not be beat,
But contrive to make both ends meet.

When his wife is in a funny way,
Then he must not go astray ;
Of all those things he must take warning,
Nor go out with the girls and stop till morning.

The last Prince of Wales was a good'un to go,
He would ride with the girls in Rotten Row,
He use to flare-up, he was no joker,
He was as fat as a Yarmouth bloater.

He must look to his stock and cultivation,
He must be a father to the nation ;
He must begin to reap and sow,
Be a rum'un to look at, but a good'un to go.

He wants six maids as light as fairies,
To milk the cows and look to the dairy,
To his wife the household affairs confiding,
While the Prince of Wales goes out riding.

Long life to the Prince and his fair lady,
May she have health and bouncing babies,
May the Prince be King, we want no other,
And take the steps of his father and mother.

H. Disley, Printer, 57, High Street, St. Giles, London, W.C.

A SCENE IN THE ELECTION.

A NEW FARCE.

Performed in various parts of the United Kingdom by His Majesty's Servants.

SCENE.—*A Cobbler's Stall.* CRISPIN *at work hammering a sole.*

Crispin. By the lord of the manor, thou art a tough piece, and not much unlike the hide of my wife Bridget; for though I should beat her hide with all my might and main, I cannot shape the vixen to my fancy: Oh, you hard soles (*hammering*) are the most useless of all others, except to the wearer. If I was a leading man in the state, I should move for a law to be enacted, that good *leather* and good *hemp* should only be employed for smuggling courtiers, purse-proud citizens, and for parliament-men — if such a law should pass, it would be a rare thing for trade in general.

Enter PANDER and SIR BILBERRY DIBBLE.

Pand. Here's a psalm-singing cobbler, Sir Bilberry; he has a vote for the borough, as good as the best; do not let us pass honest Crispin.

Sir B. By the essence of lillies, thou'rt right, Pander; the scum of mobility, as well as the scum of gentry, at this time, must be attended to; 'tis a sacrifice that's due to necessity. Therefore, may I never more breathe the mellifluous air of Montpellier, if I do not descend to request his suffrage; the controverted occasion carries a pardon for the humiliating and filthy condescension.—Master Shoe-maker, your most devoted humble servant (*bowing*), I am, sweet sir, yours to the ground. (*still bowing.*)

Cris. Master Shoe-maker! do you mean to mock me?—No, no, I am no shoe-maker, but like some of your very fine gentlemen at the head of affairs—a poor cobbler at best.

Sir B. This fellow, Pander, has been commended by some blockhead, like himself for his insufferable bluntness, or he would never presume to be so shocking to the feelings of delicacy.

Pan. Bear with him, Sir Bilberry; this is a time when men will say whatever comes uppermost, paying no more respect to delicacy than Æsops's cock to his diamond. If you would succeed, Sir Bilberry, you must descend to be perfectly reconciled to their oddities.

Sir B. I will be reconciled. Well, honest cobbler.—Do you love money?

Cris. Yes; but I love honesty better—

Sir B. Honestly said. If you do me a favor, you shall have as much honesty as you please, and money into the bargain.

Cris. Who are you, and may it please you?

Sir B. I am Sir Bilberry Dibble, knight and baronet, of Dibble Hall, in this county; come to offer myself for your most ancient borough of Steady-town; should I be so happy as to obtain the ultimate zenith of my wish, you, Mr. Cobbler, shall soon find an alteration in the price of good ale; bread shall be but half the rate it stands at now; and above all, your trade shall flourish and your taxes fall; so that the cobbler as well as the prince shall have a glorious opportunity of saddling his spit with a fat sirloin; your right of common shall soon be restored, and without excise, or the doctor's tithe; pigs, poultry, and plum puddings, shall crown your cupboards all the year. Now give me your vote, friend Crispin, and as you puff your fragrant essence from your stall in merry glee, you heel the shoe, and bless the hour you gave your vote for Dibble.

Cris. Oh, you fine powdered gentlemen are something like my codling tree last spring.

Sir B. How's that, cobbler?

Cris. It then dealt a wonderful show of blossom, so much that I concluded a rare autumn; but, alas! I was mistaken; I had not so much as a crump. So 'tis with you who are candidates for boroughs, you promise very fair in the spring of your canvass, but in autumn of election, when we should expect the fruit of good works of you, we too often find you worthless, base, and barren.

Sir B. Nay, Mr. Cobbler, you are too severe in the conclusions; a man of my honour can never deceive you;—Can I, Pander?

Pand. No, Sir Bilberry. I have known Sir Bilberry from a child, and never knew a dishonest thing of him, upon my honour, friend Crispin.

Cris. That's the last lie you told, Friend Pander. Well, Sir Bilberry Dibble, knight and baronet of Dibble-hall, in this county, you are come to ask a vote of a poor cobbler.

Sir B. I am, friend Crispin, and you may assure yourself that there is not a man in the whole borough I respect so much as yourself, though but a poor cobbler.

Cris. Indeed!—that's strange—why you never saw me before.

Sir B. Oh, that don't signify! I tell you, friend Crispin, I respect you equal to the mayor himself.

Cris. That's kind. Come into my stall and sit down, and let's have a little chat together; there, that's hearty; give us your fist. (*Here Dibble takes up his clothes, gets into the cobbler's stall, and sits down.*)

Sir B. Pshaw! how he stinks. (*aside.*)

Cris. So you love me as well as the lord of the manor himself?—that's kind, and so we'll have a glass of gin together.

Sir B. Oh, no! 'pon honour.

Cris. Oh, yes; when this is gone, there's enough at the Three Norfolk Dumplins and Horse Shoe over the way! Come, here's the North-country cobbler's health, who refused to mend the shoe of the man that was inimical to his country's interest. (*drinks.*) A glass of as good maximus as e'er tip't over an exciseman's tongue. Here, take hold. (*presents it to Dibble.*)

Sir B. Dear, Mr. Cobbler, you must pardon me.

Cris. No, no; you, who love me as well as the lord of the manor himself, must drink with me, or I shall take it unkind, and perhaps give my vote where I think I am more respected.

Sir B. Resistance is in vain—to get his vote I must submit and take the poison. (*aside.*) Well, friend Crispin, to show that I respect you, here's yours and the King's good health. (*drinks.*) Pshaw, pshaw, it's a nauseous draught. (*aside.*)

Cris. That's well (*throws his arms round Dibble's neck.*) My dear friend, that loves me as well as the mayor himself, kiss my cheek, and then I will believe you are sincere in your friendship.

Sir B. There, Crispin. Pshaw, how he stinks of those vile spirits and tobacco. (*aside.*)

Cris. Give us your fist again (*holding him by the hand*), my dear friend, Sir Bilberry, who loves me as well as the mayor himself, who can descend to drink gin with, and kiss a poor cobbler in his stall. I heartily thank you, and now I'll finish my shoe.

Sir B. Well, honest Crispin! you promised to vote for me?

Cris. Who told you so?

Sir B. Oh! my dear, I understand you (*taking out his purse*) here are corianders that will purchase hides enough to heel-piece the whole borough—here Crispin.

Cris. What! a bribe;——out of my stall, or by Jingo I'll stick my awl to the head in your——

Dibble leaves the stall, Crispin follows.

Sir B. Here's a transition, Pander.

Cris. What! shall Crispin Heel-tap, the cobbler of Steady-town, give his vote to such a thing as you? A mean-spirited rascal who can stoop to drink gin in a stall, and to kiss the sweaty cheek of a poor cobbler? No, no; to serve your purpose you would not mind stooping to kiss my——, make off while you're safe. I'll vote for none of your Jack-a-Dandy's, but for my faithful master, Sir Thomas Trueman—so away, Sir Fop, you have your answer.

Exeunt Dibble and Pander.

RYLE & CO., Printers, 2 and 3, Monmouth Court, 7 Dials, London.

A New Edition of the Universal
SPELLING BOOK,
OR A
Lesson for the Unions.

TUTOR. Now my Scholars, all of you that renounce the Whigs and all their works, stand up, and I will hear you say your lessons. —Know my children, that those who we hailed as friends a short time back, were but wolves in lamb's clothing, and are now about to attack you, the children of the Unions and members of the flock of the good Shepherd of Birmingham; but my good children, be firm, and you will yet escape their devouring jaws. Know you, my children, that ferocious wolf of Winchelsea is about to disunite you?

PUPIL. (Laughing.) Ah! ah! ah!

T. What are you laughing at, you young dog?

P. Why, sir, I really thought you was joking, when you said ferocious wolf, for I think he is more like a skulking Fox.

T. Aye! you young dog, do you mean to call the big and noble animal of Winchelsea, a skulking Fox?—Did he not bravely challenge the Tiger of Waterloo at Battersea?

P. That he did, sir, and bravely skulked away.

T. What sir! did he not nobly fight, and return the fire?

P. That he did, sir, in the air.

T. But do you mean to say that he flew from the shot?

P. Oh no, sir, for he received a mortal wound in the tail.

T. Well, come come, I find you are a good lad, and learn your lesson.—But I was about to say that this big Battersea Hermit said a short time back that your Unions must be suppressed, for that, while you are united, the Wolves of St. Stephens cannot easily prey upon you.—But, my good children, you that are of the flock of the Unions, be firm, and Attwood your Shepherd, will defend you from their avaricious jaws. Now, you sit down, while I hear little Radical his lesson.—Now Radical——

P. Here, sir.

T. Let me hear you say the lesson I set you—now, go on.

P. A—was an Addled-egg, of a pension most rare,
B—was one B....y, that call'd her his dear.

T. That's right, my boy.

P. C—was a Chapel, St. Stephens by name,
D—was the Dukes who sit there in shame.
E—was an Eldon, who'd put down penny papers,
F—was one Franky, who now can cut capers,
G—was the Gammon for the people invented,
H—was one Hobby with cabbage stumps pelted.

T. Very good, my lad.

P. J—was a Jury, whose verdict was right.
K—it was Knowledge, that's power and might.
L—it was Loyalty, that once reigned in each breast,
M—was the Millions that now are oppress'd.

T. Very true, my boy.

P. N—was a Noble, a mad Scottish fool,
O—was O'Connell, of the Patriot's school.
P—was the Peelers, whose glory is past,
Q—was a Question—how long will they last?
R—was Reform, that was spoilt in the nursing,
S—it was S——y, that old Ireland's cursing.
T—was the Times of Old England's distress.
U—is the Unions Placemen wish to suppress.
V—is the Verdict of a few honest men,
W—is the Whigs, who'd that verdict suspend,
X—is the cross with which it will end.

I can't say any more, sir.

T. There's a good boy, now get your spelling book, and I will hear you read the Fable of the Ministers in Danger.

P. (Reading.) There was a Ministry in Danger of a Turn-out, and many were their opinions concerning the best plan to be adopted to secure their seats, when a noble Hermit said there was nothing so good as a Coercion Bill; an Ex-Chancellor (called Bags) said a Coercion Bill might do very well, but there was nothing so good nor so essential as the Suppression of the Penny Press; but their Wise and Grey old Leader being present said, gentlemen, you can do as you please, but take my word there is nothing like the Destruction of the Unions.

T. There's a good child—now you sit down, and I'll hear young Anti his spelling and meanings. Now Anti.

P. Here, sir.

T. Spell me Attwood. (The boy here spells the words, and gives the meanings as follows.) A tough wood of a good grain, grows in Birmingham, and is used as the principal material in building up the Unions.

Brougham. A broom worn to a stump, formerly the Queen's own, but now owned by none.

Callthorpe. A word despised by the Whigs, but will ever live in the hearts of the People.

Dan. A Patriot of the land of Coercion, where St. Patrick banished the toads, and Stanley the freedom.

Eldon. Old Bags, one that shed an abundance of crocodile tears without one drop of pity.

Frank. A pretended friend to the people, arrived at his second childishness, and plays at Shuttlecock with the Electors of Westminster.

Grey. A dealer in humbugs: who behaved as a father to the people by giving them that which they asked for—The Bill, the whole Bill, and *Nothing but the Bill!*

Hobby. A Westminster Rat, who had so often received the favours of the people that at last they had nothing to give but cabbage stumps, which he received in showers at Covent Garden.

Justice. A balance between Might and Right, but always leaning to power and riches.

King. A title of Monarchy, and Idol of an immense weight.

Loyalty. A word nearly threadbare in some countries.

Mouth. A part of the human body padlocked by law.

Peelers. A body of great Force. Brave and noble conquerors of an un-armed and peaceable people.

Reform. A word that filled the mouths of thousands, but the stomachs of few; a thing without benefits.

Truncheon. A knock-down argument of power, an instrument of the Whigs.

Union. A word despised by all Oppressors.

Verdict. A word lately known as a Terror to the Blues, but the Glory of others.

T. There's a good boy, now read me the Fable of the Mountain and the Mouse.

P. (Reading.) There was a Bill which made a great noise in a certain country for many years, and they said it was in Labour, and the People looked with hopes for a Production of great Benefits, and great was their joy at the thoughts, when after many months pain and anxiety, it produced a Mouse.

T. I hope my children, this will be a warning to you, never build your hopes on the promises of those who are reaping the harvest of your labour, for they will take away your Substance, and leave you the Shadow to feed upon.

You trusted to Whigs, and the Tories turn'd out,
Now which of the two is the best there's a doubt;
For the Tories and Whigs are all birds of a feather,
May the D——l come soon and take both together.

J. MORTON.

QUICK, Printer, 42, Bowling Green Lane, Clerkenwell, and at 8, Little Paternoster Row, Spitalfields.

NEW DIALOGUE

AND

SONG ON THE TIMES.

Bill.—Good morning, Jack, I'm glad to see you. What's the meaning of all these Spinners, Piecers, Weavers, Winders, Grinders, Strippers, Carders, Doffers, Stretchers, Throstle Spinners, Bobbin Winders, Frame Tenders, and all those folk that work in these places with big chimneys at top of um' walking about?

Jack.—Why, if thou recollects, a few months back there wur great talk about the Corn Laws going to come off, and all these big chaps in the Parliament House, and all these Factory Lords of Lancashire, said if the Corn Laws wur repealed that poor people would get plenty of bread for little money, work would be plentiful, and wages would be a great deal higher; but instead of that, bread's dearer, wages is lower, and factories are on short time.

Bill.—Yes, Jack, I recollect hearing people talk about a lot of chaps that wur going to bring such times as wur never seen before, they said that Bobby Peel and Dicky Cobden, and a great many chaps was going to give us cheap bread, and they said that we should have plenty of work and get good wages for it, but I've only work'd ten weeks since that corn bill as they call it past, and I got less wages for it too, Jack.

Jack.—These big cotton masters of Lancashire want to drop poor people's wages, so to accomplish it they're only working four days a week, so that when they start full time again, they can drop the people's wages.

Bill.—Well, but Jack, don't you know when the corn bill passed, these Masters gave a great sum of money to rejoice and have grand processions in honour of it passing.

Jack.—Don't you see, Bill, it is poor people that must pay for it now, for they must work for less wages, or else for short time.

Bill.—Yes, but Jack, there's several factories that's stopping for a month or two, and some working none at all, and a great deal breaking down; what's the reason of that, eh Jack?

Jack.—Why the reason of them stopping a month or two is, they want to get rid of their old hands; so that when they start again they can have all fresh hands, and reduce their wages. As for them that are breaking down, it's a scheme they've got, it's these chaps that rejoiced so much at the time the bill passed, and they are ashamed to tell the people that they'll have to work for less wages or short time, so they are breaking down on purpose.

Bill.—Well, I think you're somewhere about right, Jack, for there is a deal of factory hands that are walking about and has nothing to do, so you've learnt me something, Jack.

Jack.—I bought a new song about these Factory Masters and their short time system, and if you'll stop you shall hear it too.

You working men of England one moment now attend,
While I unfold the treatment of the poor upon this land,
For now-a-days the Factory Lords have brought the labour low,
And daily are contriving plans to prove our overthrow.

CHORUS.

So arouse you sons of Freedom the world seems upside down,
They scorn the poor man as a thief in country and town.

What a fuss there was in England, Ireland, and Scotland too,
On the passing of the Corn Bill and the good that it would do,
But since it's past Meat got so high which makes poor people
    pine.
If it would do good it's time it did for factories are on short
    time.

For when the bill was in the house they said it would do good,
To the working man it has not yet, I only wish it would,
For factories are on short time wherever you may go,
And the masters all are scheming plans to get our wages low.

There's different parts in Ireland, it is true what I do state,
There's hundreds that are starving, for they can't get food to
    eat,
And if they go unto the rich to ask them for relief,
They bang their doors in their faces as if they were a thief.

Alas! how altered are the times, rich men despise the poor,
And pay them off quite scornful at their door,
And if a man is out of work his parish pay is small,
Enough to starve himself and wife, his children and all.

In former times when Christmas came we had a good big loaf,
Then beef and mutton plenty were, and we enjoyed them both,
But now a days such altered ways and different is the times,
If starving and ask relief you're sent to a Whig bastile.

So to conclude and finish these few verses I have made,
I hope to see before it's long men for their labour paid,
Then we'll rejoice with heart and voice and banish all our
    woes,
But before we do old England must pay us what she owes.

JOHN HARKNESS, Printer, 121, Church Street, Preston.

THE OLD ENGLISH BULL JOHN

v.

THE POPE'S BULL OF ROME.

"My good Child as it is necessary at this very important crisis; when, that good pious and very reasonable old gentleman Pope Pi-ass the nineth has promised to favour us with his presence, and the pleasures of Popery—and trampled on the rights and privilages which, we, as Englishmen, and Protestants, have engaged for these last three hundred years—Since Bluff, king Hal. began to take a dislike to the broad brimmed hat of the venerable Cardinal Wolsey, and proclaimed himself an heretic; It is necessary I say, for you, and all of you, to be perfect in your Lessons so as you may be able to verbly chastize this saucy prelate, his newly made Cardinal Foolishman, and the whole host of Puseites and protect our beloved Queen, our Church, and our Constitution.

"*Q.* Now my boy can you tell me what is your Name?

"*A.* B—— Protestant.

"*Q.* How came you by that name?

"*A.* At the time of Harry the stout, when Popery was in a galloping consumption the people protested against the surpremacy and instalence of the Pope; and his Colleges had struck deep at the hallow tree of superstition I gained the name of Protestant, and proud am I, and ever shall be to stick to it till the day of my death.

"*Let us say.*

"From all Cardinals whether wise or foolish. Oh! Queen Spare us.

"*Spare us, Oh Queen.*

"From the pleasure of the Rack, and the friendship of the kind hearted officers of the Inquisition. Oh! Johnny hear us.

"*Oh! Russell hear us.*

"From the comforts of being frisled like a devil'd kidney. Oh! Nosey save us.

"*Hear us, Oh Arthur.*

"From such saucy Prelates, as Pope Pi-ass. Oh! Cumming save us.

"*Save us good Cumming.*"

"And let us have no more Burnings in smithfield, no more warm drinks in the shape of boiled oil, or, molten lead, and send the whole host of Pusyites along with the Pope, Cardinals to the top of mount Vesuvius, there to dine off of hot lava, so that we may live in peace & shout long live our Queen, and No Popery!"

"*The Lesson of the Day.*"

"You seem an intelligent lad, so I think you are quite capable of Reading with me the Lessons for this day's service.

"Now the Lesson for the day is taken from all parts of the Book of Martyr's, beginning at just where you like.

"It was about the year 1835, that a certain renagade of the name of Pussy—I beg his pardon, I mean Pusey, like a snake who stung his master commenced crawling step by step, from the master; he was bound to serve to worship a puppet, arrayed in a spangle and tinsel of a romish showman.

"And the pestilance that he shed around spread rapidly through the minds of many unworthy members of our established Church; even up to the present year, 1850, inasmuch that St. Barnabus, of Pimlico, unable to see the truth by the aid of his occulars, mounted four pounds of long sixes in the mid-day, that he might see through the fog of his own folly, by which he was surrounded.

"And Pope Pi-ass the nineth taking advantage of the hubub, did create unto himself a Cardinal in the person of one Wiseman of Westminster.

"And Cardinal broadbrim claimed four counties in England as his dioces, and his master the Pope claimed as many more as his sees, but the people of England could not see that, so they declared aloud they would see them blowed first.

"So when Jack Russell heard of his most impudent intentions, he sent him a Letter saying it was the intention of the people of England never again to submit to their infamous mumerys for the burnings in Smithfield was still fresh in their memory.

"And behold great meetings were held in different parts of England where the Pope was burnt in effigy, like unto a Yarmouth Bloater, as a token of respect for him and his followers.

"And the citizens of London were stanch to a man, and assembled together in the Guildhall of our mighty City and shouted with stentarian lungs, long live the Queen and down with the Pope, the sound of which might have been heard even unto the vatican of Rome.

"And when his holyness the Pope heard that his power was set at naught, his nose became blue even as a bilberry with rage and declared Russell and Cummings or any who joined in the No Popery cry, should ever name the felisity of kissing his pious great toe.

"*Thus Endeth the Lesson.*"

A POLITICAL CATECHISM

FOR

CHILDREN OF RIPER YEARS.

Question.—Now my child, what is your Name?

Answer.—Weathercock Johnny, alias Jack the Reformer, of the tribe of Russellites.

Q.—Who gave you that Name?

A.—My Godfathers and Godmothers, the People of England, who are called the great unwashed.

Q.—And what do the People of England want you to do?

A.—First, they want to amend my ways, which they say are in a most shaky condition. Secondly, to take a few of Palmerston's pills, which they say will invigorate my Political system. And, Thirdly, to stick up for the Rights of the People, and speak up according to my size, as long as I remain in office.

Q.—And do you think that you are capable of holding firm by the reins, and steer the good coach Constitution, in safety through the mud and mire of these macadamized times, and not as you have done before, getting your unlucky feet in a plug-hole.

A.—Yes, I do, so help my tater,
Try me, and I'll prove a first-rater.

There's a good lad! now stir your young self, and let your conduct be a shade better than it has been, and you will earn our praise, and the nation will reward your services with a putty medal.

So be it.

Now let us sing for the amusement of this respectable congregation, and the benefit of own pockets, a few lines written to uncommon metre.

Now attend to good advice,—Little Johnny, O,
And I'll tell you what is right,—Little Johnny, O,
Hold your head up like a man,
Keep the whip in your right hand,
And be honest, if you can,—Little Johnny, O.

Curtail the ladies crinoline,—Little Johnny, O,
And save us from broken shins,—Little Johnny, O,
And as Gladstone gave us cheap tea,
From heavy taxes set us free,
And crush monopoly,—Little Johnny, O.

Save us from starvation's evil,—Little Johnny, O,
And from meat that's got the measles,—Little Johnny, O,
Let the poor have wholesome food,
And a loaf that's cheap and good,
Gain our praise I'm sure you would,—Little Johnny, O.

Now Johnny dear, be brave,—Little Johnny, O,
From the Fenians, pray us save,—Little Johnny, O,
If at bogey's game they play,
They will better know some day,
It will end in the cabbage garden way,—
                    Little Johnny, O.

In Yankee Land, I hear,—Little Johnny, O,
They talk big with privateers,—Little Johnny, O,
You had better send word out,
If they get Johnny Bull's shirt out,
He will put them to the rout,—Little Johnny, O.

Then put your shoulder to the wheel,—Little Johnny, O,
Then it's pressure you won't feel,—Little Johnny, O,
Flare up and be a brick,
And none of your shuffling tricks,
Or you had better cut your stick,—Little Johnny, O.

Let us say,

And now Johnny, thou most excellent of all state coachmen, to thy Fatherly care, we, an overtaxed, ill-paid, and half-starved people do consign ourselves, trusting that you will take our lamentable condition into thy kind consideration, and spare us from being poisoned with meat that has had the measles, and from being cheated by a set of greedy butchers; and save us from the Fenianites, we implore you; and grant us most merciful Johnny, that at the forthcoming Christmas, every mother's son of us may be plentifully supplied with beef, pudding, and stout, so that we may boldly shout, slap bang, here we are again, and sing in thy praise now and for evermore. Amen.

Thus endeth the Lesson of the day.

HENRY DISLEY, Printer, 57, High Street, St. Giles.

THE
FAMINE FAST DAY.

Sam—Well Tum, how did tha get on oth' Fast day.

Tom—Ta' Fas day! bye gum awe think nowt oth' fast day, for its a fast day every day wi' us.

Sam—Nay mon, not every day, awe shud think yo've summat to eat sum time.

Tom—Aye, we have summat to eat, but it's very lettle tha may depend on't, thick porrich un' sour milk for brekfast, un' potatos and suit, un sum toime a red yarrin un brown bread for dinner, an we go to bed awebewt supper, un if that's feasting aw dunna know what you cawn fasting.

Sam—Well but Tum, con yor tell me what this fast day wur kept for.

Tom—Aye by gum con aw, they sen it's to drive famine away.

Sam—Famine, wot dost mean mon, why all this clemming eh England, Ireland, an' Scotland.

Tom—Aw con there be a famine ith' land, un th' warehouses an th' tommy shops aw breaking down wi' stuff.

Sam—Aw think eth' Lords un Bishops, un Parsons an such like folks had ony goodness in um, they'd gie poor folks a feast day, instead of a fast day.

Tom—Now do you think that these Parsons and Bishops kept th' fast day.

Sam—Not they mon, they an fish, eggs, turtle soup, and such like, but if th' poor could live as they done, they might fast for one day.

Tom—I'll tell thee how aw did, aw sent owr Nell th' day afore to borrow some brass, un hoo geet sixpence, an' hoo went to Shade Hill, un hoo bought a sheep's pluck, but it had no heart toot, un hoo geet a penoth o'th bacon, un hoo stew'd it aw together, un it wur rare un good, aw dunna think th' queen had such a dinner, it's the best flesh meat dinner I've had this six months.

Sam—Aw reckon yo stuff'd yore guts so full, you'd no more to eat that day.

Tom—Why we wur hungry ageen next morning, un had to fall to our thick porrich an' sour milk, but if fasting will drive famine away, I should like it to drive poverty away so that poor folk could geet plenty of plum pudding and dumplins, an' sich like, but stop, I've bowt a song about it, un you shall hear it:—

Ye working men both far and near,
　　Unto my song pray lend an ear,
While I the wonders do declare,
　　About this famine fasting day,
The Bishop of London that godly saint,
　　Who preaches in the Parliament,
He said it was their full intent
　　For to have a fast day,
He told the Parliament he'd a call,
　　For to come and tell them all,
The Devil would fetch them great and small,
　　Unless they kept a fast day.

CHORUS.
Singing higlety pickelty fast who will,
　　I wish poor folk it's had their fill,
Good beef and pudding the famine to kill,
　　Much better than a fast day.

Some of them laugh'd, some fell asleep,
　　And out of the house some did creep;
To please the Bishops and black sheep,
　　They did appoint a fast day,
The twenty-fourth of March it was the day
　　That some did fast and some did pray,
Some made a feast as I've heard say,
　　To drive this famine far away,
I sent our Nell as I'm a sinner,
　　To get some liver and bacon for dinner,
We fasted so long we are quite thinner,
　　We thought we'd have a feast day.

To walk about that day in the street,
　　Thousands of poor folk I did meet,
Because they had got nothing to eat,
　　And so they kept the fast day.
Some who had money spent it free,
　　While others had a jovial spree,
Some pawned off their smocks they say,
　　All for to get a dinner that day,
Some went to the alehouse it is true,
　　Got drunk and fought till all was blue;
On Saturday night thousands will rue
　　The general famine fast day.

The Bishops and the Parsons too,
　　They seldom fast I tell to you,
Their paunches they well stuff it's true,
　　Yet preach about a fast day,
With fish and eggs, and Rhenish wine,
　　On turtle soup each day they dine,
Till their guts are poking out like swine,
　　As though it was their last day,
But if poor folks like them could live,
　　Or if good wages they did receive,
The storms of life they then could brave
　　Without this famine fast day.

So to conclude my fast day song,
　　Pray do not think I've kept you long,
But whether it be right or wrong
　　I'd rather have a feast day,
But if a fast would drive this famine away,
　　I've only got one thing to say,
I wish it would drive poverty
　　Into the middle of the sea,
The Parsons and Bishops are afraid,
　　Church and tithes cannot be paid,
And except they learn some other trade
　　They will have many a fast day.

John Harkness, Printer, 121, Church Street, Preston.

NEW FORM OF PRAYER
AND BELIEF.

To be said by all true Liberals, at all outdoor or indoor Meetings, at all Committee Rooms, and in front of all Hustings on which the Gladstonites and the Dizzeyites are to contend for the Managership at the forthcoming Elections, and to see who is to gain the belt, and rule the roast at St. Stephen's.   To be said without Barrel Organ or Grindstone accompaniment.

Now, my boy, as the Great Election is about to take place, and it becomes us all to sail under true colours, be so good as to tell me what you are, a Gladstonite, or a Dizzyite ?

Boy.—Why a Gladstonite to the backbone, and no mistake.

There is a good lad; now let me hear you rehearse the Gladstone or Liberal Belief.

I believe in Bill Gladstone to be the true Champion of Reform, and that he is a perfect game cock, and that he will stick his spurs into the comb of any tory mountebank who shall attempt to set the working-man's rights and privileges at naught; and I believe at the coming election that all true liberals will put their shoulders to the wheel and obtain a first-rate majority, not only in Church Reform, but in all things where reformation is wanted; and that Gladstone and his friends will reach the tip top of the poll, and start the tories off like scalded cocks, and this I firmly believe. So help me John Brown.

There is a good boy, now let us enlighten our friends on events, past, present, and future.

Now in the first place, there is Gladstone's Irish Church Question! it is a stickler to many, more especially to Dizzey, the Isrælite, for it is to him like the carpenter's saw, which the black cook said stuck in his gizzard.

For the Dizzeyites were sorely vexed by a political squib, which was recited by some of the unwashed in Hyde Park, who made a goodly collection, which went into the pockets of the Collectors in the usual manner.

And behold the Dizzeyites and Adullamites were alarmed, and they said who hath done this evil which is so likely to rob our fat shepherds of the golden wash they have so long fed upon.

And Sarah Gamp of the Standard did cause large bills to be posted in every corner, equal in size to the top of a large dining table, headed with these words, "Gladstone and his Friends," showing how the needle had pricked their tender feelings.

And Dizzey was down on his luck, when he found that his nose was compared to double size, and he hid himself in a corner and wept.

And behold there arose a loud cry from the ladies of England, saying, we are man's better half, why not let us have a voice in the affairs of our country, and not have our tongues muzzled like D— M— as served our dogs.

And moreover it is expected that when the Election takes place that the vendors of dog's meat, headed by Jack Atchley and some of the nobs from Sharp's alley will proceed to Scotland yard to petition D— M— to revoke the sentence on our blessed tykes ; for they say if it goes on much longer, instead of skewing up meat for the dogs they will be skewered up themselves—in some union house washing their blessed inside with water-gruel.

Now behold B— S— of penny newspaper notoriety is again attempting to poke his nose in for Westminster, but he will find it is no go, for with Mill and Grosvenor before him, he will have no chance to walk in for our ancient and much respected borough.

And all tories and adullamites are hereby cautioned not to have any dirty tricks, at the coming Election, as they had at the Guildhall Meeting, when they hired land rats and water rats at two bob a nob to disturb the peace, or they may find something in the seat of their small clothes more than their shirt tails.

Thus endeth the morning's address.

LET US SAY.

From all back-sliding liberals, or slop made adullamites, Friends of Reform spare us,

      Spare us we implore thee.

From all tories who would give us such quarters as the wolf gives the lamb. Gladstone, the father of the people, save us !

      Gladstone, look down upon us.

From being gobbled up by Dizzey's ' No Popery " bogey, noble army of liberals defend us.

From Dizzey's Guy Faux keep us we beseech thee.

And oh, Lawrence, when you are made king of the city, let us have no more unseemly brawls in Guildhall.

From all paid ruffians, save us good Lawrence.

And may it please you, good Richard, to look down with an eye of pity on all distressed dog's meat sellers, and take the harness from off the dogs, so that we may obtain food to supply the worms that now gnaw our hungry bowels.

      Grant this, there's a dear Dickey.

And oh, Dizzey, make your will, there's a good boy, for at the forthcoming election, Gladstone and the whole host of Liberals will be at the top of the poll, and then farewell to all your greatness.

      And I say so be it.

Henry Disley, Printer, 57, High Street, St. Giles, London.—W.C.

A POLITICAL LITANY

ON THE

TIMES.

When the present ministry shall cease their humbuging tricks, and do that which is lawful and right for the benefit of the working classes, then, and not till then, shall they receive our praise.

Dearly Beloved Brethren—Hunger moveth us at various times and in sundry places, to make known unto our Most Gracious Majesty, the Queen Victoria, our dreadful wants and sufferings, and although we ought at all times humbly to acknowledge our Most Gracious Majesty the Queen, yet the cry of our starving children prevent us from so doing.

The Lesson for the Day is taken from the present hard times.

And it came to pass in the year '65, that there was a great stoppage in the tide of politics, and the steersman, Pam, gave up the helm ; and the Queen sent unto the Land o' Cakes for a certain little man of the tribe of Russellites, well known by the name of Financial Jack, by some called Little John, who being fond of lollipops, and having a sweet tooth, it will be remembered he called out lustily for cheap sugar.

And when he arrived at the Castle, which is situated near unto the great park at Windsor, the Queen said unto him, Johnny, Johnny, thy friend Pam has cut his stick, and if thou thinkest thyself strong enough, the place is thine.

Whereupon the little man bowed and bowed till the rim fell off his hat; but when he tried on the garments of Pam, the coat fitted him like unto a purser's coat on a marlin-spike.

And the people murmured, saying, this man is totally unfit for the berth, but for the want of a better he was accepted.

Amen.

And about this time there arose in the Land of Spuds tribes of men who call themselves Feenanites, who promised to march unto the house of St. Stephen's straightway, to get something taken from them by honest John Bull.

But a messenger came from that land to the house of St. Stephen's straightway, to inform the inmates thereof they were in danger.

And there was great trouble in the House, and the servants arose and went out to meet them.

But when they arrived near unto that part of the land, behold, they had flew, leaving nought behind them to take back but a few sticks, like unto popguns, with which they had been learning to play at soldiers, so they returned home.

Amen.

And O, Gladstone, thou good and faithful servant of the late Steersman Pam, take unto thyself the helm of the good ship Great Britain, and steer it safely through the troubled waters that now surround it.

Amen.

Let us say,

From all impositions of unjust stewards,

O Queen deliver us,

We beseech thee to hear us, O Queen.

And O Johnny, if thou take unto thyself the helm of the good ship Great Britain, steer her safely through the troubled waters of poverty that now surround her.

Hear us, O Russell.

We beseech thee to hear us, O Jack.

And from being slaughtered by the Fenians,

O Queen deliver us.

We beseech thee to hear us, O Vick.

And from all heavy taxation,

O Johnny, save us.

We beseech thee to hear us, O Russell.

And from all bad meat, O Queen deliver us.

We beseech thee to hear us, O Queen.

And O thou mighty Queen, grant that we may have a cheap loaf, and each man paid justly for his daily labour, that we may live in peace and happiness both now and for evermore.

Amen.

Printed for Author and Vendor.

POLITICAL LITANY

On the Present Session of Parliament.

When the Whigs shall cease to be a milk and water set, and prove to the people of England, that like good and trusty servants they will stick up for their rights, and pass such measures as will be for the benefit of the nation at large : then, and not till then, shall we consider them as trumps, and look upon them with confidence.

Dearly bought and never-to-be-forgotten Johnny.— To your noble and all-powerful self, do we, an over-taxed, poorly-fed people appeal, trusting that, O most merciful Johnny, that by the virtue of thy most exalted position, that you will be pleased to intercede with our Most Gracious Majesty, that she will reside amongst us, and so improve the condition of the tradesmen and mechanics of this mighty metropolis, whose affairs now are in a most shaky condition. Grant this, O most mighty John, and we will pray for the well-being of thy favourite bantling, Reform, that you have nursed with such care for so many years, and will sing praises unto thee, now and evermore. Amen.

Now the Services for the Day is taken from unprinted Bills that lay on or under the tables of the House of Incurables, better known by the name of St. Stephen's.

Now it came to pass in the second month of the year '66, and on the first day of the month, that the Dictators who formed the seventh Parliament in the reign of Good Queen Vic, assembled together to consider the weighty affairs of the nation, and after relating their rigs and sprees during the holidays, adjourned to crack a bottle and a joke at the expense of patient John Bull.

And again on the 6th they met in the presence of our Good Queen, and after bestowing six thousand a-year out of the pockets of the people as a trifle for pin money for a certain little lady, they wished the Queen good day, shook their heads, and went to lunch, entirely worn out with their morning's labour.

And they held long discussions on the plague among the cattle, and soon came to the sage conclusion, that beasts that were ill could not be in good health ; but whether it was the cow or chicken pock they were not prepared to say.

But the people cried aloud that it was done to raise the price of meat, and those who used to treat themselves to a joint on a Sunday were compelled to put up with a few ornaments from off the block.

Now near unto the commencement of the year, great excitement was caused through the land, of strange revelations concerning a certain tribe of persons called paupers, whose treatment in the Whig Bastiles, or Union-houses, were likened unto swine ; and the rate-payers of Lambeth, and people in general, cried out sorely against the Poor Law nabobs, and the ratepayers cried, Turn off the unworthy servants of the poor and give the inheritance to others.

And behold, great alarm is being caused in different parts of this mighty city, on account of the many rail-roads in course of construction ; and numbers of Her Majesty's most loyal subjects, such as the small shop-keeper and poorer classes, are being driven from their homes, and by being deprived of the means of obtaining their living, will be compelled to find shelter in the workhouse, and so swell the rates imposed upon the hard-working tradesman.

And they pray the present ministry now assembled, to stay the progress of this destructive juggernaut ; and as there has been day by day great outcry about the many accidents caused by them, they beg of them to pass a clause in the acts for the regulation of railways, that they shall supply a sufficient number of surgeons with splints and bandages to each train, and a goodly supply of coffins at each station for the use of those who are headstrong enough to travel by them.

Thus endeth the morning lesson.

LET US SAY.

O most noble Johnny, pull yourself together, and spare us the necessity of selecting another steward.

Hear us, O Russell.

And O, most Gracious Queen, gladden the hearts of thy people by dwelling amongst them, and so improve the trade of thy most loyal subjects in this mighty city.

We beseech thee to hear us, O Queen.

From having our roads turned into honeycombs, and endangering our lives by being swallowed up by the underground railways, spare us we implore thee.

Railway Committees, spare us.

And O, much respected Chancellor of the Exchequer, repeal the duty upon malt, as thou hast done upon tea, so that we may refresh ourselves with a good and wholesome pot of beer, to the glory of thy good name.

O Gladstone, hear us.

And we implore thee to spare our poorer brethren from being compelled to pig upon dirty floors in Union Bastiles, or by being poisoned by bathing in a dirty soup kettle.

Good Farnell, and the whole host of parish nabobs, spare us.

Be just before you are liberal, and waste not the public money in useless expenditure.

Minister of Finance, we beseech thee to hear us.

Spare us from being starved in the land of plenty, Good Bright.

O Bright, have mercy upon us.

And O Gladstone, thou brightest star in the political hemisphere ; keep thy weather-eye open, and jog the memory of thy fellow-servant John, and guide his little feet if he should by chance to stray from the right path.

O Gladstone watch over the welfare of the people.

And now, Johnny, we implore thee to act with jus-tice to the country, and give us the benefit of Reform which is so much needed, and grant in all thy works, that you study the interests of the most patient and in-dustrious people in the world, so that they may be blessed with peace and plenty, then will they sing, Long live the Queen, and good luck to her ministers. Amen.

Henry Disley, Printer, 57, High Street, St. Giles's.

The Life, Trial, and probable Sentence of the
DERBYITES, DIZZYITES,
AND
ADULLAMITES,
AND THE
WHOLE HOST OF TORY CABINET MAKERS,

Who were tried at St. Stephen's, for conspiring to burke the People's Reform, and attempting to pass a Counterfeit Bill instead of a Genuine Article; thereby imposing upon a certain respectable firm, well-known as Messrs John Bull and Company. The prosecution was conducted by those able Advocates for Reform, Bright and Gladstone. The offenders were undefended, as no one could be found willing to take their cause in hand on account of their previous bad character.

Now the trial of these Anti-Reformers was highly amusing, owing to the singular conduct of some of the offenders.

And the proceedings was prefaced by that old-stock farce called the Struggle for Reform, or John Bull mesmerised.

And the advocates for the people said unto the Derbyites and their companions, what have you to say in your behalf concerning this fraud on the working classes of England?

Now behold one of them was a clever mountebank of the tribe of Dizzyites, and like many of his kind he had a happy knack of saying a great deal which amounted to nothing; and he commenced his defence with a mock speech on Reform, which seemed to say: If you Reformers do not unbutton your eyelids, and expand your understandings, I shall most certainly mystify you with my high presto, cockalorum jig!

And he had as many tricks as those amusing little marmozettes that are to be seen in the gardens of the Regent's Park.

And when he had concluded he turned to the people and said, how do you like me now?

And there arose a murmur through St. Stephen's, saying, Not at all, you are not in our style.

And Dizzy the mountebank was much grieved for he thought he had caused a great sensation, and he exclaimed, Dizzy, Dizzy, thy occupation's gone.

And Lowe the Adullamite, surnamed the moonraker, pleaded guilty to his offences against the people, and prayed for a mitigation of his sentence, on the plea that he could not have been in his right mind.

And the poor gentleman could not have been sane for he rambled on with some nonsense about the mark of Cain being set upon some people's brows; and asked the good citizens of London to order mass to be said for his own sins, or the success of the Bill; his strange manner left us in a fog to understand which.

Now the chief of the Derbyites being alarmed at the meetings in Trafalgar Square and throughout England, did call a council in the privy which layeth in the neighbourhood of Downing Street, to form plans by which they might overthrow the honest Bright, and all those who were on the side of the people.

For the Tories, finding that their seats were in a shaky condition, and being fond of place and pensions, were determined to stick at nothing rather than give up their golden kitchen stuff of office.

And behold their work must have been exceedingly bad, inasmuch as some of their pals said no: we will leave your company, for we will not join with you in this plot against the working classes of England.

And it was strongly suspected that Dizzy the Mountebank, eager for a goodly share of the loaves and fishes, communed with himself, saying, I will write up no connection with the head Cabinet Maker of the Upper House, and then the whole business will be mine.

And the Reformers were well pleased, for they said the old adage will then be verified that when rogues fall out honest men will get their rights.

Now it was thought that they would have called upon D—— M——, the head of the Poleaxes, to speak in their behalf; but that hero having the remembrance of the Hyde Park battle before his eyes, declined to appear, saying, He had received striking proof of the justice of the cause.

Now it was in the 3rd month of the year, and on the 18th day of the month, being the day after St. Patrick that the Tory Cabinet Makers appeared to receive judgement; and the Council for the People said unto them, If you do not give us the bill, the whole bill, and nothing but a satisfactory bill, giving to the people what is justly their rights, the sentence of this court will be that you will get the infernal sack now and for evermore.

Amen.

H. Disley, Printer, 57, High Street, St. Giles.

A NEW LITANY ON REFORM.

When the Tories shall grant to the people a share of what is justly their own, and not take all the loaves and fishes themselves, as they always have done; like the lawyer who swallowed the oyster and gave his client the shells; then, and not till then, shall they gain our thanks.

Sorely oppressed and heavily taxed brethren, duty calls us, as the bone and sinew of this mighty nation to assert our rights and privileges, and although we at all times ought to do so, yet ought we more strongly when we assemble and meet together to take such steps as are necessary to obtain manhood suffrage, and all things likely to elevate our condition as freeborn Englishmen, and not slaves to any intolerant faction, such as now assert their despotic power in St. Stephens' Infirmary. So I charge as many of you as here present, who are friends to Reform, to act firmly in the cause, and never rest till it is gained.

Now, it was shortly after the premature death of the Russell administration, that the Tories took office, and a couple of chiefs of the tribes of the Derbyites and D'Israelites laid their heads together, to consider in what way they might destroy the substance, and bamboozle the working man.

And the D'Israelite said to the Derbyite keep your whip still, and I will pull the string, and the day will be our own. So the Derbyite was like unto the dolls in the toy shops, that say, we will cry for sixpence.

And about this time, loud shouts was heard for Reform, and the echo was carried throughout the length and breadth of the land.

And the whole host of Derbyites shook, as if struck with the palsy, and their chief was sorely alarmed, so that his hair stood out from his head like unto the quills of the porcupine, and he cried, Oh, Dizzy, save us!

And behold there sprung up on the face of the earth a new race of people called Adullamites, who were like unto their namesakes of old, a dissatisfied and two-faced people, and like the camelon could change their colour at will.

And their chief was a *Low*(e) man from the land of moonrakers; and him and his colleagues were the Reformers of to-day and the Tories of to-morrow.

And they said to the people, behold we are on thy side, at the same time they were seeking how they might destroy their cause.

And they combined with certain unprincipled electors, and by bribery and corruption made their way into the house of St. Stephen's.

But when they got into the house, the mask fell from off their unworthy faces, and instead of Reformers, they appeared as labour-grinding Tories.

And the people murmured, saying, they are like unto Esau of old, who sold his birthright for a mess of potage, and there is no trust in them.

And it was in the 7th month of the year, when the gnats bite the hardest, that the Reformers declared their intention of assembling in Hyde Park to set forth their honest claims, and hear the most truthful voices of the worthy Beale and the Delegates.

And the Tories became alarmed, and W—— sent in haste to Dicky M——, the renowned head of all the poleaxes, to march with his army, and stop the much dreaded invasion.

But the people said, who is he who stays us from meeting in a place that is justly our own? And they laid on for Reform, and lo! the rails quickly passed away, and not a vestige was to be seen.

And when the Chief of the Poleaxes saw what was done, his nose turned as blue as his coat, and he cried, On to the charge!

But behold, while he was whistling, see the conquering hero comes, a brick, hurled by no friendly hand, caught his head unexpectedly, and his charger turned and whispered, Dicky, how is your poor nob?

Thus endeth the Lesson.

LET US SAY,

From all Tory intolerance save us, Reformers.

Friends of Reform, hear us.

From bribery and corruption, and the whole host of Adullamites, and all that have not clean hands, Election Commissioners, spare us.

Spare us, we beseech thee.

From having the Park gates shut against us, save us good Walpole.

Oh, Wally, hear us.

From unjust stewards, and Israelitish cash keepers, good Queen save us.

We beseech thee to hear us, good Queen.

And oh Derby and Dizzy, make not too cock sure that your position will be lasting, for you know not what a day may bring forth.

And now to Russell, Bright, Beales, and all true friends of Reform, let your thanks be now and evermore.—AMEN.

DISLEY, Printer, High Street, St. Giles's, London.

CAPTAIN JINK'S DREAM.

A CONVERSATION

ON THE

COMING ELECTIONS

BETWEEN

BILL GLADSTONE & BEN DIZZY.

Written by John Embleton, Author of the "Political Litany on the Irish Church Question, &c."

Your attention I claim, Captain Jinks is my name, and with your permission, I hold a commission, in Her Majesty's famed horse marines.

I have lines here for your inspection, on the coming election, and I'll try to amuse, that is if you choose, by relating a wonderful dream.

It was t'other night, I got rather tight, I had been to the Alhambra, to see the grand things there, and roll'd home at two in my glory.

And I dreamt a queer dream, though strange it may seem, that I heard a conversation, or a confabulation, between Gladstone and Dizzy, the Tory.

I had a dream the other night; and the same I'll lay before ye,
A conversation on the coming election, between Gladstone and Dizzy, the Tory.

Said Gladstone, Dizzy my rum 'un, the time is a coming, though you think yourself clever, you will find so help my never, at the forthcoming general election,

That your goose will be cooked, and you must take your hook, for like a cow's tail you will find, you will be all behind, when the people they make their selection.

Then said Dizzy it is plain, Gladstone, you want the reins, and between you and me, your Reform and cheap tea, you fancy will carry you straight, sir,

But I know what your wish is, to prig my loaves and fishes, but Gladstone my hearty, I'll lick you and your party, and stick to my stall, so help me tater.

Ben, your No Popery cry, it is all my eye, and your cant and your crawling, shews you are afraid of falling, for of honesty you have not a spark, Ben.

For you and your chums dirty, got dreadful shirty, but that is not worst, sir, said I fell to the gutter, when my friends met like bricks in Hyde Park, Ben.

Says Dizzy, I know Bill, you think your Irish Church Bill, with the aid of the donovans, will make you A No. 1, but you will find in the end it's no use man.

For it is a great shame man, that with Bradlaugh and Finlen, and the rest of your Pets, should make this cabal, to capsize church and constitution.

Said Gladstone, that is it, if the cap did not fit, Sally Gamp of the Standard, would not have stuck up her placards, unless you Tories had got some queer twitches,

But they have made a mistake, sir, it's a mere waste of paper, and if they come up to the scratch, they will find the Liberals their match, and they may chance to have an earthquake in their breeches.

Says Dizzy, I know, that old Jemmy Squaretoe, to himself will you take man, for running down shovel hats and silk aprons, and I wonder you can sleep in your bed, Bill,

For in Hyde Park it was said, that a litany was read, and it said, and no flies, my nose was like double size, and my curly hair shook on my head, Bill.

Gladstone said by-the-bye, there has been a loud cry, which is nothing unkimmon, for it comes from the women, they declare they will rule if they like, Ben.

They say, at home in their houses, they can rule their spouses, and they seem rather puzzled, that their tongues should be muzzled, like D—— M—— muzzled our tykes, Ben.

Dizzy said, bless the ladies, they are well in their places, to wash and dress babbies, and lecture the daddies; and some in homes they are graceful.

They can rule in the kitchen, and cook puddings—if they can get them,—and to say they're not clever, I'd not venture, no, never! when I think upon old Madam Rachel.

Gladstone said, my Cockawax, there is that cursed income tax upon trades and professions, I'd like to sing its dying speech and confession, for it robs the poor man of his bread, Ben.

Why not tax grunting pigs, the counsellor's wigs, the little hedge-sparrows, the cat's-meat man's barrow, or the chignons they stick on their heads, Ben.

And Ben, it is said, you are politically dead, but have not pluck at present, to get buried decent, and leave the Liberals to weather the storm, Ben.

So I would advise you, and the Adullamites too, to make yourselves scarce then, at the coming election, for you are done brown as sure as you are born, Ben.

Dizzy said, Bill and I have tried, but you are not satisfied, but we will see who is the best one, at the General Election, and to do our best then we will endeavour.

Then I heard a great noise, with, We have lick'd them, my boys, and just then I awoke, and though not a soul spoke, my ears rung with

GLADSTONE FOR EVER!

Henry Disley, Printer, 57, High Street, St. Giles, London.—W.C.

A POLITICAL THANKSGIVING

FOR THE

Great and Glorious Victory Gained by the Liberals, and the Complete Defeat of the Tories!!!

Much respected and truly victorious brethren, and all who have lent a liberal hand in sticking the axe of Reform so deeply into the root of that old contemptible tree called Toryism. I have this day come amongst you to offer up a thanksgiving for the great victory gained by Gladstone and his brave army at the Great Election, and also to offer my sympathy for the alarming illness of the Tories, who are suffering from an attack of the *place fever*; and all true Liberals are invited to be present and take the front places, as Gladstone and his comrades will in the House of St. Stephen's. And all Tories and Adullamites are requested to keep in the background, where they will remain now and for evermore, and not disturb the present congregation, or they will be given into the custody of the beadle.

Now the Lesson for the Day is taken from the battle with the Gladstonites and the Dizzyites at the late Elections.

Now for many years past the Tories have been a place seeking and ease loving people, greasing their chins with the lion's share of what justly is the rights of the working classes of this mighty land.

And the people communed together, saying, who are those who toil not nor yet spin, and yet they swallow up all the grain, and leave us nought but the husks to eat.

And lo there arose a mighty host called the Liberals, whose chieftain was named Gladstone, who was in himself a tower of strength, who with the Spear of Liberty sorely wounded the Tory chief, who was surnamed Dizzy the Isrælite.

And, behold, it was in the dismal month of November,—the season so fatal to all shakey constitutions—that the Tories became alarmingly ill, and at the Great Election Battles found that their power was passing away, and that they were dead licked.

And the victory that was gained by the Liberals was sorely painful to Dizzy the Tory Chief, for he had said in the fulness of his political health, " Show me the man who will tread on the skirts of my coat." But his boasting was like unto the mountain that became pregnant, and brought forth a mouse.

For Gladstone the Liberal put forth his foot, and lo, Dizzy's Government was rent in twain.

Then went the Chief of the Tories unto the Castle which lieth near unto the Great Park of Windsor, and threw himself at the feet of our good Queen Victoria, saying, Bill Gladstone, the head boy in our school at Westminster, has given me such a fright, that I feel quite white, and I am afraid if I stay any longer, the other boys will chaff me, and say, " Dizzy, Dizzy, I'll have your curls!"

Then did the Queen send for Bill Gladstone, and said unto him, Are you afraid, too? But Gladstone spoke up boldly, saying, Not I. Then said the Lady of the Castle, Get you back to St. Stephen's, and be head teacher in the room of the boy Dizzy.

And Sarah Gamp, of the Tory cess-pool, sung quite small when she heard of the disgrace her favourite boy had got into.

And since the Great Election has taken place, it has been rumoured that certain Tories has been coming the Rachel dodge, and has been trying to make themselves beautiful for ever, by rubbing themselves with golden ointment, which has so dazzled the eyes of some of the free and independent electors, that they will not be able to see clearly until Gladstone and his friends settle the hash by giving us the ballot.

Thus endeth the Lesson for the Day.

Let us all say,

For giving the command into the safe keeping of General Gladstone, oh, Queen, we give unto thee our thanks.

We thank thee, oh, Queen.

From being left to the tender mercies of the Tories. Friends of Freedom save us.

Spare us, we beseech thee.

And oh, Lowe, since Gladstone has duly installed you as Keeper of the National Cash-box, let us have none of your hanky-panky or Adullamite tricks, as you had at the time of the great Reform Meeting, when you charged the working-men with being a vile, degenerate, and beer-swilling crew.

Now, Lowe, none of your moon-raking capers, or I shall give you another taste of my rod of correction.

And, oh, Gladstone, give them a plentiful supply of Liberal pills, to purge them of impurity.

Warm them, good Gladstone.

And, oh, Dizzy, my lad, keep up your pecker, and don't be cast down, for Gladstone is a good sort of a chap, and if you behave yourself, I dare say he will give you a job.

Do not fret, Dizzy, there's a good boy.

And, oh, D——, we thank you for paying attention to our last prayer, by kindly removing the spectacles from off the dog's noses, and when the roasted chesnuts and boys hoop question is settled, turn your great mind into another channel, and devise some means of ridding us of the garrotting ruffians that now infest our streets and highways in the open daylight.

Do D——, and we shall bless thee.

And now to Gladstone and all who have fought so nobly to gain this great victory, be all thanks due, and may they stick like bricks to the cause, and do their duty at the forthcoming Sessions of Parliament, and they shall receive our praises now and for evermore.

Amen.

H. Disley, Printer, 57, High Street, St. Giles, London.

BELIEF AND COMMANDMENTS

ON THE RIGHTS OF WOMEN.

To be read by all married women to their husbands, and by all single ones to their sweethearts.

At a meeting of women the other day, that dear old lady, Mrs. Caudle, amused the ladies present, by reading her Belief and Commandments on the rights and privileges of married women ; so after taking half-a-dozen pinches of snuff and a couple of glasses of eye-water, and coughing three times, she commenced as follows :—

I believe, that has some one has said, that woman is man's better, and sometimes his bigger half, and the best friend he has got to his back ; she should not only rule the roast at home, but have a voice in the affairs of the country to which she belongs ! and I not only believe, but I am quite sure, that it is her husband's place to obey her in everything, and patiently attend to her commandments, and then, and not till then, will curtain lectures cease.

Now my first commandment, if I was married, would be this, I would say to my husband.

1st. You must never think of, or even look at any other woman but me, for am sure the parson must have made a mistake when he said, woman, obey your husbands.

2nd. You must never make me jealous by praising those forward jades that wear those ugly things on their heads called chignons, but keep your eye wholly on me, and study my wants both day and night, or I will comb your head with a small tooth bellows, that's what I will, and no mistake.

3rd. Before going to work in the morning, you must light the fire and make me a strong cup of tea, with something nice in it in case I should have the wind, and you must not grumble if the kettle does not boil when you come home to breakfast.

4th. Six days must work from six to six, that you may provide me with the comforts of life, and on the seventh, you may scrub the floor, peel the potatoes, make the dumplings, and cook the dinner. In the afternoon. by way of amusement, you must take the children to the park and show the little darlings the ducks.

5th. If any of the children should have the measles, or the blessed baby should require weaning, you must get up without a murmer and give it the bottle, lest I might be disturbed by its crying.

6th. You must not crib a shilling from your wages on Saturday night, but fork it all out and be contented with the pocket money I shall think fit to give you.

7th. You must not get in a state of beer on any pretence whatever, or I shall compel you to sleep at the foot of the bed for six weeks.

8th. You must not take my name in vain by calling me other than my dear, or my duck, nor lay finger on me, lest I should give you six months to learn you better manners.

9th. You must not dare to grumble if your shirt should be minus of buttons, or you should be compelled to eat a cold dinner at least three days during the week, if it should be my pleasure to go out for amusement.

10th. You must not covet to be trusted with the latch key in the evening, you must not covet to visit the Alhambra or the Oxford, nor any other such like place ; you must not look at the girls' legs on a windy day, nor rule your house or your spouse, or anything this is within, but be a good boy and keep my commandments.

H. Disley, Printer, 57, High Street, St. Giles, London.

A NEW
POLITICAL AND REFORM ALPHABET.

A stands for Aristocrat, who nothing will do,
    Who says they to work was not born;
And also the Adullamites, a double-faced crew,
    The worst foes we have to Reform.

B stands for Beale, and likewise for Bright,
    True Champions are of Reform;
So may good luck attend them by day and by night,
    For nobly they battle the storm.

C stands for the Charter, and five points there are,
    And by right they belong to us all;
Tho' they'd fain keep them from us, seems pretty clear,
    But we'll gain them, my boys, or we'll fall!

D stands for Derby, and also Dizzey,
    Who talks large when there's nothing to do;
Like parsons they say, you must do as they say,
    But, mind you, don't do as they do.

E stands for England, the land of the free,
    The home of the true and the brave;
But our share of freedom is small, you'll agree,
    Though the song says we ne'er shall be slaves!

F stands for Franchise, it is our birthright,
    So we want what is justly our due;
Tho' the Tories they say, they will have their own way,
    We'll tell them, we'll be damn'd if they do.

G stands for Gammon, and plenty we've had,
    Till we are sick of that unstaple store;
But if they think to gammon us out of Reform,
    They will find we'll be gammoned no more.

H stands for Honour, there is some amongst thieves,
    The saying goes that way I hear;
The Adullamites have none, it's quite plain to me;
    And the Tories have none for to spare.

I stands for Idlers, but none must be found,
    Who wish for the success of our cause;
So boldly push forward, you'll win I'll be bound,
    When it's gained it is time for to pause.

J stands for Jacks, in office who are found,
    To look on while honest men toil;
And they tidy sums get, to keep their mouths shut,
    And blab not of the ill-gotten spoil.

K stands for Knight, and there many sorts are,
    And some with the garter are deck'd;
Who instead round the leg, where the garter they wear,
    Would look better if worn round the neck.

L stands for Lowe, both by nature and name,
    And from Wiltshire he comes I tell you;
Who the workmen of England did vilely defame,
    By calling them a drunken and ignorant crew.

M stands for Mayne, by some called Naughty Dick,
    The chief of the Bluebottle mob;
Who in Hyde Park, they say, some queer cards did play,
    Till at last he got one for his nob.

N stands for Nobles, and true nobles are they,
    Who strive for their fellow-man's good;
Not in luxury and idleness spend all their days,
    Nor care to do good if they could.

O is an O, for nothing it stands,
    And that is the working-man's share;
Next to nothing he gets while he is here in this land,
    And needs nothing when he leaves here.

P stands for Patience, so be not cast down,
    My lads, nor give way to despair;
The sun shines on you, although the world frowns,
    And good times must come it is clear.

Q stands for Question, and the Question is this,
    Are Englishmen to gain their Rights?
Or must they labour like nameless serfs,
    And allow Might to overcome Right?

R stands for Russell, and likewise Reform:
    Then for Reform shout for ever;
For let come what may, we will clear the way,
    For shall we be conquered? No, never!

S stands for Soap, some hard, and some soft,
    So let's say to our foes, just be steady;
Hard soap it is best, though it won't well digest,
    We've had enough of your soft soap already.

T stands for Tory, a set of greedy elves,
    Who take all the loaves and the fishes;
They take all the fat of the land to themselves,
    And give the poor man empty dishes.

U stands for Unity, which all of us need,
    Which no power on earth can e'er sever;
It ensures a strong pull, while we give a long pull,
    Then pull for Reform altogether.

V stands for Vultures, and many there are
    Sit in St. Stephen's, you'll own;
If the poor man is starving and can't get food for carving,
    And asks for bread, they will give him a stone.

W stands for Workhouse, the poor man's last home,
    When by sickness or age is brought down,
Tho' he's toil'd all his life till he's but skin and bone,
    To uphold the mitre and crown.

X is a letter that looks like a cross,
    An emblem of the working man's life;
He has crosses enough, he finds to his cost;
    If he dares for to ask for his rights.

Y stands for Yoke, the poor man must bear,
    'Tis an odious badge of slavery to wear;
But never mind, boys! we will weather the storm,
    And toast in a bumper, success to Reform!

Z stands for the Zeal the Reformers must use,
    If they stick back and edge to gain what's their dues.
Here is good luck to Gladstone, is now what I say,
    Here's the good cause Reform, for ever, huzza!

                                    J. EMBLETON.

DISLEY, Printer, 57, High Street, St. Giles, London.

A NEW EDITION OF THE LITANY

ON THE

IRISH CHURCH QUESTION

Not exactly sanctioned by either Bishop, Parson, Curate, or any other Prelate. It is not to be said or sung in either Church or Chapel, but to be learnt by all persons without distinction to creed, country, or colour. Composed on the Great Battle which lately took place in St. Stephen's House of Incurables.

When the rulers of this mighty Babylon shall be like unto good stewards, and render unto the people, things that are the people's, and purge the Established Church of its many impurities, not only in Ireland and Scotland, but in this mighty and loyal city, and allow every tub to stand on its own bottom, then, and not till then will this war cease, which has so long been an abomination in the land.

Sorely oppressed and heavily taxed Brethren :—

It becomes us all to be up and doing, and assist this monster question of the day—the Irish Church Bill — no matter what your creed may be, whether it be Catholic, Protestant, Quakers, Shakers, Spirit Rappers, or Tub Thumpers, who have so long forked out the golden grain which has so greedily been swallowed by Mother Church and her hungry chickens.

The lesson for the Day is taken from the late debate on on the Church Question.

Now in the days of darkness, when Fat Harry, the Bluebeard King of England, joined in unholy wedlock the Lion of State to Lady Lawn Sleeves, the people were troubled with a blindness, which has continued for upwards of three hundred years.

But of late the film has fell from off their eyes, and they murmured saying, why pay we tribute to those from whom we receive nothing, and for buildings we do not enter?

But the masters in lawn, replied, we say unto you, pay you must, for such is the law of the land.

But lo! there arose up a loud cry for Ecclesiastical Reform, and Gladstone, their Champion, arose up in the house of St. Stephen's, which is near unto Parliament Square, and with stentorian lungs, said, I intend to go the whole hog or none, and call upon the country to dissolve the banns of matrimony between the aforesaid Lion and Lawn Sleeves, which has so long been an eyesore to the country.

And, behold the words that Gladstone uttered sounded like unto a death-warrant to the ears of Dizzey and his pals, and his nose turned blue when he thought it was U. P. with his greatness.

Now in due time the Great Election Battle took place, and the Place-loving Tories, in spite of their back-sliding capers, were dead licked ; and Dizzey retired to Buckinghamshire, and fasted for three whole days, and sat up to his blessed chin in sackcloth and ashes.

For the voice of the Country was with Gladstone, for they knew well he was a Brick, and would hold the balance justly between the rich and poor.

Now it was two days after St. Valentine, that the Liberal Chief buckled on his armour, entered St. Stephen's, and prepared himself for the fight. And his war-cry was "Justice to all men," "Liberty to Ireland," and "Disendowment of the Irish Church." And the sons of the Land of Buttermilk, shouted, "More power to you, Gladstone !"

And lo, the cry caused certain prelates to curtail their shovel hats of their fair proportions and go into mourning, by converting their silk aprons into hatbands, at which the grunters nearly split their side with laughter.

And there arose a cry from the exiled sons of Erin, which sank deep into the heart of noble Gladstone, and with the battle-axe of Mercy struck off their fetters and they were free!

And there was loud cries of "Long life to noble Gladstone, the Liberator of the Land of Donovans !"

And Hardy the bosom friend of Poleaxe Dickey the hero of Hyde Park, protested loudly against Gladstone and his measure, and he and Dizzey wept bitter tears, when they saw that they were licked.

And the land of donovans and buttermilk shouted, No surrender, faugh o'ballagh ! go it Gladstone, and the Sandys danced tullochgorum round the rims of their porridge-pots, and in whiskey, success to the Church Bill.

Thus endeth the lesson for the day.

LET US SAY.

From all Church monopoly, good Gladstone, save us.
Save us, good Gladstone.

From being compelled to keep the fat shepherds of every creed. Good Queen deliver us.
Spare us, good Queen.

From maintaining such a large staff of idlers in silk aprons and shovel hats, Friends of Reform, spare us.
Friends of Reform, spare us.

From all undue taxes in the shape of tenths and sucking pigs. Common sense, save us.
Spare us our grunters, we beseech thee.

For the liberation of the exiled sons of Ireland, we thank thee, good Gladstone !
In the name of the sons of Erin, we thank thee, oh, Gladstone.

Hear that, oh, Dizzey.

And now to Gladstone, the father of Reform, and the friend of the people, be all thanks due both now and for evermore, and success to the Irish Church Bill.
So be it.

H. Disley, Printer, 57, High Street, St. Giles.

A LITANY

ON THE

IRISH LAND QUESTION.

In consequence of the gross mismanagement of John Bull's possessions at home and abroad, by unprincipled servants and dishonest stewards; especially in the land of St. Patrick, we have met together without distinction to country or creed, to consider the best means of alleviating the sufferings of that ill-used country.

When the down-trodden sons of Erin shall dig their spades into their own native soil, free from the stone and gravel of tyranny, then, and not till then, shall the wrongs of Ireland cease.

Friends and Fellow Countrymen,

The country calls us in divers places to reform abuses, and assist the unemployed, by offering new gates of labor, in place of those that have been most cruelly shut at Woolwich and elsewhere, and although the old saying says "Charity begins at home," it is no reason why we should forget our neighbour next door; therefore I pray and beseech thee, oh! John Bull and Sandy, to sympathise with poor Brother Pat, who for knocking his shillaleigh a little too hard about the heads of the varmint, was popped into quod till the Almighty will of the people shall compel the Lords of St. Stephen's to let them go free.

The Lesson for the Day is taken from one of the dark pages of Irish History.

Now it came to pass when that renowned Irish Champion, Brian O'Lynn, bequeathed his ghost to all the wakes in Tipperary, behold there arose four kings to suck up the best of the buttermilk and dance with the prettiest girls in Ould Ireland.

Then arose a Royal Judas among them, who sold his country to the Saxon Harry of Fair Rosamond notoriety.

And it came to pass, after many years, Hooknosed Billy the Dutchman, went over and deprived poor Jamie Stuart of his rights.

And he cried aloud to his redcoats, Down with the Spirit of Freedom! and eat up all the good of the land, and let it be a refuge for foreigners, and let the children of St. Patrick wander elsewhere.

Here endeth the Lesson.

The Second Lesson is taken from the Irish Land Question.

Now it is well known that the curse of Ireland or any other country is "Land Monopoly," especially in our own country, where one man has thousands of acres, and another poor fellow not enough whercon to rest his aching bones.

For in the Emerald Isle the rich Landowner cries aloud to his Steward, Steward! collect my rents in my absence, who, instead of studying the prosperity of my tenants am squandering away in debauchery and vice the hard earnings of a poor and oppressed people.

Then the Agent answers, I must put money in my purse, and straightway he cries aloud to his tenantry, Lo, this is my master's land and all that is thereon, pay more rent or skedaddle, and make room for strangers who are ready to pop into your place.

For the Irish land monopoly is like a landlord, who, when he turns his tenant out of doors, stick to his goods and furniture, saying, these are mine, are they not on my premises?

Thus endeth the Lesson.

LET US SAY,

Oh, Gladstone, Champion of Reform, and Friend of the People, intercede for the poor Fenian prisoners.
We beseech thee, oh, Gladstone.

Ye undaunted Champions of Ireland, Sullivan and Moore, agitate for the poor Fenian prisoners.
Agitate, oh, Patriots, we beseech thee!

To raise funds for the free emigration of our London poor, tax the "Upper Ten," we beseech thee, oh, Lowe!
Do, we beseech thee, there's a good Lowe!

And, oh, most thrifty Chancellor, we pray thee to reduce the pocket money of our Royal pensioners, for it is hard to pluck the poor hard working-man's pence, and let the idle children of mammon go free.
Hear that, oh, purple and fine linen!

And may it please your Majesty to grant a lease of Buckingham Palace to the old and infirm Bishops of St. Stephen's, that they may take daily exercise in St. James's Park, fill their aprons with bread crumbs, and reverently feed the ducks!
Hear that, oh, Lawnsleeves?

And now to Gladstone, Bright, and Stuart Mill, chosen of the people, let us render our thanks now and for ever!
AMEN.

H. Disley, Printer, 57, High Street, St. Giles, London.

THE NEW INTENDED
REFORM BILL

Which is expected to come into operation as soon as the Lords and Commons think fit.

The first Clause in this new intended Act is relative to Teetotalers. BE IT ENACTED:—That any teetotaler who shall be known to drink more than three gallons of cold water during the day, shall be chained to the parish pump four hours, and pay two shillings extra, in each quarter, water rate. So says the Reform Bill.

Clause 2nd. Any young lady who shall wear a crinoline more than twelve yards in circumference, or containing more than thirteen steel hoops, shall pay 5s. to the nearest hospital to where she resides to find plasters for broken shins.

3rd.—Any workhouse-master who shall neglect to skim the fat off the water in which thirty-six paupers have been bathed, shall be forced to live upon skilly for five days, and work for eight hours at the crank.

4th.—Any lady over the age of seventy, who shall drink more than three quarterns of gin before breakfast, unless she shall be suffering from the cholic, shall be kept without snuff for a fortnight.

5th.—Any man who shall be known to get drunk, and beat his wife more than once a day, shall be compelled to sleep at the foot of the bed for one month; and if that does not cure him, he shall be confined in one of her Majesty's Gaols till a reformation shall take place.

6th.—And whereas we have received numerous complaints that a great number of ladies' pet dogs having been found smothered in the mud that has been swept up and left by the roadside, the commissioners are requested to see that the said mud shall be carted away at least once a week, especially in rainy weather.

7th.—Any woman who shall bring forth more than two children at a birth, she will not be allowed to sleep with her husband for two months, unless the head-board shall be placed between them.

8.—And it having come under our notice, that many respectable females have been much annoyed by second-hand dandies' and counter-jumpers puffing the smoke in their faces from their penny pickwicks, the Reform Bill enacts that such fops shall be compelled to pay their last quarter's washing bill, and wear an unstarched dicky for six months.

9th.—And as we understand that many ladies belonging to a class known as milliners' assistants and bonnet builders, having been frequenting different music halls, and passing themselves off as ladies of fortune, on purpose to lead young men astray. Be it known to all whom it may concern, that if they do not reform their ways they will have to pay 6d. per week to the Baby clothing Association, and their mamma's will be made acquainted with their goings on.

10th.—And as Reform is the order of the day, so Reform your tailors' bills. There is a clause set apart for volunteers only :—it says that any rifle volunteer found strutting about in a new uniform, shall be compelled to produce two respectable persons not being volunteers, to make oath that he has paid for the old ones.

11th.—Butchers will be compelled to reform their ways, and cease to wag their chops about the steaks being so dear on account of the cattle disease. And butchers selling meat that has died of the scarlatina, will be compelled to live upon bullocks' liver and sawdust for the space of three months.

12th.—Any policeman who shall be known to be courting more than two cooks and three housemaids at the same time, or be found with more than five pounds of mutton in his possession, shall pay 2s. 6s. to the Servants' Aid Society, and not be allowed to look down any area for three calender months.

13th.—Any boy over the age of seven years, who shall be found with a pea-shooter concealed about him, shall be apprehended as a Fenian, and be debarred from playing at cat for a fortnight.

14.—And as we have received intelligence that in many parts of London there are lots of daring children that have been found dancing to the tune of the Jolly Butcher Boy, and Oh, Cafuzelum! thereby disturbing the public peace, they will henceforth be considered as dangerous members of society.

15th.—And lately we have been much startled by hearing that numbers of evil-disposed paupers in the parishes of Marylebone, St. Luke's and Chelsea, have refused to crack stones at 1s. 3d. per yard, unless such stones are parboild! A clause in the Beform Bill says that such paupers who offend in the like manner, shall be sentenced to penal servitude for one night in the casual ward of Lambeth work-house that being the heaviest sentence the law can inflict.

16.—And any cabman or 'bus-conductor are empowered by the new Reform Bill to charge double fare for any person or persons weighing over eighteen stone; but no cabman shall charge more than one shilling over and above his legal fare, excepting to Members of Parliament or disorderly persons.

17.—No milkman will be allowed to mix more than two gallons of water with one of milk, excepting when the said milk is over-proof, and has a creamy appearance.

18th.—And no baker shall employ any man who is capable of eating more than four pounds of meat for his dinner, as we have had many complaints about people's joints looking in a state of rapid consumption after coming from the oven, as if they had taken to fretting.

19th.—And all persons contemplating suicide, are earnestly requested not to drown themselves, as bodies lying too long in the Thames cause the water to become very unwholesome.

20th and last.—And by virtue of the Reform Bill, any married couple who can prove that they have never quarrelled since they were first married, will be entitled to the blessings of universal suffrage.

So says the Reform Bill.

HENRY DISLEY, Printer, 57, High Street, St. Giles.

THE
NEW ACT OF PARLIAMENT.

The First Clause in this new intended Act of Parliament is relating to the Bakers. It says : Be it enacted that all master bakers who shall mix, or cause to be any spurious ingredient in his bread, in the shape of bean-flour, pea-flour, starch or alum, or use more than six stone of potatoes with one sack of flour, thereby robbing the poor man of part of his hard earnings, he shall be popped in his own oven directly after the batch is drawn, and not come out till he is half-baked. And every journeyman who dips his fingers into the people's dishes, shall not be allowed to have more than three dead men for the next month.

2. Any Butcher who is known to give short weight, or sell, or cause to be sold, any part of any ox, cow, calf, sheep, or pig, that shall have died with the measles, erysipelas, hooping cough, or any other disease, he is to be fattened and fed on sheep's blood and sawdust for three months.

3. Any Publican that makes more than three butts of beer out of one ; or use nux vomica, salt, treacle, or horses' liver in doctoring the same, or not filling his pots within one inch and a half of the top, he must drink eight quarts of his stale beer, directly after a thunderstorm.

4. Any Teetotaler who drinks more than seven quarts of double stout, or one pint of gin, rum, or brandy, unless so ordered by his medical adviser, he must be chained to the nearest drinking fountain for twenty-four hours.

5. Any Tailor who is so fond of garden-stuff, as to cabbage half the cloth entrusted to him by any customer to make up, it shall be in the power of any magistrate to compel him either to walk nine times round St. Paul's with a sleeve-board tied to his back, or to sit on his hot goose for one hour.

6. Any Shoemaker, Bootmaker, or Cobler, who is known to put less than three stitches to the inch, or leave more than one score of pegs sticking up in his customers' boots, must live upon lumps of wax for three days, and pay 5s. to the hospital for cripples.

7. Any man who is known to ill-use his wife, or strike her with anything harder than a kitchen poker, or grumble if the child wet his shirt more than six times in one night, must sleep at the foot of the bed for one calendar month.

8. Any Barber, or barber's clerk, who when shaving a customer shall cut more than one inch off the said customer's chin, or cram more than a pint of soap suds into his mouth, is ordered to bite three inches off his own pole, or live upon hair shavings for a week.

9. Any Policeman who shall be known to have less than six ounces of hair on his upper lip, or fail to inspect the cupboards of the houses on his beat, must forfeit his claim to being rated sergeant, and be kept without mutton for three months.

10. Any Milliner, dress maker, or fast young girl who may be seen walking with a chignon larger than a porter's knot, and over 12 pounds in weight, she must pay a fine of 5s. a-year to find wigs for those that are baldpated.

11. Any puffing Grocer who shall be known to be so very kind as to present his customers with sugar basins or milk jugs, and try to persuade them that he is selling better tea for 2s. per pound than others can for 5s. shall be treated as a man who is off his chump and forthwith be taken to Bedlam, or the nearest lunatic asylum to where he resides.

12. Any woman who shall be known to be gadding about from house to house, attending to other people's business instead of minding her own, shall be made to stand at the door of the parish church with her nose stuck in the key hole, during the service, and wear a ticket on her back, with the words Paul Pry written thereon.

13. Any married Postman who shall be known to wink at, or squeeze the hand of any cookmaid, nursemaid, or any other pretty young girl, while delivering his letters, his wife shall be empowered to flog him with a wet dish-clout the whole length of his beat.

14. Any nursemaid or greasy cook, who shall have more than two soldiers cuddling her at one time in the kitchen, shall give her next quarter's wages to the nearest lying-in-hospital.

15. Any young man, who while riding a dandy horse or velocipede, knocking the bark from off his nose more than three times in one week, shall not be allowed to mount one again without being attended by his nurse.

16. Any young virgin over sixty, that has remained single up to that time ; and cannot make oath that she has not been kissed at least a score of times by some nice young man, shall be compelled to find meat for half the cats, no matter whether they are black, white, carrotty, or tabby, that are found within one mile of where she resides.

Lastly. And in addition to the penalties here laid down, any person failing to attend to, and breaking one or more of these clauses, they shall be taken to the nearest Union, and made to crack a bushel of unboiled stones.

Disley, Printer, 57, High Street, St. Giles, London.

THE NEW STREETS ACT.

The First Clause in this truly farcical and singular Act is relating to all 'regular' but not 'running' dustmen :—

That it be enacted that no dustman or scavenger shall dare to sing out dust oh ! in a falsetto voice, between the hours of 10 in the morning and 7 in the evening ; and that all housekeepers or lodgers shall place all their cabbage stumps, potatoe peels, or fish bones into a fryingpan, dustpan, box or basket, chamber utensil, or any other utensil that is at hand, and place them neatly along the kerb, so that children may play at leap-frog on their way to school.

2.   That no persons shall under any pretence leave any goods in the streets for more than sixteen seconds and a half ; and any baker resting his basket for a longer space of time, shall for the first offence, forfeit his basket, and for the second, be compelled to stand three hours in a flour sack.

3.   That no ox, pig, or ass, or any other kind of donkey shall be driven through the streets without an order from Scotland yard, or the Police Commissioners may detain them for ther own use.

And it is enacted that on and after the first day of November no cabman shall ply for hire, unless his cab shall be illuminated ; and moreover, it is expected that each cabman shall be furnished with a transparent hat, each hat to have a life-like photographic likeness of Sir R— M— stuck in the centre.

4.   That no 'bus driver or conductor shall allow more than twenty-four volunteers to ride on the roof at one time, and any female with a crinoline more than twelve yards round shall not be allowed as an inside passenger ; and any person with more than thirteen stone of useless fat, shall not be considered as a single fare.   And it is expected that each 'bus will be provided with a truck to transport all such live lumber te their destination.

5.   No walking sandwich will be allowed to parade the streets, and no pavement to be disfigured with, 'read Fun or Tommyhawk.'   And any dandy seen strutting about in one of Moses's Guinea Overcoats, will be considered as a walking advertisement, and will be punished as the law directs.   No play bills, show bills, sale bills, nor bills of any kind be seen in the public streets ; and any quack doctor's butler who shall be seen giving out bills relative to extraordinary cures of incurable cures shall be treated as a treasonable offender.

6.   All carts, go-carts, or donkey carts, must keep a correct line, at least four inches and a half from the kerb, and all nursemaids who are seen out with a perambulator with more than two soldiers as an escort, shall forfeit their last quarter's wages.

7.   And be it enacted that any pug-dog, lap-dog, poodle-dog, bull-dog, who shall be found lurking about the street without being well muzzled, so as to prevent them from picking up the stray bones ; and such dogs not giving their names and address to the police will be treated as bad characters, and will be taken into custody, —that is if the police can catch them—and be detained until their parents or friends can be found.

8.   And further that such dogs shall board and lodge at the nearest station-house for three days free of expence, and provided with such food a medical inspector shall think fit, but if not owned at the end of that time they shall be treated as outcasts and executed accordingly ; and their bodies sold for what they will fetch, the proceeds to go towards a fund for the relief of decayed pie shop keepers.

9.   No shoeblack will be allowed to polish up your understandings, nor use the words, " shine your boots, sir," without being duly licensed according to Act of Parliament.   And no costermonger, or costermonger's apprentice, shall dare to cry " ten a penny walnuts," within four feet of the footway ; and any donkey braying without an order from the Commissioners shall be taken into custody, and fed upon cabbage stumps for one month.

10.   With a view to suppressing all gaming, all betting men are forbidden to meet more than three together in public thoroughfares, but may victimise as many as they like in the back streets.

11.   No owners of soup or cook shops shall dare to sell any stocking pudding that has not got at least two plums and a half in a square inch, or they will be compelled to swallow three quarts of double size every day for a fortnight.   No confectioner shall make or cause to be made, any lollipops or sugar sticks measuring more than six inches in length, and any children sucking any of larger dimensions in the public streets will be considered as causing an obstruction, and punished accordingly.

12.   This Act is favourable to all cats as we find they are not mentioned, so they are empowered to plunder our cupboards, and seranade us with their nightly gambols on the tiles.

13.   No boy under twenty years of age will be allowed to trundle a hoop upon the footpath, except between the hours of twelve at night and six in the morning.

14.   No lady after the passing of this Act must wear a bonnet larger than the bottom of a halfpenny bun, lest they should be afflicted with the brain fever, nor have more hair sticking out behind than would stuff a moderate side pillow-case.

15.   No gent shall be allowed to wear whiskers that shall extend more than four inches and a half from his face under the pain of being close shaved with a carpenter's hand-saw.

16.   And all mothers will be compelled to keep a supply of soothing syrup on hand, as no child will be allowed to cry during the prescribed hours ; and this Clause refers to all persons addicted to snoring, who are hereby cautioned not to lay on their backs, for fear they should disturb the public peace.

17.   And as no one can be convicted unless seen by a policeman, the public are requested to wait till that gentlemen is out of sight before they violate any part of this Act.

18.   And as evil doers will be punished by Mayne force, a placard to that effect will be stuck on each lamp-post.   So much for the New Police Act.

God save the People !

H. Disley, Printer, 57, High Street, St. Giles, London.

THE POOR LAW CATECHISM.

Q. What is your name?

A. A Pauper.

Q. Who gave you that name?

A. The Board of Guardians, to whom I applied in the time of distress, when first I became a child of want, a member of the workhouse, and an inheritor of all the insults that poverty is heir to.

Q. What did the Board of Guardians do for you.

A. They did promise two things. First, that I should be treated like a convicted felon, being deprived of liberty, and on prison fare. Lastly, that I should be an object of oppression all the days of my life.

Q. Rehearse the Articles of thy belief.

A. I believe in the cruelty of Lord H—y B—m, the author of the present Poor Law, and I also believe that these laws have caused the death of tens of thousands by starvation and neglect.

Q. How many Commandments have you and such as you are to keep?

A. Ten.

Q. Which be they?

A. The same which the Poor Law Commissioners make in Somerset House, saying, We are thy lords and masters, who have caused thee to be confined as in bastiles, and separated thee and the wife of thy bosom, and the children of thy love. 1st, Thou shalt obey no laws but ours. 2nd, Thou shalt not make to thyself any substitute for skilley, nor the likeness of tea, or any other kind of food, or drink, except as is allowed in the workhouse; for we are very jealous men, punishing with severity any transgression against our laws. Should'st thou disobey in this, we shall teach you a lesson that shall last thee all the days of thy life. 3rd, Thou shalt labour hard, and for nothing, and none of thy earnings shall be thy own. 4th, Remember the Sabbath day: six days shalt thou labour hard, and have but little to eat; but the seventh day is the Sabbath, wherein we cannot make you work, and so we give you liberty for an hour or two, to save the parish the expense of your Sunday dinner. 5th. Thou shalt honour the Poor Laws, the Commissioners, and the Beadles; thou shalt take no offence at what they say or do, or else thy days shall be made more miserable in the workhouse wherein thou livest. 6th, Thou shalt commit murder by neglecting thy starving children, for we will give thee no assistance to get them food. 7th, Thou shalt learn to neglect the dear ties of nature, for we will separate thee from the wife of thy bosom, and the children of thy love. 8th, Thou shalt rob thyself of the society and enjoyment of her whom thou hast sworn to protect while life shall last. 9th, Thou shalt be a false witness whenever a Pauper dies, and should the coroner or jury ask you how you live, why tell them you live like lords, and are as happy as princes. 10th, Thou shalt covet all thy neighbour is possessed of, thou shalt covet his friends, his clothes, and all the comforts which thou once had; yet shalt thou long in vain; for remember, oh, pauper! that the motto of every workhouse is—"He who enters here leaves all comforts behind."

LINES ON THE DEATH OF AN OLD PAUPER.

Oh! Englishmen, come drop a tear or two,
While I relate a thrilling tale of woe,
Of one whose age demanded all the care
That love which aged pilgrims ought to share.
This poor old man, whose limbs refused to bear
The weight of more than eighty years of care,
Was brought before a beak, worse than a Turk,
And sent to gaol because he could not work,
Weep, sons of Britain, mourn your sires' disgrace!
Weep, English mothers! hug your rising race,
And pray to Him, who gave your children breath,

They may not live to die this old man's death,
In a dark dungeon he was close confined,
No friend to comfort, or to soothe his mind;
No child to cheer his loathsome dying bed,
But soon he rested with the silent dead,
Oh, ye who roll in chariots proud and gay,
Ye legal murderers! there will be a day,
When you shall leave all your riches behind,
A dwelling with the ever lost to find,
And your great Master, He whose name is good
Will hold you guilty of your brother's blood.

THE
SOLDIER'S  CATECHISM.

Question. What is your name?

Answer. Soldier.

Q. Who gave you that name?

A. The recruiting-sergeant, when I received the enlisting shilling, whereby I was made a recruit of bayonets, bullets, and death.

Q. What did the recruiting-sergeant promise then for you?

A. He did promise and vow three things in my name. First, that I should renounce all idea of liberty, and all such nonsense. Secondly, that I should be well harassed with drill. And, thirdly, that I should stand up to be shot at whenever called upon so to do; and I heartily hope our Colonel will never call me into such a perilous position.

Q. Rehearse the Articles of thy Belief.

A. I believe in the Colonel most mighty, maker of Sergeants and Corporals; and in his deputy the Major, who is an officer by commission, and rose by turn of promotion, suffered the hardships of the field-service, marching and fighting; he descended into trials; after the wars he rose again; he ascended into ease, and sitteth on the right hand of the Colonel, from whence he will come to superintend the good from the bad. I believe in the Adjutant; the punishment of the guard-room; the stopping of grog; the flogging with cats; and the certainty of these things lasting. Amen.

Q. How many Commandments may there be?

A. Ten.

Q. What are they?

A. The same which the Colonel spake in the standing orders, saying, I am thy Colonel and commanding officer, who commands thee in the field and in quarters.

I. Thou shalt have no other Colonel but me.

II. Thou shalt not make to thyself any sergeant or corporal, that is in any European regiment above, or in any Sepoy regiment below, neither shalt thou salute them; for I thy Colonel am a jealous Colonel, and visit the iniquities of my men unto the third and fourth with stripes, and promote those who obey me and keep my standing orders.

III. Thou shalt not take the name of thy Colonel in vain, for I will not call him a good man who shall do so.

IV. Remember that thou attend church parade. Six days shalt thou have for drill and field-days; but on the seventh day thou shalt have no drill, thou, nor thy fire-lock, nor thy pouch, nor thy pouch-belt, nor thy ammunition, or any of thy appointments: for six days are sufficient for these things, and I like to rest on that day; wherefore I order church parade—attend to it.

V. Honour thy Colonel and thy Major, that thy comfort may be long in the regiment you are in.

VI. Thou shalt not get drunk on duty.

VII. Thou shalt not be absent from drill.

VIII. Thou shalt not sell thy kit.

IX. Thou shalt not come dirty to parade.

X. Thou shalt not covet thy pay-sergeants's coat, nor his place, nor his pay, nor his sword, nor his perquisites, nor his wife, nor his authority, nor any thing that is his.

Q. What do you chiefly learn by these commandments?

A. I learn two things: my duty towards my Colonel, and my duty towards my pay-sergeant.

Q. What is your duty towards your Colonel?

A. My duty towards my Colonel is to believe in him, to fear him, to obey all his orders, and all that are put in authority under him, with all my heart; to appear before him as a soldier all the days of my life; to salute him, to submit to him in all respect whatever; to put my whole trust in him, to give him thanks when he promotes me, to honour him and his commission, and to serve him as a soldier. Amen.

Q. What is your duty towards your pay-sergeant?

A. My duty towards my pay-sergeant is to attend to his directions, to look to him for pay and allowances, and all supplies of clothing; to borrow four shillings and give him five in return, to sign all books and papers he may require, and to never doubt his word in any thing.

Q. Let me hear you say your prayers.

A. Our Colonel, high in rank, honoured be thy name; may thy promotion come; thy will be done by thy sergeants, corporals, and privates. Give me my daily allowance of pay; and forgive me my crimes as I should forgive my comrade soldier. And lead me not to the triangles; but deliver me from them; and thine shall be the honour, thine the power, for ever and ever. Amen.

Q. What desirest thou in this prayer?

A. I desire my Colonel, our commanding officer, to extend his kindness to me and all my comrades; that we may honour him, serve him, and obey all his orders as we ought to do. And I pray unto him that he will be merciful unto us, and forgive us our crimes; and that he will lead us on to the defence of our country and Queen. And this I trust he will for his honour and renown; and therefore I say, Amen, and Amen.

THE DRUNKARD'S CATECHISM.

Question.—What is your name?

Answer.—Drunken Sot.

Q.—Who gave you that name?

A.—As drink is my idol, landlords and their wives get all my money; they gave me that name in my drunken sprees, wherein I was made a member of strife, a child of want, and an inheritor of a bundle of rags.

Q.—What did your landlords and landladies promise for you.

A.—They did promise and vow three things in my name, first, that I should renounce the comfort of my own fire side; secondly, starve my wife and hunger my children; thirdly, walk in rags and tatters, with my shoe soles going flip flap all the days of my life.

Catechist.—Rehearse the articles of thy belief.

Answer.—I believe in the existence of one Mr Alcohol, the great head and chief of all manner of vice, the source of nine-tenths of all diseases; and I not only believe, but am sure that when my money is gone and spent, the landlord will stop the tap and turn me out.

C.—How many commandments have ye sots to keep?

A.—Ten.

C.—What be they.

A.—The same which the landlord and landlady spake in the bar, saying, We are thy master and thy mistress who brought thee out of the paths of virtue, placed thee in the ways of vice, and set thy feet on the road which leadeth to New South Wales.

I.—Thou shalt use no other house but mine.

II.—Thou shalt not make to thyself any substitute for intoxicating drinks, such as tea, coffee, ginger-pop and lemonade; for I am a jealous man, wearing the coat that should be on thy back, eating thy children's bread, and pocketing the money which should make thee and thy wife happy all the days of thy life.

III.—Thou shalt not use my house in vain.

IV.—Remember that thou eat but one meal on the Sabbath day. Six days shalt thou drink and spend all thy money, but the seventh day is the Sabbath, wherein I wash my floor, mend my fires and make ready for the company the remaining part of the day.

V.--Thou shalt honor the landlords, the landladies, and the gin-shops with thy presence, that thy days may be few and miserable, in the land wherein thou livest.

VI.—Thou shalt commit murder, by starving, hungering, and beating thy wife and family.

VII.—Thou shalt commit self-destruction.

VIII.—Thou shalt sell thy wife's and children's bread and rob thyself of all thy comforts.

IX.—Thou shalt bear false witness when thou speakest of the horrors, saying, Thou art in good health when labouring under the barrel fever.

X.—Thou shalt covet all thy neighbour is possessed of; thou shalt covet his house, his land, his purse, his health, his wealth, and all that he has got, that thou mayest indulge in drunkenness, help the brewer to buy a new coach, a pair of fine horses, a new dray, and a fine building, that he may live in idleness all his days; likewise to enable the landlord to purchase a new sign to place over his door, with "Licensed to be drunk on the Premises" written thereon.

THE DRUNKARD'S LOOKING GLASS!

What will the drunkard do for ale?
Shall I unfold my dreadful tale?
Yes, I'll unfold it if I can,
To benefit a drunken man.

What will a drunkard do for ale?
It will make a sober man turn pale,
Sell his hat and pawn his coat,
To satisfy his greedy throat.

Sell his stockings and his shirt,
Strut about in rags and dirt,
Sell his shoes from off his feet,
And barefoot go about the streets.

What will he do to gain his end?
He will deceive his dearest friend,
His crafty plans he will devise,
And tell the most atrocious lies.

What will a drunkard do for ale?
Dark and dismal grows my tale;
Sell his bedstead and his bed,
Nor leave a place to lay his head.

Sell his blankets and his sheets,
Lie in barns or walk the streets,
His thirsty soul will cry for more,
He's starved and miserably poor.

He'll beg for half-pence when he can,
And say he is a dying man;
But if three half-pence he has got,
He'll go and find another sot.

As mean and shabby as himself,
A dirty, ragged, drunken elf,
In some alehouse corner seated,
Waiting longing to be treated.

They freely enter into chat,
If they can but catch a flat;
With every one they will be friends,
If they can but gain their ends.

Then with his bosom full of strife,
Each man goes home to beat his wife,
The children beat and sent to bed,
Because the wretches have no bread.

No meat, no butter have they got,
Such is the dwelling of a sot,
The wife in tears and ragged too,
Say, drunkard, is my statement true?

THE DRUNKARD'S FAREWELL TO HIS FOLLY!

Farewell landlords, farewell jerry's,
Farewell brandy, wine, and sherry,
Farewell horrors and blue devils,
Farewell dens of midnight revels.

Farewell fires that have no coals on,

Farewell shoes that have no soles on,
Farewell children with wry faces,
Farewell to the pop-shop races.

Farewell wash and all wash vendors,
Farewell duns and all dun senders,

Farewell landlords and your spouses,
Farewell spiders and your houses.

Farewell to your noise and babble,
Farewell to your foolish gabble,
Farewell pockets that are empty,
Farewell landlords, you've had plenty.

London :—H. Such, Printer, 123, Union Street, Boro'—S.E. Established 1846.

91

NEW BEER HOUSE ACT,

To be observed by all Beer Sellers and Beer Drinkers throughout England, and to be in force as long as the people will stand it.

Now it has pleased the Lords spiritual and temporal of this miscalled free and happy England, to look with an eye of pity on the working classes ; and feeling for all those who are fond of their beer, have passed a bill called the New Beer House Act, and all persons breaking the same will have to look out for squalls.

Clause 1. Be it enacted, that any person wishing to open a place for the sale of beer, wine, ale, cider, or swankey, shall give notice of the same to the overseers, churchwardens, town crier, and parish beadle, of the parish wherein he lives, and stick one on the door of the church or chapel, if there is one, and if not, he must pin one on the seat of his breeches, and walk round the said parish from ten in the morning till five in the afternoon, for two consecutive Sundays, or live upon skilly for one month.

2. Any person keeping a house for the sale of any kind of fermented liquor, and who shall dare to keep the said house open one moment after the clock has said cut it, and sell one half pint of malt tea, he shall for the first offence have his head shaved, and for the second shall be imprisoned for a term not exceeding his natural life.

3. Any keeper of any refreshment house who shall have the cheek to sell, or cause to be sold, one glass of cooper, or one quarter of Watling's pork feed to any person, without being cock sure that his character is strictly moral, he shall not draw another drop for 12 calendar months. This clause does not refer to the tribe of Overend and Gurney's, or any one connected with the Albert Assurance Company, or, in fact, any gentlemanly swindlers whatever.

4. No chandler shop keeper, fruit shop keeper, or shop for the sale of lollipops, shall dare to sell small beer or shandy-gaff to any wayfarer during the hours stated in the act, or they will have to pay 40s., and forfeit the swankey for Her Majesty's own private use.

5. It is enacted that a body of vigilant officers from each division of police to be called the tasters, whose duty shall be to enter such houses as they may think fit, swallow all they can find, and see that none of the working classes get half seas over.

6. All brewers' grooms, or draymen, shall sponge their horses on Saturday night, lest they should smell of malt on the Sunday.

7. All persons who are in the habit of getting tight on Saturday night, are requested to drink one quart of half-and-half before closing time, lest they should be thirsty next morning.

8. All persons who have a custom of taking a stroll into the country on a Sunday to get a blow after their week's labour, or enjoy a picnic at Hampstead or Wimbledon, will do well to provide themselves with stone bottles, labelled cold tea, as there will be no such a thing as bona-fide travellers while the new Beer House Act is in force.

9. All persons are forbidden to use any bottles, jugs, glasses, or tea cups that has contained beer on Saturday night, without well scalding out on the Sunday morning.

10. And woe betide any woman who is caught with a flask containing cholic drops in her pocket.

11. All cowkeepers or dairymen are cautioned against feeding their cows on grains, lest the milk should give the tea a beery flavour.

12. All publicans and beer shop keepers are to place a wet blanket over their chimney pots, close the windows, and stop up the key holes, lest the smell should offend the framers of the New Beer House Act.

13. Any person who receives a visit from father, mother, brother, or grandmother, during the prescribed hours, they must not dare to give them one glass, they not being servants or lodgers.

And lastly, any person causing the conviction of one score of offenders against the above Act, will receive, as a reward, a free admission to the Crystal Palace at the next meeting of the Temperance League.

So says the New Beer House Act.

H. Disley, Printer, 57, High Street, St. Giles, London.

GRAND CONVERSATION ON BRAVE NELSON.

AS some heroes bold, I will unfold, together were conversing,
 It was in the praise of Nelson, as you shall quickly hear;
Said one unto the other, if we could behold another,
In old England like Nelson, we proudly would him cheer.
From Norfolk it is known he came, he was a man of noted fame,
He struggled hard for liberty, as every Briton knows,
In battle he would loudly cry, I'll gain the victory or die,
This grand conversation on brave Nelson arose.

Now at Copenhagen and the Nile, he gave command with a smile,
He said, "Stand firm, my British tars, the enemy to meet;
Prepare each gun—all terror shun, but never do surrender!
The champion of the briny waves was Nelson and his fleet;
When Capt. Hardy, you may see, who always done his duty free,
Brave Collingwood the enemy undaunted would oppose, [main,
He caused some thousands to be slain while fighting on the raging
This grand conversation on brave Nelson arose.

Many a youth, I'll tell the truth, in action have been wounded,
Some left their friends and lovers in despair upon their native shore
Others never returned again, but died upon the raging main,
Causing many a one to cry "my son" and widows to deplore,
When war was raging, it is said, men for their labour were paid,
Commerce and trade flourishing, but now it ebbs and flows,
And poverty it does increase, though Britons say we live in peace,
This grand conversation on brave Nelson arose.

Some hardy tars they did survive, in Greenwich College now
Will tell the deeds of Nelson and the battles that he won, [alive,
He never feared a cannon ball, till at Trafalgar he did fall,
No flinching from the enemy—no action he did shun;
He many powers did defeat, and never was that hero beat,
Neither would he surrender till he had thrashed his daring foes,
Altho' he lost an eye and wing, he was loyal and true to his king,
This grand conversation on brave Nelson arose.

Trafalgar I will mention, if you will give attention,
It long has been recorded where brave Nelson fell and bled,
The officers around him, all human aid was found,
But were affected to the heart to find that he was dead. [more,
The gallant tars were grieved sore to find Lord Nelson was no
All was in confusion in the 'midst of dying woes, [conveyed,
In rum they put him, it is said, and then to England him
This grand conversation on brave Nelson arose.

Now in mem'ry of that hero's loss, we understand at Charing
A monument of Nelson has been erected there; [Cross,
An ancient building was pulled down, and an open space of
To commemorate the battle, it is call'd Trafalgar Square. [ground
You British tars as do pass by, look up aloft and you will spy,
The visage of that hero respected as it shows, [day,
Tho' his remains are in decay, grim Death in action won the
This grand conversation on brave Nelson arose.

BATTLE OF WATERLOO.

'TWAS on the 18th day of June Napoleon did advance,
 The choicest troops that he could raise within the
 bounds of France;
Their glittering eagles shone around and proudly looked the
 foe,
But Briton's lion tore their wings on the plains of Waterloo.

With Wellington we'll go, with Wellington we'll go,
For Wellington commanded us on the Plains of Waterloo,
The fight did last from ten o'clock until the dawn of day,
While blood and limbs and cannon balls in thick profusion
 lay;
Their Cuirassieurs did quickly charge our squares to over-
 throw,
But Britons firm, undaunted stood, on the Plains of Waterloo.

The number of the French that at Waterloo were slain,
Was near sixty thousand all laid upon the plain;
Near forty thousand of them fell upon that fatal day,
Of our brave British heroes who their prowess did display.
It's now the dreadful night comes on, how dismal is the
 plain,
When the Prussians and the English found above ten thousand
 slain,
Brave Wellington and Blucher bold most nobly drove their
 foes,
And Buonaparte's Imperial crown was taken at Waterloo.

We followed up the rear till the middle of the night,
We gave them three cheers as they were on their flight,
Says Bony, d—m those Englishmen, they do bear such a
 name,
They beat me here at Waterloo, at Portugal and Spain.
Now peace be to their honoured souls who fell that gloriou
 day,
May the plough ne'er raise their bones nor cut the sacred clay,
But let the place remain a waste, a terror to the foe,
And when trembling Frenchmen pass that way they'll think
 of Waterloo.

London :—H. Such, Printer and Publisher, 117, Union Street, Borough.—S.E.

A NEW SONG

ON

THE TIMES.

—§—

Come old and young and rich and poor,
　And listen to our song,
I'll give to you some good advice,
　And will not keep you long :
If you have one shilling to spend,
　Go down to Mr Ward,
And there you'll get three pounds of beef,
　That's just come from abroad.

CHORUS.

So there never was such doings in Old England before.

Now beef has come to fourpence a pound,
　It's a pity you should want,
Folks talk about America !
　But don't you Emigrate.
But stop at home in England,
　If you've any work at all,
For provisions will be cheap,
　If wages be but small.

The Butchers now they may give o'er,
　Selling their stinking meat,
For there's many a hundred weight been sold
　That never was fit to eat ;
And now when you do walk the street,
　If you should happen to turn your eye,
It's how-do-you-do ? good morning, man,
　As you are passing by.

There were hundreds in this country
　O ! 'tis true what I do tell,
That could not get a pound of meat,
　Or hardly get a smell ;
But since the Tariff Bill is pass'd,
　Many hundreds will be fed,
With plenty of good pork and beef,
　And likewise good cheap bread.

Now beef and mutton has come down,
　And so is pork and flour too,
Which is what this country wanted,
　A many years ago ;
The cutlers now may go to work,
　And grind away like bricks,
For now we'll carve with knives and forks,
　Instead of porridge sticks.

The farmers do not like those laws,
　From what I've heard them say,
Because the corn will be so cheap,
　And so will straw and hay,
If you buy a pennyworth of eggs,
　You will get three or four,
And as for churning butter,
　Why they say they'll soon give o'er.

So to conclude and make an end,
　And finish up my lines,
The poor will find in England
　A difference in the times,
For work it will be plentiful.
　And provisions will be low,
And that is what a poor man wants,
　Wherever he does go.

THE

AGONY BILL.

—§—

Dear me what a change has seen our nation,
Since we've reformed our legislation,
Each M.P. as now the fashion,
Brings a new bill every session.
Because one did in the way of peace act,
By getting past the New Police Act ;
Another wants a grand reversion,
So brings you a Sabbath Bill Coercion !

　At this you'll laugh for its meant to gag you,
　This is the bill of Saint Andrew Agnew.

This worthy, pious emasculator,
Who talks of setting your morals straighter,
Vows by the Gods your pleasures to be balking,
He'll put a stop to your Sunday walking,
When persons are preaching, then will be search time
To collar them that's walking in church time,
The tenants of houses and those of floors then,
Must not venture out ot doors then.

All those who brew their home brew'd beer then,
At times I'm sure will quake with fear then,
And dread to let it in the vat lay,
Lest it should happen to work on that day,
Then if you're seized with cough or phtisic,
You must not even swallow physic !
For 'its decreed all rest that one day,
So not even salts must work on Sunday !

Dumb animals they'll be strangely puzzled,
When Sunday comes each dog must be muzzled,
The cocks must on their roosts abide up,
And to stop their crowings their beaks must be tied up,
A noise with contempt will the act be treating,
The calves and the sheep must be kept from bleating,
The dairies must close from twelve to twelve, sir,
And as to the cows they must milk themselves, sir

No duck must lay, no cat must kitten,
The hen must leave her nest through sitting,
Though painful is the separation,
She must quit the scene of incubation !
Married men will to quake be inclined then,
For fear their wives should be confined then,
For as no labour's allowed on Sundays,
Of course she must put it off till the Mondays.

John Harkness, Printer, 121, Church Street, Preston.

A NEW SONG
ON
THE REPEAL
OF THE
CORN LAWS.

Come every heart rejoice with me,
We soon will have a glorious spree,
Cheap food once more we soon shall see,
    Throughout the British Nation,
The ports they are thrown open wide,
And ships will mount the foaming tide,
And plenty to our shores will glide,
    From every foreign Nation,
For Bob and Arthur met one day,
Those words I heard them for to say.
To us the people did long pray,
    Delay it is a danger.

CHORUS.

So rejoice and sing the ports are free,
Such thumping loaves you soon will see.
With pies and dumplings, O what glee,
    Throughout the British Nation.

The Cabinet they thought it right,
To put this famine to the flight,
And not to tempt a nation's might,—
    The belly gives no quarter,
They one and all gave their consent,
Their stubborn hearts they soon were bent,
And the bread tax chains they quickly rent,
    That long oppress'd this nation,
The van was led by Bobby Blue,
And the boasting cock of Waterloo,
For a Revolution would not do,
    They dread its desperation.

The bonded grain must soon come out,
It will give monopolists the gout,
And put them to the right about,
    To meet this competition;
Their rusty bars and locks so strong,
Must open wide before it's long;
With grief they'll hear our merry song,
    For long they've liv'd in clover;
The granaries with corn and flour
Into our markets will pour,
And the bread tax loaf we'll soon devour,
    That caus'd such desolation.

So men and women and children too,
Rejoice, you'll soon have work to do,
In spite of all the bread tax crew;—
    Rejoice—they are defeated.
Your teeth must soon commence the mill,
And grind away with right good will,
Your bellies every one can fill
    With puddings, pies, and dumplings,
So women all shout out huzza.
Hot cakes at will with good strong tea,
And that honest debts you soon will pay,
    To your neglected belly.

The poor will soon have to turn about,
With corporations they'll strut out,
With American flour cheap and stout,
    Their bellies to adorn;
The bones that now are thin and small,
In loads of flesh they soon will fall,
And on a cab will have to call,
    O what an alteration!
Away with the hungry cry that's been,
Such mumping of bread was never seen!
Long life attend our gracious Queen—
    A woman rules the nation.

A NEW SONG,
OPENING THE PORTS.

(Composed by E. Wrigley for his Three Strings.)

Men, women, and children, come list to my story—
The ports are thrown open, your bellies may glory;
Provisions must drop now, to satisfy many,
Who long before this time could scarcely get any;
For bread's been so dear it was hard to be gotten,
Potatoes so scarce, and one half of them rotten,
These hard times I fear will ne'er be forgotten;
But now wag your jaws, lad, the ports are thrown open.

CHORUS.

Chaw, chaw—banish this ruin, lads;
Your grinders in motion, it's keep them a-going, lads;
Wag, wag, wag your jaws—let them be going, lads;
Provisions must fall, now the ports are thrown open.

In Ireland and Scotland the famine has raged so,
Hundreds and thousands—old, young, middle-aged, too;
Food's been so scarce and so dear through the nation,
That many grim death clam'd died through starvation.
But let us all hope now these hard times are ended,
Provisions come down fast, and trade be mended,
That poor folk may live by their labour—God send it,
Forget what is past, now the ports are thrown open.

These millers and swailers, and other corn dealers,
Their granaries well stocked with corn and meal is;
In hopes of bread rising, from market they stop it—
These clam-gutted robbers—but now they must drop it.
The grain that in warehouses years has been bonded,
Must now be brought out—it's our right to demand it;
From all foreign shores fresh supplies will be landed,
In spite of the tyrants, the ports are thrown open.

The rich, with their treasure, can roll at their leisure;
They know not, they feel not, for nothing but pleasure.
Full bellies don't know what an empty one's feeling,
Enough to set hundreds that's honest a-stealing;
And farmers, now mind it, your corn quickly grind it,
And bring it to market, or you'll be behind it;
And 'tatoes must drop, too—old chaps, you will find it,
The corn's coming free, now the ports are open.

This dropping of food, instead of its rising,
To some of the bakers has come most surprising;
Such stocks they've laid in, thinking of making riches,
Through this fall of bread some will dirty their breeches!
The stores that's hid up, now they out must be bringing,
Or else a dead weight on their hands will be ringing,
While sighing and crying we'll merrily be singing—
Come, drop your bread, bakers, the ports are thrown open.

Set your pots on the fire which of late has been empty,
Pies, dumplings, and puddings, there soon will be plenty;
And 'tatoes must fall, too, for one thing remember,
All food's to come free from the first of September;
And ships from all parts, now they are got in motion,
Their canvas well spread are a-ploughing the ocean,
To bring in cheap food from each foreign nation,
So, lasses and lads, shout, the ports are all open.

So now to conclude and finish my ditty,
This filling of bellies it sounds very pretty.
To thousands of jaws that look haggard and thin too,
So chuck away lads, your past time to regain now;
And butchers, your flesh meat may now be dropping,
Such rattling of grinders, and porridge pots wopping,
For some when they start there will be no stopping—
Shout huzza, lads and lasses, the ports are thrown open.

John Harkness, Printer, 121, Church Street, Preston.

A NEW SONG ON THE
LIBERATION
OF
DANIEL O'CONNELL.

Harkness, Printer, 121, Church Street, Preston.

Rejoice you sons of Erin's Isle throughout the British
    nation,
I hope you'll listen unto me to this my true narration.
Each spy and knave that did enslave, thank God they
    are defeated,
For our loyal Patriots are free, and Daniel's liberated.

CHORUS.

Cheer up my boys, our Parliament will soon be reinstated,
For our loyal Patriots are free, and Daniel's liberated.

When the glorious news it did arrive throughout the
    Irish nation,
Both rich and poor, high and low, of every rank and
    station,
To Harold's cross they did repair with hearts all elevated,
To see the star of Erin's Isle, brave Daniel liberated.

These forty years brave noble Dan our rights he has
    defended ;
In spite of vile Oppression, for Freedom he contended !
Our Parliament it's his interest shortly to obtain, sir,
And gain for the land St. Patrick blest, with all his
    might and main, sir.

Long life attend brave noble Dan, and all the brave
    Repealers,
They stood true to their country and their creed in spite
    of every traitor ;
Brave John O'Connell and Tom Steele we are bound for
    to remember,
With Barrat, Ray, Duffy and Gray, they never would
    surrender.

When they appeared before the court to defend their
    country's cause, sir,
Our hero Dan, that matchless man, he did explain the
    laws, sir ;
He says, my country's rights I'll defend while blood
    remains in my veins, sir,
And we'll ne'er desist, but still insist, till the Union I
    obtain, sir.

When the writ of error it was brought before the
    House of Lords, sir,
Lord Denman, Campbell and Cottingham did explain
    the laws, sir,
The Lord Chancellor and Brougham, their schemes were
    all defeated,
I'm sure the Tories will run mad since Dan is liberated.

So now my friends I will conclude these lines that I
    have penn'd, sir,
We'll drink a health unto brave Dan, long may he live
    and reign, sir,
He'll plant the Tree of Liberty once more in College
    Green, sir,
And while life remains brave noble Dan for ever he'll
    wear the green, sir.

A
NEW SONG
ON
THE TIMES.

Good people all I pray draw near,
We have entered in another year,
The markets now they must come down,
Both in country and in town ;
The farmers now begin to grin,
Their corn to market must bring in,
The ports are opened now you see,
In spite of all their roguery.

They've risen the barley, flour, and meal,
I think they must have hearts like steel,
And wages are so very low,
Fills poor men's hearts with grief and woe ;
The potatoes too, you all must know,
Have proved poor people's overthrow,
If they had been good, I am very sure
They never would have rais'd the flour.

The rich have all things at command,
While poverty rages through the land,
And bread it is so very dear,
Draws from poor people many a tear ;
The store houses are breaking down with grain,
No wonder that the poor complain,
In the midst of plenty you plainly see,
They are dying from want and poverty.

The Americans have provisions in store,
From the black sea they will send us more,
The millers and farmers will look blue,
They'll not know which way for to do ;
I hope that trade may flourish once more,
Upon this our native shore,
Then the working man will be right glad
To see his children well cloth'd and fed.

The maltsters and brewers they stamp and swear,
With sugar and treacle must brew their beer,
For all the malt that they do use,
Must all be made into barley loaves ;
So drunkards all I tell to you true,
It's old hock you must bid adieu !
No more of that will be I vow,
So you must drink all treacle now.

Now, to conclude and make an end,
I hope the times they soon will mend,
Send trade and commerce to our shore,
Then the working men will grieve no more,
In peace and unity, they will unite,
Then all the nation will be right,
I hope I have said nothing wrong,
So now I finish off my song.

A NEW SONG.

Come gentlemen listen awhile,
    And hear how they carry the jest on,
I'm sure it will cause you to smile,
    Such fun there is at the Election.
To Brentford the Voters repair,
    Two Knights of the Shire to elect,
Old Nero each Slave doth ensnare,
    Whilst the Free vote for Byng and Burdett.
        Fal de ral lal de ral lal de ral.

The mob are all silent and hush'd,
    To hear Orator Tub on the green,
Some with laughter are ready to burst,
    And others with malice spleen,
He tells you a terrible tale,
    Of a Damn'd Diabolical Crew,
Who Innocents starv'd in a Jail,
    And the worst of it is—IT IS TRUE!
        Fal lal de ral.

There's the case of poor Mary Rich,
    Indeed 'tis a horrible story,
Much about it he's not time to preach,
    But look round and you'll see it before you.
Can you such a monster approve,
    Whose voice on the Hustings doth falter?
His conduct your anger must move—
    Give your Vote—give the Rascal a Halter.
        Fal de ral.

At four the Poll closes and then
    His heart with fear bounces and capers,
'Till his carriage he's safely within,
    Surrounded by all the Thief-takers.
There's Myrmidons sturdy and bold,
    For the Quorum they care not a button,
They'd bother em all I am told,
    If led on by Commodore Dutton.
        Fal lal de ral.

But Byng is a Man you've twice try'd,
    From his duty he never did flinch,
He scorns Aristocracy's pride,
    And Despots will fight inch by inch.
Then Electors now give him a voice.
    And however the Tyrants may fret,
Join him with the man of your choice,
    Independent Sir Francis Burdett.
        Fal de ral.

Sir Francis, the Friend of the Poor,
    Ever staunch in Humanity's cause,
Disdaining a minister's lure,
    Stands forth in support of our laws,
His Mind is untainted and pure,
    Then him place at the head of the set,
In his hands Freedom's Cause is secure,
    For Liberty dwells in the soul of Burdett.
        Fal de ral lal de ral lal de ral.

J. Catnach, Printer, Monmouth Court, 7 Dials.

FLEETWOOD, STRICKLAND,

AND

REFORM TRIUMPHANT.

For Fleetwood and Strickland hurrah !
Hurrah, for the Radicals true,
Now the polling is done, and the election is
    won
By the Banners of Green and Sky-blue ;
The Tories may now go and mourn,
No longer they'll carry the sway,
For the brave Preston lads, the Whigs and
    the Rads,
Have torn all their laurels away.

For the Preston Reformers hurrah,
A glorious struggle they've made,
To pull tyranny down, and victory crown
The friends of Reform and Free Trade ;
No longer shall liberty's sons,
Crouch down to the bigotted few ;
Now the election is won Reform marches on,
In spite of what Tories can do.

So hurrah for the Black Fleet, hurrah !
For the spinners and weavers also,
Now the banners shall wave, and the music
    shall play,
And our members in triumph shall go ;
The faction that dared to oppose,
Before the voice of the people does fly ;
So the victors shall sing till the welkin does
    ring,
With voices that reach to the sky.

To the land that we live in hurrah !
Where the banner of freedom's unfurl'd,
May it soon have to wave o'er the last tyrant's
    grave,
And liberty reign o'er the world ;
The children that yet are unborn,
Shall sing of the deeds we have done,
How their fathers so brave would no longer
    be slaves,
But fought till the battle was won.

PETERLOO.

See ! see ! where freedom's noblest champion
    stands,
Shout ! shout ! illustrious patriot band,
Here grateful millions their generous tribute
    bring,
And shouts for freedom make the welkin
    ring,
While fell corruption and her hellish crew
The blood-stained trophies gained at Peter-
    loo.

Soon shall fair freedom's sons their right
    regain,
Soon shall all Europe join the hallowed
    strain,
Of Liberty and Freedom, Equal Rights and
    Laws,
Heaven's choicest blessing crown this glo-
    rious cause,
While meanly tyrants, crawling minions too,
Tremble at their feats performed on Peter-
    loo.

Britons, be firm, assert your rights, be bold,
Perish like heroes, not like slaves be sold, ;
Firm and unite, bid millions be free,
Will to your ehildren glorious liberty,
While cowards—despots long may keep in
    view,
And silent contemplate the deeds on Peterloo.

John Harkness, Printer, Preston.

THE STATE

OF

Great Britain,

OR

A TOUCH AT THE TIMES.

TUNE—Irish Molly O.

As old John Bull was walking one morning free from pain,
He heard the Rose, the Shamrock, and the Thistle to complain,
An alteration must take place together they did sing,
In the Corn Laws and Poor Laws, and many another thing.

CHORUS.

Conversing on the present time together they did range,
All classes thro' Great Britain now appear so very strange,
That England, Ireland, Scotland, and Wales must quickly have a change.

The railroads all through England have great depression made;
Machinery of every kind has put a stop to trade;
The innkeepers are weeping in agony and grief,
And the ostlers swear they'll buy a rope and go to felo-de-se.

The steam boats to old Belzebub the watermen do wish,
For they say they've nearly ruined them and drowned all the fish,
Of all their new inventions that we have lately seen—
There was none begun or thought upon when Betty was the queen.

Behold the well-bred farmer, how he can strut along,
Let a poor man do whatever he will he's always in the wrong,
With hard labour and low wages he hangs his drooping head,
They won't allow him half enough to find his children bread.

The farmers' daughters ride about well clad and pockets full,
With horse and saddle like a queen and boa like a bull,
In their hand a flashy parasol, and on their face a veil,
And a bustle nearly seven times as big as a milking pail.

The nobles from the pockets of John Bull are all well paid;
Sometimes you hardly know the lady from the servant maid,
For now they are so very proud, silk stockings on their legs,
And every step they take you think they walk on pigeon's eggs.

The tradesman he can hardly pay his rent and keep his home,
And the labourer has eighteen pence a day for breaking stones,
In former days the farmer rode a donkey or a mule,
There never was such times before since Adam went to school.

Some can live in luxury while others weep in woe,
There's very pretty difference now and a century ago,
The world will shortly move by steam it may appear strange,
So you must all acknowledge that England wants a change.

A NEW SONG

OF THE

ELECTION.

O the general Electiom is coming they say,
What an huhabolu and a bustle there'll be,
With the new candidates to be Parliament men,
And the old ones who wished for to go back again.
There'll be all sorts of shuffling and all kinds of rigs,
There's some will call Tories and some will call Whigs,
There's some will wear colours, blue, orange, and red,
And to prove which is best, they'll break each other's heads.

O the general Election is coming they say,
What canvassing, coaxing, and thumping there'll be,
While some will shout —— and —— so clever,
And others bawl ———— and free trade for ever.

O the Whigs for ten years have cut a great swell,
But now by the Tories they've been wollop'd well,
And to pay off the bad boys with a good tit for tat,
They are sending them home to see how they like that.
This has caused amongst Tories and Whigs a great rout,
And many may go tell their mothers the're out,
While some of the boobies will do a deal worse,
By loosing their election, and emptying their purse,

O the Elections are coming, what doings there'll be,
Such gutting and guzzling you never did see,
There'll be cheap beef and ale for poor voters just then,
With Wine, Turtle, and Venison for gentlemen,
There will be open houses in every street,
Where the Birds of a feather may daily meet,
And sly Booots attends to collect all their senses;
Crying, landlord, fill up now, and damn all expenses.

Then to see the great nobs, who a canvassing go,
In the house, or the garret, or the cellar below,
Altho' by infection he dreads his sweet life,
He'll shake hands with the cobbler or kiss the sweep's wife,
Or perhaps he will dandle the sweet little child,
Till he suddenly finds that his trowsers are spoiled,
Tho' his heart it is ready to come up at his throat,
Yet he'd do ten times more to secure a vote.

And then at the last, when all other means fail,
To catch them they try to put salt on their tails,
Don't think I mean bribery, my good sir, dear no !
They only give friends a small present or so.
Or perhaps if you have a nice Bird, Dog, or Cat.
To sell, they will give you five sovereigns for that,
He's a very good customer, that is quite true,
So I'll vote for ——, pray what less can I do ?

O the Election is coming, what meeting and speeching,
All their knavish tricks to all the world teaching ;
What rogues, fools, and shufflers, each other they call,
And stick their good characters up on the wall.
Each party seem ready the other to mill,
About rural policy, or the new poor-law bill.
While the Elections are on, what patriots they are,
But when they get in, the d———l may care.

LAMENTATION ON THE DEATH
OF THE
Duke of Wellington.

Britannia now lament for our Hero that is dead,
That son of Mars, brave Wellington, alas, his spirit's fled.
That general of a hundred fights, to death he had to yield,
Who brav'd the cannons' frightful blaze upon the battle
    field.

CHORUS.

Britannia weep and mourn, his loss all may deplore,
That conquering hero Wellington, alas, he is no more.

The destructive wars of Europe does not disturb him now,
Great laurels of bright victory sit smiling on his brow,
For the burning sands of India he trac'd with valour
    bright,
And against that daring Tippoo Saib so valiant he did
    fight.

Where cannons loud did rattle, spread death and sad
    dismay,
The Duke was always ready with his men to lead the
    way.
Fortified cities he laid low, that general of renown,
Intrenchments and their batteries he quickly levelled
    down.

Thro' Portugal and Spain his enemy did pursue,
With the veteran sons of Britain he march'd to Waterloo,
And there he made a noble stand upon that blood-stain'd
    day,
And fought the French so manfully and made them run
    away.

At Vittoria,—Badagoz, and Talevara too,
On the plains of Salamanca, the French he did subdue,
With the veteran sons of Britain wherever he did go,
Amidst thundering peals of cannon he conquer'd every
    foe.

On the plains of Waterloo where thousands they lay
    dead,
The iron balls in showers flew around his martial head,
While his valiant men and generals lay bleeding in their
    gore,
The laurels from the French that day brave Wellington
    he tore.

Napoleon was as brave a man as ever took the field,
And with the warlike sons of France he said he would
    not yield;
But the reverse of fortune that day did on him frown,
By Wellington and his army his eagles were pulled down.

Now let him rest in peace, and none upbraid his name,
On his military glory there never was a stain,
The steel-clad Cuirasiers of France that day at Waterloo,
He quickly made them face about and cut their armour
    through.

Brave Ponsonby and Picton they fell upon that day,
And many a valiant soldier brave in peace their ashes lay,
And that brave Duke that led them on his spirit's took
    its flight,
To see him laid down in his tomb will be a solemn sight.

DEATH
OF
WELLINGTON.

J. Harkness, Printer, 121, Church Street, Preston.

On the 14th of September, near to the town of Deal,
As you may well remember who have a heart to feel,
Died Wellington, a general bold, of glorious renown,
Who beat the great Napoleon near unto Brussels town.

CHORUS.

So don't forget brave Wellington, who won at Waterloo,
He beat the great Napoleon and all his generals too.

He led the British army on through Portugal and Spain,
And every battle there he won the Frenchmen to
    restrain,
He ever was victorious in every battle field,
He gained a fame most glorious because he'd never yield.

He drove Napoleon from home, in exile for to dwell,
Far o'er the sea, and from his home, and all he loved
    so well.
He stripped him quite of all his power, and banished
    him away,
To St. Helena's rocks and towers the rest of his life to
    stay.

Then on the throne of France he placed Louis the king
    by right,
In after years he was displaced all by the people's might,
But should the young Napoleon threaten our land and
    laws,
We'll find another Wellington should ever we have
    cause.

He's dead, our hero's gone to rest, and o'er his corpse
    we'll mourn,
With sadness and with grief oppress'd, for he will not
    return,
But we his deeds will not forget, and should we ere
    again,
Follow the example that he set, his glory we'll not
    stain.

So don't forget brave Wellington, who won at Waterloo,
He beat the great Napoleon and all his generals too.

THE FALL OF SEBASTOPOL.

There is nothing now talked on wherever you go,
Among old folks or young be them high or low,
But the Crimean heroes I vow and declare,
That has smothered the Russians in this very year,
On the 8th of September, Eighteen hundred & fifty-five
The wounded old bear from his den did arise;
He curs'd and he swore and he fell off his stool,
He lost all Malakoff and Sebastopol too.

CHORUS.

Then hurrah jolly soldiers and sailors likewise,
With the brave sons of France you blackened his eyes,
You knock'd off his muzzle and stole all his grub,
And his teeth is all rotten and he can't chew his cud.

The soldiers of France went at it like steel,
Determined to conquer and make the Russians feel,
That they were the lads that could do it like fun,
Then crack went their rifles and the Russians did run;
The hearts of oak thundered, their guns had began,
As hearts of oak only ball'd at the Redan;
The French blaz'd away with courage so cool,
Now England and France has Sebastopol.

The Russian bears did grumble and said it is no joke
To smother in rubbish with powder and smoke,
And to be without water our thirst for to quench,
When a thundering big bomb shell came in from the
    French,
They all turned dizzy some spued and some spit,
And the Russian commander in his breeches did s—t,
For he had got the skitters with Johnny Bull's pills,
Our shot is the doctors that find out their ills.

At last they retreated, these bears from their den,
They got nearly roasted with shot and with shell,
Dingdong they did trot unto to the North side,
If they'd stopt any longer we'd have tickled their hides,
The Russian commander these words he did say,
We must now all hook it without more delay,
We can stop no longer in Sebastopol;
If we do they will choke us with long iron tools.

So come my brave fellows let's sing and let's dance,
Both Turkey, Sardinnia, old England and France;
We will all have a jig while the music does play,
We have nothing to fear for the Russians will pay;
And when we come home we will all keep a pig,
Our wives shall have bustles made of Russian wigs,
We will all take a bumper and drink good health,
So down with the Russians and up with the French.

BATTLE OF ALMA

Oh! boys have you heard of the battle,
    The allies brave had on the shore,
The joybells and cannons did rattle,
    Announcing it o'er and o'er,
The total defeat of the Russians,
    Was echoed with joy everywhere;
Success to John Bull and Napolean,
    And very soon peace may we hear.

CHORUS.

Then here's to the army and navy,
    In Russia they're on the advance,
Supporting the standard of freedom,
    Success to old England and France.

It was on the heights of Alma,
    The Russians were laying entrench'd
Lord Raglan and Marshal St. Arnaud,
    Commanding the English and French;
In front of the fortified walls,
    The allies marched into the fight,
Fifty-eight thousand men in bright armou,
    Put all the wild Russians to flight,
        Then here's, &c.

On the twentieth of September,
    The desperate battle was fought,
The Russians will ever remember,
    Tho' dearly my boys it was bought
With the blood of our courageous allies,
    Who fell on the fortified plain,
They brought the flag of old England,
    Without either blemish or stain.
        Then here's, &c.

The Russians held up their position,
    And fought for the space of three hours,
Secluded behind their entrenchments,
    The balls flew around us in showers;
At last at the point of the bayonet,
    The Russians were forced to retreat,
And run in the greatest disorder,
    Compell'd by a total defeat.
        Then here's &c.

The number that lay dead and wounded,
    Is awful my friends to recite,
Let's mourn the loss of our allies,
    Who fell in the desperate fight;
They fought them with great desperation,
    And forced the wild Russians to yield,
While cannons did rattle in battle,
    They conquered and died on the field,
        Then here's, &c.

THE NIGHTINGALE IN THE EAST.

On a dark lonely night, on the Crimea's dread shore—
There had been bloodshed and strife on the morning
before—
The dead and the dying lay bleeding around,
Some crying for help—there was none to be found.

Now God in his mercy He pity'd their cries,
And the soldier so cheerfully in the morning doth rise,
So forward my lads, may your hearts never fail,
You are cheered by the presence of a sweet Nightin-
gale.

Now God sent this angel to succour the brave,
Some thousands she's saved from an untimely grave ;
Her eyes beam with pleasure, she's bounteous and good,
The wants of the wounded are by her understood.

With fever some brought in, with life almost gone,
Some with dismantled limbs, some to fragments are torn,
But they keep up their spirits, their hearts never fail,
Now they're cheered by the presence of a sweet Night-
ingale.

Her heart it means good—for no bounty she'll take,
She'd lay down her life for the poor soldier's sake,
She prays for the dying, she gives peace to the brave,
She feels that a soldier has a soul she may save.

The wounded they love her, as it has been seen ;
She's the soldier's preserver, they call her their queen !
May God give her strength, and her heart never fail,
One of heaven's best gifts is Miss Nightingale.

The wives of the wounded, how thankful are they ;
Their husbands are cared for, how happy are they ;
Whate'er her country, this gift God has given,
The soldiers they say she's an angel from heaven.

Sing praise to this woman, and deny it who can !
And all women were sent for the comfort of man ;
Let's hope no more against them you'll rail,
Treat them well, and they'll prove like Miss Nightin-
gale.

BATTLE OF INKERMAN;

OR

" There came a Tale to England."

———‡———

There came a tale to England,
 'Twas of a battle won,
And nobly had her warriors
 That day their duty done ;
They fell like sheaves in autumn,
 Yet 'mid that fearful scene,
Their last shout was for England,
 Their last breath for their queen.

There came a tale to England,
 Of suffering, want, and woe,
Of the night watch in the trenches,
 Of the sortie by the foe ;
'Mid rain, and storm, and sickness,
 With no rest, no pause between,
And there was grief through England,
 From the humblest to the Queen.

Then wrote the Queen of England,
 God's blessing on her pen.
Oh ! tell those wounded soldiers,
 Those sick, patient, suffering men,
There's no heart in England,
 Can feel a pang more keen,
That day and night her own lov'd troops
 Are thought of by their Queen.

Then rose a shout through England,
 From them 'twas wafted o'er,
From those sick wounded soldiers,
 And it rang from shore to shore ;
From Alma and Balaklava,
 And Inkerman it came,
" God bless the Queen of England "
 Again we'd do the same.

GRAND CONVERSATION

ON

SEBASTOPOL AROSE!

As the western powers of Europe united all together,
In close deliberation they did appear to be,
And all their conversation seemed a grand determination,
To seize upon Sebastopol and set poor Turkey free!
When up steps Omar Pasha, saying here I am amongst you—
My country has been oppressed by tyranny and woes,
But now England and France in tens of thousands we'll advance,
This grand conversation on Sebastopol arose.

The twentieth of September we ever shall remember,
Upon the heights of Alma we made the Russians run,
After a weary marching the day was hot and scorching,
We fought the first great battle by the setting of the sun,
Like hearts of oak we bounded and the enemy wounded,
And when the bugle sounded to charge our mighty foes,
For England's home and beauty we nobly did our duty,
This grand conversation on Sebastopol arose.

Through rivers, brooks, and fountains, up hills and lofty mountains,
Our Generals were mounted in armour bright array,
Light infantry advancing with glittering bayonets glancing,
Upon the heights of Alma we showed them British play,
The cannons roared like thunder we cut their ranks asunder,
Though not an equal number unto our mighty foes,
We drove them from their quarters and made a dreadful slaughter,
This grand conversation on Sebastopol arose.

The cannons loud did rattle all in the field of battle,
To see the dead and wounded would grieve your heart full sore,
Through fields of blood we waded the enemy invaded,
As we beheld our comrades weltering in their gore,
With one determination and one loud exclamation,
We went with desperation against our mighty foes,
We cut them in succession of their guns we took possession,
This grand conversation on Sebastopol arose.

Lord Raglan that commander was brave as Alexander,
Describes this dreadful battle the first upon record,
The legions of France by the side of old England,
The power of the Russians could not them retard,
With fire and smoke around us nothing could confound us,
We gained the heights of Alma regardless of our foes,
Though hundreds fell upon the field we made the enemy to yield,
This grand conversation on Sebastopol arose.

The brave thirty-third and twenty-third regiments,
Also the ninty-fifth and the seventh fusiliers,
Under Sir Colin Campbell the gallant highlanders,
Died on the field of battle with the brave grenadiers,
Like lions they marched in the face of the cannon,
While hundreds lay bleeding as you may suppose,
They conquered and died on the hill of the Alma,
This grand conversation on Sebastopol arose.

LITTLE

LORD JOHN

OUT OF

SERVICE.

You lads of this nation, in every station,
    I pray give attention, and listen to me,
I'm little Jack Russell, a man of great bustle,
    Who served Queen Victoria by land and by sea;
They call me a Proosian, an Austrian, a Roosian,
    And off to Vienna they sent me afar;
They'd not me believe then, they vowed I'd deceived them,
    And called me Friend of the great Russian Czar.

Chorus.

I'm little Jack Russell, a man of great bustle,
    I'm full of vexation, grief, sorrow, and care,
I have got in disgrace, and am now out of place;
    But I never broke windows round Bel-ge-rave Square.

In great London City for me they've no pity;
    And Moon the Lord Mayor to my face told me plain,
All the freemen would scout me, and old women rout me,
    If ever I went to the City again.
I'm the son of old Bedford, I'm going to Deptford
    To look for employment, and find out a friend,
And then I'll come back with a pack on my back,
    Bawling frying-pans, saucepans, and kettles to mend.

Chorus, I'm, &c.

I have lost all my riches, I have worn out my breeches,
    I am turned out of place, and have nowhere to go,
My state is most shocking, great holes in my stocking,
    And my poor tender toes peeping out of my shoe—
Why should they so serve me, and try for to starve me?
    I fought for my country and stood by my Queen.
Bad luck to the Prussians, the Austrians, and Russians,
    And jolly bad luck to old Lord Aberdeen.

Chorus. I'm, &c.

I went like a wary plenipotentiary,
    To the town of Vienna to settle the war,
Where I saw Francis Joseph, King Peter, and Moses,
    And I fought Alexander, the great Russian Czar;
And when I came back they began for to clack,
    They blamed me and gamed me and pulled out my hair,
They threatened to lick me, and nicely they kicked me,
    Bawling pickled eel's feet around Bel-ge-rave Square.

Chorus. I'm, &c.

I love Queen Victoria, I dearly adore her,
    Although at Vienna I did her displease;
I wish all the Russians and Austrians and Prussians
    Were tied in a blanket, and smothered with fleas.
Oh dear, hey down diddle, I have the Scotch fiddle,
    I know that I caught it of old Aberdeen,—
Now I will so clever sing England for ever,
    Down with the Russians, and God save the Queen.

Chorus. I'm, &c.

JOHN MORGAN.

A NEW SONG

TO THE MEMORY OF THE LATE

R. COBDEN, ESQ., M.P.,

"HE GAVE THE PEOPLE BREAD."

TUNE—"FARMER'S BOY."

Come mourn ye sons of Britain all,
   The fact that Cobden's dead :
Come sing his deeds, come praise his worth,
   "He got the people bread."

O death why didst thou snatch away
   The best of England's seed ?
Why lay thy hand upon his brow ?
   "He gave the people bread."

If ever man deserved a name,
   Who did the people lead,
'Twas Richard Cobden known to all,
   "He gave the people bread."

His generous, loving, feeling heart
   Brought blessings on his head,
Because he fought a long lifetime,
   "To give the people bread."

He lived a life of doing good,
   This was his much loved creed,
Untiring zeal his labours crown'd
   "To get the people bread."

Yes, bread untax'd that all might live,
   In every time of need ;
Amidst the strife with truth as guide,
   "To get the people bread."

He's now enshrin'd in the cold grave,
   Which Kings and princes dread ;
He died in peace, he smil'd at death,
   "He'd gained the people bread."

For ever shall his name endure,
   Tho' numbered with the dead,
His name through earth's immortalised,
   "He got the people bread."

GREAT NAVAL ACTION
BETWEEN THE
KEARSAGE & THE ALABAMA.

Come all you gallant hero's
   Of high and low degree,
And listen to the glorious fight
   Was fought upon the sea ;
The Alabama and Kearsage
   Not far from the French shore,
Met on the 19th day of June,
   Eighteen hundred and sixty four.

It was a glorious battle,
   The crews fought manfully
In the Alabama and Kearsage,
   That day upon the sea.
The English Yacht Deerhound
   Was all the time quite near,
She belonged to Squire Lancaster,
   Of Wigan in Lancashire ;
And many a gallant seaman
   So nobly did save,
Who when the Alabama sunk
   Would have met a watery grave.

About nine miles from Cherbourg
   This gallant fight took place,
The noted Alabama,
   She did the Kearsage chase,
The Alabama's guns did rattle,
   And Captain Semmes believed
That he would win the battle,
   But he was much deceived.

The men did fight like hero's,
   And round the decks did run,
Each ship did shake and no mistake,
   As they fired their powerful guns,
Brave Captain Semmes did loudly call,
   As he on the deck did stand,
Don't move or flinch a single inch,
   "Do your duty every man."

But alas ! the Alabama,
   Began to feel affright,
Her sides were dreadfully shaken,
   And she could no longer fight,
The Kearsage was chain plated,
   And her guns were fired so free,
She beat the Alabama,
   And sunk her in the sea.

The Deerhound was in readiness,
   The conquered to receive ;
And rendered great assistance,
   My friends you may believe ;
When the battle it was over,
   The conquered, void of fear,
Safe in the Steam Yacht Deerhound,
   Did to Southampton steer.

Now to conclude this gallant fight,
   Undaunted brave and bold,
As great and glorious battle
   As ever yet was told,
To the seaman and the officers,
   We drink with three times three,
Who did their duty manfully
   That day upon the sea.

John Harkness, Printer, Preston.

DIZZY'S LAMENT.

Oh dear ! oh dear ! what shall I do ?
They call me saucy Ben the Jew,
The leader of the Tory crew,
     Poor old Benjamin Dizzy.
I'd a great big house in Buckinghamshire,
My Wages was Five Thousand a year ;
But now they have turned me out of place,
With a ticket for soup, in great disgrace.
I had a challenge last Monday night,
Billy Gladstone wanted me to fight ;
The challenge was brought by Jackey Bright,
  To poor old Benjamin Dizzy,

    I've got the sack, what shall I do ?
    They call me a converted Jew,
    Bad luck to Bright and Gladstone too,
    They mean to drive me crazy.

I never thought they'd turn me out,
For well I knew my way about,
But I am licked without a doubt,
    So pity poor Benjamin Dizzy.
Oh ! if I could Bill Gladstone thump,
I'd burst his nose, and kick his r—p ;
If like Jack Heenan I could fight,
I'd wollop both him and Johnny Bright.
Gladstone will play the deuce with me,
For he's got a great majority,
And as sure as my name is Disreali,
    I am shoved out by Gladstone.

Billy Gladstone made a great big birch,
And said he'd not be in the lurch,
But he'd sweep away the Irish Church,
    And kill poor Benjamin Dizzy.

If he had his will he'd play some rigs,
He'd smother the people with Parsons' wigs ;
But if I had my will, mark what I mean,
I'd make Murphy a footman to the Queen.
Murphy and me could make it right,
If like a Lancashire lad I could fight,
I'd poke out the eyes of Jackey Bright,
    And punch the shins of Gladstone.

I tremble and I quake with fear,
For Gladstone he is so severe,
Though he was kicked out in Lancashire,
    For Greenwich he's elected.
The destructives say all over the land,
Every tub on his own bottom shall stand.
But in spite of all their joy and prate,
I will support the Church and State.
Bill Gladstone, Bright, and old Bob Lowe,
Are in the Cabinet you know,
And I will whistle not for Joe,
    To all the measures they bring forward.

Where the Shamrock, Leek and Thistle grow,
I find that I had lots of foes,
So I will stick to England's Rose,
    And never will surrender.
Last night as I lay on my bed,
Some dreadful things came in my head,
I dreamt that I was whacked with a birch,
And that I'd swallowed the Irish Church.
Oh, Bright and Gladstone go the rig,
The Irish Church the fishes and pigs,
That you may be choked with Parsons' wigs,
    Is the wish of Benjamin Dizzy·

John Harkness, Printer, Preston.

THE GREAT BATTLE

FOR

FREEDOM AND REFORM.

YOU working men of England,
  Who live by daily toil,
Speak for your rights, bold Englishmen,
  All thro' Britain's isle;
The titled tories keep you down,
  Which you cannot endure,
And the reason I to tell am bound,
  You're but working men—and poor.

With Gladstone, Russell, Beales, and Bright
  We shall weather through the storm,
To give the working man his rights,
  And gain the Bill,—Reform.

If the Hyde Park meeting had been allowed,
  No disturbance would have been.
Long life, they cried, to the Prince of Wales,
  And God bless England's Queen!
Why should the parks be ever closed
  Against the poor, who for them pay,
Work with a will for equality,
  And you will gain the day.

We want no Tory government,
  The poor man to oppress,
They never try to do you good,
  The truth you will confess.
The Liberals are the poor man's friend,
  To forward all they try,
They'll beat their foes you may defend,
  And never will say, die.

Great meetings are held in high parts,
  In country and in town,
The names of Beales and Gladstone,
  With working men resound,
Riches are but worthless dross,
  Without our working brother,

Which proves that in our national cause
  We could help each other.

Great praise is due to the Reform League,
  They have generous hearts and minds,
For the prisoners taken in Hyde Park,
  They intend to pay the fines;
At the Agricultural Hall they met,
  With band and flags so gay,
And when they meet at Lincoln's-Inn fields
  Give them a loud huzza!

Then vote for manhood suffrage,
  And the ballot too, likewise,
For Freedom of opinion,
  All Englishmen doth prize;
And why should not a working man
  Have power to give his vote,
To one that is the poor man's friend,
  Tho' he wears a ragged coat.

If the public parks of London
  Are only for one class,
They ought to put this notice up :—
  The poor they cannot pass.
It's time our laws they altered were,
  You'll say it is a bore,
That one law should be for the rich,
  And another for the poor.

An Englishman is not a slave,
  For that was never sent,
Then give the working man his rights,
  You'll find he is content;
Give us the ballot and franchise,
  It's the only boon we ask,
Then shouts will rend the skies,
  For that will end our task.

Disley, Printer, 57, High Street, St. Giles.

THE GREAT
REFORM MEETING

On Monday, December 3rd, 1866.

You true friend of Reform,
  Just listen to my song,
And some truth in these verses will be found :
  It's the talk throughout the nation,
  About the Monster Demonstration,
Announc'd to take place in Ashburnham
    Grounds.

Then, cheer for Reform, and on be marching !
  And you will find you will weather the
    storm ;
For depend on what I say, you will sure to
    gain the day,
  If you will lend a willing shoulder to
    Reform.

Now when the Tories found,
  That in Ashburnham Grounds,
England's sons were to meet—now only
    mark,—
  At their dirty work they got,
  And determined they should not,
As if they wished another scene like Hyde
    Park.

But, my lads, do not despair,
  There is the pure and open air,
Which belong to the great and the small,
  And though our foes they make a fuss,
  There our rights we can discuss,
For the song says "There's room enough for
    all."

Shall our liberties be crushed,
  And be trampled to the dust,
By men who never earnt a penny in their
    lives ?
  And yet we must not meet,
  Nor for our rights dare speak,
But if we cannot win, boys, we must try !

Now the Tories they do say,
  If we will only wait, some day
They will give us Reform upon their plan ;
  But their kindness it comes slow,
  And the quarters they would show,
Would be the sort the wolf he shows the
    lamb.

So England's working men,
  The Rights they still defend,
Of the mightiest nation in the world ;
  And thousands will be found,
  Who will gladly rally round,
So the banner of Reform we'll keep unfurled.

Then send the Adullamite crew,
  And their pals, the Tories, too,
Headlong to Old Nick altogether,
  But for men like Beale and Bright,
  Let's shout with all our might,
Here's the good cause, Reform, boys, for
    ever !

P 2

WHEN WE GET JOHNNY'S
REFORM.

Oh ! is there not a fuss and bother
    About Reform, Reform ?
From one end of England to the other,
    It's Reform, Reform.
They say it's to place us in a position,
That we may better our condition,
    And be so jolly happy
When we get Johnny's Reform.

Little Johnny, bless the darling boy,
    Love's Reform, Reform,
Long time he has nursed his favourite toy,
    Reform, Reform ;
And the dunderheads says, now really,
Is not it a fine grown baby,
    Shan't we be jolly happy,
When we get Johnny's Reform.

There is our old friend Jacky Bright,
    Says that Reform, Reform,
Is just the thing that's right,
    Reform, Reform ;
To the seven-pound franchise he will stick,
And send all opponents to old Nick,
    And make all jolly happy
When we get Johnny's Reform.

Now our pauper system loud does call
    For Reform, Reform ;
With the great as well as small
    Need Reform, Reform ;
For the poor are not the only ones,
That feed upon the nation's crumbs,
    But never mind, be happy,
When we get Johnny's Reform.

The teetotalers they will preach
    Up Reform, Reform ;
And the water-drinking dodge they teach,
    Reform, Reform ;
But the tipplers they all do say,
They will get tight three times a day,
    And be so jolly happy
When they get Johnny's Reform.

The little boys and girls they say,
    Reform, Reform,
They expect it's coming some fine day,
    Reform, Reform ;
Their bellies then they will be stuffing,
With almond rock and cakes for nuffin,
    And be so jolly happy,
When they get Johnny's Reform.

The farmers all throughout the nation,
    Want Reform, Reform,
For they stand in need of reformation,
    Reform, Reform ;
But must not they have tidy cheek,
To give their men eight bob a week,
    And tell them to be happy
When they get Johnny's Reform.

Many they aloud will shout,
    For Reform, Reform,
Scarcely knowing what about,
    Bawl Reform, Reform ;
They think no poor there will be then,
But all be ladies and gentlemen,
    And be so jolly happy,
When they get Johnny's Reform.

Now if the Bill should pass,
    This Reform, Reform ;
Now little Johnny he will laugh
    At Reform, Reform ;
His little body he will strut, sir,
Like a crow along the gutter,
    And be so jolly happy
When we get the new Reform.

Then let us hope that we may see
    This Reform, Reform,
Do some good for you and me,
    Reform, Reform ;
But liberty give to your thought,
If it don't do good, why then it ought,
    And make us jolly happy,
When we get Johnny's Reform.

H. Disley, Printer, 57, High Street, St. Giles.

FREEDOM & REFORM.

Unto these lines I've penned,
Listen, England's working men,
Be united, we shall weather thro' the storm,
Gladstone, Beales, & Bright, God save,
And your banners proudly wave,
Shout Old England for ever and Reform.

Hark to those drums so loudly beating,
See those glorious banners proudly wave,
Come men, and shout with me, Old England's
      liberty,
And Reform! for Britons won't be slaves.

Let's be firm my boys, I say,
While the sun shines make your hay,
They've promis'd it long enough I vow.
At length the die is cast,
And the Lion's woke at last,
No longer will he wait, he'll have it now.

Fellow workmen, let them know,
We won't have such men as Lowe,
Who treat the working classes all with scorn
Let them try with all their might,
For the working men are right,

And they'll gain what they're working for,—
    Reform.

What stagnation through the land,
For all trade is at a stand,
While the Tory government holds the sway.
Let us join then heart and hand,
And boldly make a stand,
If we've only got the will we'll find the way.

Then banish care and pain,
Never mind Old Dicky Mayne,
He says this time he'll not interfere;
He remembers it quite well,
How the Hyde Park railings fell
We his noble staff of Poleaxes don't fear.

Then shout with all your might,
God save Gladstone, Beales, and Bright,
Wave your banners, let your ranks closer
And let your watchword be :— [form,
    " Old England ! Liberty !
Manhood Suffrage ! Vote by Ballot ! and
    Reform !"

H. Disley, Printer, 57, High Street, St. Giles.

THE GREAT
LIBERAL MAJORITY OF 110.

The Tories they are Froze out, and got no Work to do.

Draw near all you true Liberals,
  And listen for awhile,
While I a ditty sing to you
  That will cause you for to smile ;
It's concerning of the poor Tories,
  Who are in a precious stew, oo-oo
They are out of a job, so-help-my-bob,
  And got no work to do,
For the Liberals they have gained you see,
One hundred and ten majority,
And the Tories they are all froze out,
  And got no work to do.

Through England and Ireland,
  Scotland and Wales, they cry,
Give us the brave Liberals,
  And let their colours fly ;
For you may see by the returns,
  The Tories they have cause to mourn,
They are in disgrace, and out place,
  And got no work to do;
They are a selfish crew, oo-oo,
And their noses look quite blue oo-oo,
Their day is past, done brown at last,
  And got no work to do.
        For the Liberals, &c.

Now there is the Irish Bishops,
  Must spout their shovel, hat, and wigs,
They will get no rent in shape of tenths,
  Nor get no nice tythe pigs :
And the little boys will them get at,
  I say, old boy, I'll have your hat ;
You have lost your tythes, and sarve you right,
  You will have no work to do.
Yes, they will be licked clean off their perch,
  If they capsize the Irish Church,
For Gladstone will give them the sack,
  They'll have no work to do.
        For the Liberals, &c.

Ben Dizzey, he is lamenting,
  For he is in a dreadful fix,
And from St. Stephen's Cabinet-works,
  He has had to cut his stick ;
He is grieving for the loaves and fishes,
He may say his grace to empty dishes,
For Gladstone he will cut his comb,
  Oh dear, what will he do ?
His hopes are up the flue oo-oo,
But I pity him, don't you, oo-oo ?
He is all the way from Buckinghamshire,
  And got no work to do.
        For the Liberals, &c.

Now the Tories boast in Westminster,
  They have gained a victory,
But how John Mill he has turned out,
  You all may plainly see ;
And there are more in the same state,
Who have been fishing with a golden bait,
But it is all of no use, we have cooked their goose,
  They'll have no work to do,
They dirty tricks can do, oo-oo,
  What I tell you is quite true, oo-oo,
In St. Stephen's Hall, they will sing small,
  We have got no work to do, oo-oo.
        For the Liberals, &c.

Now the working-men of England,
  May chance to get their rights,
While they have their Champion Gladstone,
  Their battles for to fight ;
For that he is a brick, you'll say I am right,
And so is that old cock Johnny Bright,
And the Tories them for to affright,
  Will have their work to do.
Then for Reform give three huzzas !
The Liberals have gained the day,
And the Tories they in grief do say,
  We have got no work to do.
        For the Liberals, &c.

H. Disley, Printer, 57, High Street, St. Giles, London.

THE
REFORM DEMONSTRATION

In Hyde Park, May 6th, 1867.

Good people come listen, I'll tell of a lark,
That happened on Monday, the 6th, in Hyde
    Park,
For brave Edmund Beales and his friends
    they did start,
    To meet the working men there.
They reached there at six o'clock, gallant
    and right,
    And when in so boldly did shout,
We're here my brave boys, and we'll show
    them this night
    We'll speak, and they shan't turn us out.

So remember, my boys, 'twas a glorious sight,
In Hyde Park, on the 6th, it was right
    against might,
With Beales for our leader, we beat them
    that night,
    At last working men they are free.

Now Dickey M— to his friend Walley said,
If you go to Hyde Park pray mind your
    poor head,
And I'm sure I expect to be taken home
    dead,
    And for me it will not be a lark.
Now don't go says Walley, to you I declare,
    Against us you know they've a spite,
The people mean business, so I shan't go
    there,
    Not in Hyde Park, on that Monday night.

In busses the Polcaxes hurried along,
And when they arrived they were **five**
    thousand strong,
But during the night you couldn't see one,
    Interfere with our friends in Hyde Park.
I heard that one said to his mate, "Bill, I say,
    If they have a row, I'll be off quick,
For I got in a bother the last reform day,
    And they measured my head with a brick."

Now Government frightened on **Monday**
    they were,
Some constables special in then they did
    swear,
Their staffs they did hide, when in the **Park**
    there,
    They thought that they would have to fight.
One went home enraged, says he, "I'll
    have a row—
    Since to Hyde Park I've been on the march,
I am almost a boiling—we have been I **vow**,
    Like dummies stuck on the Marble Arch."

So the Franchise for ever, we've beat them,
    hurra!
Long life to brave Beales, and Reformers,
    I say,
United let's be, and we'll yet gain the day,
    And always remember Hyde Park.
We do not want SPECIAL duty to be done,
    Our rights! it is all that we ask,
To meet with each other when labour is done,
    And speak out our minds in the Park.

REFORM MEETING

AT

BLACKHEATH.

For Reform, meet again, boys, on Monday I say,
Let trumpets sound loudly, we'll yet gain the day,
Your banners wave proudly, and shout, boys, hurrah!
When to Blackheath on Monday you start;
Manhood suffrage, you know, is the working man's own.
We only want that which is right,
Then raise loud your voices, the cause we shall gain,
If united we stand in our might.

Then forward for Liberty, Justice, and Right,
On Blackheath, my boys, 'twas a glorious sight,
And shout loud for Gladstone, for Beales, and for Bright,
Manhood Suffrage for ever, hurrah!

We'll have it at last, of that you may be sure,
If they had not turned tail we'd have had it before,
We must have the Suffrage on England's shore,
To be free is all that we ask;
You remember Hyde Park on the last 6th of May,
When there they boldly did shout,
Manhood Suffrage, the Franchise, we will have fair play,
Special Constables won't turn us out.

So onward to Blackheath without care or pain
In Hyde Park we have met, and will meet there again,
In spite of the Specials, or old Dicky Mayne,
I am sure he will not interfere;
With Beales for our leader, again they will show,
English workmen themselves can behave,
Without the poleaxes, we can let them know,
That we will not be treated like slaves.

If we are to be governed, let us cry far & wide,
Let us be governed well, 'tis an Englishman's pride,
And not have disturbance and bloodshed besides,
On this, our own dear native land.
Then let us have Justice, we do not want more,
We ask for our wives and our homes,
And have peace and prosperity on Britain's shore,
Then we shall have what is our own.

Then wave high your banners, your trumpets then sound,
Manhood Suffrage for ever! let Blackheath resound,
And victory, yet we shall win, I'll be bound,
If united we stand firm and true.
Long life to brave Beales & Reformers I pray,
The Reform League for ever, hurrah!
We'll all work together, united we'll be,
And, my boys, we will yet gain the day.

H. Disley, Printer, 57, High Street, St. Giles, London.

THE FENIANS
ARE COMING.

Wherever we go, wherever we be,
Some wonder of wonders we daily do see;
All classes through Britain are trembling with fear,
The Fenians are coming,—oh, don't things look queer?
The land of old Erin looks bashful and blue,
Colonel Catchem and General Doodlem doo,
Has crossed the Atlantic, poor Erin to sack,
And carry Hibernia away on their back.

There's a rumpus in Ireland by night and by day,
Old women and girls are afraid out to stray;
Cheer up and be happy on St. Patrick's day,
The Fenians are coming,—get out of the way!

Pop goes the weazel, and shoot goes the gun,
While over the mountains the Fenians do run;
As a regiment of soldiers did after them jog,
Four hundred and fifty fell into a bog!
The best of the fun was—the soldiers did shout,
We have got in a mess, and we cannot get out!
When a funny old woman so nimbly flew,
And collared great General Doodlem-doo.

Some could not fire, and some could'nt run,
One carried a reap-hook, another a gun,
They tried to kill nobody, just for a spree,
So they both went together to cut down a tree;
There was a young lady, her name it was Peg,
She'd one eye and two noses, one arm and one leg,
March on, lads, she shouted, to glory we'll steer,
The Fenians are coming, oh dear, oh dear!

Some with big stones and brickbats their pockets did
    fill,
They thought of the battle of great Bunker's Hill,
Cut away, fire away, go along Pat,
A soldier fired at a Fenian, and shot a tom cat;
Old Molly Maloney, up her chimney did creep,
Over the hills and the monntains she had a good peep,

While under her window the bagpipes did play,
To cheer Moll with the tune of St. Patrick's day.

What do you think of the Fenians? said Kit, in a joke,
Why, says Nell, it will end in a bottle of smoke,
Thousands over the mountains, like grasshoppers flew,
Be aisy, cried General Doodlem-doo:
Colonel Catch'em commanded, had a hump on his back,
Shoot away, fire away, philliloo whack,
Then a jolly old fiddler from famed Mullingar,
Struck up the bold anthem of Erin-go-bragh.

The soldiers one night when the bugle did sound,
That night going over the mountains they found,
A cat and a donkey, a pig and a dog,
And twenty old women stuck fast in a bog;
While down at Killarney, 'twas fire away whack,
At the glorious battle of herrings and sprats!
And although they fought without trousers or shirt,
I think they were really more frightened than hurt.

Cheer up, says old Barney, here comes the police:
Here's old Erin and glory, plum pudding and peace,
A glass of good whiskey twice every day,
That is better than fighting and running away!
As for me, my dear boys, if a row I was in it,
I'd rather run for a mile than fight for a minute;
And I would advise all to have done with such capers,
And just stay at home to look after the taters.

Old Dennis Mahoney got up in a tree,
His musket was loaded with skillagalee,
Blood-an-ouns, said old Denny, I'm a Fenian, here goes,
He fired, and shot two policemen under the nose;
The bough of the tree with old Dennis soon broke,
And Dennis came down like a pig in a poke.
He died as he fell, and he whistled, oh la!
Singing, farewell for ever, old Erin-go-bragh.

H. Disley, Printer, 57, High Street, St. Giles, London.

AWFUL
EXPLOSION
IN
CLERKENWELL.
DREADFUL LOSS OF LIFE.

Now mothers all pray give attention,
   And fathers listen to the tale I'll tell,
To the fearful scene at the House of Detention
   In Corporation Lane at Clerkenwell;
While parents for their children are weeping,
   And tender mothers wring their hands in pain
Do tell me, are they dead, or only sleeping,
   O shall I never see my child again.

To rescue Burke it was their intention,
   At Clerkenwell this wicked deed was done,
And such a sight as this I'll mention,
   Was never heard of beneath the sun.

Three men they say on that fatal Friday,
   At four o'clock on that afternoon,
Those villians caused that explosion,
   And hurried those poor creatures to their doom.
They from a truck took a barrel of powder,
   A female, Ann Justice was there as well,
And in one moment death and disorder
   Around the neighbourhood of Clerkenwell.

Then all around lay the dead and dying,
   Some crying, where is my mother dear,
Among the ruins in anguish lying,
   Where tender mothers and children dear;
Covered with blood and mutilated,
   And some they found, death had stilled their
   cries,

For mothers, fathers, and helpless infants,
   Now in Bartholomew Hospital lies,

Three persons there were apprehended,
   Allen and Desmond to escape they tried,
Their purpose it was frustrated,
   But destruction was spread far and wide.
The one who did this deed so cruel,
   From that sad spot he did escape,
But justice quickly will follow after,
   Be sure it will that villain overtake.

They little thought on the fatal morning,
   With hearts so light and spirits gay
That ere the sun should again be dawning,
   Their little homes would be swept away;
That little children in death be sleeping,
   Or parents for them in anguish cry,
For Minnie Abbot many now are weeping,
   Another little girl has lost her eyes.

For those that's gone shed a tear of pity,
   And God bless those who assistance gave,
Such a crime we seldom hear in London city,
   May God receive their souls now in the grave.
The government has relieved the sufferers,
   From the Queen, a message to those in pain,
And such a sad and dreadful story,
   In London may we never hear again.

SUNDAY
TRADING BILL.

Oh dear, oh lor, what shall we do?
I am sure I cannot tell, can you?
Of Lord Chelmsford's Bill, I'll tell you true—
   The Bill on Sunday trading.
The mawworms seem to try, I'm sure,
Each way they can to crush the poor,
And bring them to the workhouse door,
   By stopping Sunday trading.
I'm sure it is a lying sin,
It's no harm to say, bad luck to him,—
He might as well try to stop our wind,
   As to stop all Sunday trading.

Oh! Chelmsford, you use the poor man ill,
Starve us all, I'm sure you will,
If they should pass your infamous Bill,
   And stop all Sunday trading.

Tho' the swells they may blow out their kites,
On jellies and tarts, and all things nice,
For the poor to live it is not right,
   Says the Bill on Sunday trading.
With watercresses they must not go round,
Nor with winkles or shrimps to earn a brown,
Or else you will get fined a crown,
   Says the Bill on Sunday trading.
No cat must mew, no dog must bark,
They'll stop the warbling of the lark,
And drive them all bang out of the parks,
   Says the Bill on Sunday trading.

The poor may buy potatoes and greens,
That is if they have got the means,
But no coals to cook them, though strange it seems,
   Says the Bill on Sunday trading.
The nobs may call at the pastry shops
And with all sorts of dainties cram their chops,
But the poor must not buy a lollipop,
   Says the Bill on Sunday trading.
You must not take, at least, they say,
A dose of salts on Saturday,
Lest they should work on the Sabbath day,
   Says the Bill on Sunday trading.

If on Sunday you feel inclined to eat,
You can buy both bread and meat,
But no tea or sugar,—what a treat!
   Says the Bill on Sunday trading

But to wash it down, Lord Chelmsford say,
To the gin shop you can cut away
And get blind drunk upon that day,
   Says the Bill on Sunday trading.
And by and bye, if you have got the tin, sir,
To raise a baked joint for your dinner,
They'll say, drop that dish, you hungry sinner,
   Don't you know it's Sunday trading?

If your wife should be in the family-way,
She must not be confined upon Sunday,
But put it off till another day,
   Says the Bill on Sunday trading.
No milkman through his rounds must go,
With milk, my pretty maids, below!
Without paying a crown,—the Lords say so,
   In the Bill on Sunday trading.
Even the kittens must not play,
Nor frisk about upon that day,
Or their grub will be stopped for three whole days,
   Says the Bill on Sunday trading.

No shoeblack, he must not dare to say,
Polish your boots upon Sunday,
Or else a dollar he will have to pay,
   Says the Bill on Sunday trading.
And if you want to enjoy your pipe,
Where would you get a box of lights,
For the sellers they will be put to flight,
   Says the Bill on Sunday trading.
No Yarmouth bloaters must be sold,
Nor peppermint drops for coughs or colds,
And muffin man's bell it's clapper must hold,
   Says the Bill on Sunday trading.

You must not buy, but you must starve,
You must not sing, you must not laugh,
So you had better sow your mouth up fast,
   Says the Bill on Sunday trading.
You must not sell, you must not buy,
To earn a crust you must not try,
Nor in the streets lay down and die,
   Says the Bill on Sunday trading.
For the poor a fig they do not care,
More workhouses they must prepare,
He ought to be kicked to I know where,
   For his Bill on Sunday trading.

H. Disley, Printer, 57, High Street, St. Giles.

115

SOUTHWARK ELECTION.

ODGER

AND

VICTORY.

Now all you gallant Southwark men,
   Who does require protection,
Just mind I say, your p's and q's
   At this Great Grand Election;
Never don't elect a man
   Who your wages will be stinting,
And never have a covetuous man
   Like one who lives by printing.

Then act like men you Southwark blades,
   Have neither a printer nor a "sodger,
Vote for a man who will protect your trade,
And sing, Southwark, lads, and Odger.

Long enough the poor man has been crushed,
   Now is your time or never,
Come, now with me lads, nimble be,
   Here's Odger, lads, for ever.
Don't you elect a Waterlow,
   Whose principles are stinting,
He knows as much about the poor man's rights
   As a donkey knows of printing.

There has lately been some glorious fights,
   In Southwark, says Ben Fagan.
It beat the Battle of Bunker's Hill,
   And the glories of Copenhagen;
An old lady stood by London Bridge,
   Bawling, lick me you shall never,
She jumped complete to Toloey Street,
   Bawling, Odger, boys, for ever.

In Bermondsey there was glorious fun
   Among the girls and sailors,
It put the Borough all in mind
   Of the devil among the tailors.
A grocer's wife, full of spleen and spite,
   Doffed her chignon so clever,
Pulled her petticoat off and went aloft,
   Singing, Odger, boys, for ever.

Oh, Colonel, Colonel Beresford,
   You are a rum old codger,
Neither you or Waterlow
   Can ever cope with Odger;—
Odger is a working man,
   And as clever a man as Pompey,
Odger is a gentleman,
   And you are a pair of donkeys.

When Odger is returned, my boys,
   To the brim we'll flll our glasses,
We will drink success to the tanners' wives,
   And the blooming Kent Street lasses;
From the Bricklayers' Arms to London Bridge,
   There will be such a bustle,
Aye, and all the way from Cotton's Wharf
   To the Elephant and Castle.

Put the right man in the right place,
   Keep out the aristocratic sodger
Tell old Waterlow it is no go—
   It is victory and Odger;
The working men must have a friend,
   Who against tyranny is clever,
With heart and glee, sing liberty,
   Odger, my lads, for ever.

Odger we know is a working man,
   If he's not rich, he's noble-minded,
He will understand how the working man
   Has been crushed down and grinded.
Then send him into Parliament,
   To put a stop to their capers,
And tell them we want a good beef steak,
   Instead of herrings and taters.

Keep out the printing gentleman,
   Banish the tyrant sodger,
Strive with all your might to do what's right,
   And plump my lads for Odger.

Printed for the Vendors.

A COLLECTION

OF

"BALLADS ON A SUBJECT."

DIVISION III.

A COLLECTION OF

BALLADS ON A SUBJECT.

"What hast here, ballads? I love a ballad in print; for then we are sure they are true."—*Shakspeare.*

"Street Ballads on a Subject."—There is a class of ballads which may with perfect propriety be called *street* ballads, as they are written by street authors for street singing and street sale. These effusions, however, are known in the trade by a title appropriate enough,— "Ballads on a Subject." The most successful workers of this branch of the profession are the men described as patterers and chaunters.

The "Ballads on a Subject" are always on a political, criminal, or exciting public event, or one that has interested the public, and the celerity with which one of them is written, and then sung in the streets, is in the spirit of "these railroad times." After any great event "a ballad on a subject" is often written, printed, and sung "in honour," it was announced "of Lord John Russell's resignation." Of course there is no time for either correction of the rhymes or of the press; but this is regarded as of little consequence,—while an early "start" with a new topic is of great consequence, I am assured; "Yes, indeed, both for the sake of meals and rents." If, however, the songs were ever so carefully revised, their sale would not be greater.

It will have struck the reader that all the street lays quoted as popular have a sort of burthen or jingle at the end of each verse. I was corrected, however, by a street chaunter for speaking of this burthen as a jingle. "It's a chorus, sir," he said. "In a proper ballad on a subject there's often twelve verses, none of them under eight lines, and there's a four-line chorus to every verse; and, if it's the right sort, it'll sell the ballad." I was told, on all hands, that it was not the words that ever made a ballad, but the subject, and, more than the subject, —the chorus; and, far more than either,—*the tune!*" Indeed, many of the street-singers of ballads on a subject, have as supreme a contempt for words as can be felt for any modern composer. To select a tune for a ballad, however, is a matter of deep deliberation. To adapt the ballad to a tune too common or popular is injudicious; for then, I was told, any one can sing it—boys and all. To select a more elaborate and less-known air, however appropriate, may not be pleasing to some of the members of "the school" of ballad-singers who may feel it beyond their vocal powers; neither may it be relished by the critical in street songs, whose approving criticism induces them to purchase as well as to admire.

The license enjoyed by the court jesters, and in some respects by the minstrels of old, is certainly enjoyed, undiminished, by the street writers and singers of ballads on a subject. They are unsparing satirists, who, with rare impartiality, lash all classes and all creeds, as well as any individual. One man, upon whose information I can rely, told me that, many years ago, he himself had "worked" in town and country, twenty-three different songs at the same period and the same subject—the Marriage of the Queen. They all "sold"—but the most profitable was one "as sung by Prince Albert in character." It was to the air of "Dusty Miller;" and "it was good," said the ballad-man, "because we could easily dress up to the character given to Albert. "And what's more, sir," continued my informant, "not very long after the honeymoon, the Duchess of L—— drove up in her carriage to the printer's, and bought all the songs in honour to Victoria's wedding, and gave a sovereign for them and wouldn't take the change. It was a Duchess. Why I'm sure about it—though I can't say whether it were the Duchess of L—— or S——; for didn't the printer, like an honest man, when he'd stopped the price of the papers, hand over to us chaps the balance to drink, and *didn't* we drink it! There can't be a mistake about *that.*"

The "Ballads on a Subject" are certainly the rude uncultivated verse in which the popular tale of the times is recorded," and what may be the character of the nation as displayed in them, I leave to the reader's judgment.—*Henry Mayhew's London Labour and the London Poor.*

The writer of an able article in the *Quarterly Review*, 1867, on "The Poetry of Seven Dials," remarks that Our next section of 'Modern Events' is characterised throughout by such a general sameness of treatment as to need few examples by way of illustration. They are clearly written, for the most part hastily, on the spur of the moment; and though they may command a good sale at first, they do so not by the wit, beauty, or aptness of the verse, but by the absorbing interest of the calamity which it describes. Thus, say, an appalling accident happens in London; the news spreads like wildfire throughout the city, and gives rise to rumours, even more dreadful than the reality. Before night it is embalmed in verse by one out of five or six well-known bards who get their living by writing for Seven Dials, and then chanting their own strains to the people. The inspiration of the poet is swift, the execution of the work rapid,—how rapid may be judged from the following fact. On Thursday, February 21, a woman named Walker was brought before the magistrate and charged with robbing Mr. F. Brown, her master, a publican, to whom she had offered her services as a *man*. She was sent to prison, and there her sex was discovered. The next morning, at 10 a.m., two men and two women were singing her personal history and adventures in the New Cut, to a large but not select audience, under the title of 'The She Barman of Southwark.' It was great trash, but sold well—but the pay for such work is small. 'I gets a shilling a copy for my verses' (says one), 'besides what I can make by selling 'em.' But the verses are ready and go to press at once, A thousand or two copies are struck off instantly, and the 'Orfle Calamity' is soon flying all over London from the mouths of a dozen or twenty minstrels, in the New Cut, in Leather Lane, Houndsditch, Bermondsey, Whitechapel, High Street, Tottenham-court-road—or wherever a crowd of listeners can be easily and safely called together. If the subject admits of it, two minstrels chant the same strain

'In lofty verse
'Pathetic they alternately rehearse.'

each taking a line in turn, and each vying with the other in doleful tragedy of look and voice. A moment suffices to give out in sepulchral accents, 'Dreadful Accident this day on the Ice in Regent's Park,' &c., &c.

"These Halfpenny Sheets form almost the entire poetry of Seven Dials, and though they teach little or no history, they show, at least, what kind of poetry finds the most favourable reception and the readiest sale among our lowest classes. As far as we can ascertain, there are in London eight or ten publishers of the Fortey and Disley stamp—through not on so large a scale. Of ballad-singers and patterers of prose recitations (such as the 'Political Catechism'), there may be about a hundred scattered over the metropolis, who haunt such localities as the New Cut, Tottenham-court-road, Whitechapel, and Clerkenwell Green; and according to the weather, the state of trade, and the character of their wares, earn a scanty or a jovial living by chanting such strains as we have now laid before our readers. 'Songs if they're over religious.' says one minstrel, 'don't sell at all; though a tidy moral does werry well. But a good, awful murder's the thing. I've knowed,' says our authority, 'a man sell a ream a day of *them*.—that's twenty dozen you know;' and this sale may go on for days, so that with forty or fifty men at work as minstrels, a popular ballad will soon attain a circulation of thirty or forty or fifty thousand. Now and then the publisher himself composes a song, and in this case is saved the cost of copyright, though his expenses are very trifling, even when he has to purchase it. If one of the patterers writes a ballad on a taking subject, he hastens at once to Seven Dials, where, if accepted, his reward is 'a glass of rum, a slice of cake, and five dozen copies,'—which, if the accident or murder be a very awful one, are struck off for him while he waits. A murder always sells well, so does a fire, or a fearful railway accident. A good love story, embracing

'infidi perjuria nautæ
Deceptamque dolo nympham'

often does fairly; but politics among the lowest class are a drug. Even the famous *Ballad on Pam's death didn't do much* except among the better sort of people; and though the roughs are fond of shouting *Reform*, they don't care, it would seem, to spend money on it."

We have submitted this wretched doggrel to our readers, that they may form some idea of the kind of Street Literature which is still popular with so many of the lower classes. It is humiliating, in the midst of all the schools and teaching of the present day, to find such rubbish continually poured forth, and eagerly read. Still there are some redeeming features in this weary waste. *Taken as a whole*, the moral tone of the ballads, if not lofty, is certainly not bad; and the number of single stanzas that could not be quoted in these pages on account of their gross or indecent language is very small; while that of entire Ballads, to be excluded on the same ground, is still smaller.

THE FEMALE HUSBAND,

WHO HAD BEEN MARRIED TO ANOTHER FEMALE FOR

TWENTY-ONE YEARS.

What wonders now I have to pen, sir,
Women turning into men, sir,
For twenty-one long years, or more, sir,
She wore the breeches we are told, sir,
A smart and active handsome groom, sir,
She then got married very soon, sir,
A shipwright's trade she after took, sir,
And of his wife, he made a fool sir.

   Sing hey! sing O! 'twas my downfall, sir,
   To marry a man with nothing at all, sir,

Well Mother Sprightly, what do you think of this Female Husband; it appears to me a strange piece of business. Why, Mother Chatter, I do not believe half what is said about it—Pho, pho, do you think I would have been in bed with my husband twenty-one minutes without knowing what he was made of, much more twenty-one years, for I should never have patience to wait so long. My old man cuddles me as close as wax these cold winter nights, and if he was to turn his back to me I would stick a needle into it.

If the wife asked for a favour,
Then she flew into a fever,
Gave to her a precious thump, sir,
Which after left a largeish lump, sir,
Then her limbs so straight and tall, sir,
She turn'd her face against the wall, sir,
And oft have quarrel'd and much strife, sir,
Because he would not cuddle the wife, sir.

   Why I must say, Mother Chatter, if he had been my husband, I think after hard work all day he must have slept sound, and I would have seen what he was before I rose in the morning, or I'd know the reason why.

Was woman ever so perplex'd, sir,
And through life so grievously vex'd, sir,

And disappointments oft did meet, sir,
And instead of a kiss, I oft got beat, sir,
Sometimes cuff'd and sometimes scouted,
Because I asked what woman wanted,
And if ever that I marry again, sir,
I'll surely marry a perfect man, sir.

   Mother Chatter,—Man, indeed! yes, I hope she will take care next time she marries, and not be duped in that way again; and as she was such a bad judge I would advise her to taste and try first next time.
   Mother Sprightly,—I have no doubt but she'll examine the beard and whiskers of the next man she marries, and not take a beardless thing at his own word.

With this pretty handsome groom, sir,
She went and spent the honey-moon, sir,
The very first night my love should cuddle,
Up in the clothes he close did huddle;
And with his face against the wall, sir,
He never spoke a word at all, sir,
A maid to bed I then did go, sir,
And a maiden am now, heigho! heigho! sir.

   Well, Mother Frisky, how is your old man? Why he is quite hearty, and every inch a man, none of your sham husbands; give me the real man or none at all. Well, I am of your way of thinking, and I hope the next husband she has she will have thumping children.

Pretty maidens list I pray, sir,
Unto what I now do say, sir,
Taste and try before you buy, sir,
Or you'll get bit as well as I, sir;
See he's perfect in all parts, sir,
Before you join your hand and heart, sir,
You then with all your strength may try, sir,
To be fruitful, increase, and multiply, sir.

Printed by T. Birt, No. 10, Great St. Andrew Street, Seven Dials.

SHAKESPEARE'S HOUSE.

"Pulling down and building up is all the go,
And the scene changes like a raree show,"
Yet is it not disgraceful to the nation,
That Shakespeare's house is doomed to mutilation?
The house in which that great man first drew breath,
A spot renowned before and after death—
Where pilgrims from every land have come,
To see his birth place, Nature's learned home—
Where first shone forth, a pale, an infant light,
A spreading brilliancy, which still burns bright.
Oh, who shall have the writings on the walls,
Oh, who can save the house that's doomed to fall?
True genius, of which we vainly boast,
By our rulers seems neglected most.
How we took the kernel, and threw by the shell,
    Profanation, degradation,—Oh, England, thou art
      a tardanation!

Time-hallowed spot, could we call back those days,
When Shakespeare here in thoughtless boyhood plays.
Before his plays had graced the mimic scene,
Since which three hundred years have been
Food for reflection, here the thinking mind,
"And good in everything" we ought to find.
From out the walls in fancy we might trace
Macbeth, Hamlet, and King Richard's face;
And all the clouds that on this house have lowered,
Look frowningly, as 'twere upon a coward,
Who thus stands meekly by this sacred wood,
Nor helps to save it for its country's good.
But let it go, our Shakespeare needs no fame,
'Tis but a house! a house! "What's in a name?"
Let it be sold, or in the sea be tossed—
His loved and mighty labours ne'er will be lost.
    Altercation, dilapidation,—Time steps in and cheats
      the nation!

Great Premier,—Oh, King John,—grant this our charter,
Why in this land should genius be a martyr?
The Tempest's rising, if we fail we fall;
And time may tell you a sad Winter's Tale.
Come, As you like it, make this house a treasure,
Do not divide it, Measure for Measure.
Methinks in sadness I can see the Moor,
Othello, looking blacker than before;
Therefore, good John, we look to you
To put this house in order, and to Tame the Shrew.

The very age and body of the time (reflecting mirrors)
Proclaims this sale a Comedy of Errors,
While England wastes her thousands, 'tis not soothing,
To say this is Much Ado about Nothing;
For to the wise and thoughtful this would seem
A summer cloud or Midsummer Night's Dream.
    Moderation, preservation,—Is all we're asking of
      the nation!

Robins, at knocking houses down so fond,
Exclaims, with Shakespeare's Jew, I'll have my bond.
Put down your hammer, Mr Robins, stop;
You take my house when you do touch the prop.
Hard-hearted man, such antique relics ridding,
With hammer soon to fall and looks for-bidding,
Shakespeare by you has been puffed up and praised,
To sell his house you have a story raised.
And is it true this house is coming down,
To be put on wheels and dragged about the town?
Can such things be, can it be so!
What, make this classic pile a travelling show?
Tis true; 'tis pity chaps from Yankee land
Are coming over with the cash in hand.
Blow winds, crack cheeks, their paltry lucre spurn,
To what base uses may we not return.
    Speculation—British nation, Oh, save the house
      from exportation!

Time was, and it seems but t'other day,
When we could see a real Shakesperian play,
With Miss O'Neill, Siddons, or the great John Kemble,
Could laugh at Munden, or at old Kean tremble.
Macready does Shakespeare now, with Kean's son
    Charlie,
And Drury Lane holds legitimate with Harley;
Shakespeare inside has long been quite neglected,
His statue outside looks forlorn, dejected;
For great folks now run after Greas or All-bony,
Tamburini, Jenny Lind, or Taglioni,
Which John Bull's dire indignation rouses,
Till he exclaims, "A plague on both your houses."
Portia, Miranda, Juliet for him plead,
Preserve this house, thy potent spell we need."
My song is done, and you I pardon crave—
All's well that ends well, if this house we save.
    Determination, stimulation,—and Shakespeare's
      house an honour to the nation.

E. Hodges, Printer (from the late J. Pitt's), Wholesale Toy Warehouse, 38, Dudley Street, 7 Dials.

A NEW SONG

ON

THE BLOOMER COSTUME.

Oh, did you hear the news of late,
　　According to the rumours,
The pretty ladies one and all,
　　Are going to join the bloomers.
Since Mrs Dexter's come to town,
　　She says, oh, what a row, sir,
The men shall wear the petticoats
　　And ladies wear the trousers.
　　　　　　Oh, did you hear, &c.

Now Mrs. Dexter's come to towu,
　　She says, she'll not be lazy,
But quickly turn the ladies' brains,
　　And set the men all crazy.
Old maids and lasses fine and gay,
　　Short, stumpy, tall and bandy,
Long petticoats now throw away,
　　And beat the yanky dandy.

Prince Albert and the Queen one day,
　　Had such a jolly row, sirs,
She threw off her petticoats
　　And put on boots and trousers ;
Won't it be funny for to see
　　Ladies possessed of riches,
Riding up and down the town
　　In Wellingtons and breeches.

Now you with ancles short and thick,
　　Of every rank and station,
Oh, won't you cut it fine and slick,
　　By this new alteration.
And landladies that creep about,
　　Well known as twenty stoners,
Come shove your bustles up the spout,
　　And join the dashing bloomers.

The bloomers dress, the people say,
　　Is getting all the go now,
The pretty factory lasses they,
　　Will cut a gallant show now,
In petticoats above their knes,
　　And breeches too you'll fit them.
Nice jackets made of velveteen,
　　All button'd up behind them.

Now married men take my advice,
　　Step out and spend your riches,
And buy your wife all in a trice,
　　Short petticoats and breeches,
For in the fashion she will hop,
　　Whene'er she's out of humour,
I wonder if her tongue will stop,
　　When she becomes a bloomer.

Last night my wife she said to me,
　　Tom, when we've got the notes in,
I'll have a pair of gaiters, and
　　Breeches made of goat's skin.
A pair of boots and silver spurs,
　　For I have got such bad legs,
I cannot hide I'll have to ride,
　　The donkey now a strad-legs.

The men must go out selling fish,
　　And deal in shrimps and mussels,
Dress'd up in ladies' petticoats,
　　Fine flounces and big bustles,
You'll have no call to work at all,
　　But walk out in your broaches,
The ladies are determined, for,
　　To drive the cabs and coaches.

The tailors now must all be sharp
　　In making noble stitches,
And be sure and clap their burning goose
　　Upon the ladies' breeches ;
Their pretty little fingers will
　　Be just as sore as mutton,
Until that they have found the way
　　Their trousers to unbutton.

You factory lasses, one and all,
　　Your dresses all reform now,
Buy a jacket and a trousers for
　　To keep you snug and warm now ;
Short petticoats and garters too,
　　No matter how the time goes,
A billycock and feather for
　　To see which way the wind blows.

M. O'LOUGHNAN.

R

MANCHESTER'S
AN
ALTERED TOWN.

Once on a time this good old town was nothing but a village,
Of husbandry, and farmers too, whose time was spent in tillage ;
But things are altered very much, such building now allotted is,
It rivals far and soon will leave behind the great Metropolis.
    O dear O, Manchester's an altered town, O dear O.

Once on a time were you inclin'd, your weary limbs to lave, sir,
In summer's scorching heat in the Irwell's cooling wave, sir ;
You had only got to go to the Old Church for the shore, sir,
But since those days the fish have died, and now they are no more,
    sir.

When things do change you ne'er do know what next is sure to
    follow,
For mark the change in Broughton now, of late 'twas but a hollow
For they have found it so snug, and chang'd its etymology,
They have clapt in it a wild beast's show, now call'd the Gardens
    of Zoology.

A market on Shudehill was, and it remains there still, sir,
The Salford old bridge is taken away, and clapt a new one in, sir,
There's Newton lane I now shall name, has had an alteration,
They've knock'd a great part of it down, to make a railway station.

There's the Bolton railway station in Salford, give attention,
Besides many more too numerous to mention ;
Besides a new Police, to put the old ones down stairs, sir,
A mayor and corporation to govern this old town, sir.

There's the Manchester and Salford old bridge, that long has stood,
    the weather,
Because it was so very old they drown'd it altogether ;
And Brown street market too, it forms part of this sonnet,
Down it must come, they say, to build a borough gaol upon it.

Not long ago if you had taken a walk thro' Stevenson's square, sir,
You might have seen, if you look'd, a kind of chapel there, sir,
And yet this place, some people thought, had better to come down,
    sir,
And in the parson's place they put a pantaloon and clown, sir.

In former times our cotton swells were not half so mighty found, sir,
But in these modern times they everywhere abound, sir,
With new police and watchmen, to break peace there's none dare
And at every step the ladies go, policemen will cry, move on there'

In former days this good old town was guarded from the prigs, sir,
By day constables, by night by watchmen with Welsh wigs, sir ;
But things are alter'd very much, for all those who are scholars,
May tell the new policemen by their numbers on their collars.

A NEW SONG ON THE
PRESTON GUILD,
1842.

J. Harkness, Printer, 121, Church Street, Preston.

You lads and lasses far and near,
Unto my song pray lend an ear,
The time is come for mirth and glee,
To Preston Guild let's haste away,
For Tom and Sal with Jim and Peg,
And daddy with his wooden leg,
And grunting Jack with Sam and Will,
Are all gone off to Preston Guild.

There lords and ladies, Kings and Queens,
At Preston Guild they may be seen,
Yes, Merchants, Tradesmen,—a grand show,
With ladies walking in a row ;
And then the trades they do appear,
By gum it makes one feel quite queer,
Some walking,—others standing still,
This is the fun at Preston Guild.

The tailors they lead up the van,
With Adam and Eve they look so grand,
Then Robin Hood's men and gardeners,
Who represent Mars the God of Wars,
Shopkeepers, Publicans so free,
Will follow up for liberty,
The grandest show in England still,
Is the jubilee at Preston Guild.

The factory folks are next in view,
Spinners, weavers, and carders too,
The piecers do not lag behind,
Brickmakers at the Guild we find,
Bricksetters, masons two and two,
To see them walking in a row,
The men who houses and factories build,
You'll see them walk at Preston Guild.

When at the Guild you do arrive,
Like bees they're swarming all alive,
All kinds of trades are working still,
You'll see, now you're at Preston Guild.
There's swinging boxes, likewise shows,
And soldiers 'listing drunken fools,
Both drunkards and teetotallers will,
Enjoy a peep at Preston Guild.

Its toss or buy for cakes or nuts,
Sweet meats or ORMSKIRK, stuff your guts,
Or take a trow at civil will,
Now lads you've come to Preston Guild,
Or see the sports that's up and down,
At Preston Guild in Preston town,
Two shillings a bed pay with good will,
If you stop one night at Preston Guild.

The times are hard, the wages low,
Some thousands to the Guild can't go,
From Blackburn, Burnley, and Chorley still,
They will roll on to Preston Guild,
From Wigan, Bolton, Lancaster,
From Liverpool and Manchester,
The Railroad brings them on it still,
To see the fun at Preston Guild.

So young and old I'll tell you true,
It's different now since twenty-two,
The men did labour with good will,
It's not so now this Preston Guild.
But let us hope the times will mend,
When the poor man can the poor befriend,
We want our rights and then we will,
Have plenty of sport next Preston Guild.

PROPHECY

FOR 1850——

John Harkness, Printer, Church St. ;—Office, North Road, Preston.

Now Christmas it is gone and past, throughout the British nation,
Come list to me and you will see a wonderful alteration;
In the new year there will appear, or I may cause a blunder,
Some curious changes that will fill you with amaze and wonder.

CHORUS.

So listen to me of all degree, both single, wise, and thrifty,
While I prophecy what you will see, in eighteen hundred and fifty.

The Queen will have another son, he will be a steam-loom weaver,
And Prince Albert he is going to be a wopping big coal-heaver;
Old Wellington as I've heard say, with his great whacking nose, sir,
With a donkey cart is going out a gathering old clothes, sir.

Russell and Grey, as I've heard say, are going to be sailors,
And Bobby Peel will make, of steel, new thimbles for the tailors;
Cobden and Bright will have a fight, and conquer in dirch man,
Without protection, in a crack, knock down the Duke of Richmond.

The muck carts they will go by steam, no horses will be wanted,
We will have four pound loaves for threepence each, then we shall be undaunted,
Girls must new fashioned whiskers wear, fine lawns they must adorn her,
Their stockings must be made of gold brought home from California.

All females over seventeen, that out of doors are flocking,
Will sadly rue if there should be, a hole seen in their stocking,
Either in the leg or heel, the law to nothing flinches,
Each bustle must be stuffed with straw full nine feet eleven inches.

And very soon, in May or June, we will be amaz'd with wonder,
For it will either rain or freeze, with heavy claps of thunder,
The free hall is going to fall, believe me it's no fable,
And legs of mutton from the clouds will fall upon the table.

No little boys must smoke cigars, nor yet be seen a courting,
Male and female under twenty-two, must not be seen a flirting,
Any factory lass that has a child until she is married really,
Must serve twelve months in —————— or else in the New Bailey.

If any landlord call for rent upon a Monday morning,
His tenants shall be authorised without a moment's warning
To strip him naked to the skin in any sort of weather,
Daub him with tar from head to foot, and cover him with feathers.

And Scotchmen, too, mark what I say, you may roll in soot and cinders,
And after that take him up stairs, and throw him through the windows,
They will take the duty off the gin, and clap it on the mussels,
And lay an extra shilling on the gutta-percha bustles.

The old women they will dance with glee, and if I'm not mistaken,
They will take the duty off the tea, the sugar, and the bacon;
Morning and night they'll have fat cakes, the frying pans will flourish,
With mutton chops and good beef steaks, their stomachs for to nourish.

R 2

GRACE DARLING.

I pray give attention to what I shall mention,
    There was a young damsel liv'd by the sea side,
Her name was Grace Darling, a good hearted heroine,
    And she with her father alone did reside,
She was brave and undaunted, possess'd of great courage,
    Her heart often beat in her breast we are told,
While the seas were commotion, she ventured the ocean,
    Grace Horsely Darling, a female so bold.

On the 6th of September, the Forfarshire steamer,
    Sailed from Hull to the port of Dundee,
With her crew on board and forty-one passengers,
    All hearts light and merry we put out to sea;
With her full crew and passengers sixty in number,
    The vessel proceeded so gallant we're told,
They thought not of storms, nor even of danger,
    Though rescu'd from death by Grace Darling so bold.

In the dead of the night on the 6th of September,
    The crew and passengers felt dreadful shocks,
Against Longstone Island with force so tremendous,
    The Forfarshire steamer she went on the rocks,
Asunder she rent while the crew fell a weeping.
    And some from the deck to deep they were roll'd,
But the shrieks and the cries met the ears of that female,
    Grace Darling—that gallant young woman so bold.

In the dead of the night this undaunted young female,
    Oh! father, dear father, awake she did cry,
Arouse from your slumber and launch the boat quickly,
    Poor creatures to save, our efforts let's try,
I fear there's a wreck, let us strive then to rescue
    Some part of the crew from the deep sad and cold,
Their shrieks do appal me, their cries she said pierce me,
    Grace Darling—that gallant young female so bold.

Says her father, dear daughter, this night it is stormy,
    'Tis cold, and the seas they do run mountains high,
It is folly my child to attempt on the billow,
    I fear not the danger, dear father, she cried!
The boat was launched quickly, the seas loudly roaring,
    To the wreck with her father she ventur'd we're told,
And nine of the sufferers she saved from drowning,
    Grace Darling—that gallant young female so bold.

When the danger was past her bosom beat lightly,
    Yet tears from her eyes in large torrents did fall,
And saying we've only saved nine out sixty,
    Oh! I wish dearest father we could have saved all.
Since her life she did hazard through tempests to save them
    Her name shall be written in letters of gold,
With health and long life to that gallant young damsel,
Grace Horsely Darling--that female so bold.

SAYERS' & HEENAN'S GREAT FIGHT
FOR THE CHAMPIONSHIP.

Upon the seventeenth day of April,
  All in the morning soon,
The Yankee and the champion Sayers
  Prepared to meet their doom.
The train it ran along like wind,
  Coaches and cabs did fly,
Both men appeared determined
  To conquer or to die.

They fought like lions in the ring,
  Both men did boldly stand,
They two hours and six minutes fought,
  And neither beat his man.

Tom hit at the Benicia boy
  Right well you may suppose,
Heenan returned the compliment
  Upon the champion's nose.
Like two game cocks they stood the test,
  And each to win did try,
Erin-go-bragh, cried Heenan,
  I will conquer, lads, or die.

Cried Sayers, I will not give in,
  Nor to a Yankee yield,
The belt I mean to keep my boys,

Or die upon the field.
They together stood it manfully,
  Surprised all in the ring,
There was never such a battle, since
  Jack Langham tackled Spring.

Such fibbing and such up and down
  Lor, how the swells did shout,
Their ribs did nicely rattle,
  And their daylight near knocked out,
Tom Sayers let into Heenan,
  Heenan let into Tom,
While the Fancy bawled and shouted,
  Lads, my jolly lads, go on.

Two long hours and six minutes
  They fought, and the claret flew,
Sayers proved himself a brick, so did
  Yankee doodle doo.
The bets did fly about, my boys,
  And numbers looked with joy
On Sayers, the British champion,
  And the bold Benicia boy.

They both had pluck and courage,
  Each proved himself a man,

None better since the days of Spring
  In the British ring did stand.
Erin-go-bragh, cried Heenan,
  I want the English belt,
When Tom let fly, saying, I will die,
  Or keep the belt myself.

At length bounced in the peelers,
  And around the ring did jog,
So those heroes were surrounded
  By a lot of Hampshire hogs,
Who caused them to cut their stick,
  And from the fight refrain,
That they were both determined
  In the ring to meet again.

We admit Tom Sayers had his match
  One who did him annoy,
With lots of pluck and courage,
  Was the bold Benicia boy.
And when two heroes fight again,
  For honour and for wealth,
He that's the best man in the ring,
  Shall carry off the belt.

H. Disley, Printer, 57, High Street, St. Giles, London.

TERRIBLE ACCIDENT

ON THE ICE

IN REGENT'S PARK,

AND

LOSS OF FORTY LIVES.

Of all the dread calamities you ever yet did hear,
　　Either in history or story;
If pity is within your breast, you will shed a silent tear,
　　And mourn for those drowned, now in glory!
The 15th of January, that Tuesday afternoon,
　　Some hundreds on the ice took their station,
Young men and boys, in youth and bloom,
　　To the park went for healthy recreation.

But soon it gave way, more than 40 lost their lives,
　　The widows and poor orphans 'twill distress them;
God bless those gallant hearts, to save life did strive,
　　And those now in Heaven,—God rest them.

'Twas near four o'clock, how dreadful to relate,
　　The ice it broke up in every quarter;
Two hundred then fell in, oh, what a sad fate,
　　All struggled for their lives in the water.
The cries of the people, as they stood upon the shore,
　　To witness such a scene most distressing,
Some clung to each other, but now are no more,
　　In grief are the friends of the missing.

What must have been the feelings of those standing by,
　　Unable to save and madly raving?
The women rushed about, and bitterly did cry,
　　My children, my children, oh save them!
Wives calling to their husbands,—children, father dear,
　　But few that were able to assist them,

Now all will miss their own, for them shed a tear,
　　Kind fathers, the children will miss them.

They clung to the ice, until benumbed with cold,
　　The ice in their grasp broke asunder;
One lady on the shore, in grief did behold
　　Her husband, exhausted, go under;
Two sisters were screaming and calling for aid,
　　Their sorrow, poor girls, could not smother,
In anguish wrung their hands, and franticly said,
　　For God's sake save my poor brother.

The most mournful part remains to be told,
　　As the bodies to the dead-house were taken,
At the workhouse gate two thousand young and old,
　　The scene it was truly heart-breaking;
One body was owned by an old gentleman,
　　My son can't be dead, he said, while crying,
He left me but two hours, was strong and cheerful then,
　　For a father so old it's very trying.

The doctors did their best in saving many lives,
　　Of those that were in this sad disaster;
Officials one and all, Mr Douglas and his wife,
　　Long life to that kind workhouse master.
A poor faithful dog saw his master disappear,
　　And never left the park since that evening,
No food will he take, by the water stays near,
　　For it's master the poor dog is grieving.

H. Disley, Printer, 57, High Street, St. Giles.

FOREIGNERS IN ENGLAND.

What wonders we do daily see,
Enough to fill our hearts with glee,
Britannia now will merry be,
   With the foreigners in England ;
John Bull does foreigners adore,
Here's the Viceroy from Egypt's shore,
Here's the Turkish Sultan blythe and gay,
And the Belgium Volunteers huzza !
The bells shall merrily ring, huzza,
Britannia sing and the band shall play,
Old Jacky Bull will the piper pay,
   For the foreigners in England.

They are come to see the grand review,
And England's Roberts', dress'd in blue,
Hokey pokey parleyvous,
   All the foreigners in England.

You pretty English maids, heigho,
If you don't mind you'll have to go
To the Sultan's grand Seraglio,
   And bid adieu to England.
Yes, and all old women, so you must mind,
Under the age of seventy-nine,
Will be taken away in the morning soon,
In a wooden cane bottom air balloon,
You must marry the Turk and danger drive,
Till to Constantinople you do arrive,
For the Turks have eleven hundred wives,
   And he'll take you all from England.

Now the other day, you know its true,
There was a terrible great to do,
About the grand Hyde Park review,
   And the foreigners in England.
The reason they stopped, the papers said,
Poor Maximilian had lost his head,
And he could not come with the jovial crew
To have a look at the grand review.
But Britons you must understand,
There'll be a grand review by sea and land,
No power in Europe beat it can,
   With the foreigners in England.

They're going to dine with a great Lord
   Mayor
And they'll sit in a new mahogany chair,
Such lots of dainties are prepared,
   For the foreigners in England.
They'll have sausages seasoned high
Soused mackerel and rabbit pie,
Rashers of bacon nicely done,
Lobster sauce and donkey's tongue,
Lots of crabs and pickled sprats,
Cabbage and onions covered in fat,
Skillygolee and paddywhack,
   For the foreigners in England.

To the Crystal Palace they will go,
The Museum and National Gallery too,
To Windsor, Aldershot, and Kew,
   All the foreigners in England.
They are going to visit Charing Cross,
To see old Charley sit on his horse,
Then to Buckingham Palace to have a game,
Then off they go to Petticoat Lane,
Where life in splendour they will see,
Fried fish and liver, and shockerhorsey,
Then have a bathe in the river Lea,
   The foreigners in England.

Let us welcome them with a loud huzza,
You pretty maids get out of the way,
Old Jacky Bull will expenses pay,
   For the foreigners in England :
Here's the Viceroy from Egypt's land
And Turkey's Sultan hand-in-hand.
If he wants some wives for the ottoman
   plains
He can have all the women in Drury Lane.
So all pretty girls in London chaste
Go home to your mothers and wash your face,
Or perhaps they will collar you round the
   waist,
   The foreigners in England.

When the foreigners reach their native shore,
They may say, we never saw before,
Such glorious sights, and we may no more,
   As we beheld in England.

H. Disley, Printer, 57, High Street, St. Giles, London.

WHAT SHALL
WE DO FOR MEAT!

Old England, once upon a time,
  Was prosperous and gaily,
Great changes you shall hear in rhyme,
  That taking place is daily.
A poor man once could keep a pig,
  There was meat for every glutton,
Folks now may eat a parson's wig,
  For they'll get no beef or mutton.

The times are queer, and things are dear,
  Well, it really is alarming;
Up and down, country and town,
  I think we'll all be starving.

Although the times are very queer,
  Some old women have a way got,
To raise themselves a drop of beer.
  Or a drop of gin in the teapot.
If meat was seven shillings a pound,
  Old Polly, Kit, and Sally,
Would find the means to guzzle down,
  A little cream of the valley.

The butchers now, oh dear! oh dear!
  Declare no meat they can sell,
Five thousand is gone to Colney Hatch,
  And seven thousand to Hanwell.
Sixteen jumped in the water-butt,
  Lamenting they did shiver,
Three ship-load sailed down to Gravesend
    town,
  And went to sleep in the river.

Bullock's head will be two shillings a pound,
  And if I'm not mistaken,
We shall have to pay a half-a-crown
  For a slice of rusty bacon.
I wonder what they do put in
  The faggots and the sausages?—
Cold donkeys' dung, says Biddy Flinn,
  Candle ends and rotten cabbages.

The butchers now are gone to pot,
  Crying, oh! such times was never,

They lay their heads on a greasy block,
  Saying, we are done for ever.
They cannot cry, who'll buy! who'll buy!
  Their marrow bones are aching,
For want of beef they seek relief,
  And will be sent stone breaking.

Old Molly Bayton had a cat,
  So handsome and adorning,
She would be moll-rowing all the night,
  And mewing in the morning.
Last Friday night she killed a bird,
  To death old Moll did beat it,
She put it in the pot to fry,
  And her son Bill did eat it.

From a foreign land has come a man—
  He really is a wonder—
He can raise mutton, veal, and lamb,
  And veal by steam and thunder.
He the world to please, cures cattle disease,
  His skin is a blueish yellow,
He carries a wand to banish the bugs,
  Is he not a curious fellow?

Friends, never fret, there will be yet,
  Good things, plenty and stunning,
Good beef to sell, we'll all live well,
  For there's right good times a coming.
Lots of bulls with horns are being born,
  Large buffaloes are standing,
New milk and cream will be made by steam,
  And in Ireland pigs are lambing.

Though butchers' meat to the poor's a treat,
  Just look at Ned and Nelly,
How they strut along, so says my song,
  With a flashy back and hungry belly.
Have patience, folks, though 'tis no joke,
  Smell at the cook shop windows,
If you want relief, and have got no beef,
  Have a jolly blow out of cinders.

H. Disley, Printer, 57, High Street, St. Giles, London.

FIFTEEN
SHILLINGS A WEEK.

Air :— " King of the Cannibal Islands."

A MAN and his wife in —— street,
    With seven children young and sweet,
Had a jolly row last night complete,
    About fifteen shillings a week, sir.
He gave his wife a clumsy clout,
Saying, how is all my money laid out,
Tell me quickly he did shout,
And then she soon did set about
Reckoning up without delay,
What she had laid out from day to day,
You shall know what's done, the wife did say,
    With fifteen shillings a week, sir.

Seven children to keep and find in clothes,
And to his wife he did propose,
To reckon how the money goes,
    His fifteen shillings a week, sir.

Threepence-halfpenny a week for milk is
    spent,
One-and-ninepence a week for rent,
For the children a penny for peppermint,
    Out of fifteen shillings a week, sir ;
For tobacco eightpence every week,
A half-a-crown for butcher's meat,
And to make your tea complete,
A three-farthing bloater for a treat,
A penny a week for cotton and thread,
Last Sunday, tenpence a small sheep's head,
Ninepence-halfpenny a day for bread,
    Out of fifteen shillings a week, sir.

Potatoes for dinner there must be found,
And there's none for less than a penny a
    pound,
And I must have a sixpenny gown,
    Out of fifteen shillings a week, sir.
A pennorth of starch, a farthing blue,
Twopence-halfpenny soap and potash too,
A ha'porth of onions to make a stew,
Three-halfpence a day small beer for you,
A quartern of butter, sixpennorth of fat,
And to wipe your shoes a twopenny mat,
One halfpenny a day to feed the cat,
    Out of fifteen shillings a week, sir.

Ninepence a week for old dry peas,
Sixpence sugar, eightpence tea,
Pepper, salt, and mustard, farthings three,
    Out of fifteen shillings a week, sir.
One and tenpence-halfpenny, understand,
Every week for firing out of hand,
Threepence-halfpenny candles, a farthing
    sand,
And threepence to bottom the frying-pan ;
A twopenny broom to sweep the dirt,
Three-ha'porth of cloth to mend your shirt,
Now don't you think you're greatly hurt,
    Out of fifteen shillings a week, sir.

Clothes for Tommy, Dick, Sal, Polly, and
    Jane,
And Jimmy and Betty must have the same ;
You had a sixpenny jacket in Petticoat Lane,
    Out of fifteen shillings a week, sir.
For shaving, a halfpenny twice a week,
A penny to cut your hair so neat,
Threepence for the socks upon your feet,
Last week you bought a tenpenny seat
Besides, old chap, I had most forgot,
You gave a penny for a kidney pie, all hot,
And threepence for an old brown chamberpot,
    Out of fifteen shillings a week, sir.

So now, old chap, you plainly see,
If you can reckon as well as me,
There is little waste in our family,
    Out of fifteen shillings a week, sir.
There's many a woman would think it no sin,
To spend the whole in snuff and gin !
When again to reckon you do begin,
Recollect there's a farthing a week for pins,
To make things right my best I've tried,
That's economy can't be denied.
Dear wife, said he, I'm satisfied,
    Out of fifteen shillings a week, sir.

So you women all the kingdom through,
To you this might appear quite new,
Just see if you the same can do,
    With fifteen shillings a week, sir.

London : H. SUCH, Machine Printer, aud Publisher, 177, Union street, Borough.—S. E.

THE GREAT AGRICULTURAL SHOW.

Hurrah, my lads, this is the day,
When tens of thousands haste away;
Rich and poor, high and low,
Are off to the Agricultural Show.

CHORUS.

Sing the ploughboy's song,
Dance the milkman's dance,
What glorious fun, away they run,
　Kicking up their heels in the morning.
Heigho! away they go,
Jolly young fellows all of a row,
Don't get kissing the girls you know,
　At the Agricultural Show.

Now at the Show some sights you'll find,
To delight the eye and improve the mind,
Carts, waggons, patent ploughs,
Horses, bulls, and Alderney cows.

There's scythes, sickles, forks and rakes,
Ganders, turkeys, ducks and drakes,
Chickens, hens, and cocks that crow,
Is seen at the Agricultural Show.

There's buckets, churns, milk-pails,
Washing tubs, and Chowbent nails;
All sorts of flowers and fruit that grow,
At the Agricultural Show.

There is some young men got on the
　spree,
And lushey got as they could be,
An old cobler they met, they made him so
　drunk,
That he went to smoke his short pipe at
　the pump.

A man from London brought his wife,
Indeed it is true upon my life,
To tell you all that she can do,
She can lick Jem Mace and Heenan too.

From miles around they come by train,
Into the town to see the game;
And the country lads are always right,
They won't go home till broad daylight.

Two or three machines of every kind,
To go by water or by wind;
Some to stop old people's tongues,
And one to grind old people young.

There are Lancashire clogs and Cheshire
　cheese,
London bugs and Suffolk fleas,
You cannot sleep a wink at night,
They are such devils for to fight.

There's a farmer's daughter, — sweet
　eighteen,
With nineteen hoops in her crinoline;
It's just a mile round the brim of her hat,
She has got a cock-eye and a hump on her
　back.

Triumphal arches I'll be bound,
Decorating ————— town;
With hearts so light and spirits gay,
Hark! how the bands of music play.

Some young ladies dress'd in white,
Will be stopping out all night;
If you should wink why they will wait,
Upon the road by the turnpike gate.

Oh, lovely night, when all alone,
The lads and lasses toddling home;
In a few months' time the girls will show
The game was played coming from the
　Show.

The farmers' lads will you not mind,
The factory girls will dress so fine,
They'll go and leave the silk machine,
To make little boys and girls by steam

THE WINDHAM
LUNACY CASE.

THE COVE THAT WANTED THE MONEY.

Oh, dear! what a rumpus and bother,
From one end of England right bang to the other,
The lawyers their wigs pelted one at the other,
  Young Windham has conquered them all.
They swore he was mad, that he acted quite funny,
Imitated the cat, and stood just like a dummy,
The fact was, you see, that they wanted his money,
  But now the old soldier is licked.

Oh, dear! what can the matter be?
Swearing and humbugging, jawing and flattery,
They may now go and hang themselves up to an apple
      tree,
  Young Windham has conquered them all.

Before there was never such pulling and tearing,
The tales that was told was really unbearing,
Such bawling, such pushing, such talking, & swearing,
  To prove that young Windham was mad.
Because he thought proper to marry a wife, sir,
Because he was happy and cheerful through life, sir,
'Twas money, the money, that caused the strife, sir,
  But young Windham has conquer'd them all.

Sometimes he would Mackney be imitating,
I wish I was with Nancy! he oft would be stating,
In the Strand, in the Strand! as I am relating,
  And then they all swore he was mad.
Because on the engine he went fast and slow, now,
And with the ladies he used for to go now,
Then holloa like winking, Bob Ridley, O! now,
  Well, but that wouldn't make him be mad.

Not far from St. James's some coveys were dwelling,
They such wonderful tales to the jury was telling,
And there was a lot that was named Llewellin,
  Who spun a most wonderful yarn.

THE LADY WHO GOT THE JEWELS.

That sometimes he was naked, & drunk too, I vow, sir,
That he crowed & moll rowed, & kick'd up a row, sir,
And wetted sometimes the back part of his trousers,
  And they swore to be sure he was mad.

Now young Windham has conquered them all, and is
      right, sir,
He may fight, drink and sing, be enjoying his pipe, sir,
And he with his money can do as he likes, sir,
  He has licked the old soldier right well.
The weeping old soldier is beat, he is done, sir,
He may slip on his knapsack and follow the drum, sir,
Or march thro' the country, and shoulder his gun, sir,
  It's a chance if he doesn't go mad.

Through all the set speeches of Montague Chambers,
If he carried the day we should all be in danger,
They'd have made us all mad, and there's nothing more
      stranger,
  But into the madhouse we'd go!
Oh, the money, the money, they wanted the money,
And that was the thing made the parties feel funny,
There was rough tales, and smooth tales, and tales told
      like honey,
  But it didn't make young Windham go mad.

Here's success to the jury who acted so clever,
Do you think they'd be bias'd, oh no, they would never,
Drink their health in a bumper, may they live for ever,
  And we hope they will never go mad.
When the trial was over, young Windham not fear'd
      them,
And the public as soon as ever they near'd him,
Hurrah'd him right well, and so heartily cheer'd him,
  And declar'd that he never was mad.

H. Disley, Printer, 57, High Street, St. Giles, London.

THE OLD MARQUIS
And His Blooming Wife.

Oh, here's a jolly lark,
　Some strife perhaps there may
　　be,
A Marquis had a wife,
　Oh, such a blooming lady;
She married him they say,
　For title, and remember,
'Twas lovely Miss May,
　And old Mister December.

Old Fidgets lost his wife,
　And sorely now does grumble
When he goes to bed at night,
　He's nobody to fumble.

The old man is seventy eight,
　As sprightly as a donkey,
Such a noble friend is he
　To the Italians & the monkeys.
The lady he did wed,
　He married her one Monday,
Blooming, young, and fair,
　Only seventeen come Sunday.

He cuddled her so sweet,
　The damsel he did flatter,
Singing I for Bobbing Joan,
　And she for stoney batter;

An angel from above,
　The poor old man did think
　　her,
But oh dear, she ran away
　One morning with a tinker.

The old Marquis lost his wife,
　And he was in a sad mess,
Miss was a lady gay,
　An Irish Marchioness;
Lovely seventeen,
　He could not discard her—
Wedded she thought she'd been
　Unto her great grandfather.

Five hundred bright pounds,
　The damages, that got he,
Against the naughty man
　Who robbed him of his lady.
The lawyers they did chaff,
　What fun in court, oh law there
They caught her snug in bed,
　In Sheffield town, in Yorkshire.

This blooming damsel fair,
　Has such a lovely pimple,
Such pretty chesnut hair,
　And nigh her mouth a dimple;

A bustle made of gold,
　And I can now remember,
A crinoline to hold
　Poor old Mister December.

Old men, take my advice,
　Or taken in you may be,
If you should wed a nice,
　Sweet frolicsome young lady;
A gay, young Mister June,
　Perhaps they may connive at,
To play to her a tune,
　Just now and then in private.

The poor old man is mad,
　Though he has lots of riches,
He wants another wife,
　Or a larger pair of breeches;
Though past three score and
　　ten,
　If one should meet his fancy,
He says he'll marry again,—
　Oh! don't I love my Nancy.

When he married his sweet wife
　He didn't care for nothing,
He used to lace her stays,
　And then tie up her stockings
He kissed her lovely lips,
　What a darling he did think
　　her,
But she soon gave him the slip,
　And bolted with the tinker.

A single man again,
　His lordship now will be, sirs,
Just threescore and eighteen,
　But another wife wants he,
　　sirs,
To cuddle him at night,
　And his old knees be warm-
　　ing,
What a lark if his next wife
　Should cut away in the morn-
　　ing.
She got old Fidgets off,
　Made cock sure all right,
And with the Yorkshire blade
　She danced a jig at night.

H. Disley, Printer, 57, High Street, St. Giles, London.

131

MARRIAGE OF THE
Blooming Lady and the Groom.

There was a beauty bright,
　At Woking she did dwell,
Her father had a handsome groom,
　And his daughters loved him well.
They used to trot away,
　Conversing on the land,
Oh ! Alice Caroline dearly loved
　Her father's servant man.

Alice loved her father's groom,
　She longed to take his hand,
No one can separate her
　From her father's servant man.

She is twenty years of age,
　As blythe as e'er was seen,
And George, the groom, was a youth in bloom,
　Is aged but eighteen.
She dearly loved her George,
　She by his side would stand,
She vowed no one should part her,
　From her father's servant man.

George and Caroline would toy,
　Each other they would please,
Each other they would kiss,
　And tiddle each other's knees.
They swore by all above,
　Did together fondly plan,
To dear each other, lovely
　Alice and her servant man.

From Woking they set out,
　Thinking e'er they far had got,
A lovely chance they'd have
　To tie the lovers' knot.
They disappointed was,
　And they amazed did stand,
Then young Alice went to Wandsworth
　With her father's servant man.

The banns they did put up,
　Alice and her father's groom,
And in Love Lane, in Wandsworth,
　They together took a room :
Saying they were man and wife.
　As the young lady blythe did stand,

Vowed she would lose her life,
　Or wed her father's servant man.

But mark ! young men and maids,
　Sad was the lovers' fate ;
They were by her father took
　Before the magistrate ;
Alice boldly faced them all,
　As she at the Bar did stand,
And swore she ran away
　With her father's servant man.

Have her Georgy Smith she would
　For he had gained her heart ;
No power in the world,
　She and her groom should part.
Like a maiden in despair,
　She would wander through the land,
If they would not let her wed,
　Her father's servant man.

May they both united be,
　And live a happy life,
May the pretty sweet Miss Crosse,
　Be a kind and loving wife ;
And may she ne'er regret
　She did at the altar stand,
By the side of Georgy Smith,
　Her father's servant man.

You Weybridge pretty girls,
　You Chertsey lads and lasses gay,
Can you blame me 'cause from Woking
　With my love I run away ?
You girls of Guildford town,
　Together we will trill,
To see the pleasant fair,
　At the place called Catharine Hill.

This lovely pretty maid,
　The parson's daughter all in bloom,
Declares she'll never have another man,
　Unless she has her groom.
She loves him as her life,
　And may she dance a jig,
And may she have a little boy,
　Marked with a parson's wig.

Printed for the Proprietors, Messrs. Saville, Lucky, & Co.

YELVERTON MARRIAGE CASE.

THE LADY BEAT THE SOLDIER.

YOU are all aware as well as me,
   There has been great consternation,
In Dublin has a trial been
   Which excited all the nation;
There was a blooming lady, who
   Did wed a soldier laddie,
And he was afraid of his mamma,
   And he dare not tell his daddy.
     The lady licked the soldier well,
      Cause he refused to take her,
     And the Irish lads were all so glad,
      To see her beat the Major.

He is the son of a great lord,
   Stand at ease, and order;
He took a bonny, blooming maid
   Over the Scottish border;
He told her pretty tales of love,
   Embraced her round the middle,
And when they were at Gretna Green
   The Major caught the fiddle.

He took then to Paddy's land,
   So gentle, meek, and clever,
He disgraced the Holy Church of Rome,
   He did, the naughty fellow;
He vowed that she was not his wife,
   And caused a pretty bother,
He clapped his knapsack on his back,
   Then went and married another.

Brave Serjeant Sullivan was the man,
   No lawyer could be bolder,
With gallant Whiteside went to work,
   And fired away at the soldier;
While every upright person there
   The lady pitied, who was round her,
The sheepish Major droop'd his head,
   And pop went the powder.

He was a Major, a Lord's son,
   As evil as a monkey,
All the religion that he cared about,
   Was who had got most money;

The fool was of no creed at all,
   The Church of Rome defied a sad way,
He could swear a lie thro' a nine inch wall,
   And cover his nob with pipeclay.

Now like a brick the soldier's licked,
   And his coronet is troubling,
She shamed him in the Four Courts,
   In the good old town of Dublin;
They made the naughty soldier jump,
   If the ladies could have caught him,
They would have ducked him underneath
     the pump,
And better manners taught him.

He drove the lady round and round,
   While riches she had any;
To Waterford and to Belfast,
   To Bantry and Kilkenny;
He disgraced the Holy Church of Rome,
   The naughty soldier laddy,
And all because he was afraid
Of a flogging from his daddy.

He has made a pretty kettle of fish,
   He has lost his wife and baby,
The Dublin lasses shout huzza!
   May Heaven bless the lady;
She like a brick the Major licked,
   The naughty wicked soldier,
He bolted out of Dublin town,
   With his firelock on his shoulder.

If to Gretna Green he goes again,
To play his hey down diddle,
Let the ladies pray both night and day,
That he may get the fiddle!
And then go mad to Ballinafad,
   Where they will stand no parley,
So cut your stick, your Irish licked,
   And a regular guy is Charlie.

He married a wife and then made strife,
   Such terrible tales he told her,
It was such sport in the Dublin court,
   To see Sullivan drill the soldier.

THE
NAUGHTY LORD & THE GAY YOUNG LADY,
DAMAGES, £10,000.

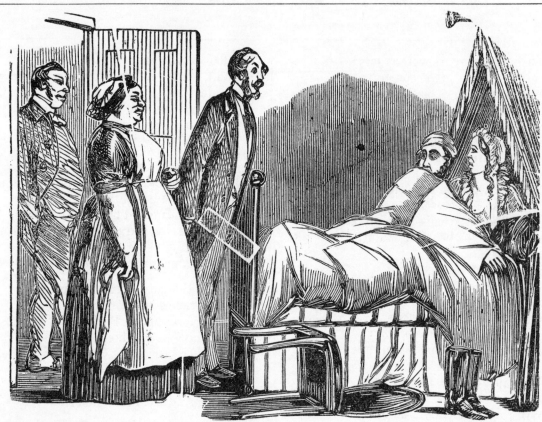

There is a pretty piece of work,
  It is up in high life,
Upon my word an amorous lord,
  Seduced another man's wife;
She was a lady of title,
  She was charming, young, and fair,
With her daddy and her mammy once
  She lived in Belgrave Square.

The trial now is over,
  And his lordship, with a frown,
For kissing Lady Nelly
  Has to pay ten thousand pounds.

Lord G—— was a naughty lord,
  Oh! how could he engage,
To seduce young Lady Ellen,—
  He is sixty years of age.
The verdict of the jury
  Made his lordship quake and jump,
Ten thousand pounds he has to pay,
  For playing tiddly bump.

Lady Nelly left her husband,
  And would with his lordship be,
She would trim his lordshlp's whiskers
  As she sat upon his knee.

Some said oh, lack-a-daisy,
  She was in a comical way!
His lordship was bald-pated,
  And his hair and whiskers grey.

My lord was very fond of lamb,—
  The cook said so at least,—
And neighbours you must understand
  He liked the belly piece.
His lordship loved the lady,
  And the lady she loved he,
His lordship played by music,
  The tune called fiddle-de-dee.

His lordship when he heard the news,
  Caused his eyes to flash like fire then
He looked around, ten thousand pounds
  His lordship holloaed, " wire-em."
He sold his hat, he pawned his coat,
  To pay the browns, we find,
And then he run round Hyde Park sqre,
  With his shirt hanging out behind.

Sweet Ellen was a daughter
  Of my Lord and Lady C——
And once lived in a mansion,
  Yes she did in Belgrave Square,

Sweet Ellen had an husbund,
  An honest upright man,
And his lordship went a trespassing
  Upon her husband's land.

My lord was fond of sporting,
  And hunting of the hare,
He has to pay ten thousand pounds,
  The damage to repair;
His lordship played the fiddle,
  Down in Scotia's land, 'tis said,
And his lordship must have fiddled well
  Both in and out of bed.

Now all young lords take warning,
  When a hunting you do go,
In the evening or the morning
  Pray beware of "Tally-ho!"
If you are caught a trespassing
  On other people's ground,
Perhaps you'll be like old Lord G——
  Made to pay ten thousand pounds.

The lady's injured husband,
  Has nobly gained the day,
And beat old Mr December,
  Who seduced young Lady May.

H. Disley, Printer, 57, High Street, St. Giles, London.

STRIKE OF THE
JOURNEYMEN TAILORS.

Oh have you heard the jolly row,
In London all around, just now,
If not, I'll tell you all, I vow,
    It is the strike of the Journeymen Tailors
The masters and the men you see,
They cannot very well agree,
The masters they won't alter the log,
The men say they shall, so help their bob ;
The masters say the men are wrong,
But the men say they are too strong,
So I suppose they must settle it themselves
    among,
    This strike of the journeymen Tailors,

The sleeveboard and goose may idle lay,
The needle and bobkin is stowed away,
Oh, is there not the devil to pay,
    Thro' the strike of the Journeyman Tailors

Now ever since the world began,
They say nine tailors makes a man,
But do without them they never can,
    The host of the Journeymen Tailors.
For indebted to their work 'tis clear,
Is kings and dukes, and lords and peers,
They are wanted here, and wanted there,
And all they want is to play fair.
And they must get it, these men of stitches,
Or what shall we do for coats and breeches,
We must black and go naked, or hide in
    ditches
    Thro' the strike of the Journeymen Tailors.

Now the tailors are of ancient date,
Believe it's true, what I now state,
And I'll tell you the time if you'll only wait
    When the world was first blessed with a
    tailor
The first there was, tho' I never see'd him,
Had his workshop in the garden of Eden,
And I tell you he was not a green 'un,
Tho' he grew lots of cabbage to feed on ;
He stitched away when the world began,
And made fig leaf togs, A No. 1,
He was a regular Flint, and never a Dung,
    It was Adam, the first of the tailors.

What we shall do, I do not know,
If the men to work they will not go,
We shall walk about just like scarecrows,
    Thro' the strike of the Journeymen Tailors.
We shall be all rags and jags,
And only fit for the ragman's bags,
Or to make a sign for some rag shop,
With just enough left to make a mop ;
Oh wont it be a funny go,
To see the swells in Rotton Row,
With their shirt tails flying in the wind, as
    they go,
    Thro' the strike of the Journeymen
    Tailors.

An old lady the other day did run,
Into the shop of Moses and Son,
Saying, please Mr Mo, are you a Dung ;
    Don't you know there's a strike with the
    tailors !
Then round the corner she did pop,
Saying, is this not a sweating shop,
Then he holloa'd police, but it was no use,
For she flattened his nose with a ten pound
    goose,
Now they tell me the sleeveboards looked
    quite big,
And round old ——— they danced a jig,
Saying, we shall have a rest, so please the
    pigs
    Thro' the strike of the Journeymen
    Tailors.

Now let us hope we soon shall see,
The masters and the men agree,
For fair play is the style for me,
    With all classes, as well as the tailors.
If they don't go in, I do declare,
We soon shall have no breeches to wear,
But that my friend is only a joke,
So, if I offend, I am sorry I spoke.
We all for the biggest shilling fight,
And I think you will own that I am right,
But jolly good luck I say, blow me tight,
    To the whole of the Journeymen Tailors.

H. Disley, Printer, 57, High street, St. Giles.

WONDERFUL MR. SPURGEON.

Oh! there is such a wonderful man,
   Just listen to my sequel,
I'm sure throughout the British land
   There never was his equal.
He's such a chap to preach and teach,
   Father, mother, son, and daughter,
And for to hear this wonderful man
   They run from every quarter.

This wonderful man surprises the land,
   Parson, lawyer, snob, and surgeon,
From every place they run a race,
To the wonderful man call'd Spurgeon.

He can please the duke, the lord, & squire
   And ladies with gold lockets,
He can make the very sovereigns jump
   Out of old women's pockets.
He can look above, and look below,
   And deeply groan, and sigh, ah!
He can shake the rocks and swallow the
   He's a greater man than Jonah. [whale

Oh, such a sermon he can preach,
   And the congregation harras,
He has a tabernacle twice
   As big as the Crystal Palace.

He can make a Bishop jump Jim Crow,
   Turn a peeler into a carter,
He can make a parson's daughter jump
   Right bang out of her garters.

He can shake the damsels' crinoline,
   And cure a cobbler's sore throat;
He bangs the country east and west,
   And licks Johanna Southgate.
There never was since Sampson lived,
   A man on earth to match him;
Spurgeon is an out and outer, lads,
   To act the game of cadging.

If Spurgeon went into St. Paul's,
   I'm sure he'd not dissemble,
His voice would make the dome to rise,
   And St. Paul's church for to tremble.
And what do you think he does it for?
   Why, for money, I supposes;
Some say Spurgeon is a greater man,
   Than Soloman or Moses.

Oh, can't he spin a tidy yarn,
   And trick the ladies handsome,
He makes you think he's twice as strong
   As that old covey Sampson.
They'll say by and bye that he can fly,
   To kingdom come, and stop there,
Dance a hornpipe in the clouds,
   And jump to Ballinahoker.

Punch says he is a wonderful man,
   And causes many a row, sirs,
Oh, can't he make the joey's fly
   From the pockets of your trousers,
And when not vexed, he gives the text,
   He alarms the congregation;
A better beggar can't be found,
   All over this great nation.

Well, every man unto his trade,
   The cobbler, snip, and surgeon,
Many a good day's work he's made,
   So much for Parson Spurgeon.
He can make the money fly like rain,
   No man on earth can stop it,
His wonderful voice will make it jump
   Like winking out of your pocket.

H. Disley, Printer, 57, High Street, St. Giles.

A NIGHT

IN A

LONDON WORKHOUSE.

All you that dwell in Lambeth, listen for awhile,
　To a song to enlighten and amuse you,
In the workhouse only mark, there's queer doings
　after dark.
　And believe me it is true I now tell you;
It's of the ups and downs, of a pauper's life,
　Which are none of the best you may be sure, sir.
Strange scenes they do enact, believe me, it's a fact,
　In Lambeth workhouse among the casual poor,
　sir.

Oh my, what a rummy go, oh crikey, what a strange
　revelation,
Has occurred in Lambeth workhouse a little while
　ago,
And through the parish is causing great sensation.

Now a gent, with good intent, to Lambeth workhouse
　went,
　The mystery of the place to explore, sir,
Says he, without a doubt, I shall then find out,
　What treatment they give the houseless poor, sir.
So he went through his degrees, like a blessed brick,
　Thro' scenes he had never seen before, sir,
So good luck to him, I say, for ever and a day,
　For bestowing a thought upon the poor, sir.

Says he, when you go in, in a bath you are popt in,
　To flounder about just like fishes,
In water that looks like dirty mutton broth,
　Or the washings of the plates and the dishes;
Then your togs are tied up tight, to make sure all is
　right,
　Like parcels put up for a sale, sir,
A ticket then you get, as if you are for a trip,
　And a-going a journey by the rail, sir.

Then before you go to bed, you get a toke of bread,
　Which, if hungry, goes a small way to fill you,
And if not too late at night, you may chance to be all
　right,
　To wash it down with a draught of skilley;
Some they will shout out, Daddy, mind what you are
　about,
　And tip me a comfortable rug now,
And be sure you see it's whole, for I'm most jolly
　cold,
　And mind you don't give us any bugs now.

Then you pig on a dirty floor, if you can, you'll have
　a snore,
　And pass away time till the morning.
Then you're muster'd up pell mell, at the crank to take
　a spell,
　Just to give your cramp'd up body a good warming.
Then see them all in rows in their torn and ragged
　clothes,
　Their gruel and their bread they swallow greedy,
Then through London streets they roam, with neither
　friends or home,
　It's the fate of the suffering and the needy.

Now a word I've got to say, to all you who poor rates
　pay,
　Tho', of course, offence to none is intended,
Before you your poor rates pay, just well look to the
　way,
　And inquire how your money is expended;
Do as you'd be done to, that is the time of day,
　And with me you'll agree, I am sure now,
As you high taxes pay, it is but fair I say,
　To look a little to the comforts of the poor now.

Disley, Printer, 57, High street, St. Giles, London.

THE GHOST

OF

WOBURN SQUARE.

Strange doings in London there is I declare,
So listen to me and a tale you shall hear,
Some hundreds each night flock to Woburn
    Square,
   To just get a peep at the Ghost
Great consternation it has caused all around,
   And each one to his neighbour declares,
Have you seen the Ghost that each night is
    found
   A dancing round Woburn Square.

They toddle along, the lame and the blind,
The deaf and the dumb they will not stay
    behind,
Saying, to Woburn Square, hasten lads, let's
    be in time,
   And have a good look at the Ghost.

Some say that his Ghostship that walks there
    at night,
It is Mrs. Chang the Chinaman's wife,
And some say it's Muller again come to life,
   To look for the cabman his friend.
But whoever it is he has no business there,
   And he'll stand a good chance, so help my
    bob,
For disturbing the good folks of Woburn
    Square,
   To find himself some day in quod.

But whoever he is he is togg'd all in white,
And such antics he plays in the square every
    night,
Like a long scaffold pole he stands bolt up-
    right,
   This naughty Ghost of Woburn Square,
As large as the soup plates is his glaring
    eyes,
   The sight of which puts you in dread,

He's a smart little fellow about ten feet high,
   With a monstrous donkey-like head.

He escaped from St. Pancras churchyard I
    hear,
Not liking the company he had got there,
He stalks out at night just to take the fresh
    air,
   And get a drop for to moisten his clay;
He is not at all quarrelsome you must allow
   For the devil a word does he speak,
But when he is tired his Ghostship I vow
   In a jiffey he beats a retreat.

The women did holloa, the boys they did
    shout,
Mr. Ghost, how's your mother, does she know
    you're out?
The peelers was sent to put them to the
    rout,
   And clear them away from the square.
They collared some boys, but the Ghost was
    not found,
   Though they looked for him everywhere,
And some will remember the time I'll be
    bound—
   The Ghost's visit unto Woburn Square.

In my time I have heard queer ghost stories
    told,
How through keyholes they'd pop in the
    days of old,
But I can't think men such fools to come out
    in the cold,
   On purpose the people to scare;
So if it's a live ghost playing a trick,
   And you can his Ghostship come near,
The best way to pay him is with a thick stick,
   And he'd never trouble again Woburn
    Square.

H. DISLEY, Printer, 57, High Street, St. Giles's.

THE
WICKED WOMAN
OF
CHIGWELL.

Come one and all, and listen to
  This funny little song,
Concerning Mrs Harrison,
  I will not keep you long;
She in Chigwell Road resided,
  With her husband, so it's said,
She swore that Saunders on the 12th of
    March,
  Assaulted her in bed.

So listen to this funny tale,
  She tried to cause much strife,
Did this false swearing woman,—
  The Chigwell Station master's wife.

At Epping Sessions, there this case occurred.
  And she said, now only think,
That the docter, Mr. Saunders,
  With her played at tiddly-wink;
That he went into her chamber,
  When her husband left the room,
How far her story there was true,
I'll let you know full soon.

She refused to say one word about
  Her former course of life;
Oh, is she not a beauty!
  This Chigwell Station-master's wife

When the Counsel for the Docter,
  Soon put this lady down,
By asking her the manner
  She lived in Peterborough town.

Now a witness he was called,
  And when he did pop in:
Pray, do you know this gentleman?
  She cried, yes, all serene!
But whether it is true or not,
  At least the folks do say,
That he with this famed Mrs. H—
  Some funny games did play.

Round Ilford and round Epping,
  And Romford too it seems,
That she was very fond of pork,
  And she dearly loved her greens!
But to swear that Docter Saunders
  Assaulted her, 'twixt me and you,
She must tell it to the devil,
  For with us that tale won't do.

One word for Docter Saunders—
  That kind and skilful man—
She ought to be well bonneted
  And put in the prison van;
Such disgraceful dirty conduct—
  It really was too bad,
And when the Docter was discharged
  The people were right glad.

Smith, Printer, High Street, London.

T 2

MARY NEWALL,
The Artful Girl of Pimlico.

Come all you ladies list to me,
  And give me every attention,
It's all about a servant girl,
  That I am going to mention,
Mary Ann Newall is her name,
  She possessed herself of riches,
She collar'd all her master's tin,
  And swore she'd wear the breeches

Mary Newall is a nice yound girl,
  She possessed herself of riches,
In the Vauxhall Road she crack'd the crib
  And put on the pegtop breeches.

Her master went out for a walk,
  And as he abroad did roam,
I will tell you what Miss Newall did,
  While her master was from home;
She turned the house near inside out,
  Indeed I am no joker,
She cut the hair from off her head,
  And stuck it on the poker.

She got a lot of bullock's blood,
  And mixed up in a pail, Sir,
So to think that I am murdered, now
  Master will not fail, Sir;
She smashed the poker right in two,
  That no one should doubt it,
With a bit of glue, now this is true,
  She stuck the hair about it.

She in the wainscoat cut a hole,
  Just the size of a man, sir,
She smashed a window from the inside,
  Saying, I'm the girl that can, sir,
Crack a crib with any chap,
  And back up all the riches,
Then she pulled off her crinoline,
  And put on the pegtop breeches.

With new spring boots, & fine cloth vest
  And overcoat to match, sir,
With the lodger's hat & nice gold guard,
  She was up to the scratch, sir,
She had the cheek to call a cab,
  With boxes in rotation,
Saying, Cabby, old boy, as quick as you like,
  Drive off to Shoreditch Station.

Now her master soon returned home,
  The truth I do declare, sir,
Saying the house is rob'd and Mary's dead,
  Here's the poker cover'd with hair, sir
To the station-house he quick did send,
  Murder and robbery, who could doubt it,
But Detective Sheen, a clever chap,
  Soon told them all about it.

The telegraph was set to work,
  The best thing for to track her,
It was soon found she at Yarmouth was
  A smoking of her tobacco;
Drest up in slap togs, you're sure,
  Like the greatest swells of the day,
She got dead nuts on her landlady,
  And took her to the play.

Sheen, the detective, soon found her out
  And the place where she dwelt, sir,
The landlady told him, her nice young man
  Was walking with the girls, sir
But she was nabbed, cigar in hand,
  She swore she fight a duel,
Sheen says, where is your petticoats?
  I know you Mary Newall.

She sold her togs, both stays and shift,
  Hair bag, dresses, and bustle,
She had bought a pair of pegtop tights,
  To go off in a bustle;
To the Magistrate she was brought up,
  And stripped of all her riches,
The Magistrate said, take her away,
  And pull off this lady's breeches.

H. Disley, Printer, 57, High street, St. Giles.

SHE HE BARMAN
OF SOUTHWARK.

You bonny lads and lasses gay,
  Who like a bit of chaff,
I'll tell you of a She He Barman,
  And I'm sure 'will make you laugh.
She did not like the petticoats,
  So she slipped the trousers on,
She engaged herself as a barman,
And said her name was Tom.

At the Royal Mortar Tavern, London Road,
  She served the customers all round,
The She He Barman was engaged
  By Mr Frederick Brown,

She popped around the bar like steam,
  The girls and chaps did wink,
When they went in for a drop of gin,
  But little did they think
That Tommy Walker was a maid,
  When they together met,
Last night a costermonger said,
Who'd thought Tom's name was Bet.

In the morning she put on her shirt,
  Her trousers, coat, and boots,
She He Tommy Walker
  A regular swell did look ;
She could drink a little drop of stout,
  And smoke a mild cigar,
Tommy Walker, the female barman,
  Was a clever chap, oh ! la !

She had neither beard or moustache,
  And her belly was not big,
But Tom the He She barman
  Turned out to be a prig ;
She nailed the sixpences and shillings,
  And she prigged the half-a-crown ;
She three months was Tom the barman
  At Mr Frederick Brown's.

She Tom had been a sailor,
  Two years upon the main,

She was dropped from the Royal Mortar,
  On board the ship Horsemonger Lane
Three years she doffed the petticoats,
  And put the trousers on,
She served behind the counter,
  And the people called her Tom.

For years she plough'd the ocean,
  As steward of a ship,
She used to make the captain's bed,
  Drink grog and make his flip.
She could go aloft so manfully,
  This female sailor Jack,
But if she slept with a messmate,
  Why of course she turned her back.

Now tired of a sailor's life,
  She thought she'd be a star,
She got a crib at Mr. Brown's,
  To serve behind the bar,
This pretty female barman—
  Her modesty don't shock—
It is better than handling of the ropes,
  To be turning on the cocks.

If you'd seen her take them in her hand,
  You'd have said she was a caulker,
So nicely she handled them—
  She said her name was Walker.
To see her put on a butt of beer,
  And when the brewers come,
She nicely drove the spigot in,
  And then out came the bung.

The ladies like the trousers,
  Of that there is no doubt.
Many would be a barman,
  But fear they'd be found out.
Tom was not a handsome female,
  She too long had been adrift,
Since she put on the Gurnsey,
  And chucked away her shift,

H. Disley, Printer, 57, High Street, St. Giles.

141

BEAUTIFUL FOR EVER.

Well, here I am, as you may see,
A buxom lady fair and free,
I don't care what they say of me,
  I am the charming Madame Rachel;
I am the girl can carry the sway,
Make the ladies handsome, fair, and gay
To beauty I can lead them on,
I can curl and dress their sweet chignons.
I can please them all upon my word,
To say I'm wrong is quite absurd,
I can splice an old woman to a lord,
  So much for Madame Rachel.

I will stand my trial like a brick,
And to my business I will stick,
I will all the silly old ladies nick,
  My name is Madame Rachel.

Now there was an old woman, list to my
    tale,
Her name was Mrs Sparrowtail,
I promised her a husband without fail,
  She bothered Madame Rachel.
She came to me with money in hand,
She said she wanted a nice young man,
I saw the old fool had plenty of browns
She had just fifteen thousand pounds,
It was very tempting, upon my word,
I looked at her like a strayed bird,
I said I'll marry you to a lord,
  My name is Madame Rachel.

To please the old woman I did not fail,
I flattered and coaxed Mrs Sparrowtail,
Got all her money by telling a tale,
  She was pleased with Madame Rachel.
I got her a man, lawks how he did laugh
He saw Mrs Sparrowtail in the bath,
He viewed her chignon when he did her
    see,
And said that old woman won't do for me,
But I wheedled out of her money so fine,
I dressed her old chignon behind,
A lord for a husband did her fine,
  That suited Madame Rachel.

Now let the world say what they will,
I will be Madame Rachel still,
Ladies, lovely, I make you will,
  If you'll come to Madame Rachel;
To polish up, my dear, I'm clever,
I will beautify you girls for ever,
I will enamel your face, your legs and
    hands,
If you want a husband I'll yet you a
    man,
Yes, my dears, if a husband you desire,
I'll get you a marquis, a lord, or squire,
Who will look in a bath and you admire,
  Now listen to Madame Rachel.

Why should I disturb my mind,
They to punish me a way can't find,
I shall leave my ticket at Number Nine,
  Enquire for Madame Rachel;
I am the woman who can you please,
I can polish your skin, anoint your knees,
I can enamel your pretty chignons so
    clever,
I can make you all sweet beauties for ever.
I say Mrs Sparrowtail was a fool,
And of the old woman I made a fool,
To polish old ladies shall be my rule,
  It shall, says Madame Rachel.

My trial is not ended yet,
Then why should Madame Rachel fret,
I think acquitted I shall get,
  They can't hang Madame Rachel;
I think next sessions all be right,
And while I live I will do as I like,
If an old fool with plenty of browns
Only say about fifteen thousand pounds,
I will tickle her up upon my word,
I'll make her as lovely as a bird,
And if she wants a husband get her a lord.
  Am I not right, says Madame Rachel.

Disley, Printer, High Street, St. Giles,
London.

FUNNY DOINGS
IN THE CONVENT.

Strange things every day we hear,
So one and all pray draw near,
Of a strange trial you shall hear,
   Concerning life in a Convent.
In Hull, as I to you will tell,
Within a Convent I did dwell,
A Mother, as you know well,
   And a Sister of Mercy.
Her name is Starr, as I now state,
She's a perfect star, and no mistake,
So I will tell you if you will wait,
   How they treated a Nun in a Convent.

Now the trial is o'er, and the Judge did say
Mistress Starr, you have lost the day,
And five hundred pounds you'll have to pay
   For tricks that are play'd in the Convent.

Now this Nun's name it is S——n,
Who wished to lead a life serene,
And has for years an inmate been,
   And led a nice life in the Convent.
For Mrs. Starr—that merciful mother—
In her some faults would oft discover,
And led her a life, a regular drudger,
   When she was in the Convent.
This Nun she could do nothing right,
She was always wrong, both day and night,
To be a Nun is'nt nice,
   How happy they live in a Convent!

She made her on her knees to go,
Black-lead the stoves, scrub the floor,
Empty them things the name I don't know,
   And that's what she did in a Convent.
She dare not keep thimble, cotton, or rag,
Her clothes were not fit for a bone-picker's
   bag,
And would make her walk about, isn't it sad,
   When she was in the Convent.
If she snored in bed that was not right,
Or picked gooseberries that was not ripe,
This duck of a mother led her a fine life.
   Oh, who would live in a Convent?

If she dared to write, or too loud speak,
Or if of grub too much did eat,
She must lay for a month without blanket
   or sheet,
   Oh, that was a treat in a Convent!
Mrs. Starr said she once met her with a ham
And her mouth was like turkey's crammed,
And she said, sister, what are you at,
   I declare your mother is smothered in fat,
Did you ever see such an hungry glutton,
Upon sawdust you must be put on,
You put away ham if you're baulk'd of mutton,
   Said kind Mother Starr of the Convent.

When her stocking was the Judge before,
He said they're old, I'm certain sure,
Why they've been well patched behind and
   before,
   Is that what they wear in a Convent?
Yes, said the Nun, and it is a great scandal,
She says grease is dear, and I must not use
   candle,
And as for the grub I could'nt handle,
   Whilst I was in the Convent.
It would puzzle Old Nick with her to agree,
And as for mercy, small share she gave me,
So I think my Lord Judge, you plainly may
   see,
   It's no joke to live in a Convent.

So ladies all, don't think it a sin,
If your husband at night you can't keep in,
Send for Mrs. Starr, and bundle him in,
   And give him a month in a Convent;
He'll miss his wife to tuck in the clothes,
To make him gruel and tallow his nose,
For one dose will cure him I do suppose,
   If he only gets in a Convent.
Now you young lasses, my song is near done,
And I would advise you everyone,
To ask Mrs Starr to make you a Nun,
   And have a peep at her Convent!

W. S. Fortey, General Steam Printer and Publisher, 2 & 3, Monmouth Court, Bloomsbury.

THE DUNMOW
FLITCH OF BACON.

Come all you married couples gay,
Get up before the break of day,
To Dunmow then pray haste away,
    To gain the flitch of bacon ;
There is such pleasure, mirth and glee,
The married folks will have a spree,
They'll try for love and victory,
    And the Dunmow Flitch of Bacon.

So lads and lasses haste away,
And do not make the least delay,
And to Dunmow town pray haste away,
    And carry off the bacon.

There's special trains from distant parts,
Young and old, with joyful hearts,
In coaches, gigs, and donkey carts,
    Have come to the flitch of bacon ;
Sound the trumpets, beat the drums,
See how the lads and lasses run,
To Burton's meadow they have come,
    To view the flitch of bacon.

A man and wife must married be,
Just a twelvemonth and a day.
And never have a quarrel they say,
    To get the flitch of bacon ;
And when they gain the prize, we hear,
They'll carry them round the town on a chair,
And give them many a lusty cheer,
    And show the flitch of bacon.

There's a grand procession through the town,
And Mr. Smith, he has come down,
We'll drink his health in glasses round,—
    Success to the flitch of bacon ;
Young men and maids like summer bees,
We'll roam beneath the shady trees,

Come marry me quick now, if you please,
    And next year we'll get the bacon.

Some will laugh, and some will shout,
Some on the grass will roll about,
While smart young men, without a doubt,
    Will dance with the pretty ladies ;
Bands of music sweetly play,
Smart young men and maidens gay,
To Burton's meadow they will stray,
    To talk of the flitch of bacon.

The velocipedes will races run,
The fight with clowns will cause some fun,
And maypole dancing will be done,
    To please the folks of Dunmow ;
There's punch and judy, all so gay,
The clowns they will at cricket play,
To the circus the folks will haste away,
    To see Bluebeard at Dunmow !

Now when the sport it is all done,
And the flitch of bacon carried home,
Some scores will to the pop-shop run,
    With bolsters, quilts, and blankets ;
Coats and waistcoats, gowns and shawls,
Shirts, chignons, and parasols,
Will have to go to the golden balls,
    To pay for the spree at Dunmow.

So now to finish up my lay,
Take my advice, young ladies gay,
Get married now without delay,
    And try for the flitch of bacon ;
For the Essex lads they are so sly,
And you had better mind your eye,
Or next year you may have a girl or a boy,
    Marked with a flitch of bacon !

H. Disley, Printer, 57, High Street, St. Giles, London.

LAST DYING SPEECH

And Farewell to the World

OF THE

LORD MAYOR'S SHOW,

**Who suffered the extreme penalty of the law, Saturday,
November 9th, 1867.**

Come one and all, pray listen to my ditty,
Good times have gone by,—oh dear what a pity !
The procession this year I have to relate,
And how on the ninth they will all go in state.

They all shake their heads and say it's no go,
It's the last dying speech of the Lord Mayor's Show.

At half-past eleven, by the word of command,
From Guildhall will tumble a big German Band ;
With mounted police,—to you it is plain—
On their hats stuck a lamp with a portrait of Mayne

Old Alderman Gobble with a large Chinese gong,
Six girls with six shoelacks stuck on their chignons
They set backside before, and so on you will find,
And for reins hold the ribbons that hang down behind.

There's the old Lord Mayor stuck on a blind horse
Like an old turtle, with his fat legs across ;
It will make him sore behind if he has a long ride,
He has lost the key, or he would creep inside.

Then the sword-bearer he will make a start,
He sits like a king in an old donkey cart ;
He sold his hairy cap to make him a muff,
And he has broke his sword on the old donkey's duff.

The great City Marshall, he is not much use,
He is flying about like a one-legged goose ;
He is here and he's there, and he's off in a crack,
You would think he had swallowed the New Streets Act.

The poor men in armour are not here to day,
Through last year's exertion they sweated away ;
They are selling fusees—it's a very bad trade,
And all the poor horses into sausages are made.

There's old Parson Spurgeon, as sly as a fox,
On a chair with two sticks, just like a Guy Faux ;
With tracts in his hand, you soon will him spy,
And a dish of fine sprats and a tear in each eye.

There's poor Gog and Magog, so it appears,
With a pail in each hand to catch their own tears,
They both weep in anguish and been heard to say
The days of our pastime are faded away.

Then comes the Lord Mayor—he makes it a rule,
He rides on the back of an Abyssinian mule ;
The great Lady Mayoress, if her sight does not fail,
She sits on behind, aud holds on to his tail.

All the old Companies have gone to the wall,
No old blokes in livery was there at all ;
The flags and the banners, as I'm a sinner,
Were put in the rag scale to get them a dinner.

Now where's the old coachman with his powdered wig ?
Who drove the state carriage so noble and big ?
If I tell you the truth, it will break your heart,
They have sold the old coach to make a muck cart,

They're stopping all pleasure, except for the swells,
In the course of time, there'll be no pretty girls ;
No pleasure for children, but you can let them know,
That a thing of the past is the Lord Mayor's Show.

For in the year '67, how funny you know,
There's a New Streets Act, and there's no Lord Mayor's
    Show.

W. Garbutt.

H. Disley, Printer, 57, High Street, St. Giles, London.

INTERNATIONAL
BOAT RACE.

Hark ; the bells are merrily ringing,
          Doodah, doodah,
The lads and lasses gaily singing,
          Oh doodah day.
With turban hair, and slender waist,
          Doodah, doodah !
They are off to see the Great Boat Race !
          Oh ! doodah day.

They pull with all their might,
  One must pull it off to day,
Through thick and thin, let the best men win,
  But give them both fair play.

Such sights were never seen on land or river,
Such wonderful things you will discover
The girl of the period—like clothes props.—
Like a stick stuck on the head of a mop !

Then a fat old lady bought a barge
To see the sight so grand and large,
Some one told her it was rotten,
So they tarr'd her bows and cork'd her
    bottom.

The next was a skiff, a gent and his daughter
Oh Pa' the boat is making water !
They were in a mess, depend upon it,
She bailed her out with her plate bonnet.

Here they come and there they go,
Quite as good as the Lord Mayor's Show ;
A scream !—what's the matter ?—that's
    something good.
A girl's heels stuck up, and her head in the
    mud.

The Americans, some say, will win it,
Look at their move, forty strokes a minute,
So you chaps you'd better look to it
Just tell me the chap or girl that can do it.

On the road some thousand lads and lasses,
Singing, laughing and drinking their glasses,
With legs as thick as cabbage stumps,
Some wearing horns like the handle of a
    pump.

Some of the girls will stop out all night,
Just to look at the stars and stripes,
Standing on tiptoe, in such a bustle,
Just to look at the men's big muscle.

The Oxford lads look good and clever,
Go it, lads, now or never !
We know what you can do if you like
Just keep down the stars and stripes.

Mr Caudle and family went on the water,
Twelve in family, sons and daughters ;
The boat went down, by hook or by crook,
They pulled them out with a boat hook.

Such a glorious sight was never seen,
But we did not expect to see the Queen ;
The Prince rode in a donkey cart,
He wack'd the moke till he made him start.

Success to the Havard, do the best they can
And the Oxford too and every man,
Let every one keep his place,
No matter to us who wins the race.

To get lodging, oh, such a bother,
They all pig in with one another,
They all lay down all of a lump,
One pillows his head on another's rump.

So rolling home so tight,
  So happy and so gay,
Success to all rowing men,—
  May the best men win the day.

H. Disley, Printer, 57, High Street, St. Giles, London.

ENGLISH
LADIES' NEW FASHIONED PETTICOATS.

Search all the world over I vow and declare,
With the ladies of England there's none can
    compare
With the sleeves on their arms like a coal-porter's
    sack,
Their cockleshell bonnets and Jack Sheppard hats.
The ladies hooped petticoats dragging around,
Just cover a mile and three-quarters of ground.

Oh, I must have a husband young Jenny did say,
I will be in the fashion so buxom and gay,
With a bustle before and another behind,
And under my trousers a big crinoline.

When I'm married, my husband upon me will
    doat,
Looking so fine in a hooped petticoat.
To have one, I'll just go a week without grub,
Or else knock out the staves of our big washing-
    tub.
There was an old lady went down through the
    Strand,
She was linked in the arms of a dashing young
    man,

Her hooped petticoat caught a coal-heaver's
    clothes.
Down he went like a donkey wop bang on his nose.

The lasses that wander the streets in the dark,
Swear they cannot get custom unless they're
    smart,
If their skin is as black as a Welch Billy Goat,
They must have a wonderful hooped petticoat.

An old farmer's wife an hooped petticoat wore,
'Twas as wide as an haystack behind and before,
The wind caught the bottom as you may suppose,
Then up in the clouds in a moment she goes.

I knew a young milkmaid at old Farmer Days,
She sold her frock and trousers, her stockings
    and stays,
From her master's beer barrel, a hoop then she
    took,
And she had it sown round her new red petticoat.

She got up one morning, so buxom and fine,
She quickly went folding her new crinoline,
She holloaed and swore such a terrible oath,
For the old cow had calved in her hooped petticoat.

A young lady of Aldershot was when it rained,
And a regiment of soldiers going over the plain.
Popped into a place, just for shelter they took,
The whole regiment stood under her hooped
    petticoat !

Good people, beware ! as you pass through the
    streets,
If a girl with a crinoline you chance for to meet,
Take care as you ramble along in a group,
Or, you may get caught in a hooped petticoat.

There was a sweet duchess a lap dog had got,
She had lost it one morning and cried such a lot,
But oh, lack-aday, she beheld in a group,
A bitch and nine pups in her hooped petticoat.

They say that the queen has a crinoline on,
And so has Prince Albert and buxom Lord John,
We expect to see Palmerston next week afloat,
Strutting up round May Fair in a hooped petticoat.

H. DISLEY, Printer, 57, High Street, St. Giles.

THE
SUPPRESSION OF CRINOLINE.

Tune—"A Kiss and Nothing More."

Good people give attention, and listen to my
    rhyme,
I'll sing about the fashions that's in vogue
    the present time,
The ladies now have bustles, now don't they
    cut it fine,
With their dandy hat and feathers, and fancy
    crinoline?

As I walked through the streets, not many
    days ago,
I met a girl who said, she was looking for a
    beau,
She invited me to go with her, I said I did
    not mind;
She looked just like a lady, dressed up in a
    crinoline.

She took me to a splendid house, with cush-
    ions on the chairs,
She treated me to brandy—and took me up
    the stairs,
She undressed me so kindly, and said she
    would be mine;
But I cursed the hour I admired her hand-
    some crinoline.

I had a splendid watch and chain, I'd gold
    and silver, too,
But in the morning when I woke I scarce
    knew what to do,

For in the middle of the night, after treat-
    ing me so kind,
She stole my money, watch and clothes, and
    left me her crinoline.

There's a pretty bobbin winder, they call
    her Mary Jane,
She's courting a snob! so help my bob, that
    lives in —— lane;
Last Sunday afternoon, she thought to cut
    it fine,
With the hoop of her mother's washing tub,
    she made a crinoline

I knew a steam loom weaver so cunning and
    so sly,
She had got a hump upon her back, and
    she squints with one eye,
She works at —— factory, her name is
    Anne O'Brian,
Her smock's as black as a chimney back and
    wears a crinoline.

There's a woman lives up —— road, they
    call her mother ——,
She wants to buy a crinoline, to wear under-
    neath her gown?
But her husband would not let her, and when
    she was confined,
She had a son mark'd on the bum, with a
    lady's crinoline!

London :—H. SUCH, Printer, 123, Union Street, Boro', and at 83, White Cross Street, St. Luke's.

THE DOWNFALL OF
CHIGNONS.

You lasses of ——— come list to my song,
'Tis concerning the fate of the fancy chignon;
The ladies of Paris are determined 'tis said,
To wear their own hair at the back of their head.
They have given o'er wearing such queer looking lumps
Of nasty old rubbish screw'd up in great bumps,
To cast them adrift they have made up their minds,
To be ugly for ever they don't feel inclined.

CHORUS.

The Chignons are going we're happy to hear,
From the young Ladies they must now disappear,
They are not in the fashion and soon must be gone,
It's all up the spout with the saucy chignon.

'Tis a good job they're going, for the darling young girls
I am sure would look better in natural curls;
Madame Rachel has worn such a wopper 'tis said,
She is quite bandy-leg'd thro' the weight of her head:
Girls that want to be married before Whitsuntide,
Pull off your Chignons and throw them aside,
If you practice economy you'll find it true,
That a fancy chignon will make bustles for two.

Those buxon old ladies who like to be gay,
At the change in the fashions are out of the way,
For with wig and chignon they all come the grand,
Tho' their heads are as bald as the palm of my hand.
The ladies at first will feel rather strange,
They will get light-headed I hope by the change,

It will seem rather awkward at first I suppose,
To wear hats on their heads now, instead of their nose.

Now what's to be done with the left off chignons,
They are sure to amount to some millions of tons!
To set them on fire would make all the world sneeze,
And slaughter some thousand industrious fleas;
For bachelors they would do very fine,
Or three in a bunch for a pawnbroker's sign;
They'd pay very well to boil down for grease,
Or they would make some good beds for the country
        police.

If the chignons were gathered, it would be a treat
To see them made use of for pitching the street,
Or perhaps they would do, either black, red, or brown,
To fill up the quaries about the ———Downs:
If the Volunteers had them they'd make cannon balls.
And tell ——— enemies to look out for squalls,
If a foe should come here to do us a wrong,
They'd get blow'd to old Nick with a charge of
        chignons.

The poor cows and horses will welcome the change,
And pigs with their bristles on freely will range,
No more county crops for the women in jails,
Nor donkeys lamenting the loss of their tails.
No more bags of sawdust to way down your heads,
Nor rags tied in bundles as big as a bed,
The ladies declare that the fashion is gone,
They've clapp'd the bumbailiffs on all the chignons.

London :—H. SUCH, Machine Printer and Publisher, 177, Union Street, Borough, S.E.

THE DANDY HORSE, OR THE WONDERFUL
VELOCIPEDE.

Queer sights we every day do find,
  As the world we pass along,
The ladies hoops and crinolines,
  And then their large chignons;
To come out in French fashion,
  Of course we must indeed,
And have a dandy horse,—
  The famed Velocipede.

The dandy horse Velocipede,
  Like lightning flies, I vow, sir,
It licks the railroad in its speed,
  By fifty miles an hour, sir,

The lasses of the period,
  Will cut along so fine,
With their hair just like a donkey's tail,
  A hanging down behind;
Upon a dandy horse will go,
  And behind them footman John,
Whose duty will be to cry, gee-wo!
  And hold on their chignon.

The Velocipedes are all the go,
  In country and in town,
The patent dandy hobby-horse
  It every where goes down;
A wheel before and one behind,
  Its back is long and narrow,
It's a cross between the treading mill,
  And a Razor Grinder's barrow.

All the world will mount velocipedes,
  Oh wont there be a show
Of swells out of Belgravia,
  In famous Rotten Row;
Tattersall's they will forsake,
  To go there they have no need,
They will patronise the wheel wright's now
  For a famed Velocipede,

All kinds of Velocipedes
  Will shortly be in use,
The snob will have one like a last,
  The tailor like a goose!

Bill Gladstone he will have one,
  To ride, so-help-me bob,
The head will be the Irish Church,
  The tail Ben Dizzy's nob

Old Sal Brown to her husband said
  There is no use of talking,
I must have a dandy hobby-horse,
  For I am tired of rocking;
Your leather breeches I will spout,
  And send you bare on Monday,
If I don't have a Velocipede
  To ride to church on Sundays.

What will the poor horse-dealers do,
  I am sure I cannot·tell,
Since the dandy horses have come up
  Their horses they can't sell;
Oh, won't the cats and dogs be glad,
  Their grub they will get cheap,
Or else it will be all bought up
  To sell for Paupers' beef.

The Velocipedes are rode by swells,
  Tinkers too and tailors,
They will be mounted, too, by the police,
  The soldiers and the sailors;
An old lady who lives in————
  At least the story goes, sir,
Is a going to race the omnibus,
  All down the————road, sir,

The railways they will be done brown,
  The steamboats too, beside,
For folks when they go out of town,
  The Velocipedes will ride;
But I'd have you look out for squalls
  Or else you may depend,
You will go down, dandy horse and all,
  And bruise your latter-end.

Disley, Printer, 57, High street, St. Giles, London.

THE
LORD MAYOR'S SHOW.

Now all you gay people, be off in a jiffy,
To see this grand sight in London city,
If you do not go, it will be a pity,
  Such a beautiful Lord Mayor's Show;
If my Lord Mayor should give up the old
    coach,
In an old dung cart he will approach,
As sleek as an eel, as sly as a roach,
  Such a big bellied man is the mayor.

Ride a cock horse to old Charing Cross,
To see the Lord Mayor on an old horse,
But where is the Mayoress we are at a loss,
  Such a beautiful Lord Mayor's Show.

The Queen won't be there, as I am sinner,
She has gone to Scotland to get a dinner,
Scotch oatmeal and burgoo, to make her
    thinner,
  So much for Vickey our Queen.
To travel the highlands her little feet itches,
To see them big men without any breeches,
With such fine looking fellows with big legs
    to match it,
  They would look very well at the show.

Here comes the lady, we thought not so fast,
By the side of the Night Mayor on a jackass;
Her head through Temple Bar cannot pass, sir,
  Something new at the Lord Mayor's Show.
Then the old watermen, wicked old sinners,
One eye on the Mayor and one on their dinner,
As for the mock birds, they're wonderful
    thinner,
  So make haste to the Lord Mayor's Show.

As for Old Lawrence his hopes is all blighted.
A few weeks ago he was quite delighted,
He thought he was going to be knighted,
  He'll look like a pig at the New Cattle
    Show.
They go on the bridge instead of going under,
Perhaps dance on the viaduct, or else it's a
    wonder,
Gog and Magog won't stand it, they bawl
    out like thunder,
  And weep for the good old show.

God bless the Queen, for her we may mourn,
But we think she might give England a turn,
And then perhaps she might something learn
  By going to the Lord Mayor's show.
Such sights as these enliven the nation,
Puts trade into hands, and keeps off starvation;
And every man ought to have a good situation,
  So to visit the Lord Mayor's show.

Some is fond of a load of oatmeal & cabbages,
Some take a delight in the bare legg'd
    savages,
While England crime and poverty ravages,
  So welcome the Lord Mayor's show.

H. DISLEY, Printer, 57, High Street, St. Giles's.

OPENING OF THE VIADUCT
BY THE QUEEN.

Come lads and lasses, be up in a jiffy,
The Queen is about to visit the City,
That her visits are so scarce, we think it a pity,
   She will open the Viaduct and Bridge.
With the Lord Mayor Elect like a porpoise,
Big round as an elephant is his old corpus,
To see this great sight nothing shall stop us,
   Gog and Magog shall dance with the Queen.

Oh dear, what can the matter be,
The Queen she is coming on a velocipede,
How nicely she treads it with high heels and
      buckles.—
She will open the Viaduct and Bridge.

The Mayor, Mr Lawrence will take off his hat,
He would like to be Whittington without
    the cat,
There's old Alderman Besley, all blubber and
    fat,
   They are going to welcome the Queen,
Girls of the period, of every station,
With hair down their backs of all occupations,
That would frighten Old Nick out of this
    nation,
   It's all just to please our good Queen.

All the good clothes that is got upon tally,
They'll put on this day as they look at the
    valley,
Dusty Bob, Tom, and Jem, and African Sally,
   These bye-gones will visit the Queen.
All the old horses will jump for joy,
'Twas up Holborn Hill that did them annoy,
I remember truck dragging when I was a boy,
   Good luck to the Viaduct and Bridge.

There will be all nations ashore and afloat,
Old Jack Atcheler will cut his throat,
No horses are killed, no cat's meat afloat,
   All through this great Viaduct and Bridge.
The cabman will dance in every passage,
Cow Cross is done up, you wont get a sassage,
You can travel the Viaduct like a telegraph
    message,
   Now they've opened the Viaduct & Bridge.

The banners and flags will go in rotation,
Emblems of things of every nation,
The workmen of England and emigration,
   And old Besley fighting for Mayor.
Lawrence is down as flat as a flounder,
On his belly stands the trumpet type founder,
The Aldermen in rotation playing at rounder,
   When they open the Viaduct and Bridge.

Next comes the Queen, so pretty indeed,
How nicely she sits on the velocipede,
With high heels and buckles she treads with
    ease,
   She's getting quite young is our Queen.
That Alderman Salomon out of the lane,
He holds up so stately poor Vickey's train,
Prince of Wales and Prince Tick will come
    if they can,
   Just to open the Viaduct and Bridge.

Horses and donkeys will caper like fleas,
No more sore shoulders and broken knees,
The animal Society may take their ease,
   Good-bye to the once Holborn Hill.

H. Disley, Printer, 57, High Street, St. Giles, London.

CABMEN
AND THEIR NEW FLAGS.

Oh dear, what a fuss and a bother,
From one end of this great city bang to the
    other,
The Cabmen all say they shall live in
    clover
    Now they have the Free-trade in cabs;

This Act, it is Bruce's, the Home Secretary,
And it came into force the 1st of February,
That his ideas are grand, of course you'll say
    very,
    Especially the dodge of the Flags!

Oh my, is there not an uproar
About the new regulations of Bruce's New
    Cab Law,
First the Cabby's, the badge, like school-
    boys they wear now,
    Now it's a Flag and a Ticket for Soup!

The Cab-horses now at their good luck are
    laughing,
To think their nose bags will have more
    corn and chaff in,
And cock up their noses as by us they're
    passing,
    Saying, what do you think of our Flags?

The phillibeloo of the Cab-strike, I'll never
    forget ye,
Nor who brought out the Badge, oh no, what
    a pity?
Or the Cabman's best friend, poor lamented
    dear Dickey,
    But he never thought of the Flags!

They must mount their banners up in the
    air, sir,
Nor stir from the rank till hail'd by a fare,
    sir,
And dub up their Tickets, its true I declare,
    sir,
    Yes, that is the rules of the Act.

To see their Flags stuck up, it's strange for
    to see now,
Like those that they stick on a Christmas
    tree, now,
They're stuck full of letters and on it just see
    now,
    You can ride just for sixpence a mile!

Now a man and his wife in the old fashioned
    manner,
Could ride side by side just a mile for a tanner
And two or three kids besides they could
    cram there,
    But now it's just two for a bob;

For a young one in napkins, it's true what I
    tell you,
Is considered a person, though a small one,
    it is true,
Butt, a pot-bellied Alderman is counted as
    two, now,
    To help them to pay for the Flags!

Now the Act is in force, I should not at all
    wonder
That dustmen and nightmen and coster-
    mongers
Will apply for a license and take out a number
    And mount on their foreheads a flag;
And the people they shout, tho' it's really
    too bad, sir,
As over the stones they go with their cabs, sir,
I say, old pal, I'll have your flag,
    And where is your ticket for soup.

Now cabs of all kinds they must be inspected
To see that no sand cracks are in them detected
And all the shofle shofles they will be rejected
    Now won't they look after the flags.

Now I think of the Act to say more it no use is,
They'll rechristen the cabs, & stand no excuses,
There'll be no four wheelers or hansoms,
    they'll all be called Bruce's,
    Tho' it does not say so in the act.

Disley, Printer, High Street, St. Giles's.

THE FUNNY
DIVORCE CASE.

Now list to me awhile,
   And I'll sing you a ditty,
It will cause you for to smile,
   If not, it is a pity.
It's of a crim con case,
   And it has caused sport,
Which lately did take place,
   At Westminster Divorce Court.

So all classes high and low,
   Make out this case I well can't,
But it is a funny go,
   Of rummy Lady ——.

Now this gay Lady ——
   Cannot be right, or hardly,
She said she loved other men,
   Much better than her Charley.
Some say it was her dodge,
   And nothing but hanky panky.
While others say all fudge,
   She is trying to act cranky.

But whether she is so or not,
   This Lady —— so clever,
A propensity has got,
   She has, so help me never !
She is so fond of sport,
   She has a mighty knack then,
Of proving every sort,
   Lords, Prince's too, and Captains.

When the case was in the Court,
   It caused a deal of bother,
Some said her head was hot,
   She could not tell one from t'other.
The Doctor he looked grand,
   And said censure she did not merit,

For the poor dear Lady
   Was subject to hysterics.

Now Lady ——, the dear,
   As we may understand her,
Could play the German flute,
   The organ and piano.
But she oft made a mistake,
   As some letters to us tell will,
She was in a weakly state,
   Since she has had the measles.

Charley said to her one day,
   As some queer doubts there may be,
Do tell me dear, I pray,
   How about the baby ?
Then Charley dear, said she,
   I really have forgot dear,
Whether it belongs to me,
   Or whether to the doctor.

This lady's appetite
   It really is enormous,
But whether wrong or right,
   The papers will inform us ;
She is fond of veal and ham,
   To feed she is a glutton,
She got tired of Charley's lamb,
   And longed for royal mutton.

Now husbands mind I pray,
   The lesson you have got here,
If your wives should go astray,
   Be sure you call the doctor.
Though I mean not to offend,
   I've proved the fact, and said it,
That like poor Lady ——,
   They might be troubled with hysterics.

Disley, Printer, 57, High street, St. Giles.

BRIGHTON
GRAND
VOLUNTEER REVIEW.

Lads and lasses, blithe and gay,
From town and country far away,
The young and old will come, they say,
To see the grand review, sir
There is Polly Pluck and Ginger Blue,
For fun they are always right on,
Such shaking hands and how-do-you-do
With the volunteers from London.

Such sights before has never been,
Drinking healths in wine and gin,
And the pretty girls a winking then
At the volunteers of England.

There is special trains from every part,
Old and young with joyful hearts,
With coaches, gigs, and donkey carts,
Will drive to the review, sir.
The pretty girls will dress so fine,
With their frizzly hair all down behind,
With a hat and feathers cut a shine
When at the grand review, sir.

The Cockney lads are fond of fun,
When on the downs are strolling,
And down the hill in the afternoon
The lasses will be rolling.
Blow the trumpet, beat the drum,
Away with melancholy,
Shoulder arms and fire the guns,
Let every one be jolly.

One young lady of sixty-two,
With high-heeled boots and buckles, too,
And with a crutch she had to go
To see the grand review, sir,

She on the hill was pushed about
By some great ugly fellow,
Her crutch soon broke and she fell down,
And she lost her umbrella.

There'll be Ikey Bill from Petticoat Lane
His sherbet will be selling,
And gipsies come from far and near
Your fortune to be telling.
The gents that on the stools will stand,
And in your faces smiling,
Hear's three half-crowns and a purse, my lads,
And the lot is but a shilling.

All sorts of games will be that day,
To please both old and young, sir;
If the volunteers should want a rest,
The girls will hold his gun, sir.
For good-tempered girls there will be there,
No better in England found, sir,
For if you ask them there to sit,
They're sure to tumble down, sir.

The flags so gay the bands will play,
And thousands will be mingling,
And welcome with a loud huzza
The volunteers of England.
May Queen Victoria happy be,
And all the royal family,
The Prince of Wales, cheer three times three
And the Princess Alexandra.
Now merry Punch with voice so strong,
He is all for fun and chaffing,
If you listen to his song
You'll burst your sides with laughing.

THE FROLICSOME PARSON OUTWITTED.

Come all you hearty roving blades, and
    listen to my song,
A verse or two I will unfold, and will not
    keep you long,
It is of a frolicsome parson, as you shall
    quickly hear,
That dwelt in the town of Ledbury, in the
    county of Herefordshire.

The parson being a rakish blade, and fond
    of sporting games,
He fell in love with the pretty cook, as I
    have heard the same ;
The parlour-maid found out the same, and
    in the fruit room looked,
And there she saw the parson sporting with
    the cook.

It was in nine months after she brought him
    forth a child,
Within the rectory it was born, it drove him
    nearly wild :
It proved to be a male child, at least they
    tell us so,
Then this damsel from the rectory was
    quickly forced to go.

Then the secret to unfold, it was her full
    intent,
During the time of service into the church
    she went,
Holding the child up in her arms, and on
    the parson gazed,
Saying, lovely babe, that is your dad, which
    filled him with amaze.

The congregation they all stared, the parson
    seemed confused,
And many a lad and lass no doubt, within
    them felt amused ;
Such a scene as this was never known within
    this church before,
Let us hope that it will be the last, and the
    like shall be no more.

'Twas then a court was called in town, for
    to invest the case.
There the parson, cook, and parlour-maid
    they met face to face,
And many more in court appeared, to hear
    the sport and fun,
This damsel swore the parson was the father
    of her son.

Your reverence ; you are found to blame
    the Justices declared,
Although some honest country lad you
    thought for to ensnare ;
So with all your doctrine and your skill
    unto him they did say,
A half-a-crown each week to the child
    you've got to pay.

His reverence felt dissatisfied with such a
    glorious treat,
To a higher court he did proceed, and there
    was quickly beat,
So this damsel she's victorious, the truth I
    now declare,
And his reverence is suspended for the period
    of five years.

Come all you blooming servant maids a
    warning take by this,
When in service with the parsons don't be
    treated to a kiss ;
Or it may cause much jealousy, as you may
    all well know,
Then you from service must be gone your
    sorrows for to rue.

Now to conclude and make an end and finish
    up my song,
All you young men that's deep in love, be
    sure don't stay too long ;
Join hand in hand in wedlock's band without
    the least delay,
Before the fairest of all girls is by parsons
    led astray.

THE FUNNY
HE-SHE LADIES!

We have had female sailors not a few,
And Mary Walker the female barman, too,
But I never heard such a sport, did you,
   As these swells tog'd out as ladies.
They are well known round Regent Square.
And Paddington I do declare,
Round Bruton street, and Berkeley Square,
Round Tulse Hill, and the lord knows where

At my opinion I pray don't gig,
I'll speak my mind so please the pigs,
If they are nothing else, they might be prigs
   This pair of he-she ladies.

At Wakefield street, near Regent Square,
There lived this rummy he-she pair,
And such a stock of togs was there,
   To suit those he-she ladies.
There was bonnets & shawls, & pork pie hats
Chignons and paints, and Jenny Lind caps,
False calves and drawers, to come out slap,
To tog them out, it is a fact.

This pair of ducks could caper and prance,
At the Casino they could dance,
Ogle the swells, and parle vou France,
   Could this pair of he-she ladies
They'd sip their wine and take their ice,
And so complete was their disguise,
They would suck old nick in and no flys,
Would these beautiful he-she ladies.

One day a cute detective chap,
Who of their game had smelt a rat,
Declared he would get on the track,
   Of these two he-she ladies.
So he bolted up to Regent Square,
And soon espied this worthy pair,
They hailed a cab, who took his fare,
Says the police, I am after you my dear.

They bolted off at such a rate, sir,
And in they went to the Strand Theatre,
But the game was up, so help my tater,
   Of this pair of he-she ladies.
You would not suppose that they were men,
With their large Chignons and Grecian bend,
With dresses of silk, and flaxen hair,
And such a duck was Stella dear.

When they were seated in the stalls,
With their low neck'd dresses a flowing shawl
They were admired by one and all,
   This pair of he-she ladies.
The gents at them would take a peep,
And say they are duchesses at least,
Lor ! what a fascinating pair,
Especially she with the curly hair.

The detective, Chamberlain by name,
Upon these two sham ladies came,
And said what is your little game,
   My beautiful he-she ladies.
Oh, was it not a cruel sell,
That night they must remember well,
When they had to pig in Bow Street cell,
   What a change for them he-she ladies.

When first before the magistrate,
Oh, what a crowd did them await,
It was a lark and no mistake,
   To look at them he-she ladies.
Lor ! how the people did go on,
With, I say I'll have your fine chignon,
Another cried out, Stella dear,
Pull off those togs, and breeches wear.

Now I think behind there is a tale,
Which will make this bright pair to bewail,
For on skilly and whack they might regale,
   Those beautiful he-she ladies.

H. Disley, Printer, 57, High Street, St. Giles.

"The gallows does well : but how does it do well ? It does well to those that do ill."

THE EXECUTION.

DIVISION IV.

THE "GALLOWS" LITERATURE OF THE STREETS.

PUBLIC EXECUTIONS, DYING SPEECHES. CONFESSIONS, AND COPY OF VERSES.

"There's nothing beats a stunning good murder after all."—EXPERIENCE OF A RUNNING PATTERER.

Of accounts of Public Executions, Dying Speeches, and Confessions we have those before us, stretching from the Execution of Sir John Oldcastle in 1417, to the Trial and Execution of F. Hinson, who suffered the extreme penalty of the law, at the Old Bailey, Monday, December 13th, 1869, for the wilful murder of Maria Death, to which is attached the all-important and necessary "Copy of Verses," and by way af supplement, we add a *verbatim* copy of the Full, True and Particular Account of the Execution of J. Rutterford, at Bury St. Edmunds, for the murder of J. Hight, with copy of "Death-verses." But the convict was NOT hanged after all. As the gaol surgeon having reported that Rutterford had a malformation which might cause an unusual degree of suffering on death being inflicted by strangulation, whereupon the Secretary of State for the Home Department ordered a special examination to be made by some medical men of the immediate neighbourhood, and on whose report the sentence of death previously recorded was commuted to transportation for life !

All the modern examples of THE "¡GALLOWS" LITERATURE OF THE STREETS come not only from different printers and publishers, but from distant towns,—London, Birmingham, Lincoln, and Preston, but they have all the same stamp. And the whole of the last dying speeches and confessions, trials, sentences from what ever part of the country they come, run in the same form of quaint and circumstantial detail, appeals to heaven, to young men, to young women, to christians in general, and moral reflections. The narrative, embracing trial, biography, &c., is usually prepared by the printer, being a condensation from the accounts in the newspapers. It is then necessary to add the "copy of verses." Many of these are clearly by the same hand, probably one of the five or six well-known authors, who also chaunt their own verses in the streets. And with regard to this matter—"Time being the essence of the contract,"—it must also be noted that many of the most popular "Death-verses" being composed on the spur of the moment for the purpose of being sung while all the town is ringing with the event, all niceties of rhyme, metre, and orthography have to be utterly disregarded. "I gets," says one of the fraternity, "I gets a shilling a copy for the verses *written by the wretched culprit* the night previous to his execution." "And I," says another, "did the helegy on Rush. I didn't write it to horder ; I knew that they would want a copy of verses from the wretched culprit. And when the publisher read it ; 'that's the thing for the streets,' he says. But I only got a shilling for it." "It's the same poet as does 'em all," says a third authority, "and the same tip : *no more nor a bob for nothing.*" This was paltry pay under any circumstances, but still more so when we find that in the case of the chief modern murders these "Executian Ballads" commanded a most enormous sale, thus :

Of Rush's murder	2,500,000 copies	Of the Five Pirates (Flowery Land)..	290,000 copies.
Of the Mannings	2,500,000 "	Of Müller	280,000 .,
Of Courvoisier	1,666,000 "	Of Constance Kent (trial only)	150,000 .,
Of Greenacre	1,650,000 "	Of Jeffery (1866)	60,000 "
Of Corder (Maria Martin)	1,166,000 "	Of Forward (Ramsgate)	30,000 "

So that the printers and publishers of "Gallows" Literature in general, and "The Seven Dials Press" in particular, must have reaped a golden harvest for many a long day, even when sold to the street-folks at the low rate of 3d. per *long* dozen. Mr. W. S. Fortey, the successor of the late celebrated Jemmy Catnach, stated to us during a recent conversation with him on the sale number of modern dying speeches. "Well, *I* never in *my* time printed so many as *I* did of the Five Pirates of the Flowery Land, and *I* sold them at the rate of 3,000 copies per hour, and did altogether 90,000,—that was my share. What the others did of course I can't say. I know I got a new machine out of the job !—which we now call the "Pirates," or sometimes "The Flowery Land."* Mr. Fortey furthermore informed us that his share of the "Execution Papers" of recent popular murders was as follows :—Müller, 84,000 ; Constant Kent, 15,000 ; Jeffery, 10,000¡; Forward, 5,000. Mr. Fortey's trade announcement runs thus :—"The Catnach Press." (Established 1813.) William S. Fortey, (late A. Ryle, successor to the late J. Catnach, Printer, Publisher, and Wholesale Stationer, 2 and 3, Monmouth Court, Seven Dials, London, W.C. The cheapest and greatest variety in the trade of large coloured penny books ; halfpenny coloured books ; farthing books ; penny and halfpenny panoramas ; school books ; penny and halfpenny song books ; memorandum books ; poetry cards ; lotteries ; ballads (4,000 sorts) and hymns ; valentines ; scripture sheets ; Christmas pieces ; Twelfth-night characters ; carols ; book and sheet almanacks ; envelopes, note paper, &c., &c. W. S. Fortey begs to inform his friends and the public generally, that after 19 years' service, he has succeeded to the business of his late employers (A. Ryle and Co.), and intends carrying on the same, trusting that his long experience will be a recommendation, and that no exertion shall be wanting on his part to merit a continuance of those favours that have been so liberally bestowed on that establishment during the last 46 years.

As far as can be ascertained, the sale of Broad-sheets in the Mannings and Rush's case far exceed that of any now before us. Even that of Müller did not amount to more than two hundred and eighty thousand copies—though no modern murder ever surpassed it in atrocity, or in the profound interest which it excited throughout England. And this difference is no doubt to be explained by the fact that since Mannings and Rush's day the daily penny newspapers have almost forestalled the "Dying Speeches and confessions "—with or without the "copy of verses "—by giving a full account of the different enormities in all their minute and hideous details. The force of public opinion, too, thus exerted through the Press, has been brought to bear on the question of crime, and much of the morbid sympathy which found expression in the case of such a monster as Rush, had died away in 1864, when detectives tracked Muller across the Atlantic, and brought him back to be hanged by an English hangman, in the presence of an Englsh mob. To every one of the murderers, Constance Kent at

---

* "The Pope, God bless him ? he's been the best friend I've had since Rush. Then Cardinal Wiseman. They shod me, sir." "*Who's* they ?" "Why the Pope and Cardinal Wiseman. I call my clothes after them I earn money by to buy them with. My shoes I call Pope Pius ; my trowsers and braces, Calcraft ; my waistcoat and shirt, Jael Denny ; and my coat, Love Letters. A man must show a sense of gratitude in the best way he can.—EXPERIENCE OF A RUNNING PATTERER.—*Mayhew's London Labour and the London Poor.*

Road hill house, Jeffery, Forward, at Ramsgate, and the Pirates of the "Flowery Land,"—one and all alike,—stern justice is meted out with inflexible severity, The wretched girl who at Salisbury confessed her crime to the judge, makes no excuse for her guilt, but tells only of the intolerable remorse that would give her no rest—

> "My infant brother so haunted me,
> I not one moment could happy be ;
> And if for the murder they do me try,
> I declare I'm guilty, and deserve to die."

"Scoundrels," "malefactors," "villains," are the gentlest names for this Newgate gallery, and the gallows in every case is promised, with a sort of grim satisfaction that augurs strongly for a deep popular belief in the justice of those solemn words, "Whoso sheddeth man's blood, by man shall his blood be shed."

With the recent Act of Parliament abolishing the execution of criminals in sight of the public. Halfpenny and penny newspapers, and the capriciousness of Home Secretaries, the Dying Speech trade has in its turn received its death-blow. Still old memories and customs yet cling to the "Affectionate Copy of Verses."—"The (cooked) Love Letters" and "Confessions"—made only by the Street-Patterer, and are found sufficiently remunerative to author, printer, publisher, and vendor—But for THIS DAY ONLY !

The following is the style of "gag" and "patter" of a man formerly well-known in the "Dials" as "Tragedy Bill "—" Now, my friends, here you have, just printed and published, a full, true, and pertickler account of the life, trial, character, confession, behaviour, condemnation, and hexecution of that unfortunate malefactor, Richard Wilbyforce, who was hexecuted on Monday last, for the small charge of one ha'penny, and for the most horrible, dreadful, and wicked murder of Samuel—I means Sarah Spriggens, a lady's maid, young, tender, and handsome. You have here every pertickler, of that which he did, and that which he didn't. It's the most foul and horrible murder that ever graced the annals of British history(?) Here, my customers, you may read his hexecution on the fatal scaffold. You may also read how he met his victim in a dark and lonesome wood, and what he did to her—for the small charge of a ha'penny ; and, further, you read how he brought her to London,—after that comes the murder, which is worth all the money. And you read how the ghost appeared to him and then to her parents. Then comes the capture of the *willain* ; also the trial, sentence, and hexecution, showing how the ghost was in the act of pulling his leg on one side, and the 'old gentleman' a pulling on the other, waiting for his victim (my good friends excuse my tears !) But as Shakspeare says, 'Murder most foul and unnatural,' but you'll find this more foul and unnatural than that or the t'other—for the small charge of a ha'penny ! Yes, my customers, to which is added a copy of serene and beautiful werses, pious and immoral, as wot he wrote with his own blood and skewer the night after—I mean the night before his hexecution, addressed to young men and women of all sexes—I beg pardon, but I mean classes (my friends its nothing to laugh at), for I can tell you the werses is made three of the hard-heartedest things cry as never was—to wit, that is to say namely—a overseer, a broker, and a policeman. Yes, my friends, I sold twenty thousand copies of them this here morning, and could of sold twenty thousand more than that if I could of but kept from crying—only a ha'penny !—but I'll read the werses.

Come all you blessed Christians dear,
  That's a-tender, kind, and free,
While I a story do relate
  Of a dreadful tragedy,
Which happened in London town,
  As you shall all be told ;
But when you hear the horrid deed
  'Twill make your blood run cold.—
    For the small charge of a ha'penny !

'Twas in the merry month of May,
  When my true love I did meet ;
She look'd all like an angel bright,
  So beautiful and sweet.
I told her I loved her much,
  And she could not say nay ;
'Twas then I strung her tender heart,
  And led her all astray.—
    Only a ha'penny !

I brought her up to London town,
  To make her my dear wife ;
But an evil spirit tempted me,
  And so I took her life !

I left the town all in the night,
  When her ghost in burning fire,
Saying, "Richard," I am still with you,
  Whenever you retire.—
    Only a ha'penny !

And justice follow'd every step,
  Though often I did cry ;
And the cruel Judge and Jury
  Condemned me for to die,
And in a cell as cold as death,
  I always was afraid,
For Sarah she was with me,
  Although I killed her dead.—
    For the small charge of a ha'penny !

My tender-hearted Christians,
  Be warned by what I say,
And never prove unkind or false
  To any sweet la'-dy.
Though some there, who wickedness
  Oft leads 'em to go astray,
So pray attend to what you hear.
  And a warning take I pray.

THE LIFE & EXECUTION
OF
SIR JOHN OLDCASTLE
AT THE
NEW GALLOWS,
AT
ST. GILES'S IN THE FIELDS,
ON
THE 19TH OF DECEMBER, 1417.

Who was Hang'd as a Traytor, and Burnt as a Heretick.

At the beginning of the reign of Henry V., about the year 1413, the anger of the clergy was excited against the *Lollards*, and they fabricated a report of a pretended conspiracy among them, headed by Sir John Oldcastle, or, as he was called by courtesy, Lord Cobham, in his wife's right.

Lord Cobham has the honour of being the first author and the first martyr among the nobility of England. He was a man of considerable natural abilities, proficient in literature, of a ready wit, and skilled in the affairs of the cabinet or in the field. In his love for philosophy, he had perused the writings of Wickliffe, and in so doing unconsciously absorbed the leaven of evangelical and spiritual religion. When persuaded of the truth of those doctrines he enrolled himself as a disciple, and did all in his power for their spread, both by his gifts and personal efforts. He transcribed the works of Wickliffe; he supported various preachers, and became the acknowledged leader of the rising reformation. The hostility of the church was, of course, an inevitable result.

Sir John being convicted of heresy, the Archbishop waited upon the King, and gave him an account of the proceedings against him, and moved his Majesty that the execution might be respited for 50 days, which was readily granted by the King, as well as the Archbishops, being desirous to preserve Sir John Oldcastle.

Sir John before the fifty days expired, made his escape out of the Tower, and endeavoured to secure himself by making an insurrection. To this purpose he wrote letters to his friends, to engage their Party, and make them ready for the Field, to surprise the King, and overturn the Government.

The King being apprised of the danger, on the 6th of January, 1414, removed from Eltham to his palace at Westminster, but without any appearance of alarm. The Rebels were just upon the execution of their design, being drawn together by Sir John Acton, Knight, John Brown, Esq., and John Beverly, a priest, in Ficket-field, on the backside of St. Giles's; hither they came in the dead of night, expecting to join their General, Sir John Oldcastle.

The King came into the field before Day, where several of the Rebels, mistaking their party, fell in with the King's forces; and it being demanded whither they were going, they answered, to my Lord Cobham. The King, to prevent their getting together, had ordered the City Gates to be shut and guarded, without which precaution 'tis thought the Londoners would have reinforced their party to a very formidable body, but being disappointed of this succour they soon dispersed, and several of them were killed or taken prisoners.

And the King set a thousand Marks upon Sir John Oldcastle's head, with a promise of great Privileges to any town that should deliver him up. An Indictment of High Treason was found against Sir John in the King's Bench, for conspiring the Death of the King, the Subversion of the Established Religion and Government, and Levying War, whereupon he was outlawed.

Sir John Oldcastle was near being surprised in the neighbourhood of St. Alban's, at a farmhouse belonging to the Abbot of that town, *anno* 1417; for the Abbot being informed Sir John lay concealed at one of his Tenants, sent some of his servants, in the night, to beset the house, and though they missed of Sir John, they seized some of the principal men of his party. They found also several religious Books, adorned with paintings, which the *Lollards* esteeming superstitious, cut off the Heads of the Figures, and also erased the Names of the Saints out of the Litanies; they also found scandalous Papers in Dishonour of the blessed Virgin. These Books were sent over to the King into Normandy, and by him returned to the Archbishop.

Upon the occasion the *Lollards* were loudly disclaimed against at St. Paul's Cross, and a tragical Representation made of the Matter, and not long after Sir John Oldcastle was taken in Powis Lands in Wales. He stood upon his Defence, fought those that came to apprehend him, and refused to surrender his Person till he was wounded and disabled.

Sir John Oldcastle having been outlawed upon an Indictment for High Treason, for that he with divers others called *Lollards*, to the number of Twenty Thousand, had assembled themselves at *St. Giles's in the Fields*, levyed War, and conspired the Death of the King and the Subversion of the Religion and Government established, and standing also excommunicated for Heresy, he was brought before the Parliament on the 18th of December, 1417, and it being demanded what he had to say why Execution should not be awarded against him according to Law, he ran out into a Discourse foreign to the matter, concerning the Mercy of God, &c., whereupon the Chief Justice required him to answer directly, if he had anything to object against the Legality of the Process; he replyed, *he could not own them for his judges, as long as his Sovereign Lord King Richard was living in Scotland.* Upon this Answer a Rule was made for his Execution, *viz.,* That he should be carried back to the Tower, and from thence drawn through London to the New Gallows at St. Giles's in the Fields, and there be hanged, and burnt hanging, which Sentence was executed with Rigour. He was hanged as a Traytor, and burnt as a Heretick.

The DYING SPEECHES and EXECUTION of John Ballard, priest; Anthony Babington, Esq.; John Savage, Gent.; Robert Barnwell, Gent.; Chidiock Titchborne, Esq.; Charles Tilney and Edward Abington, Gent. (Seven of the Conspirators against Queen Elizabeth) for High Treason

On the 20th of September, 1586, a Gallows being set up on purpose in St. Giles's Fields, where they us'd to meet, these seven were drawn thither to their Execution.

John Ballard, the Priest, the principal Conspirator, confess'd, that he was guilty of those things for which he was condemned, but protested they were never enterprised by him upon any hope of preferment, but only, as he said, for the advancement of true Religion. He craved pardon and forgiveness of all persons, to whom his doings had been any scandal, and so made an end; making his prayers to himself in Latin, not asking her Majesty forgiveness, otherwise than if he had offended.

Anthony Babington, Esq., also confessed, That he was come to die, as he had deserved; howbeit that he (as Ballard before) protested that he was not led into those actions upon hope of preferment, or for any temporal respect; nor had ever attempted them. For his wife, he said, she had good friends, to whose consideration he would leave her: And thus he finished, asking Her Majesty forgiveness, and making his prayers in Latin.

John Savage, Gent., confessed his guilt, and said (as the other two before) that he did attempt it, for that in conscience he thought it a deed meritorious, and a common good to the weal publick, and for no private preferment.

Robert Barnwell, Gent, confessed that he was made acquainted with their Drifts, but denied that ever he consented, or could be in conscience persuaded that it was a deed lawful. I crave forgiveness; if the sacrifice of my body might establish her Majesty in the true religion, I would most willingly offer it up. Then he prayed to himself in Latin.

Chidiock Titchbone, Esq., began to speak as followeth, *viz.*, Countrymen and my dear Friends, you expect I should speak something; I am a bad Orator, and my text is worse: It were in vain to enter into the discourse of the whole matter for which I am brought hither, for that it hath been revealed heretofore, and is well known to the most of this company; let me be a warning to all young gentlemen, especially *generosis adolescentulis* I had a friend, and a dear friend, of whom I made no small account, whose friendship hath brought me to this; he told me the whole matter, I cannot deny, as they had laid it down to be done; but I always thought it impious, and denied to be a dealer in it; but the regard of my friend caused me to be a man in whom the old proverb was verified; I was silent, and so consented. Before this thing chanced, we lived together in most flourishing estate; of whom went report in the Strand, Fleet street, and elsewhere about London, but of Babington and Titchbone? No threshold was of force to brave our entry. Thus we lived, and wanted nothing we could wish for; and God knows, what less in my head than matters of State? Now give me leave to declare the miseries I sustained after I was acquainted with the action, wherein I may justly compare my estate to that of Adam's, who could not abstain one thing forbidden, to enjoy all other things the world could afford; the terror of conscience awaited me. After I consider'd the dangers whereinto I was fallen, I went to Sir John Peters, in Essex, and appointed my horses should meet me at London, intending to go down into the country. I came to London, and there heard that all was bewrayed; whereupon, like Adam, we fled into the woods to hide ourselves, and there were apprehended. My dear countrymen, my sorrows may be your joy, yet mix your smiles with tears, and pity my case. This done, he prayed first in Latin, and then in English, asking Her Majesty, and all the world, heartily, forgiveness, and that he hoped, stedfastly, now at this his last hour, his faith would not fail.

Charles Tilney said, I am a Catholick, and believe in Jesus Christ, and by his Passion I hope to be saved; and I confess I can do nothing without him, which opinion all Catholicks firmly hold. He prayed in Latin for himself, and after he prayed for Queen Elizabeth, that she might live long; and warned all young gentlemen, of what degree or calling soever, to take warning by him.

Edward Abington said, I come hither to die, holding all points firmly that the Catholick Church doth; and for the matters whereof I am condemned, I confess all, saving the death of Her Majesty, to the which I never consented. He feared, as he said, great bloodshed in England before it were long.

Ballard was first executed. He was cut down and bowell'd with great cruelty while he was alive. Babington beheld Ballard's execution without being in the least daunted; whilst the rest turned away their faces, and fell to prayers upon their knees. Babington being taken down from the gallows alive too, and ready to be cut up, he cried aloud several times in Latin. *Parce mihi Domine Jesu*, spare or forgive me O Lord Jesus! Savage broke the rope, and fell down from the gallows, and was presently seized on by the Executioner, his privities cut off, and his bowels taken out while he was alive. Barnwell, Titchborne, Tilney, and Abington were executed with equal cruelty.

The DYING SPEECHES and EXECUTION of Thomas Salisbury, Henry Donn, Edward Jones, John Charnock, John Travers, Robert Gage, Jerome Bellamy, for High Treason, the 21st of September, 1586. Being drawn to the place of Execution.

Thomas Salisbury, Esq., since it hath pleased God to appoint this place for my end, I thank his infinite goodness for the same; I confess that I have deserved death, and that I have offended her Majesty, whom to forgive me I heartily beseech, with all others whom I have any way offended; I desire all true Catholicks to pray for me, and I desire them, as I beseech God they may, to endure with patience whatsoever shall be laid upon them, and never to enter into any action of violence for remedy. Thus done, he cried in English and Latin, Father, forgive me.

Henry Donn, Yeoman, said, Do the people expect I should say anything? I was acquainted, I confess, with their practices, but I never did intend to be a dealer in them: Babington oftentimes requested me to be one, and said, for that he loved me well, he would bestow me in one of the best actions; which should have been the delivery of the Queen of Scots, to which I could not for a long time agree; at length, by many urgent persuasions he won me, so as I told him I would do my best: And being asked, as he was ascending the ladder, whether he thought it lawful to kill her Majesty: He answered, No, no. No soul was more sorrowful than his, nor none more sinful; and prayed for her Majesty, wishing she might live in all happiness, and after this life, be eternized in everlasting bliss; and so he prayed in Latin and English.

Edward Jones said, I come hither to die, but how rightfully God knows; for thus stands my case: At Trinity Term last, Mr Salisbury made me acquainted with their purposes; and for that he knew me to be well horsed, he thought me as fit as any to attempt the delivery of the Queen of Scots, and requested me to be one; which I utterly denied, altogether misliking their practices, and persuading him, by what means I might, from it; and told him, this was the haughty and ambitious mind of Anthony Babington, which would be the destruction of himself and friends, whose company I wished him to refrain; and for that I would have him out of his company; I have divers times lent him money, and pawned my chain and jewels to buy him necessaries to go into the country, and so concluded with his prayers, first in Latin, and then in English, that the people might better understand what he prayed.

John Charnock and John Travers having their minds wholly fixt on prayer, recommended themselves to God and the Saints. Gage extolled the Queen's great grace and bounty to his father, and detested his own perfidious ingratitude towards his Princess. And Jerome Bellamy, with confusion and deep silence, suffered last.

The Queen being informed of the severity used in the executions the day before, and detesting such cruelty, gave express orders that these should be used more favourably; and accordingly they were permitted to hang till they were quite dead before they were cut down and bowell'd.

THEIR CHARACTERS.

The Conspirators were most of them gentlemen of good families, whom nothing but the specious pretence of religion could probably have prevailed upon to turn affairs.

THE EXECUTION OF BALLARD, &c.

The history of the plot in which Ballard, Babbington, Tichbourne, and others, were engaged in 1586, is well known. The subsequent ballad, by the celebrated Thomas Deloney, (his initials T.D. being at the conclusion of it) was no doubt printed immediately after the execution of the " fourteen most wicked traitors," on the 20th and 21st September. At the top of the broadside are woodcuts of fourteen heads, but they are not likenesses, but merely engravings which the printer happened to have in his possession, and which had been already used for Hill's work on Physiognomy, and perhaps for other publications requiring illustrations.———*

A proper new Ballad, breefely declaring the Death and Execution of 14 most wicked Traitors, who suffered death in Lincolnes Inne Fielde, neere London : the 20 and 21 of September, 1586.

TO THE TUNE OF "WEEP, WEEP."

REJOYCE in hart, good people all,
　Sing praise to God on hye,
Which hath preserved us by his power
　From traitors tiranny ;
Which now have had their due desarts,
　In London lately seen ;
And Ballard was the first that died,
　For treason to our Queene.

　　O praise the Lord with hart and minde,
　　Sing praise with voices cleare ;
　　Seth traitorous crue, have had their due
　　To quaile their partener's cheere.

Next Babington, that caitife vilde,
　Was hanged for his hier ;
His carcasse likewise quartered,
　And hart cast in the fier.
Was ever seen such wicked troopes
　Of traytors in this land,
Against the pretious woord of truthe,
　And their good Queene to stand ?
　　Oh praise, &c.

But heer beholde the rage of Rome,
　The fruits of Popish plants ;
Beholde and see their wicked woorks,
　Which all good meaning wants :
For Savage also did receave
　Like death for his desert,
Which in that wicked enterprise
　Should then have doon his part.
　　O praise, &c.

O cursed catifes, void of grace,
　Will nothing serve your turne,
But to behold your cuntries wrack,
　In malice while you burne?
And Barnwell thou, which went to view
　Her grace in each degree,
And how her life might be dispatcht,
　Thy death we all did see.
　　O praise, &c.

Confounding shame fall to their share,
　And hellish torments sting,
That to the Lords annointed shall
　Devise so vile a thing.
O Techburne, what bewitched thee
　To have such hate in store,
Against our good and gratious Queene,
　That thou must dye therefore ?
　　O praise, &c.

What gaine for traitors can returne,
　If they their wish did win ?
Or what preferment should they get,
　By this their trecherous sinne ?
Though forraine power love treason well,
　The traitors they dispise,
And they the first that should sustaine
　The smart of their devise
　　O praise, &c.

What cause had Tilney, traitor stout,
　Or Abbington likewise,
Against the Lords annointed thus
　Such mischeef to devise ?
But that the Devill inticed them
　Such wicked woorks to render ;
For which these seven did suffer death,
　The twentith of September.
　　O praise, &c.

Seven more the next day following
　Were drawen from the Tower,
Which were of their confederates
　To dye that instant hower :
The first of them was Salsburie,
　And next to him was Dun,
Who did complaine most earnestly
　Of proud young Babington.
　　O praise, &c.

Both lords and knights of hye renowne
　He ment for to displace,
And likewise all the towers and townes
　And cities for to race ;
So likewise Jones did much complaine
　Of his detested pride,
And shewed how lewdly he did live
　Before the time he died.
　　O praise, &c.

Then Charnock was the next in place
　To taste of bitter death ;
And praving unto holy saints,
　He left his vitall breath.
And in like maner Travers then
　Did suffer in that place,
And fearfully he left his life,
　With crossing brest and face.
　　O praise, &c.

Then Gage was stripped in his shirt,
　Who up the lather went,
And sought for to excuse him selfe
　Of treasons falce intent.
And Bellamie the last of all
　Did suffer death that daye ;
Unto which end God bring all such
　As wish our Queenes decay.
　　O praise, &c.

O faulce, and foule disloyall men,
　What person would suppose
That clothes of velvet and of silke
　Should hide such mortall foes ?
Or who would think such hidden hate
　In men so fair in sight,
But that the Devill can turne him selfe
　Into an angell bright.
　　O praise, &c.

But soveraigne Queene, have thou no care,
　For God, which knoweth all,
Will still maintaine thy royall state,
　And give thy foes a fall.
And for thy Grace thy subjects all
　Will make their praiers still,
That never traitor in this land
　May have his wicked will.
　　O praise, &c.

Whose glorious daies in England heere
　The mighty God maintaine,
That long unto thy subjects joye
　Thy Grace may rule and raigne.
And, Lord, we pray, for Christes sake,
　That all thy secret foes
May come to naught, which seeke thy life
　And Englands lasting woes.
　　O praise the Lord with hart & minde, &c.

The names of 7 Traitors which were executed on Tuesday, being the xx of September, 1586.

John Ballard Preest.	Chodicus Techburne.
Anthony Babington.	Charles Tilney.
John Savage.	Edward Abbington.
Robert Barnwell.	

The names of the other vii which were executed on the next day after.

Thomas Salsbury.	John Charnock.
Henry Dun.	Robert Gage,
Edward Jhones.	Harman Bellamy.
John Travers.	

Finis.　T.D.

* OLD BALLADS, Edited by J. Payne Collier, Esq., F.S.A.—*The Percy Society.*

Imprinted at London at the Long Shop adjoyning unto Saint Mildreds Churche in the Pultrie by Edward Allde.

THE EXECUTION OF LUKE HUTTON.

A TRACT by Luke Hutton, of which there were two editions, the first without date, and the last in 1638, is very well known, and an account of it may be found in the Bridgewater Catalogue, (privately printed for Lord Francis Egerton) p. 149. Hence it appears also that Hutton was the author of an earlier production, called his "Repentance." He seems to have been a highwayman and house-breaker, who, being condemned and pardoned, dedicated an affected piece of contrition to Lord Chief Justice Popham; and on subsequent liberation, returned to his old courses, and was hanged at York in 1598. Whether what follows, or indeed anything that goes under his name, were really written by him is very questionable.*

Luke Hutton's Lamentation: which he wrote the day before his death, being condemned to be Hanged at Yorke this last Assises for his robberies and trespasses committed.

TO THE TUNE OF "WANDERING AND WAVERING."

I AM a poore prisoner condemned to dye,
  Ah woe is me, woe is me, for my great folly!
Fast fettred in yrons in place where I lie.
  Be warned yong wantons, hemp passeth green holly.
My parents were of good degree,
By whom I would not counselled be.
Lord Jesu forgive me, with mercy releeve me,
Receive, O sweet Saviour, my spirit unto thee.

My name is Hutton, yea Luke of bad life,
  Ah woe is me, woe is me, for my great folly!
Which on the high way did rob man and wife,
  Be warned yong wantons, &c.
Inticed by many a gracelesse mate,
Whose counsel I repent too late.   Lord, &c.

Not twentie yeeres old, alas, was I,
  Ah woe is me, woe is me, &c.,
When I begun this fellonie.
  Be warned yong wantons, &c.
With me went still twelve yeomen tall,
Which I did my twelve Apostles call.   Lord, &c.

There was no squire nor barron bold,
  Ah woe is me, woe is me, for my great folly!
That rode the way with silver or gold,
  Be warned yong wantons, &c.
But I and my twelve Apostles gaie
Would lighten their load ere they went away.   Lord, &c.

This newes procured my kins-folkes griefe,
  Ah woe is me, woe is me!
They hearing I was a famous theefe,
  Be warned yong wantons.
They wept, they wailde, they wrong their hands,
That thus I should hazard life and lands.   Lord, &c.

They made me a jaylor a little before,
  Ah woe, &c.
To keep in prison offenders store;
  Be warned, &c.
But such a jaylor was never none,
I went and let them out everie one.   Lord, &c.

I wist their sorrow sore grieved me,
  Ah, woe is me, &c.
Such proper men should hanged be,
  Be warned yong, &c.
My office ther I did defie,
And ran away for company.   Lord, &c.

Three yeeres I lived upon the spoile,
  Ah woe is me, &c.
Giving many a carle the foile,
  Be warned yong, &c.
Yet never did I kil man nor wife,
Though lewdly long I led my life.   Lord, &c.

But all too bad my deedes hath been,
  Ah woe is me, &c.
Offending my country and my good queene,
  Be warned yong, &c.
All men in Yorke-shire talke of me;
A stronger theefe there could not be.   Lord, &c

Upon S. Lukes day was I borne,
  Ah woe, &c.
Whom want of grace hath made a scorne,
  Be war, &c.
In honor of my birth day then,
I robd in a bravery nineteen men.   Lord, &c

The country weary to beare this wronge,
  Ah woe is me, &c.
With huse and cries pursude me long,
  Bé war, &c.
Though long I scapt, yet loe at last,
London, I was in Newgate cast.   Lord, &c.

There did I lye with a grieved minde,
  Ah woe is me, &c.
Although the keeper was gentle and kinde,
  Be warned yong, &c.
Yet was he not so kinde as I,
To let me be at libertie.   Lord, &c.

At last the shiriffe of Yorke-shire came,
  Ah woe is me, &c.
And in a warrant he had my name.
  Be warned yong, &c.
Said he at Yorke thou must be tride,
With me therefore hence must thou ride.   Lord, &c.

Like pangues of death his words did sound:
  Ah woe is me, &c.
My hands and armes full fast he bound.
  Be warned, &c.
Good sir, quoth I, I had rather stay,
I have no heart to ride that way.   Lord, &c.

When no entreaty might prevaile,
  Ah woe is me, &c.
I calde for beere, for wine and ale;
  Be warned, &c.
And when my heart was in wofull case,
I drunke to my friends with a smiling face.   Lord, &c

With clubs and staves I was garded then;
  Ah woe is me, &c.
I never before had such waiting men;
  Be warned, &c.
If they had ridden before amaine,
Beshrew me if I had cald them againe.   Lord, &c.

And when into Yorke that I was come,
  Ah, &c.
Each one on me did passe their doome;
  Be war, &c.
And whilst you live this sentence note,
Evill men can never have good report.   Lord, &c.

Before the judges when I was brought,
  Ah woe is me, &c.
Be sure I had a carefull thought,
  Be, &c.
Nine score inditements and seaventeene
Against me there was read and seene.   Lord, &c.

And each of these was fellony found,
  Ah woe is me, &c.
Which did my heart with sorrow wound.
  Be, &c.
What should I heerein longer stay,
For this I was condemned that day.   Lord, &c.

My death each houre I do attend;
  Ah woe is me,
In prayer and tears my time I spend:
  Be, &c.
And all my loving friends this day
I do intreate for me to pray.   Lord, &c.

I have deserved long since to die:
  Ah woe, &c.
A viler sinner livde not then I,
  Be, &c.
On friends I hopte my life to save,
But I am fittest for my grave.   Lord, &c.

Adue my loving friends, each one:
  Ah woe is me, woe is me, for my great folly!
Thinke on my words when I am gone.
  Be warned yong wantons, &c.
When on the ladder you shall me view,
Thinke I am neerer heaven then you.   Lord, &c.

                                        Finis.   Hutton.

Printed at London for Thomas Millington. 1598.

* OLD BALLADS, Edited by J. Payne Collier, Esq., F.S.A.—*The Percy Society.*

EXECUTION OF THE CONSPIRATORS.

On Thursday, the 30th of January, 1605, Sir Everard Digby, Robert Winter, John Grant, and Thomas Bates, were executed at the West End of St. Paul's ; and the next day, January 31, Thomas Winter, Ambrose Rookwood, Robert Keyes, and Guido Fawkes, were executed in the Old Palace Yard, over against the Parliament House, Westminster, Conspirators in the Powder Plot.

The prisoners, after their condemnation and judgment, being sent back to the Tower, remained there till the Thursday following, on which day four of them, viz., Sir Everard Digby, Robert Winter, John Grant, and Thomas Bates, were drawn upon sledges and hurdles to a scaffold erected at the western end of St. Paul's churchyard. Great pains were taken in the city to render the spectacle of the execution as imposing as possible. Among other arrangements made in order to be prepared against any popular tumult, a precept issued from the Lord Mayor to the Alderman of each ward in the city, requiring him to " cause one able and sufficient person, with a halbard in his hand, to stand at the door of every several dwelling-house in the open street in the way that the traitors were to be drawn towards the place of execution ; there to remain from seven in the morning until the return of the Sheriff."

Now these four above-named being drawn to the scaffold, made on purpose for their execution, first went up Digby, a man of goodly personage, and a manly aspect ; yet might a wary eye, in the change of his countenance, behold an inward fear of death, for his colour grew pale and his eye heavy ; notwithstanding that he enforced himself to speak, as stoutly as he could. His speech was not long, and to little good purpose, only, that his belied conscience being but indeed a blinded conceit, had led him into this offence, which in respect of his religion, alias indeed idolatry, he held no offence, but, in respect of the law, he held an offence, for which he asked forgiveness of God, of the King, and the whole kingdom ; and so, with vain and superstitious crossing of himself, betook him to his Latin prayers, mumbling to himself, refusing to have any prayers of any but of the Romish Catholics : went up the ladder, and with the help of the hangman, made an end of his wicked days in this world

After him went Winter up the scaffold, where he used few words to any effect, without asking mercy of either God or the King for his offences ; went up the ladder, and, making a few prayers to himself, staid not long for his execution.

After him went Grant, who abominably blinded with his horrible idolatry, though he confessed his offence to be heinous, yet would fain have excused it by his conscience for religion ; a bloody religion, to make so bloody a conscience ; but better that his blood, and all such as he was, should be shed by the justice of the law, than the blood of many thousands to have been shed by his villainy, without law or justice. Having used a few idle words to ill effect, he was, as his fellows before him, led to the halter ; and so, after his crossing of himself, to the last part of his tragedy.

Last of them came Bates, who seemed sorry for his offence, and asked forgiveness of God and the King, and of the whole kingdom ; prayed to God for the preservation of them all, and, as he said, only for his love to his master, drawn to forget his duty to God, his King, and country, and therefore was now drawn from the Tower to St. Paul's churchyard, and there hanged and quartered for his treachery. Thus ended that day's business.

The next day, being Friday, were drawn from the Tower to the old palace in Westminster, over against the Parliament House, Thomas Winter the younger brother, Ambrose Rookwood, Robert Keyes, and Guido Fawkes, the miner, justly called " the Devil of the Vault ;" for had he not been a devil incarnate, he had never conceived so villainous a thought, nor been employed in so damnable an action. Winter first being brought to the scaffold made little speech, but seeming, after a sort, as it were, sorry for his offence, and yet crossing himself, as though those were words to put by the devil's stoccadoes, having already made a wound in his soul ; of which he had not yet a full feeling, protesting to die a true Catholic, as he said ; with a very pale and dead colour went up the ladder, and after a swing or two with a halter, to the quartering-block was drawn, and there quickly despatched.

Next him came Rookwood, who made a speech of some longer time, confessing his offence to God in seeking to shed blood, and asking therefore mercy of his Divine Majesty ;—his offence to the King, of whose majesty he likewise humbly asked forgiveness, and his offence to the whole state, of whom in general he asked forgiveness ; beseeching God to bless the King, the Queen, and all his royal progeny, and that they might long live to reign in peace and happiness over this kingdom. But last of all, to spoil all the pottage with one filthy weed, to mar this good prayer with an ill conclusion, he prayed God to make the King a Catholic, otherwise a Papist, which God for his mercy ever forbid ; and so beseeching the King to be good to his wife and children, protesting to die in his idolatry, a Romish Catholic, he went up the ladder, and, hanging till he was almost dead, was drawn to the block, where he gave his last gasp.

After him came Keyes, who like a desperate villain, using little speech, with small or no show of repentance, went stoutly up the ladder, where, not staying the hangman's turn, he turned himself off with such a leap, that with the swing he brake the halter, but, after his fall, was drawn to the block, and there was quickly divided into four parts.

Last of all came the great devil of all, Fawkes, *alias* Johnson, who should have put fire to the powder. His body being weak with torture and sickness, he was scarce able to go up the ladder, but yet, with much ado, by the help of the hangman, went high enough to break his neck with the fall ; who made no long speech, but after a sort, seeming to be sorry for his offence, asked a kind of forgiveness of the King and the state for his bloody intent ; and with his crosses and idle ceremonies, made his end upon the gallows and the block, to the great joy of the beholders, that the land was ended of so wicked a villainy.

EXECUTION of Sir WALTER RALEIGH,

Knight, at Westminster, on the 29th of October, Anno 16°, Jacobi Regis, 1618.

Upon Wednesday, the 28th of October, *anno dom.* 1618, the Lieutenant of the Tower, according to a warrant to him directed, brought Sir Walter Raleigh from the Tower to the King's Bench Bar at Westminster, where the record of his arraignment at Winchester was opened, and it was demanded why execution should not be done upon him according to law.

He began, in way of answer, to justify his proceedings in the late voyage.

But the Lord Chief Justice told him, That he was therein deceived, and that the opinion of the Court was to the contrary.

Master Attorney General, requiring in the King's behalf, that execution might be done on the prisoner, according to the aforesaid judgment: the Sheriffs of Middlesex were commanded for that purpose to take him into their custody, who presently carried him to the Gatehouse.

From whence, the next morning, between the Sheriffs of Middlesex, Sir Walter Raleigh was brought to the old Palace Yard in Westminster, where a large scaffold was erected for the execution.

Whereupon, when he came, with a chearful countenance, he saluted the Lords, Knights, and gentlemen there present.

After which, a proclamation was made for silence, and he addressed himself to speak in this manner.

I desire to be borne withal, for this is the third day of my fever, and if I shall shew any weakness, I beseech you to attribute it to my malady, for this is the hour in which it is wont to come.

Then pausing a while, he sat, and directed himself towards a window, where the Lord of Arundel, Northampton, and Doncaster, with some other Lords and Knights, sate, and spake as followeth:

I thank God, of his infinite goodness, that he hath brought me to die in the light, and not in darkness; (But by reason that the place where the Lords, &c., sat, was some distance from the scaffold, that he perceived they could not well hear him, he said) I will strain my voice, for I would willingly have your honours hear me.

But my Lord of Arundel said, nay, we will rather come down to the scaffold, which he and some others did.

Where being come, he saluted them severally, and then began again to speak as followeth, *viz.*

As I said, I thank God heartily, that he hath brought me into the light to die, and that he hath not suffer'd me to die in the dark prison of misery and cruel sickness; and I thank God that my fever hath not taken me at this time, as I prayed to God it might not.

Then a proclamation being made, that all men should depart the scaffold, he prepared himself for death: giving away his hat, his cap, with some money, to such as he knew that stood near him.

And then putting off his doublet and gown, he desired the Headsman to shew him the Ax; which not being suddenly granted unto him, he said, I prithee let me see it, dost thou think that I am afraid of it? so it being given unto him, he felt along upon the edge of it, and smiling, spake unto Mr. Sheriff, saying, this is a sharp medicine, but it is a physician that will cure all diseases.

Then going to and fro upon the scaffold one very side, he intreated the company to pray to God to give him strength.

Then having ended his speech, the Executioner kneeled down and asked him forgiveness, which laying his hand upon his shoulder he gave him.

Then being asked which way he would lay himself on the block, he made answer, and said, so the heart be straight, it is no matter which way the head lieth; so laying his head on the block, his face being towards the east, the Headsman throwing down his own cloak, because he would not spoil the prisoner's gown, he giving the Headsman a a sign when he should strike, by lifting up his hands, the Executioner struck off his head at two blows, his body never shrinking nor moving; his head was shewed on each side of the scaffold, and then put into a red leather bag, and his wrought velvet gown thrown over it, which was afterwards conveyed away in a mourning coach of his lady's.

The EXECUTION of
SIR THOMAS ARMSTRONG,
A TRAYTOR,
AT TYBURN,
On FRIDAY, the Twentieth of June, 1684.

The Sheriffs of London and Middlesex, about nine o'clock in the morning, coming to Newgate, and demanding their prisoner, he was forthwith delivered to them, and put into a sledge, and drawn to the place of execution, attended by a numerous guard, and as great a number of spectators, of all degrees and qualities, as have been seen on such occasions. Tho' he affected an air of courage, yet something of sullenness and reserve appeared in his countenance.

He employed the time he was drawing to Tyburn in reading *The Whole Duty of Man*, till he came within sight of the gallows, and then he laid it by, and with lifted up hands and eyes, addressed himself to Heaven, till he came beneath the tree, where he remained about a quarter of an hour in the sledge; before he ascended the cart that stood ready for him, he desired the Sheriff to admit Dr. Tenison to come to him; and having delivered a paper to the Sheriff, the Doctor kneeled down with the prisoner, and prayed with him about a quarter of an hour, during all which time the prisoner preserved a becoming and heroick countenance, little daunted with the terror of that fate he was in view of; but rising from his devotions, he pulled off his cravat and hat, which he gave to his servant who attended him, and had followed him by the sledge-side, when kneeling down himself, he prayed for a short time with fervency and devotion, begging pardon of his God for those manifold and crying sins he had been too often guilty of, and concluded with a resignation of himself to the God of heaven and earth, before whose judgment seat he was forthwith to appear, desiring that the whole world would forgive him, with whom he hoped to die in peace and charity. Having thus ended these devotions, he again stood up, and putting off his periwig, he had a white cap delivered to him, which he put on; and being soon ty'd up, the chief of his discourse was addressed to a gentleman who stood by him; and after a short space, holding up his hands, he again renewed his prayers; his visage little changing all the the time, till the very moment the cart drew away; the Executioner having pulled the cap over his eyes, he continued his prayers all the time, and even whilst he hung, as long as life was in him, and he had the command of his lips; after he had hung about half an hour, and the Executioner had divested him of his apparel, he was cut down according to his sentence, his privy members burnt, his head cut off, and shew'd to the people as that of a traitor, his heart and bowels taken out and committed to the flames, and his body quartered into four parts, which, with his head, was convey'd back to Newgate, to be dispos'd of according to his Majesty's pleasure.

LIFE, TRIAL, & EXECUTION

OF

WILLIAM NEVISON,

THE HIGHWAYMAN, AT YORK GAOL.

William Nevison, the great robber of the north, was born at Pomfret in Yorkshire, 1639, and his parents being in good circumstances, conferred upon him a decent education. But he was badly disposed, and commenced his depredations by stealing cash to the amount of £10 from his own father, then, taking a saddle and bridle, hastened to the paddock and stole his schoolmaster's horse, and rode with all speed towards London. About a mile or two from the capital he cut the throat of the poor horse, for fear of detection. Arrived in London he changed his name and clothes, and commenced his wild career which at length brought him to an untimely end.

In all his exploits, Nevison was tender to the fair sex, and bountiful to the poor. He was also a true loyalist, and never levied any contributions upon the Royalists. His life was once spared by the royal clemency. He then returned home, and remained with his father until the day of his death. But soon after returned to his former courses, his name became the terror of every traveller on the road. He levied a quarterly tribute on all the northern drovers, and in return not only spared them himself, but protected them against all other thieves, and the carriers who frequented the road willingly agreed to leave certain sums at such places as he appointed, to prevent their being stripped of them all,

After committing a robbery in London, about sunrise, he rode his mare to York in the course of the day, and appeared upon the bowling green of that city before sunset. From this latter circumstance, when brought to trial for the offence, he established an *alibi* to the satisfaction of the jury, though he was in reality guilty. At length his crimes became so notorious, that a reward was offered to any that would apprehend him. This made many waylay him, especially two brothers named Fletcher, one of whom Nevison shot dead. But though he escaped for a time, he was afterwards apprehended in a public-house at Sandal-three-houses, near Wakefield, by Captain Milton, sent to York gaol, where on the 15th of March, 1685, he was tried, condemned, and executed, aged forty-five.

BOLD NEVISON, the HIGHWAYMAN.

Did you ever hear tell of that hero,
  Bold Nevison that was his name?
He rode about like a bold hero,
  And with that he gained great fame.

He maintained himself like a gentleman,
  Besides he was good to the poor;
He rode about like a bold hero,
  And he gain'd himself favour therefore.

Oh the Twenty-first day of last month,
  Proved an unfortunate day;
Captain Milton was riding to London,
  And by mischance he rode out of his way.

He call'd at Sandal-Houses by the road-side,
  The one known by the sign of the Magpie,
There Nevison he sat a drinking,
  And the Captain soon he did spy.

Then the captain did very soon send for,
  And a constable very soon came;
With three or four men in attendance,
  With pistols charged in the King's name.

They demanded the name of this hero,
  "My name it is Jobsons," said he,
When the captain laid hold by his shoulder,
  Saying, "WILL NEVISON thou goeth with me.'

Oh! then in this very same speech,
  They hastened him fast away,
To a place called Swannington bridge,
  A place where he used to stay.

They call'd for a tankard of good liquor,
  It was the sign of the Black Horse,
Where there was all sorts of attendance,
  But for Nevison it was the worst.

He call'd for a pen, ink, and paper,
  And these were the words that he said:
"I'll write for some boots, shoes, and stockings,
  For of them I have very much need."

'Tis now before my lord judge,
  Oh! guilty or not do you plead;
He smiled unto the judge and jury,
  And these were the words that he said.

"I never robb'd a gentleman of twopence,
  But what I gave half to be blest,
But guilty I've been all my life time,
  So gentleman do as you list.

"It's when that I rode on the highway,
  I've always had money in great store,
And whatever I took from the rich,
  I freely gave to the poor.

"But my peace I have made with my Maker,
  And to be with Him I'ready to draw;
So here's adieu! to this world and its vanities,
  For I'm ready to suffer the law."

THE TRIAL & EXECUTION

OF

JAMES LOWRY,

By the High Court of Admiralty, at the Old Bailey, on the 18th day of February, 1752, and the

SESSIONS GAOL DELIVERY.

James Lowry was put to the bar and arraigned on an indictment which set forth that he, James Lowry, late commander of the merchant ship *Molly*, did, on the 24th day of December, in the 24th year of the reign of his present Majesty, on board the said ship *Molly*, in latitude 49 degrees, 50 minutes, cruelly and violently assault, strike, and beat Kenith Hossick, a mariner, on board the said ship, with a rope the thickness of one inch and a half, over the back, loins, shoulders, head, face, and temples; of which beatings, wounds, and bruises he instantly died. To which indictment the prisoner pleaded not guilty, and put himself upon his country for his trial. To prove which several witnesses were called. After which the prisoner was informed that now was his time to make his defence.

The prisoner then said he had no witnesses as to the fact, but that he thought the log-book would sufficiently support what he had said in his defence, as that the witnesses who had been produced against him had sworn with halters about their necks, in order to screen themselves from their wicked acts of mutiny and piracy, well knowing that if he escaped they must be hanged. And then called several persons to his character; who gave him that of a quiet, humane, good-natured man.

The witnesses being all examined, the judge very impartially summed up the evidence, and gave a most excellent and learned charge to the jury, who withdrew, and in about half an hour returned with a verdict, finding the prisoner "Guilty," DEATH.

THE SESSIONS GAOL DELIVERY.

On the 19th began the sessions of goal delivery at the same place, and continued till Wednesday, when the following malefactors received sentence of death:

James Hays, Richard Broughton, and James Davis, for street robbery; John Powney, for house-breaking; Bernard Angua, Thomas Fox, and Thomas Gale, for forging a note of twenty-four guineas; Ann Lewis, for forging a seaman's power of attorney; Antonio de Rosa, for the murder of Mr. Fargues, at Hoxton; Joseph Gerardino, for the murder of Christopher Alboni; Thomas Huddle, for returning from transportation; John Andrews, for forgery; and Ann Wilson, for the murder of Ann Ellard.

THE EXECUTION.

On the 25th Capt. Lowry was executed at Execution Dock, pursuant to his sentence in the High Court of Admiralty, upon which occasion was the greatest concourse of spectators that ever was known; and though some of the meanest of the populace were ignorant and impudent enough to insult him as he was carried through the streets in a cart, he behaved with great temper, composure of countenance, and with a manly as well as Christian courage. He declared himself innocent of any intention of murder: said that he had just reason to punish the person for whose death he was to suffer; and that he gave no more than five or six stripes at the most, with the end of a rope; and that he believed his death was occasioned by drinking excessively of rum just before he ordered him to be tied up. On the place from whence he was turned off, he asked the officer in waiting, "If he had not a reprieve for him?" and said he forgave his enemies. His body was carried directly down the water and hung upon a gibbet in the gallions below Woolwich, on the river Thames.

THE TRIAL, CONFESSION, AND EXECUTION

OF

JOHN SWAN AND ELIZABETH JEFFRYES,

Who were found guilty at Chelmsford Assizes for the murder of Mr. Joseph Jeffryes, at Walthamstow, in Essex, on the 3rd of July, 1752.

THE TRIAL.

On Tuesday, March 10th, 1752, at the Assizes at Chelmsford, a bill of indictment was found by the Grand Jury for petit treason, against John Swan, for the cruel and wicked murder of his late master, Mr Joseph Jeffryes, of Walthamstow, in the county of Essex, and against Elizabeth Jeffryes, spinster, niece of the deceased, for being, aiding, helping, abetting, assisting, comforting, and maintaining him, the said John Swan, to commit the said murder.—GUILTY DEATH.

THE CONFESSION·

On Thursday, the day after her conviction, Miss Jeffryes made a confession, That what Mathews had swore was true, except that part of his being in the house at the time the pistol went off: And that she had had this murder in her thoughts for two years past, but never had a proper opportunity of getting it executed before, till she engaged Swan, and together with Swan, she offered Mathews money to execute it, who agreed to do it; that upon the night the murder was committed, it was agreed between Swan and her, that they should both go up to their chambers, as if they were going to bed, and as soon as the maid had locked her door, and was supposed to be in bed, Miss Jeffryes came out of her own room and went to Swan's, and said, "Holloh! are you awake?" he answered, "Yes," and he was not undressed; then she went into her uncle's room to see if he was asleep, and took a silver tankard, a silver cup, and some silver spoons, from off a chest of drawers in the deceased's room; then she and Swan went down stairs, and Swan took out a new sack from under the stairs, and she and Swan put the plate, and some pewter and brass which they took off the shelves in the kitchen, into the sack, till she said, I can do no more. Swan and she then drank each a large dram of brandy; then she went upstairs into her own chamber, where it was agreed she should undress herself, and lie till a signal was given by a knock at her door or wainscot, that her uncle was murder'd, then she was to open her window, and cry out, "Diaper! fire and thieves," to alarm the neighbourhood. She farther says, she accidentally fell asleep as soon almost as in bed; but on a sudden was waked by some noise in a fright, when she laid and listen'd, and heard a violent breathing or gasping, as if somebody was under a difficulty in drawing their breath; then she concluded her uncle was murder'd; and then open'd her window, and made the agreed alarm; directly after which she came down stairs, and Swan let her out of the street door in her shift, when she ran to Mrs Diaper's door, in the same

court-yard; Swan then shut the street-door, and as soon as he heard the neighbours were coming, and thought a sufficient alarm was made, he opened the street-door again in his shirt, and run out as if he was just come out of bed in a fright. She further says, that previous to the excuting this diabolical design, they had taken care to cut the wire of the bell on the outside, which went from the master's to the maid's room, to prevent his calling the maid.

Swan says that he did not do the murder, but that Mathews, who came in at the garden gate, which Swan left open for that purpose, actually did, with one of the deceased's pistols, which was hanging up in the kitchen; and Swan cut a bullet, which he took out of a draw in the kitchen to make it fit the pistol. And he is implacable against Miss Jeffryes for having made any confession of this melancholy and wicked affair.

On Saturday, March 14th, they received sentence of death; and while the judge was making a moving and pathetic speech before the sentence, Miss Jeffryes fainted away several times, and at last recovered herself, pray'd for as long a time as possible to prepare herself for a future state.

THE EXECUTION.

On the 28th, Swan and Jeffryes were executed on Epping-Forest, near the six milestone in the parish of Walthamstow. Swan was drawn on a sledge, and Miss Jeffryes in a cart, in the midst of the greatest concourse of people of all ranks and conditions, in coaches, &c., on horseback and a-foot, that ever had been seen in the memory of man. At the place of execution Swan was put into the same cart with Miss Jeffryes, She acknowledged to a gentleman, one of the jury, there present, "That her sentence was just." But, being asked whether Mathews was in the house at the time the murder was committed, she said, "She believed he was not." She also added that she died in charity with all the world. Swan also confessed to the same gentleman, "That he committed the murder." And that he believed Mathews was not in the house at the time of the committing the murder, but that he had been there just before. It was observed that these criminals did not so much as speak, touch, or look at one another, during the whole time they were in the cart. Miss Jeffryes fainted when the halter was tied up; and again when placed on a chair (she being short) for the better conveniency of drawing away the cart. Miss Jeffrye's body was carried away in a hearse to be interred. Swan's body was immediately after cut down, and hung in chains on the same gibbet.

EXECUTION

OF

Six Unfortunate Malefactors,

AT TYBURN,

YESTERDAY MORNING, AUGUST 30, 1783.

Yesterday the six following malefactors were executed at Tyburn, viz., William Wynne Ryland, for publishing a bill of exchange, purporting to be drawn at Fort Marlborough, in the East Indies, with intent to defraud the Hon. East India Company in London—John Lloyd, otherwise John Ferdinando Lloyd, for a robbery in the dwelling house of John Martin—James Browne, alias Oatley, for burglary—Thomas Burgess, for robbing Thomas Tool, in the Willow Walk, Tothil Fields, of a watch and money—James Rivers, alias Davis, for assaulting Nathaniel Thwaits, at the house of Paul Maylor, Agent, in Broad street, and stealing a bag containing thirty eight guineas—and John Edwards, for personating William Madden, a Marine, with intent to receive his prize-money.

Ryland and Lloyd went each in a mourning coach, and were followed by the others in two carts. Ryland, who led the procession, was dressed in black, and accompanied by the Rev. Mr. Villette and two more persons.

The gallows was fixed about fifty yards nearer the Park wall than usual. About five minutes before eleven o'clock, Ryland's coach drew on the right of the gallows, as did Lloyd's on the left, and between them the cart; soon after which a violent storm of thunder, lightening, and rain came on, when the Sheriffs gave orders for a delay of the execution. When the storm had subsided, and some time had been employed in prayer, River was lifted from one cart into the other, which backing to Lloyd's coach, he alighted therefrom, and entered the vehicle. After the ropes had been fixed about their necks, Ryland stepped from the coach to join his unhappy fellow-sufferers. After a conversation of at least ten minutes between Ryland and Mr. Villette, Ordinary of Newgate, and the same time employed in an earnest discourse between Lloyd and Burgess, all the Malefactors joined in singing the hymn, called "The Sinner's Lamentation." The cart was then driven away, and all were nearly at the same instant motionless.

At the place of execution, Lloyd confessed to the Ordinary of Newgate, that he was the person who robbed Mr. Worters, near Woodford, in company with Chesterman, alias Jones, (who was executed last week at Chelmsford) and that Thomas (who is now under sentence of death at Chelmsford) is innocent of that robbery. Three people swore that they saw Thomas in company with Chesterman a few minutes before and after the robbery, and one man positively swore that Thomas was one of the men who turned round to shoot at Mr. Jones, the Surgeon, who was pursuing them. Mr. Jones, in his evidence before Sir Sampson Wright, said, that he did not belive that Thomas was one of the highwaymen, but had no doubt about Chesterman. The Rev. Mr. Villette requested Mr. Jones to attend yesterday morning in Newgate, to hear Lloyd's confession: Mr. Jones did attend, and Lloyd, in the most solemn manner, assured him that he was the man who robbed Worters, with Chesterman, and that Thomas was innocent of that robbery.

THE LAMENTATIONS OF A SINNER.

O Lord, turn not thy face from me,
  Who lie in woeful state,
Lamenting all my sinful life
  Before thy mercy-gate;

A gate which opens wide to those
  That do lament their sin :
Shut not that gate against me, Lord,
  But let me enter in.

And call me not to strict account,
  How I have sojourn'd here;
For then my guilty conscience knows
  How vile I shall appear.

I need not to confess my life
  To thee, who best can tell
What I have been, and what I am ;
  I know thou know'st it well.

The circumstances of my crimes,
  Their number and their kind,
Thou know'st them all; and more, much more
  Than I can call to mind :

Therefore, with tears, I come to beg
  Of my offended God,
For pardon, like a child that dreads
  His angry parent's rod.

So come I to thy mercy-gate,
  Where mercy doth abound,
Imploring pardon for my sin,
  To heal my deadly wound.

O Lord, I need not to repeat
  The comfort I would have :
Thou know'st, O Lord, before I ask,
  The blessing I do crave.

Mercy, good Lord, mercy I ask,
  This is the total sum ;
For mercy, Lord, is all my suit ;
  Lord, Let thy mercy come !

ACCOUNT OF THE
TRIAL AND EXECUTION
OF
JOHN AUSTIN.

Convicted at the OLD BAILEY on Saturday, Nov. 1st, 1783, of a Cruel Highway Robbery on JOHN SPICER, a Poor Man.

This robbery was so peculiarly inhuman and aggravated, that the circumstances attending it are too interesting to the public not to be given in the detail; nor perhaps can the Old Bailey afford an instance more odious, or more reflecting on the depravity of human nature.

John Spicer, the prosecutor, of Cray, in Kent, a poor labouring man, was coming to town on the Tuesday before, with his bundle, where he was a total stranger, in order to get into work, and met with the prisoner at Ilford, where they joined company, and travelled to town together. The prisoner, during their travelling together, sifted the prosecutor, and got out of him the nature of his journey, and what little property he was possessed of, undertook to get him a lodging, provide him a master, and to show him about London. After eating, drinking, and sleeping together on the road at different places, they arrived in town on the Thursday, when the prisoner took Spicer to a public house in Whitechapel, and left him there, pretending to go out after a lodging.

Under this specious shew of friendship, Spicer was left for three or four hours, when a man whose name is Patrick Bowman (who also stands indicted, but is not yet taken) came to Spicer with a plausible apology for Austin's leaving him so long, and desired Spicer to go with him to Austin, who had got him a lodging. This the credulous prosecutor assented to, and Bowman took him to another public-house, where they joined Austin, and from thence they all went out, as Spicer thought, towards the lodging; but when he found himself in the middle of a field, out of the high road, by the side of a ditch, no house near, nor anything to be seen but the lights of some distant lamps, he observed that it was a very comical place to look after a lodging; upon which Austin retired a little, and Patrick Bowman drew a cutlass, with which he kept chopping at the hands, wrists, arms, body, and head of the prosecutor, and mangled him in a most shocking manner. Spicer resisted this attack, and would have got the better of Bowman, if Austin had not come up to Bowman's assistance; for when the poor wretch, thinking he had a firm friend in Austin, called out, "O John, won't you come and help me!" Austin immediately seized him by the collar with one hand the inside of his handkerchief, and with the other caught hold of his legs, and threw him down, when they rifled him of the things mentioned in the indictment, Spicer crying out, "O John, I hope you won't be against me."

This cruel attack on the prosecutor happened to be overheard by one James Story, a servant to Mr. Wells, a gardener, who rushing out to the poor man's assistance, Austin and Bowman made off, and Story ran after to apprehend them, and overtook them, but Bowman and Austin facing about, one with a stick, the other with a cutlass, in order to attack him, he retreated to Spicer, whom he found in a most mangled condition, and took him to his master, from whence he was sent to the hospital, without hopes of recovery.

This was confirmed by Mr. Wells, who did everything in his power to comfort, assist, and stop the bleeding and wounds. Early the next morning, Story saw the prisoner coming towards the spot where this brutal scene took place, and looking about him; Story asked him what he was looking for, to which Austin replied, for some money that had been lost there; upon which Story, who before had some suspicions, apprehended Austin, and secured him in his master's stables; he was observed by Mr. Wells to secret a silk handkerchief and a pair of stockings in the rack, which turned out to be the prosecutor's property, and on Austin being shown to Spicer, was fixed on by him. This was the evidence, except the prisoner's cloaths being wet with blood when apprehended, which

was proved by Story and Mr. Wells, and one Yardly, a constable, proved that Bowman and Austin has been companions on board the lighters together.

Being called on for his defence, he said, that he acted from the impulse of fear, and that he should not have assisted in the robbery but for the dread and threats of Bowman. The Jury without hesitation found him guilty; and the Recorder, who tried the prisoner, first consulting with Baron Eyre and Judge Nares, said he thought the case of such a nature that he should immediately pass sentence of death. Austin being asked the usual question of what he had to say why judgment of death should not be pronounced against him, replied, "I don't fear death, as I am not guilty, and shall die innocent."

The Recorder then addressed the prisoner as follows:—

John Austin, you have been tried and convicted by a just and yet merciful jury, upon the most clear and satisfactory evidence. So horrid a crime as you have been guilty of, in its nature so audacious and inhuman, calls aloud for the very severe and immediate interposition of justice. It has been the declared intention of our merciful Sovereign, that he will never shew any compassion to such wretches as you, who add cruelty to robbery, and whose attacks on the property of his peaceable and honest subjects are accompanied with acts, whereby the crime of murder may be added to that of robbery. Everybody must applaud a resolution founded on the strictest justice and necessity. It is peculiarly my duty to further his royal intentions, by making my report of such criminals as you the first opportunity after conviction; and, therefore, to carry his Majesty's purpose into effect, I shall report you as a fit object of punishment with all possible speed. Your crime has been accompanied with every speices of aggravation. Under the mask of friendship you have robbed a poor innocent man, deluded by your treacherous designs, and your false friendship: it is further aggravated by the baseness and inhumanity of your deceit, which cannot intitle you to any instance of mercy, but requires that you may be made an example of immediate justice. On Monday, therefore, I shall make the report of you to his Majesty. I advise you to prepare your soul for that fate which I am now about to pronounce against you.

The Recorder then pronounced the usual sentence, and the prisoner was taken from the bar.

THE EXECUTION.

Yesterday morning was executed, at Tyburn, John Austin, convicted last Saturday of robbing John Spicer in a field adjoining the highway at Bethnal green, and cutting and wounding him in a cruel manner. From Newgate to Tyburn the convict behaved with great composure. While the halter was tying, the unhappy wretch trembled in a very extraordinary manner, his whole frame appearing to be violently convulsed. The Ordinary having retired from the cart, the convict addressed himself to the surrounding populace in the following words, "Good people, I request your prayers for the salvation of my departing soul; let my example teach you to shun the bad ways I have followed; keep good company, and mind the word of God." The cap being drawn over his face, he raised his hands, and cried, "Lord have mercy on me, Jesus look down with pity on me, Christ have mercy on my poor soul;" and while uttering these exclamations, the cart was driven away. The noose of the halter having slipped to the back part of his neck, it was full ten minutes before he was dead.

THE TRIAL & SENTENCES

OF ALL THE

PRISONERS,

WHICH COMMENCED

On WEDNESDAY, the 11th of APRIL,

AT

JUSTICE HALL IN THE OLD BAILEY,

WITH AN

ACCOUNT OF THE PILLORY

OF

JOHN LINGARD,

FOR PERJURY.

On the 14th, The sessions ended at the Old-bailey, when fourteen prisoners were tried, seven were cast for transportation, and seven acquitted. Seven received sentence of death. One transported for fourteen years. Twenty-nine transported for seven years. Two branded. Three whipp'd. One pillory'd, imprison'd, and transported.

——o——

JOHN LINGARD,
PILLORY'D FOR PERJURY.

On the 18th. A few minutes after twelve at noon, Lingard, found guilty of perjury in swearing Mr. Coleman's life away, was brought from the New Goal to the pillory, near St. George's church, Southwark, were the executioner was several minutes before he could get his head fix'd; as soon as he had done his business and left the scaffold, the people, who universally expressed their detestation and abhorrence of the criminal, began their attack upon him in a very furious manner, by throwing at him mud, stones, and sticks, so that it was imagined he would not get off alive; however, the mob, which was very great, moderated their rage, and though the pelting never entirely ceased, it, at last, considerably abated: he got his head twice out of the hole, but it was soon fixed again by some who used him but roughly. He waved his hands in a suppliant manner, begging for mercy, and though he had a tin scull plate under his cap, he was cut in the left side of his head, and the blood ran down his face, He was taken down in a dirty condition, about a quarter before one, and had not been kept in the pillory above half an hour. This perjured villain formerly kept a public house near Newington, in Surry; was a marshall's court officer, and frequently employed as crier of the court.

TRIAL AND EXECUTION

OF

JOHN HOGAN,

FOR

MURDER,

JANUARY 13th, 1786.

THE TRIAL.

In the course of the trial on Friday, the 13th, of Hogan, the mulatto, for the murder of the servant maid of Mr Orrell, of Charlotte street, Portland place, the following circumstances appeared:—That as soon as Mr. and Mrs. Orrell got into their house, the latter found her servant reclining against the wall of the kitchen, besmeared with blood; and on screaming out, Mr. Orrell ran into the kitchen, and seeing the girl in this situation, said, "Nanny! for God's sake what have you been doing?"—She however being unable to make any answer, Mr. Orrell alarmed his next door neighbour, and a surgeon was sent for, who however pronounced her too much wounded to recover: she was however sent to an hospital, where she expired. Her head-dress had been entirely torn off, and thrown on the ground, which was covered with blood, as were her handkerchief, gown, &c. Her skull was fractured violently; her left eye was beaten almost out of its socket; her cheekbones were both broken; her chin was cut; her neck and throat both cut; several wounds on her breast, particularly a large circular one; her left arm broke, and her right arm and wrist both cut. The instrument with which the wounds had been made was a razor; and notwithstanding it had been thrown into a fire, the spots of blood were not erased. It appeared in the course of the evidence, that on the prisoner (after very strong suspicions had been formed of his guilt) being taken to the body of the deceased, he appeared not in the least agitated, but putting his hand on her breast, said, "My dear Nanny, I do remember you very well: I never did you harm in my life?" These expressions very forcibly added to the suspicions of his guilt, because her face was so exceedingly cut and mangled, that Mr. Orrell declared he himself could not possibly have known her. Two other circumstances which tended to criminate him were a spot of blood on a waistcoat which he wore, and some slight marks of blood on one of the sleeves of his coat; which coat had been washed, though the blood on the sleeve remained; and an effort seemed to have been made, but in vain, to rub out the spot of blood from the waistcoat. The principal evidence against him was the woman with whom he cohabited, who deposed that he brought her home a cloak, which he said he had bought on condition of paying for at the rate of so much a week. The cloak was produced in Court, and Mrs Orrell swore to it as her property. The deponent further said, that after Hogan had been twice taken before a magistrate, and discharged for want of sufficient evidence, he at intervals appeared to me very uneasy; that, particularly, he could not sleep in his bed; that she finding him thus restless, said to him one night, "For God's sake what is the matter with you? Surely you are not guilty of what you have been taken up for?" That his answer was, "Yes, I am!—I am guilty!—I did it!—She then was much troubled in mind, and apprehended fatal consequences to herself from having been connected with him; particularly as he said to her, "You must say nothing:—you must be quiet; for if I be hanged, you will be hanged with me."

The circumstances which afterwards providently contributed, in conjunction with the above, to lead to the discovery of the horrid deed, are well known to the public. It is only necessary to observe that on the last mentioned evidence asking him why he had murdered the young woman, he answered, "Because he wanted to be great with her, and she resisted him."

The razor with which the murder was committed was produced in Court, and the heart of every spectator shuddered at its appearance.

———o———

THE EXECUTION.

On Monday morning Hogan was executed on a gibbet erected opposite Mr. Orrell's house. A great concourse of people attended the execution; but it has been seldom seen that a malefactor has died so little pitied as Hogan. Before being turned off, the prisoner bowed four times to the populace, and in an audible voice, confessed himself guilty of the murder, for which he was to suffer.

The Trial, Confession, and Execution

OF

JOSEPH RICHARDS,

For the Cruel and Wicked Murder of Walter Horseman.

THE TRIAL.

Old Bailey, February 24th, 1786.

Joseph Richards was arraigned for the wilful murder of Walter Horseman, milkman, in Kentish Town. The deceased's widow deposed, that the prisoner was formerly a servant to her husband; that he was discharged for negligence; that he had frequently threatened vengeance on the deceased; that on the morning the murder was committed, she was awakened by a noise, and on entering the room her husband slept in, she found him sitting up in the bed, and as far as his waist in blood; that a stick which the prisoner had cut some time before, lay in the room, and an iron bar, covered with blood; that her husband was mangled in a shocking manner: —he lingered a few days, and died a shocking spectacle.

Four other witnesses were examined, whose testimony proved certain corroborating circumstances; such as, being from his lodging the night the murder was committed, being seen to melt lead, and to pour it into the stick that was found in the deceased's room, &c.

The prisoner confessed the murder to one of the magistrates who committed him for trial; but pleaded Not Guilty at the bar.

The jury, after a few minutes' consideration, brought in their verdict Guilty.

Mr. Recorder pronounced judgment. He said the voice of innocent blood cried to heaven for vengeance. He dwelt upon the atrociousness of the crime of murder, observing, that the Divine Law had ordained, that whoever sheddeth man's blood, &c., and then expatiated on the peculiar circumstances of the murder, the murder of an innocent master, to whom he owed duty and reverence.

The sentence was then passed as usual, that he be hanged till dead, and anatomized; and an order of Court was made out, to execute him on Monday, at Kentish Town, as near as possible to the house of the deceased.

THE EXECUTION.

Joseph Richards, a youth about eighteen, who was convicted on Friday last, for the wilful murder of Walter Horseman, with whom he lived servant, was executed at Kentish Town, opposite the house where the horrid fact was perpetrated. The malefactor came out of Newgate about twenty minutes before eight o'clock, and with some alertness stepped into the cart, which conveyed him through Smithfield, Cow Cross, and by the two small-pox hospitals to the spot, where he was removed from that society of which he had proved himself a most unworthy member, at a time of life when such atrocity of guilt as he possessed has been seldom known to degrade humanity. In his way to the place of execution, the convict appeared to be in a state of mind bordering upon stupefaction; he had no book, nor did he employ the short remnant of time in those preparations for eternity which his miserable situation rendered so indispensably necessray.

Before being turned off, the prisoner desired to see the widow of the deceased; she was sent for to her house, but was gone to London; he declared he had no accomplice in the fact, and that he was induced to the perpetration thereof by the supposition, that after the decease of his master he should succeed to his business as a milkman. Just before coming to the village, he burst into tears, and when he came to the place of execution, wept bitterly; his expressions of sorrow and contrition being only interrupted by fervent appeals to Heaven for mercy till the last moment of his existence.

Old Bailey Intelligence.—Execution of Six Unfortunate Malefactors, and the Barbarious Execution and Burning of Phœbe Harris, for Coining Silver, on the 21st of June, 1786.

The following male convicts, viz., Edward Griffiths, George Woodward, William Watts, Daniel Keefe, Jonathan Harwood, and William Smith, were executed pursuant to their sentence, on the scaffold usually erected opposite Newgate. They were brought out at half-past seven in the morning, and the platform dropped about eight o'clock. Woodward was so exceedingly weak, that he was obliged to sit down till the executioneer had tied up the rest, and was then supported by two men.

The Barbarious Execution and Burning of Phœbe Harris.

Soon after the above execution, Phœbe Harris, convicted the session before last of coining silver, was brought out at the debtor's door, from whence she walked to a stake fixed in the ground, about half way between the scaffold and Newgate street. She was immediately tied by the neck to an iron bolt fixed near the top of the stake, and after praying very fervently for a few minutes, the steps on which she stood were drawn away, and she immediately became suspended. The executioner, with some assistants, put a chain round her body, which was fastened by strong nails to the stake. Two cart-loads of faggots were then piled round her, and after she had hung about half an hour, the fire was kindled. The flames presently burning the halter, the convict fell a few inches, and was then suspended by the iron chain passed over her chest and affixed to the stakes. Some scattered remains of the body were perceptible in the fire at half-past ten o'clock. The fire had not quite burnt out even at twelve. The unhappy woman was so exceedingly affected on Monday night, that it was generally supposed (and indeed wished) that she could not have survived.

Phœbe Harris was a well made little woman, something more than thirty years of age, of a pale complexion, and not of disagreeable features. When she came out of prison she appeared languid and terrified, and trembled greatly as she advanced to the stake, where the apparatus for the punishment she was about to experience seemed to strike her mind with horror and consternation, to the exclusion of all power of recollectedness in preparation for the approaching awful moment. A great concourse of people attended on the melancholy occasion.

THE GAOL DELIVERY,

AND THE

TRIALS AND SENTENCES

OF ALL THE PRISONERS

AT THE OLD BAILEY SESSIONS,

TOGETHER WITH A FULL ACCOUNT OF THE

EXECUTION OF FIFTEEN UNFORTUNATE CONVICTS.

The April sessions ended at the Old Bailey, on the 25th, when 13 convicts received judgment of death; 60 were sentenced to be transported, two of whom, for stripping children, are to be sent to Africa, the other women to New South Wales; 8 to be imprisoned in Newgate; 1 to hard labour in the house of correction; 5 to be whipped; and 31 discharged by proclamation.

Elizabeth Kirvan, a convict for forgery, whose execution was respited on her plea of pregnancy, is referred to her former judgment, she not being pregnant.

The sessions of the peace is adjourned until Monday the 21st day of May next. at Guildhall; and the sessions of Goal-Delivery of Newgate, until Wednesday, the 23rd day of the same month, at the old Bailey.

APRIL 26.

EXECUTIONS.

The following 15 convicts were brought out of Newgate on the platform erected before the Debtor's-door, and executed pursuant to their sentence, viz., Francis Parr, for personating Isaac Hart, the proprietor of £3,900 3 per cent. consolidated annuities, with intent to defaud the said Isaac Hart and the Govenor and Company of the Bank of England; William Trapshaw, for breaking open, in the day-time the apartments of James Linney, in a house let to several tenants, and stealing a linen gown and an apron, no person being then therein; Joseph Mullagan, James Coleman, and John Williamson Halfey, for breaking and entering the dwelling house of Joseph Stokes, in the parish of St. Catherine, and stealing a sheet, a blanket, and other things; Charles Baker, for breaking and entering the dwelling house of William Watson, in the parish of St Matthew, Bethnal-green, and stealing several small casks, containing a quantity of spirituous liquors; William Dwyre, for feloniously and traitorously counterfeiting the current coin of this kingdom, called six-pences, by coloring certain pieces of brass with a certain liquid composition producing the color of silver; Charles Shaw, for assaulting John Hughes on the highway in St. Paul's Churchyard, and robbing him of a silver watch, &c.; John Walker and John Evans, for assaulting William Stevenson on the highway, in Old-street, and robbing him of a silver watch, two guineas and a half, some silver, and a dollar; Elizabeth Sedgewick, for setting fire to the premises of her master, Mr. John Taylor, at Feltham-hill, Middlesex; Michael Daily and Elizabeth Connolly, for stealing in the dwelling-house of Mrs. Catherine Plomer, in Howland street, Oxford road, a gold watch, a silver watch, several articles of plate, and a quantity of wearing apparel; John-Pousarque Dubois, for breaking into the dwelling-house of John Grant, in Cockspur street, and stealing a gold watch, a silver watch, a metal watch, and other things; and John Adamson, for assaulting Samuel Horne, on the highway, near the Opera-house, in the Haymarket, and taking from him, by force, a metal watch in a shagreen case. They all behaved very penitent.

D. W. Murcutt, Printer, Stationer, &c., Long Acre, London.

EXECUTION

OF

EIGHT CONVICTS

ON THE

NEW SCAFFOLD FOR EXECUTING CRIMINALS

IN THE

OLD BAILEY.

April 24, 1787.

Yesterday morning the following convicts were executed on the newly-invented temporary scaffold, placed before the debtors' door of Newgate:—John Burn, Daniel Gunter, James Francis, and John Green, convicted in January sessions; and William Ludlam, William Oakes, John Bishop, alias John Buller, and James Haylock, alias Hullock, formerly a runner at a public office, convicted in February sessions.—After divine service in the chapel of Newgate, the prisoners were brought out of the gaol, and six of them having joined the ordinary in devout prayer, and chaunted the usual psalm (the others, being two Roman Catholicks, were attended by a priest of that persuasion). At nine o'clock the platform dropped, and in a few moments they showed no signs of life. They were fervent in their devotions, and all of them appeared to die sincerely penitent.

The scaffold on which these miserable people suffered is a temporary machine, which was drawn out of the yard of the sessions-house by horses; it had this day only one beam fixed; and upon a bolt being drawn, the platform dropped, leaving the malefactors suspended in a manner similar to that of the scaffold lately in use.

After the convicts were cut down, the gallows was drawn back to the sessions-house yard; and the whole cleared away in half-an-hour's time.

An Account of the new-invented Scaffold for Executing Criminals in the Old Bailey.

We imagine that an accurate representation of the new mode of executing criminals in the Old Bailey, which does so much honour to the present worthy Sheriffs, will hardly fail of giving satisfaction to such, at least, as do not reside near the metropolis.

The whole of this temporary erection is hung in black. The criminals are attended by the proper officers and the Ordinary of Newgate, from their cells to the centre part of the scaffold, which is a platform raised about two or three inches above the general floor, and directly under the gallows: here, after the usual prayers and solemnities, the rope is tied up, and, at the Sheriff's signal, the executioner pulls away a staple, which loosens a bar that supports the platform, and the platform then falls in: and this, being much more sudden and regular than that of a cart being drawn away, has the effect of immediate death. During the whole time of this awful spectacle, a full-toned bell, which is suspended above the roof of this part of the prison, is solemnly tolled; but as it is fixed so far on the roof as not to be in sight, it does not appear. The scaffold is supported by strong posts, fixed into grooves made in the street, and the whole is temporary, being all calculated to take to pieces, which are preserved within the prison.

FULL ACCOUNT OF THE
EXECUTION OF
FIVE UNFORTUNATE SAILORS,

VIZ.,–

MICHAEL COX,   **MARTIN EALEY,**

JOHN SULLIVAN,

ROBERT M'LAURIN,   and   **WILLIAM MORRIS.**

AND HIS MOST GRACIOUS MAJESTY'S ROYAL PARDON

OF

JOHN FLINT,   **JOHN LAWSON,**
     and
GEORGE WYTHICK,   **WILLIAM HANDY.**

And the Sentence passed on Capt. Affleck, late of the Amethyst.

At Sheerness, on the eighth day of this month, at about nine o'clock in the morning, the signal for EXECUTION was made on board of the DEFIANCE man-of-war by firing a gun, and hoisting a yellow flag at the fore-top-gallant-mast head: a lieutenant, in a boat manned and armed, was sent from each ship to witness the awful scene: the crews of the respective ships were called on deck, and the articles of war read to them by their captains, who afterwards warned them to take examples from the fate of the unhappy men who were about to suffer. The Rev. Dr. Hatherall, chaplain of the *Sandwich*, administered the sacrament to all of them, except Michael Cox and Martin Ealey, who were Roman Catholics; after praying with them for some time, they were brought on deck, and the ropes fixed around their necks, when John Flint, George Wythick, John Lawson, and William Handy were made acquainted that His Majesty had been pleased to pardon them.

Handy, who had a wife and child on board, immediately ran down to her, and fainted in her arms, which presented a most affecting scene. The tear of thankfulness and joy adorned the cheeks of the hardy tars; and Lawson addressing the clergyman, said, "I am afraid I shall never again be so well prepared for eternity."

At a quarter past eleven, the signal for the execution of the remainder was made, by firing a gun, when Michael Cox, Robert M'Laurin, John Sullivan, Martin Ealey, and William Morrison, were launched into eternity. After hanging the usual time, their bodies were sent on shore, to the agent at sick quarters, for interment.

These unhappy men suffered for a mutiny on board the *Defiance*, then in Leith roads, in the month of October last.

Portsmouth, March 16th, 1796.

The following is the sentence passed yesterday at Portsmouth, on Captain Thomas Affleck, late of the *Amethyst* frigate, for the loss of that ship: "That the loss of His Majesty's ship *Amethyst* was occasioned by her striking on a rock near the island of Guernsey, and by a hole being thereby beaten in her bottom; and that the same was attributable to the misconduct of the said captain, Thomas Affleck; and the court do adjudge him to be reduced from his rank on the list of post captains to the bottom of the said list, and to be incapable of being again employed in His Majesty's naval service for the remainder of his life; and the court further agree, that the loss of the said ship was not attributable to any misconduct in any other of the officers or company of the said ship, and do adjudge them to be acquitted."

W. PARKER, Printer, Portsmouth and Gosport.

THE TRIAL AND EXECUTION

OF

MARTIN CLINCH & SAMUEL MACKLEY,

For the Wicked Murder of Mr. Fryer, in Islington Fields.

THE TRIAL.

At the Old Bailey, Martin Clinch and Samuel Mackley were capitally convicted of the wilful murder of Mr Fryer, in the parish of St. Mary, Islington. It appears by the evidence, that the deceased and his cousin, Miss Fryer, were walking across the fields in their way from Southampton Buildings, Holborn, towards Islington : that, when they arrived at the field called the cricket field, near White Conduit house, they heard a noise, as of some person in distress ; this induced the deceased to go to the spot. At this time, Miss Fryer, the principal witness on this occasion, was at some distance from him. By the time she came to the stile, which she had crossed in his way to the place, she saw Clinch fire, when the deceased fell into a small pond. Clinch then took his watch out of his fob, and a sum of money out of his pocket. By this time Miss Fryer had got on the other side of the stile, when the prisoner, Mackley, held a pistol to her head, and took her cloak from her. They then went away, and Mr. Fryer was taken to a house at a short distance from the spot, where he died at eleven o'clock the same evening. The evidence in support of the above statement, as given by Miss Fryer, was clear, artless, and unembarassed. When asked if she really believed Clinch to be the man who shot Mr Fryer, she said she believed from her soul he was ; with regard to Mackley, she seemed not quite so positive ; several witnesses, however, proved his being seen in the same field within a few minutes of the time the murder happened, who all had noticed him, on account of his having red hair. The prisoners being called on for their defence, they only said they were innocent, but could give no account where they were at the time the murder was committed. The jury went out for about half an hour, and returned with a verdict —Guilty.

The sessions being ended, the same were adjourned until Wednesday, July 12, 1797.

THE EXECUTION.

Yesterday morning were executed at the front of Newgate, Martin Clinch and Samuel Mackley, for the daring robbery and cruel murder of Mr Fryer, in Islington fields. An extremely disagreeable circumstance occurred shortly before the period which is usually allowed to men in their unfortunate situation. The floor of the scaffold, from some previous misarrangement, gave way, and precipitated into the area of the apparatus, Messrs Vilette and Gaffy, the latter a Catholic priest, who attended Clinch, and the two executioners ; Mr. Sheriff Stains had himself a very narrow escape. Mr. Gaffy being a lusty man was severely hurt, as were both the executioners ; Mr Vilette escaped with a slight bruise. The two unfortunate malefactors swung off with their distorted features exposed to the view of the distressed spectators. By the laudable activity of Mr. Ramsden, the prison surgeon, however, the cap was drawn over their faces afterwards. Their bodies were removed to a proper place for the purposes of dissection and exposure. They both denied to the last moment having had any concern in the murder.

Pitts, Printer, Toy and Marble Warehouse, 6, Great St. Andrew Street, London.

AN ACCOUNT OF THE
COURT MARTIAL, SENTENCE, AND EXECUTION
OF
RICHARD PARKER FOR MUTINY,

Held on board His Majesty's ship the NEPTUNE, lying in the river Thames, off Greenhithe.

The Court was formed on Thursday, June 22, 1797, and the prisoner was charged with making, and having endeavoured to make, a mutiny among the seamen of His Majesty's ships at the Nore; with having caused assemblies of these seamen to meet frequently, and with having behaved himself contemptuously toward and disobeyed his officers.

Captain Moss, of the Sandwich, was the prosecutor, and after the whole of the evidence had been gone through, the prisoner was ordered to withdraw, and the court was cleared for the purpose of leaving the members to deliberate on the sentence.

In two hours and a half the Court was re-opened, and the prisoner being called in, the sentence of the Court was read by the Judge Advocate to the following purport:—"That Richard Parker do suffer death, and to be hanged by the neck on board of one of His Majesty's ships, and at such time as the Lords of the Admiralty may think proper."

On Friday, June 30, at eight o'clock in the morning, a gun was fired from on board His Majesty's ship L'Espion, lying off Sheerness garrison, Vice-Admiral Lutwidge's flag ship, and the yellow flag, the signal of capital punishment, was hoisted, which was immediately repeated by the Sandwich hoisting the same colour on her fore-top. At half-past eight Parker was told the chaplain was ready to attend him. He now requested a minute to collect himself, and knelt down in prayer, then, rising up, said, "I am ready," and holding his head up, said to the boatswain's mate, "take off my handkerchief," which being done, the Provost-Marshal placed the halter over his head (which had been prepared with grease), but doing it awkwardly, the prisoner said rather pettishly to the boatswain's mate, "Do you do it, for he seems to know nothing about it!" The halter was then spliced to the reeved rope; all this being adjusted, the Marshal attempted to put a cap on, which he refused; but on being told it was indispensible, he submitted, requesting it might not be pulled over his eyes till he desired it. He then turned round for the first time, and gave a steady look at his shipmates on the forecastle, and, with an affectionate kind of a smile, nodded his head, and said, "Good-bye to you!" He now said, "Captain Moss, is the gun primed?" "It is." "Is the match alight" "All is ready." He now ascended the platform, repeated the same questions about the gun, then the cap being drawn over his face, walking by firm degrees up to the extremity of the scaffold, he dropped the handkerchief, put his hands in his coat pocket with great rapidity, and at the moment as he was springing off, the fatal bow-gun fired, and the reeve rope catching him, run him up, though not with great velocity, to the yard arm. When suspended about midway, his body appeared extremely convulsed for a few seconds, immediately after which no appearance of life remained. He suffered exactly at half-past nine, and was lowered down, after hanging at the yard-arm a full hour, when the yellow flag was struck, and his body instantly put into a shell that had been prepared for it, with all his clothes on; and soon after it was taken in one of the Sandwich's boats and rowed to the east point of the garrison, and there being landed was carried to the new naval burying ground, out of the Red Barrier Gate, leading to Minster; the coffin lid was here taken off to the spectators for a few minutes; his countenance appeared not much altered, but his eyes were wide open. He was interred exactly at noon. His body was afterward secretly taken up, and conveyed to London, and decently interred in Whitechapel church yard.

THE DEATH OF PARKER.

Ye Gods above protect the widow,
　And with pity look on me,
Help me, help me out of trouble,
　And out of all calamity.
For by the death of my brave Parker,
　Fortune has proved to me unkind,
Tho' doom'd by law he was to suffer
　I can't erase him from my mind.
Parker he was my joyful husband,
　My bosom friend I love so dear;
At the awful moment he was going to suffer
　I was not allowed to come near.
In vain I strove, in vain I ask'd
　Three times o'er and o'er again,
But they replied you must be denied,
　You must return on shore again.
First time I 'tempted my love to see
　I was obliged to go away,
Oppres't with grief and broken hearted
　To think that they should me stay.
I thought I saw the yellow flag flying,
　A signal for those who was to die;
A gun was fired as they required,
　As the time it did draw nigh.
The boatswain did his best endeavour
　To get me on shore without delay,
When I stood trembling and confounded,
　Ready to take his body away.
Though his trembling hand did wave
　As a signal of farewell,
The grief I suffered at this moment
　No heart can paint, no tongue can tell.
My fleeting spirit I thought would follow
　The soul of him I lov'd most dear,
No friend or neighbour would come nigh me,
　For to ease me of grief or care.
Every moment I thought an hour
　Till the law its course had run;
I wished to finish the doleful task
　His imprudence first began.
In the dead of the night 'tis silent,
　And all the world are fast asleep;
My trembling heart that knows no comfort
　O'er his grave does often weep.
Each lingering minute that passes
　Brings me nearer to his grave,
Where we shall shine in endless glory,
　Never to be parted more.
Farewell Parker, thou bright genius,
　That was once my only pride;
Tho' parted now it won't be long
　E'er I'm buried by thy side.
All you that see my tender ditty,
　Don't laugh at me in disdain,
But look down with eyes of pity,
　For it is my only claim.

Pitts, Printer, Toy and Marble Warehouse, 9, Great St. Andrew Street, Seven Dials.

Trial and Execution of Mary Nott, for the dreadful Murder of a French emigrant; and the Trial and Execution of Richard Ludman and Eleanor Hughes, for the Murder of George Hebner in a Brothel.

Mary Nott was tried at the Old Bailey, for the wilful murder of the Count de Greffiere de Laval, a French emigrant. It appeared in evidence, that she had the care of a house, which was let out in lodgings, in Monmouth court, Whitcomb street, the front room on the first floor of which was occupied by the count. The lodger in the room adjoining, not hearing the count as usual, had, for several mornings, enquired after him; when the prisoner said she supposed he was gone into the country with a French man and woman who used to call on him, but had not been there since his absence, for she had not seen him; that the key was not in his door, and, upon looking through the keyhole, she observed the room was just as she left it.—To another witness, who had called to see the count, she said that he had gone out very early that morning, and that she did not expect him home until it was late. Some doubts, however, arising from his absence, a ladder was procured, perfectly with the consent of the prisoner, to look into the room of the deceased; and upon the person's calling out that there was a man upon the bed, she cried out, that she would not have remained there last night if she had known there was a man dead in the house; and upon which she, in fact, alarmed the neighbourhood. A smith was sent for, and the door forced open: the deceased was found lying on the bed with all his clothes on but his coat; he was wrapped up in the bedclothes, and pillows covered his head: there was a great deal of blood in the room, a wound was observed in the neck, and the body was nearly in a state of putrefaction. A woman, who lived in an opposite house, and who had observed the prisoner shut one of the windows, which prevented her seeing into the prisoner's room, on the day the murder was supposed to have been committed, went up with her at the time the door was opened, and observing his right hand pocket was turned out, said, "He has been robbed;" to which the prisoner instantly replied, "He did it himself;" upon this witness made a similar remark that he must have been murdered, she again said, "He did it himself;" and upon her noticing a wash-hand basin with some water in it tinged with blood, as if some person had wrinsed their hands therein, the prisoner said, "It is not strange, not strange at all; what do you come here to raise suspicion for?" Another neighbour had heard a scream about two o'clock on that day, but could not say whence it came. The deceased was seen coming toward home between twelve and one o'clock, and as the lodger in the next room went home as early as five, the supposition was that the murder had been committed in that time. The surgeon who examined the body swore positively there was no wound in the side of the deceased, but that the raised skin, supposed to be such, was from the putrefaction; nor would he undertake to say what was the cause of his death, although a considerable quantity of blood might have issued from the wound in his neck.—Beside this testimony, which included all that related to the prisoner, it appeared that the deceased's portmanteau had been cut; that there was a knife upon the table, which was by no means bloody; that in his left-hand pocket he had a knife and a key, the latter of which opened a drawer, wherein were several pieces of French coin and three guineas; that the deceased had been possessed of a very considerable property in France, and upon emigrating to this country, an agent in the city had allowed him twenty pounds per month: but affairs taking such a turn there, that pittance had been stopped, and he was so reduced, that a friend had forced upon him the loan of four guineas; he having no other clothes than those on his back. The prisoner denied the charge generally, and called three persons to her character, one of whom said she was of so humane a disposition, that if a worm lay in her way, she would turn aside rather than do it an injury. The jury returned a verdict of guilty. She is aged 63.—Richard Ludman, Ann Rhodes, Eleanor Hughes, and Mary Baker, were likewise indicted for the murder of George Hebner. This murder was committed in King street, East Smithfield, in one of those obscure receptacles of debauchery with which this metropolis abounds. The body of the deceased was found on the morning of Sunday, the 22nd of May, suspended by the neck from a bed-post, in a room on the second floor, with his hands tied behind his back. It was proved that the four prisoners were in the house (which belonged to Eleanor Hughes) on the evening of Saturday, the 21st, and next morning. They were seen, and some of their conversations heard, by two women who lived in an adjoining house; this house was separated from that in which the deceased was found by only a lath partition, perforated in several places, and the holes and crevices affording a distinct view of almost all the apartments of the latter.—The manner in which the hands of the deceased were bound with a piece of tape was described in the court. The knot that had been used was what seamen call a timber hitch, and it was obviously such could not have been done by himself. There was no direct and positive proof of the guilt of the prisoners; but there was a chain of most suspicious circumstances pointing strongly against Ludman and Hughes. The lord chief baron summed up the evidence with great precision, candour, and humanity. It was on the expressions used by the prisoners that the proof chiefly rested, and his lordship nicely discriminated between those which seemed to arise from surprise, on the discovery of the situation of the deceased, and those which could be supposed to proceed only from a knowledge of the murder. The jury returned a verdict, finding Richard Ludman and Eleanor Hughes guilty. Ann Rhodes and Mary Baker not guilty.—Eleanor Hughes pleaded pregnancy, to stay the execution of her sentence. On which a jury of matrons was collected and sworn, to examine her, and report their opinion to the court. They retired with the prisoner about half-an-hour, and at their return declared her to be "with child, but not quick with child."

THE EXECUTION.

Yesterday, Mary Nott, convicted of the murder of Le Comte de Laval, an emigrant nobleman; and also Richard Ludman and Eleanor Hughes, convicted of the murder of George Hebner, were executed on a temporary platform in the Old Bailey, before the gaol of Newgate, pursuant to their sentence; after which the bodies were delivered at Surgeons'-hall for dissection.

John Clarke, Printer, Swan Street, Minories, London.

EXECUTION

OF

JAMES NESBETT

FOR THE

HORRIBLE MURDER

OF

MR. PARKER & HIS HOUSEKEEPER.

This wretched criminal surrendered his life to-day to the outraged laws of his country, From the complication of crimes of which he was convicted, and from the probability that the murder of Mr. Parker and his housekeeper was not the first instance in which he had been guilty of a violation of the laws, great curiosity prevailed to witness his execution, in the expectation that, if he had not previously made any confession he would in his last moments be induced to reveal the particulars of his guilt.

After his family had taken leave of him, he made a full confession of his guilt. Some of the particulars which he communicated are said to be very important, and the whole of his statement is, for the present, kept strictly secret. Various rumours are, of course, in circulation respecting the nature of his confession to which it would be equally improper to give publicity, whether they be ill or well founded.

After his mind had been disburdened of the load of guilt which had pressed so heavily on it, he became more composed, and joined in the exercises of devotion with more fixed attention, and apparently with a greater degree of intelligence, than he had hitherto evinced. On Sunday night he slept for more than two hours; and this morning he was more tranquil than usual. The Rev. Mr Harker, whose humane exertions in administering to him the consolations of religion, have all along been unremitted, attended him at 6 o'clock, and remained with him till eight. He returned again at nine o'clock, to assist him in preparing for the last awful trial of his fortitude.

At a quarter past eleven the unhappy culprit was placed in a waggon, to be drawn to the place of execution, on Pennenden heath, about a mile from Maidstone gaol. The executioner was placed by his side, and two officers with loaded carbines were also seated in the waggon. fronting the criminal. His dress was the same that he had worn during his trial, consisting of a blue coat, a yellow waistcoat, a white neck cloth, and top boots. The procession moved slowly towards the heath, the criminal frequently turned up his eyes to heaven, and ejaculating "O Lord, have mercy upon me! Christ, have mercy upon me!"—About 100 yards from the prison gate his mother caught his eye in the crowd. He did not appear to be much moved at seeing her, but bent his head to one of the officers who sat before him, and said, "Mind, tell Mr Bowen to do something for my family." The procession arrived at the place of execution about 10 minutes before 12, and the waggon was drawn up along the side of the scaffold. The chaplain then joined the criminal in prayer, and the stillest silence pervaded the immense crowd, who stood uncovered while the service was reading. The criminal, who had knelt down by Mr Harker's side, joined in the prayers with as much fervour as his agitation would permit. His hands were clasped together and uplifted, and his eyes were sometimes directed downwards to the book in the chaplain's hand, as if he did not understand what was read; occasionally they were turned up to heaven, but during the greater part of the time they wandered unconsciously over the crowd without any definite direction.

When the devotions were closed, and the criminal was about to be removed from the waggon, he observed near him Mr Hay, the barrack master of Woolwich, and said he wished to speak to him. Mr Hay come forward and said, "For God's sake, Nisbett, be sincere; consider what you are about, and tell the truth." He replied, "I have told the truth already, and nothing but the truth. My family knows nothing of my guilt, and I hope you will do something for them." Mr Hay asked him if he had confessed his guilt; and he replied, "I have confessed it to another person." He then mounted the stage with a firm step, and the executioner proceeded to put a cap over his eyes, and to adjust the rope round his neck. Having seen Mr Bowen, of Woolwich, near the scaffold, he called to him and said, "Mr Bowen, I hope you will have some regard for my family. Poor things! they are innocent. None that belongs to me know anything of my doings." Mr Bowen called to him to confess his crime, on which he replied, "I have made all the confession I had to make. That will be known after I am gone. The people is convenient that has it. It is enough for one person to know."

At 5 minutes after 12 o'clock the fatal signal was given. He did not seem to suffer more than one minute. The body, after hanging the usual time, was cut down, and conveyed in a shell to Messrs. Day and Watman's to be anatomized, pursuant to his sentence.

Previously to his trial, Nesbett had prepared the following declaration, in his own hand-writing, to be delivered to Mr Hay, the barrack master of Woolwich, an intelligent and humane gentleman, who was anxious to have it ascertained that the family of the murderer were not implicated in his guilt :—

"Maidstone, the 24th July, 1820

"This is the truth, as I have God to meit it in the next world, let me Be Guilty or Not, none of my family, father or mother wife or Children or any Relation of mine knows whether I am Guilty or Not of the Crime that is laid to my Charge, that is the murder of Mr Parker and his House-keeper, or any other part of that Crime that is laid to my Charge, or any other crime that is laid to me, As God has my soul in his Charge this Day to try my Guilt that is the truth, and I hope no one will Cast it up to my wife or Children, for the Do not deservit. I sine this to be truth.

"JAMES NISBETT."

Addressed for "Mr Hay, Barrick Master, Woolwich, Kent."

Endorsed in the handwriting of Mr Hay, but the diction of the prisoner :—

" As I have this Bible in my hand, and God to meet, I declare the contents of this paper are true.

JAMES NISBETT "

" Witness, STEPHEN PAGE, Turnkey.

Maidstone Goal, 26th July,'1820,"

J. Catnach, Printer, Monmouth Court.

THE SENTENCES OF ALL THE PRISONERS,

WHICH COMMENCED ON

WEDNESDAY,

11th Sept., 1822.

—§—

BEFORE

Justice Hall, Mr Baron Graham, Mr Justice Best, and Mr Justice Richardson, the Lord Mayor, Recorder, and Sheriffs of London, Mr Alderman Ansley, &c.

IN THE OLD BAILEY.

DEATH.

Richard Mitford, alias Captain Stracy, for forgery; William Adams for cutting and maiming; William Callaghue, for returning from transportation; Samuel Wilson, Isaac Knight, and James Simpson, for horse-stealing; Samuel Greenwood, John Bridgeman, Robert Ramsey, Thomas Gordon, William Milton, and John Levy, for highway robbery; Thomas Hayes, William Williams, Joseph Williams, Francis Waddel, Mary Gyngell, Daniel Coltrel, John Brown, Walter Blanchard, Alexander Brown, Frank Purdon, William Corbett, alias Watson, Charles Robinson, and Joseph Mackarell, for stealing in dwelling houses; William Reading, for burglary; Edmund Mustoe, James Gardner, William Bright, and George Vergenton, for robbing near the highway; and John Partier, John Roberts, and Stephen Tool, for burglary.

During the time the Recorder was passing sentence of death, the culprits behaved with great propriety. The prisoner, R. Mitford, alias Captain Stracey, for forgery, was attired in a very elegant manner, his youthful and very gentlemanly appearance interested every one present in his lamentable situation. He is the son of a Clergyman.

Holland, King, and North for an unnatural crime.

TRANSPORTED FOR LIFE.

John Boyle, Cornelius Reading, Joseph Haybury, John Lewis, Thomas Trinder, William Smith, John Strange, and Thomas Harris,

FOR FOURTEEN YEARS.

Thomas Luby, T. L. Robinson.

FOR SEVEN YEARS.

William Garrard, Matthew Fennett, James Hicker, James Nicholas Moore, Eliza Davis, David Davis, otherwise Barnard, Rosina Davis, Thomas Long, James Moore, Julia Witherell, Mary Mushton, Christopher Gromer, Edward Fordem, Harriet Wyse, Thomas Jefts, William Needham, Edward Ford, Sarah West, James Harris, George King, Elizabeth Bool, Mary Smith, James Kellerin, William Tuck, John Mackay, George Hilsey, Luke Higgins, Joseph Hunt, George Wiggis, William Jupennan, John Williams, John Card, Hedges, and Willoughby.

—Imprisoned two years, and kept to hard labour.— Thomas Williams, John Pavey, Robert Wilson, John Bankes, and William Tuck, the two latter to be publicly whipped.——Imprisoned one year and kept to hard labour—John Haughton, Joseph Johnson, Joseph Moore, Thomas Letford, Eliza Godfrey, Bridget Callagan, Thomas Burke, and William Coulson,—imprisoned one year in Newgate.—Mary A. L. Butler,—imprisoned six months and kept to hard labour.——Thomas Best, Eleanor Jackson, Mary Barnes, John Hitchen, Sarah Jones, Thomas Griffiths, Eleanor Smith, P. H. Nielle, Ann Hay, Harriet Lee, Richard Spragg, Joseph Thirk, William Jones, James Sidebotham, Thomas Jones, Charles Askew, and James Easthill.

Catherine Rouke, John Gidling, John Wignal, and George Malsby, for felony, to be imprisoned for six months in the House of Correction, and kept to hard labour.—M. Gerard, W. Mayne and M. Pedlard for minor offences, to be fined one shilling and then discharged.— W. Smith and Ann Aldridge for felony, to be imprisoned two months in the House of Correction, and kept to hard labour during that period.—H. Browne, for a felony, to be publicly whipped, and kept to hard labour in the House of Correction for one year.—John Smith and Eliza Lewis, for felonies, to be imprisoned three months in the House of Correction, and kept to hard labour.— T. Worcester and John Jones, for felonies, to be publicly whipped and kept to hard labour for three months in the House of Correction.—Edmund Barber and William Burrell, for a misdemeanour, to be imprisoned six months and kept to hard labour during one month.

Judgment respited on John Parkes, James Hicker, James Nicholas Moore, (whose father is sentenced to transportation) and Thomas Wilbraham.

An immense number were sentenced to various minor periods of imprisonment, some to be publicly and some privately whipped. —— A considerable number were discharged by proclamation.

The number of prisoners tried this Sessions has been between 400 and 500. Adjourned to the 23rd of October.

London: Printed by Charles Pigott, 52, Compton Street, Clerkenwell.

A mournful and affecting
COPY OF VERSES
on the death of
ANN WILLIAMS,
Who was barbarously and cruelly murdered by her sweetheart,
W. JONES, near Wirksworth, in Derbyshire, July, 1823.

William Jones, a young man aged 20, has been fully committed to Derby gaol for the murder of his sweetheart, under circumstances of unheard of barbarity. The poor victim was a servant girl, whom under pretence of marriage he seduced. On her proving with child the villain formed the horrid design of murdering her, and carried his diabolical plan into execution on Monday evening last. The following verses are written upon the occasion, giving a complete detail of this shocking affair :—

Come all false hearted young men
  And listen to my song,
'Tis of a cruel murder,
  That lately has been done
On the body of a maiden fair.
  The truth I will unfold,
The bare relation of this deed
  Will make your blood run cold.
Near Wirksworth town in Derbyshire,
  Ann Williams she did dwell,
In service she long time had lived,
  Till this to her befel.
Her cheeks were like the blushing rose
  All in the month of May,
Which made this wicked young man
  Thus unto her did say :
Nancy, my charming creature,
  You have my heart ensnared,
My love is such I am resolved
  To wed you I declare.
Thus by his false deluding tongue
  Poor Nancy was beguil'd,
And soon to her misfortune,
  By him she proved with child.
Some days ago this damsel fair
  Did write to him with speed,
Such tenderness she did express
  Would make a heart to bleed.
She said, my dearest William,
  I am with child by thee;
Therefore, my dear, pray let me know
  When you will marry me.
The following day at evening,
  This young man did repair,
Unto the town of Wirksworth,
  To meet his Nancy there.
Saying, Nancy dear, come let us walk,
  Among the flowery fields,
And then the secrets of my heart
  To you I will reveal.
O then this wicked young man
  A knife he did provide,
And all unknown to his true love
  Concealed it by his side.
When to the fatal spot they came,

These words to her did say :
All on this very night I will
  Your precious life betray.
On bended knees she then did fall,
  In sorrow and despair,
Aloud for mercy she did call,
  Her cries did rend the air ;
With clasped hands and uplift eyes
  She cried, Oh spare my life,
I never more will ask you
  To make me your wedded wife.
O then this wicked young man said,
  No mercy will I show ;
He took the knife all from his side,
  And pierced her body through.
But still she smiling said to him,
  While trembling with fear,
Ah! William, William, spare my life ;
  Think on your baby dear.
Twice more then with the bloody knife
  He ran her body through,
Her throat was cut from ear to ear,
  Most dreadful for to view ;
Her hands and arms and beauteous face
  He cut and mangled sore,
While down upon her milk white breast
  The crimson blood did pour.
He took the shawl from off her neck,
  And round her body tied,
With pebble stones he did it fill,
  Thinking the crime to hide.
O then into the silver stream
  He plunged her straightway,
But with her precious blood was stained,
  Which soon did him betray.
O then this young man taken was,
  And into prison sent,
In ratling chains he is confin'd,
  His crime for to lament,
Until the Assizes do come on
  When trembling he must stand,
Reflecting on the deed he's done ;
  Waiting the dread command.
Now all you thoughtless young men
  A timely warning take ;
Likewise ye fair young maidens,
  For this poor damsel's sake.
And Oh beware of flattering tongues,
  For they'll your ruin prove ;
So may you crown your future day,
  In comfort, joy, and love.

Printed at J. Pitts, Wholesale Toy and Marble Warehouse, 6, Great St. Andrew Street, Seven Dials.

THE CONFESSION AND EXECUTION OF
JOHN THURTELL
AT HERTFORD GAOL,
On Friday, the 9th of January, 1824.

THE EXECUTION.

Hertford, half-past twelve o'clock.

This morning, at ten minutes before twelve, a bustle among the javelin-men stationed within the boarded enclosure on which the drop was erected, announced to the multitude without that the preparations for the execution were nearly concluded. The javelin-men proceeded to arrange themselves in the order usually observed upon these melancholy but necessary occurrences. They had scarcely finished their arrangements, when the opening of the gate of the prison gave an additional impulse to public anxiety.

When the clock was on the stroke of twelve, Mr Nicholson, the Under-Sheriff, and the executioner ascended the platform, followed on to it by Thurtell, who mounted the stairs with a slow but steady step. The principal turnkey of the gaol came next, and was followed by Mr Wilson and two officers. On the approach of the prisoner being intimated by those persons who, being in an elevated situation, obtained the first view of him, all the immense multitude present took off their hats.

Thurtell immediately placed himself under the fatal beam, and at that moment the chimes of a neighbouring clock began to strike twelve. The executioner then came forward with the rope, which he threw across it. Thurtell first lifted his eyes up to the drop, gazed at it for a few moments, and then took a calm but hurried survey of the multitude around him. He next fixed his eyes on a young gentleman in the crowd, whom he had frequently seen as a spectator at the commencement of the proceedings against him. Seeing that the individual was affected by the circumstance, he removed them to another quarter, and in so doing recognised an individual well known in the sporting circles, to whom he made a slight bow.

The prisoner was attired in a dark brown great coat, with a black velvet collar, white corduroy breeches, drab gaiters and shoes. His hands were confined with handcuffs, instead of being tied with cord, as is usually the case on such occasions, and, at his own request, his arms were not pinioned. He wore a pair of black kid gloves, and the wrists of his shirt were visible below the cuffs of his coat. As on the last day of his trial, he wore a white cravat. The irons, which were very heavy, and consisted of a succession of chain links, were still on his legs, and were held up in the middle by a Belcher handkerchief tied round his waist.

The executioner commenced his mournful duties by taking from the unhappy prisoner his cravat and collar. To obviate all difficulty in this stage of the proceedings, Thurtell flung back his head and neck, and so gave the executioner an opportunity of immediately divesting him of that part of his dress. After tying the rope round Thurtell's neck, the executioner drew a white cotton cap over his countenance, which did not, however, conceal the contour of his face, or deprive him entirely of the view of surrounding objects.

At that moment the clock sounded the last stroke of twelve. During the whole of this appalling ceremony, there was not the slightest symptom of emotion discernible in his features; his demeanour was perfectly calm and tranquil, and he behaved like a man acquainted with the dreadful ordeal he was about to pass, but not unprepared to meet it. Though his fortitude was thus conspicuous, it was evident from his appearance that in the interval between his conviction and his execution he must have suffered much. He looked careworn; his countenance had assumed a cadaverous hue, and there was a haggardness and lankness about his cheeks and mouth, which could not fail to attract the notice of every spectator.

The executioner next proceeded to adjust the noose by which Thurtell was to be attached to the scaffold. After he had fastened it in such a manner as to satisfy his own mind, Thurtell looked up at it, and examined it with great attention. He then desired the executioner to let him have fall enough. The rope at this moment seemed as if it would only give a fall of two or three feet. The executioner assured him that the fall was quite sufficient. The principal turnkey then went up to Thurtell, shook hands with him, and turned away in tears. Mr Wilson, the governor of the gaol, next approached him. Thurtell said to him, " Do you think, Mr Wilson, I have got enough fall?" Mr Wilson replied, "I think you have, Sir. Yes, quite enough." Mr Wilson then took hold of his hand, shook it, and said, " Good bye, Mr Thurtell, may God Almighty bless you." Thurtell instantly replied, " God bless *you*, Mr Wilson, God bless *you*." Mr Wilson next asked him whether he considered that the laws of his country had been dealt to him justly and fairly, upon which he said, "I admit that justice has been done me—I am perfectly satisfied."

A few seconds then elapsed, during which every person seemed to be engaged in examining narrowly Thurtell's deportment. His features, as well as they could be discerned, appeared to remain unmoved, and his hands, which were extremely prominent, continued perfectly steady, and were not affected by the slightest tremulous motion.

Exactly at two minutes past twelve the Under-Sheriff, with his wand, gave the dreadful signal—the drop suddenly and silently fell—and

JOHN THURTELL WAS LAUNCHED

INTO ETERNITY.

Printed at J. Pitts, Wholesale Toy and Marble Warehouse, 6, Great St. Andrew Street, Seven Dials.

TRIAL, CONFESSION, & EXECUTION

OF

C. T. WHITE, FOR ARSON, & AMELIA ROBERTS, FOR A ROBBERY,

AT THE OLD BAILEY.

THE

Horrible & Appaling Spectacle

WITNESSED ON THE FATAL GALLOWS.

Yesterday morning, before 8 o'clock, an immense assemblage of spectators, in numbers equal to those who witnessed the fate of Fauntleroy, crowded the Old Bailey, from one end to the other, to witness the execution of Charles Thomas White, late a bookseller in Holborn, for the crime of arson, and Amelia Roberts, for an aggravated robbery. The unfortunate man White had excited an extraordinary interest.

The young woman, Roberts, who was convicted of robbing Mr Austin, of Red Lion-street, Clerkenwell, with whom she lived as cook, of property to the amount of £400 and upwards, and Patrick Riley, her sweetheart, was convicted of the same offence. The conduct of this unhappy creature has been such, during her confinement, as to excite the respect, pity, and commisseration of those who visited her. She has been extremely attentive to her religious duties, and the principal thing that engrossed her attention relative to this world was to exculpate Riley, and hear that he was converted from what she deemed Papistical errors. On the evening of Sunday she was amazingly cheerful, and said, as her punishment was just, she would rather undergo it than return into a world of temptation.

The conduct of White was very different, the bare contemplation of the awful moment of execution unmanned him. He totally disregarded religious exercises, and sat day after day brooding over his past life, and occasionally starting upon his feet, bitterly inveighing against his sentence. Immediately after his trial, and for a long time subsequent, the unfortunate young man persisted in his entire innocence, and strove to convince others of it, by that sort of sophistical reasoning of which his defence consisted. He has asked over and over again what could have been his motive to commit so flagrant a crime, when his circumstances were not embarrassed, and his prospects flattering?

At length, however, he confessed his guilt, but in excuse pleaded that he was of unsound mind at the time. Finding, at length, that in all probability the door of mercy would be closed against him, he had recourse to many ingenious measures to effect his escape; and it appears quite clear, that he must have some powerful auxiliaries, both among his fellow prisoners and outside of the prison.

When the warrant of death arrived, which included his name, the wretched man at first raved like a maniac, his fondly cherished hope being cut off, but when he regained composure, his thoughts and conversation were again engaged upon an attempt to escape. A few days before that fixed for his execution, he said, "I know that I am a sinner, but God is merciful, and I hope to go to Heaven. I know, too, that I must suffer, but I never allow myself to think of the day."

THE EXECUTION.

White ascended the platform with an unsteady and tremulous step. Slark, the Sheriff's attendant, with a black wand, accompanied him, and said something to the executioner, who called his assistant, and they immediately conducted White to the west end of the platform, and while one adjusted a rope through the chain attached to the beam, the other held his hands and arms. White trembled, and his agitation seemed to increase; he raised his arms, and extended his chest, as if desirous of bursting the cords, and by the effort loosened his wrists. The cap was drawn over his eyes, but the restlessness of the unhappy man seemed to increase; and, just as the woman was ascending the steps, he bent his head down, and pushed off the cap, accompanying this action by a violent movement of the body, as if to break or get his head out of the fatal

noose. The action was made with so much strength and violence, and his struggling appearing to increase, that a dreadful yell, and cries of the utmost horror burst from the crowd. The two assistant executioners were called to ascend the platform, and they held the unhappy man while a handkerchief was tied over his eyes. They endeavoured to draw a cap over his face, but he struggled hard with the executioner, and repeatedly forced it off. The executioner seized the unhappy man with some violence, to induce him to desist from proceeding to loosen his hands, and the crowd renewed their former cries and yellings.

Amelia Roberts was then brought upon the scaffold, and a cord having been tied round her lower garments, the rope was adjusted round her neck. White again got the handkerchief off, and turning to the woman and crowd alternately, by his gestures, appeared as if desirous of exciting universal sympathy. The arrangements of the executioner being complete, he removed the woman to a position immediately under the fatal beam, and then placed White by her side; but the unhappy man gradually moved forward, until he gradually got his toes upon the ledge, where Mr Cotton and Mr. Baker were reading the Burial Service. The handkerchief was again placed over his eyes, but it was evident, from the fineness of its texture, and what occurred soon afterwards, that he must have seen through it. At the moment Mr Cotton drew a white handkerchief from under his surplice, he leaped upon the platform, and by sinking his head was able to grasp that part of the cord which was affixed round his neck under his chin. It appeared to be a desperate effort to prolong that life which he so fondly clung to. At this moment the spectacle was most horrifying—he was partly suspended, and partly standing on the platform. During the violence of his exertions, his tongue was forced out of his mouth, and the convulsions of his body and contortions of his face were truly appalling. The cries of displeasure from the crowd were again renewed, and they continued till the executioner had forced the wretched man's hands from the cord, and moved his feet from the platform, when in an instant the rope had its full tension; and, by pulling the man's legs, he ceased struggling, and in a few minutes was dead. It is thought, that if his arms had not been fastened by a cord, the handkerchief would have given way, and the most painful consequences would have resulted. As it was, his sufferings were considerably protracted. The distortions of his countenance, in the agonies of death, could be seen by the crowd; and, as he remained suspended without any covering to his face, the horrible spectacle was most terrific. The shrieks of the women, and the cries of the men, rendered the scene more painful than any one we had ever witnessed before; and but for the wise precaution of erecting extra barriers across the street, much mischief would have been done in the confusion.

The sufferings of the poor woman were momentary.—When she was brought into the dock, at the bottom of the stairs leading to the scaffold, she took a seat on a bench. Mr. Baker attended her, while Mr. Cotton attended White on the scaffold. Her eyes were closed, and her resignation was surprising. She ejaculated, "Into thy hands, oh Lord! I commit my soul;" and just before she ascended the scaffold, she said, "God have mercy, save my soul! and pity and pardon my poor friend Patrick" (alluding to Riley). Whilst on the scaffold, she continued praying, in which she was in some degree disturbed by the extraordinary conduct of her fellow culprit.

The crowd were greatly affected by the horrid sight which they had witnessed, and we trust that this example will have its due effect upon the minds of the thoughtless and wicked.

J. Catnach, Printer, 2 and 3, Monmouth Court.

CONFESSION AND EXECUTION OF
WILLIAM CORDER,
THE MURDERER OF MARIA MARTEN.

Since the tragical affair between Thurtell and Weare, no event has occurred connected with the criminal annals of our country which has excited so much interest as the trial of Corder, who was justly convicted of the murder of Maria Marten on Friday last.

THE CONFESSION.

"Bury Gaol, August 10th, 1828.—Condemned cell. "Sunday evening, half-past Eleven.

"I acknowledge being guilty of the death of poor Maria Marten, by shooting her with a pistol. The particulars are as follows :—When we left her father's house, we began quarrelling about the burial of the child: she apprehended the place wherein it was deposited would be found out. The quarrel continued about three quarters of an hour upon this sad and about other subjects. A scuffle ensued, and during the scuffle, and at the time I think that she had hold of me, I took the pistol from the side pocket of my velveteen jacket and fired. She fell, and died in an instant. I never saw her even struggle. I was overwhelmed with agitation and dismay :—the body fell near the front doors on the floor of the barn A vast quantity of blood issued from the wound, and ran on to the floor and through the crevices. Having determined to bury the body in the barn (about two hours after she was dead. I went and borrowed a spade of Mrs Stow, but before I went there I dragged the body from the barn into the chaff-house, and locked the barn. I returned again to the barn, and began to dig a hole, but the spade being a bad one, and the earth firm and hard, I was obliged to go home for a pickaxe and a better spade, with which I dug the hole, and then buried the body. I think I dragged the body by the handkerchief that was tied round her neck. It was dark when I finished covering up the body. I went the next day, and washed the blood from off the barn-floor. I declare to Almighty God I had no sharp instrument about me, and no other wound but the one made by the pistol was inflicted by me. I have been guilty of great idleness, and at times led a dissolute life, but I hope through the mercy of God to be forgiven. WILLIAM CORDER."

Witness to the signing by the said William Corder, JOHN ORRIDGE.

Condemned cell, Eleven o'clock, Monday morning, August 11th, 1828.

The above confession was read over carefully to the prisoner in our presence, who stated most solemnly it was true, and that he had nothing to add to or retract from it.—W. STOCKING, chaplain ; TIMOTHY R. HOLMES, Under-Shertff.

THE EXECUTION.

At ten minutes before twelve o'clock the prisoner was brought from his cell and pinioned by the hangman, who was brought from London for the purpose. He appeared resigned, but was so weak as to be unable to stand without support; when his cravat was removed he groaned heavily, and appeared to be labouring under great mental agony. When his wrists and arms were made fast, he was led round towards the scaffold, and as he passed the different yards in which the prisoners were confined, he shook hands with them, and speaking to two of them by name, he said, "Good bye, God bless you." They appeared considerably affected by the wretched appearance which he made, and "God bless you!" "May God receive your soul!" were frequently uttered as he passed along. The chaplain walked before the prisoner, reading the usual Burial Service, and the Governor and Officers walking immediately after him. The prisoner was supported to the steps which led to the scaffold; he looked somewhat wildly around, and a constable was obliged to support him while the hangman was adjusting the fatal cord. There was a barrier to keep off the crowd, amounting to upwards of 7,000 persons, who at this time had stationed themselves in the adjoining fields, on the hedges, the tops of houses, and at every point from which a view of the execution could be best obtained. The prisoner, a few moments before the drop fell, groaned heavily, and would have fallen, had not a second constable caught hold of him. Everything having been made ready, the signal was given, the fatal drop fell, and the unfortunate man was launched into eternity. Just before he was turned off, he said in a feeble tone, "I am justly sentenced, and may God forgive me."

The Murder of Maria Marten.
BY W. CORDER.

COME all you thoughtless young men, a warning take by me,
And think upon my unhappy fate to be hanged upon a tree ;
My name is William Corder, to you I do declare,
I courted Maria Marten, most beautiful and fair.

I promised I would marry her upon a certain day,
Instead of that, I was resolved to take her life away.
I went into her father's house the 18th day of May,
Saying, my dear Maria, we will fix the wedding day.

If you will meet me at the Red-barn, as sure as I have life,
I will take you to Ipswich town, and there make you my wife ;
I then went home and fetched my gun, my pickaxe and my spade,
I went into the Red-barn, and there I dug her grave.

With heart so light, she thought no harm, to meet him she did go
He murdered her all in the barn, and laid her body low :
After the horrible deed was done, she lay weltering in her gore,
Her bleeding mangled body he buried beneath the Red-barn floor.

Now all things being silent, her spirit could not rest,
She appeared unto her mother, who suckled her at her breast ;
For many a long month or more, her mind being sore oppress'd,
Neither night or day she could not take any rest.

Her mother's mind being so disturbed, she dreamt three nights o'er,
Her daughter she lay murdered beneath the Red-barn floor ;
She sent the father to the barn, when he the ground did thrust,
And there he found his daughter mingling with the dust.

My trial is hard, I could not stand, most woeful was the sight,
When her jaw-bone was brought to prove, which pierced my heart quite ;
Her aged father standing by, likewise his loving wife,
And in her grief her hair she tore, she scarcely could keep life.

Adieu, adieu, my loving friends, my glass is almost run,
On Monday next will be my last, when I am to be hang'd ;
So you, young men, who do pass by, with pity look on me,
For murdering Maria Marten, I was hang'd upon the tree.

Printed by J. Catnach, 2 and 3, Monmouth Court.—Cards, &c., Printed Cheap.

189

THE TRIAL, SENTENCE, FULL CONFESSION, AND EXECUTION OF
BISHOP & WILLIAMS,
THE BURKERS.

BURKING AND BURKERS.

The month of November, 1831, will be recorded in the annals of crimes and cruelties as particularly pre-eminent, for it will prove to posterity that other wretches could be found base enough to follow the horrid example of Burke and his accomplice Hare, to entice the unprotected and friendless to the den of death for sordid gain.

The horrible crime of "Burking," or murdering the unwary with the intention of selling their bodies at a high price to the anatomical schools, for the purpose of dissection, has unfortunately obtained a notoriety which will not be soon or easily forgotten. It took its horrifying appellation from the circumstances which were disclosed on the trial of the inhuman wretch Burke, who was executed at Edinburgh in 1829, for having wilfully and deliberately murdered several persons for the sole purpose of profiting by the sale of their dead bodies.

APPREHENSION OF THE BURKERS.

On Tuesday, November 8th, four persons, viz., John Bishop, Thomas Williams, James May, and Michael Shield, were examined at Bow Street Police Office on the charge of being concerned in the wilful murder of an unknown Italian boy. From the evidence adduced, it appeared that May, *alias* Jack Stirabout, a known resurrection-man, and Bishop, a body-snatcher, offered at King's College a subject for sale, Shield and Williams having charge of the body in a hamper, for which they demanded twelve guineas. Mr Partridge, demonstrator of anatomy, who, although not in absolute want of a subject, offered nine guineas, but being struck with its freshness sent a messenger to the police station, and the fellows were then taken into custody, examined before the magistrates, when Shield was discharged and the others ultimately committed for trial.

THE TRIAL.

Friday, December 2nd, having been fixed for the trial of the prisoners charged with the murder of the Italian boy, the Court was crowded to excess so early as eight o'clock in the morning.

At nine o'clock the Deputy Recorder, Mr Serjeant

Arabin, came into the court, when the prisoners severally pleaded "Not Guilty."

The Jury were then sworn, and at ten o'clock Chief Justice Tindal, Mr Baron Vaughan, and Mr Justice Littledale entered the Court, with the Lord Mayor and Sheriffs.

The Bench was crowded with persons of rank, amongst whom was the Duke of Sussex.

Mr Bodkin having opened the case, Mr Adolphus proceeded to state to the Jury the leading facts, as they were afterwards stated in the evidence produced. The case for the prosecution having closed, the prisoners were called upon for their defence.

The prisoner Bishop in his defence stated that he was thirty-three years of age, and had followed the occupation of carrier till the last five years, during which he had occasionally obtained a livelihood by supplying surgeons with subjects. He most solemnly declared that he had never disposed of any body that had not died a natural death.

Williams' defence beiefly stated that he had never been engaged in the calling of a resurrectionist, but had only by accident accompanied Bishop on the sale of the Italian boy's body.

May, in his defence, admitted that for the last six years he had followed the occupation of supplying the medical schools with anatomical subjects, but disclaimed ever having had anything to do with the sale of bodies which had not died a natural death. That he had accidentally met with Bishop at the Fortune of War public house on the Friday on which the body was taken for sale to Guy's Hospital.

At eight o'clock the jury retired to consider their verdict, and on their return they found the prisoners were Guilty of Murder.

The Recorder then passed the awful sentence upon them, "That each of them be hanged on Monday morning, and their bodies be delivered over for dissection and anatomization."

The prisoners heard the sentence as they had the verdict, without any visible alteration. May raised his voice, and in a firm tone said, "I am a murdered man, gentlemen."

THE FULL CONFESSION OF BISHOP AND WILLIAMS.

On Saturday morning Williams addressed a note to Mr Wontner, stating that he and Bishop wanted particularly to see him and Dr. Cotton, the Ordinary. In the course of the interview which immediately followed, both prisoners made a full confession of their guilt, both exculpating May altogether from being party to any of the murders. Having received the confessions, Mr Wontner immediately waited upon Mr Justice Littledale and Baron Vaughan, and upon communicating to them the statements, they said they would at once see the Home Secretary on the subject.

On Sunday morning the Sheriffs visited all three of the prisoners in succession, and with the Under-Sheriffs were engaged between three and four hours in taking down the statements of the convicts. The result of all these investigations was that the same afternoon a respite during his Majesty's pleasure arrived at Newgate for May, and his sentence will be commuted to transportation for life.

THE EXECUTION.

During the whole of Sunday crowds of persons congregated in the Old Bailey, and the spot on which the scaffold was to be erected was covered with individuals conversing on the horrid crimes of the convicts, and in the course of the day strong posts were erected in the Old Bailey and at the ends of Newgate street, Giltspur street, and Skinner street, for the purpose of forming barriers to break the pressure of the crowd.

At half-past twelve o'clock the gallows was brought out from the yard, and drawn to its usual station opposite the Debtor's door. The crowd, as early as one o'clock amounting to several thousand persons, continued rapidly increasing.

By some oversight three chains had been suspended from the fatal beam, and this led the crowd to suppose that May had not been respited. Mr. Wontnor, on hearing of the mistake, directed that one of the chains should be removed. The moment this was done an exclamation of "May is respited," ran through the crowd, and, contrary to the expected tokens of indignation, distinct cheers were heard amongst the crowd on witnessing this token that mercy had been shown to May.

At half-past seven the Sheriffs arrived in their carriage, and in a short time the press-yard was thronged with gentlemen. The unhappy convicts were now led from their cells. Bishop came out first, and after he was pinioned he was conducted to a seat, and the Rev. Mr. Williams sat alongside of him, and they conversed together in a low tone of voice.

Williams was next introduced, and the wonderful alteration two days had effected in his appearance astonished everyone who was present at the trial. All the bold confidence he exhibited then had completely forsaken him, and he looked the most miserable wretch it is possible to conceive. He entered the room with a very faltering step, and when the ceremony of pinioning him commenced, he was so weak as to be scarcely able to stand.

Everything being ready, the melancholy procession moved forward. Bishop was then conducted to the scaffold, and the moment he made his appearance the most dreadful yells and hootings were heard among the crowd. The executioner proceeded at once to the performance of his duty, and having put the rope round his neck and affixed it to a chain, placed him under the fatal beam. Williams was then taken out, and the groans and hisses were renewed. The dreadful preparations were soon completed, and in less than five minutes after the wretched men appeared on the scaffold the usual signal was given, the drop fell, and they were launched into eternity. Bishop appeared to die very soon, but Williams struggled hard. Thus died

THE DREADFUL BURKERS OF 1831.

Printed in London for the Vendors.

191

LIFE, TRIAL, CONFESSION, & EXECUTION

OF

JAMES GREENACRE,

FOR THE

EDGEWARE ROAD MURDER.

On the 22nd of April, James Greenacre was found guilty of the wilful murder of Hannah Brown, and Sarah Gale with being accessary after the fact. A long and connected chain of evidence was produced, which showed, that the sack in which the body was found was the property of Mr. Ward; that it was usually deposited in a part of the premises which led to the workshop, and could without observation have been carried away by him; that the said sack contained several fragments of shavings of mahogany, such as were made in the course of business by Ward; and that it contained some pieces of linen cloth, which had been patched with nankeen; that this linen cloth matched exactly with a frock which was found on Greenacre's premises, and which belonged to the female prisoner. Feltham, a police-officer, deposed, that on the 25th of March he apprehended the prisoners at the lodgings of Greenacre; that on searching the trowsers pockets of that person, he took therefrom a pawnbroker's duplicate for two silk gowns, and from the fingers of the female prisoner two rings, and also a similar duplicate for two veils, and an old-fashioned silver watch, which she was endeavouring to conceal; and it was further proved that these articles were pledged by the prisoners, and that they had been the property of the deceased woman.—Two surgeons were examined, whose evidence was most important, and whose depositions were of the greatest consequence in throwing a clear light on the manner in which the female, Hannah Brown, met with her death. Mr. Birtwhistle deposed, that he had carefully examined the head; that the right eye had been knocked out by a blow inflicted while the person was living; there was also a cut on the cheek, and the jaw was fractured, these two last wounds were, in his opinion, produced after death; there was also a bruise on the head, which had occurred after death; the head had been separated by cutting, and the *bone sawed nearly through*, and then broken off; there were the marks of a saw, which fitted with a saw which was found in Greenacre's box. Mr. Girdwood, a surgeon, very minutely and skilfully described the appearances presented on the head, and showed incontestibly, that the head had been severed from the body *while the person was yet alive;* that this was proved by the retraction, or drawing back, of the muscles at the parts where they were separated by the knife, and further, by the blood-vessels being empty, the body was drained of blood. This part of the evidence produced a thrill of horror throughout the court, but Greenacre remained quite unmoved.

After a most impressive and impartial summing up by the learned Judge, the jury retired, and, after the absence of a quarter of an hour, returned into court, and pronounced a verdict of "Guilty" against both the prisoners.

The prisoners heard the verdict without evincing the least emotion, or the slightest change of countenance. After an awful silence of a few minutes, the Lord Chief Justice said they might retire, as they would be remanded until the end of the session.

They were then conducted from the bar, and on going down the steps, the unfortunate female prisoner kissed Greenacre with every mark of tenderness and affection.

The crowd outside the court on this day was even greater than on either of the preceding; and when the result of the trial was made known in the street, a sudden and general shout succeeded, and continued huzzas were heard for several minutes.

THE EXECUTION.

At half past seven the sheriff arrived in his carriage, and in a short time the press-yard was thronged with gentlemen who had been admitted by tickets. The unhappy convict was now led from his cell. When he arrived in the press-yard, his whole appearance pourtrayed the utmost misery and spirit-broken dejection; his countenance haggard, and his whole frame agitated; all that self-possesion and fortitude which he displayed in the early part of his imprisonment, had utterly forsaken him, and had left him a victim of hopelessness and despair. He requested the executioner to give him as little pain as posiible in the process of pinioning his arms and wrists; he uttered not a word in allusion to his crime; neither did he make any dying request, except that his spectacles might be given to Sarah Gale; he exhibited no sign of hope; he showed no symptom of reconciliation with his offended God! When the venerable ordinary preceded him in the solemn procession through the vaulted passage to the fatal drop, he was so overcome and unmanned, that he could not support himself without the aid of the assistant executioner. At the moment he ascended the faithless floor, from which he was to be launched into eternity, the most terrific yells, groans, and cheers were vociferated by the immense multitude surrounding the place of execution. Greenacre bowed to the sheriff, and begged he might not be allowed to remain long in the concourse; and almost immediately the fatal bolt was withdrawn, and, without a struggle, he became a lifeless corse.—Thus ended the days of Greenacre, a man endowed with more than ordinary talents, respectably connected, and desirably placed in society; but a want of probity, an absolute dearth of principle, led him on from one crime to another, until at length he perpetrated the sanguinary deed which brought his career to an awful and disgraceful period, and which has enrolled his name among the most notorious of those who have expiated their crime on the gallows.

On hearing the death-bell toll, Gale became dreadfully agitated; and when she heard the brutal shouts of the crowd of spectators, she fainted, and remained in a state of alternate mental agony and insensibility throughout the whole day.

After having been suspended the usual time, his body was cut down, and buried in a hole dug in one of the passages of the prison, near the spot where Thistlewood and his associates were deposited.

T. Catnach, Printer, 2 and 3, Monmouth Court.

TRIAL, SENTENCE, CONFESSION, & EXECUTION
OF
F. B. COURVOISIER,
FOR THE
Murder of Lord Wm. Russell.

THE VERDICT.

OLD BAILEY, SATURDAY EVENING,
June 20th, 1840.

After the jury had been absent for an hour and twenty minutes, they returned into court, and the prisoner was again placed at the bar.

The names of the jury were then called over, and the clerk of the court said—"How say you, gentlemen, have you agreed on your verdict? Do you find the prisoner Guilty or Not Guilty of the felony of murder with which he stands charged?"

The foreman of the jury, in a low voice, said—"We find him GUILTY!"

The Clerk of the Court then said: François Benjamin Courvoisier, you have been found Guilty of the wilful murder of William Russell, Esq., commonly called Lord William Russell; what have you to say why the court should not give you sentence to die according to law?

The prisoner made no reply. The usual proclamation for silence was then made.

SENTENCE.

The LORD CHIEF JUSTICE TINDAL, having put on the black cap, said: François Benjamin Courvoisier, you have been found guilty by an intelligent, patient, and impartial jury of the crime of wilful murder. That crime has been established against you, not indeed by the testimony of eye-witnesses as to the fact, but by a chain of circumstances no less unerring, which have left no doubt of your guilt in the minds of the jury, and all those who heard the trial. It is ordained by divine authority that the murderer shall not escape justice, and this ordination has been exemplified in your case, in the course of this trial, by the disclosure of evidence which has brought the facts to bear against you in a conclusive manner. The murder, although committed in the dark and silent hour of night, has nevertheless been brought clearly to light by Divine interposition. The precise motive which induced you to commit this guilty act can only be known to your own conscience; but it now only remains for me to recommend you most earnestly to employ the short time you have to live in prayer and repentance, and in endeavouring to make your peace with that Almighty Being whose law you have broken, and before whom you must shortly appear. The Learned Judge then passed sentence on the prisoner in the usual form.

The court was very much crowded to the last.

THE CONFESSION OF THE CONVICT.

After the Learned Judge had passed sentence on the convict, he was removed from the bar, and immediately made a full confession of his guilt.

THE EXECUTION.

At eight o'clock this morning, Courvoisier ascended the steps leading to the gallows, and advanced, without looking round him, to the centre of the platform, followed by the executioner and the ordinary of the prison, the Rev. Mr Carver. On his appearance a few yells of execration escaped from a portion of the crowd; but the general body of the people, great as must have been their abhorrence of his atrocious crime, remained silent spectators of the scene which was passing before their eyes. The prisoner's manner was marked by an extraordinary appearance of firmness. His step was steady and collected, and his movements free from the slightest agitation or indecision. His countenance indeed was pale, and bore the trace of much dejection, but it was at the same time calm and unmoved. While the executioner was placing him on the drop he slightly moved his hands (which were tied in front of him, and strongly clasped one within the other) up and down two or three times; and this was the only visible symptom of any emotion or mental anguish which the wretched man endured. His face was then covered with the cap, fitting so closely as not to conceal the outlines of his countenance, the noose was then adjusted. During this operation he lifted up his head and raised his hands to his breast, as if in the action of fervent prayer. In a moment the fatal bolt was withdrawn, the drop fell, and in this attitude the murderer perished. He died without any violent struggle In two minutes after he had fallen his legs were twice slightly convulsed, but no further motion was observable, excepting that his raised arms, gradually losing their vitality, sank down from their own lifeless weight.

After hanging one hour, the body was cut down and removed within the prison.

AFFECTING COPY OF VERSES.

Attention give, both old and young,
　Of high and low degree,
Think while this mournful tale is sung,
　Of my sad misery.
I've slain a master good and kind,
　To me has been a friend,
For which I must my life resign,
　My time is near an end.

Oh hark! what means that dreadful sound?
　It sinks deep in my soul;
It is the bell that sounds my knell,
　How solemn is the toll.
See thousands are assembled
　Around the fatal place,
To gaze on my approaching,
　And witness my disgrace.

There many sympathising hearts,
　Who feel another's woe,
Even now appears in sorrow,
　For my sad overthrow.
Think of the aged man I slew,
　Then pity's at an end,
I robb'd him of property and life,
　And the poor man of a friend.

Let pilfering passions not intrude,
　For to lead you astray,
From step to step it will delude,
　And bring you to dismay.
Think of the wretched Courvoisier,
　Who thus dies on a tree,
A death of shame, I've nought to blame,
　But my own dishonesty.

Mercy on earth I'll not implore,
　To crave it would be vain,
My hands are dyed with human gore,
　None can wash off the stain,
But the merits of a Saviour,
　Whose mercy alone I crave;
Good Christians pray, as thus I die,
　I may his pardon have.

PAUL & CO., Printers, 2, 3, Monmouth, Court, Seven Dials.

TRIAL, SENTENCE, AND EXECUTION

OF

ROBERT BLAKESLEY,

For the Wilful Murder of JAMES BURDON,

in Eastcheap.

~~~~~~~~~~~~~~~~

This morning soon after eight o'clock, Robert Blakesley was executed in the Old Bailey for the murder of James Burdon, on the 21st of September, by stabbing him on the left side of his belly. The prisoner was tried at the Central Criminal Court before Lord Abinger and Mr Baron Gurney. Mr Payne appeared for the prosecution. Mr C. Phillips and Bodkin conducted the defence. The Jury after an absence of half an hour returned into court finding the Prisoner GUILTY. The officer of the court then asked the prisoner if he had anything thing to say why sentence of death should not be passed upon him?

The Prisoner: So help me God I am innocent of all intention to murder James Burdon.

Proclamation was then made to keep silence in the court.

Lord Abinger, having put on the black cap, addressed the prisoner as follows:—Robert Blakesley, you stand convicted by a jury of your countrymen of the atrocious and abominable crime of murder. Though you appeal to God to bear witness of your innocence, yet it is by human tribunals that you must be judged. If you are innocent God will not hear that appeal in vain, but we can judge only by human testimony, and the means we have of investigating guilt. Upon that investigation no doubt can be entertained that you are guilty of the crime laid to your charge. You intended to commit another murder; the first person whose life you aimed at taking away was your wife. You then aimed at taking away that of the unfortunate man who became the victim of your anger, and his life has been taken by you, who gave it not, and who cannot restore it. You have, to a certain extent, by your remorse, appeared conscious of your offence. It is impossible for me, sitting in this place, to take any other notice of that remorse than to express a hope that it may be genuine, and that you may, in the short time you have to pass in this world, endeavour to make your peace with God, whose laws in this life you have violated by your crime.

An attempt has been made to excuse you on the ground of temporary insanity. You have had a merciful and deliberate jury, who have paid the greatest attention to to the evidence adduced before them upon that subject, and your own father, who appears to be a person highly respectable, has come forward to endeavour to prove that, as far as he could do so consistently with the truth on your behalf. But, notwithstanding, all the inclination which the jury must have felt to yield, if possible, to the anxious wish of your parent, we have all found it impossible to doubt that you committed this act with malice, with deliberation, and with an intention you had no right or authority to feel, much less to execute. You have taken away the life of one of your fellow-creatures; another, that of your own wife, still remains in jeopardy. What can you expect from human tribunals but that the law should be executed with the utmost severity against you? Its sentence, and I pronounce it with pain and sorrow, is, that you be taken to the place whence you came, to be thence removed to the place of execution, then that you be hanged by the neck till you are dead, and that your corpse be buried in the place of your imprisonment, and may the Lord have mercy on your soul.

The prisoner, who had preserved the same coutenance and demeanour unmoved, was then taken from the dock.

THE EXECUTION.

The moment the culprit appeared on the scaffold, there was a yell from the multitude, but he took no notice of it, but muttering a few words in prayer, he was launched into eternity. For the first couple of minutes, the wretched man struggled very much, to the great gratification of the crowd, at the pain he was supposed to be suffering. After hanging the usual time, the body was cut down, and deposited in a shell, in which he is to be buried to-night within the precintes of the gaol.

PAUL & CO., Printers, 2, 3, Monmouth Court, Seven Dials.

VERSES ON DANIEL GOOD,

Who was executed this morning May, '42, for the Murder of Jane Jones

Of all the wild deeds upon murder's black list,
Sure none is so barbarous and cruel as this,
Which in these few lines unto you I'll unfold,
The recital's enough to turn your blood cold.

In the great town of London near Manchester square,
Jane Jones kept a mangle in South street we hear,
A gentleman's coachman oft visiting came,
A cold-blooded monster, Dan Good was his name.

As a single man under her he made love,
And in course of time she pregnant did prove,
Then with false pretences he took her from home,
To murder his victim and the babe in her womb.

To his master's stables in Putney Park Lane,
They went, but she never returned again,
Prepare for your end then the monster did cry,
You time it is come for this night you must die.

Then with a sharp hatchet her head did cleave,
She begged for mercy but none he would give,
Have mercy dear Daniel my wretched life spare,
For the sake of your own child which you know I bear.

No mercy, he cried, then repeated the blow,
Alive from this stable you never shall go,
Neither you nor your brat shall e'er trouble me more,
Then lifeless his victim he struck to the floor.

And when she was dead this sad deed to hide,
The limbs from her body he straight did divide,
Her bowels ript open and dripping with gore,
The child from the womb this black monster he tore.

He made a large fire in the harness room,
Her head, arms, and legs in the fire did consume,
But e'er his intentions were fulfilled quite,
This dark deed by Providence was brought to light.

To a pawn-shop the coachman he did go one day,
A boy said some trowsers he did take away,
A policeman followed unto Putney Lane,
The coachman and trowsers to bring back again.

When in searching the stable the body he spied,
Without head, legs, or arms, and ript open beside,
Then a cry of murder he quickly did raise,
And the coachman was taken within a few days.

And when he was tried, most shocking to state,
The evidence proved what I now relate,
That Daniel Good murdered his victim Jones,
Then cut up and burnt her flesh and bones.

He soon was found guilty and sentenced to die,
The death of a murderer on the gallows high,
The blood of the murder'd must not cry vain,
An we hope that his like we shall ne'er see again.

J. Harkness, Printer, Preston.

2 c 2

THE EXECUTION OF
JAMES BLOOMFIELD RUSH
AT
NORWICH CASTLE, APRIL 23rd., 1849,
For the murder of Isaac Jermy, Esq., the Recorder of Norwich, and his son, I. Jermy Jermy, Esq.,
AT
STANFIELD HALL.

Between 11 and 12 o'clock the bell of St Peter's, Mancroft, tolled the death knell of the criminal. When conducted to the turnkey's room to be pinioned he met Calcraft, whereupon he said to Mr Pinson "Is this the man that is to do the business?" The reply was "Yes." When he was pinioned he shrugged up his shoulders, saying "This don't go easy; it's too tight."

Within two or three minutes after 12 o'clock the mournful cavalcade proceeded from the interior of the Castle to the spot on which the gibbet was erected. The chaplain, who headed the procession, read, as he passed along, part of the burial service.

When the procession left the Castle gate to proceed to the gibbet, Rush presented a most melancholy and dejected appearance. He was dressed in a plain suit of black, wearing no neck-hankerchief. His shirt collar was turned down. For about twenty yards he walked with a firm unwavering step, but in a moment afterwards he raised his pinioned hands to his face and trembled violently. He then removed his hands from his face, and turning up his eyes to heaven, assumed the attitude of penitence and prayer. On reaching the gallows the rev. chaplain offered up a prayer. While this prayer was being read the condemned convict seemed to be deeply impressed with the awful character of his situation. Immediately on the close of the prayer he beckoned to Mr Pinson, the governor of the Castle, when the following brief conversation ensued:

Rush: Mr Pinson, I have a last request to make to you. It is that the bolt may be withdrawn while the chaplain is reading the benediction—"The grace of our Lord Jesus Christ, and the love of God, and the fellowship of the Holy Ghost, be with us all, evermore."

Mr Pinson: I will communicate your wish to the chaplain, and I have no doubt it will be attended to.

The hangman then placed the unhappy convict under the beam on which he was to hang, and affixed the fatal rope around his neck. Rush said, "For God's sake give me rope enough. Don't be in a hurry; take your time." Then moving his head about, he said "Put the knot a little higher up, don't hurry." The rev. chaplain proceeded with the prayers, and on arriving at the words "The grace of our Lord Jesus Christ," &c., Calcraft withdrew the bolt, the platform went down, and all was over. His death was greeted with loud applause by an immense crowd who had assembled to witness the execution.

Good people listen unto my song,
And girls to whom honest hearts belong,
Pay great attention to what I say,
And by the wicked be not led astray.

Poor Emily Sandford was learned well,
Yet mark what to her fatal lot befel,
The serpent's tongue caused the tears to gush,
For she was betrayed by James Bloomfield Rush.

She begged most pleadingly to be his wife,
And lived with him a most unhappy life,
And though the hot tears down her cheeks did flow
The monster heeded not Miss Sandford's woe.

But seeing that she now was ruined quite,
She stood upon her feet in female might,
And with her pale hand stretched towards his face
Said, " God will curse thee for my deep disgrace."

Forboding were the words Miss Sandford said,
For murderous thoughts were in the wretch's head.
He set to work, and speedily did plan,
The death of servants, husband, wife, and son.

A five barrelled pistol he soon did buy,
And then a mask upon his face did try,
Put on his hat and cloak and pistols drew,
Within its fold a bloody deed to do.

For Stanfield Hall he quick did start,
And old Squire Jermy he shot through the heart !
And while the grey-hair'd man lay bleeding there,
He shot his son and lovely wife so fair.

Eliza Chestney to her Mistress ran,
Saying, " dearest mistress, who is this man ?"
And, while she pressed her mistress to her heart,
A bullet pierced in a dangerous part.

James Bloomfield Rush was then to prison sent,
Miss Sandford against him a witness went,
She was well avenged—for on the gallows high,
The base seducer was condemned to die !

The Judge soon told him that his race was run,—
That he must die for murderous deeds he'd done,
To use the time that yet on earth was given,
In making peace with his God in heaven.

O had you witness'd the parting hour,
Of this wretched man and his nine children dear,
Your hearts would break to think that they might see,
Their father hung upon a gallows tree.

J. Harkness, Printer, Preston.

EXECUTION OF
JOHN GLEESON WILSON,

At Kirkdale Gaol, on Saturday, September 15th, 1849, the Murderer of Mrs. Hinrichson, her Two Children, and Female Servant.

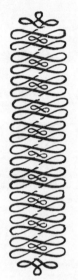

One of the most appalling murders which has for years startled and disgusted society took place on the morning of Wednesday, March 28th, 1849, at No. 20, Leveson Street, Liverpool, at mid-day. A miscreant in the most brutal manner murdered two unprotected women and two helpless children.

In due course Wilson was committed for trial, which took place before Mr Justice Patteson and a respectable jury, who, in less than five minutes, returned a verdict of GUILTY.

On Saturday morning, a few minutes before twelve o'clock, the iron gate leading to the drop was opened, and the prisoner appeared between two priests—the Rev. Mr Duggan and the Rev. Mr Marshall. A general feeling of horror seemed to pervade all present, which found expression in the most distant part of the assemblage by bursts of execration.

Calcraft, the London executioner, was unable to be present from illness, and the office was performed by Howard, from York, who was especially brought to Liverpool by the Under Sheriff. The priests read in English, the service of the Catholic Church for a departing soul until the bolt was drawn, and the wretched culprit was launched into eternity.

Thus terminated the life of one of the greatest criminals that ever disgraced the human family. Upwards of 100,000 persons were present, the railway company running cheap trains from all available parts.

THE LIVERPOOL TRAGEDIES.

Come all you feeling christians and listen unto me,
The like was not recorded in British history,
It's of three dreadful murders committed, I am told,
By one John Gleeson Wilson, for the sake of cursed gold.

On Wednesday the 28th, consternation did prevail,
In Leveson Street in Liverpool, where thousands did bewail,
The fate of this poor family, who we're left to deplore, [more.
Snatched from a father's fond embraces, who ne'er will see them

This monster in human shape did go there to dwell,
And that he went for plunder to all it is known full well,
And when this callous villain saw their defenceless state,
He did resolve them all to kill and rob them of the plate.

His bloody work he did commence all in the open day,
By striking at the children while their mother was away,
The servant girl did interfere, said, "should not do so,"
Then with a poker in his hand he gave her a severe blow.

Numberless times he did her strike till she could no longer stand,
The blood did flow profusely from her wounds, and did him brand,
Then the eldest boy of five years old, in supplication said,
"Oh master, spare our precious lives, don't serve us like the maid."

This darling child of five years old he brutally did kill,
Regardless of its tender cries, its precious blood did spill,
The youngest child to the kitchen ran, to shun the awful knife,
This villain followed after and took its precious life.

The surgeon thus describes the scene presented to his view,
A more appalling case than this he says he never knew,
Four human beings on the floor all weltering in their gore,
The sight was sickening to behold on entering the door.

The mother's wounds three inches deep upon her head and face,
And pools of blood as thick as mud, from all of them could trace,
None could identify the boy, his head was like a jelly;
This tragedy is worse by far than Greenacre or Kelly.

To the hospital in this sad state they quickly were conveyed,
The mother with her infant dear, and faithful servant maid,
Thousands did besiege the gates, their fate for to enquire,
But in three days from incise wounds, both of them did expire.

'Twill cause the captain many a pang to know their awful doom,
His loving wife and children sent to an untimely tomb, [save,
'Twill make his hair turn grey with grief, no skill their lives could
And he did go, borne down with woe, in sorrow to the grave.

But now he's taken for this deed, bound down in irons strong,
In Kirkdale Jail he now does lie, till his trial it comes on,
May God above receive the souls of those whom he has slain,
And may they all in heavenly bliss for ever with him reign.

J. Harkness, Printer, Preston.

THE EXECUTION OF

FRED. GEO. MANNING,

AND

MARIA, HIS WIFE.

At Horsemonger Lane, November 13th, 1849,

For the MURDER and Robbery of PATRICK O'CONNOR.

This morning the last act in the tragedy of the Mannings' was performed on the roof of Horsemonger Lane Gaol, in the presence of an immense assemblage.

The gardens in front of the houses opposite the prison, and from which the best view could be obtained, commanded high prices, and were occupied by persons of apparent respectability, and amongst them were many well-dressed females.

A few minutes before the clock struck nine, the bell of the prison chapel was heard to give forth the fatal toll, and those who had collected in the vicinity of the scaffold were observed to uncover, which was taken up by the populace below as a signal to do the same, and to call for silence. Immediately the roar of voices which had previously prevailed became hushed and still, and the mournful cavalcade ascended the steps of the scaffold, —Calcraft first, then the Chaplain, followed by the wretched man Manning, who ascended the stairs with a firm step, but appeared pale and emaciated. He was dressed in deep black, with a long frock-coat. The rope having been adjusted and the cap drawn over his face, Mrs. Manning, the female partner in his crime was brought up. She was dressed in black satin, tightly bound round the waist, with a long white collar fastened round her neck. On advancing up on the drop, and observing her husband at her side, as if acting upon the sudden impulse of the moment, she seized his right hand and shook it for several minutes. The hangman then hurriedly completed his deadly preparations, the next minute the slam of the drop was heard, and the dread sentence of the law had been accomplished. Manning gave a few convulsive jerks, and all was over, but his wife had a long struggle with death, and it was some moments before the immortal spirit had quitted her body for ever.

THE BERMONDSEY TRAGEDY.

BY J. CLARKE.

Come all you good people of every degree,
I pray you give attention and listen to me,
'Twas in the county of Somersetshire where I was bred and born,
And my wife she is a foreigner,—with her must die in scorn.

For the murder of O'Connor we are condemned to die ;
My wife she said I'm innocent of that sad tragedy,
But 'twas she who shot O'Connor and swore she would shoot me,
Unless I would assist her to bury his body.

Four months before his murder his doom was ready sealed,
His grave made ready under ground his body to receive,
He little thought his death so near when to the house he came,
But his death was plann'd all by our hands his money to obtain.

For murder and plunder they both were fully bent,
They shot him with a pistol, and to his lodgings went,
They got his cash and jewels and quickly did repair,   [pair
To hide the guilt for the blood they'd spilt—oh! what a wretched

At the Old Bailey, London, the trial it came on,
They were arraigned before the judge and English jurymen,
The counsel for the prisoners they nobly did defend,
And tried to prove their innocence, this point they did contend.

After the trial, Mrs Manning said,
I do protest I'm innocent and been unfairly tried,
Though you've pronounced me guilty, and doom'd me to be hung,
More like a dog than Christian, to a being thus undone.

With rage and desperation the keepers by them stood,
And to their gloomy prison they quickly were removed,
The coolness and courage which they before displayed,
Had now forsook them for a time, and they look'd quite dismay'd.

This wicked woman taken was unto Horsemonger Gaol,
Her husband followed after, and very soon did feel
Contrition for his guilty deeds, and to his wife he wrote,
Begging of her to think how soon she was to meet her fate.

The end of poor O'Connor will long in memory reign,
And shew the vice and folly which followed in its train.
Oh! may it thus a warning prove to shun bad company,
Never like the Mannings commit such a tragedy.

Now in their gloomy prisons bound down in irons strong,
Awaiting for the fatal morn when they will meet their doom,
For the murder of O'Connor—oh! what a horrid crime,
Now they are both cut off in the height of their prime.

Stewart, Printer, Botchergate, Carlisle.

THE ESHER TRAGEDY.

Six Children Murdered by their Mother.

You feeling christians give attention,
　　Young and old of each degree,
A tale of sorrow I will mention,
　　Join and sympathise with me ;
It's of a sad and dreadful murder,
　　I shall quickly let you hear,
Which was committed by a mother,
　　On her six young children dear.

The perpetrator of this murder,
　　Mary Ann Brough it is her name,
And formerly as you may see,
　　She nursed the blooming prince of Wales.
But now her days of happiness,
　　Are vanished like the evening's sun,
Good people all, both great and small,
　　Reflect upon the deed she's done.

One night she could not rest in slumber,
　　So her own confession says,
Her little children, six in number,
　　Thus she took their lives away.
'Twas with a sharp and fatal razor,
　　She committed this foul deed,
And one by one she cut their throats,
　　Which causes each kind heart to bleed.

The first and eldest whom she murdered,
　　Sad and dreadful to unfold,
Was a sweet and blooming girl,
　　Something more than ten years old,
And in her wrath and indignation,
　　Thus she slew them one by one,
Causing death and desolation,
　　What on earth could urge it on?

One little pretty boy amongst them,
　　Of the name of Henry,
He cried aloud with eyes of pity,
　　'Mother, dear, don't murder me,'
She heeded not his prattling tongue,
　　But like a demon fierce and wild,
'My dear,' said she, 'it must be done,'
　　And thus she slew her other child.

From bed to bed, and to each chamber,
　　This wretched woman she did go,
While all around her own dear children,
　　Streams of crimson blood did flow.
The dreadful sight was most surprising,
　　To behold these children dear,
How their cruel hearted mother,
　　Cut their throats from ear to ear.

Oh ! what must be the woman's motive,
　　Did she think she'd done amiss,
Or did she think of death and judgment
　　To perpetrate a deed like this?
But now the wretch she is committed,
　　To a prison's gloomy cell,
Where midnight dreams to her will whisper
　　And her deeds of blood will tell.

Within the prison's massive walls,
　　What anguish will torment her breast.
When phantoms of her six dear children,
　　Will disturb her of her rest.
Such a sad and dreadful murder,
　　On record there is no worse,
Committed by a cruel mother,
　　Once the Prince of Wales' Nurse.

CONFESSION OF THE MURDERESS.

The following confession was made by the murderess, to Mr. Biddlecombe, chief superintendent of the Surrey Constabulary :—"On Friday last, I was bad all day ; I wanted to see Mr. Izod, and waited all day. I wanted him to give me some medicine. In the evening I walked about, and afterwards put the children to bed, and wanted to go to sleep in a chair.—About nine o'clock, Georgy (meaning Georgianna) kept calling me to bed. I came up to bed, and they kept calling me to bring them some barley water, and they kept calling me till nearly 12 o'clock. I had one candle lit on the chair—I went and got another, but could not see, there was something like a cloud, and I thought I would go down and get a knife and cut my throat, but could not see. I groped about in master's room for a razor—I could not find one—at last I found his keys, and then found his razor. I went up to Georgy, and cut her first ; I did not look at her. I then came to Carry, and cut her. Then to Harry—he said, ' don't mother.' I said, 'I must' and did cut him. Then I went to Bill. He was fast asleep. I turned him over. He never awoke, and I served him the same. I nearly tumbled into this room. The two children here, Harriet and George were awake. They made no resistance at all. I then lay down myself." This statement was signed by the miserable woman.

J. HARKNESS, Printer, 121, Church Street, Preston.

EXECUTION AT NEWGATE

OF

WILLIAM COGAN,

For the barbarous and cruel murder of his own wife.

The execution of William Cogan for the murder of his wife took place this (Monday) morning at Newgate. The circumstances under which the crime was committed will be fresh in the recollection of the public. The prisoner and his wife were in the habit of getting drunk, and while in that state quarrels took place between them. They had been to a funeral on the day the occurrence took place, and they both drank freely, and when they got home they quarrelled. About two o'clock in the morning he rushed into the street with his throat cut. The prisoner endeavoured to make it appear that his wife had first cut his throat and then destroyed herself. Ever since his condemnation the culprit has continued to assert his innocence, and on Friday last, when he parted for the last time with his father and his sisters, he again positively declared he was innocent. The condemned man slept soundly his last night. On the fatal morning the executioner, Calcraft, was admitted into the cell a few minutes before eight o'clock, and the culprit the moment he entered appeared to recognise him, and rose from his seat and submitted to the operation of being pinioned with the utmost composure; and just as the clock of St. Sepulchre's church chimed the hour the mournful procession moved towards the scaffold. The culprit was then placed under the fatal beam and the rope was adjusted, and after the executioner had retired he prayed most earnestly with the Ordinary for a short time, and almost the last words he uttered were a prayer to God to forgive him. The drop fell almost at the same moment, and the wretched man, after one or two convulsive struggles, ceased to exist. After hanging an hour, according to the terms of the sentence, the body was cut down and placed in a shell and removed to the interior of the prison.

The crowd that was assembled to witness the execution, was very great. During the whole of Sunday afternoon the Old Bailey was thronged, and crowds of persons had assembled so late as twelve o'clock at night, some of whom remained until the period of the execution. The officials of the prison stated that it was one of the noisiest and most disorderly crowds they ever remember to have seen upon a similar occasion. The moment the wretched man made his appearance on the scaffold there was a general cry of "hats off," and the upturned faces of the thousands of spectators presented a most extraordinary spectacle. The culprit was twenty-six years old, and he was apparently a strong muscular man.

A COPY OF VERSES.

Come, all you feeling Christians,
  Give ear, I pray, to me ;
It's of a dreadful tragedy—
  Explained it shall be.
In London town it happened,
  As I can truly say,
William Cogan, the barbarous murderer,
  With a razor his wife did slay.

CHORUS.

Kind friends, now a warning take—
Poor William's life is now at stake.

Oh ! drink—thou cursed beverage—
  What acts thou prompts us to do ;
To make me kill my loved wife,
  Just as a fiend would do !
I once had love, as other men,
  But on my heart a brand ;
Entangled with loose company,
  Committed now I stand.

Heart-rending 'tis to know it,
  My orphan's left behind,
That had a fondling mother,
  Who unto them was kind :
But now she's dead and buried,
  Gone to that rest above,
Where all is joy and happiness—
  Blest with that sacred love.

Oh, cold and stormy was that night,
  And fast the snow did drop,
When Mary Ann was forced to fly
  All from her father's cot.
Though thinly clad, with her chemise on,
  Her shawl upon her swung,
"My God ! my God !" she thus did cry,
  As thus her hands she wrung.

Exposed to wind and weather,
  In a passage there she stood ;
Her limbs were shivering with the cold,
  And freezing was her blood ;
But then she dare not enter
  Where her demon father lay,
Fearful lest, as her mother,
  She might become his prey.

So now, kind friends, take warning,—
  A lesson let this be
Unto those drunken fathers
  Who think of nought but "spree ;"
And pray may God have mercy,
  And show it to him soon ;
And prepare this wicked person
  To meet his awful doom.

Taylor, Printer, London.

EXECUTION OF THE WARWICKSHIRE MURDERER,
GEORGE GARDNER,
For shooting his sweetheart, Sarah Kirby.

The condemned criminal, George Gardner, a ploughman, on Monday suffered the last penalty of the law at Warwick. The execution took place at ten o'clock, before the county gaol, and was performed by Smith, of Dudley. The murder was a most unprovoked and cold-blooded one, by which Sarah Kirby, his fellow-servant, was shot dead while she was standing at her washing-tub, on the 23rd of April last. Both she and the man Gardner were employed at a roadside farm, on the confines of the county, and she was a very good-looking, well-conducted, pious girl. He was a very great blackguard and a sot. Soon after he went to the farm where the murder took place she complained to Miss Edge, the housekeeper, that he annoyed her very much by his attentions, and his attempts to kiss her. Mr Edge, her master, hearing of this, called them both into the parlour, and told him he must not repeat his conduct to her, whereupon Gardner said, "Well, if I can't have her, no one else shall." No further complaints were made after this, though there is reason to believe he continued his suit. He amused himself by looking at her as she undressed at night through a chink in the wall which separated their bedrooms. The only complaint he had against her was that she would not draw him the proper quantity of beer; but the truth was that he wanted more than his fair share. On the morning of the murder he was at work in the plough-field, his master being absent at a cattle fair, and he made remarks to the other labourers which showed him to be contemplating some act of violence, saying he wished he had "some one" before him—he would kill them, and so on; but he appears to have left his work and returned to the house without causing any suspicion to arise in their minds that he was about to commit the crime of murder. Having reached the house, he asked this poor girl to fetch him his master's double-barrelled gun for shooting rooks. He had been in the habit of using it for this purpose before, and no surprise was felt by the girl or by Miss Edge, the housekeeper, who saw her hand the loaded gun to him, Miss Edge remarking, "Mind, it is loaded, George." He said, "Yes, ma'am, I know it is," and tried it by taking off the cap and letting the hammer down. Finding it all right, he followed Kirby to the wash-house, and shot her in the back of the neck. He afterwards threatened Miss Edge, and there is no doubt that if she had not concealed herself he would have shot her. He then escaped with the gun, and was taken by the police on his way to Oxford. Some delay took place in the execution; and from the bad adjustment of the rope or some other cause, the criminal died very hard, struggling much, until at last he hung motionless in the air. The crowd contained a large proportion of women, but was orderly in the extreme, and began to disperse as soon as the drop fell. Gardner died penitent, confessing his crime. The following confession was made by Gardner before his execution:—"I did not want to pay my addresses to Sarah Kirby, but she would never draw me the proper quantity of beer, and that vexed me. I did not know the master was away on the 23rd of April, and the witness who said I asked him where he was will have to suffer for his perjury. I tried my luck in the field by throwing up the "spud" of the plough, which came down with the point in the earth. If it had fallen flat I should not have killed her, but as it came down point foremost I left the field with the determination to do it. I should have killed Miss Edge if I had got near her, and it's a good job no one stopped me before I sold the gun."

VERSES ON THE EXECUTION OF
GEORGE GARDNER,
FOR SHOOTING SARAH KIRBY.

Harkness, Printer, 121, Church Street, Preston.

The solemn knell does most awful sound,
Oh God in pity on me look down,
Forgive my sins and compassion take,
And grant me fortitude to meet my fate.

Oh what numbers approach to see
A wretched man upon the tree,
My time is come, and I must be soon,
A prey to worms in the silent tomb.

When I was scarce eighteen years of age,
As ploughman to Mr Edge I did engage,
He unto me was both good and kind,
But murder entered my wicked mind.

She would't give me beer enough for weeks,
When to take her life I a plan did seek,
I pointed the gun one fatal day,
And with the same took her life away.

When from my labour I did return,
To do her harm my heart did burn,
I took the gun right speedily,
But little thinking she was to die.

Though fellow-servants I did not her like,
That was the reason I took her life,
That was the reason I did her kill,
Maidens never marry against their will.

My bosom heaves and borne down with woe,
The grave lies open and I must go,
To sleep with death till the Judgment day,
When God will pardon me I firmly pray.

It was cursed Satan led me astray,
It was Satan tempted me one day,
It was Satan prompted my guilty mind,
So slay Sarah Kirby both good and kind.

Young men and maidens ere 'tis too late,
Oh take a warning by my fate,
Trust in your Saviour who reigns above,
And never kill whom you cannot love.

It was well for me had I never been born,
To die a death of public scorn,
In youth and bloom on the fatal tree,
Oh God in mercy look down on me.

Petitions have in my favour been
Sent from Warwick town to my gracious Queen,
But alas no mercy is there for me,
And I must die on the fatal tree.

Three weeks I have lain in a gloomy cell,
Where my dreadful sufferings no one can tell,
To gain me pardon my friends have tried,
But oh, alas, it has been denied.

2 D

LIFE, TRIAL, AND EXECUTION OF
WILLIAM G. YOUNGMAN,
The Walworth Murderer.

On Thursday, August 16th, William Godfrey Youngman was placed at the bar of the Central Criminal Court to take his trial for the murder of his mother, two brothers, and his sweetheart.—Shortly after ten o'clock the learned judge, Mr Justice Wilhams, took his seat on the bench. The prisoner, who was described as a tailor, and 25 years of age, was then placed at the bar. He exhibited perfect coolness and self-possession, and did not seem in the slightest degree affected at his awful position. The indictment that was proceeded with was the one charging him with the wilful murder of his sweetheart, Mary Wells Streeter.—Mr James Bevan said : I reside at 16, Manor place, Walworth. The prisoner's father occupied the top floor of the house. On the 31st of July his family consisted of his wife, two little boys, the prisoner, and the deceased. I understand the prisoner had come to see his father on a holiday, and he would sleep there. About ten minutes to 6 in the morning I was in bed, and heard a noise and a heavy fall on the top floor of the house. I got up to see what was the matter, and before I could get to the door Mr Beard knocked at it and said, " For God's sake come here—here is murder." I went upstairs directly, and when I got to the top of the stairs I saw the elder boy lying dead upon the landing, I did not see anything more then, but went down and dressed myself, and I then saw the prisoner standing in his nightshirt on the staircase. He said to me " My mother has done all this—she murdered my two brothers and my sweetheart, and I, in self-defence, believe I have murdered her." I went out and fetched the police.—Susannah Beard said : Me and my husband occupied the back room as a sleeping room. About one o'clock in the morning of the 31st of July, I heard a noise overhead like something very heavy falling on the boards of the bedroom above ours. My husband went out to see what was the matter, and he called out " Murder !" and came downstairs. He afterwards went up again with the landlord. I went to the door of our room and saw the prisoner standing on the staircase. He said, Mrs. Beard, my mother has done all this. She has murdered my sweetheart and my two little brothers, and I believe in self-defence I have murdered her."

Philip Beard, the husband of the last witness, said, I had seen the prisoner in our house a few days. I remember being awoke by my wife, and I heard a rambling on the landing. The noise was like that of children running about. I went out of my room, and I heard a slight scream. When I got to the outside of my room, I saw some blood on the stairs, and on the top of the staircase I saw the little boy lying on the landing. His throat was cut and he was dead. I then saw the body of the deceased lying a little beyond that of the boy. I did not observe any other bodies at the time, as I was very much alarmed, and I went down and called the landlord, and we went upstairs together; and I went to dress. I then fetched a policeman and a surgeon. I saw the prisoner upon the stairs, and he told me that his mother had done it all, and that he had murdered her in self-defence.

After the further examination of a number of witnesses, who corroborated the evidence already given, Mr. Best, in a powerful and touching speech, addressed the jury for the prisaner.

The jury retired, and in about 25 minutes returned into court, and amid breathless suspense gave a verdict of Guilty.

The judge then put on the black cap, and delivered the following sentence : Prisoner at the bar, you have been convicted of the crime of murder, and one of the most heinous ever committed, but it is no part of my office to dwell on the enormity of your guilt. It is my only duty to pass upon the sentence of the law, and that sentence is—That you be taken to the prison from whence you came, and then to the place of execution, and there be hanged by the neck until you are dead. May the Lord have mercy on your miserable soul !

EXECUTION.

Tuesday, September 4th, was the day appointed for the execution of Youngman, the perpetrator of four murders at Walworth. At an early hour people of the lowest order began to assemble in the neighbourhood of the prison, and by five o'clock every available space was occupied. At seven o'clock the chaplain entered the condemned cell to administer religious consolation to the criminal, and remained with him until the time of his execution. In reply to exhortations addressed to him by the chaplain, he repeated substantially the story he had always told as to his share in the crime. The chaplain urged him not to leave the world with a lie in his mouth. " Well, if I wanted to tell a lie it would be to say that I did it." He, nevertheless, conducted himself towards the chaplain with respect, listened to him with attention, and joined in prayer ; but, beyond those mechanical observances, he showed no evidence whatever of feeling.

The minutes which remained to him to live might now be numbered. He was then conducted to a gateway ; in which a corridor he had to traverse terminated, and there, a few minutes before nine, he was pinioned. The procession then formed, the gates were opened, the chaplain commenced reading the burial service, and, so escorted, the convict proceeded to the beam. On arriving at the drop and confronting the mass of human beings he looked wild and startled, but, recovering his composure he allowed himself to be placed on the drop, and, with evident fervency and an audible voice, he followed the chaplain in a prayer, clasping his hands in unmismakeable devotion. For a moment he paused to request the exeeutioner, who was adjusting the noose, to pinion his legs, which was done; and his parting words addressed to the chaplain—were, " Thank you, Mr. Jessop, for your great kindness; see my brother, and take my love to him and all at home."

The drop fell, and he died in a few minutes.

H. Disley, Printer, 57, High Street, New Oxford Street.

THE WIGAN MURDER.

EXAMINATION AND CONFESSION

OF

JOHN HEALEY.

John Healey, who stands charged on his confession with having been concerned with four others in the murder of James Barton, at the Button or Bawkhouse Pit, Haigh, near Wigan, on the morning of the 3rd of January, 1863, was re-examined at Wigan, yesterday. The confession having been read over, Mr. Lamb asked the prisoner if it was correct. He said: it is not all correct, sir. I own to it that I had liquor with the men, but then I do not recollect where I went.—Mr. Lamb: But that portion about the murder?—Healey: I can then recollect the men and then getting drunk, but I do not know what occurred after.—Mr. Lamb: Well, then, how was it that you made that statement?—A man may be in drink and not know what he is doing.—Mr. Lamb: You were not in drink when you made the statement.—The prisoner: No.—Mr. Lamb: Then how was it you made it? The prisoner made no reply. Evidence was then tendered as to the discovery of the few remains of Barton, but nothing fresh was elicited. The only evidence bearing upon the confession of Healey, was that of Jane Little, a collier girl. She deposed that on the morning of the murder she was assisting to load a boat with coal at the Bridge or Pigeon Pit, situated on the canal bank, between the Bawkhouse Colliery and Wigan. The towering path was on the opposite side of the canal to the colliery, and the path was lighted by a light on the pit bank. About a quarter-past two she was in the boat, and a man, named Jordan, was above lowering the coals. He was approaching with a full tub, when she saw four men come in the direction of Haigh. Jordan was just lowering a tub as they came near, and when the men saw him they stopped suddenly by a heap of ashes. Whilst he was fetching another tub they walked sharply past and over the bridge, where they waited till Jordan had gone away again. The men had caps on.—Having been charged in the usual way, the prisoner said he had nothing to say, and he was committed for trial at the next Liverpool assizes.—The evidence of Little is, so far as it goes, corroborative of Healey's confession, and as it was never made public till yesterday, there is no probability that the story of the prisoner with regard to the four men can have been manufactured from the newspapers or from hearsay.

Come all you wild and wicked youth,
Listen to me, I will tell the truth
For that sad and dreadful deed
Has caused my very heart to bleed,
I could not sleep or take my rest,
I compelled was to confess.

CHORUS.

Though justice strictly searched about,
They could not find the murderer out.

Two long years have gone and pass'd,
And I, John Healey, have confessed.
At last to my grief and sad downfall,
I was takon to Wigan Town Hall,
Where I had to face Justice Lamb,
To answer was I the guilty man.

John Healey is my name,
It was strong whiskey did my head inflame,
With four companions at their desire,
At Button Pit near Wigan
To thrust poor James Barton in the furnace flames of
    fire.

              Though, &c.

A warning take young men I pray,
For fear like me you should be led astray,
For nights rambling is my downfall,
And strong drink is the ruin of all;
I have taken father,
The mother left orphans to deplore,
May the Lord have mercy on his soul,
They will never see him more.

  Alas in Kirkdale Gaol I lay,
  A-waiting for the trial-day.

Harkness, Printer, Preston.

EXECUTION

OF

PRISCILLA BIGGADIKE,

at Lincoln, for the

WILFUL MURDER OF HER HUSBAND.

Priscilla Biggadike, who was sentenced to death at the recent Lincoln Assizes, for the wilful murder of her husband by poisoning, at Stickney, a village near Boston, in Lincolnshire, was executed on Monday morning, at nine o'clock.

The unfortunate woman has appeared to pay considerable attention to the ministrations of the chaplain, but she declined to make any confession of her guilt. On Saturday, she was visited by a brother and three sisters, who remained with her upwards of three hours, and strongly urged her to confess, but still she refused, and at length became passionate at their repeated entreaties. George Ironmonger, one of the persons who lodged at her house, also applied for permission to to see her on Saturday, but was refused.

On Sunday she attended Divine service in the prison. She slept well during the night, and was visited at seven o'clock yesterday morning by the Rev. W. Richter, the chaplain, who again, without avail, implored her to confess her guilt. At a quarter to nine she was pinioned by Askerne the executioner, and although she fainted under the operation, she immediately recovered. Five minutes afterwards, the sad procession left the prison for the scaffold, which was erected within the castle walls, on the east side of the Crown Court, a distance of nearly 200 yards from the prison door.

The unfortunate woman, who was supported by two of the warders, moaned piteously, and appeared to take little heed of the chaplain, while reading the solemn service of the dead. On her way to the place of execution, she said to the warders, I hope my trubles are ended, and then asked, 'Shall we be much longer?' to which a warder gave a negative reply. The service was brought to a close at the foot of a drop, and the chaplain turning to the prisoner, asked her whether she still persisted in the declaration of her innocence? whether she had anything to do with the crime, in thought, word, or deed? In a firm voice she replied, 'I had not, sir.' She was then accommodated with a chair, and the chaplain addressed her as follows: —I have spent an half an hour with you this morning, in endeavouring to impress upon you, a proper sense of your condition, for you are about to pass from this world into another, and to stand before God, to whom the secrets of all hearts are known, I implore you not to pass away without confessing all your sins; not only generally, but especially this particular one, for which you are about to suffer. I had hoped that you would have made that confession, and thus have enabled me, as a minister of Christ, to have pronounced the forgiveness of your sins, under the promise that Christ came into the world to save sinners. It has grieved me much to find that still persist in the declaration, that you are not accountable for your husband's death; that you still say that you did not administer the poison yourself; that you did not see any other person administer it, and that you are entirely free from the crime. Do you say so, now?

The Prisoner, still in a firm voice, said, Yes.

The Chaplain.—There is only one left, that you have endeavoured to confess your sins to God, though you will not to you fellow creatures. All I can now say is, that I leave you in the hands of God; and may he have mercy on your soul. What a satisfaction it would be to your children, to your friends, to your relations, to know that you had passed from death into life, in the full persuasion that your sins were forgiven you, and that you were admitted into the blessed kingdom of God. I fear that I can hold out no further consolation to you—the matter rests between you and the Almighty. Had you made a declaration of your sins, I should have done what, as a minister of Christ, I am entitled to do—I should have told you that " your sins though many were forgiven." I am sorry I cannot exercise that authority at the present moment. I must leave you to God.

The condemned woman was then assisted up the steps to the platform, and placed on the trap door. When the fatal rope was being affixed, she stood firm without assistance. The cap was then drawn over her face, and she the exclaimed " All my troubles are over;" then suddenly "Shame, you are not going to hang me !" "Surely my troubles are over." The bell of the cathedral here tolled forth the hour of nine, at that instant the bolt was drawn, and the wretched woman was launched into eternity.

W. Smith, Printer, Lincoln.

EXECUTION
OF
FREDERICK BAKER.

This morning, the wretched criminal, Frederick Baker, suffered the extreme penalty of the law at Winchester Gaol, for the atrocious murder of Fanny Adams, at Alton, on the 24th of August last. It is satisfactory to state that since his condemnation, the conduct of the unhappy man underwent a total change for the better, and he began to realize the awful condition in which he was placed, and his callous demeanour was changed into one of deep dejection. The prisoner has been assiduously attended by the chaplain of the prison, and to such a state of religious feeling had he been brought, that he fully acknowledged the justice of his sentence. The sheriffs arrived at an early hour. When the operation of pinioning had been performed, the wretched man thanked the chaplain, the governor, and the other officials for their kindness. The procession was then formed, and slowly took its way towards the scene of execution. The cap and rope was adjusted, the bolt drawn, and the prisoner was launched into eternity.

You tender mothers pray give attention,
  To these few lines which I will relate,
From a dreary cell, now to you I'll mention,
  A wicked murderer has now met his fate;
This villain's name it is Frederick Baker,
  His trial is over and his time was come!
On the gallows high he has met his Maker,
  To answer for that cruel deed he'd done.

Prepare for death, wicked Frederick Baker,
  For on the scaffold you will shortly die,
Your victim waits for you to meet your Maker,—
  She dwells with Angels and her God on high.

On that Saturday, little Fanny Adams,
  Near the hop-garden with her sister played,
With hearts so light they were filled with gladness,
  When that monster Baker towards them strayed;
In that heart of stone not a spark of pity,
  When he those halfpence to the children gave
But now in gaol in Winchester city,
  He soon must die and fill a murderer's grave.

He told those children to go and leave him,
  With little Fanny at the garden gate
He said, come with me, and she believing,
  In his arms he lifted her as I now state;
Oh do not take me, my mother wants me,
  I must go home again, good sir, she cried;

But on this earth she never saw thee,
  In that hop-garden, there, poor child, she died

When the deed was done, and that little darling,
  Her soul to God her Maker it had flown,
She cannot return at her mother's calling,
  He mutilated her it is well known;
Her heart-broken parents in anguish weeping,
  For vengeance on her murderer cried,
Her mother wrings her hands in sorrow grieving,
  Oh would for you, dear Fanny, I had died.

The jury soon found this monster guilty,
  The judge on him the awful sentence passed,
Saying, prepare yourself for the cruel murder,
  For in this world, now, your die is cast;
And from your cell you will mount the scaffold,
  And many thousands will you behind,
You must die the death of a malefactor,
  May the Lord have mercy on your guilty soul.

What visions now must haunt his pillow,
  As in his cell he lays now almost wild,
She points at him, and cries, oh tremble, murderer!
  'Tis I, your victim here—that little child!
The hangman comes, hark, the bell is tolling,
  Your time has come, nothing can save you,
He mounts the scaffold, the drop is falling,
  And Frederick Baker fills a murderer's grave.

DOUBLE EXECUTION AT DURHAM.

TRIAL AND EXECUTION OF

M'CONVILLE & DOLAN

For the Murder of Philip Trainer, of Darlington, and Hugh John Ward, of Sunderland, in the County Prison, at Durham, on the 22nd instant.

Yesterday the two murderers, Dolan and M'Conville, were executed within the precints of the goal at Durham. M'Conville, who who was 23 years of age, worked as a furnace-man at Darlington, and was convicted of the murder of Philip Trainer, on the 30th of January last, Dolan murdered a man named Hugh John Ward, at Sunderland, on the 8th of last December. The two convicts left the condemned cell shortly after eight o'clock, each supported by a couple of warders, and attended by the Rev. Canon Consett and Rev. G. Waterton, Roman Catholic priests. A procession, headed by the under sheriff, moved to the west wing of the prison, where the scaffold was erected. The warders conducted the men chained from their cells, and they were taken through the corridors to the pinioning room, where Calcraft commenced his duties. Both men submitted quietly, and prayed unceasingly with the priests. Canon Consett ministered to M'Conville, and the Rev. Waterton to Dolan. At 6 minutes to eight the prison bell began to toll, the hour had scarcely struck before the outer door of the pinioning room opened and the procession issued into the inner court of the prison. It passed along a narrow passage between two wards and abruptly turning to the left, come into the open work yard, where the low gallows was erected. In passing across the yard neither criminal seemed to notice the slight swelling among the cinders and gravel close to their path, which indicated the spot where their graves already dug were lightly covered until the tenants for them were ready. Close to the gallows Calcraft stepped forward and conducted M'Conville under the beam. The criminal was deadly pale, but with upright bearing and steady steps advanced without faltering, Calcraft completed his work in full view of Dolan, who shuddered perceptibly, but never ceased joining in the prayers & responses with the Rev. Waterton. At length Calcraft finished with M'Conville, and then conducted Dolan under the beam. In a few seconds this convict was made fast to the beam, the Clergy and Calcraft crept off the drop, and while petitions for mercy were spoken aloud by both the victims, the bolt was drawn. Dolan died almost instantaneously, but M'Conville struggled for several seconds. After hanging an hour the bodies were cut down, and an inquest was held at eleven.

COPY OF VERSES.

A double murder we have to tell,
  Most dreadful to relate,
Dolan and M'Conville named,
  Who met an awful fate.

Philip Trainer, of Darlington,
  Was by M'Conville slain;
And Hugh Ward, of Sunderland,
  Dolan murdered in the lane.

Two Roman priests attended them
  In prayer the night before,
Who begged for mercy from on high,
  And their sad crime deplore.

At eight o'clock precisely,
  The prison bell did toll;
Each being led and supported,
  Under the warders' controul.

Where the gallows was erected,
  And loosened from their chains;
Their graves too was constructed,
  To receive their sad remains.

Within the prison they met their fate,
  Now according to the law;
And Calcraft performed his duty,
  For crimes mankind abhor.

A black flag was hoisted,
  On the prison walls,
Denoting all was over,
  The death that men appals.

May the Lord have mercy on their souls,
  For their most dreadful crime;
And a warning let it be all
  To the end of time.

W. Smith, Printer, Lincoln.

CONFESSION AND EXECUTION OF
SAMUEL WRIGHT,
For the MURDER of MARIA GREEN.

At an early hour on Monday evening the people began to congregate in front of the gaol and in the public-houses in the vicinity of Horsemonger-lane Gaol, but as the night wore on they gradually dispersed, until towards three o'clock there were only a few stragglers to be seen. About this time the last of the barricades was erected, and every precaution was taken to prevent any disturbance. It had been reported to the prison authorities and the police that an attempt would be made to rescue Wright, and in consequence 500 of the reserves from the A, C, H, K, L, M, and P divisions were on the spot keeping the ground round the prison clear. The arrangements made by Mr. Superintendent Bradford were well carried out by his colleagues, Superintendents White, Bray, Payne, and Gibbs, and Inspectors Silverton, Fyfe, and Turpin, As the hour for the execution approached the crowd began to increase, but all maintained the utmost decorum. At times men were seen pervading the place with a flag, on which was printed in large letters " Man's Cry," and several religious extracts, while some of them read aloud from the Scriptures. After them followed a number of young men singing psalms, the tunes of which were taken up by the populace.

As the hour of seven o'clock approached, the public-houses on each side of the gaol were cleared of their customers, and the doors and windows entirely closed, and at Mrs. Wrangham's, the Masons' Arms, a number of policemen took their station on the leads at the back and front of the house. When daylight began to break the morning was chilly, damp, and foggy; but, as the sun rose, it became more cheerful, and it was then observed that nearly every private house opposite the gaol had all the blinds down, as close as if a person lay dead within. Very few of the windows were occupied, and they seemed to be the inhabitants of the houses. The gardens were kept clear by the police.

Great surprise was felt as the hour of execution arrived at finding that there were so few persons to witness the awful tragedy. Many had refused to stay, saying they would have no hand in the murder of John Wright, and all felt that he was undergoing a penalty that ought to have been remitted. There were not on the whole more than 4,000 or 5,000 persons present, and being scattered round the avenues leading to the place of execution, there was no difficulty in walking about freely.

The unfortunate man slept soundly during the night, and rose about six o'clock. He was visited by the chaplain, who remained with him to the last.

Shortly before nine o'clock the governor of the gaol, Mr. Kean, the sheriffs, Calcraft, and other authorities, entered the cell and pinioned the culprit. They proceeded to the gallows, Wright walking under the drop with a firm step, followed by Calcraft, a warder, and the chaplain. He bowed to the crowd while the cap was put over his head and the rope adjusted round his neck. There were then loud shouts of " Shame," " Murder," " Disgraceful," " Townley," and other manifestations of displeasure on the part of the populace. Wright understood the feeling of sympathy in his favour, and several times bowed his acknowledgments, raising his hands spasmodically.

The fatal hour at length arrived, but there was some little delay before the doomed man ascended the scaffold. Since his condemnation he has behaved throughout with great decorum, and has seen the members of his family several times. The Rev. Mr. Jessop, the chaplain, has been unremitting in his attention to the unhappy man, and his ministrations have been received with the most happy results. Wright, it appears, was brought up a Roman Catholic at a place called Cossey, in Norfolk, and since he has been in prison he has received a letter from the Roman Catholic priest of that place, asking him not to desert the faith in which he was educated. Mr. Jessop asked him if he would like to see the Rev. Dr. Doyle, a Catholic priest, but he was perfectly satisfied with the instruction he was receiving from the chaplain. He took the sacrament on Monday at his own request.

At length the fatal bolt was withdrawn, and in a few moments the unhappy man was launched into eternity.

Wright saw his family and friends a few days ago, and took an affecting leave of them. He has also written two letters, of which the following are copies :—

" Jan. 10, 1864, Horsemonger-lane Gaol.

" Dear Mother,—I feel it my duty to write a few lines to you before I leave this world, although it is under such painful circumstances. Although I have not written to you before, you know how I am situated. I never thought that I should add to your sorrow. Dear mother, I call you by that name, for you have been to me as one, and I may say I to you as a son. I received a kind and welcome letter from Mr. Hazembeth, and was glad to hear that my Cossey friends showed so much sympathy towards me. It is a great crime that I have committed, and I feel that Almighty God will forgive me, and then I hope to join them that's gone before me. Dear mother, it grieves me very much to think that my dear children will be left fatherless and motherless, but there's one above that has promised to be a father to the fatherless.

" Since I have been here I have been treated with the greatest kindness, and I am visited daily by the chaplain, from whom I feel great comfort. I have but a few hours longer to live on this earth, and they will be taken up with reading and prayer. Dear Polly is quite well, and I will leave you to judge my parent's care ; I have seen them several times, but my dear mother does not know that I am condemned to die. I have had a great number of friends who have tried to save me from this end, and have failed ; but thank God, I feel quite prepared to meet it. Dear mother, I conclude with my kindest love to you and my dear daughter. May the blessing of God Almighty be upon you now and for ever. No more from your unfortunate son,

" SAMUEL WRIGHT."
" Good-bye."

" Jan. 11, 1864.

" Dear Mother,—I feel that I must write a few lines before I leave this world, as Almighty God has given me strength so to do. Dear Mother, although I am present here under a heavy crime, I feel as if the Almighty God had freely forgiven me, after all my sins. And what a blessing that is to think that your dear son feels so glorified—that he dies in peace with God, where I hope to meet them that are dear to us. I leave one with you, my dear child, in remembrance of me, and may the Almighty God give you health and strength to bring her up in the ways of the Lord. Dear mother, I feel as if I cannot last but a few days longer, and now I again take a farewell of father, mother, sisters, and brother, and wishing the blessing of God Almighty may be upon you, now and for ever, amen.

" Father's blessing and a kiss for his child.

" SAMUEL WRIGHT."

He made a free confession of the whole of the shocking transaction. He said he could not exactly say how the murder originated, but it was something in this way : That he was asleep in bed, and that the woman came and took him by the waistcoat and said he should not lay sleeping there. Some words ensued, and she threatened to leave him and go with some other man with whom she had previously cohabited. Upon that he jumped out of bed, and as the razor with which he had recently shaved himself was lying on the table he took it up and cut her throat. It was all the work of a moment. The father, the brother, and the brother's wife saw him for about an hour on Monday, and he has also seen his daughter, a little girl about four years old.

He was aware of the efforts that were being made out of doors to save his life, and appeared to feel very grateful to those who took so kind an interest in him. Mr. S. Gurney, M.P., and Mr. J. Phillips, one of the visiting justices, waited upon Mr Justice Blackburn on Monday, and had an interview of about half an hour with him, urging everything they could in Wright's favour, but he refused to accede to their request, and said the law must take its course. Mr. Ebsworth, a surgeon, of Newington, took a petition to her Majesty at Frogmore Lodge. While he was presenting the petition to Colonel Knollys her Majesty passed up the stairs, and he saw Colonel Knollys deliver it into the Queen's hands, but the answer he received to it was that the Queen could not undertake to advise her advisers.

Taylor, Printer, Brick Lane, London.

207

THE EXECUTION OF
JAMES CLITHEROE,
Of St. Helen's, for the Murder of Mary Woods, this day.

James Clitheroe, the culprit in this remarkable case, suffered death on Saturday, in front of the Kirkdale gaol, near Liverpool, though efforts had been made to secure a reprieve. The circumstances in connexion are of a somewhat peculiar description. Clitheroe was a married man with a family, but his affections appear to have been divided between his wife and Mary Woods, a poor paralytic woman, who earned a living by keeping a school and selling small beer. The prisoner was in the habit of sharing the murdered woman's bed, and as his neighbours knew of this he was twitted by them, in the intensely acrimonious manner peculiar to vulgar and uneducated people, as to "the poor cripple Mary Woods" being *enciente* by him. This seems to have annoyed Clitheroe very much, and his mortification and chagrin acting upon a morbid temperament prompted him to murder. On the night of the 28th of December last he visited Mary Woods' house, and went to bed with her as was his wont, but early next morning he cut her throat and his own too, though the wound was only fatal in the case of the woman. Later in the morning the school children were unable to gain admission to the house as usual, and, as no one answered the door after repeated knocks, an entrance was effected at the rear of the premises, and an investigation took place. In an up-stairs room the police found Mary Woods and the prisoner in bed together—the woman quite dead, and with her throat cut, and the man in an exhausted condition, with his throat cut also. The blood upon the woman's throat was dry, and she had evidently been dead for several hours; whereas the blood upon Clitheroe was fresh, and his wound must have been recently inflicted, because the blood was flowing freely from the arteries of the neck when the police first entered. The prisoner, when asked what he had been doing, stated that he and Mary Woods had agreed to cut their throats, saying, "We made it up to cut our throats, She told me that the razor was in the drawer, under the looking-glass. I fetched the razor, got into bed, and first cut my own throat." The prisoner never deviated from this account of the transaction, either before or after the trial, but it must have been untrue in point of fact, because the strong and irresistible probability is, that the woman's throat was cut at five o'clock in the morning, and that she was dead several hours before the prisoner made the attempt upon his own life. When the prisoner was on his trial, Mr Justice Willes directed the jury that if the prisoner counselled, assisted, or directed the woman to destroy herself, he was guilty of murder.

THE EXECUTION.

The culprit, who was pinioned by Calcraft in the usual way, struggled hard. To the last he persisted in the story of suicide. The crowd was not so great as had been expected.

After hanging the usual time, the body was cut down, and the crowd soon after dispersed.

J. Harkness, Printer, Preston.

HORRID MURDER
OF
A GENTLEMAN,
IN A
RAILWAY CARRIAGE.

Another base and dreadful murder,
  Now again, alas, has been,
One of the most atrocious murders
  It is, as ever yet was seen;
Poor Thomas Briggs, how sad to mention,
  Was in a first-class railway carriage slain,
Between Old Ford and Hackney Wick,
  Which caused excitement, care and pain.

Oh, listen to this railway murder
  Poor Briggs received the fatal wound,
Between Old Ford Bridge and Hackney Wick
  And very near great London town.

They found a hat in the railway carriage,
  Made in Crawford-street, St. Marylebone,
In which poor Thomas Briggs was riding,
  On his journey to his home ;
Alas, poor man, he little thought
  That he would be deprived of life,
In the railway carriage, by a villain,
  At ten o'clock that fatal night.

Oh, little did he think they'd kill him,
  He had no thought he was to die,
Upon that fatal Saturday evening,
  On the 9th day of July ;
The villains in the carriage slew him,
  For plunder Thomas Briggs was killed,
In a first-class carriage they did rob him,
  And all around his blood was spilled.

Thomas Briggs was a faithful servant,
  To Robarts, Lubbock and Company,
Three hundred pounds rewards is offered,
  Soon may the murderer taken be,

And brought to justice for the dreadful
  Deed he done, as we may hear,
And glad we are there is before us,
  A clue to the wicked murderer.

They have traced his watch-chain in the city,
  The very key, as we are told,
Stole from poor Briggs that fatal evening,
  Albert curb, with swivel seal in gold.
Robbed of nearly all that he possessed,
  He was, upon that fatal night,
Between Old Ford and Hackney Wick,
  In the Railway Carriage in daylight.

This sad affair has caused excitement,
  Far and near, for miles around,
And thousands to the spot are going
  From all around great London town.
And on the spot they look with horror,
  Where poor Thomas Briggs was killed,
They view with grief, with pain and sorrow,
  Where his crimson blood was spilled.

Oh, God above, look down from Heaven,
  Point the murdering villains out,
Let stern justice close pursue them,
  Never let them roam about ;
On him, or them, we all are certain,
  Has on the brow the mark of Cain,
Thus ends the brutal horrid murder,
  Which has caused such grief and pain.

On that fatal Saturday evening,
  They left him in his crimson gore,
July the 9th, in a railway carriage,
  Eighteen hundred and sixty-four.

Murder in the Railway Train.

Listen to my song, and I will not detain you
    long,
  And then I will tell you of what I've heard.
Of a murder that's been done, by some wicked
    one,
  And the place where it all occurred ;
Between Stepney and Bow they struck the
    fatal blow,
  To resist he tried all in vain,
Murdered by some prigs was poor Mr Briggs
  Whilst riding in a railway train.

Muller is accused, at present we cannot refuse
  To believe that he is the very one,
But all his actions, you see, have been so very
    free,
  Ever since the murder it was done ;
From his home he never went, but such a
    happy time he spent,
  He never looked troubled on the brain,
If he'd been the guilty man, he would have
    hid all he can,
  From the murder in the railway train.

Muller he did state that he was going to
    emigrate
  Long before this dreadful tragedy ;
He often used to talk, about travelling to
    New York,
  In the Victoria, that was going to sea.
Mr. Death, the jeweller, said, he was very
    much afraid,
  He might not know the same man again,
When he heard of the reward, he started out
    abroad,
  About the murder in the railway train.

If it's Muller, we can't deny, on the Cabman
    keep your eye,
  Remember what he said the other day,
That Muller a ticket sold for money, which
    seems so very funny,
  When he had no expenses for to pay.
They say his money he took, and his name
    entered on the book,

Long before this tragedy he came ;
Like Muller's, the Cabman had a hat, and it
    may be his, perhaps
  That was found in the railway train.

Would a murderer have forgot, to have de-
    stroyed the jeweller's box,
  Or burnt up the sleeve of his coat,
Would he the chain ticket have sold, and
    himself exposed so bold,
  And to all his friends a letter wrote,
Before Muller went away, why did not the
    cabman say,
  And not give him so much start on the
    main
If the cabman knew—it's very wrong—to
    keep the secret up so long,
  About the murder in the railway train.

When Muller does arrive, we shall not be
    much surprised,
  To hear that that's him on the trial ;
Give him time to repent, though he is not
    innocent,
  To hear the evidence give no denial.
Muller's got the watch, you see, so it proves
    that he is guilty,
  But like Townley don't prove that he's
    insane
For if it should be him, on the gallows let
    him swing,
  For the murder on the railway train.

Now Muller's caught at last, tho' he's been
    so very fast,
  And on him they found the watch and hat,
Tho' across the ocean he did roam, he had
    better stayed at home,
  And hid himself in some little crack,
Tho' he pleads his innocence, but that is all
    nonsense,
  For they'll hang him as sure as he's a man,
For he got up to his rigs, and murdered Mr.
    Briggs
  While riding in a railway train.

London: Printed for the Vendors.

CHASE, CAPTURE, AND ARRIVAL OF
MULLER,
FOR THE MURDER OF MR BRIGGS, IN A RAILWAY TRAIN.

The clue to the murderer of Mr. Briggs was obtained as follows:—A little girl, the daughter of a cabman, was playing with a small card box, such as jewellers put small trinkets in, and upon exhibiting it to her father, he remembered the name of the jeweller with whom the chain of the late Mr. Briggs had been exchanged, and upon questioning the girl, she said that Franz Muller had given it her four days ago. Muller, who is a German, a tailor's cutter, had previously lived at the house of the cabman. The police were immediately communicated with. On the box being shown to Mr. Death, he at once identified it. Mr. Death then accompanied the cabman and the police to a cottage at Bow, where Muller had lived, and upon seeing a photograph Muller had given the child, he at once recognised the features of the man who changed the chain. The cabman identified the hat found in the railway carriage as the one he had purchased for Muller about four months ago. Inquiries were made, and it was ascertained that the suspected murderer had sailed for New York, on board the Victoria. Inspector Tanner and other officers immediately started for New York, to await the arrival of Victoria. The Victoria, after a passage of forty days, arrived on the 24th of August, when Muller was arrested, and the missing property found in his possession. After certain forms were gone through, Muller started for England, Sept. 3rd, on board the Etna, and arrived at Queenstown on the 15th.

On Friday evening, September 16th, Muller arrived at Liverpool. Upon landing he was taken to the central police-station, Liverpool, and there remained till seven o'clock on Saturday morning. To avoid the crowd Inspector Tanner took the prisoner to Edgehill station. He was taken to a private room till the arrival of the nine a.m. train from Lime-street, when he walked between Inspector Tanner and Superintendent Wide to the carriage. When the train moved off attempts were made at groaning, but cries of "Good bye, Muller," prevailed. At twenty-five minutes past three o'clock on Saturday afternoon the Liverpool express train drew up to the ticket platform at the London and North Western Railway, near Camden Town. Muller was taken to Bow-street police-station, and the charge formally entered against him by Inspector Tanner.

What a consternation there has been,
 And time has swiftly gone by,
What great excitement has been seen,
 Since the ninth of last July,
In Eighteen-hundred and sixty-four,
 When Thomas Briggs was slain,
And found welt'ring in his crimson gore
 Upon the railway train.

When Muller did the dreadful deed,
 He flew across the main,
But Justice followed him with speed,
 And brought him back again.

It was to New York, in America,
 That wretched man did sail;
And justice for one moment,
 To find him did not fail.
They followed the Victoria ship,
 Unto Columbia's land,
Determined, if 'twas possible,
 To take that wicked man.

While the ship was on the ocean,
 The stormy winds did blow,
She could not get a headway,—
 A murderer was below;
The passengers did oft remark,
 We all must rest assured;
There must something dreadful have
 been done,—
 A murderer is on board.

On the twenty-fourth of August,
 The Victoria was espied,
And the officers of justice,
 On board her quickly hied;
All things were planned so cleverly,
 Just as it ought to be,
That Muller had not the least chance
 From Justice for to flee.

They soon had him in custody,
 All on the raging main,
And found upon the murderer,
 Poor Briggs's watch, 'tis plain;
Although the crime he did deny,
 When the property was found,
The murderer was landed
 Upon America's ground.

In New York he was examined,
 Then in the Etna, o'er the main,
They brought the wretched murderer
 To England again.
News flew like wind the country round
 Franz Muller had arrived,
They ran from every quarter,
 To behold him they did strive.

Conversations on the murder,
 Has by thousands taken place;
Though the circumstances are as clear
 As the nose upon his face:
His flying to America,
 Across the ocean wide,
They found on him poor Briggs's hat
 And the gold watch besides.

Franz Muller now is landed,
 Once more on England's ground,
A verdict of wilful murder
 Against him has been found.
He has caused great consternation,
 Great agony and pain, [done
And he must answer for the deed he
 All on the railway train.

H. DISLEY, Printer, 57, High street, St. Giles, London.

2 E 2

THE EXECUTION AND CONFESSION OF
FRANZ MULLER,
For the Murder of Mr. BRIGGS, November 14th, 1864.

At two o'clock on Saturday afternoon Sir George Grey returned an answer to the memorial presented to him, praying for a respite of the convict Muller, by the German Legal Protection Society. Previous to the delivery of his decision he had a long conversation with the Lord Chief Baron Pollock and Mr. Baron Martin, which terminated in his arriving at the conclusion that the memorial did not warrant his interfering with the verdict of the jury.

Immediately upon the receipt of the letter, Mr. Beard, with Alderman Wilson, proceeded to communicate to Muller the result of the efforts that had been made on his behalf. They were received by Mr. Jonas, the governor of Newgate, who conducted them to the condemned cell. They found the prisoner engaged in writing. He immediately rose, and extended his hand to Mr. Beard, who asked him how he was. The convict said, "I am very well." Mr. Jonas then informed the prisoner of the efforts that had been made to save his life, and that Mr. Beard had just received a reply from the Secretary of State, which he read to him. At the conclusion the convict said, in a low voice, "I did not expect anything else." Mr. Beard then said to the prisoner, "Did you know that any efforts had been made on your behalf?" The prisoner replied, "Yes, I did think so." Mr. Beard then said, "Have you any statement that you wish to make?" The prisoner, "No, nothing." "Because," continued Mr. Beard, "now that all has been done that can be done for you, and there is no hope in this world, if you have anything to acknowledge, you had better do so." In reply to this Muller said, "I should be a very bad fellow if I had done it. I have no other statement to make than that which I have already made." Mr. Beard then asked him if he had made his peace with God. The prisoner said, "Yes;" and in every respect appeared resigned to his fate. Mr. Beard then shook hands with him, and said, "Good-bye Muller; God bless you;" The prisoner returned the pressure of his hand, and was left to himself.

The prisoner on Sunday attended Divine service in the chapel, both in the morning and the afternoon, and listened apparently with deep attention to the discourse delivered by the Rev. Mr. Davis, the Ordinary. He was visited in the evening by Dr. Walbaum and Dr. Cappell.

PREPARATIONS FOR THE EXECUTION.

Up to Sunday night Muller preserved the same quiet, firm demeanour, and although he occupied some of his time in writing, he did not lie down till considerably after his usual time, and slept but little. He rose at five o'clock on Monday in good spirits, and was soon afterwards joined by the Rev. Mr. Davis, the chaplain of the gaol, and the Rev. Mr. Walbaum. He in every respect appeared calm and resigned to meet his fate. He joined devoutly in prayer with the rev. gentleman, and otherwise conducted himself in a manner becoming his awful position. A little before seven o'clock he was visited by Mr. Jonas, the governor of the gaol, to whom he extended his hand, and feelingly thanked him for the kind attention he had received since his incarceration. Calcraft arrived at six, but was not recognised by the mob, and thus escaped the usual hooting.

Although the fixing of the scaffold was completed by four o'clock, still the clang of hammers in putting up barriers continued till day had dawned.

At five o'clock a heavy drenching rain set in, which had the effect of driving the majority of those who during the night had taken up positions, from their strongholds, and to hastily beat a retreat to the now open public-houses and coffee-shops, as well as to other places offering anything like shelter. At this time there could not have been more than five hundred people actually upon the scene. But at six o'clock the rain abated, and from this time the crowd was recruited by an increasing flow of new comers.

At six o'clock the main body of police, under Mr. Inspector Duddy, was stationed at the approaches to, and in the Old Bailey, and preserved throughout the morning in the strictest order.

Soon after seven o'clock, Mr. Alderman and Sheriff Besley, Mr. Alderman and Sheriff Dakin, and the Under Sheriffs, Messrs. Davidson and De Jersey, arrived at the Sessions House, where they remained until summoned to the prison by the governor. About twenty minutes to eight they were informed that the condemned man would soon leave his cell. Upon receiving this intimation these officials left the Sessions House. A few minutes after this, the procession reached the door which opens into the chapel-yard. Here they awaited the arrival of the culprit.

THE EXECUTION.

While the officials were on their way from the Sessions House to this spot, Mr. Jonas had gone to the cell of the prisoner, and informed him that it was time for him to leave. The prisoner, who was deadly pale, trembled with emotion, but sought to bear the awful announcement with all the fortitude possible. He rose up, shook hands with the gaolers who had been principally with him since his incarceration, and with a firm and rather quick step left his cell, accompanied by Mr. Jonas, followed by two or three other officials. As soon as they left the cell the shouts and cries of "They are coming," "They are coming," "Hats off." At this moment the most intense excitement and confusion prevailed, in the midst of which terrible din reverberated the echoes of the solemn knell, which, from its increased rapid tolling, indicated that the mournful procession had gained the steps of the hideous, cloth-draped gibbet. A moment afterwards Calcraft, the hangman, made his appearance on the scaffold, and then withdrew to see that all was right. He had no sooner disappeared than Muller, accompanied by the Rev. J. Davis, chaplain, and Dr. Cappell, followed by other officials, made his appearance. This was a signal for the renewed excitement and clamour of the swerving multitude, who had largely, and as it were imperceptibly increased, and whose upturned anxious faces met the gaze at all points.

The culprit ascended the scaffold with a firm step, and placed himself under the drop. He cast his eyes once up towards the beam, and his lips quivered with emotion, but this he evidently sought to check. After the cap had been drawn over his head and the rope put round his neck, Dr. Cappell took hold of his hand and again prayed with him. This he did for some minutes, and concluded by addressing the following words to the now fast dying man:—"In a few moments you will be before your God. I ask you, for the last time, are you innocent or guilty?"

Muller: I am innocent.

Dr. Cappell: You are innocent?

Muller: God Almighty knows what I have done.

Dr. Cappell: Does God know that you have done this deed?

Muller was silent.

Dr. Cappell: I ask you now, solemnly, and for the last time, have you committed this crime?

Muller: Yes, I HAVE DONE IT.

Almost at the same instant, and while the words were upon the lips of the wretched man, the drop fell, and Muller died without a struggle.

Dr. Cappell nearly fainted.

Immediately after the execution the sheriffs despatched a communication to Sir George Grey, informing him that the culprit had confessed. A similar communication was made to Sir R. Mayne, at Scotland-yard.

The following despatch was immediately after the execution forwarded to the Home Secretary:—

"Gaol of Newgate, 14th day of November, 1864.
"To the Right Hon. Sir George Grey, Bart.
"Sir,—By direction of the sheriffs I have the honour to acquaint you that the prisoner Muller has at the last moment, just before the drop fell, confessed to the German minister of religion attending him that he was guilty of the deed for which he suffered.
"I have the honour, &c.,
"SEPTIMUS DAVIDSON, one of the under-sheriffs."

London; Printed for the Vendors.

LAMENTATION & EXECUTION OF
JAMES LONGHURST,

At Horsemonger Lane Gaol, on Tuesday, April 16th, for the wilful murder of Jane Sax, a little Girl seven years old, at Shere, in Surrey,

Terrible Scene in the Prison with the Culprit.

James Longhurst was executed this morning, April 16, on the top of Horsemonger-lane gaol. Since his condemnation he has expressed contrition for his crime, and hoped that God would forgive him. Notwithstanding, the prisoner appearing to be in a state of mind becoming his awful position, when he was taken down from the condemned cell to the yard to be pinioned, a frightful scene ensued. The moment the culprit saw Calcraft, the executioner, approach him with the straps to pinion his arms, he started back with an aspect of terror depicted on his countenance, and began to struggle violently with the turnkeys. The chaplain spoke to him and endeavoured to calm him, and this for a moment appeared to have the effect, but upon the executioner requesting that the culprit might be taken outside, as he could not see to fasten the straps properly, another fearful struggle ensued, and it required five warders to hold him on the ground while he was being pinioned, and one or two of the turnkeys were very much hurt by the kicks they received. The prisoner's conduct seemed to be actuated by an uncontrollable horror of the executioner and the apparatus of death. After he had been secured he walked quietly by the side of the chaplain until he arrived at the steps leading to the scaffold, and immediately he caught sight of the gibbet his horror appeared to return. He again struggled violently as well as he was able, and was forcibly dragged up to the steps and held under the beam by several turnkeys while the rope was adjusted round his neck, and as speedily as possible the bolt was drawn, and after a few struggles the wretched youth ceased to exist.

Good people all I pray draw near,
And my sad history you soon shall hear,
And when the same I do relate,
I trust you will a warning take.

At Horsemonger lane on the scaffold high,
For a cruel murder I was doomed to die.

James Longhurst, it is my name,
I've brought myself to grief & shame
Through the dreadful deed that I had done,
At Churchill field, near Guildford town

It was in last June, the twenty-eighth
I did this deed as I now state;
An innocent child I there did slay,
And with a knife took her life away.

Poor Jane Sax, on that fatal day,—
A child scarce seven years of age;
In Churchill field I her did meet,
And shamefully did her illtreat.

Then coward-like I drew my knife,
To rob this helpless child of life:
I stabbed her in the throat—her blood did pour,—
Then left her welt'ring in her gore.

Then I was taken for this cruel deed,
And sent for trial, as you may read;
At Kingston assizes, tried and cast,
Oh, would I could recall the past.

She cried for help, did poor little Jane,
David Ensor to her assistance came;
Whilst I, a guilty wretch did stand,
And licked her blood from off my hand

The Judge said, James Longhurst,
you are guilty found,
You will go from here to London town
And there you'll die a death of shame,
And meet your fate at Horsemonger lane.

While I lay in my prison cell,
My state of mind no tongue can tell!
I could not rest by day or night,
Poor Jane was always in my sight.

My tender parents came to visit me,
My heart was breaking their grief to see,
Tears from their eyes did in torrents fall,
While for mercy to my God did call.

I hope that none will them upbraid,
While I am in my silent grave;
Farewell to all—the bell does toll,
Have mercy, God, on my sinful soul.

H. Disley, Printer, 57, High Street, St. Giles, London.

MILES WEATHERHILL,
THE YOUNG WEAVER,
And his SWEETHEART, SARAH BELL.

The prisoner, Weatherhill, was Executed at Manchester, on Saturday, April the 4th, for the Murder of Jane Smith, at Todmorden, a fellow-servant of Sarah Bell.

Oh give attention, you pretty maidens,
    A tale of love I will here unfold,
And you will say, when the same is mentioned,
    'Tis as sad a story as ever yet was told;
Miles Weatherhill was a brisk young weaver,
    And at Todmorden did happy dwell,
He fell in love with a pretty maiden,
    The parson's servant named Sarah Bell.

It was at Todmorden where these true lovers,
    At the parson's house, tales of love did tell,
And none on earth could be more constant,
    Than Miles the weaver and young Sarah Bell.

Deep in each heart was true love engrafted,
    They had sworn for ever to happy be,
No power on earth could those lovers sever,
    They met in joy and felicity ;
But they was parted, and broken hearted,
    Separated was those true lovers far,
Those constant lovers adorned each other,
    And love will penetrate through iron bars.

Miles Weatherhill was but three and twenty,
    His mind was noble, he good did mean,

And Sarah Bell was fair and virtuous,
    Young blooming, aged seventeen ;
They would have married, but tales were carried,
    Which caused displeasure, as you shall hear,
Miles was refused to meet his lover,
    And she left Todmorden, in Lancashire,

She left her true-love quite broken hearted,
    And to her mother at York did go,
And when such a distance from each other parted,
    Caused them sorrow, grief, pain, and woe ;
In a fit of sadness, overcome with madness,
    He made a deep and solemn vow,
If separated from his own true lover,
    He would be revenged on Parson Plow.

With four loaded pistols, in a fit of frenzy,
    Miles to the Vicarage did haste forthwith,
And with a weapon wounded the master,
    And shot the maiden, named Jane Smith ;
To the lady's bedchamber, in rage and anger,
    Bent on destruction, with intent to kill,
He did illtreat her, with a poker beat her,
    And her crimson blood on the floor did spill.

Oh, God, in mercy guide evil passions,
    Thou seest all things from heaven above,
Three innocent lives has been sacrificed,
    And one serious injured, all through true love,
If they'd not been parted, made broken-hearted,
    Those in the grave would be living now,
And Miles would not have died on the gallows,
    For slaying the maiden and Parson Plow.

Young men and maidens, you constant lovers,
    If true and honourable you make a vow,
Be just and upright, and oh, remember,
    Todmorden Vicarage, and Parson Plow ;
And all good people, oh, pray consider,
    Where true love is planted, there let it dwell,
And recollect the Todmorden murder,
    Young Miles the weaver, and Sarah Bell.

Miles and the true-love by death is parted,
    In health and bloom, he the world did leave,
And his true love, quite broken-hearted,
    For Miles the weaver, in pain do grieve ;
At the early age of three and twenty,
    In the shades below, with the worms do dwell,
On the fatal drop, he cried, broken-hearted,
    May we meet in heaven, my sweet Sarah Bell.

H. Disley, Printer, 57, High street, St. Giles, London.—W.C.

TRIAL AND SENTENCE
OF
CONSTANCE KENT.

On Friday, July 21st, Miss Constance E. Kent was placed at the Bar of the Salisbury Assize Court, charged with the murder of her brother, Francis Saville Kent.

The Clerk of the Assize, addressing the prisoner, said: How say you, are you guilty or not guilty? The prisoner in a voice scarcly audible, said—Guilty.

A profound silence then ensued in court, which was broken by Mr Coleridge, the prisoner's counsel, standing up and saying, I desire to say three things before your Lordship pronounces sentence. First, solemnly before Almighty God, she wishes me to say that the guilt is her own alone, and that her father and others, who have so long suffered most unjust and cruel suspicions, are wholly and absolutely innocent; and secondly, that she was not driven to this act by unkind treatment at home, as she met with nothing there but tender and forbearing love, and I may add that it gives me a melancholy pleasure to be the organ of these statements for her, because, on my honour, I believe them to be true.

The Judge, with much emotion, then said—Constance Kent, it is my duty to receive the plea which you have deliberately put forward. I can entertain no doubt that the murder was committed under great deliberation and cruelty. You appear to have allowed your feelings and anger to have worked in your breast, until at last they assumed over you the influence and power of the Evil One. It remains for me to pass the sentence which the law adjudges. The learned Judge then passed upon her the usual Sentence of Death. During the passing of the sentence, prisoner burst into a violent flood of tears, sobbing aloud.

Oh, give attention, you maidens dear,
My dying moments are drawing near,
When I am sentenc'd alas to die,
Upon a gallows gloomy and high.
  Oh what s sight it will be to see,
  A maiden die on the fatal tree.

I am a maiden in youth and bloom,
I a wretched murderer to die am doom'd,
And in the city of Salisbury,
My days must end on a dismal tree.

My little brother, a darling sweet,
That fatal morning did soundly sleep,
I was perplexed. I invented strife,
Fully determined to take his life.

To the dirty closet I did him take,
The deed I done caus'd my heart to ache,
Into the soil I did him thrust down,
Where asleep in death he was quickly found.

My own dear father they did suspect,
That he would suffer they did expect,
I was apprehended, but I got clear,
Tho' I was the murderess of my brother dear.

Long, long I pined in deep distress,
At length the murder I did confess,
The vile Road murder, as you may see,
Committed was no one but me.

Farewell my father, my father dear,
I know for me you will shed a tear,
Yes, your wicked daughter in shame must die,
For that cruel murder on a gallows high.

How many maidens will flock to see,
A female die upon Salisbury's tree.
Constance Emily Kent is my dreadful name,
Who in youth and beauty dies a death of shame.

I must go to my silent grave,
Father. is there no one your child to save,
Oh the awful moments are drawing near,
Father, forgive your daughter dear.

Oh, God in heaven, look down on me,
As I stand on the dreadful tree,
Forgive the crime, I, alas, have done,
Wash me with the blood of thy blessed son.

I must not live, I am bound to go,
I must be hurried to the shadows below,
My guilty heart long did quake with fear,
Why did I kill my little brother dear.

I see the hangman before me stand,
Ready to seize me by the law's command,
When my life is ended on the fatal tree,
Then will be clear'd up all mystery.

Disley, Printer, High street, St. Giles, London.

LIFE, TRIAL, CHARACTER, CONFESSION, AND EXECUTION OF
STEPHEN FORWARD,

For the Horrid Murder of THREE CHILDREN near Holborn, also of his WIFE AND CHILD at Ramsgate.

Murder of Three Children by Poison, near Holborn.

On Wednesday, August 9th, 1865, the neighbourhood of Red Lion Square, was thrown into a state of excitement owing to a report that three brothers had been murdered at the Star coffee-house, Red Lion street.

It appears that on the Saturday, a man called at the above hotel, and inquired if three children could be accommodated with a bed for a few nights. Having been informed that there was one room unoccupied, he said the children were aged respectively six, eight, and ten years, and that accommodation would be suitable. He called again on the Monday evening with the three children, and saw them to bed.

Half-past eight, when one of the chambermaids entered the first room in which the two younger children were in bed, and to her extreme horror found they were dead. She immediately raised an alarm, when the proprietor and others entered the room in which the eldest child had been placed, and there found that he also was in the sleep of death. Medical assistance and the police were instantly summoned, the surgeon firstly arriving, and upon his examination of the bodies, pronounced life to have been extinct for some hours, the limbs being rigid and cold.

From information gained by the police, it appears that the person who left the children at the coffee house went by the name of Southey.

Murder of Mother & Daughter at Ramsgate, by the person who committed the other Murders.

On Thursday morning, August 10th, Ramsgate was thrown into a state of intense excitement by a report that a man named Stephen Forward had committed a double murder in a dyer's house in King street. It appears that Forward, who was formerly a baker in the town, left Ramsgate some eight years ago, leaving his wife and a little girl behind him in a state of almost total destitution. On Wednesday evening Forward suddenly appeared in Ramsgate, and made his arrival known to his wife. On Thursday morning, about twenty minutes past eight, Forward went to Mr Ellis's house. His wife was there, having some breakfast with Mr Ellis and his daughter. He was asked if he would take any breakfast, but he declined. He sat down and commenced talking. Shortly before nine Ellis went into his workshop, and while there his daughter told Forward and his wife if they had anything to say in private they might go up stairs. They both went up stairs, and had not been there many minutes before the daughter of Forward went up with them. She had hardly got there when Mr Ellis and his daughter were startled by two rapid reports of a pistol, and on the latter rushing up stairs she arrived at the landing just in time to see Forward's daughter fall down dead, she having been shot by her father. Miss Ellis then called out to her father, who came in, and he saw Forward standing at the top of the stairs. He said, "What have you done, Forward?" and seeing that he had a pistol in his hand he called on him to give it him, which he did. Forward at this time had a black moustache and dark whiskers on. Ellis then saw the feet of Forward's wife, and on looking over the table he saw her head, and that blood was oozing therefrom. He told Forward to sit down, and he then perceived that he had neither moustache nor whiskers on. He asked Forward where they were, and he replied that they were under the grate. He looked there, but could not find them, and Forward then gave them to him. He then called out to send for the police and a surgeon. Forward added, "Yes; send for a policeman." He was then given into custody.

At twelve o'clock at noon Forward was brought before the magistrates, charged with the murder of his wife and child.

Previous to the calling of any witnesses, the prisoner, addressing the magistrates, said : I have here a paper to Sir Richard Mayne, which I hope you will permit me to read to you. I have a reason for it. If you will grant me a favour, I think you will see that my reason justifies me in asking it. Immediately I was brought to the station-house I asked for some paper, a pen, and some ink, that I might draw up this statement, but it is not finished. I also made a statement to the inspector in charge. I inquired whether he had heard of the murder of three children in London. My reason for asking this question was, that previous to my being charged with this crime I was guilty of the murder of the three children in London. I hope this may be taken as a communication to Sir Richard Mayne, and also that it is made quite voluntarily.

The evidence having been gone through, he was fully committed to take his trial at the next Assizes for wilful murder, when he was found guilty of the murders, and was EXECUTED THIS MORNING and died without a struggle.

COPY OF VERSES.

Of all the crimes we ever heard, of all the crimes we read,
Sure none on earth did ever know, a more sad dreadful deed ;
Five murders were committed—he with Satan did connive—
It was in the month of August, eighteen hundred and sixty-five.

The murderer's name is Forward, he led a wicked life,
Living with a married woman, whose husband's name was White ;
She had four little children, three of which he vile did slay,
In Red Lion street, in Holborn, then he did from London stray.

The cruel murderer Forward, at Ramsgate had a wife,
She had a youthful daughter ; but the murderer lived with White,
Who of his cruel usage, had cause oft to complain,
Not long ago she left him, and sailed o'er the briny main.

When he had killed the little boys, from London he went down,
Where dwelt his wife and daughter, in peace, in Ramsgate town.
He shot his wife and daughter dear, it cruel was, and sad,
And wanted to make it appear the villian, he was mad.

Five innocents he did destroy, how dreadful to unfold,
Mrs. White's three little boys, his wife and child, were told ;
The boys he killed in London, which caused great excitement round,
And his wife and lovely daughter he killed in Ramsgate town.

When Mrs White's dear children he did in London slay,
He with a dreadful weapon to Ramsgate went straightway ;
His own wedded wife and daughter, so maliciously he shot,
And thousands flocked from far around to view the dreadful spot.

For those five cruel murders, may the villian punished be,
And die a malefactor upon the fatal tree ;
More cruel dreadful murders we very seldom hear,
And wonderful excitement it has caused both far and near.

H. Disley, Printer, 57, High street, St. Giles, London.

The Execution of Five Pirates, for Murder, which took place on Monday, February 22nd, at the Old Bailey.

This morning, Monday, February 22nd, 1864, will long be remembered by the inhabitants of the city of London, as one of the most remarkable in the annals of hanging, by the execution of five foreign sailors, viz.: John Lyons, Francisco Bianco, Mauriccio Durranna, Marcus Watter, Miguel Lopez, *alias* Joseph Chances, *alias* The Catelan, for the wilful murder of George Smith upon the high seas. The attendance of persons to witness the execution was enormous, being greater than was ever remembered by the oldest inhabitant in the City, and was much of the same class as usually attend these exhibitions, with the addition of a fair sprinkling of seafaring men. The prisoners have been very assiduously attended by the worthy Priests of the Catholic persuasion, to which creed the prisoners belong, and they had been brought to a full knowledge of the enormity of the crimes which they had committed; and to such a state of religious feeling had they been brought, that they all fully acknowledged the share each one took in the horrible crime, and recognized the justice of their punishment. The sheriffs, with their usual attendants, arrived at a very early hour at the prison, and immediately visited the various criminals in their cells. The worthy priests who had been attending the criminals since their condemnation, was in the prison the whole night, and were early in their attendance on the unhappy criminals. After the usual formalities had been gone through of demanding the bodies of the prisoners into their custody, the executioner, with his assistants, commenced pinioning the prisoners, which operation was quickly performed, considering the number of prisoners. The arrangements having been completed, the mournful procession began to move towards the scaffold, the worthy priests praying fervently with the wretched prisoners, who appeared to have been fully brought to a thorough state of penitence. The prisoners ascended the scaffold in an orderly manner, and directly they appeared on the drop, the immense multitude gave a deep and loud groan, which seemed to make some of the wretched men tremble. The executioner having adjusted the fatal ropes, and drawn the caps over their eyes, left the platform, and the priests administered the last parting words of scriptural consolation to them. The signal was then given, the bolts were withdrawn, and the wretched murderers were launched into eternity.

COPY OF VERSES.

Is there not one spark of pity,
For five poor unhappy men,
Doomed, alas! in London city,
On a tree their lives to end?
The dreadful crime which they committed,
On the raging, stormy sea,
By every one must be admitted,
They each deserved to punished be.

Five poor unhappy sailors
On the drop did trembling stand,
And their lives did pay a forfeit,
For their deeds on board the Flowery Land.

Sometimes at sea there's cruel usage,
And men to frenzy oft are drove,
They're always wrong by men in power,
And that there's many a sailor knows.
But those unhappy seven sailors,
Did commit a dreadful deed,
Killed and slaughter'd, sad to mention,
On board the Flowery Land, we read.

Great excitement through the nation,
This most sad affair has caused,
Sent across the briny ocean,
To be tried by English laws;
Seven tried and there convicted,
And sentenced each to hanged be,
For the dreadful murders they committed,
When sailing on the raging sea.

For two of them they did petition,
Alas, there nothing could them save
Sad indeed was their condition,
To lie side by side in a murderer's grave;
Far away from friends and kindred,
They unpitied on the drop did stand,
Sad was the deed that they committed,
On board the fatal Flowery Land.

Thousands flocked from every quarter,
Seven unhappy men to see,
Sailors from distant foreign nations,
Suspended on a dreadful tree.

The fatal signal soon was given,
The awful drop at length did fall,
It caused a groan—it caused a shudder,
May God receive their guilty souls.

May this to sailors be a warning,
The dreadful sight the world did see,
In London, that fatal morning,
The seven died on Newgate's tree.
Was there not a tear of pity,
While trembling they in death did stand,
To die for crimes in London city.
Committed on the Flowery Land.

Their victims they did show no mercy,
No time for to prepare did give,
They kill'd them in a barbarous manner,
And though they were not fit to live,
We pity to them on the gallows,
Englishmen could not deny,
Now, alas, their days are ended,
They died on Newgate's gallows high

H. Disley, Printer, 57, High Street, St. Giles.

2 F

CONDEMNATION & EXECUTION

OF

LEIGH,

For the Murder at Brighton.

On Thursday, March 22nd, J. W. Leigh was indicted at the Lewes assizes for the wilful murder of Mrs. Harton, at Brighton, on the 1st of February, 1866.

The first witness, Charles Hastings, deposed—On Thursday night, February 1st, I was in the bar parlour of the Jolly Fisherman tavern with another person named Manuel, and Mrs. Harton, the landlady. She was sitting near the fire, and furthest from the door. Prisoner came into the bar with a revolver in his hand, and as soon as Mrs. Harton saw him she ran to witness for protection. While coming towards witness prisoner fired the pistol at her and shot her, the ball grazing the forehead of witness. Mrs. Harton fell on the shoulder of witness, and asked him to save her. Prisoner followed her, and placing the revolver within two feet of the woman's back fired again. Mrs. Harton then left the bar and ran down into the cellar. Witness went for a doctor.

Stephen Loveday, a dyer, deposed he was in the bar, outside the bar-parlour, and saw the prisoner come. Prisoner fired at Mrs. Harton, who ran down the cellar steps. Witness followed her, and found her lying half-way down the stairs, groaning. He got her up stairs into the back room, where he left her.

Serjeant I. Barnden said—From information I received, I went to the Jolly Fisherman tavern about 11 o'clock on the night of February 1st. I saw Mrs. Harton there wounded, and in a fainting state. I went out and saw the prisoner standing in the street, leaning against a house near the King's road end of Market street. Some one told me not to go near the prisoner, or he would shoot me. I went towards the prisoner and said, "What's all this about?" He said, "Stand off, or I'll shoot you," at the same time bringing the pistol from his breast pocket. I said, "Will you?" At that moment the pistol went off, and I closed with him. I must have touched his arm at the precise instant, for the ball went through my overcoat and trousers, so that it just missed me. I threw him down, and several people assisted me to take him to the Town Hall.

After the examination of several other witnesses, the prisoner's counsel addressed the jury for the defence, and the judge having summed up, the jury returned a verdict of Guilty. The judge passed the usual sentence of death upon the prisoner, and he was executed this day in front of Lewes Gaol, before an immense crowd of spectators, who came for many miles round.

On the first of February,
  In Brighton we see,
There did appear a murderer,
  By name John William Leigh.
He led a dissipated life,
  To wickedness gave way,
That fatal night he left his wife,
  And he did her sister slay.

For this cruel murder he must die,
And end his days on the gallows high.

With a six barrelled revolver,
  He went on Thursday night,
To the Jolly Fisherman, in Market st.,
  To take away the life
Of the landlady, Mrs. Harton,
  He was by Satan led—
Where her husband, Mr. Harton,
  Had been ten months ill in bed.

He fired the fatal weapon,
  Oh, twice he fired the shot,
His victim soon lay bleeding,
  Upon that fatal spot;

Her husband, ill, ran trembling,
  And there beheld his wife,
By the hand of a wicked murderer,
  Deprived of her life.

John William Leigh, the murderer,
  In Brighton town did dwell,
A very wicked troublesome man,
  And many knew him well;
He, mad with desperation,
  If he could but had his way,
The police, and all around him,
  The murderer would slay.

In the American service,
  A Confederate, he had been,
Though aged only twenty-eight,
  Much villany had seen;
There is nothing now can save him,
  For that atrocious deed.
Of such an audacious scoundrel
  We scarcely ever read.

Leigh left his wife and entered
  The Jolly Fisherman;

He looked just like a demon,
  With the revolver in his hand;
He killed his own wife's sister,
  Alas! she soon lay dead,
And her poor afflicted husbsnd,
  Lay consumptive in his bed.

He had no consideration,
  No pity in his breast,
His wicked desperation
  Caused horror and distress
Confined in Lewes dungeon,
  For a short time he must be,
Then for the Brighton murder,
  They will hang the prisoner Leigh.

Leigh a native was of Brighton,
  To the family a disgrace,
By every one detested,
  Who knew him in the place;
She was his own wife's sister.
  Who received the fatal wound,
Which has caused such consternation,
  Many miles round Brighton town.

C. Phillips, Printer, Market Street, Brighton.

BARBAROUS
MURDER OF A CHILD
BY A
SCHOOLMISTRESS.

A child murder has been committed at Park Horner, in the parish of Hampreston, under circumstances of the most shocking barbarity. At the Coroner's inquest it was given in evidence that the child had been beaten on the head with a heavy flint stone, and its tongue cut completely out at the root. It was found wrapped up in another part of a drawer where the body was discovered. The inquiry lasted four hours and a-half, and resulted, in the first instance, in a verdict, "That the child was born alive and murdered by someone." The Coroner pointed out that the evidence was conclusive against Emma Pitt, the national schoolmistress, who was the mother of the child; and he expressed his surprise that such a verdict should have been returned. The Jury after reconsidering their previous finding, returned a verdict of "Wilful murder against Emma Pitt."

We have read of sad and dreadful deeds
　Of mothers cruel and unkind,
But in the annals of history
　Such as this we seldom find;
In the parish of Hampreston,
　This deed was done we hear,
Near to the town of Wimborne,
　In the county of Dorsetshire.

This Emma Pitt was a schoolmistress,
　Her child she killed we see,
Oh mothers, did you ever hear,
　Of such barbarity.

With a large flint stone she beat its head
　When such cruelty she'd done,
From the tender roof of the infant's mouth
　She cut away it's tongue;
Sad and wicked, cruel wretch,
　Hard was her flinty heart,
The infant's tongue from the body was
　Wrapped in another part.

The murderess placed in a drawer,
　And it there, alas! was found,
The news of this dreadful murder,
　Soon spread for miles around;
And first upon the inquest,
　She expected to get free,

Although she was the author
　Of this dreadful tragedy.

A schoolmistress too, how sad to tell,
　Well known for miles around,
Who had many children under care,
　In and near to Wimborne town.
Oh, what a sad example,
　To children she did set,
There was never such a cruel wretch,
　As the barbarous Emma Pitt.

She committed is for murder,
　Soon her trial will take place,
And if she is found guilty,
　How sad will be her case.
If she has a woman's feelings,
　She surely will go wild,
She in such a barbarous manner killed
　Her tender infant child.

The hour is approaching,
　The moments near at hand,
When before a Judge and Jury,
　This monster soon must stand;
And if she is found guilty,
　She her deserts will get,
And mother's, miles round Wimborne,
　Will remember Emma Pitt.

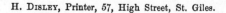

H. Disley, Printer, 57, High Street, St. Giles.

2 F 2

FAREWELL TO THE WORLD

OF

RICHARD BISHOP,

Who now lies under sentence of Death in Maidstone Gaol,
For the Murder of Alfred Cartwright.

In Maidstone Gaol, I am lamenting,
　I am borne down with grief and pain,
I for my deeds am now repenting,
　I shall Sydenham never see again ;
I have been tried for wilful murder,
　No power on earth can me now save,
I am doomed to die, my time's approaching,
　And I must lie in a silent grave.

Now I, alas ! must die for murder,
　Oh, how awful is my doom,
Richard Bishop, one and twenty,
　In youth and vigour, health and bloom.

Alfred Cartwright was my neighbour,
　We both at Forest Hill did dwell,
Alfred, servant was at the Swiss Cottage,
　Where he was respected well ;
I went with others to annoy him,
　It was upon that fatal night,
Ere he returned from his day's labour.
　Unto his home and loving wife.

I never did intend to kill him,
　Why should I my neighbour slay,
He never gave me any reason,
　To take his youthful life away ?
I was given in charge, and in a passion,
　I drew the awful, deadly knife,
And plunged it in poor Alfred's body,
　And there deprived him of his life.

The solemn funeral of my victim,
　Caused consternation miles around,
Thousands flocked from every quarter,
　The funeral dirge did mournful sound ;
Poor Alfred, to his grave respected,
　Proceeded by a solemn band,

And I must die upon the gallows,
　A wicked and degraded man.

Farewell, vain world, I now must leave you,
　Farewell, my friends and neighbours all,
Around Forest Hill no more you'll see me,
　The hangman's voice on me does call ;
Saying, Richard Bishop, now be ready,
　To die upon the fatal tree,
Oh, aged only one and twenty,
　What a dreadful sight to see.

Poor Alfred's friends,　will you forgive me,
　His father, mother, tender wife,
I him did kill, his blood did spill,
　And I pay a forfeit with my life ?
And God, look down from heaven upon me,
　Forgive the crime that I have done.
I see grim death standing before me,
　Saying, Richard Bishop's glass is run.

Oh, pray, young men, by me take warning,
　Remember me and what I done,
Ponder, yes, oh ! and consider,
　Let passion you not overcome ;
I did the deed in the heighth of passion,
　I had no　animosity.
Little thought my tender parents,
　I should die upon a gallows tree.

When the Judge did pass the awful sentence
　Saying, Richard Bishop, you must die,
For the murder of young Alfred Cartwright,
　On Maidstone's tree so awful high ;
Oh think, dear friends, what was my feelings,
　Sad and wretched and forlorn,
Doomed at the age of one and twenty,
　To die a dreadful death of scorn.

H. Disley, Printer, 57, High street, St. Giles, London.

LAMENTATION OF
J. MAPP,

Who now lies under Sentence of Death in Shrewsbury Gaol, for the Murder of Catherine Lewis.

On Monday, March 23, at the Shrewsbury Assizes, John Mapp, a labourer, was placed at the bar, charged with the wilful murder of Catherine Lewis, on the 22nd of December, 1867, at the parish of Longden.

Jane Richards deposed that after leaving chapel she accompanied deceased and John Mapp as far as Wood Farm, where she left them together going down Long lane.

Edward Lewis, the father of the deceased, deposed to Mrs. Hutchins bringing him his daughter's hat covered with blood. I at once started in search through several fields till I saw a hovel. There were marks at the door as if something had been dragged along, and on entering saw the body of my child in a little bin, covered with straw and loose litter.

Mr. Harris, surgeon: I made a *post mortem* examination of deceased. I found a shawl tied round her neck, and about eight inches shoved tightly into her mouth. There were five incisions on the right side of the throat, finishing in one deep wound on the left. The windpipe was cut through. I attribute her death to loss of blood and suffocation.

Edward Jones, police-constable, produced a brooch belonging to deceased, which was found on the prisoner when he took him into custody.

John Aston, a waggoner, deposed to finding the hat of the deceased in a holly bush.

Mrs. Davies: I reside at Longden. I knew the deceased. The brooch produced is the one she wore.

The counsel for the prisoner then proceeded to address the Jury for the defence, and the counsel for the prosecution having replied,

The Judge then summed up, and the Jury without retiring from the box returned a verdict of Guilty. The usual Sentence of Death was then pronounced upon the prisoner.

John Mapp, in Shrewsbury, does now bewail,
Doomed to die for murder in a dreary gaol;
Such a dreadful murder, as you may see,
Which we may compare to the Alton tragedy.

In Shrewsbury Gaol, now in grief do lie,
John Mapp, the murderer, condemned to die.

The cruel monster was not afraid,
To kill a youthful and innocent maid.
Little Catherine Lewis on a Sunday night,
Mapp, without a reason, deprived of life.

Returning home from chapel, he embraced her fast,
'Twas the twenty-second of December last;
He cut and mangled her, took her from the road,
And her murdered body in the hovel throwed.

Oh! how could any one so vile engage,
To kill a child but nine years of age;
Her clothes he scattered over ditch and field,
For which he finds now his fate is sealed.

The child was missed—news spread far and wide,
John Mapp was questioned, he the deed denied,
He prevaricated—untruths did state,
And he must meet his untimely fate.

Little Kitty's brooch that was found on Mapp,
And he took her ribbon from her Sunday hat;
He had a heart harder far than steel,
He was quite composed, working in the field.

Mapp was apprehended and sent to gaol,
And in a dungeon does now bewail;
On the tree a forfeit he must pay, his life,
His murdered victim haunts him day and night.

Now Mapp is cast and condemned to die,
Although the murder he does now deny;
The jury found him guilty, the case was clear,
And his last moments are drawing near.

How sad and dreadful it is to state,
The horrid murders that have been of late;
In every quarter both far and near,
Such atrocious deeds before this no one did hear.

Little Catherine Lewis, as I unfold,
Was but a little more than nine years old,
Innocent and charming, pious and kind,
Sweet disposition, and amiable mind.

What motive could the horrid murderer have,
To send the child to an early grave?
It was not for lucre, he could nothing gain,
To cause such horror, such grief and pain.

When he appears on the fatal tree,
Not a a spark of pity will there be for he;
He must die a murderer, nothing can him save,
Aged thirty-five, lie in a murderer's grave.

H. Disley, Printer, 57, High Street, St. Giles, London.

LAMENTATION OF H. LINGLEY.

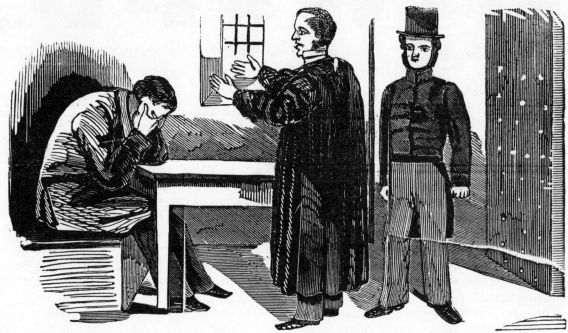

Within a dungeon in Norwich gaol,
One Hubbard Lingley in grief bewails,
His own kind uncle he did kill and slay,
On a Friday morning in the month of May.
   For that cruel murder he's doomed to die
   On Norwich fatal sad gallows high.

He is doomed to suffer as I relate
On the very tree where Rush met his fate
In health, in vigour, in youth and bloom,
The murderer Lingley must meet his doom.

In the morning early at four o'clock
He fired a sad and dreadful shot
Which caused his uncle's fatal death wound
Where he fell bleeding upon the ground.

A kind good uncle as may be seen
To his wicked nephew he had been;
Reared him up tenderly and used him well,
And in his cottage with him to dwell.

But he resolved he his blood would spill
His uncle Benjamin he wished to kill;
On Friday morn, the seventeenth of May,
The nephew did his kind uncle slay.

Early in the morning, at four o'clock,
To attract his uncle he fired a shot
And by that spot received the fatal wound.
The murderer flew and left him on the ground

Some labouring men who were passers by,
Saw the murdered in his blood to lie;
Suspicion did on his nephew fall,
And innocent blood did for vengeance call.

Many excuses did Lingley make,
Not having courage to meet his fate;
He before a jury for the deed was tried,
And condemned to suffer on the gallows high.

Hubbard Lingley thought when his uncle died
His place to him would not he denied;
So he was determined to kill and slay,
His uncle dear the seventeenth day of May.

He is doomed to die, nothing can him save,
By the side of Rush in a murderer's grave;
His bones will moulder till the Judgment day,
How could he take his uncle's life away?

At Norwich castle he was tried and cast
And his last moments approaching fast;
The hangman anxious does now await
To terminate Hubbard Lingley's fate.

Oh! all young men a warning take
Think and consider ere it is too late;
How could he dare lift his murderous hand,
Base, vile, ungrateful, and cruel man.

H. Disley, Printer, 57, High-street, St. Giles.

TRIAL, CHARACTER, CONFESSION, BEHAVIOUR, & EXECUTION OF
ALICE HOLT,
In front of Chester Gaol, this day, for the Wicked Murder of her own Mother.

This day the extreme sentence of the law was carried into effect on Alice Holt, at Chester Gaol, for the murder of her mother by poison. The evidence at the trial showed that prisoner, her mother, and a man named Holt, with whom she cohabited, lived together at Stockport. In February last the deceased, Mary Bailey, was taken ill, and the prisoner insured her life for £26, at a premium of 6d. per week. She induced a woman named Betty Wood to personate her mother before the doctor, telling her that the agent said "Any one would do." The proposal was accepted by the Wesleyan Assurance Society, and from that time the mother became worse. Prisoner called in the parish surgeon and the infirmary visiting officer, both of whom were ignorant of the other's visits, and complained of their medicine not being given. On the 25th and 26th the prisoner bought some arsenic—a quarter of a pound each time —which she put in a jug with some boiling water, and sprinkled about the room where her mother lay to kill vermin. The night of the 26th deceased had some brandy-and-water, and complained of "grounds" being at the bottom. Prisoner said, "You ought to have drunk grounds and all." Mary Bailey died in the morning with all the symptoms of arsenical poison, and was buried. The personation came to the ears of the office, and the body was disinterred, when it was found perfectly fresh, but "saturated with arsenic," of which no less than 160 grains were found in the stomach and adjacent parts.

The unfortunate woman was not tried at the Summer Assizes, in consequence of her being in the family-way. The child has since been adopted by Holt's uncle, the only person who has visited her since during her imprisonment. She has been sullen, and strongly protested her innocence.

CONFESSION.

On Sunday, the prisoner made the following statement:—On the Monday before mother died, I brought the insurance paper home, insuring my mother's life for £26, and mine for £28. He then proposed I should get some charcoal and put it under mother's bed alight, when she was asleep, and she would never wake more. On Wednesday night Holt and I never went to bed. He said it would be a great release-ment if she was in her grave, and he would buy some stretchnine (strychnine) if I would give it her. I said, "Thou'lt be found out." He said, "They cannot find it out by that." I said, "Thou hast brought me to destruction, and now thou wants to bring me to the gallows" He then beat me. In the beer of which I spoke, I saw, after my mother had drank it, a quantity of blue arsenic grounds. I said, "Thou hast given my mother arsenic." He said, "If thou tell aught, I will have thee up for defrauding the insurance," and said, "Nobody will believe but what thou hast done it thyself." This was the only arsenic my mother ever had.—Another statement was afterwards made by the prisoner.

THE EXECUTION

Took place this morning. When near the drop her courage failed her, and she was half dragged, half carried to the scaffold. On the platform she fell on her knees, and moaned piteously, "The Lord have mercy upon me," which she continued to do whilst Calcraft pulled the bolt. The drop fell, and the culprit was launched into eternity before a great many people, particularly women-folks.

COPY OF VERSES.

A dreadful case of murder,
  Such as we seldom hear,
Committed was at Stockport,
  In the County of Cheshire.
Where a mother, named Mary Bailey,
  They did so cruelly slaughter,
By poison administered all in her beer
  By her own daughter.

The daughter insured the life of the mother,
  For twenty-six pounds at her death,
Then she and the man that she lived with
  Determined to take away her breath.
And when Betty Wood represented the mother,
  She did'nt act with propriety,
For the poor mother lost her life,
  And they all swindled the Society.

Now that the old gal's life's insured,
  Holt to the daughter did say,
Better in the grave she were immured,

And the money will make us so gay.
Now that you have got me in the family way,
  And from me my virtue you've wrung,
You'll never be happy a day,
  Till on the gallows I'm hung.

She laid a plan to murder her,
  As we now see so clear,
To put a quantity of arsenic
  Into her poor mother's beer.
To see her lay in agony,
  Upon that dreadful night,
With a dreadful dose of arsenic,
  Oh, it was a dreadful sight.

She lived but just six hours,
  Then the poor woman did die,
And this base murdering wretch,
  The dreadful deed did deny.
On the man Holt she laid the blame,
  Vowed he did her mother slay,

Holt on her did the same,
  Saying she took the mother's life away.

The father of her unborn infant,
  Whom she vowed to love most dear,
And when confined in prison,
  She was overcome with fear,
She made a rambling statement
  'Bout the arsenic in the beer
Laid all the blame on Holt and Betty Wood
  Expecting for to get clear.

But there's no doubt the base wretch
  Did her poor mother slay,
For which on Chester's scaffold,
  Her life did forfeit pay,
So all young women a warning take,
  By this poor wretch you see,
A hanging for the mother's sake
  On Chester's fatal tree,

W. Smith, Printer, Chester.

CRUEL AND INHUMAN MURDER

Of a little Boy, by his Father.

COMMITTAL OF THE PRISONER.

On Monday morning a cruel and inhuman murder was committed by the father on a child aged six years, in Neal's passage, Seven Dials. The father has been separated from his wife for some time, and the boy had been brought up by its maternal grandmother, a poor old woman. The child being an unusually intelligent and nice-looking boy was a great favourite with the grandmother and an aunt who lived in the same room. It appears the mother had been living with another man as his wife, and the father also had formed an illicit connection with another woman. The poor boy had consequently become a source of trouble to both of them, although the merest trifle was required for its maintenance.

On Sunday evening the father (Jeffery) called at the grandmother's for the boy. She asked him what he wanted with the child, but he became very violent, ordered the child to dress himself, and swore that "he would do for her and the child too," if she did not mind. Jeffrey then went to his sister, in White Lion street, taking the child with him, and asked for a bed. He was accommodated with one, and went to bed with the boy; but at two o'clock in the morning he rose, and took the child away. He could not have walked many yards away —for Neal's passage, where the body of the deceased was found, is close at hand. The child was found suspended from a projecting beam or bracket in a cellar to which all the residents had access for water, &c. Horrible as it seems, it is apparent from the condition of the body, that the cruel father tied its hands behind, and had literally enacted the part of executioner of his own child, holding its legs, and forcing down its body to complete the strangulation of the poor boy. The child remained in this position till about half-past six o'clock, when it was seen by a girl who had occasion to go to the cellar, and who gave the alarm. Dr. Harvey, the parish surgeon, attended directly, and pronounced the child to have been dead about three or four hours.

Dr. Lankester, the coroner, held an adjourned inquest on Wednesday, and there being no further evidence the jury returned a verdict of wilful murder by hanging and suffocation of Richard A. Jefferey, by his father, John R. Jefferey. The prisoner was examined at Bow street yesterday, and committed to Newgate.

You kindest fathers, tender mothers,
 To this sad tale, oh! list awhile,
Hark you, sisters, too, and brothers,
 To a murder on the Seven Dials;
Such a crime indeed,—no never!
 Its baseness I can scarce reveal,
In Neal's Passage, Earl Street, Seven Dials,
 In St. Giles's-in-the-fields.

In all your troubles and your trials,
 You never knew, as I reveal,
Such a murder, on the Seven Dials,
 In St. Giles's-in-the-fields.

In Earl Street lived a wretch named Jefferys,
 Who a tailor was by trade we find,
A sad, a base, and cruel villain,
 Wickedness ran in his mind ;
A child, the villain ought to cherish,
 His offspring which he should adore,
Seventeen weeks ago he left him,
 At his old Grandmother's door.

His little boy named Richard Arthur,
 By the wretched father, we are told,
Was cruelly and basely murdered,—
 The child was only seven years old ;
The villain took him to a cellar,
 Resolved his offspring to destroy,
Tied his little hands behind him,
 And hanged the pretty smiling boy.

Vengeance against the boy he threaten'd
 Determin'd for to take his life,
And to commit the dreadful action,
 He often did produce a knife ;
'Twas his only child, he had no other,
 A rogue in grain, devoid of fear,
He'd been separated from the mother
 Of the little boy for three long years.

The grandmother, his mother's mother,
 Her little grandchild long did keep,
Receiving nothing from the father,
 For the space of seventeen long weeks,
And then the villain did demand him,
 He clandestinely took him away,
That fatal evening he determined
 Was his little boy to slay.

Then he to the cellar took him,—
 His heart was harder far than steel,
The wicked, base, inhuman monster,
 His actions no one can reveal.
His only chlld, to hold beside him,
 With rope he bound his little hands,
When behind his back he placed them,
 He in the cellar did him hang.

He flew, but Justice close pursued him,
 And taken he has been we see ;
When tried, no doubt, they'll find him guilty,
 And he'll be hanged on Newgate's tree ;
Hanging is too good for such a villain,
 He who would his flesh and blood destroy,
The child, we are told, was six years old,
 A pretty little prattling boy.

We all have got our cares and trials,
 And unto fate compelled to yield,
This deed was done on the Seven Dials,
 In St. Giles's-in-the-fields.

H. DISLEY, Printer, 57, High street, St. Giles, London.

LAMENTATION & CONFESSION

OF

J. R. JEFFERY,

Who now lies under sentence of death, for the wilful murder of his little boy.

Within a dreary cell I lie,
A wretched murderer, condemned to die
For the murder of my darling boy,
Whose precious life I did destroy.

I am doomed to die, my glass is run,
For the murder of my darling son.

John Richard Jeffery, it is my name,
Why did I do that deed of shame?
I confess my crime, but do declare,
No ill feeling to my child did bear.

From my wife I long had parted been,
Which disturbed my mind, as may be seen ;
And Satan's doubts they filled my mind,
Which led me to this dreadful crime.

I could not bear the child to see,
It seemed to increase my misery,
While thinking of my absent wife,
I form'd a plan to take his life.

At his grandmother's he found a home,
And with fiendish thoughts I'm asham'd to own ;
Quick dress that child, to her did say,
For I was determined the boy to slay.

Poor little boy, it seemed filled with fear,
And cried, don't dress me granny dear ;
Don't let father take me away,

With you, dear granny, I'd rather stay.

But to his wishes I paid no heed
But left with the child, as you may read ;
Then proceeded in the dead of night,
To a lonely spot to take his life.

To a dismal cellar I took the helpless child,
The thoughts of which now drives me wild ;
Poor boy, he fainted with affright,
And in that state I took his life.

With a handkerchief I bound his hands,
And to the cistern I did him hang ;
Poor innocent, unconscious quite,
Knew not his father had took his life.

When this fearful act the hand had done,
From the fearful scene away did run ;
With stricken conscience, like the murderer Cain,
But peace of mind could not obtain.

I strove to forget it for a time,
But my murdered boy so haunted my mind,
I gave myself up, as you may read,
To make some atonement for the deed.

I soon upon the drop must stand,
A guilty and heart-broken man ;
My darling boy I shall no more behold,
Have mercy, God, on my guilty soul !

H. Disley, Printer, 57, High Street, St. Giles.

2 G

MURDER OF A WIFE

AT ASHBURNHAM, NEAR HASTINGS.

A shocking murder of a wife was committed on Sunday, at Ashburnham, a village near Hastings. Near the village is a quantity of land called Gardener's Farm, which is farmed by an old man named Stubberfield and his son Jeremiah. The son, who is married, has a separate residence about sixty yards from that of his parent. There were living in the same house with the son, his wife Matilda, their son, Mary Deeprose (a companion to Mrs Stubberfield), and several farm labourers and servants. The boy, eight years old, who occupied the same room with his parents, states that early on Sunday morning he saw his father kneeling upon his mother, and squeezing her throat. Hearing his mother say, "Oh!" feebly, as is in pain, he said to his father, "Your hurting mother." "You hold your tongue," replied the father, "I'm only tickling her." The boy again made a similar remark, upon which the father said that if he didn't hold his tongue he would "see to him." Stubberfield then dressed himself, and having kissed his wife and child, went down stairs. The boy immediately aroused the other inmates of the house, who were soon in the bedroom of the murdered woman. The police were sent for, and in a short time, some two hundred persons were scouring the neighbourhood in search of Stubberfield, and it was not till the afternoon he was discovered, and then he was making his way towards home. He had secreted himself in a pit, and tried to drown himself, but could not do so, for he always floated on the top of the water.

A dreadful deed, as you may read,
   I am going to unfold,
A base and cruel murder,
   That will make your blood run cold;
At a village called Ashburnham,
   A few miles from Hastings town,
Where the family of the Stubberfields
   Was known for miles round.

Jeremiah Stubberfield killed his wife,
   At Ashburnham, we see,
Which caused many a tear both far and near,
   The Sussex tragedy.

There lived old Farmer Stubberfield,
   An aged, wealthy sire,
At Gardner's Farm, and near him lived,
   His son, named Jeremiah;
Who had a wife, Matilda,
   Virtuous, good, and kind,
Who had a son, and her companion,
   Labourers and servants, too, we find.

On Sunday morn, the twenty-third of May,
   The little boy, but eight years old,
Saw his father squeeze his mother's throat,
   Most awful to unfold;
He called unto his father,
   While trembling with fear,
Saying, oh, cruel father,
   You are killing mother dear.

The murderer kissed his wife and child,
   After that he did slay,

Then placed his coat upon his arm,
   And from the farm did stray;
The servants and the labourers,
   Went to the fatal bed,
And there beheld Matilda
   Quite cold, and lying dead.

They did pursue the murderer,
   They in numbers went along,
Searched the hedges and the ditches,
   Dragged the rivers and the ponds;
But late on Sunday afternoon,
   As they in numbers on did stray,
They saw him wandering to his home,
   Where his murdered wife did lay.

He says he dearly loved her,
   A kind, good, and tender wife,
Oh, whatever could possess him,
   To take away her life;
It has caused great excitement,
   Far round the country,
A farmer's son the murder done,—
   The Sussex tragedy.

To end this dreadful tale of woe,
   Confined within a gaol,
Lies Jeremiah Stubberfield,
   In anguish to bewail;
He loved his wife, far more than life,
   He her corpse sweet kisses gave,
He has brought his aged parents,
   In sorrow to the grave.

H. Disley, Printer, 57, High street, St. Giles, London.

LAMENTATION & FAREWELL ^{TO THE} WORLD

OF

JOHN FLETCHER

AND

ANN LAWRENCE

Who now lies under Sentence of Death at Maidstone Gaol.

A poor unhappy man and woman,
　Does in agony bewail,
Sentenced to die, alas for murder !
　In separate cells, in Maidstone gaol.
Ann Lawrence aged eight-and-twenty,
　For the wilful murder of her child,
And John Fletcher, only twenty,
　For the dreadful murder of James Boyle.

In agony, now lies lamenting,
　John Fletcher, who is frenzy wild,
In Chatham prison killed the warder,
　And Ann Lawrence her own darling child.

Ann Lawrence is a married woman,
　Who with a man named Highams did
　　dwell;
He also had a wife still living,
　Highams and Lawrence lived at Tunbridge
　　Wells,
They lived unhappy, often quarrelled,
　Faults on both sides we may see,
Ann Lawrence in a fit of frenzy,
　Overpowered with jealousy.

Determined was to kill her offspring,
　Revengeful, shocking to unfold,
To aggravate her own paramour,
　Her little boy but four years old;
At Tunbridge Wells she basely murder'd.
　Wickedness ran in her mind,
When her child she'd slain, said with disdain,
　The innocent child was killed by Highams.

The little boy named Jeremiah,
　Looked in his mother's face with tears
When her little boy she did destroy,
　Aged only four years ;

Her counsel for her pleaded clever
　To free her every way he tried,
When the Judge the sentence passed upon
　her,
　The dreadful murder she denied.

John Fletcher who must die beside her,
　A convict was for seven years,
He in Chatham prison killed the warder,
　To give the blow he was prepared,
He says the warder did illuse him,
　And tantalized him day by day,
And in a fit of desperation,
　He with a hammer did him slay.

At Maidstone they were tried and sentenc'd
　To die a murderer's death of scorn,
In youth and health they are lamenting,
　In grief and agony forlorn ;
The awful moments are approaching,
　And there is nothing can them save,
They soon must leave this world of sorrow,
　And sleep within a murderer's grave.

Oh male and female curb your passions,
　Think and consider ere too late,
Passion, jealousy, and vengence,
　Has caused those wretched person's fate ;
Let their fate be an example,
　Oh! pray be guided one and all,
Think of John Fletcher and Ann Lawrence,
　Remember what caused their downfall.

Passion, jealousy, and vengeance,
　Was the cause, we plainly see,
Of bringing John Fletcher and Ann
　Lawrence
　To die on Maidstone's dismal tree.

Disley, Printer, High street, St. Giles, London.

EXECUTION OF
MICHAEL BARRETT,
Who was executed this morning at the Old Bailey, for the wilful murder of Sarah Ann Hodgkinson, one of the sufferers at the Clerkenwell Explosion.

This morning the unfortunate Fenian convict, Michael Barrett, suffered the extreme penalty of the law at the Old Bailey. The prisoner has been attended by the Rev. Mr. Hussey, a Roman Catholic priest, who has remained with him a considerable time every day. He was very taciturn, and although he was no doubt aware of the efforts that were being made to obtain a reprieve, it was a noticeable fact that he never attempted to declare his innocence. Down to recently he used to attend the service in the prison regularly, but after Mr. Hussey had been with him he entirely refrained from doing so. He has not been visited by any one since his conviction. All his relations appear to reside in Ireland, and he does not seem to have had any connexions or friends in this country.

The sheriffs of the prison arrived at an early hour, and immediately proceeded to the condemned cell, where they found the prisoner in devotional exercises with the Rev. Mr. Hussey. He declared himself ready to die, and seemed to consider himself a martyr. The time having arrived, Calcraft, the executioner, was introduced to the prisoner, who immediately commenced pinioning him, which operation having been gone through, the prisoner thanked the governor and other officials of the prison for their kindness towards him. The procession was then formed, and slowly took its way towards the scene of execution. The prisoner ascended the scaffold with a firm step. Everything having been prepared, the cap was drawn over his eyes and the rope adjusted, the bolt was drawn, and he appeared to struggle but slightly before life was extinct.

COPY OF VERSES.

Adieu, vain world, I now must leave you,
  Here I cannot longer dwell,
I have been tried, and I am sentenced
  To die for the deed in Clerkenwell ;
Oh ! that dreadful sad explosion,
  Which did so much destruction cause,
Brought me to the tree at Newgate,
  My sufferings sure no one knows.

I must leave this world of sorrow,
  On earth I must no longer dwell,
Sentenced to be hanged for murder,
  For the sad affair in Clerkenwell.

Alas ! my name is Michael Barrett,
  Born and brought up in Erin's isle,
I did adore my native country,
  Whereon I oft did sweetly smile ;
Oh yes, my own dear native Erin,
  Behold me on the fatal tree,
A miserable malefactor,
  In a murderer's grave I soon shall be.

A traitor did swear hard against me,
  A wretch, Mullany known by name,
Worse by far than any other,
  And many persons know the same ;
Only one amongst the prisoners,
  And that poor one, alas ! was me,
Poor unhappy Michael Barrett,
  Condemned to die upon a tree.

I twice have been respited,
  I did not expect to die,
But I must go in grief and woe,
  On Newgate's tree so high ;
That I should gain my liberty,
  Some thousands did believe,
But, oh, alas ! all hope is passed.
  And I have been deceived.

Farewell, my friends, I'm doomed to leave
  With you I can no longer stay, [you,
Let not my departure grieve you,
  I die upon the twenty-sixth of May,

On the fatal tree at Newgate,
  For the affair at Clerkenwell,
Called a Fenian, Michael Barrett,
  Friends and kindred, farewell !

I see the hangman now before me,
  Standing on the fatal drop,
In the prime of life and vigour,
  Hard is Michael Barrett's lot :
Only one of all the number,
  All the rest, alas ! but me,
Acquitted was, but Michael Barrett
  Dies on Newgate's fatal tree.

A last adieu, vain world, I leave you,
  I am going to the silent bourne,
Lovely Erin, I grieve for you
  But I never shall return ;
Approaching is the Tuesday morning,
  I am summonsed far away,
Erin, remember Michael Barrett,
  Who died upon the twenty-sixth of May.

EXECUTION OF
ALLEN, GOULD, & LARKIN,

At the New Bailey Prison, Manchester, on Saturday, November 23rd, charged with the Wilful Murder of Sergeant Brett, at Manchester, on September 18th, 1867.

the authorities, who had erected barricades about every thirty yards, and so prevented the great pressure that would have been. The prisoners were astir at an early hour, and partook of the holy communion, and at the appointed time. Calcraft, the executioner, was introduced, when the operation of pinioning was gone through. The prisoners the meanwhile showed wonderful confidence, and appeared to be the least concerned. They all shook hands together and affectionately embraced one another, and declared themselves ready. The mournful procession was then formed, and at once proceeded towards the scaffold, where on their appearance there was a slight manifestation of applause. Everything having been prepared, the ropes adjusted, the signal was given, and the unhappy men were launched into eternity. The prisoners appeared to die very easy.

You true friends of liberty, and sons of the Emerald Isle,
   Attend with an ear of sympathy to what I now relate,
And to my sad story, I'd have you to list awhile,
   Its of those poor unhappy men who now have met their fate;
Its Allen, Larkin, and Gould I mean, who of treason have convicted been,
   Coupled with the crime of murder, for which we all deplore,
To the scaffold were condemned we see through struggling for liberty,
   Of that poor unhappy country, the poor old shamrock shore.

Now its well known that Irishmen have oft upon the battle field,
   Nobly fought our battles, against old England's foes.
And with the hearts of lions have forced her enemies to yield;
   But to friends they are warm-hearted, as all the world well knows.
Its but for their rights they crave, old Ireland's honour for to save,
   That has led to this calamity, for which we all deplore,
But by treachery they were betrayed, and these poor men have the forfeit paid,
   And Allen, Gould, and Larkin, alas! are now no more.

It was at Manchester, as I now state, they sought their comrades to liberate,
   And where is the man in such a state, would not have done the same?
Those poor men they were taken, for whom many hearts are aching,
   For there is no one in reason their conduct can well blame.
It was in the midst of that strife, that poor Brett he lost his life,
   That has caused the sons of Ireland most deeply to deplore,
And through that sad unhappy day, there's many a pitying heart will say,
   Poor Allen, Gould, and Larkin, alas! are now no more.

These men they were convicted, and by the judge was sentenced,
   And for murder and treason they were condemned to die,
And left to meet their fate to the gaze of all spectators,
   Tho' that their lives would be spared it was the country's cry.
To God I recommend them, in his mercy to defend them,
   May their souls shine in glory upon that blessed shore,
Safe within his keeping where there will be no weeping,
   Now Allen, Gould, and Larkin, alas! are now no more.

   This morning, Saturday, November 23rd, the three unfortunate convicts, Gould, Allen, and Larkin, suffered the extreme penalty of the law at the New Bailey prison, Manchester. Since their condemnation the culprits have behaved in a most exemplary manner, and have paid great attention to the Rev. gentlemen who attended them. They continued to declare their innocence to the last, and appeared to think themselves martyrs to a grand cause, and appeared quite ready for the event. The mob was very great, but not so large as it might have been, but for the precautions taken by

H. Disley, Printer, 57, High Street, St. Giles, London.

The Last Moments and Confession
OF
WM. SHEWARD.

On Tuesday, April 20, the last dread sentence of the law was carried out in the case of Wm. Sheward convicted at the last Norwich Assizes for the murder of his wife. The culprit died without any very painful struggles. He showed a considerable amount ef nerve, although he trembled a good deal at the drop, to which he had to be carried on account of his rheumatism. In the prisoner's confession he stated that he killed his wife in June, 1851, and that he afterwards mutilated the body. He placed the head in a saucepan, and put it on the fire to keep the stench away. He then broke it up, and distributed it about Thorpe. He then put the hands and feet in the same saucepan, in hopes they might boil away. Carried portions of the body away in a pail and threw them in different parts of the city. The long hair on my return from Thorpe, he cut with a pair of scissors in small pieces and they blew away as he walked. The blankets, where there was any blood he cut in small pieces, and distributed them about the city, and made off with anything that had the appearance of blood about them. The prisoner also stated that he never saw or knew his present wife until June 21, 1852, twelve months after the occurrence.—The confession was taken in the presence of a magistrate, and the governor and chaplain.

I am a sad and wretched man,
  Borne down in care and woe,
I am doomed to die for a murder done
  Near eighteen years ago ;
A dreadful deed, as you may read,
  I long kept in my breast,
I'had no comfort day or night,
  Until I did confess.

With the dreadful knife I slew my wife,
  And her body round did throw,
Now I must die for a murder done,
  Near eighteen years ago.

I her body into pieces cut,
  And scattered it around,
Here and there, I scarce knew where,
  I placed it on the ground.
I now must die for that foul deed,
  And in a murderer's grave lie low,
I did her kill, her blood I spilled,
  Near eighteen years ago.

I boiled her head, how sad to tell,
  I was mad without a doubt,
I threw it in the different parts,
  I placed it round about ;
Kept the secret eighteen years,
  Within my guilty breast,

And till the same I did divulge,
  I day nor night could rest.

For eighteen years, in grief and tears,
  I passed many a dreary night,
I had not one moment's happiness,
  Since I killed my own dear wife ;
At length I did confess the deed,
  For which I now must die,
For a mnrder eighteen years ago—
  The which I don't deny.

There was letters sent from different parts,
  To say my wife did live,
To save me from the gallows,
  But none would they believe ;
I could not from Justice flee,
  I do deserve my fate,
No pen can write, or tongue can tell,
  My sad and wretched fate.

My moments they do swiftly pass,
  I soon shall sleep below,
I done that dreadful awful deed,
  Near eighteen years ago ;
I cut and mangled that poor soul,
  My heart was flinty steel,
Her limbs and body strewed about,
  In hedges, lanes, and fields.

H. Disley, Printer, 57, High street, St. Giles, London.—W.C.

THE EXECUTION OF
JOHN DEVINE,

In front of Newgate, for the Murder of JOSEPH DUCK, at Marylebone.

THE EXECUTION.

On Monday morning, at Eight o'clock, John Devine suffered the extreme penalty of the law, in front of Newgate. Not so much excitement was created as we have noticed on similar occasions, although a very large concourse of persons had assembled to witness the shocking spectacle. In fact, we might say every available spot was occupied by both male and female, all of whom were anxious to get a "good place," to see the wretched culprit on the drop. Precisely at the appointed time the sheriffs, with their usual attendants, arrived at the prison, and, after the necessary ceremonies had been observed, of demanding the body of the prisoner to be delivered into their custody, they were conducted to the waiting room. The executioner then commenced pinioning the arms, which operation he quickly dispatched. During the awful preparations the unhappy prisoner appeared to feel his sad position deeply.

At length the arrangements having been completed, the bell of the prison commenced tolling and the chaplain read in a distinct tone the burial service for the dead. When the bell commenced tolling, a movement was heard from without, and the words "Hats off" and "Silence" were distinctly heard, from which time no sound, excepting the sighs of the unhappy prisoner, interrupted the chaplain as the procession moved along the subterranean passage. The prisoner, on arriving at the scaffold, hastily glanced around at the immense concourse of persons assembled. After which he was placed in the proper position for Calcraft to adjust the ropes. The executioner having drawn the cap over his face retired from the scaffold, and the signal having been given the bolt was withdrawn, and the unhappy criminal was launched into eternity.

CONFESSION OF THE CULPRIT.

On Thursday the unhappy criminal was visited by the worthy chaplain, to whom he made a confession, and fully admitted the justice of his sentence.

COPY OF VERSES.

Young Devine was a graceless youth,
　And bold in every sin,
In early years with petty thefts,
　His life he did begin.

But God whose vengeance never sleeps,
　Though he delays the blow,
Can in a single moment lay
　The prosperous villain low.

One night was in the King's Head,
　Joseph Duck he did meet,
Whom he then robbed of all he had,
　And cruelly did him beat.

Suspicion fell on young Devine,
　So well they knew his face,
Imprisoned, tried, condemned to die,
　So he now has run his race.

Of gambling and theft pray beware,
　Let me beseech you in time,
Lest you like me should be cut off,
　Whilst you are in your prime.

It was these that caused me to run,
　From virtuous paths astray,
Deaf to advice and every good,
　I sought destruction's way.

The 10th day of March last,
　I went to the King's Head,
And there I met an aged man,
　Joseph Duck he was named.

I cruelly did him use,
　And on the ground him cast,
He cried for help, but no one came,
　So now he has breathed his last.

Those deeds I mournfully repent,
　But now it is too late,
The day is past, the die is cast,
　And fixed is my fate.

Young men be taught by this dreadful fate,
　Avoid the paths I have trod,
And teach yourselves in early years,
　To love and fear your God.

231

LIFE, TRIAL, CONFESSION, AND EXECUTION OF

MARTIN BROWN,

FOR THE DIABOLICAL MURDER ON NEWMARKET HILL NEAR, LEWES.

The facts of this deliberate and cruel murder must be fresh in the minds of all persons. The deceased was a labourer (in the employ of Mr Hodson, farmer, at Kingston, near Lewes), and lived in a cottage on New-market Hill, about a mile and a half from the village. Martin Brown worked for the same employer, and lodged with the deceased and his family, and left about six weeks before the murder, but continued in the same service, lodging with the farm bailiff, named Wickham. The deceased was paid fortnightly, and on the 9th of October he left home for Kingston, to receive the wages of himself and two sons, boys; and he was paid £2 11s. He was also paid 24s. by another son at Kingston, and he had 5s. 3d. in his tobacco-box when he left home, at half-past six o'clock in the evening. He never returned; and early the next morning he was found dead on the hill, about a quarter of a mile from his home. His pockets were then empty. It was discovered that he had been shot through the back—three small bullets were taken from the body—and that he had been severely beaten about the head with some heavy instrument, but after death had taken place. The trigger of a gun and a small piece of gun-stock were found close to the body, and in a copse not far from the spot there was subsequently found a broken gun-stock, to which the pieces found close to the body accurately fitted. This gun-stock belonged to a gun which the prisoner had purchased three weeks before the murder; and which he took out on the night of the murder, stating that he was going to take it to his brother at Brighton, and should not be back till the next day. He returned,

however, the same evening, and in less time than it was possible for him to go to Brighton and get back again; and on the following evening,—the murder was freely talked of, and prisoner was even suspected,—he absconded.

He was apprehended by Mr Superintendent Crow-hurst, at Maidstone, where he had enlisted under the name of Reuben Harvey.

He was tried at the Sussex Winter Assizes, found guilty, and sentenced to death.

THE EXECUTION.

The execution took place this morning, at eight o'clock, It was the first execution at Lewes since the passing of the recent act of Parliament; which is car-ried out in private, within the prison walls. Shortly before eight o'clock, the black flag was hoisted, and the prison-bell began to toll. All the arrangements being completed, Calcraft began the process of pinioning the condemned man, who appeared to be quite calm. At eight o'clock, the mournful and melancholy procession began to move towards the gallows; the culprit walked slowly, but firm, and having arrived at the foot of the gallows, he mounted the steps on to the top of the platform, and placed himself on the trap-door, under the fatal beam; Calcraft then put over his head the cap, and placing the rope round his neck, he then shook hands with him, and instantly the bolt was withdrawn, and the unhappy man was launched into eternity. After a few short struggles, life was extinct. After hanging an hour, the body was cut down, and buried within the precincts of the prison.

COPY OF VERSES ON THE CONFESSION OF MARTIN BROWN.

I am a wild and wicked youth,
    And my name is Martin Brown,
I was brought up by honest parents,
    I once did dwell in Brighton town;
And for a horrid and cruel murder,
    I am condemned, as you may see,
It's for the murder of poor old Baldey,
    I shall be hanged upon a tree.

Poor and honest David Baldey,
    In a lonely spot his cottage stands,
For many years did happy dwell there,
    Has fallen by a murderous hand:
Poor Baldey, he was much respected,
    In Kingston and for miles around,
They little thought on Hodson's farm,
    Of such a villain as Martin Brown.

'Twas a fatal day I did waylay,
    Poor Old Baldey on Newmarket Hill,
I with my gun did shoot him through,
    His harmless blood I did there spill.
And then his pockets soon I rifled,
    And took from him all his gold,

I left him dead where he was found,
    A sight most shocking to behold.

My victim then, I from him fled,
    But the eye of God did on me frown,
Oh, what a wretch I must have been,
    To strike the poor old shepherd down;
I for a soldier soon enlisted,
    When I arrived in Maidstone town,
But justice soon did overtake me,
    In Maidstone barracks I was found.

My wicked career now is run,
    I'm taken, and in irons bound,
In a dismal cell in Lewes gaol
    To wait my trial, young Martin Brown.
My guilt I strongly did deny,
    Until my strength it did give way,
My guilty conscience, I must confess
    I took poor Baldey's life away.

'Twas at the Assizes I took my trial,
    For two long days at the bar did stand.
The jury they did find me Guilty,

For murdering of this poor old man.
So sad a crime, and so revolting,
    The judge did say there could not be,
The sentence is, that you be hanged,
    Young Martin Brown, upon a tree.

My parents, when they heard my doom,
    Their eyes with tears did fall like rain,
When death was passed on Martin Brown,
    It filled their hearts with grief and pain.
In my dismal cell I am now lamenting,
    Strange visions they do appear to me,
My troubled mind, both night and day,
    My victim's blood I often see.

Now to this world I bid adieu,
    For on the gallows I must die,
To meet my God I must prepare,
    My sentence just I can't deny;
And when my history you do read,
    It will make your very blood to chill,
And for ages will not be forgotten,
    The Murder on Newmarket Hill.

C. Phillips, cheap and expeditioius Printing Office, Market Street, Brighton.

EXECUTION OF ALEXANDER MACKAY
For the Wilful Murder of Mrs. Grossmith.

This morning the unfortunate convict, Alexander Mackay, suffered the extreme penalty of the law at Newgate, for the murder of Mrs. Grossmith, at Norton Folgate.

This is the second execution that has been carried out in private, under the provisions of the recent statute, and it, of course, necessitated the making of a great many alterations with regard to the details. It was at first proposed that the scaffold should be erected in one of the yards adjoining the scaffold, upon the level; but, although the original plan was adhered to, it was decided that the scaffold should not be on a level, and the culprit, as was the case before, had to reach the drop by ascending a ladder.

It is due to the prisoner to state that he seems to have conducted himself very well since his condemnation, and as far as outward appearance can be relied upon, he seems to have felt severe remorse for his crime. He was visited last week by his father, his brother-in-law, and two sisters, and these interviews, as may be readily imagined, were of a most painful character.

The sheriffs of the prison having arrived, immediately proceeded to the condemned cell. The executioner was shortly afterwards introduced to the prisoner, who immediately commenced pinioning him. During this very trying operation, the wretched criminal only once he exclaimed, "May the Lord have mercy on my soul!" Everything having been completed, the prisoner thanked the chaplain and officers of the prison for their kindness towards him. The procession was formed, and slowly took its way towards the scaffold, which the prisoner ascended with a firm step; the rope was then speedily adjusted, the bolt was drawn, and the wretched man after a few struggles ceased to exist.

The bell of St. Sepulchre tolled as the prisoner left his cell; and immediately on the drop falling a black flag was raised, announcing that the last dread sentence of the law had been carried into effect.

COPY OF VERSES.

My dying moments are approaching,
　Inside of Newgate's gaol I die,
Nothing now, alas! can save me,
　I see the hangman standing by;
A dreadful murder I committed,
　Upon the fatal eighth of May;
At No. 11, Artillery Passage,
　My own kind mistress I did slay.

Barbarously I did her murder,
　I cruelly her blood did spill,
With a rolling pin and bar of iron,
　I did Mrs. Grossmith kill.

Farewell my parents, friends and kindred,
　Adieu! a last and fond adieu!
Your unhappy son, that deed has done,
　Don't let it bring disgrace on you;
The day I killed my dearest mistress,
　Sudden, in anger, spleen, and rage,
Upon the floor, I shed her gore,
　I die now eighteen years of age.

My master was away on business,
　My mistress offended me,
I seized the rollig pin and iron,
　Killed Mrs. Grossmith, then did flee,
I knew, alas! that I was undone,
　I knew not where to hide my face,
I went away some miles from London,
　Covered with shame and great disgrace.

Justice closely did pursue me,
　In agony I did bewail,
In Woolwich I was apprehended.
　And sent from thence to Maidstone Gaol;
Although I was an unknown murderer,
　I did not feel the least surprised,
When by a photograph description,
　I in the gaol was recognised.

Then, oh dear, sad was my feelings,
　What pain and anguish filled my breast,
I found that Justice overtook me,
　And I did the deed confess;
The dreadful sufferings I endured,
　I sufficient cannot unto you state,
From Maidstone Gaol I was conveyed,
　To a prison cell in Newgate.

I was tried for the dreadful murder,
　The Jury they convicted me,
The Judge he passed the dreadful sentence,
　Which was to die on the gallows tree;
I left the Bar in grief and sorrow,
　Went to my cell for to deplore,
Inside the Gaol I die to-morrow,
　Where no one ever died before.

My dying moments are approaching,
　The authorities me do surround,
The hangman by me is preparing,
　My limbs by him will soon be bound;
No one but those inside a prison,
　A poor unhappy youth can see,
Young and old pray take a warning,
　And while you live remember me·

Printed by Talyor, Brick Lane, Spitalfields, London.

2 H

SHOCKING MURDER

OF

A WIFE AND SIX CHILDREN.

On Monday morning last, a terrible tragedy took place in Hosier-lane, City, in which a man named Duggin, his wife, and six children were found poisoned. On Saturday evening Duggin returned from his work, and he then looked rather sad, and his wife told a female neighbour that her husband had been dismissed his employment, and they had also received notice to leave their lodgings at 12 o'clock on Monday. On Sunday evening Duggin took his wife and children out for a walk, and on his return went to the Wheatsheaf-tavern, Hosier-lane, and asked the landlord for a quart of ale. He then left, and was not seen again until half-past 4 o'clock on Monday morning, when a man saw him drop a letter in the Hospital pillar letter-box, and then walked towards his home. Two hours afterwards the police received a letter signed James Duggin, stating that he had murdered seven persons, and that he was about to destroy his own life. In it he said the police would be able to obtain further particulars of his brother at Sheffield. Constables were immediately despatched to 15, Hosier-lane, where they found the writer of the letter lying dead upon a bed in a room by himself. In another room they found lying on a bed, a boy aged 4, and a girl aged 3, lying upon the arms of the dead body of the mother. At the foot of the bed was the dead body of a girl aged 12, and on another bed lay the dead body of another child.

Attend you feeling parents dear,
While I relate a sad affair;
Which has fill'd all around with grief and pain
It did occur in Hosier Lane.

On Monday, June the 28th,
These crimes was done as I now state,
How horrible it is to tell,
Eight human persons by poison fell.

In London city it does appear,
Walter James Duggin lived we hear,
And seemed to live most happily,
With his dear wife and family.

They happy lived, until of late,
He appear'd in a sad desponding state,
At something he seem'd much annoy'd
At his master's, where he is employed.

He was discharged, and that we find,
It preyed upon his anxious mind,
Lest they should want, that fatal day,
His wife and children he did slay.

Last Sunday evening, as we hear,
To the Wheatsheaf he did repair,
Then homewards went, as we may read,
For to commit this horrid deed.

To the police he did a letter send,
That he was about this life to end,

And that he had poisoned, he did declare
His wife, and his six children dear.

To Hosier Lane in haste they flew,
And found it was alas, too true,
They found him stretched upon the bed,
His troubles o'er—was cold and dead.

They searched the premises around,
And they the deadly poison found;
And the shocking sight, as you may hear,
Caused in many an eye a tear.

They found upon another bed,
The ill-fated mother, she was dead,
While two pretty children we are told,
In her outstretched arms she did enfold,

It is supposed this wretched pair,
First poisoned their six children dear,
Then took the fatal draught themselves,
Their state of mind no tongue can tell.

Of such an heartrending affair,
I trust we never more may hear,
Such deeds they make the blood run cold,
May God forgive their sinful souls.

This wholesale poisoning has caused much pain
It did take place in Hosier Lane.

H. Disley, Printer, 57, High Street, St. Giles.

THE HEROES OF THE GUILLOTINE

AND GALLOWS,

OR, THE

AWFUL ADVENTURES

OF

Askern, Smith and Calcraft, the Three Rival Hangmen

Of York Castle, Stafford Gaol and Newgate;

And SANSON, the Executioner of Paris,

With his Cabinet of Murderer's Curiosities.

FULL OF ASTONISHING DISCLOSURES

Concerning their Private and Public Lives, and Startling Incidents before and after
the performance of their dreadful office.

LONDON:—FREDERICK FARRAH, 282, STRAND, W.C.
And all Booksellers.

PRICE ONE PENNY.

THE HEROES OF THE GALLOWS AND GUILLOTINE.

" One murder makes a villain, a million a hero."

THE above words of our illustrious bard may well be re-applied to the professional manipulators of the gallows and the guillotine, in England and France. In both countries, said to be the head of European civilization, the executioner seems to be a beloved and venerated object, and regarded as a hero worthy of the support of majesty and power, while smaller and less pretending kingdoms around are, one by one, abolishing his hideous and useless office.

It is a most striking and instructive anomaly, and worthy of the statesman, the philanthropist, the Christian, and all who wish for the moral progress of society, to consider and seriously examine the seeds of evil it is sowing broadcast among the human family. France is a huge nation of contradictions, never to be thoroughly understood, and England is now, in a threefold sense, her sister ! Every since their first sanguinary revolution some classes of the French people have *fondly hugged* the guillotine as a national toy of great worth, and petted three generations of SANSONS as their most excellent scientific headsmen ; they have also at every execution followed the criminal sitting in a cart, bound and bare-necked, on his coffin, beside his confessor, and gloated with open mouths and staring eyeballs upon the descending blade and the head rolling into the basket of sawdust ; and have dipped their handkerchiefs in the bloodsplashes that appeared to fall beyond the bounds of the gibbet. Other classes, of which judges and juries are made, have tried murderers of the most demoniac nature, and to the amazement of the whole woard, by the fiction of "extenuating circumstances" appended to their verdicts, have saved them from capital punishment and consigned them to the galleys ; in violation of their own consciences and oaths and the law, which sustains the guillotine as an engine of terror and example !

In our own country within the last few months we have witnessed the passing of a law abolishing public executions, on account of the demoralization that always attended their exhibition in the public highway, and which was complained of for many years by the virtuous and good of every class, who could discern the evils they generated and their inefficiency for either terror or example !

But oh ! most singular inconsistency, with the passing of that law, and the substitution of private strangling within the prison-yard, the last tatters of the old worn-out argument in favour of executions as a terror to evil-doers and an example to embryo-offenders, are completely torn away, and yet England at this time nurses three rival hangmen in her official lap for performing her secret hanging business ! The three worthies are ASKERN, of York Castle, SMITH, of Stafford-gaol, and CALCRAFT, of Newgate, in London. Three heroes of the gallows— three professional stranglers—yes, " three servants of the law," England can now boast of, against France's single hero of the guillotine to hang up their fellow sinners for a terror and an example ! Let us now enquire of the advocates of death punishments how secret executions can terrify or afford an example in the eyes of those they are intended to influence, when they are permitted no longer to witness them ?

It needs not a waste of words to prove clearly, that what was before a barbarous and demoralising exhibition, and an inefficient preventative of crime, is now a useless operation and a ghastly tragedy for sickening and tor-turing all those whom the law compels or the authorities permit to be personal spectators. As the daily and weekly papers published since Calcraft's and Smith's joint essays with the first private strangling machine at Maidstone, have proved, murders and other sanguinary offences tending to the same end, do not in the least decrease ; but on contrary, the graphic accounts of the first private execution, and the form and action of the new method that were afterwards given in every morning and evening journal, served only to *entertain* and amuse the lovers of horrors, and were followed by a repetition of capital crimes in several places, as if no such punishment awaited the perpetrators of them. And so will it be after the second trial of the new system, on the boy MACKAY, at Newgate, for the Norton Forgate murder, until society to its lowest depths is more moralised and humanised ; and a more exacting retribution is enforced against the hardened classes, whom no law of capital punishment will now terrify into submission.

As the Star's special reporter's description is worth preserving in its entirety, both for what it says, and for *what it does not say*, in favour of our argument, *at its conclusion*, we shall transcribe it into this part of our book:

The first execution within the prison walls, and in presence only of a limited number of spectators, in accordance with the new Act of Parliament for the better regulation of capital punishment, took place on Tuesday morning, August 13th, at Maidstone Gaol. The culprit who suffered sentence was Thomas Wells, late a porter in the employ of the London, Chatham, and Dover Railway Company, who was left for death after the last assizes for the murder of Mr. Walsh, the station-master at Dover. In the course of his duties Mr. Walsh had occasion to find fault with Wells, who took reproof in very ill part, and revenged himself on the first available opportunity on the unfortunate station-master by shooting him dead as he sat alone at his work in his office. The alarm was raised, and Wells was found hiding close at hand. The proofs of his crime were so positive that he scarcely attempted to deny it, and on his trial he was at once found guilty and condemned to death. The reports which from time to time have appeared in the public prints since his condemnation have described the young man—he was little more than eighteen years of age—as sincerely penitent, and these reports are borne out by the prison officers, who seemed to have been much impressed by his quiet and decorous conduct.

The curious in such matters will note as an odd coincidence the fact that Maidstone—a town so notorious for its anti-capital punishment feeling, that lawyers will tell you it is most difficult to get a jury to return an adverse verdict against a prisoner on trial for his life—should have been the first place in which the arrangements of the death sentence under the new law should have been carried out. Whether in pursuance of this feeling the inhabitants wilfully ignored the tragedy which was about to be enacted in the immediate outskirts of their own, or whether they were indifferent to it, or whether the exact period of the execution has been hidden from them, it is impossible to say ; but it is certain that, amongst the people freely scattered about the broad and handsome streets on Wednesday evening, there was not the slightest indication that anything unusual was to take place among them the following day. A travelling menagerie, which had pitched its tent close by the borders of the canal, was thronged with delighted gazers, among whom the private-soldier element was strongly represented. The local volunteers, headed by their band, were attended in their march by many of the youthful population, and a still larger gathering followed the band of the militia regiment, and grouped round while they played in front of their headquarters, the Mitre Hotel. But in none of the crowds, composed as they were of old and young, male and female—did one hear the least allusion, either in earnestness or ribaldry, to the criminal who was spending his last hours within a few hundred yards of the place where this gaity was being carried on, and to whose ears, deafen them how he might, abstract his senses how he would, the clangour of the drums must have been painfully audible. Nor was there any remarkable difference yesterday morning. It had been expected that a large majority of the shops would remain closed until after the execution, which was fixed to take place at half-past ten, but the shutters were taken down at the usual hour, men proceeded to their usual avocations, and there was not the smallest sign—not even that most ordinary sign of men and women conversing in knots and groups—of anything unusual being about to happen, until one reached the immediate neighbourhood of the gaol, and there, on the far side of the broad road running round by the court-house, was a thin fringe of humanity, some fifty persons in all, in one long line, looking towards the great gate of the gaol, and talking among themselves. Emphatically a "bad lot" this, tramps out on hopping excursions, beggars, a female gipsy or two,—men and women, too, the lowest scum of the population, and a dozen eager-eyed, wolfish, cunning-looking blackguard boys. They gape and stare, though there is nothing for them to look at as yet ; the gaol-gate is closed, and there is no one in the immediate neighbourhood, so they take stock of the flagstaff, on which, in accordance with official injunctions, the "black flag" is to be run up at the moment of the execution, and find matter for comment in the exit from the gaol of certain stonemasons who have been at work inside the prison walls.

At half-past nine exactly a four-wheeled cab drives rapidly up the street, and pulls up at the door of the New Inn, immediately opposite the Court house. The cab door and the inn door open simultaneously ; from the former descends a man, who inters the inn, the door of which is again immediately closed upon him, while the cab drives off. In two minutes this man emerges from the inn and makes for the gaol. He is an elderly man, with white hair and white beard, broad and thick-set, and dressed in black, with a peculiar tall hat, and carries a small carpet bag in his hand. This is Calcraft, the hangman. As it were intuitively the little crowd becomes aware of this, a whisper runs round among it that the bag contains his "tackle" of pinioning straps, &c., and the blackguard boys, excited beyond bearing, spring to their feet and start in pursuit. The man, taking no notice and looking doggedly before him, crosses the road, and getting close to the gaol railings, half slinks, half shambles along till he reaches the gate which opens at his approach and closes behind him. Five minutes afterwards another man issues from the inn and makes for the gaol—a tall, thin, wiry man, with a keen eye, with his cheeks and part of his forehead closely shaved, dressed in a velveteen shooting coat, loose trousers, and billycock hat, and looking like an acrobat who had donned his private clothes over his professional costume. The little crowd does not know this man, though he is almost as notorious as the other. He is Smith, of Dudley, the hangman of the Birmingham district, who hanged Palmer, and who occasionally assists Calcraft on great occasions.

At ten o'clock the representatives of the press, who have been provided by the authorities with proper credentials, are admitted into the prison, and are first ushered into the round-house, a building in the debtors' division, where the turnkeys on duty pass the night. It is fitted with a desk and benches, is glazed on all sides, and overlooks the front court and several of the exercise yards. Several of the warders are here, and from them one learns that the prisoner passed a quiet night, sleeping from half-past ten till half-past four, but that the extraordinary equanimity which he had hitherto displayed is failing him now, and that he is beginning to "break down." This conversation is carried on in a low whisper ; the silence of the place is singularly oppressive ; and this, combined with the knowledge of what one is about immediately to witness, renders this period one of the most painful suspense. There are five hundred prisoners within the gaol, but one might as well be in the City of the Dead for all one hears of them, the only sound, the jingling of the warders' keys, grating on the ear. A little excitement is caused by the hurried entrance of a warder from the direction in which the prisoner is known to be, and his equally hurried disappearance bearing some brandy in a tumbler, but the silence sets in afresh, and one is reduced to watching two little knots in the fore court. One of these consists of the under-sheriff (who is deeply affected), the medical officer, and a nonchalant person in a wideawake hat, who is said to be the governor, but who takes no part in the proceedings, and who is poking up the ground with his walking-stick in a very degagé manner. The other knot is formed of Calcraft, his assistant. and two of the warders who are chatting together. At twenty-five minutes past ten the party—consisting of four reporters of the London journals, six from various local papers, a carpenter who is in attendance lest his service should be required in connection with the arrangements of the drop, and a warder in plain clothes who has been sitting up all night with the prisoner—is summoned from the round-house and ushered into a narrow vaulted ante-room, whence, after five minutes' delay, they are led through a narrow passage into the presence of the gallows.

There it stands, erected under a shed at the further end of a small yard some thirty feet square, the old square gallows formed of two uprights and one crosebeam, and whose form has been familiar to us from woodcuts and description for years, only in this instance it is painted buff instead of the ordinary dead black. The uprights across have iron supports fixed into the wall, and in the crossbeam there is a hook, immediate under which stands Thomas Wells, with the rope round his neck. There is no built scaffold ; the drop on which the prisoner stands is flush with the ground, and the public (if the little representative party can be so called) is placed behind a barrier breast-high, yet so close to the prisoner that they can see every movement of his face, and hear every word he utters. He looks a mere youth, short, yet strongly built. He is dressed in his railway porter's uniform of velveteen, with the company's initials in red on the collar, and in his waistcoat, just above his pinioned hand, wears a small flower. He evidently knows little of anything of what is going on around him. He is absorbed in prayer—his face, of a livid hue, is upturned, and his eyes are looking upwards. Standing by him, the chaplain, the Rev. W. C. F. Sugden Frazer, reads, in a voice broken with emotion, the burial service. Suddenly the prisoner begins, in a low, thick, trembling voice, to sing a hymn— one, as we afterwards learn, which he has been recently repeating in his cell—and continues to sing it after Calcraft has pulled the cap over his face, and the chaplain has shaken hands with him—is singing it when, at a signal from his superior, Smith pulls the bolt, and then, with a sickening rattle, the drop falls, Calcraft standing behind, and, as it were, guiding the falling figure. In our belief, life was not wholly extinct for three or four minutes after the falling of the drop. It is usual on these occasions to speak of the movements of the limbs as being "merely muscular," in this instance there was scarcely any muscular contortion, but there were undoubtedly deep respirations and other undeniable evidence that asphyxia did not immediately happen.

Such is the history of the first private execution in England. Anticipated with just horror by those who were compelled to be present, it was carried out with every decency and all decorum, in a manner calculated to give the least pain to those whose duty it was to witness it. The presence of the representatives of the press at a private execution is a guarantee to the public, whose delegates they are, that the sentence of the law which has been passed upon a certain criminal is duly carried out. But there is no occasion to inflict upon them, as was the case at Newgate, the horror of witnessing the pinioning, the procession, and all the awful details of the scaffold. These, thanks to the visiting justices and to the under-sheriff of Kent, Mr. Furley, of Ashford, were spared at Maidstone, and will, it is to be hoped, be spared in future. Meanwhile, so far as this one instance affords means of judging, IS THE EXECUTION UNDER THE NEW LAW MORE IMPRESSIVE THAN UNDER THE OLD ? We answer, decidedly, in the affirmative. The applause or censure of the mob, the desire to "die game" before his friends had, it is acknowledged, the worst influence on the prisoner, and the solemn stillness of the little yard, with its handful of spectators, must have been IMPRESSIVE in the most awful degree, while a peaceful provincial town is left to its usual avocations, entirely free from the influx of pestilent blackguardism, drunkenness, and obscenity which always attended a public hanging.

For the moral purpose of our theme, there are but three items worth noticing in the above account ; they are 1st.—The black flag, hoisted as a terror and example to the "bad lot" of "tramps out on hopping excursion, beggars, a female gipsy or two, men and women, the lowest scum of the population, and a dozen eager-eyed, wolfish, cunning-looking boys !" 2nd.—The officials and representatives of the press who "anticipated with just HORROR" the coming scene at which they "were compelled to be present, and then when it is enacted as the primary NATIONAL PLAY for the time being, staring at the prisoner in his "railway porter's uniform of velveteen," roped to the fatal beam, with a faded flower "in his waistcoat, just above his pinioned hands," absorbed in prayer—his face of a livid hue, upturned, and his eyes looking upwards; at the same time singing a hymn " in a low, thick, trembling voice," " after Calcraft has pulled the cap over his face," and the Chaplain, who had been reading " in a voice broken with emotion, the burial service," has shaken hands with him ;" and then *listening* to the " SICKEN-ING RATTLE " in the criminal's throat, mixed with the whirring sound of the collapsing machinery, as " Smith pulls the bolt," and " the drop falls," while " Calcraft is standing behind, and, as it were, guiding the falling figure " into the newly-dug pit below; and 3rd—the summing-up question and answer of the reporter, after making one of a group at this disgusting performance. " Is the execution under the new law more *impressive* than under the old ?" " We answer decidedly in the affirmative. The applause or censure of the mob, the desire to 'die game' before his friends, had, it is acknowledged, the worst influence on the prisoner, and the solemn stillness of the little yard, with its handful of spectators, *must have been impressive* in the most awful degree."

Impressive upon whom let us here ask? Not upon the "bad lot" contemplating the black flag ! The very class who needed some wholesome impression of fear, and who never realised it at public hangings, were shut out and left to indulge their idle fancies and curious promptings—a kind of pleasure to them ! If it were impressive upon the " gentlemen of England," and the representatives of the press, while looking upon a drama so horrible, we should imagine that it was in a sense different from that for which capital punishments were enacted; unless we were to believe that, notwithstanding their high refinement, they were susceptible of murderous emotions.

Then there remains only what the conclusion of the report seems to point at, that it was impressive upon the dying criminal, thus leaving only one poor miserable pretence for sustaining the existence of the gallows as a moral preventative, and a wholesome example. Of what use to society is the transitory impression of an agonised wretch about to die unobserved by the world? None whatever, and therefore the advocates of death punish-ments must soon give way to those of our opinion, that the gallows is an effete institution, unfit for its purpose; and that solitary confinement and hard labour for life would not only be a greater and more deterring punish-ment, but a security against prematurely hurrying into eternity, as in days of old, *innocent* persons, wrongly convicted through some vile perjury of the wicked, mistaken identity, or imperfectly unravelled circumstances.

Amongst the earliest converts, we expect soon to number the reporter of the above quoted narrative, and most of his literary brethren. For promoting the cause of abolition, we have issued this pamphlet, and although we notice the awful adventures of the heroes of the gallows and guillotine in our progress, we have no wish to pander to the taste of the illiterate and depraved, but to point a moral that shall leave a trace of some good impression behind.

As we have placed ASKERN foremost in our list of modern living British hangmen, the most unknown and least experienced, we shall first give a short biographical notice of his life and professional career.

Except in the performance of their dreadful office, and the associations it brings them into, before and after every execution, there is nothing in their private antecedents and habits above the common run of men of their class. No extraordinary genius has ever been manifested by either of our gallows-heroes, beyond the horrible calling which fate has marked out for them. But under the irresistable spell of an evil destiny, they are com-pelled by fate to perform deeds which all other men shudder at, although they know their legal necessity; and in their endeavours to become proficient in their strangling art, so as to earn the praise of their official superiors, and the admiration of the multitude, they stand out from the rest of society with more than ordinary prominence, and in that respect are regarded as the chief of remarkable public characters. From the most reliable informa-tion current amongst the old friends and associates of Askern about York and adjacent districts, also from officials of the castle, which is now used as a gaol, a career of abject poverty, want of employment, ill-luck in almost every one of his undertakings, and a too-fast life whenever his chequered destiny placed money, in small sums at a time, within his power, led him into *temptation*, and from that temptation came the *commission* of a deed which consigned him a prisoner to York Castle, from the sombre scenes of which he never emerged, except as a convict, whom evil fate had long marked for her own ! In charity, we throw a veil over his particular offence, as our object is only to here show cause and effect, and warn the yet pure and innocent from evil courses.

It was while a convicted prisoner and when an execution was pending without any hangman to do the " job," after an unsuccessful application to Calcraft of London, who was then fully engaged, that an offer of pardon was made to him on condition that he performed the office on the doomed man.

Moved by the love of liberty, which like life is said to be sweet to everyone, and promises of remuneration and perquisites, Askern accepted without much hesitation the office of public executioner, and to qualify himself in his new and ominous business, he diligently employed his time (as all others in the same line have done before him) in tying and knotting several lengths of rope after the hangman's fashion, and testing their tightening effects upon an effigy suspended to a rope stretched across the private room where he lodged. To acquire speed and precision in the tying of a hangman's "noose," also in the "turning off and cutting down" without the least blundering and rousing the execrations of the depraved mobs which generally assemble to view such ghastly sights, many trials he had to make upon the suspended figure to fit him for the work of the scaffold.

At length the fatal morning came for his first practical essay on the neck of a human being over the top of the castle wall, and in the presence of a vast hideous-looking concourse of people, who hissed at the culprit when he appeared; and strange inconsistency, also hooted the man who was employed to execute the bidding of justice on the object of their detestation !

ASKERN, at a scene so horrible and new to him, trembled, and would have rushed at once from the scaffold the very moment he had stepped upon it, if he had possessed the power and freedom to do so; but alas! for him there was no chance, his apprenticeship to the strangling trade must be fulfilled according to the prescribed con-ditions previously mentioned.

Therefore, *nerveless* as he felt, and ready to sink into the death-trap beneath, amongst the machinery of the drop, he had to summon up all the courage and fortitude which draughts of intoxicating liquor then plentifully supplied to him, could instil into his drooping frame.

At one bound he approached the pinioned wretch, roughly seized him, placed him under the cross-beam of the gallows quickly, with blanched features and trembling hands, hurriedly pulled the white cap down over his livid face, placed the rope over his neck, and drew the noose most scientifically as he thought, in the true Calcraft style, and as his preceding lessons had taught him; but, lo, and behold! a turnkey had no sooner hastened down and drawn the bolt that lets fall the flooring on which the murderer stands, and sets him swinging in the air, than the culprit's awful convulsions and desperate struggles to clutch the rope and free himself from the tortures he was suffering, showed the ghastly fact, that his first attempt did not succeed, and that the yelling multitude around and below, all horror-stricken at the sickening spectacle, were clamoring against the unfortunate servant of the law! Speedily he had to release the quivering half-strangled wretch, and do his work of hanging over again, ere death terminated the writhings of the doomed man, and at the same time quieted the unearthly cries of the heaving and seething crowds of men and women who had come from various distances, near and far, to behold the great NATIONAL SHOW!

Subsequent experience "got his hand in" as the saying is, and made him more adroit at strangling, but except among a very few relatives and old acquaintances, he was a man shunned and despised, and often liable to insults and desperate encounters in public company, when once the whisper went round that he was the hangman of York Castle.

Another unhappy being, fated to follow the same horrible vocation, is SMITH, of Dudley. On the outskirts of the town there used to be seen the old half-tumbled down cottage, surrounded by a marshy piece of ground, where "Dudley Smith," as he is often called, resided at the time he took it into his head to become a second rival to London's famous hangman. The news of ASKERN'S exploits gave SMITH courage, but made CALCRAFT only laugh and wonder how many more fools, ambitious of a black notoriety, were going to compete with him. Events soon followed to settle the question, and afford SMITH the opportunity he sought.

"Red-handed guilt, the child of woe" then made rapid progress, and cast a gloom over many a household in Staffordshire, and throughout the adjacent "black country." The difference of a few guineas settled the matter in the minds of the authorities of Stafford gaol, and struck the balance against the pecuniary demands of the skilful CALCRAFT, and in favour of the lesser price of the inexperienced SMITH, who, however, supplemented the want of experience with that species of brazen impudence and animal confidence which men of his class possess. Mentally and physically he was of rougher mould than either of the two former gallows heroes. Nurtured from birth among miners, the companion of the most illiterate pottery hands, and with bull-dog tastes and habits, he was well fitted for the office of public executioner. A man being wanted for the coming "job," he applied, sent in the "lowest tender," and was accepted. Visions by day and night now haunted his mind; asleep or awake the gallows and all its appurtenances dwelt strongly upon his imagination, and flitted before his eyes in his drunken moments. Coils of rope here, there, and everywhere rose up before him, and sometimes twined about his own neck in his midnight dreams, like fiery serpents. Time was getting brief, and he must prepare to perform his task neatly and expeditiously, and in dexterity equal the renowned William Calcraft. So, accordingly, after being shown the sort of rope he must use, he set himself to the work of experimenting and forming slip knots round logs of wood, knobs of furniture and fixtures, the tops of his garden rails, and sometimes round his own neck, close under the ear, and sufficiently tight to satisfy himself that it would answer at the proper time. He practised also the pinioning process on his "young woman" in secret; who, not at all enamoured at his intended profession, at first stoutly resisted, but his importunities and determination made her submit to his strange proceedings.

Without overburdening our confined space with an enumeration of the criminals he afterwards executed at Stafford and elsewhere, suffice it to say, that after a few blunders and the usual violent outcries of the brutal multitudes, he became tolerably expert, and was considered a fit assistant to Calcraft, when a change of the law and private executions were determined upon. As we have been informed in the before quoted narrative of the first private execution, on account of Calcraft's great age, and in obedience to the overtures of the authorities, SMITH performed the subordinate part of moving the bolt that supported the platform on which the criminal stood; preliminary, it is supposed, to taking Calcraft's place, if death or inability should ere long necessitate a change.

Such a change may be nearer than people suppose, for Calcraft is expected to be a successful applicant for a retiring pension, on account of his infirmities, now too plainly visible, in which event Smith might have for a competitor the notorious "LONG TOM COFFIN," a costermonger of old Clare Market, lately pulled down, and a quaint character about town, who addressed an epistle in the following form to the authorities of Newgate, which we give in its original orthography, and "with all its blushing honours" and beauties "thick upon it":—

"Wild Street, March 1st, 1868.

"To the Gaol Committee of Newgate,"

"Gentilmen,—As Ive heerd Calcraft yure ould hangmon iz goin to leeve iz plaise, Ive just takin the libertee too ask yu too chuse me, as I am villin too do the jobs on murdrers for the same pay, and vill ever bee punkshal hat it, ven ever yu vant to hang em up at the gallers. Ive no objecshun to exshecute any vun yu pleese, without feer or favur too any relashun or aquanetense, but vill do my dooty imparshul, for vich I can git a goood karacter,"

I am Gentilmen,
Yure humbel sirvent,
THOMAS COFFIN."

"P.S.—Nevyew by my granmuther's side to the late Doctur Coffin."

The secret execution of Wells, the railway porter, at Maidstone, on August 13th, 1868, marks in the criminal calendar William Calcraft's disappearance from public life. He will henceforth be surrounded by the mystery becoming his terrible office, and the rising generation of criminals who take an interest in the matter, will have to ask their seniors what kind of man he was, and to trust to their imaginations for the picture of him. To no man probably will this mystery be more welcome than to Calcraft himself. He has shown, on more than one occasion, that his dread of facing the crowd was equal to his victim's dread of facing the gallows.

At the execution of the Manchester Fenians, and of Barrett in London, he was seen to manifest more fear and nervous weakness than any of the men whom he was to put to death. On both occasions he received violent threatening letters from the fenian friends of the culprits. He therefore shuffled about the prison yard, and seemed afraid to mount the gallows-steps, while the sweat fell from his face, and stood in large drops upon his brow. It is a great relief to him for his few remaining years, and a moral gain in every sense to society, to have lost sight of him; for after all, he constituted perhaps the most revolting part of a public execution. The strong prejudice, and the intense savage hatred of the crowd against him was, no doubt, a most unjustifiable feeling, seeing that as the mere instrument of justice and of judgment, he was neither to be hated nor to be loved; but it existed in such intensity that there was no prospect of its ever being lessened. The effect was extremely injurious even to the poor kind of morality that public executions were supposed to promote. The passive feeling of awe with which men might be disposed to look on a criminal going to a righteous doom, was changed into an active feeling of disgust and horror, when they beheld the man by whom he was publicly strangled; and there was too much reason to believe that they left the precincts of the gibbet with more of this unjust feeling uppermost in their minds, than that which open-air executions were meant to inculcate.

All this is now changed by the private system of hanging, but it also destroys every plea for retaining the use of the gallows, as we have before argued in previous pages.

In sketching the career of Calcraft, much is necessary to be said respecting his predecessor, Tom Cheshire, to whom he acted for some years as an assistant hangman, and who gave him during that time repeated instructions in the art of putting criminals to death.

The commencement of his professional life reaches back far into the reign of George the Third, when Tom Cheshire first employed him, and was in the height of his fame. A very remarkable character was old Cheshire, who used to wear always a snuff-brown coat reaching down to his heels, and on that account was often hooted at wherever he was seen, as the "snuffy skull thatcher!" Many of the ancient customs of Newgate he was an eye-witness of, and which will be interesting to mention here.

When the last night of some poor condemned wretch had arrived, at midnight, and from hour to hour, till the dawn of the execution morning, a bell man used to parade outside the prison walls under the grating of the condemned cell, and in loud solemn tones accompanied the harsh sounds of his bell with his warning-cries, to "prepare for death." With a blush of shame for our forefathers, we are obliged to confess that, MURDER BY LAW on the gallows was then so common for burglary, highway robbery, forgery, horse and sheep stealing, shop-lifting to the value of forty shillings, and other minor offences, that "hanging Monday" was regularly looked for, after every Old Bailey sessions, when a batch of males and females, sometimes amounting to half a dozen, would be hung up like so many dogs and cats on a Monday morning, although only found guilty and sentenced on the preceding Friday. Simple stealing from a house or the person was then oftener punished with death than were murderous offences. And so awfully unscrupulous were the "Bow-street runners," as the officers of police were termed, that the innocent used to be "planted" with stolen property, entrapped, sworn positively against, and put to death for the sake of the £40 "blood money" then given for every one capitally convicted. Then the horror of the "condemned cell, and pew, and press yard" were kept continually going, and the blood-thirsty monsters afterwards held their nightly saturnalias together, with spies, informers, bawdy-house pimps of both sexes, and the master and deputy-hangman amongst them; who revelled and toasted the success of their trade of blood-spilling. Then also, the "press yard" witnessed every sessions the torturing of its many youthful victims by the lead-knotted lash; and the "press room" resounded with the piercing shrieks of a prisoner under-going the punishment awarded to those who refused to plead. Whenever a prisoner at the bar declined to say whether he was guilty or not guilty (a formality required by the law before he could be tried), he was taken to the "press room," laid on the stone floor naked, and with arms and legs extended, chained fast by the wrists and ancles; and a stout board was placed on the front of his body, on which heavy iron weights, one by one, were gradually placed, after every time he was asked if he would plead to the question first put to him, "guilty or not guilty?" Some poor tortured wretches, after a certain number of ponderous weights, never less than half-hundreds or hundreds, had been heaped upon them, would be terrified into pleading and standing the chance of their trial; but others would be obstinately dumb till such a pile of weights was added, that they were, according to the sentence of the law, crushed to death! The murderer's pew in the chapel, on the sabbath day, often presented a spectacle, that once seen, never was forgotten. While the late Rev. Dr. Cotton, then the prison chaplain, was preaching the "condemned sermon" one time scowling assassins deep-dyed with the blood of many victims would be seen grouped together; at another time youth and innocence, wrongfully condemned to die a felon's death on the gallows (as history has since proved), through perjury, or misconstrued circumstances and uncertain evidence. Amongst these we must not forget the fair and beautiful Eliza Fenning, a virtuous maiden servant of a tradesman's family in Fleet Street, who suffered death on the public gibbet for an offence which she called God to witness that she was totally innocent of! She was convicted on doubtful circumstantial evidence of attempting to poison the whole family, by putting arsenic into the flour of some dumplings she made for their dinner. All her solemn asseverations of innocence availed her not, and the best of characters was entirely useless: sentenced to die she was, and she was ruthlessly hanged by her fair neck, before a vast sympathising multitude of men, women, and children in the Old Bailey, all melted to tears, and crying out "shame," "shame!"

The beauteous innocent creature appeared on the gallows platform in a new white dress from head to foot, as spotless as her own purity; and we doubt not her soul, the moment it was released by the executioner's vile hands, was caught up by attending angels and carried to the haven of eternal bliss.

Long after it was too late to wipe out the stain of her judicial murder, her master's son confessed on his death bed that he secretly mixed the arsenic in the flour she used, during her brief absence from the kitchen, as an act of revenge for refusing to submit to his embraces.

Tom Cheshire and Newgate has witnessed other ghastly scenes, and his predecessor has had adventures with " Sixteen-string-Jack, Jerry Abershaw, Jonathan Wild, Jack Shepherd, Betsy the bank-note forger and foot-pad, who was half executed and restored to life; when the CONDEMNED used to go in an open cart, sitting on their coffins, from Newgate all through Holborn to a public half-way house in St. Giles's, where they were allowed to stop and drink their " parting draught " with their friends, and be presented with their " last nosegay," and then resume their procession through Oxford Road, and at the top of it, in the open space facing the gates of Hyde Park, near the turnpike that then existed, to be at once executed on Tyburn's three-corner'd gibbet.

Passing to later times, CHESHIRE and his man Calcraft knew something about the noted Dr. Brooks and the dreadful secrets of old surgeon's hall at the back of Newgate. Subjects for dissection being very scarce, "BODY-SNATCHERS," sometimes called *"resurrectionists"* used to watch funerals during the day time in the church-yards of London, mark where the youngest and plumpest subjects were interred, and at night, with digging tools take them up and bag them in sacks, which they would speedily convey to a hired hackney coach standing conveniently near, and drive off with them to the said hall, or to St. Bartholomew's, according to orders. As body-snatching did not always supply enough subjects for the numerous doctors and students who required them for lectures and experiments, a viler class of offenders sprang to way-lay the friendless and unfortunate, entice them into some lonely out of way house surrounded by vacant ground walls, and there poison and smother them. These horrible villains were called Burkers, who contrived for a long time to sell the bodies of their victims undetected for large sums, as persons who had died naturally and been buried. At last a poor Italian boy who exhibited white mice in the streets, was burked by Bishop, May, and Williams, in a lone house in Bethnal-green, and one night was offered at Bartholomew's hospital. The doctor to whom they took it, feeling certain after a minute examination, that the corpse had died a violent death, quietly sent for the officers of justice, and gave them into custody. They were tried and found guilty on the clearest evidence of Italians who identified the boy, and were hanged by Calcraft and his master amidst the loudest execrations ever heard in the precincts of Newgate.

During the earlier times of that awful looking gail, the classification and administration were so loose as to render it a perfect HELL ON EARTH. Depravity, ribaldry, drunkenness, gambling and debauchery there reigned unchecked in its dark dungeon, between gaolers and the lowest of their male and female prisoners. The latter sex often times exchanged clothes with their keepers, when the govener was, at night, fast asleep, and in their cells they carried on whatever lewd revels they had a fancy for, and made a pandemonium of the prison. At the death of Cheshire, Calcraft became principal executioner. He was previously a private watchman at Reid's brewery, Liquorpond Street, and by trade a lady's shoemaker. He is also celebrated as a first-class rabbit-fancier, whose breed has won prizes, and unknown, has graced the festive board of many London families. At the Tiger public house, corner of Devizes Street, near the Rosemary Branch, Hoxton, next door to his old resi-dence in his younger days, he used to meet great numbers of his brother snobs, rabbit-breeders, and skittle players, and there held jollifications and played skittles with them. On account of the prejudice of the neighbours, and the too-great freedom of impudent boys in calling out " Jack Ketch," his habit was to go out very early in the morning and after dark. He is married, and is the parent of a goodly number of sons and daughters, morally brought up and schooled, who have sometimes, been unjustly annoyed by ignorent people on account of their unfortunate parentage. To show the full force of this prejudice we will mention a curious circumstance that happened to one of his daughters.

She was accustomed to meet and court a young mechanic at a friend's house. One night a supper was ap-pointed to be held there, and the sweetheart had promise of a good merry-making with mutual acquaintances of both sexes, not one of whom knew Miss Calcraft by her paternal name. Through some mysterous cause we have never had explained, just as all were comfortably seated around the smoking viands on the table, and were pledg-ing the lovers and each other in preliminary bumpers of beer and gin, strange footsteps were heard on the stairs, followed by a knock at the door, and when it was opened, the whole company, especially Miss Calcraft's lover, were suddenly petrified with horror. No sooner was the fatal name pronounced and a recognition passed between father and daughter, than the young man at one bound cleared the table, rushed down the stairs, ran fast away from the house and was seen no more: thus proving again to the deserted hangman's daughter, that " the course of true love never runs smooth."

A parallel to the iniquities of the old Bow Street runners are to be found in the records of our modern police force of London. " Jack Ketch's warren" was well supplied by police scoundrels from many quarters of the poverty stricken districts. One of the most infamous was the " prig's haunt" in Tyndal's Buildings, Gray's Inn Lane, inhabited by low Irish, where KING, a policeman in disguise, attended daily when off duty, to teach pocket-picking and all the arts of burglary to poor outcast boys. Between experiments with various instruments, and lessons on the way to use them, a coat was swung across a line, and the young ones were shown how to pick the pocket single-handed when a thief was by himself, and when they went together in twos and threes. As fast as they became adepts in the art and went into the streets to obtain their living by it, King, who always knew their walks, watched them in his uniform, and the moment they committed a robbery, pounced upon them and pro-cured their conviction, for which he obtained the praise of his superiors for extraordinary vigilance, and rewards, besides court-fees at the sessions. At last this vile thief-trainer became too clever ; he was denounced by some boys sharper than himself, and some of his honester brother-constables took the clue up, unravelled it to the end, and on the clearest evidence got him sentenced to penal servitude for life. A more recent proof, while we are penning this, has come out, that perjury is still rife in the Metropolitan police force. Three policemen have been wrongfully procuring the conviction of a drover on the charge of stealing several sheep from a field at Tottenham, and have received their " blood money" from the County of Middlesex funds. Since their poor victim has been suffering his conviction, the real thief, at the trial of one of his confederates, has confessed to his own guilt, and declared the entire innocence of the man formerly sworn to by the said policemen. May justice soon overtake them.

Returning to Calcraft and his latter days, we have to congratulate our readers upon his religious conversion, and regular Sunday attendance with his wife, at a church near Poole-street, Islington. He has long ceased to love his office and make money by sales of the clothes of the numerous culprits, and bits of the ropes that hanged them. The ancient ceremony of swearing in the executioner was an awful one. Amidst a collection of ropes, fetters and handcuffs, with his hand upon the bible, he was required to solemnly swear that he would execute every criminal condemned to die, without favouring father or mother, or any friend whatsoever; and when he had taken the horrible oath he was dismissed with the ominous words—"GET THEE HENCE WRETCH!"

The latest performance of Calcraft is reported below, and shows that the first private execution at Newgate was like the one at Maidstone, privately barbarous and publicly useless.

At nine o'clock in the morning of September 8th, the first private execution in London took place in the interior of Newgate Prison. The culprit was Alexander Arthur Mackay, a youth of only eighteen years of age, who, on the 8th of May last murdered a woman Emma Grossmith in whose service he was, at 11. Artillery-passage, Norton Folgate. It now only remains to tell how he expiated his crime upon the scaffold in the presence not of a roaring, surging mob, but in the solitude of a prison, and before a few persons, whose number did not much exceed a score.

Inside the gaol the scene was solemn to the last degree. The representatives of the morning newspapers whose duty it was to witness the execution were admitted to Newgate at half-past eight, and after traversing several gloomy corridors found themselves in an inclosed yard near the prison chapel, in front of the scaffold. A few words will enable the reader to picture for himself the scene.

The yard is a square one, entered by a wicket gate at the south-east corner, and in the corner to the north-west stands the scaffold. In the south-west corner, near the grating through which prisoners undergoing punishment hold converse with their friends at periods arranged for by the prison rules, is a space railed off for the representatives of the press, and standing at intervals of a few yards apart are men of the City police, occupying the remainder of the yard. Behind the scaffold the prison buildings rear their massive walls, and from the roof peers down upon the solemn scene below a stolid warder stationed there in order that, so soon as the ghastly business is at an end, he may signal the man in whose hands are the ropes to hoist the black flag, as a witness to the outside world that justice is satisfied; on the opposite side of the yard are other prison buildings with grated windows, but no outward sign of the life within, while flanking the yard north and south are walls—the one is topped by a terrible cheveaux de frise, and over the other hangs suspended a large cloth, the sound of whose rustling, as shaken by the wind—it beat against the prison wall,—was as the flapping wing of a huge bird of prey. The silent expectation of the twenty minutes spent in that dreadful yard was the most painful experience of the present writer's life. Absence of sound when a man is alone in the heart of a trackless forest is said by travellers to be fearfully oppressive, but the involuntary silence of twenty men waiting the entrance of the messengers of death and their victim becomes painful to the last degree. Sometimes there is a slight murmur heard from the outside of the prison, with now and again the clanking of a latch or the grating of a bolt within the gaol itself, and occasionally a low hum of conversation in the yard—these are the only sounds heard, and they only serve to intensify the oppressiveness of the silent intervals that intervene. What was going on within the prison during this time was not known to the representatives of the press. Under the new Act of Parliament they are excluded from what was known as the pinioning room, and only see the very last scene of all, an alterat on very agreeable to the feelings of gentlemen upon whom is imposed a most painful duty. They learned after the execution that Mackay had since his condemnation conducted himself with great decorum, had frequently expressed his great sorrow for the crime he had committed, and his perfect readiness to die. The poor youth, we were told, lost his own mother when he was about the same age as one of his victim's children, and this deepened in his own mind the intense feelings of poignant regret he seemed to experience between his sentence being pronounced and carried into effect. He was most attentive to the ministrations of the Rev. Mr. Jones, ordinary of Newgate, and took the sacrament at his hands on Sunday. The condemned youth slept soundly until about six o'clock in the morning, when he rose and remained in communion with his spiritual adviser until the last. So much for the interior of the prison; outside the silence remained unbroken, save by the sounds of which we have spoken, until within a quarter of an hour of nine, when from the neighbouring church of St. Sepulchre a passing bell began to toll, and a slightly increased murmur from the outside world reached the ears of those who waited within the prison. At about this time Mr Sheriff M'Arthur, with his under sheriffs, Messrs Roche and Davidson Mr. Jonas, the governor; and Mr. Gibson, the surgeon of Newgate, entered the yard, and having satisfied themselves that all the arrangements were complete, retired, leaving the space again to the reporters and policemen, one of the latter body having some few minutes earlier turned sick and left the yard. This almost unbearable suspense lasted until the clocks in the neighbourhood were heard to strike the hour, and then the clanking of a latch behind the black screen surrounding the scaffold was followed by the appearance of the Rev. Mr. Jones, who supported the doomed man as he ascended the few steps leading from the ground to the drop. The chaplain, whose voice trembled with emotion, read the Litany from the Church of England Prayer-book, and Mackay joined with a loud, clear voice in the responses, his voice being heard distinctly over the yard, even after he was capped and noosed. Just at this supreme moment the young man's firmness seemed about to forsake him, and he tottered as though to fall, but the hand of the chaplain laid upon his arm sustained him, and in another second the trap on which the unhappy man was standing fell, and he hung suspended. The fall was a very short one, and signs of life were visible for a longer time after the bolt was drawn than we remember to have seen on any similar occasion. As soon as possible every one concerned in the ghastly business was glad to make his escape from this last act in a doleful drama. To the spectators, judging from our own experience, and the appearance of many persons present, nothing could have been more terrible than this sight of a man, calmly, methodically strangled under shadow of a prison wall, without any of the frothy excitement that has up to within a very short time formed part of an execution ceremony. Few things could be more impressive, so far as the outside spectators were concerned (by reason of its fearful suggestiveness) than the silent running up of a black flag from the gaol wall just as the murderer passed down into the valley of the shadow of death; and nothing we should say could have been more awful than the sight of those four high, hard, pitiless walls to the wretch brought forth to die. Such is an account of the first execution of a murderer in London that has taken place out of sight of such as chose to brave the horrors of an execution crowd in order to see a fellow-creature die a shameful death.

The body, after hanging an hour, was cut down, and a coroner's inquest, as prescribed by the Act of Parliament, was held in the course of the afternoon, previous to burying it.

The last personage we shall record here as a fit companion to all the before-mentioned, is SANSON, the renowned HERO OF THE GUILLOTINE. On the outskirts of old Paris, in a small neat cottage overlooking the banks of the Seine, surrounded by palings at the front, and thick hawthorn hedges at the sides and back, lives secluded from vulgar gaze a descendant of three generations of the Sansons, who from father to son have inherited the office of public executioner. He is a grim-looking old man of strong build, and is complacent to all visitors whose curiosity leads them to see and converse with him, and view his curious cabinet of murderers' relics and criminals' curiosities; and who make their request with becoming civility. He is full of anecdotes about the exploits of his ancestors at chopping off the heads of Louis the XVI, Maria Antonette, Charlotte Corday, the authoress of the famous saying " O! liberty, what crimes are committed in thy name," as she was about to put her neck under the guillotine knife. He will exhibit at the same time, models of guillotines, instruments of torture, amongst them spokes of the blood-stained breaking wheel of former days, locks of the hair of various nobles and their ladies, rings, brooches, and other trinkets of the victims of the bloody Robespierre, with pieces of the robes and surplices of the bishops and priests who were then brought out of dungeons and guillotined in multitudes early every morning for weeks together, till the ground where the scaffold stood ran with blood. A few skulls and finger-bones of remarkable persons he will also show, and tell how he obtained them. We will now spare our reader's feelings, and conclude by hoping that the day is not far off, when the awful adventures of the heroes of the gallows and guillotine will be numbered among the things of the past.

THE END.

ELLIOT, Printer, " The West-End News" office, 475, Oxford Street, W.C.

EXECUTION
F. HINSON,

Who suffered the extreme penalty of the law, at the Old Bailey, this morning, Monday, December, 13th, 1869, for the Wilful Murder of Maria Death.

This morning Frederick Hinson suffered the extreme penalty of the law at the Old Bailey, for the murder of Maria Death.

The prisoner previous to his trial behaved in a most sullen manner, scarcely heeding anything that was said to him. It is satisfactory to state that since his condemnation the conduct of the unhappy man underwent a total change for the better, and he began to realize the awful condition in which he was placed, and his callous demeanour was changed into one of deep dejection. The prisoner has been assiduously attended by the chaplain of the prison, and to such a state of religious feeling had he been brought, that he fully acknowledged the justice of his sentence. He has frequently alluded to his great affection for the unfortunate woman, and his regret at having sent her before her maker totally unprepared. Since his condemnation, the prisoner has been visited by his children, and also his father, the final parting from whom was of the most affecting character, and will not be forgotten by those who witnessed it.

The sheriffs arrived at an early hour, and immediately proceeded to the condemned cell, where they found the prisoner earnestly engaged in his religious duties with the chaplain of the prison. The time had now arrived for the prisoner to be pinioned, the operation of which was quickly performed, and the wretched man having thanked the chaplain, the governor, and other officials for their kindness towards him, the procession was then formed, and slowly took its way to the scene of execution. The cap and rope having been adjusted, the bolt was drawn, and the wretched man ceased to exist. Simultaneously with the drop falling, a black flag was hoisted at one corner of the prison, announcing that the last dread sentence of the law had been carried into effect.

Young men and maidens pay attention,
  You married and you single all,
List to my sad lamentation,
  And pity, pity my downfall ;
For those double Wood Green murders,
  I alas am doom'd to die,
How can I meet my heavenly father,
  Or dare to him for mercy cry.

So all young men I pray take warning,
  Your passions curb, 'ere 'tis too late,
My dying prayer do not be scorning,
  Think of Frederick Hinson's wretched fate.

At Wood Green I was respected,
  With all around in peace did dwell,
Now broken-hearted and dejected,
  I pine within a gloomy cell.
With Maria Death I lived contented,
  'Till Boyd he caused her for to stray,
And by the tales that he invented,
  He affection stole from me away.

When I found she was false-hearted,
  Jealousy fill'd my mind, 'tis true,
I grieved from her for to be parted,
  For I loved her, and our offspring too ;
Poor darling orphans, let none upbraid them,
  When my soul is gone, I know not where,
That God above from harm may save them.
  Shall be my last, my earnest prayer.

When at the station on her did gaze there,
  In company with that treacherous man,
One kindly word from her would saved her
  And stay'd alas my murderous hand ;
But she braved my anger, and in madness,
  Recall the dead I never can,
I saw her fall, and gazed in sadness,
  A guilty and heartbroken man.

Now for my crimes I was convicted,
  And the dreadful sentence on me pass'd,
Condemn'd by some, by many pity'd,
  And in a dreary cell was cast ;

The Judge said on passing sentence,
  Frederick Hinson you must prepare,
Ask God to grant you true repentance,
  And bend to him in heartfelt prayer.

My days are spent in lamentation,
  My sleepless nights were spent in prayer,
My mind was filled with agitation,
  For Maria's shade was always there.
But I trust her soul is now in heaven,
  But a little time she's gone before,
This sinful world I must be leaving,
  And so my sad end will deplore.

A last farewell, I must be going,
  To meet with my offended God,
My state of mind there is no knowing,
  My soul's bow'd down with deeds of blood.
Now once again I pray take warning;
  For me the fatal bell does toll,
My dying prayer do not be scorning,
  May the Lord have mercy on my soul.

H. Disley, Printer, 57, High-street, St. Giles.

236

Execution of J. Rutterford,

At Bury St. Edmunds, for the MURDER of J. HIGHT.

This morning, at the county prison, Bury St. Edmunds, James Rutterford underwent the last dread sentence of the law, for the wilful and deliberate murder of John Hight, a gamekeeper, in the employ of Maharajah Dhuleep Singh, at Eriswell, Suffolk, on the 31st of December last. The prisoner, since his condemnation, has displayed a perfect indifference as to his awful situation, and when spoken to about the murder, always tried to avoid it. He has been constantly attended by the worthy chaplain, and has paid particular attention to what he said, but in a quiet surly mood. The prisoner was visited last week by a government inspector, for the purpose of examining the neck of the prisoner, the gaol surgeon having reported that he had a malformation, which might cause an unusual degree of suffering on death being inflicted by strangulation. The inspector came to the conclusion that there was nothing in the neck of the convict to prevent his being hanged in the usual manner.

The sheriffs arrived at an early hour, and immediately proceeded to the condemned cell, where they found the prisoner earnestly engaged in his religious duties, with the worthy chaplain of the prison. The time had now arrived for the prisoner to be pinioned, the operation of which was quickly performed, and the wretched man thanked the parson, the governor, and other officials for their kindness towards him. The procession was formed, and slowly took its way to the scene of execution. The cap and rope having been adjusted, the bolt was drawn, and the wretched man soon ceased to exist. Simultaneously with the drop falling, a black flag was hoisted at one corner of the prison, announcing that the last dread sentence of the law had been carried into effect.

You Suffolk lads of each degree,
And all young men of each degree,
And when my mournful tale you hear,
For my sad end shed a silent tear.

    Upon the dreadful scaffold high,
    A murderer's death I am doom'd to die.

James Rutterford it is my name,
I now must end my life in shame ;
Repentance, alas! it is too late,
I must prepare to meet my fate.

My parents reared me tenderly,
And good advice they gave to me ;
If to my dear mother I did attend,
I should not have met a murderer's end.

On the 31st of December last,
Oh would I could recall the past,

With Heffer I went in search of game,
Which led to that deed I dread to name.

When poor John Hight, on that fatal day,
To the plantation came that way,
I owed him no spite, I tell you true,
It was but his duty he did do.

I know you Rutter, poor John Hight said,
Those words filled my mind with dread,
To secure my safety, I did him kill,
And his precious blood on the ground did spill.

As Heffer says, I then struck him down,
And covered him with deadly wounds,
I stopp'd his mouth I do declare,
For his dying groans I could not bear.

And then I dragg'd him in his gore,
His mangled body then covered o'er,

As my mate said, it was a sickening sight
But the eye of God brought my crime to light.

Of that deed alone I am to blame,
Heffer is innocent, I declare the same,
With my dying breath, I do him forgive,
And trust he a better life may live.

Since I have taken poor Hight's life,
I cannot rest by day or night,
His form is ever before my eyes,
And for vengeance on his murderer cries.

That my sentence it is just, I own,
Farewell to friends, farewell to home,
How can I meet my offended God,
With my soul bow'd down with guilt and blood.

☞ "**This man was to have been hung, but they let him off because they thought it would hurt him, good Christians**."—MSS. NOTE *attached to our copy of the above by the intended Printer and Publisher.*